AFTER CAPONE

After Capone

THE LIFE AND WORLD OF CHICAGO MOB BOSS

FRANK "the Enforcer" NITTI

Mars Eghigian, Jr.

Cumberland House
Nashville, Tennessee

AFTER CAPONE
PUBLISHED BY CUMBERLAND HOUSE PUBLISHING, INC.
431 Harding Industrial Drive
Nashville, TN 37211-3160

Cover design: Gore Studio, Inc.
Text design: John Mitchell

Library of Congress Cataloging-in-Publication Data
Eghigian, Mars.
  After Capone : the life and world of Chicago mob boss Frank "the Enforcer" Nitti /
Mars Eghigian Jr.
    p. cm.
  Includes bibliographical references and index.
  ISBN-13: 978-1-58182-454-4 (hardcover : alk. paper)
  ISBN-10: 1-58182-454-8 (hardcover : alk. paper)
  1. Nitti, Frank, d. 1943. 2. Criminals—Illinois—Chicago—Biography. 3. Organized crime—Illinois—
Chicago—History. I. Nitti, Frank, d. 1943. II. Title.
  HV6248.N625E44 2005
  364.1′092—dc22
                                                                    2004030480

Printed in the United States of America

1 2 3 4 5 6 7—12 11 10 09 08 07 06

To my late grandfather, Ara Eghigian Sr.,
an immigrant illiterate in the English language who earned an honorary
doctorate from Golden State University and inspired me to write;
my late mother, Darlene, who encouraged me to read;
and Alesa Wilson, whom I hope to encourage to read.

CONTENTS

FOREWORD

Al Capone is easily the most famous gangster in history; a great deal has been written about him and also about Prohibition-era Chicago.

But what happened after Capone, from 1932 to the trial in the Browne-Bioff Hollywood extortion case in 1943 that sent the leadership of the Chicago mob to prison? Sadly, very little has been written about this period, with the exception of perhaps Virgil Peterson's *Barbarians in Our Midst* and my own short history of the Chicago Outfit. The Capone biographies are largely silent on this era, leaving Chicago almost completely behind when Capone himself boards the train for the U.S. Penitentiary in Atlanta in early 1932. The Prohibition-era gangland histories dealing with Chicago, many of which are also centered on Capone, either end with his departure or were published just before 1932.

⟨0/0/0⟩

In many ways 1932-43 is the Dark Ages of Chicago mob history, a period we know little about. This is partly because the Nitti-led Syndicate kept out of the limelight and partly because gangland violence decreased dramatically after the Prohibition-era gang wars ended, both of which kept the underworld under the radar. Also, other events, such as the Great Depression, Franklin Roosevelt's New Deal and international disputes that eventually involved the United States, pushed the mob out of the public eye. There is little useful material available from the federal government, which at the time believed the Capone gang broke up after Scarface Al went to prison. All in all, the organized-crime historian has much less to work with during this period than during most other periods after 1920 and, therefore, for years many interesting questions have gone unanswered.

Just who was Francesco Raffele Nitto, more commonly known as Frank Nitti, the man who succeeded Al Capone? Where did he come from and what role did he play in the Capone gang while its leader was still in Chicago? Was he Al Capone's cousin? Was he Capone's underboss? Was he "the Enforcer," the fearsome nickname commonly given to him by the press, who dispensed violence to enforce Capone's orders? Was he really the Boss during the years after Capone, or was he just a puppet fronting for Paul Ricca and others? Why did Nitto commit suicide in 1943?

What happened to the Capone gang after Al Capone went away? How did it move against the allies of the North Side Gang led by George Moran, after the Moran gang finally broke up in late 1930? When and how did the Chicago Outfit, to use the common label for the post-Prohibition criminal enterprise that still exists today, come into existence? How did the Outfit keep operating and retrench itself after the repeal of Prohibition, keeping its doors open, its "employees" employed, and its members from killing one another? Just how was it able to extort—at the height of the Depression—$1 million from major Hollywood film studios, and how did that episode backfire on the Outfit?

This book answers these questions and many others. It is the product of more than twelve years of research by Mars Eghigian, who dug through the extensive files of the Chicago Crime Commission and other archives around the country. He has also carefully examined what was written by probably the foremost experts on Chicago organized crime during this period, the reporters for Chicago's daily newspapers. The latter sources are especially important because for years Chicago's crime writers, with sources in the Chicago Police Department and in the underworld, kept "their fingers on the pulse" of the mob and relayed the details to the public. This material has been largely unexplored, except by a handful of dedicated Outfit historians, because few writers were willing to pay the price of examining the primary sources in detail.

In the process the author has left no stone unturned while exploring Nitti's life and the evolution of organized crime in Chicago. Because he has paid the price, Mars Eghigian is able to not only tell us what happened but, to the extent possible (given the fog that hangs over the history of organized crime in general), also *why* it happened. This book, therefore, goes well beyond the usual mob histories that are incident driven—relating who probably shot whom on a given day or who was convicted of what crime when—and instead gives insight into how this unusual entity created under Frank Nitti, the Chicago Outfit (which has been the most successful of the Cosa Nostra crime families in the United States), was formed and why it did what it did at various points in time.

— John J. Binder

ACKNOWLEDGMENTS

I am immensely grateful to the late FBI agent Bill Roemer, who, after my initial inquiry on the lack of Nitti information, suggested I write about the one Chicago mob boss who was always overshadowed by Capone and who, in his words, "fell through the cracks" of history. He unhesitatingly provided the initial leads to obtain information for this book.

My most profound thanks to the Chicago Crime Commission. Their files, dating back to 1919, contain many of the contemporary newspaper clippings, observer reports, and notes from Nitti's time that provided the basis for my research, which would have been infinitely more exhausting without these items. I am especially grateful to Director of Operations Jeanette Callaway, President Bob Fuesel, Executive Vice President Katherine Kirby, and the many interns for their infinite patience and kindness during my research trips to the commission office. I would also like to thank retired Chief Investigator Jerry Gladden for sharing his vast knowledge on the history of Chicago organized crime. Certainly, this book could never have been realized without them all.

Most generous and helpful was John J. Binder, organized crime researcher and author of *Images of America: The Chicago Outfit*, whose knowledge and understanding of Chicago organized crime is arguably among the best. John provided key information that filled in the gaps and greatly increased my understanding of many of Nitti's associates. John also possesses one of the most extensive private collections of gangster photographs available. If one picture is worth a thousand words, then John's collection is certainly responsible for several thousand words in this text, as his photos were most helpful in providing countless descriptions in this book. Additionally, many photographs from his collection appear in this book.

I am exceedingly grateful to Arthur J. Bilek, former chief of the Cook County Sheriff's Police and co-author of *The St. Valentine's Day Massacre: The Untold Story of the Gangland Bloodbath That Brought Down Al Capone*, for sharing his vast knowledge of the era and providing the introduction to Cumberland House Publishing. He is the reason this book exists. Look for his next title, *The Scarlet Sisterhood*, a view of Chicago's Levee district and Big Jim Colosimo.

Also of immense assistance in Chicago was organized-crime researcher Jeff Thurston, whose tireless efforts provided many key details, especially the seldom-mentioned assassination attempt on State's Attorney Thomas J. Courtney in 1935 and the difficult-to-find "whatever happened to" details in the final chapter. I would also like to thank Matt Luzi for sharing his expertise on the era, especially about the Chicago Heights gangs (which, in itself, is a particularly interesting area of organized crime).

I am extremely indebted to New York attorney Boris Kostelanetz, who in 1943 was the young special assistant to the U.S. attorney who prosecuted Louis Campagna, et al., in the Hollywood extortion case. Mr. Kostelanetz provided me with transcripts from that trial which proved invaluable in separating fact from fiction in subsequent historical accounts relating to the case. He and his longtime legal secretary Evelyn Wyckoff also shared some of their recollections of those involved in the trial.

My heartfelt and sincere acknowledgment to all of those who took time to share their expertise, knowledge, and experiences of Nitti and his era. No matter how great or small they considered their information, their assistance proved invaluable in preparation of this book. More often than not, the small details they provided and deemed insignificant were those that made all the difference. These individuals include William Balsamo, Anthony Berardi, Walter Spirko, Howard Browne, Senior Judge Abraham Lincoln Marovitz, George Meyer, George Murray, and all those who talked with me who wish to remain anonymous.

With regard to everyone mentioned above, any errors interpreting Nitto history are due solely to the author.

Considerable recognition is due those authors of previous books on the people and events of the Nitti era who readily and unselfishly shared information and research experiences and provided many valuable leads necessary for the completion of this book. Thank you very much to Robert J. Schoenberg, Charles Rappleye, Ed Becker, and Blaisé Picchi. A very special acknowledgment is due the late George Murray, who is possibly the only person who attempted to piece together at least part of the Nitti story. His 1975 book, *The Legacy of Al Capone: Portraits and Annals of Chicago's Public Enemies*, provided the foundation and point of departure for my research.

Much of the information located on Frank "the Enforcer" Nitti was not in files bearing his name or alias but rather in the numerous disparate files of those associates and events linked to Nitti. These records are literally scattered all around the United

Acknowledgments

States—sometimes in the most unlikely locations—in various collections and governmental agencies and are chiefly composed of professional papers, legal documents, and press accounts. The many newspaper articles used were retrieved the old fashion way—by plowing through reels of microfilm. Every attempt was made to locate and retrieve all known information and records about Nitti so as to leave no stone unturned. In that quest, I wish to thank the many organizations that were helpful:

Brooklyn Public Library, especially the microfilm staff
Chicago Historical Society—the entire library staff, especially Archie Motely curator of archives;
Chicago Public Library, especially the microfilm staff
Circuit Court of Cook County, Criminal Division
Circuit Court of Cook County, Chancery Division
Circuit Court of Cook County, Probate Division
Cook County Office of the Medical Examiner
Cook County Recorder or Deeds
Clerk of the County Court, Dade County, Florida
Dallas County Clerk of Vital Records, Dallas, Texas
Newberry Library of Chicago, especially the microfilm staff
Herbert Hoover Presidential Library, West Branch, Iowa, especially Dale Meyer
Kings County Court House, Brooklyn, New York
National Archives, Great Lakes Region in Chicago
National Archives, Northeast Region in New York
National Archives at College Park, Maryland, especially Fred Romanski for his patience and guidance in locating textual records within Justice Department Record Group 60
New York Municipal Archives, especially Kenneth Cobb
New York Public Library, especially the staff in the U.S. History, Local History, & Genealogy Division
St. Louis City Marriage License Bureau
St. Louis Mercantile Library at the University of Missouri at St. Louis, especially Charles Brown
St. Louis Post-Dispatch, especially Ken Roberts
St. Louis Public Library, especially the microfilm staff
U.S. Department of Justice, Bureau of Prisons
U.S. Department of Justice, Civil Division
U.S. Department of Justice, Criminal Division
U.S. Department of Justice, Executive Office for the U.S. Attorneys
U.S. Department of Justice, Federal Bureau of Investigation
U.S. Department of Justice, Immigration and Naturalization
U.S. Department of the Treasury, Bureau of Alcohol, Tobacco, and Firearms

Special thanks to Mike Webb, owner of www.crimewebcollectibles.com. Mike collects and sells various crime antiquities such as wanted posters, mug shots, and the like. It was Mike who happened across Nitto's 1930 wanted poster and notified me.

Key to the book was New York genealogist Rhoda Miller, who chased down some of those vital details in New York for the early chapters of the book that appear probably for the first time anywhere. A job well done!

Crucial to obtaining photographs were John J. Binder, through his personal collection; the research staff of the Chicago Historical Society, particularly Colleen Becket of the Legal Department; Tom Gilbert of AP/Wide World Photos; Kenneth Cobb of the New York City Municipal Archives; and Charles Brown of the St. Louis Mercantile Library.

Many thanks to Publisher Ron Pitkin and Editor John Mitchell at Cumberland House for taking on a project in which few other publishers saw value.

I sincerely thank all my friends and relatives, those along the way whom I may have overlooked, and the many who provided generosity and hospitality during my travels.

And anyone who professes to complete such a project without support in all ways from family is not being honest with him- or herself. Thank you, Mars, Maresa, Bill, Alesa, and especially Skip and Arpina Stanton, for your endless support of a project many may have questioned from the beginning—you had no doubt.

INTRODUCTION

It was 1932. Celebrated Chicago gangland boss Al Capone had been shipped off to federal prison only the previous May, and rampant guesswork followed as to who would succeed to the throne of the most powerful Chicago gang in history. The answer was revealed nearly seven months later in a most unusual way.

With a World's Fair only months away, the Chicago police force was given the green light to raid all known gangster enclaves large or small to rid the city of its hoodlum element, especially the old Capone Outfit. Police strikes the previous month netted eighteen Capone hoodlums, including some of the upper echelon. Nearly every important member within the organization had been arrested since then . . . except one.

For a December day less than a week before Christmas, the thirty-two-degree temperature wasn't too appalling for Chicago. About 1:15 p.m., a car with two plainclothes detectives pulled to the front curb of the nearly new LaSalle-Wacker Building at 221 North LaSalle Street. An hour earlier they phoned for a back-up detail.

They were there ready to go in. To the reinforcements, the raid appeared more or less routine—more hoods, more evidence, and the usual arrests. But not that day. The lead detectives knew better.

Up on the fifth floor, the men crashed through the door of Room 554. A number of hoodlums were immediately taken. In another room, a swarthy man with dark, slicked- backed hair sat in a supervisory position behind a desk with two companions at either side. As he stood up, this central figure revealed no apparent forceful physical presence; he was a rather dreary-eyed individual, standing only five feet, six inches tall at best. But the detectives were taking no chance with *him*. His companions were escorted out. Only this man and one detective were left in the room. Ordered up against a nearby wall, the swarthy character was shot three times by the detective for no apparent reason. Had this man, a known gangster, died there or even in a hospital, the officer might have become a hero and the hood just another statistic in the war on crime. He did not, and the local crime crusade that precipitated the shooting dissolved, never again to seriously challenge him.

That a detective would attempt to kill this man above all the others previously taken suggested that some in the police department knew the wounded man was Capone's successor. The shots fired that day validated his crown. The man was Frank Nitto, better known as Frank "the Enforcer" Nitti. The old Capone mob under his leadership weighed heavily on Chicago, Cook County, and the nation for the next eleven years.

In September 1984, the popular myth regarding his name still endured. That month the press reported the acquittal of a twenty-two-year-old man on charges of murder. He was, however, found guilty of conspiracy to cover up the death. Hardly an exceptional news story in any large metropolitan area, unless the name of those involved is thought to be noteworthy. Unfortunately for this man, his name was Nitti.

After the trial, his attorney was pressed by reporters to acknowledge young Mr. Nitti as the grandnephew of the late Frank "the Enforcer" Nitti. The attorney replied, "Don't believe it."

They should have listened.

This is the real story of Francesco Raffele Nitto, the Enforcer.

AFTER
CAPONE

———◇———

1

THE LAST NITTO:
ITALY TO BROOKLYN

HE MAIN COASTAL ROAD RUNNING south from Naples will eventually pass between and afford a magnificent view of both the Gulfo de Napoli and the great Mount Vesuvius. The road continues a short distance to the coastal town of Torre Annunziata and the ruins of ancient Pompeii. Here, the road forks. To the right, less than five miles down the coast to the east is Castellammare di Stabia, native village of Gabriele Capone, father of Alphonse Capone, the most powerful Chicago gang leader of the 1920s. The main road continues to the left into the mountains, and roughly the same distance inland on the way to Salerno is the town of Angri, once the home of Luigi Nitto and his son Francesco Raffele Nitto, later known as Frank "the Enforcer" Nitti, leader of the same mob after Capone's reign and his clear Number Two during the gang's Prohibition heyday. The paths of both sons of these fathers never seemed to stray; they converged in Brooklyn, New York, and subsequently joined again in Chicago, Illinois. Nitto's road would end there in the suburb of North Riverside—and so would the family name.

Luigi Nitto and the people along Italy's southwest coast probably suffered as much as anyone else in the south during the mid-1860s. But then again, chaos, exploitation, and economic ruin—unremitting misery—were nothing new to the region. They were simply a way of life. Ironically, the residents of Angri owed their anguish in part to the very element responsible for the town's origin and development.

3

Key to the success of the ancient Roman Empire was its creation of a fundamental network of roads that gave it the ability to move armies and develop commerce throughout the boot of Italy. From Rome, they branched out: the Via Aurelia to the northwest; the great Via Flaminia routed Emperors Augustus and Hadrian north; Via Valeria stretched east to the Adriatic coast; the Via Appia, the queen of the roads, or Appian Way, led south. Emperors steadily built a network of secondary arteries. Those tracks south of Naples snaked up through the Lattari Mountains, a chain of the great Apennines, stretching to the Amalfi coast. It was during the empire's later years, along one of those well-worn mountain footpaths nineteen miles south of Naples, that the ground on which Angri rests was first settled. Unfortunately for the local populace, those same narrow cart tracks provided a natural course for other armies marching up and down Italy's lower west coast between the rugged mountains and the turquoise waters of the Tyrrhenian Sea.

First, the Goths tramped through. Then, to reclaim the western empire, the Byzantine Emperor Justinian marched in. His peoples established a permanent settlement as a stopover for their knights on the advance which became known as the present-day Angri. (The name derives from the knights then known as *Angari* from the Greek word *Aggaroi*.) A few years later, Justinian's knights defeated the Goth king Teias once and for all near Angri. The area was far from secure, however, and was later raided by Arabs.

In the centuries preceding the Arab invasion, the site sprouted a citadel, then a town. Wealthy families alternated as lords over Angri, though they seemingly always bowed to one external jurisdiction or another. Lombards, Saxons, and Normans came and went. For the next 300 years, the southern Italian boot, including Angri and the island of Sicily, were ruled together by the Spanish Bourbon monarchy as the Kingdom of Two Sicilies. The port of Naples, long the provincial seat of power for aristocrats, served as the Bourbon capital and nerve center. Bourbon rule was loose and corrupt, the government remaining invisible to most southern *contadini* (peasants) except when collecting taxes and quelling rebellions. The primarily agricultural south remained quite primitive. Further compounding the area's plight, criminal and political brigandage swarmed throughout southern Italy. Calls for social reform were ignored. Popular uprisings ignited but were quickly crushed, with the peasants bearing the brunt of the suppression again and again.

The departure of the Bourbons from Naples and the unification of the peninsula in September 1860 changed conditions in the south not one iota. As one historian observed, the union "was not a nation in the hearts of many of its citizens." Wealthy, more educated northerners guided Rome's politics, and it was not long before they displayed a dualism unfavorable to the south. They imposed taxes far in excess of the previous Bourbon rate; the taxes were, in fact, the highest in Europe, far beyond the proportion of the region's share of national income. Agriculture and fishing gradually collapsed. Jobs in the north were either economically or geographically out of reach. Isolated, there was little chance for a southern peasant to improve his lot. The armies came again. The church seemed indifferent. All the age-long passion, doubt, and hatred still remained.

Nitto's hometown of Angri suffered, but because the town straddled a main artery south from Naples, it probably did so to a slightly lesser degree than the surrounding rural villages. The through road was well-trafficked, and the town grew as a key communication and transportation link for points south. By the 1800s, Angri was generally a busy place filled with passers-by, townsfolk, tradesmen, and farmers. The population stood at a few thousand, but Angri remained more primitively communal than urban. In this sense, it was really no better off than neighboring, truly rural villages, which were usually characterized as miserable places to live.

The typical southern family establishment resembled little more than a shanty, described by one contemporary observer as "consisting of only one room that served as kitchen, bedroom, and usually as quarters for the barnyard animals as well." The rooms were oftentimes windowless, with light only from the open door. Sparse, feeble furnishings might fill open spaces. Small charcoal braziers provided a cooking surface and the only means of heat. News clippings and crucifixes—symbols of hope—ordinarily adorned the walls. Construction materials were frequently crude and deteriorated. Worn stone served as floors. Plaster on walls was primitive and imperfect. Life in Angri was a relatively meaninglessly existence that offered little more than a magnificent mountain view of sunny Mediterranean skies and *la miseria*.

This was the world into which Frank Nitto was born. Pure survival, an experience few of his fellow mobsters could claim, was what made him different.

———— ⚍☙☙☙☙ ————

In 1870s Angri, Luigi Nitto reportedly earned a living as a barber, a skill probably dictated by family tradition and acquired through long youthful apprenticeship. Ordinarily, it might allow a somewhat more comfortable lifestyle than that of his agricultural brethren. About that time he met and subsequently married teenaged Rosina Fezza. Coincidentally, that decade marked the beginning of a trend of increased birth rates throughout southern Italy—and newlyweds Luigi and Rosina Nitto did not buck that trend.

Family life and its accompanying responsibilities began for the Nittos in 1880 with the birth of a daughter, Giovannina, later Americanized as Anna. The family expanded in the following years at least three times and possibly for one last time in the mid 1880s. On January 27, 1886, a dark-haired, brown-eyed boy of dusky complexion was born and christened Francesco Raffele Nitto, Americanized as Frank Nitto. The new arrival to the Nitto clan, however, came at a time of even greater austerity for those living on the southern Italian peninsula.

During the 1880s, government economic policies caused life in the agrarian south to deteriorate even more harshly than before. Agriculture collapsed, and the effects trickled down. The Nittos understood this hardship firsthand, as the family lost at least three children during that decade. Yet, Luigi Nitto stubbornly persevered with the remainder of his family. His strength of *famiglia* (family), the closely knit web which encompassed not only blood kin but also certain villagers, and which was his society and means of continued existence, was in Angri. By custom, and like many of his family before him, there Luigi Nitto lived and there he would die.

But for others in an environment that showed little prospect for improvement, and especially a national culture that provided no real chance for upward social mobility, southerners' traditional resistance to moving from one's birthplace began to erode. "If I could have worked my way up in my chosen profession in Italy, I would have stayed in Italy," one immigrant candidly remarked. "Repeated efforts showed me that I could not."

Southerners began to look for something better—somewhere else. Their aspirations coincided with expanding opportunities for unskilled labor in other countries, especially America, whose needs in the midst of an industrial revolution were most urgent. At least there, those willing to work might have a chance to improve their lot.

Such a possibility certainly must have penetrated the Nitto household, perhaps from chatter heard along Angri's well-traveled road, or from a male villager who had worked abroad and saved enough money to take his family to the new country, or from word that large steamship companies were recruiting workers for American companies (such labor contracts were later made illegal by U.S. authorities). Steamships served the nearby port of Naples at least once or twice a month, three or more times in the busy spring and early summer, and offered inexpensive third-class or steerage quarters affordable to southern *contadini*. Once on board, if all went well, the peasants would set foot in America in about two weeks. After years of having no real political representation or input in their affairs, southerners could now vote—and they did so with their feet. In the 1880s, they began a mass migration to America.

Just as the Nittos may have begun contemplating a move to America, those thoughts were extinguished in 1888 when father Luigi passed away, leaving widow Rosina Fezza with daughter Giovannina and two-year-old Francesco.

Despite deplorable conditions, the trio survived. Giovannina, now almost nine, likely abandoned her childhood to keep up the household, as was expected of most females that age. Another role—that of a fatherly authority figure—also needed filling for the family. This was accomplished a little less than a year later when Rosina Fezza married Francesco Dolendo. She chose well, for Dolendo was a better-than-average wage earner, possessing the talents of an *illusatore*, or painter. Nonetheless, life for the Dolendos would prove to be just as difficult as it had been for the Nittos. After two years of marriage, none of the children born to Rosina and Francesco survived.

With ever more southerners departing for America, the couple decided they too would take their chances in the New World. He might find respectable work with fitting pay, and she might find a more hospitable, less repressive place to raise Giovannina and Francesco and begin a new Dolendo family. In July 1890, after scraping together enough money, Francesco Dolendo boarded the aging Prince Line steamer *Elysia* in Naples harbor and departed for New York. There he would test the possibilities, find work, and hopefully save enough money to bring the rest of the brood over later. In the meantime, Rosina would have to fend for the children herself. She had managed once before without a husband; she could do so again.

It was nearly three years before Dolendo could save enough money to bring Francesco Nitto, his mother and his sister to America. In the spring of 1893, with sufficient funds from America and passports and possibly prepaid tickets from Dolendo in her possession, Rosina packed what family belongings she and her children could carry on their shoulders and left Italy behind. By now age seven and a half, Francesco Nitto was certainly old enough to recognize the hopeless situation they were exiting—the injustice, mistrust, dire need, and death that permeated southern Italy in the late nineteenth century, just as they had for much of the region's history. These were indelible memories for a boy entering his formative years, and like his father, he had learned the hard life and had lived it firsthand. However, in America he learned to cast off much of that baggage, and this was part of his success. It bore greatly on his determination to rise above his awful beginnings.

In early June 1893, the North German Lloyd liner *Werra* arrived in Naples harbor from the port of Genoa. A recent transfer from her original ten-year stint on the Bremen-Southampton-New York run, the *Werra*'s one thousand third-class passenger capacity made her an ideal moneymaking candidate for shifting the Italian masses. Not terribly imposing at 4,817 gross tons, even harbor tugs in New York made her look undersized. But she was durable. Of iron construction, with a single screw and two funnels flanked by masts at the bow and stern, she could make sixteen knots on the open ocean, not bad at the time. With flags whipping atop each of her masts and thick black smoke pouring from her funnels, she may have been impressive to the inhabitants of Naples's smaller harbor as well as those about to board her that summer day, especially a young boy.

Rosina, Giovannina, and young Francesco boarded the *Werra* as third-class passengers and were directed to Steerage Compartment IV for the two-week journey to New York. Later, as ship's crew made their rounds, the three were duly registered in the *Werra*'s manifest as passengers number 798, 799, and 800, respectively. Rosina, traveling without her husband, gave, as was customary of most Italian women in the same situation, her maiden name, Fezza, to the registrar. Francesco Nitto was simply recorded as "Raffaele," a misspelled version of his middle name. They were part of a near-record 70,000 compatriots leaving Italy that year, many of them also from the south.

Among those leaving later that same season was Gabriele Capone. He packed up his wife, Theresa, and newborn son, Vincenzo, and left Castellammare di Stabia, their destination also New York.

After roughly a two-week passage in typical steerage conditions—tight spaces, foul air, and unclean conditions in the lowest compartments, often just above the ship's screw—Francesco Nitto, his mother, his sister, and 794 steerage passengers arrived in New York City on Monday, June 26, 1893. They disembarked from the harbor ferry under the gaze of the Statue of Liberty for processing at the enormous Ellis Island facility built and opened the previous year.

Constructed by the federal government because of local corruption (states ran immigration facilities until that time) and concerns about the new immigration crunch, the Ellis Island station through which Francesco Nitto and his family entered America was not the French Renaissance structure that stands today. The administrative complex consisted of twelve wooden buildings, including a small hospital, restaurant, and powerhouse, and was built almost entirely of Georgia pine. The largest building was the three-story, 400-by-150-foot Main Processing Building, whose four square, pointed towers commanded an excellent view of the channel and its traffic. The sight of the immense processing building, as viewed by newcomers in the harbor, was described by one contemporary observer in a rare account: "It looks like a latter-day watering place hotel; presenting to the view a great many-windowed expanse of buff painted walls, of blue slate roofing, and of light and picturesque towers." Thousands of immigrants could now be processed more quickly and more comfortably than ever before. Francesco Nitto entered this great hall.

The disheveled immigrants made their way into the main-floor hall, its sheer size and thirteen-foot ceilings allowing for the storage and handling of baggage from as many as twelve thousand arrivals. The Dolendo-Nitto family, along with the other dazed, excited, and grateful new arrivals, entered the cavernous hall ringing with the mass cacophony of humanity. Most were dressed in their bedraggled best for the occasion, carrying their luggage and tattered possessions to begin the regimen of registering for a new life: stow baggage in the main entrance hall; ascend stairs to the second floor for medical inspection; if not detained for health reasons, proceed to the second-floor processing room; enter one of the ten available aisles and anxiously wait to reach a clerk for one final imposing interrogation.

Passing or failing depended on one's ability to explain one's self sufficiently; therefore, many an informed immigrant nervously spent the two-week voyage rehearsing critical answers. No slip-ups. Undesirables such as criminals or even simple, unskilled persons were sent back home since they had no apparent means to earn a living. And while there technically was no monetary requirement for entering the United States, immigrants had to produce sufficient currency to prove that they could initially sustain themselves. In the early years, the sum required was $50 (the average Italian immigrant family arrived with approximately $17). Fortunately for many, this parameter alone did not dictate expulsion, especially when skills and work destinations were considered, but for single women with (or without) children and no means of support or money, it could mean the end of the line and a return trip home. This was not a problem for Rosina since she and husband Francesco had wisely followed the common routine for immigrants at the time—he came over first.

After passing inspection and exchanging currency, those heading for New York and its surrounding communities would move to one side of the terminal to catch the next ferry to the city, while those traveling elsewhere would move to the other side, purchase train tickets, and catch a ferry to New Jersey. From start to finish, without any glitches, the process could take as little as three to four hours. After enduring the Ellis Island ordeal and clearing all inquiries, the reunited Dolendo-Nitto clan may have caught a ferry to Harrison, New Jersey, for a brief period. But ultimately the journey ended in New York City. Francesco Raffele Nitto would grow up in Brooklyn.

Perhaps his inaugural three-year experience in America taught him well, or perhaps it was simply fate that led Francesco Dolendo to settle the family in Brooklyn and not in the slums of Manhattan's Lower East Side like so many of his countrymen. Conditions were far from ideal for an Old World Italian family, but the potential for a good life was a great deal better there than across the East River. Brooklyn offered the new Italian immigrant two basic requirements for living: housing that was, if not of the best quality, at least affordable and less overcrowded, and a central location within easy walking distance of work.

Italians first settled south and east of Union and President streets in the waterfront area abutting the Brooklyn docks. There they formed the first Italian colony. Desirable work on the waterfront was close at hand, albeit difficult to come by due to the long-standing Irish monopoly on dockside labor. Eventually, Italians would gain a foothold there, and they spread steadily eastward along Union and President toward the last sluggish stretches of the Gowanus Canal. Those who gained any subsequent measure of prosperity relocated east across Fourth Avenue to brownstones in the much better Park Slope neighborhood and beyond.

By the time Dolendo and family arrived, Italians had just begun to move into the area surrounding the sprawling U.S. Naval Yard (Brooklyn Navy Yard) near the east end of the Brooklyn Bridge. Navy Street was a major north-south artery that abutted the west side of the Navy Yard from its start at York Street, turned south past Sands Street to Flushing Avenue, then bent slightly southeast past a large city park, skirting just a block west of Fort Greene and the Raymond Street Jail before ending at DeKalb Avenue. It was near the naval yard, just south of Flushing and close to the confluence of Tillary and Navy streets, that Dolendo planted the clan in a multi-unit flat they shared with another Italian family at 113 on Navy Street's east side. Rent was cheap at $3-$4 a month, but that still amounted to half a week's pay for an unskilled immigrant laborer.

The neighborhood dwellings were either deteriorating wooden flats, some with ramshackle, flimsy rear additions to house even more people, or ancient and worn brick structures, some of which had been built almost a hundred years before. Houses crowded shoulder to shoulder along Navy Street, confining the neighborhood and obscuring distant views. Streets were cluttered and dirty but teeming with horse-drawn carriages that plodded slowly back and forth, peddlers selling their wares, and children at play. Despite the comparable physical condition of the neighborhood to that of the Lower East Side, the family's chances of survival here were certainly better than in the dense squalor across the river.

Much like the growing Italian colony to the south, the Navy Street district offered an array of work possibilities—factories, warehouses, and small businesses—just the thing for the unskilled Francesco. Other essentials for family life were also present—public schools were a few blocks away, and at the corner of Tillary and Lawrence stood St. Michael the Archangel Catholic Church. A simple community house of worship eclipsed by the surrounding construction, it was later described as "an odd little white stucco building partly constructed below street level so that one had to descend a flight of stairs to enter it." Father Gioachino Garofalo was the priest, and as the congregation enlarged, twice a year he would lead the parishioners in vibrant festivals to the glorification of the archangel, the climax of which included a flag-waving parade down Tillary, very near the doorstep of Nitto's building, before turning north on Navy and circling back on York Street. The processions ended at St. Michael's with Father Garofalo celebrating mass. As daylight faded, the festivities included fireworks, with dancing in the streets beneath the glowing Bengal lights and the colorful detonations while resonating bursts echoed all around.

No matter how refreshing, the area surrounding the Navy Yard in 1893 was not without its shortcomings to a newly landed Italian family. Navy Street was a world away from anything the Dolendo-Nitto clan had experienced before. Most noticeably, the vicinity provided little of the communal ethnicity and Old World ambience usually sought by Italian immigrants at the time. Even as the Brooklyn Bridge increasingly deposited the Lower East Side's Italian overflow on Sands Street to the north of Tillary, no real Italian colony existed there at the time. The Dolendos' neighborhood just south of Flushing Avenue was largely populated by Irish and resident Americans, with a smattering of Scandinavians, English, Scots, and Italians. Even fewer Italians resided to the east toward North Portland Avenue. Thus, the family was among the original pioneers who formed some of the first islands of Italian presence that far south on Navy Street.

In addition to the medley of nationalities in the area, blatant vice, predictably, lurked on the periphery of the nearby docks. "The Navy Yard area was loaded with bars and entertainment," according to longtime Brooklyn historian William Balsamo. In particular, the tract along Sands Street at the Navy Yard gate provided sailors with some of the roughest dives in Brooklyn. Day or night, fresh off the ships, they only had to proceed out the gate, cross Navy Street, and stroll down Sands to quench their thirst. They could also patronize any of the numerous bawdy houses nearby whose female staffs could lay claim to some of the world's most colorful names. Raunchy tattoo parlors, gambling dens, and dance halls were in abundance, and not far away were several bowling alleys that might entertain the less adventurous. At any time the streets might be swarming with sailors whose volatile mix of desires often spelled trouble for the less worldly-wise, especially the minority Italians.

The wild nature of the Sands Street area and the hustle and bustle of Brooklyn in general was the polar opposite of the literal step-by-step, rhythmic lifestyle of rural Italy. Not surprisingly, young Francesco Nitto's early life on Navy Street, as he related years later, was steeped in strong Old World parental authority. Stepfather Francesco Dolendo, as the main provider, reigned supreme, while mother Rosina unofficially ruled over domestic matters. Just as in the Old Country, their survival depended on this highly structured way of life.

Times had changed for the worse since Dolendo first came over. A national recession in 1893 threw many out of work, and now Francesco had to spend long hours away from home scavenging junk for resale to support the brood. Rosina and daughter Anna no doubt tended to their quarters and, in accordance with tradition, may well have been on the lookout for a prospective husband for Anna among the area's small Italian population. Anna was now nearly fourteen and, like most Italian girls her age, found that formal education was most likely out of the question. The immediate future for young Francesco Nitto was compulsory schooling and work. None of the family claimed the ability to read or write English, and with the possible exception of Francesco Dolendo, none could speak English proficiently, although he probably learned no more than broken English in the three years after his arrival.

Though Rosina, like most conservative Italian parents, might have complied only minimally with compulsory education requirements for her children—especially her son, who was an economic asset—she observed the law long enough so that Francesco would at least be literate. Subsequently, the seven-year-old Nitto was enrolled in Brooklyn Public School 14, conveniently nearby at the corner of Concord and Navy streets, no more than a short two- or three-block walk north of their neighborhood. Under the tutelage of school administrator Harriet H. Coffin, Nitto became the first in his family to read and write English. After school hours he worked to assist the family.

While Nitto trudged back and forth to school, Dolendo-Nitto family events bustled (throughout Nitto's youth, family events always seemed fluid) and may very well have affected his perception of the family unit. Within a year of their landing in Brooklyn, Nitto's sister Anna became acquainted with one Vincenzo Vollaro. He was at least nine years her senior and a native of Gragnano, a village in the hills a few scant miles southwest of Angri. It was a joining if not by chance then surely by prearrangement. Vincenzo had arrived in New York with the males of his family just days before Rosina and the children. The Vollaro family also settled on the Brooklyn side of the East River.

Vincenzo worked in the shoe-repair and barbering trades to assist his clan. Those talents, plus the child-rearing skills acquired by Anna as a teenager in Italy, provided an excellent foundation for marriage. Although they were not from the same village, as Old World protocol might demand, they were matched well enough for marriage in America. They were wed in Brooklyn on October 21, 1894, in a simple ceremony performed by Father Garofalo. After the wedding, the newlyweds moved a mile southwest to Van Brunt Street, near the Brooklyn docks and the Italian colony near Union and President streets. The Vollaros immediately set out to establish a family, and the following year, Anna gave birth to a son, Gennaro, making Francesco Nitto an uncle at age nine.

Earlier that same year, Nitto had gained a half-brother when Rosina gave birth to her first child in America—a son, Raphael, born at the family's home at 113 Navy Street. Two years later, she delivered another son, Gennaro. In the meantime, the Vollaros added yet another nephew to the clan. Thus, in the span of four short years, Francesco Nitto, who had not yet reached his twelfth birthday, had seen the demographic of his family change significantly, but no more so than on the day he gained a brother-in-law three times his age—for on that October day, he became the last Nitto family member in name.

A few doors north on Navy Street, another Italian isle popped up. When Gabrielle and Theresa Capone disembarked with son Vincenzo (Americanized to Jim) in New York in late 1893, they too elected to put down roots in the Navy Street area. The couple soon added another son, Raffaele (Ralph), to the brood, and in 1895, Theresa gave birth to a third son, Salvatore (Frank). To support the growing brood, Gabrielle worked at a grocery store in the area, and until he could ply his trade as a barber, the family remained on Navy Street, just south of Francesco Nitto and the Dolendos.

Given the circumstances, it is difficult to fathom how these two families did not know each other. In the mid-1890s, the Capone boys were too young to become socially acquainted with the much older Francesco Nitto, but as they grew up, according to at least one Brooklyn historian, the sons of the two families came to know each other.

By century's turn, the growing Dolendo family moved a block south into a multi-family flat at 142 Navy Street. Two more mouths to feed added to the strain on Francesco Dolendo to provide and on Rosina to parent, now that daughter Anna had moved from the household. The additional burden of contributing to the family's upkeep inevitably fell on the slight shoulders of young Nitto. Francesco worked at various jobs before and after school, bringing most, if not all, his earnings home to help the family. A typical day for the adolescent Nitto probably began with an early morning hike to a nearby shop to perform some menial tasks, then a walk to school for a day of lessons, and finally a late-afternoon return to the store to finish his chores. He may even have helped his stepfather with his many entrepreneurial pursuits on the streets as the family struggled to get by.

The long days likely left little time for studies, and how well Nitto performed in school is unknown (the records of P.S.14 prior to World War I are long gone). After six or so years of trudging back and forth to school, and upon completion of the seventh grade at age fourteen, he left school for good. Part of the reason was increasing financial hardship at home, or, as Nitto would later explain, he left school simply because he "had to work." This was typical in that Italian sons were often pulled out of school early to help their families. In Nitto's case, the move was evidently critical, as stepfather Dolendo had not been able to find more lucrative work and was still scraping up shreds off the street to support his brood. Clearly, the time had come for Nitto to work full time. His valued education—he could read and speak English—might allow him to obtain the sort of semi-dignified job that was unavailable to his stepfather. The remainder of his education—including his later legendary flair for bookkeeping, if true—was likely acquired through self-study, tutoring by another, or at work and on the streets.

By his own account, Nitto spent the next handful of years working a variety of jobs in the Navy Yard area, including stints as a pinsetter in the nearby bowing alleys and as a laborer in the local factories, to support the family. It was at some point during this time that Nitto claimed he was introduced to the one skilled profession that would allow him to eke out a living anywhere he might go—barbering. It was a profession that would later provide him with a cloak of legitimacy in time of need.

Just how and where Nitto learned the trade, he never made clear, although there were several shops in the neighborhood serving the community and the sailors from the Navy Yard. It's quite possible that he picked up some vocational tidbits while working part-time in a barbershop while still in school, though it's more reasonable to presume that he learned the rudiments of the trade from his much older brother-in-law Vincenzo Vollaro or from James LaFernina, an acquaintance of Vollaro, both of whom cut hair at least part time.

It was an ideal occupation to take up at the time. Barbers were valued by their clients not only for their tonsorial skills but also because many could read and speak English and thus serve as interpreters for the new arrivals. With the bulk of Italian immigrants yet to settle Brooklyn, this proved a perfect opportunity for Nitto, although it doesn't appear to have been a full-time endeavor. It was, however, the one skill that he would revert to and become famous for much later.

Streets in the Dolendo neighborhood could be dangerous for a young outsider like Nitto, who was hardly physically imposing (at maturity, he stood only five feet, six inches tall and weighed 145 pounds). With Irish youth gangs prowling the Navy Yard periphery, Jewish gangs roaming Williamsburg to the north, and the Sicilians—who were hostile to everyone—becoming a force on Flushing Avenue to the east, it was not unusual for Italian youngsters like Nitto to band together for security. There was safety in numbers, a physical and psychological reassurance, and a sense of kinship and autonomy. This was their *famiglia*. Safe within a circle of their peers and away from domestic responsibilities, they might play stickball or other games in the dingy streets or enjoy some extravagant delicacy pilfered from a street-side stand.

Unfortunately, at home, such independence often resulted in New World-Old World friction. Many boys, feeling stifled by the Old World traditions observed by their families, looked for adventure with their pals on the streets. Later, these juvenile gangs might progress to more daring mischief—knocking over milk cans, tipping over pushcarts or pulling more serious pranks for thrills. Some of the older and more hardened gangs staked out and defended territories, usually along ethnic lines. Fistfights settled the most pressing disputes between rival gangs or members within a gang, and in general, the gang members were little more than delinquents. According to one ex-gang member, the majority of youngsters dropped out of gangs around the age of fifteen or sixteen to go to work or return to school.

For some, though, the rough streets provided an array of illegal enterprises that offered, as one Italian immigrant noted, "the chance to make money without working." Those inclined to crime as a profession often joined bands of older youths that mimicked the adult gangs of New York City—essentially serving a form of internship. A stepping stone for ambitious youngsters around the turn of the twentieth century was to join the South Brooklyn Rippers or the junior affiliate of the Five Points Gang, whose members could be as young as eleven. If they proved their worth there, they frequently graduated to the more virulent adult gangs.

The Five Points Gang of Lower Manhattan was one of New York's most promi-nent street gangs. Its members were always on the lookout for up-and-coming young talent to replace those who had fallen in inter-gang battles over rights to control extortion, prostitution, or gambling. Youngsters knew these illicit enterprises pro-duced abundant and easy money and were avenues to requiring respect. As one youngster from the era later observed, "We all knew what a big-time crook was, and most of us looked up to them." Many of Nitto's later acquaintances gradually filtered through some similar process, showing sufficient proficiency in physical brutality, viciousness, or organizational wit to achieve celebrity.

When Nitto actually got his start in crime or how long he may have tramped about the Navy Yard streets is not documented. One reporter who later attempted to trace Nitto's extracurricular activities stated that the youngster may have embarked on his criminal career with an unnamed gang of prowlers. More specifi-cally, according to Brooklyn historian William Balsamo, Frank Nitto's juvenile gang career began with the original Navy Street Boys, a group of mostly neighborhood Italian youths who stirred up minor mischief and did occasional favors for the "big guys." The youth gang, however, was not unruly enough to draw police attention, or perhaps its members had enough clout to remain off the blotters, for no police records of their escapades remain.

The dark-haired, dreary-eyed Nitto, though slight of build, apparently did not lack temper, ferocity, or the willingness to involve himself in a street brawl, as he eventually came to demonstrate as leader of the group. By then, the Capone boys would enter the picture.

⸺◦◦◦⸺

On January 17, 1899, just ten days shy of Nitto's thirteenth birthday and only a block away (at 95 Navy Street), Theresa Capone gave birth to her fourth son, Alphonse (Al). The event and the Capone family's proximity to the Dolendo-Nitto clan gave rise to a genealogical exaggeration which may have aided both Capone and Nitto later in life when contemporary reporters stated the two men were cousins. In fact they were not, but they did share a sense of la famiglia. Both fami-lies shared similar tribulations on their journeys from Italy to America, and both lived in close proximity in Brooklyn. Three weeks after Alphonse's birth, the Capones bundled the infant off to St. Michael the Archangel Church to be bap-tized—by the same Father Gioachino (now Joseph) Garofalo who had married Nitto's sister to Vincenzo Vollaro.

Soon afterward, the Capones moved to an apartment at 69 Park Avenue, just a couple of blocks around the corner from their Navy Street abode, where Gabriele Capone opened a barbershop downstairs to support his family. Given the relatively small number of Italians who lived near the Navy Yard at the time, it is possible that Nitto may have heard of the oldest Capone sons, six-year-old Vincenzo (known as James or Jim) and five-year-old Raffaele (called Ralph), and eventually teamed up with them on the streets. In a couple of years, Salvatore (Frank) would join them, as would a very young Alphonse.

Brooklyn historian William Balsamo confirms that "Nitti hung around the older Capone boys Vincenzo and Salvatore" and much later with Al as a tag-along, the "mascot" of the group because of his age. It is perhaps because the Capone name is attached to it that the only surviving account of Nitto's early gang career exists. The date was probably around 1903-05, in the waning years of Nitto's term on the streets and at a time when local Irish toughs thought it an amusing pastime to taunt anyone who got in their way, particularly newcomers to America. Balsamo recounts the story of a woman who grew up in the Navy Street area at the time:

> One day a local Irish thug pulls the skirt of Rocky Mangano'a aunt as she is walking down the street. That night Nitto gets the boys together in front of the Capones' at 69 Park Avenue next to the doorway of the barbershop. Mangano, Nitto, Nitto's brother Lolly, Vincenzo and Salvatore Capone, and the rest of the Navy Street Boys including a young Alphonse. They got together pulling slats off nearby picket fences for weapons. They borrow one of the Capones' metal wash basins for battle and strap it to young Al. Theresa Capone sees the meet, so the boys put the pickets on their shoulders like soldiers and Al beats the basin to pretend a marching parade.
>
> The Navy Street Boys march over to Tommy's Bar on Sands Street knowing the Irish they were looking for hung out there. Along the way a German boy named Knapp who hung around with them sees the procession, gets his bugle, an heirloom from the Civil War, and marches with them. They stop in front of the bar and begin making noise, blowing the bugle and beating the basin all the while singing, *"We are the boys of Navy Street, touch us if you dare!"* The Irish guys come out and have words with Nitto. Nitto cracks the offender over the head and begins fighting. Nitto kicks the shit out of him all the while mentioning the Mangano dress incident and further picking on the Chinese coolies and cutting their ponytails.

If accurate, the story illustrates Nitto's early character, curiously upholding the pride of not only the local Italians but also other local inhabitants targeted by the Irish toughs. Rallying the youthful troops into action, he demonstrated leadership, a lack of prejudice, and tolerance of diversity; it appears he cast off his Old World baggage.

After his exploits with the Navy Street Boys, however, Nitto's early gang career dead-ends. Later reports would describe him as an established member of the notorious Five Points Gang in "good standing," a prime endorsement for any ruffian wishing to move up the ranks of organized crime, yet Nitto apparently never was a climber in New York. He is not mentioned in any New York gang histories. The Five Points Gang was by this time on the decline after years of warfare had reduced its ranks, and it is for this reason that federal investigators later doubted that Nitto had advanced any further in the gang. For Nitto, the Navy Street Boys were apparently nothing more than an outlet for juvenile hooliganism that he apparently outgrew.

Instead of committing crimes, he continued to engage in honest work to support himself and the Dolendo family.

The economic status of the Dolendo-Nitto household hardly appeared to improve, however, and it's not surprising that certain bonds among the family members began to disintegrate. Frank's sister Anna Vollaro would occasionally stop by Navy Street with her brood for a visit with mother Rosina—Anna's Old World habits apparently never wavered. Anna likewise remained devoted to her brother Frank, and he reciprocated in kind for years.

On the other hand, the Nitto-Dolendo relationship declined into disagreement. Though Nitto gave no explanation for the troubles, their root cause is not difficult to surmise. The family was by now a Dolendo unit of four plus one Nitto, and stepfather and junk collector Francesco Dolendo's inability to support the brood probably inspired little Old World respect in the nearly twenty-year-old Frank, who had obtained much more respectable employment (Nitto toiled in several small Brooklyn factories, none very far from either the Dolendo or Vollaro homes). That his stepson could obtain decent jobs which he could not must have been a stinging blow to Dolendo's Old World pride, as was the fact that the young Nitto had become a major, if not the main, contributor to the family's livelihood. As a result, Dolendo surely lost any aura of authority he might have had over his stepson.

The members of the family increasingly must have seemed like strangers to Nitto, whose only blood tie to the clan was through his mother. And the running dispute with his stepfather no doubt intensified when Francesco Dolendo finally obtained a respectable job a couple of years later. The strain proved too much for even Rosina to resolve, and Nitto finally left the Dolendo household for good. After exiting the Dolendo home, Nitto claims he moved in with his sister's family. When the Vollaros moved away from the Brooklyn dock neighborhoods, they rented a house in the Park Slope neighborhood at 17 Garfield Place, just off Fourth Avenue and a mile south of the Dolendos' Navy Street address. Four years later, the Vollaros moved to 34 Garfield Place, and in 1907 they shuffled back down the street to 19 Garfield Place. The only available census record shows no trace of Nitto there either, but sister and brother were close. At about the same time Nitto obtained a job in shoe factory not very far from Garfield Place, possibly upon recommendation of the Vollaros, both of whom were then in the shoe business.

However long Nitto lived with his sister's family, the span is certainly worth mentioning. In 1907, the Capones, now a family of eight, moved from the Navy Street area to 21 Garfield Place, shifting later to No. 38. They lived just a few houses away from the Vollaro family for quite some time, which perhaps provided Nitto with the opportunity to expand his social contacts with the older Capone boys. Jim had recently run away from home (the family would not hear from him again for more than forty years), but Frank and Ralph, now in their teens, were still around and beginning to pursue various moneymaking efforts. Just two blocks north, at the corner of Fourth Avenue and Union Street, was the headquarters of up-and-coming hoodlum Johnny Torrio, the gilt letters on a window facing the street proclaiming "The Johnny Torrio Association." The business and its activities evidently made little impression on Nitto and the others; they were older now and had pretty much outgrown their tendencies toward waywardness.

Al, however, nearing the age of ten, was different. Perhaps it was his earlier stint with the Navy Street Boys, or perhaps Torrio and the glitz of his nearby club influenced his decision, but young Al began to gravitate toward crime as a profession. When Torrio left town circa 1909, it was his friend Frankie Yale who introduced Al to the South Brooklyn Rippers and later, more significantly, to the Forty Thieves Juniors. When his toughness was confirmed, Capone was initiated into a senior Brooklyn gang under the tutelege of Yale while working a humble bar job for his criminal tutor. He now stood on the first rung of the gangland career ladder.

Nitto probably remained only a short time with his sister. The Garfield Place apartment was becoming cramped; by 1910, Anna and Vincenzo's brood numbered seven, with another on the way. Nearing the age of twenty-four and detached from the Dolendo clan, he had no wife, no one of any real importance to him except his sister, and he was working a string of ordinary jobs. There was really nothing for him in New York City, and so, simulating Jim Capone's earlier exodus from the city, Francesco Nitto left Brooklyn circa 1910—destination unknown.

2

AN ENIGMATIC
CHICAGO GENESIS

FRANCESCO NITTO'S MOVEMENTS FOR THE decade immediately after his departure from his family in Brooklyn are nothing less than wraith-like and are mostly lost to time. Reporters never asked Nitto later of his whereabouts during this period, and it isn't likely that he would have volunteered such information—he never really talked to the press and very few direct quotes from him ever made it into print. Further, he never detailed this period of his life when dealing with various governmental agencies, and they didn't seem to think it was particularly important. The Federal Bureau of Investigation and its predecessors obtained some information, but even after almost seventy years, it will not share what it learned. Perhaps his sister Anna knew where he was, yet she was apparently never called upon to reveal that or any other information about him, which was odd since federal authorities knew of their kinship. Journalists, however, seemed to be ignorant of that fact and left Anna alone.

On only one occasion was Nitto officially required to account for his whereabouts during this time period, but corroborating information is scarce and sometimes conflicts with his statements. For example, Nitto said that he stayed with his sister in Brooklyn until at least 1918 or 1919, but this is almost certainly not true; no documentation exists to suggest he was there anytime after 1910. He is not listed as a resident at any of the Vollaro addresses on the U.S. Census in 1910 and 1920, the New York State Census in 1905 and 1915, or in any of the city directories. Circumstances suggest otherwise as well—Anna's family included eleven children by 1918. If Nitto was in New York City as he claimed, he must have remained there somehow undetected as an itinerant local resident or perhaps as an in-and-out-of-town floater.

On two other official occasions much later, Nitto claims to have been much farther west, in Chicago, Illinois, during this time. In one instance, he gives December
1913 as his arrival date there, while in the other, he claims residence there possibly
as early as 1911. Supporting his claim of Chicago residence, two later acquaintances
independently testified to his presence in the city since 1913, and at least one
reporter noted a Chicago arrival about that time. However, another reporter said
Nitto arrived in Chicago in 1919 or 1920, after Capone. Unfortunately, just as with
New York City, no city or state records exist to indicate his presence there, and the
federal census turns up empty. Given the time frame, war records might reveal Nitto's
whereabouts, but there is no evidence he served this country during World War I, nor
was he in the service at any other time. Although he was an alien (neither Nitto nor
his mother evidently became U.S. citizens), he did fill out a draft registration card just
two months before the armistice was signed in September 1918. Still, in spite of
sparse evidence, there are enough clues to confirm his 1913 Chicago claim and at
least restore a historical watermark to Nitto's life picture during this period.

Remarkably, from 1900 in New York until 1918 in Chicago, the only location where
Nitto can be unquestionably documented is Dallas, Texas, in the autumn of 1917.
There, he occupied one of two apartments at 902 Evergreen Street for perhaps no
more than a month or two with a Russian woman of vague origins who was at least
a year his senior. This temporary sojourn resulted in Nitto's first marriage. In a simple civil ceremony performed by Justice of the Peace S. J. Barnett on Thursday,
October 18, 1917, thirty-three-year-old Frank Nitto married Rosa (Rose) Levitt,
sometimes known as Levy. The newlyweds, however, vanished soon thereafter and
reappeared in Chicago at 914 South Halsted in late 1918.

The obvious question arises: how did Italian native and Brooklynite Frank Nitto
end up getting married in Texas? Could there have been another reason besides mat-
rimony, such as an employment opportunity, for Nitto to be in Dallas? Located forty-
five miles south of Oklahoma and nestled in the heart of cotton country, yet near the
Gulf Coast, southern railroads naturally converged on Dallas at the time. Here, agriculture—particularly cotton—was king, and its economic peak was still not realized by
the time of Nitto's appearance. Railroad construction was also booming, luring many
nationalities including the Italians. Further, a short trip along the tracks to the southeast led to several growing Gulf Coast harbor communities like the warm-water port
of Galveston, which was in its building heyday. New Orleans also attracted immigrants
of all ethnicities. It was here on the coast of the Gulf of Mexico that many southern
Italians gained familiar employment as fisherman or longshoreman, while others peddled fish and fruits in the streets or at the markets. Eventually, a few made fortunes.

The adaptability and ambition of some immigrants to succeed in the face of the
often trying circumstances of their early days in America were remarkable. Nitto's
probable acquaintance from Brooklyn, James Capone, ran away from his family as a
teenager prior to Nitto's own departure. When he returned to his family much later,
James said he worked in the circus and traveled throughout the U.S. before landing

in one of the most unlikely of states for a city dweller—Nebraska. Another later and much younger Nitto associate, also from Brooklyn, joined a traveling theatrical troupe which toured through remote corners of Texas and California.

Nitto's motives for being in Dallas may never be known, but obtaining employment seemed to be no problem in New York, and the agricultural South appears distinctly out of character for Frank Nitto. He was not new to America and was twenty-plus years inured to the big-city environment when he married. Furthermore, the Dallas city directory for the years prior to and including 1917 fail to reveal either Nitto or his bride, and their names do not appear in the directories of other Texas cities or in any census listings. Such invisibility was not uncommon for many Italians prior to and during the war years, as employment in the transient railroad and construction sectors kept many workers from cities or towns for long periods of time and did not permit them to register to vote or maintain a permanent address. Still, this sort of transient construction work appears to be out of the ordinary for urbanite Nitto, who was used to more humdrum, less labor-intensive factory tasks. He may have been down south for some sort of economic opportunity, but it was probably of a variety far from the agriculture field and whose origins were perhaps in another location. In any event, evidence and conditions generally rule out a long-term residency in Dallas or any other part of Texas.

Nitto may have shifted around the country in search of fresh employment opportunities during the decade, but thoughts of marriage suggest some type of stable residence somewhere. Closer scrutiny of the woman he married and her background might provide the answer, but almost nothing is known of Rose Levitt in these years. Only one reporter in Nitto's time wrote about this marriage, but no details, not even her name, were given in the account. A lawyer who later handled her affairs recalled that she was Russian, ostensibly Jewish, a year or so older than Nitto, and may have been from New York City. It is possible that the pair met on the East Coast, for when Nitto worked along the Williamsburg shorefront in Brooklyn, immigrants, particularly those of the Jewish faith, were increasingly settling in the area. Still, it is quite unlikely that he and Rose met while in New York. By Nitto's account, he worked in the Williamsburg area somewhere between 1900 and 1911, but he was likely absent from Brooklyn by 1905 and was almost certainly gone by 1910. Thus, this narrows the possible employment period at Williamsburg to the years from 1900 to 1905. Even if he had maintained his residency with the Dolendo family undetected until 1911 and worked in Williamsburg, six years would pass before their wedding. Would or could the pair really carry on a romance that long before marriage?

Cultural obstacles tend to discredit the theory as well. Generally, Nitto's early Brooklyn haunts were not necessarily congenial to courting someone so far removed from his own ethnicity. He was no stranger to the strong antagonisms among the various groups of immigrants and knew very well that strict Old World influences dominated many households, producing an unfavorable atmosphere for such a mixed marriage. In time, these barriers were overcome when, for example, some men in the first American-raised generation of Italians eventually married Irish women. In Brooklyn, the Irish lived in close proximity to Italians, and such unions were strengthened because the two nationalities shared a common faith. On the other hand, a Nitto-Levitt connection would appear irregular here since there were few Russians in the immediate area. Further, due to the distinct sets of beliefs and traditions of the families involved, the marriage of a Catholic Italian man to a Jewish Russian woman would raise serious protests among family members from the old country.

Outside of a possible chance meeting in Williamsburg, there is no solid evidence to link Nitto and Levitt together in New York City. Even if Nitto had been an anonymous member of the New York populous, had he hooked up with Levitt after 1910 or so, they could have conveniently married and avoided domestic disapproval by quietly settling down in any New York or nearby New Jersey location. So why, then, should Nitto elope to Texas? Economic opportunity in the East was plentiful and the surroundings familiar, so why chase a job and marry in a dusty cotton town in Texas, seemingly miles away from anything traditional at the time, even if they wished to maintain some anonymity? It simply doesn't add up. Both Frank and Rose may have been from New York City, but a meeting there appears dubious at best.

Where, when, and how, then, did Nitto come to meet Rose Levitt? Chicago represents a more agreeable and calculating draw for urbanite Nitto during this transitory period than any dusty Texas locale. In 1913, Chicago was still ballooning economically and physically, and opportunities there were plentiful, especially for the type of light work to which Nitto was more accustomed. Most important, Chicago demographically provided a more suitable environment for meeting his first spouse than Brooklyn. From 1890 to 1910, the city's foreign-born population had increased by over 300,000, and as in New York, many of these new immigrants were of southern and eastern European origin, i.e., Poles, Russians, Greeks, and southern Italians.

As in many other metropolitan areas, the newcomers settled into exclusive enclaves, but in Chicago these groups settled close to one another, particularly the Russians, Greeks, and Italians. The fringes of their societies enmeshed in such a way that a hostel full of Russians might be right next door to a Italian boarding house. Across the street might be Greeks, and either the Italian or Jewish communities might be a block away in one direction or the other. As one resident of the time, Samuel Paynter Wilson, commented, "No city on the continent is so thoroughly American as this." He saw Chicago as a place where younger generations of foreigners lost Old World habits and ideas in such a way that others see "them as genuine and devoted Americans as any in the city." Three years prior to Nitto's 1913 arrival Wilson observed: "Chicago is to the West what New York is to the East. It is not only the Great Metropolis of the western states, but is the chief attraction upon this continent, the greater center to which our people resort for business, and pleasure, and as such, is a source of never-failing interest." New York and Chicago are strikingly similar giants, but it was unquestionably the city of the west that drew Nitto in and likely provided both the setting for him to meet Rose Levitt and the formula for his future calling.

Nitto arrived in Chicago in 1913. His choices for a place to live were generally limited to either the city's racy First Ward or its Nineteenth Ward hellhole. This had been the case for at least the past twenty years for many Italians, partially due to the fact that there were prospects for work in both wards, perhaps more so in the First Ward. Convenience also fueled the decision. Chicago, though long a commercial rail center, lacked a principal station for detraining rail passengers, as Nitto may have been. By the time of Nitto's arrival in the city, passengers might arrive at either the North West Station, completed in 1911 and located west of the Chicago River, or Dearborn Station, made of rose-colored stone and serving as a drop-off point for rail traffic just south of the Loop. From these stations, new arrivals made their way to the hospitable confines of nearby ethnic areas much as they did in New York when they arrived via ocean steamers, and the First Ward blocks directly east of Dearborn Station initially contained the heaviest concentration of Italians in the city.

Until 1890, Chicago's First Ward generally embraced the area south of the Chicago River where it joined Lake Michigan down to the 1200 block at Roosevelt Road and from the lakefront west to the South Branch of the Chicago River. Later, legislation shifted its southern frontier to Twenty-ninth Street and, in a few places, to Thirty-first Street. Most importantly, the city's most notorious vice districts always remained within its bounds. Foremost among them was the Levee. Here, for forty years, two aldermen—the flamboyantly dressed, buff, hearty John Coughlin and the diminutive, calculating, and piercing Mike Kenna—would cement all First Ward departments of immorality into one alliance so that all could be exploited to their benefit.

A few Italians prospered here under their aegis, one of whom was perhaps the most significant Italian ward icon of the time, James "Big Jim" Colosimo. He landed in the First Ward as a strapping youth before the turn of the century and employed himself in various honest labors before dabbling on the other side of the law as a pickpocket and minor pimp. Perhaps after a close brush with the law, he returned to honest work, this time as a member of the district's street sweepers. He astutely organized that group into a social and athletic club, and at election time he delivered their block of votes to Coughlin and Kenna. In return, the duo appointed Colosimo precinct captain, a position that virtually insulated him from legal trouble, convenient since at about that time he married a plump bawdyhouse madame and managed her house.

Eventually, Colosimo's ambition lifted him to the position of lead spokesman and bagman for the vice district. All paid him tribute and delivered their votes to the aldermen, and everyone profited handsomely. Increasingly wealthy and a major power within the Kenna-Coughlin machine, Big Jim's headquarters were in a recently opened plush café, aptly named Colosimo's, in the heart of the Levee district at 2126-2128 South Wabash.

The residential attraction of the First Ward for Italians had largely diminished, though, by the time of Nitto's arrival. Gradual commercial and industrial development around Dearborn Station forced a shift—a few residents went north, while the bulk headed westward across the South Branch of the Chicago River into the

Nineteenth Ward. This precinct was bounded to the east by the river, to the north by Van Buren Drive, to the south by West Twelfth Street, and to the west by Throop Street (in 1914 most of the western boundary shifted farther west to Hermitage Avenue). The main Italian community or Little Italy emerged here, centered in the area between Halsted Street on the west and the Chicago River to the east and between Taylor Street and Polk Street to the north and south, respectively. Here, Italians were chiefly from the southern mainland, unlike those smaller colonies north of the Chicago River on Wells Street (whose residents chiefly hailed from Genoa and Lucca) and in "Little Hell" around Oak Street (where the residents were primarily from Sicily).

The local potentate of the Nineteenth was Alderman John "Johnny De Pow" Powers. Thoroughly corrupt and possessing gruff physical features accentuated by bushy eyebrows and a thick, walrus-like mustache, Powers (with his First Ward associates) typified a comment made at the time by one resident who thought he could put his finger on the source of the city's foul smell, claiming Chicago's politicians had as much to do with it as the city's famed stockyards. An Irishman in a predominantly Irish ward, Powers used his saloon proprietorship as the stepping stone to a political career when he was elected alderman in the late 1880s. Powers's rise to prominence in the city council ranks was swift and complete, his rule thereafter absolute.

His election coincided with one of the greatest orgies of council graft in Chicago history, the 1890s. During this decade, roads were being built and paved, lighting was installed, and subways and elevated train lines were constructed. Powers finagled his way into the dominant position in the city council, from which he ruthlessly refined his grafting technique so that all who wished to benefit from a project could do so with minimum quarrel. Often, his methods included selling the same favors more than once to more than one interested party, but always with Powers in control to avoid aldermanic in-house disputes. Even if another alderman was against such graft, he often voted with the majority out of necessity. The most recalcitrant and honest aldermen were bluntly warned by Powers, "Either you go along with us, or you won't get a can of garbage moved out of your ward till hell freezes over." And most knew he could make good on such threats.

Besides enriching himself appreciably through city council shenanigans, Powers improved his financial standing through shady activities within his Nineteenth Ward as a gambling boss. Powers, along with the other ward alderman, ran a gambling dive above his Nineteenth Ward saloon, and he naturally protected gambling and vice within his district. Though his ward lacked the advertised raunchiness of the neighboring First Ward, it did contain a concentrated vice district known as the West Side Levee in the area of Sangamon, Green, and Morgan streets, later to be moved to the safe haven along Thirty-first Street farther south. Gamblers, prostitutes, and others could operate in the district for a price—set by Powers. One contemporary investigating Chicago vice claimed the price list rated protection fees as follows: $50 a month for gambling houses; $50-$200 for houses of prostitution; and $100 for saloon licenses, which were under the direct control of the alderman of each ward.

Preoccupied with making money, Powers often neglected his ward's social needs, and community conditions, for the most part, remained dreadful. Thoroughfares and lighting were in disrepair, trash and garbage overflowed from collection boxes into the streets, and accommodations in this part of the Nineteenth Ward were described as "some of the worst housing in the city." Even after the Great Fire, more than half of the houses facing the street here were frame rather than brick, with the ratio as high as four to one on some streets. Many of the tenements were dark, stagnant, teetering, two- or three-story-high edifices, often without plumbing and always overcrowded. Each floor typically contained two apartments of four rooms each which were shared by multiple families who lived and slept in shifts. Nearby lots reeked of poor sanitation. For those who were not fortunate enough to rent one of these hovels, numerous boarder lodgings or hotels that probably offered little more in comfort dotted the ward's main streets. Fold into this mix crime in the form of the numerous individual Black Hand extortionists (not the Mafia) threatening mayhem against store owners, street peddlers, and newcomers.

It was into this milieu that Frank Nitto, with few belongings, arrived. It hardly looked like the favorable beginning he was seeking—from the slums of Brooklyn to the slums of Chicago, one wretched hole to another. Mere survival was his early priority, but from this stew, people instrumental to his progress would gradually surface.

Initially, his work must have been humble, just enough to pay rent and survive. There are no indications that he came to Chicago for anything other than a lawful job; no police records from either end of the New York-Chicago connection indicate otherwise. During these first Chicago years, some have suggested he fell back upon the barbering skills he possessed as a dependable means of survival. Though never licensed as a barber, as required by the State of Illinois, Nitto could likely ply the trade without any real threat from officials as long as he shifted from shop to shop. In particular, as he may have observed in Brooklyn, demand for Italian barbers like himself seemed insatiable in the big cities, and Chicago was no exception where, as far back as 1871, barbering ranked among the top occupations of Italian-born residents. Italians were a "people thought to possess some special gift for snipping hair, patronized by all." Though monetary rewards may have been small, there was no better place to network among influential persons than the neighborhood barbershop.

Where he actually plied the barbering trade is unknown, but it is likely that he originally worked alongside another Italian somewhere in the Nineteenth Ward. Nitto himself credited three barbers as employers: Luigi Esposito of 849 West Taylor Street, resident and barber at least since 1910; Richard Russo of 850 South Halsted since at least 1914; and Nate Romano at 852 South Halsted. Another barber who was critical to his introduction to Chicago was Mack Ronga, resident of 904 West Taylor and possible relative of one of the most respected of Nitto's later Chicago acquaintances. All these men were mere doors away from each other, allowing Nitto to canvass them quite conveniently.

Working chairs within shops naturally afforded Nitto the opportunity to meet and quickly become familiar with many locals, and he established lifelong friendships and associations throughout the community. Besides Esposito, Russo, and Romano, with whom he maintained acquaintance at least through the following decade, another confidant in his earliest Chicago years who was roughly the same age as Nitto and was almost certainly a future employer was Joseph Vicedomini. A half block south of Russo's barbershop on Halsted, Vicedomini operated the Dante Theatre, a small neighborhood show house whose clientele was almost exclusively Italian and whose location changed in the succeeding years, though it was always near the intersection of Halsted and Taylor. Here, dusty *pisans* took in the latest silent films, a temporary reprieve from the everyday stress and misery of the streets. Additionally, Vicedomini and his two brothers sometimes operated a restaurant in the same vicinity. Whether the two first met as Nitto snipped his hair or patronized his nickelodeon or restaurant, the two would become close enough for Vicedomini to act as a witness on some of Nitto's legal documents and to allow Nitto to use him as a personal reference years later.

Not all of Nitto's valued associates were Italian, however. Just as in Brooklyn, the neighborhood around South Halsted and West Taylor streets harbored an ethnic mix, but here, the groups seemed to be more receptive to each other. The Nineteenth Ward, in which the Italian community was the majority at the time, included significant German and Irish populations. To his credit, Nitto allowed little of the Old World suspicion or bias to interfere with his finances or his social acquaintances, and he almost immediately began what proved to be a long-term relationship with a German couple, the Gottloebs.

More momentously for him, newer immigrants to Chicago—the Eastern Europeans, Russians, and Greeks—increasingly infiltrated the ward, filling vacancies directly in and around the Italian community, including the city ward just to the south where, by 1914, the Russian population was second only in number to the Italians. Sprinkled throughout the vicinity of the Esposito and Russo barbershops, particularly on Halsted south of the 900 block, were entire tenements of Russians, and just four blocks further along the main Halsted trolley line to the south at Maxwell Street was the hub of the Eastern European Jewish quarter. Given the close positioning of these groups, Nitto couldn't avoid interaction with people of various ethnicities, and some individuals from these communities made as much impact on his life at this time as any Italian.

Nitto's first barbering job, according to *Chicago Sun-Times* writer Dale Harrison many years later, was performed beside a Russian youth named John "Jake" Factor in a shop owned by the Factor family. Maybe this is the case. The Factors (originally Factorovitz) came from a small village near Warsaw in what was then Czarist Russia. The family was large; Jake was the youngest of ten children, a brood that included a much older half-brother, Max. The brothers would progress through life in notably opposite directions. Eventually, most of the family landed in Chicago. They, like many of their countryman, were inclined to settle within the mayhem of humanity on South Halsted near Maxwell Street. Jake's early Chicago résumé included employment as a newspaper vendor, a bootblack, a washroom attendant, and, somewhere along the line, a brief stint as a barber. One story surfaced that his family possessed a shop on Halsted for which Jake only ran errands. His later and lasting sobriquet, "Jake the Barber," appears to have been the result of creatively "clipping" individuals of their coins at least as much as whatever minor barbering duties he may have performed. (He later graduated to phony stock schemes and real estate deals.) Conceivably, though, as Nitto surveyed the local streets in search of a job, he may have tumbled into one where he worked a chair alongside Jake.

Nonetheless, one noteworthy Russian remembered the Italian barbering in a shop farther north near the vicinity of Centre Street (now Racine) and McAllister Place (now Lexington), four blocks west of Halsted but still well within the Nineteenth Ward. The residents here were, more often than not, well-established American citizens, and their housing was among the trendiest within the ward. Residential property sold at an exorbitant $100 per foot of frontage. Due to the higher rents and property values, only a few established and affluent immigrants could settle here—a couple of Russians, the longtime Irish ward boss Johnny Powers at 1284 McAllister, and just down the block near Centre Street, an Italian doctor. The shop where Nitto worked at 712 South Centre was Italian owned, but Russians were certainly part of the clientele.

The noteworthy Russian patron remembers Nitto as "a very good barber," and the two quickly became friends. The customer, an up-and-coming saloonkeeper, later a financial and real estate investor occasionally on the periphery of some shady transactions, was most certainly the common denominator linking Nitto to most of his early non-Italian associations. In fact, he served as the catalyst in Nitto's career, instigating financial opportunity and providing for a long-term fiduciary, personal, and business relationship. In turn, his association with Nitto allowed him to tap into his future gang affiliation. Thus, throughout Nitto's life, he was perhaps more important than even the biggest man in Chicago, Al Capone. Further, he may very well have been the intermediary connecting Nitto to Rosa Levitt. The man was Alex Louis Greenberg.

⚜

Alex Louis Greenberg claimed a rags-to-riches life story, beginning as a near-penniless young immigrant and ending with him described as a millionaire in some newspapers at the time of his death. During his lifetime he came to know many of the important gang figures in Chicago, even those on opposites sides of the battlefield, such as Dean O'Banion and Al Capone. For them, Greenberg handled great sums of money, eventually figuring into the major tax-evasion cases of several gang members in 1930-31. In several of the showcase trials of Chicago gangsterdom during the 1940s, he was called as an identifying witness. During the early 1950s, Estes Kefauver thought Greenberg was prominent enough to call him as a witness for his proceedings into organized crime during a trip to Chicago.

Greenberg seemingly was always on the periphery of the law and often in the proximity of hoods, though he was not a hood himself and was not even physically menacing. He stood just five feet, seven inches tall, weighed perhaps 150 pounds, and possessed dopey yet gruff facial features. He definitely did not fit the hoodlum stereotype, but financially he was as big as any of them.

As Greenberg told the story, he hopped off a ship in New York with no more than a few cents, left New York a short time later, and ultimately arrived in Chicago with approximately $10,000. A good tale, but not quite true. Alex Louis Greenberg, son of Jacob, was born in Yanove, Russia, in 1891. In April 1906, while Nitto was leading the Navy Street Boys into mischief, Greenberg, at age fourteen, shipped off alone to New York City via the port of Bremen, Germany. Settling in Brooklyn with an uncle, he may have worked briefly as a machinist, but it seems doubtful that he would have had such skill at such a young age. He did, however, work two to three years at his uncle's restaurant near Coney Island as a manager, claiming enough of, as he called it, "a percentage" to eventually save a couple of thousand dollars. A later writer apparently took the term *percentage* as a euphemism for stealing, opining that the uncle, supposedly after finding his profits missing, proceeded to kick Greenberg out of the business; however, there is no substantiation for this account. At any rate, it's highly unlikely that he saved any significant amount of cash, and for whatever reasons, Greenberg left New York with no more than a few coins, arriving on Chicago's West Side in 1909 or 1910 to visit another uncle and some cousins who ran a small retail shop there.

Greenberg's long-term career was not within the family shop, and his stay there must have been fleeting. Perhaps he was dishonest, his reputation preceding him, but regardless, what his family did not fully realize was his concentrated resolve not only to survive but also prosper. While his family toiled on the West Side, Greenberg independently settled across the river in the Market and Van Buren Street area of the First Ward, working first in the restaurant business and later in a workingman's saloon. Here, he started as a swamper or porter, the lowest and sloppiest rung in the saloon hierarchy. In exchange for mopping floors, cleaning spittoons, and performing general janitorial duties, he received room, board, and meals. In time, Greenberg proved himself capable for promotion to the positions of bartender and part-time cook, serving meals and drinks to the working stiffs after shifts. All the while, patrons' tips provided his only real cash.

Not surprisingly, Greenberg looked for other avenues to increase his personal wealth. Fortunately for him, he eventually made the acquaintance of Samuel J. "Nails" Morton (born Markowitz). At the time, a youthful Morton rallied together a tough group, a defense society of sorts, renowned in its efforts to defend community honor. Among their dignified communal deeds, however, Morton and company did not exclude enriching themselves through occasional use of thuggery. Such brutish behavior earned him later police notoriety as a suspect in several murders, including that of a policeman. Greenberg, though, was never mentioned as part of a Jewish gang or of any other gang, for that matter—he was too independent for such liaisons. He was not, however, above forming associations when it came to making money.

Significantly for Greenberg, he met an unlikely individual named Charles Dean O'Banion, who was short in stature and walked with a limp but was just as feral as any of Morton's thugs. O'Banion, twice transplanted from his birthplace of Aurora, Illinois, had grown up just north of the river in a small industrial patch called "Little

Hell" near the Sicilian enclave around Wells Street. Like many kids maturing in hell-holes, O'Banion soon took to the streets and, stature and noticeable limp notwithstanding, proved to be quite a ruffian with an erratic and vicious temper, a necessity for survival on the streets. As a youth, he hawked newspapers during the city's violent circulation wars.

Hardened by his exploits, O'Banion was later thought to have joined up with a marauding Market Street gang operating along the north branch of the river. With such hoodlums, he tuned his skills in relieving unfortunate drunks along the Clark Street Levee district of their cash and valuables by blackjacking and jackrolling, the preferred ruffian methods. Blackjacking involved slipping a grip device attached to an elongated piece of hard material around the hand and knocking the victim senseless from behind, usually in a dark alley between cramped buildings for concealment. Jackrolling the victim required a certain amount of finesse. One closed on his victim from behind and clamped a forearm around his throat while pinioning an arm and putting a knee in his back. After forcing the unfortunate to the ground and grinding his face into the pavement, the jackroller would relieve the dazed victim of any property and scamper off. Gang finishing school included perfecting the more advanced arts of larceny and armed holdups. By winter 1909, O'Banion, still just a teenager, earned his first term in jail, nine months for burglary of a local post office. Less than two years later, he was back in jail again, this time for assault.

How Greenberg and O'Banion hooked up is anyone's guess. Their meeting may have occurred after World War I when Greenberg, having already established himself on the North Side near O'Banion's haunts, accumulated enough wealth to begin a sideline business as a bond agent for local crooks, a service for which the Irishman seemed to have a constant need. An equally plausible story, and the one given more often, is that O'Banion's travels, either through his gang exploits or during one of his on-again, off-again ventures as a newspaper vendor, led him into the Maxwell Street domain of Nails Morton, where the two thugs immediately struck up a friendship based on unlawful exploits and remained allies throughout Morton's lifetime. Tagging along with O'Banion was a childhood friend, a lean and savage hoodlum named Earl Wojciechowski, a Catholic Pole who was known by the more Jewish-sounding name Hymie Weiss. As partners in crime, the two meandered through the Market Street area, sometimes slugging drunks, some of whom may have stumbled from the bar where Greenberg worked, for cash and valuables.

It was Morton who introduced Greenberg to O'Banion and Weiss while they were on one of their forays through Market Street. A colorful yarn suggests a chance encounter on the streets as Greenberg and O'Banion separately but simultaneously eyed an intoxicated patron teetering down a dark alley, an easy jackroll long after hours. To the intoxicated and unwary, neither O'Banion, with his soft features and his limp, nor Greenberg, a man of average size, looked threatening, which made them all the more successful. However they met, the alliance of the two created a business relationship that was to last not just for a few sporadic sluggings but for well over a decade. They split the take on jobs, with O'Banion, the action man, taking the cash, and Greenberg, the fence, keeping the valuables. The arrangement, apparently an equitable one, was witnessed by Weiss and provided Greenberg with the extra capital he longed for while he maintained his legitimate saloon job.

Greenberg was quickly on his way to building a nest egg from his moonlighting as a thug, fencing stolen jewelry for good hard cash. And while O'Banion and Weiss continued to pursue careers of contemptuous lawlessness, for Greenberg, any illegal extracurricular messiness such as hooliganism was apparently a temporary means to a more enriching and somewhat more respectable end. Greenberg strived for more than just a barkeeping job—he desired a saloon of his own. But first he had to clear several hurdles. In addition to startup costs such as rent for the first month and cash for the beer and whiskey, such a privilege as saloon ownership in the First Ward required sanction from the powers to be—in this case, the politicos Kenna and Coughlin. The pair was sought out, and in exchange for the saloon authorization, of course, Greenberg was expected to deliver votes to the appropriate First Ward political candidates as well as provide beat cops with a free lunch and the desk sergeant with a $2 retainer each week. Not yet twenty-one years of age, Greenberg selected a hole-in-the-wall location on Market Street just north of Van Buren for his grand opening.

Greenberg quickly turned the saloon into a success, in part by greatly reducing costs, purchasing stolen liquor and supplies at half price. At the same time, he continued to enjoy the company of Morton, O'Banion, and Weiss; and the group may have continued for a short time to jackroll drunks from Greenberg's bar, splitting the take equally. With a small accumulation of cash from his businesses, Greenberg was said to have started a loan sharking operation on the side, the real basis for his future success and a career for which he apparently was well-suited—a contemporary described him as "the kind of man one felt comfortable coming to for a favor." Though congenial and easily approachable in his saloon, the standard weekly street rate of 20 percent or $5 for $6 in interest was apparently not difficult to collect since Greenberg could occasionally call on ruffians O'Banion and Weiss to assist in collections. Later, with both the bar and the loan sharking enterprise highly successful, Greenberg branched into the bail bond business—a perfect fit for him since the individuals with whom he associated had an inherent need for this service.

In 1912 Greenberg married a Romanian woman five years his junior, and by the next year the couple had become a family of three with the addition of a baby girl. Also around that time, he resided near McAllister Place in the Nineteenth Ward, and his child was delivered by a prominent Nineteenth Ward Italian physician, Gaetano Ronga. Greenberg lived near the doctor's residence on McAllister near Centre Street, sometimes in the same buildings at either 1204 or 1208 McAllister, while tending to business in the Loop, where he continued to operate until 1914-15. By 1915, Greenberg had expanded his saloon venture and moved his family to 4346 North Lincoln Avenue near Montrose Avenue in the more pleasant neighborhood of the North Side. He still maintained his contacts on the West Side and, just as importantly, expanded his saloon business westward to include an operation in the newly developing, but not entirely Jewish, Lawndale community. Jake Factor may have lived right around the corner from the new saloon in Lawndale as well.

Greenberg, the now relatively well-off, immigrant saloon proprietor, probably encountered Frank Nitto in the barbershop at Centre and McAllister streets during the 1913-15 period.

The Nitto-Greenberg friendship sprouted quickly and rooted deeply in a very short period, and by 1915 Nitto was spending a considerable amount of time in Greenberg's North Side saloon. The trust between the two grew until Greenberg brought Nitto into a sideline business immensely more profitable than barbering, a break he really needed. Greenberg, still in contact with thugs O'Banion, Weiss, and Morton, was thought to have accumulated a significant amount of stolen valuables, mainly jewelry, that needed to be fenced. Nitto, as a barber with many public contacts within the shop, was thought an ideal distributor. At first Nitto may have worked with one or two customers, gathering a commission here or there on the side. After proving competent as an apprentice fence, Greenberg gave him more loot to dispose of. His work schedule included barbering by day and conducting jewelry transactions by night, and he maintained his daytime job in order to scout businesses and retain contacts for his night work. Nitto was now one of Greenberg's many business associates, and thanks to the business the Russians and Italians were conducting, this "thoroughly American" city was paying Nitto his first dividends.

Additional early rewards from Nitto's association with Greenberg included social acquaintances. In all likelihood, thanks either to his nearby barbering duties or his acquaintance with Greenberg, Nitto forged a lifelong affiliation with the tenant next door to Greenberg. Three doors west of Centre Street at 1204 McAllister, amidst a block of three-story gray stones, lived Dr. Gaetano Ronga. The doctor—dark, handsome, refined, and with a mild-mannered appearance—was one of the few Italians prosperous enough to be able to afford the pricey rents on McAllister Place.

Born in 1874 to a doctor's son in Nola, Italy, east of Naples, Ronga emigrated during the 1890s. In Chicago, Ronga graduated with an A.B. from the University of Chicago and later earned his M.D. at Rush Medical College. He set up shop in Chicago's Nineteenth Ward as a neighborhood physician at an address more convenient to the Italian masses than his more upscale McAllister home. Various rooms on Polk Street and Blue Island Avenue provided office space early on, but he later transferred his office closer to his home, perhaps at 1200 McAllister. This address was a three-story gray stone building with a ground floor entrance conveniently facing the corner of Centre Street as if intended for a neighborhood business of some sort, while the upstairs provided residential lodging.

In addition to being a physician, Ronga maintained a pharmacy with changing locations and various partners in the early years of his practice until 1915. These early medical services of his never seemed to stray far from the heart of the Italian community, always on or near Blue Island Avenue or around the intersection of Polk Street and Morgan. Just as he remained loyal to his community, Ronga's affiliation with Nitto was lifelong.

Undoubtedly, the most important social benefit Nitto derived from his alliance with Greenberg appears to be the introduction to his future wife, Rosie Levitt. There are many possible scenarios for their meeting, but it is impossible to say which scenario is true. The relationship may well have had its beginnings simply as a brief encounter as the pair's paths crisscrossed in the Nineteenth Ward, which was, as noted earlier, home to many Russians and Eastern Europeans. Rose, like Nitto, may have come to Chicago on her own and lived in one of several lodges or Russian-filled rooming houses in the well-traveled area around Halsted. It appears likely that Nitto was introduced to her, and any additional meetings between the couple may have been promulgated through other early Eastern European links of Nitto's. However, none of his associates had the consistent proximity to and enduring influence on Nitto that Louis Greenberg had.

How might Rosie Levitt and Alex Louis Greenberg have known one another? From 1915 through the early war years, Greenberg maintained his saloon on the West Side at Sixteenth Street and Lawndale Avenue. Though he hired a local man to manage his saloon there while he shuttled back and forth from the North Side and Market Street districts, Greenberg was quite familiar with those in the West Side community—several of his relatives lived no more than a couple of blocks from his Lawndale saloon, and he may have dropped in from time to time for a visit after making a business inspection.

Living with the Greenberg family at the same address were the Leavits, evidently close friends. Was Rose part of this family? Perhaps, or she may simply have been one of Greenberg's acquaintances from the neighborhood. It's not hard to believe that, with their shady business partnership cemented, Nitto and Greenberg established a more social relationship, and the then-married family man Greenberg might have concerned himself with thirty-one-year-old bachelor Nitto, now age thirty-one, and introduced him to family friend Rosie Levitt. Now able to support himself, Nitto would be an attractive matrimonial candidate, and his fortunes were about to improve further. Greenberg's saloon business was expanding to include shady liquor dealings which would eventually grow to interstate proportions, and he cut Nitto in for at least a small part of this business. This may be the most plausible explanation for Nitto's presence in Dallas and the mysterious marriage to Rose Levitt.

—◁/◁/◁—

With stokes of luck, there are also misfortunes.

Just how much Nitto was able to or desired to maintain contact with his family in Brooklyn is unknown. The Vollaros still shuffled from rental to rental about the Garfield Place and First Street neighborhoods, the moves made increasingly difficult by their numerous and still-growing brood. Nitto seems to have been equally nomadic, and it is therefore likely that he was unaware of extreme family events unfolding back east.

Ironically, just as Nitto's life showed signs of economic buoyancy, the mood suffusing the Dolendo family home as well as the home of his sister back in Brooklyn was quite the opposite. In 1914, Rose Dolendo's mental state declined rapidly. She was troubled by periods of acute, intense excitement, perhaps as result of the severe day-to-day strain of raising children in unremitting squalor combined with the knowledge that so many of her children did not survive. Stress of this nature was not an uncommon malady afflicting poor immigrant women of the time. Rose was apparently treated locally at first, and institutions in the heart of Brooklyn were regularly full in those years, with many patients suffering from similar ailments.

Despite therapy, she continued to decline. Late in the year, as an indicator of the gravity of her worsening condition, husband Frank Dolendo, now a fruit vendor, and her doctors elected to send her to the King's Park Hospital on a remote stretch of rural Long Island for treatment. Originally established by the City of Brooklyn on nearly eight hundred acres of meadowland, the first of three sprawling two- and three-story wooden structures opened to thirty-two male and twenty-three female patients in 1885. By the time Rose arrived, the complex had added several buildings, including a bakery, laundry, library, amusement hall, repair shops, solarium, and nursing school. A railroad spur directly on the grounds provided the hospital with its own locomotive and nursing car to import patients directly from the city. All the while, the institution maintained its serene atmosphere surrounded by the still numerous open fields and farmlands. All in all, King's Park Hospital was a noticeably finer facility for treating her condition except that, as noted New York genealogist Rhoda Miller points out, "It was no short-term place to be." For many, it was the last stop.

Regardless of the illness, treatment then was still primitive and fairly universal. The first step was simple if not logical: remove the patient from agitating external surroundings, thereby providing sanctuary from the bustling commotion in any city infirmary. Then, as one physician who worked there remarked, the primary treatment regimen consisted of "O&O and R&R"—occupation and oxygen, rest and recreation. This was, sadly, the best they could do for anyone; physicians had little else in their arsenal of remedies since drug-based treatments such as insulin shock were at least twenty years away.

Rose remained at King's Park through Christmas and into the spring of 1915. Despite O&O and R&R, her condition remained unchanged, and it became clear to those family members nearest her that she would not return to Brooklyn. In late spring, the durations of her frenzy grew longer and longer, and for the next three months, the intensely exasperating condition persisted, taking a toll on her physical well-being. Her strength gradually ebbed away, and finally, in the very early morning hours of July 27, 1915, Rose Dolendo, mother of Francesco Raffele Nitto, weary and exhausted from her protracted illness, departed life.

Back in Chicago, ripening conditions signaled nothing but prosperity for Nitto.

3
INTO WARTIME PROHIBITION

AFTER HIS MOTHER'S DEATH, NITTO apparently continued to fence jewelry, and he may have continued barbering. Investigation suggests he did well enough monetarily to sock away at least some of his liquid assets with confidant and now financial mentor Louis Greenberg who acted for Nitto as he would for many others, as an unofficial, one-man Federal Reserve. As a safety deposit of sorts, Greenberg would pool their respective reserves together and invest them in his money-making ventures, the saloons and loan sharking, and then return any portion as needed to his clients or reinvest the sum, possibly compounding the amount—or so the story goes. Because he invested his money in a street-side banker like Greenberg rather than in an ordinary banking institution, credence is lent to the suspicions that the glittery adornments Nitto hawked in the Italian slums of the Nineteenth Ward were pilfered property. It also demonstrated very early on an unquestionable, enduring trust between two characters of such far removed backgrounds.

Nitto could have easily invested his money with one of his own kind; private Italian bankers on the street were commonplace. Generally, they were people who previously handled money while working in other occupations such as steamship ticket agents, labor agents, or various small business owners. Some cheated and shortchanged clients, and some absconded back to Italy with the money. Pilfered sums of $10,000 were not uncommon. Others, inexperienced and inefficient, quite frequently went broke investing in crazy schemes. Nitto's choice of banker provides a keen insight into his persona at this mostly undocumented period in that

35

he wasn't taken in by any of his own breed and that he recognized Greenberg's saloon and moneylending business, whatever their legal or illegal slant, as a solid business enterprise.

A move up the economic rung was close at hand. The source of his future prosperity might be traced to Chicago's 1915 mayoral elections, the results of which worked hand in hand with reformist attitudes seeping into the national political climate. This squall of countrywide proportions has been described as "the means by which young ethnics entered the mainstream of American entrepreneurial crime." These circumstances made many an ordinary person in either a legal or illegal career quite a bit better off economically. The political talk was about alcohol prohibition, which took the form of legislation in the late war years, not the Roaring Twenties. Frank Nitto jumped the bandwagon early and, in effect, got an enormous head start on most of his contemporaries. And once again, he would thank Louis Greenberg.

—⟜⟊⟊⟞—

Nitto may have heard talk on the street or from Greenberg, who was well-informed because of his saloon businesses, but the political landscape in Chicago was about to undergo an advantageous transformation at the highest level. For the last few months prior to the 1915 mayoral election, Chicago was, in the words of one writer, "as free from organized vice as at any time in its history." The infamous red light district had been shuttered, and Mayor Carter Harrison II had gone so far as to revoke select saloon liquor licenses—most notably that of now-First Ward Italian power broker Jim Colosimo. Cancellation of saloon licenses was far from enduring, however, as the 1915 mayoral election demonstrated by tipping the balance back toward businesses that catered to human frailties as well as the booze interests Greenberg was interested in.

In the January 1915 mayoral primary, Democratic machine-backed candidate Robert Sweitzer trounced incumbent Mayor Harrison by nearly 80,000 votes. Harrison, despite serving a total of ten-plus years in several stints as mayor, was never really popular with some Democratic powers. On the Republican side, the field had remained wide open throughout the previous fall. Speculation remained rampant as to who might run on the Republican slate, and many names surfaced. Nearly all speculators, including the major city papers, overlooked the one individual who would ultimately outshine all—a fellow of immeasurable "rascality" who eventually befriended many of those in need of vice—William Hale "Big Bill" Thompson.

By 1915, Thompson was nearly forty-eight years old. The athletic son of a historically prominent and wealthy real estate family and a millionaire, he was nearly unknown politically in 1915. As a former alderman, he entered politics years before only on a bet, and Thompson did not stir much recognition among his colleagues. After his term as alderman, Thompson became an indiscernible part of the Cook County Board. Even now, with a decade of politics under his belt, he was still an enigma. Candidate Sweitzer pursued his campaign precisely along that line, asking "Just who is this Bill Thompson? Who ever heard of Bill Thompson doing anything worthwhile?" Sweitzer soon found out.

Pushed to the fore by political opportunists in a divided Republican Party, Big Bill could bellow with the best. This was his supreme weapon, and as "the Babe Ruth of promisers," he knew just how to tickle everyone's fancy, even if those promises contradicted one another. Most importantly for harassed saloonkeepers like Louis Greenberg, Thompson saw "no harm in a friendly little drink." This is exactly what they wanted to hear. Who cared about what he pledged the reformers?

In response, a self-assured Sweitzer castigated Thompson at every turn, continually noting for his audiences the dichotomy of Bill's various platforms. Assuredly, Sweitzer could count on the many Democratically controlled city and county offices for support. Others who lined up behind him were of the more notorious variety—anti-Harrison Democrats, including hoodlum bondsman Billy Skidmore, North Side boss John F. O'Malley, West Side political fixer and saloonkeeper Barney Grogan, as well as stockyards gambling czar Big Jim O'Leary. Accordingly, First Ward betting parlors made Sweitzer the unofficial favorite at 8-to-1 odds. On April 6, 1915, not only did dark-horse candidate Bill Thompson beat the odds, he won by the largest plurality given to a Republican up to that time—140,000 votes. The *Chicago Tribune*, which refused to endorse either candidate, noted before the election that, regardless of who won, "we do not believe there will be a loose and disorderly city . . . we do not believe that we are headed for the bowwows."

The *Tribune* prognostication was not wholly incorrect. For a time, despite the plethora of impossible-to-keep campaign promises, Thompson glowed as the new mayor. He again promised to clear out the criminals and crooks to make Chicago a safe place to visit. Much to Greenberg's chagrin, Big Bill even enforced Illinois's often-ignored Blue Laws prohibiting the serving of alcohol on Sunday. "Dry" was the term of the day reserved for those who supported increased legislation restricting alcohol sales and supply in some form or another. Those who generally opposed such legislation were tagged as "Wets."

After saloon operation was limited to six days a week, Alderman Kenna let it be known to those in his Workingman's Exchange, "I guess the only thing to do is to get loaded Saturday if you're gonna try to last till Monday morning." Those in Greenberg's saloons no doubt had the same thought. Saloon windows showed signs of the times: "Don't forget to stock up, tomorrow's Sunday!" The reference was to bottled beer, a commodity only recently accepted by beer patrons and then enjoying upward sales momentum. They took their bottles home to ice up for consumption anytime, Blue Laws or not.

Fortunately for Greenberg and others, this inconvenience was short-lived. Political pressure forced the mayor to retreat on the Blue Law issue and announce, "I'm no reformer!" And though he would become known admiringly as "Big Bill the Builder" for the abundance of infrastructure improvements made during his administration, his attitude toward certain areas of law enforcement leaned more toward nonchalance. As they were not under Harrison, during much of Thompson's first term as mayor, Chicago's drink and vice businesses were alive and well.

Chicago might be a Wet town, but nationally the sentiment was growing considerably dustier. The slant against alcohol seemed to be winning, thanks in part to The Anti-Saloon League. Founded by Ohioan Reverend Howard Hyde Russell in 1893, the League had already achieved political and legislative successes against alcohol in Ohio. The anti-alcohol movement grew from its primarily rural and evangelical roots to advance its ideology in larger cities, including Chicago. As early as 1907, they tried, without success, to bully Chicago's mayors into supporting a prohibition of Sunday saloon hours. Allied with the League in their prohibition cause was the Progressive Movement. Like the league, they saw in Prohibition a chance to nobly eliminate the evils they associated with saloons, among them, low standards of living, corrupt politics, and what they viewed as an organized underworld. Together, the groups pressed local politicians, rewarding and punishing them according to their Prohibition plank. They also fervently worked parishioners from the pulpit on Sundays where they could spread the word as well as rake in financial aid.

Progress was slow but steady, and by 1912, the Dry cause could count a half-dozen state legislative victories. However, the Anti-Saloon League desired some form of national compliance and soon pushed for federal enforcement of alcohol prohibition. By March 1913, their first national triumph, the Webb-Kenyon Act prohibiting interstate transportation of alcohol, was passed by Congress and, though vetoed by the president, had sufficient congressional support to see the veto overridden. However, the legislation was a limited victory for the Dry agenda, making it illegal only to transport intoxicating beverages into Dry states. Following up on this first national victory, in three year's time, the total number of states with enacted and enforced prohibition laws was up to twenty-three. Riding victory further, the resolution for a future Prohibition amendment to the U.S. Constitution banning the "manufacture for sale, transportation for sale, importation for sale, and exportation for sale" of intoxicating liquors was first introduced in Congress in late 1913, just about the time Nitto arrived in Chicago. Congress debated the amendment's merits, but in the end, it received less than the necessary two-thirds vote for ratification.

The war changed everything. The national movement for alcohol prohibition began to gather greater momentum when the United States declared war on Germany in 1917. With a sizable portion of the population away from home, widespread resistance to prohibition was gradually overwhelmed as the Anti-Saloon League remained in the thick of the prohibition battle on the homefront and was responsible for the results. The Dry forces railed against the wasteful conversion of good grain into alcohol when the people of Europe were starving, and they patriotically stressed the need to keep our fighting men sober by creating dry zones around military establishments—bread will help win the war more than whiskey, and prohibition will at the same time sober up America.

Nonetheless, there was plenty of high-profile opposition to the crusade. Samuel Gompers, head of the American Federation of Labor, argued against prohibition for employment reasons, estimating the amendment would throw approximately two million people out of work. A compromise measure to allow President Wilson the discretion to limit or stop manufacture of beer or wine was passed in August 1917. Much to the relief of the consumers of those products, Wilson did not choose to exercise the option. However, a rider attached to the compromise bill mandated the cessation of the manufacture of distilled alcohol the following month on September 8; however, merchants of ardent spirits could sell remaining stocks until they were exhausted.

It was at about this time that Frank Nitto came into the alcohol business through saloon owner Louis Greenberg. The early Prohibition legislation created no hardship for Greenberg; it only made him wealthier by leaps and bounds. By 1917 Greenberg operated at least three saloons in the north and west areas of the city, and they provided a substantial segment of his income. He knew people would always pay to drink distilled alcohol spirits, wine, or beer regardless of the law, but now in order to sustain his business, he needed an adequate, reliable supply of now-illegal liquor.

This proved to be no great problem, however, for since he began his operations, Greenberg had stocked his saloons at least partially through illegitimate sources. From his view, stolen or not, using illegal liquor made good business sense—reduce costs, increase profits. Why pay full price for what he could get at a discount? The word on the street said that for every piece of hot merchandise Greenberg purchased, he received another at no cost. Some shipments he arranged through "questionable friends," presumably hijackers or fences who, by virtue of his North Side saloon, may have included nearby light-fingered acquaintance Dean O'Banion and his crowd. Soon Greenberg personally oversaw delivery of wagonloads of hijacked whiskey.

Eventually, as laws required permits to access and move liquor stocks, he graduated with the times to more sophisticated means to waylay those inventories via forged or counterfeit paperwork. Greenberg soon had more than enough to supply his saloons, but demand beyond his saloons was endless. Greater opportunities beckoned. The gravity of the approaching Dry climate dictated short supplies of liquor everywhere, and Greenberg astutely fenced the remainder of his stocks to those in need. He was now a liquor salesman in his own right, and in turn, he opened this door of opportunity for Frank Nitto.

Greenberg sought some means for unloading his extra merchandise just as he had with his past jewelry capers. The person(s) he used had to be trustworthy and reliable thanks to the illegal nature of the job. Nitto had already learned to handle business transactions of commodities on the underside of the law first by fencing for Greenberg, and as part of his duties, he reliably handled sums of money. He proved capable of solving business dilemmas amidst the acrimonious street environment. Amounts due were paid in full regardless of the collection method, and Nitto's battle scars—a broken nose, a readily-noticeable scar from a split lip, as well as other small facial pockmarks—proved he was not averse to using violence when necessary.

Though Nitto's specific role went unrecorded, by 1918 he was involved in some type of distributorship of liquor, though not beer distribution for beer was still legal and abundant. From late 1917 to early 1918, only distillers were forced to cease producing grain alcohol, and grain liquors were what Greenberg and Chicago now needed. Nitto became a fence responsible for dispensing some of Greenberg's hot booze, probably through previous street-side contacts. The volume and scope of his territory were unknown, but he was thought to be banking nice sums of cash with Greenberg.

As the business evolved, another individual believed to be involved in part of the Greenberg-Nitto booze operation in the Nineteenth Ward was mutual friend Dr. Gaetano Ronga. His role, like Nitto's, is vague, though it's not hard to surmise, nor was it necessarily unlawful. As a physician, Ronga was in a unique position during this early phase of Prohibition in that he could legally dispense various amounts of medicinal liquors through prescriptions. He might regularly prescribe wine or spirits as a non-specific medicinal remedy, if only for therapeutic reasons.

Despite the research at the time, exemplified by the succinct declaration of Dr. Howard Kelly of Johns Hopkins University that "there is no single disease in the world of which alcohol is the cure," cultural traditions are hard to modify or regulate by reason or law. Even as this early Prohibition evolved to become more encompassing as a national law, it was still written to accommodate physicians for such treatment. All they had to do was apply for the required permits in order to legally dispense vinous or spirituous alcohol via prescription. Each doctor under permit was allotted one hundred prescriptions every ninety days to legally draw on government warehouse stocks of those liquors, and physicians could obtain more blank prescriptions if they could show extenuating or extraordinary circumstances.

Conveniently for Greenberg's operation, Ronga had long owned and/or had access to just the right vehicle to dispense medicinal liquor, for hand-in-hand with his physician duties he had operated small neighborhood pharmacies in the poor Italian sections along Polk Street or Blue Island Avenue in the Nineteenth Ward. With the advent of Prohibition, pharmacies and their operators, much like doctors, functioned on a government permit system to distribute medicinal liquors. In theory, authorities compared amounts withdrawn legally by the druggists under license with the amount totaled on prescriptions, but just as it was in the 1920s, the scant number of enforcement squads had little way to determine amounts actually kept in stock or what transactions really took place. A druggist might honestly overdraw on government stocks or might forge a script to do so. In one district, agents by chance discovered the pharmacies there had drawn nearly twice the allowed amount from government stocks.

Other druggists, while dispensing amounts within legal limits, circumvented the law by distributing untold amounts of illegal product off the record. A doctor or pharmacy owner could write scripts and dispense his entire legal allotment to anyone he desired, including bootleggers, and for an inflated price, if he so demanded. In the first six months of 1920, a half-million scripts for whiskey were issued in the Chicago area. Of that, according to the Treasury Department whose responsibility it was initially to enforce the laws, about half seemed to evade "the spirit or letter" of the law. The risk to doctors and pharmacists was low, for they were seldom bothered. All the operator needed were reliable, discretionary clients.

One result of Prohibition was that it placed doctors in the difficult position of upholding the law and refusing treatment to an individual even if he genuinely believed that alcohol would not cure but would at least relieve the patient's condition. A doctor who turned away legitimate clientele ran the risk of losing patronage from and stature in the community along with a loss of income. Not wanting to risk loss of practice in the face of something so apparently brainless as liquor prohibition, many otherwise law-abiding doctors without permits by default became bootleggers in a sense, at least by government definition. With only paper records, how could the government differentiate between genuine patients in need and bootleg customers? In either case, at the going rate of $3 a pint, medicinal or not, alcohol could be a very lucrative business for those with connections to suppliers. Whether Dr. Ronga shaded over the legal line to do his friends Greenberg and Nitto any favors is not certain, except to say he was apparently never arrested for any such misdeeds.

⚜

Over in the First Ward, Big Jim Colosimo reigned as the ranking name in vice for nearly a decade, thanks primarily to former Brooklynite Johnny Torrio. Having arrived in Chicago circa 1909-10, Torrio established himself as a strategic and efficient manager of Colosimo's affairs. Torrio, too, needed supplied of alcohol. He expanded Colosimo's vice and saloon business to the southeast suburbs of Burnham, South Chicago, and Posen near the Indiana border. Roadhouses, a generic term for establishments that included gambling and just about anything else, sprouted, and these franchises not only took in the traveling public but also acted as a parachute in case of reform pressure in the city. Expansion was carried out in a reasonable, businesslike fashion by reaching out to the town pols and making deals. Most town pols were willing, but if the saloon/roadhouse owners encountered resistance elsewhere in the community, they used money to pry favor from the resistance. Violence was always a rare last option since knocking people about and spilling blood was simply bad business. Further, violence invited bothersome police investigations and raids as well as unwanted publicity, all of which usually translated into lower receipts. This was the Torrio trademark approach to business, and it seldom failed.

Given this business-like temperament, few if any atrocities occurred in their domain at the time. More importantly, here was a real business-criminal organization whose leadership was focused on business and understood the burden that bloodshed imposed. It was a mindset very similar to Louis Greenberg's, but there were no similar outstanding business organizations in Frank Nitto's ward.

⚜

Ironically, though Nitto was not a mover in the beer business, outlawing the froth furthered his business web. Dry forces never abated their efforts for all-encompassing prohibition on alcoholic products, and in 1917, playing politics and anxious to get some form of absolute alcohol interdiction legislation passed, they hastily packaged a proposal for a national constitutional amendment that included beer and wine. The loopholes within the amendment were glaring. Manufacturing and selling would be illegal, posing a risk for those who might supply alcohol producers in that they could be arrested, but the legislation did nothing to outlaw the purchase or use of intoxicating beverages, making possession still legal. Further political maneuvering provided a one-year grace period for those in business to dispose of their stocks if the amendment passed. The amendment cleared both the Senate and the House of Representatives, and the news that the National Prohibition Act or Eighteenth Amendment was being sent to the states for ratification hit the newspaper headlines December 17. Thirty-six states needed to approve the measure for it to become effective.

Still, the Anti-Saloon League wasn't through muscling. Their congressional allies pushed until allowed to enact a total wartime prohibition measure forbidding the manufacture and sale of all intoxicating beverages of more than 2.75 percent alcohol content until de-mobilization was complete, a measure which included beer and wine. Ironically, with the war nearly at its end, Wartime Prohibition, as it was called, was passed in late 1918 as part of an agriculture appropriations bill. Too weak politically to resist, Woodrow Wilson signed the measure, and Wartime Prohibition became reality. The new deadline for the last legal retail sale date for alcohol products of greater than 2.75 percent alcohol was set for June 30, 1919.

Later that year, Congress approved the Volstead Act to shore up the Eighteenth Amendment. Named after Minnesota Representative Andrew J. Volstead, who truly believed "law does regulate morality," this legislation decreed the alcohol content of intoxicating beverages to be greater than 0.5 percent. There was no scientific merit in terms of actual alcohol needed for intoxication for this figure; however, the Anti-Saloon League liked it, petitioned for it as the standard, and obtained it. The act also provided grit for enforcement and penalties lacking in previous legislation, and whereas the states were responsible for at least token compliance, according to the Eighteenth Amendment, the Volstead Act provided for federal action as well. Thanks to wartime Prohibition and the Volstead Act, beer was now lumped together with whiskey, wine, and all other alcoholic beverages as "booze," the chic, risqué slang term coined by the Drys.

Any strategic efforts mustered by the Wet forces and their allies to fight passage of the Eighteenth Amendment proved futile, and it steamrolled at nearly unprecedented speed through the necessary number of state legislatures in only thirteen months. With Nebraska's clinching vote on January 16, 1919, real Prohibition, the intention to mop up all intoxicating alcohol in the United States, was a done deal.

———

As the clock began ticking down toward January 17, 1920, when the Eighteenth Amendment was to take effect, it was also ticking off time on Thompson's first term as mayor. In the spring of 1919, he was fighting for his political life, and those Chicagoans of the Wet persuasion had plenty to worry about. Thompson's first tenure as mayor created some weighty liabilities for the candidate. The city's $2.8 million treasury surplus had become a $4.6 million deficit, and many 1915 election promises still remained unfulfilled, gathering political dust, especially his promise to the first women voters to appoint a woman to the school board. Four years later, they still held no such appointment. Thompson had also promised that body of voters he'd clean up crime, but in his first term, crime escalated. Chicago newspapers commonly ran headlines about vice and gambling operators who held sway with little or no interference from police during Thompson's term.

Nonetheless, Thompson cleared the first hurdle once again, gaining the Republican nomination by 40,000 votes, while on the Democratic side, his old nemesis Robert Sweitzer was back to take up the challenge. This time Thompson prevailed by a bare miracle 21,000-vote margin. The town would remain wide open and Wet.

A good thing, since the great majority of Chicagoans clearly did not support Dry legislation. They were given a say on the matter as they were voting in the mayoral election. Ironically, the referendum was thrust upon them at the urging of the Anti-Saloon League as part of their overall Dry campaign. The Dry strategy backfired miserably with Wet votes out-polling Dry votes by a greater than three-to-one majority.

As a matter of contingency, long-respected Chicago brewers—the majestic, deep-rooted Joseph Stenson types of the Stenson Brewing Company, as well as the smaller entities, all of whom had considerable investments in property and equipment—considered how to cut their losses. They could legally continue producing low-alcohol-content beer, but public demand for this substitute for the real thing was not proven, and hence, the brewer could still lose big. A shift in production to non-alcoholic beverages, malt syrups, ginger ale, cider, or root beer was feasible, if undesirable and unprofitable. A brewer might just make ends meet in hopes of holding onto facilities until a shift in public sentiment brought real beer consumption back in favor. Those who could not afford to exercise one of these options gave up hope, shutting down and selling their equipment and property for whatever they could get.

From the start, Johnny Torrio hardly viewed Dry legislation as a threat, but rather as a prospect. The previous liquor measure had done little to hinder demand or operations; neither would a new one. Beer was already an integral part of the voluminous Colosimo-Torrio business conglomerate of countless saloons, bordellos, gambling joints, and roadhouses. As expected, manager Torrio needed to supply these dives in order to keep the blue-collar customers happy and the empire functioning. Now that legislation was striking fear into the hearts of brewers, the manufacturing apparatus was available as well. That's when he made his move on behalf of Colosimo.

Scouting the beer industry to satisfy those needs, Torrio began seeking out agreements for outright purchase or investment partnership with "brewers with larceny in their hearts." Such brewers opted neither for alternative non-alcoholic beverages nor for closing, but rather for some type of continuing enterprise free from blame. With a less scrupulous partner, they might continue operations under the guise of a near-beer brewer, while churning out a good deal of the real stock instead. As part of any deal, much of that original product would be barreled and shipped out to Colosimo operations. The brewer had nothing to fear; the final arrangement was entirely trouble-free. Torrio and his company would front for the brewer, managing production, protecting shipments from rogue hijackers, and taking the fall in the event of legal entanglements, while the brewer enjoyed a hefty percentage of the earnings as an investor.

Torrio found such a partner in the person of Gold Coast brewery magnate Joseph Stenson. A veteran brewer, the youngest and most active of four brothers in the business since the turn of the century, he owned at least two breweries in Chicago. Examining his business alternatives for Prohibition, the confident Stenson, not wasting any time, added two more closed city breweries to his holdings. As a result of his potential production volume and his petty, iniquitous heart, the brewer came to the attention of Johnny Torrio and received the bulk of Colosimo's beer business in the First Ward.

In spring 1919 Charles Schaffner, another brewery owner, sought to sell the group of block-long, brick behemoths at the corner of Union and South Emerald avenues on the South Side that were home to the independent Manhattan Brewing Company. Torrio, with Stenson, quickly snatched up the opportunity, buying the facilities and, in December, changing the name to Malt Maid. Then Louis Greenberg came in.

"The booze business," Greenberg later admitted, "put me in touch with the people who were just people when I first met them, but who became beer barons after Prohibition." Quite possibly, earlier liquor networking put him in touch with Johnny Torrio in the First Ward. Both men were in booze commerce, both needed liquor stocks, and both knew Coughlin and Kenna. Not long after the purchase of the Manhattan Brewing Company, sources cite Louis Greenberg as the manager. Greenberg's experience as a moneyman was a perfect fit. His previous bond business and money-lending schemes had mushroomed into Roosevelt Finance Company on Roosevelt Road, which, among scattered legitimate transactions, now handled loads of bootleggers' cash. He was now financially fat. Soon after Torrio's new purchase, Greenberg bought a 25 percent interest in the brewery. With Greenberg now into beer, Frank Nitto's web, no matter how remote, extended into the First Ward.

—————

Unknowingly, Torrio provided the next link in Frank Nitto's career when, in late 1919, Torrio added another asset to his holdings with the arrival of twenty-year-old Al Capone. Capone left New York at the behest of his benefactor Frankie Yale for his own protection on what was supposed to be a temporary deferment. Back in Brooklyn, young, thick, and burly Capone had worked as a bouncer in clubs owned by Yale. One day, using only his fists, Capone hammered a member of a rival Irish gang into unconsciousness; death was given as the victim's prognosis. Although the injured party was low on the ladder, the incident provoked great anger in the Irish gang boss. To him, it was a matter of principle to protect his own kind, hunt down the offender, and inflict the deserved punishment.

The Irishman survived, as it turned out, but Frankie Yale was fully familiar with the fierce disposition and reputation of the Irish chief and took the appropriate action of sending his valued young tough out of harm's way to his associate Johnny Torrio in Chicago. Torrio would put Capone to work in Colosimo's organization just long enough, maybe a year or so, for the Irishman's fury to cool of for leadership of the gang to change so that Yale could bring Capone back. In the meantime, Capone's role in the Colosimo-Torrio vice combine was humble—working as a bar bouncer and drumming up customers for bordellos in the wintry weather, his pay was maybe $35 a week. Hardly a career, but it would do for the planned layover. Of course, he would not remain lowly for long, nor would he return to gang duties in Brooklyn.

Prohibition came in like a lamb. For the third year running, the nation's capital rang in the new year without great fanfare. Only the foreign diplomats seemed to be toasting champagne. Many Chicagoans, however, celebrated New Year's Day 1920 with all the usual intoxicating indulgences. One reporter surveying the town found, "They were drinking their champagne from satin slippers behind closed doors and were foregoing their dips in the fountain." When Prohibition became official on January 17, 1920, it stirred little in the way of headlines in the Windy City. The *Chicago Tribune* noted one local mock funeral of John Barleycorn with a photo of a glove clasping a liquor bottle in a small coffin. The pronouncement above the photo read: "Born. Almost with the first Man. Died January 16, 1920, at Nick's Buffet."

Of their elected state officers who voted accordingly, Chicagoans very well may have echoed Will Rogers sage commentary: "voted wet by the people and dry by their misrepresentatives." At least Chicagoans knew there was no such travesty in their city. As long as Thompson sat as mayor, citizens who considered themselves Wet had little to fear even from a national decree, just another sign of encouragement for bootleggers. Thompson's law and order sputtered off and on for a short time before belching out of steam for good—another campaign promise down the drain.

With the top echelon of county and city law enforcement indifferent, Greenberg, Torrio and other bootleggers faced little interference from the numerous men in blue patrolling the streets. To many of them, Prohibition initially was more of a practical means to solve their personal economic concerns than a reason to enforce an apparently absurd moral issue. Of even the high-ranking police officials at the time, one notorious bootlegger observed: "Just because a police captain looks dignified, guys get the idea that he don't need anything. That's crazy. Gold badges look swell, but you can't eat 'em. They're in a spot where they earn some and they're nuts if they pass it up. Damn few do."

At a time of a national fiscal recession, this was understandable. From the outset of Prohibition, many city policemen—some honest, others not—hired themselves out to protect shipments of beer and whiskey. Piecemeal work paid according to the volume and value of the cargo. Others were regularly compensated to turn a blind eye. In one particularly efficient operation, the stipend collected depended on rank or work shift. The payoff in one district included as many as 400 uniformed policemen and five captains from the local station, police headquarters on Clark Street, and even the state's attorney's office. They would line up weekly at one local gang warehouse, just like payday, where badge numbers were cross-checked and the appropriate cash doled out. More enterprising policemen reached agreements to buy booze from distributors at wholesale prices for resale to increase their income. Transactions were so pervasive that it was later estimated that half the police force at the time was in the booze business. "It was such a common thing," a patrolman later claimed, that even if you were honest, "it came as a matter of course." A squad car parked near or in front of a speakeasy generally received an envelope full of cash tossed through the window without the bat of an eye. Who could refuse that kind of treatment?

Torrio might expect little trouble from the federal side either. In preparing to put Prohibition into practice, Congress asked the U.S. district attorney for the southern district of New York in New York City what his manpower needs for enforcement might be in his district; he replied that to keep tabs on the number of saloons and related businesses that currently existed, an estimated force of 1,500 men was needed. A district attorney for a three-state district nearby predicted his needs at 12,000 men. Both estimates proved to be very low. In fact, Congress budgeted for just over 1,500 agents for the entire United States (that was decreased by a hundred agents the next year). Given the minuscule allotment of 134 agents for the Midwest section covering Illinois, Iowa, and part of Wisconsin, enforcement would be no less sieve-like than the Eighteenth Amendment itself.

Even if the hard work and diligence of the enforcers paid off by nabbing a suspect, seldom did a violator risk viewing the interior walls of any jail. The so-called teeth of Prohibition, the Volstead Act, commanded a first offense penalty of a fine of not more than $500, while a second offense demanded not less than $100 but no more than $1,000 or up to ninety days in jail; only on the third offense was jail time certain. These penalties might deter the average person but were paltry to those with political affluence like Torrio or Greenberg.

⸺◦◦◦⸺

That Torrio was a visionary and, in a very expansive way, a strategic planner was plain to his biographer Jack McPhaul. In his words, Torrio "knew exactly where he was going. His course had been chartered months back. . . . He concentrated on the heart of the matter." Torrio knew the potential profits to be made from real beer and alcohol sales far outweighed any obstacle law enforcement might provide. That's why he cut deals with Stenson earlier. Now, immediate shortages drove the price of a barrel of beer to $17 wholesale, and it might go for two or three times that much retail. With beer costing perhaps as little as $5 a barrel to produce, and with consumption in Chicago estimated at 20,000 barrels a week, this was a windfall. The same scarcity was a boon to Greenberg and Nitto, who might command as much as $10-$20 per fifth of whiskey. At bars, the price per shot increased fivefold (from fifteen cents to seventy-five cents per shot). Who knew how high the prices would rise?

Given that kind of potential, the illegal beer and whiskey trade was a sure bet to bring in money that would dwarf anything Torrio and Colosimo were now making. Their realm already had a major distribution apparatus in place and was expanding. For Torrio, this was a convenient opportunity for still greater horizontal expansion. He could increase the number of outlets for his wares, and if he didn't do so through ownership, he might supply the beer that others needed. He might also expand the business vertically. He was already manufacturing the product, but in between product manufacture and retail sale, he might control the distribution via trucking concerns. He had contacts in certain cartage companies to haul the products. This big picture vision was Torrio's bona fide genius. Moreover, he was well positioned as operating manager of Colosimo's empire to see this concept to fruition. All the pieces for Torrio were in place. All he needed was his boss's blessing.

By 1920, Colosimo preferred the trappings of notoriety that his renowned café offered and increasingly disdained the raunchy details of his empire, leaving those for Torrio. The problem for Torrio was obvious; as long as Jim remained in his debilitating stupor, his vision of enjoying the spoils offered by such ludicrous Dry legislation remained thwarted. Their loss would be someone else's gain. Such complacency could only "encourage the jackals to turn on the lion."

Among the jackals, Capone had performed admirable work for Torrio during his stay. In turn, Torrio tutored the twenty-one-year-old further in the ways of the business—diplomacy first, violence as a last resort. Capone returned the tutelage with a reverent loyalty; the young tough had decided to stay on with Torrio. With a hopeful young stalwart in the wings and untold riches beckoning, Torrio, probably with heartfelt reluctance but keen awareness that his planned expansion could no longer be put off, determined that Jim Colosimo must go. Emotions aside, it was purely a business decision.

On Wednesday, May 11, 1920, Frank Nitto could hardly have missed such a notorious citywide event that was passed by word of mouth and trumpeted in the headlines that appeared on street corners the next day: "COLOSIMO SLAIN; SEEK EX-WIFE, JUST RETURNED." The police came down hard, for this was no ordinary murder. Most higher-up police officials were at the scene. Naturally, Torrio was among those hauled in, but he expected that, and the questions asked, the clues analyzed, all came to nothing. Many suspected Torrio's involvement but lacked proof. Hence, as Torrio was instantly set free, Nitto's old boyhood acquaintance and Torrio's new protégé Al Capone became number two in the entire organization.

—⁂—

Observers noted their complimentary styles: the older Torrio with his organizational mind, reserved demeanor, and urbanity; the young, spirited Capone, with his brute force, physicality, and gregariousness, was an appropriately intense and complimentary understudy. Capone became Torrio's chief gunman. In return, Torrio rewarded young Capone's efficiency and reliability. Initially, Torrio remunerated Capone's prowess and loyalty with a 25 percent share of the brothel profits, which in 1920 were estimated to be about $25,000. Torrio further promised 50 percent of the bootleg profits as soon as they became available. He was also given management of

Torrio's old headquarters, a block south of Colosimo's at 2222 South Wabash, appropriately named the Four Deuces.

Conveniently adjoining the four-story brick building, with an address of 2220 South Wabash, Capone established his headquarters under the guise of an antique dealer. He stocked the dominant window front with junk for passersby to see and printed appropriate business cards for legitimacy, but that was it. The real business remained as it had under Torrio's management—a notorious First Ward hot spot. A saloon was in back on the first floor, general management offices occupied the second, a gambling den was on the third, and a brothel was on the fourth. Torrio still maintained his office there while he forged ahead with his plans.

Despite the Dry law and the national economic recession, the number of speakeasies by 1921 blossomed to nearly 20,000 (from roughly 13,000 saloons before Prohibition). Saloon owners facing the gloom and doom of sort beer supplies needn't fear, Torrio announced; he was equipped and ready to supply all those in need. Personally supervising his next operation of horizontal expansion, Torrio hatched a plan for development by bloating the holdings of the organization until no others were ready or able to venture into the as-yet unclaimed areas of the western suburbs like Stickney and Forest View and east into the Indiana suburbs of East Chicago, Gary, and Whiting. There, he increased his brothel and gambling franchises while simultaneously increasing his needs for prohibited supplies. He might also expect to target a good number of now-illicit saloons or speakeasies in those towns for supply as well.

He expanded his brewery holdings to fill increased orders. By 1921, the Torrio-Stenson alliance added a mammoth eleven-building brewery complex in West Hammond, Indiana, to their collection of breweries, now perhaps five in number (Stenson signed over the deed to Torrio on this one). Their Manhattan brewery, under the eye of Louis Greenberg, was particularly efficient. Upon one of the rare police raids there, the employees, previously tipped off, dumped the entire production of illegal beer on-hand down a nearby sewer. So much of the frothy stuff was drained into the overloaded pipe that the resulting pressure popped a nearby manhole cover, and a geyser shot up approximately four feet above the street level, flooding the road surface with illicit beer. While such raids did occur, much of Torrio's beer production, perhaps up to 16,000 barrels a week, was consigned to eager vendors, shipped primarily in trucks also owned by Torrio. Capone's many duties included buying trucks for just such a purpose. With his organization neatly in place and expanding, Torrio was thought to be raking in millions of dollars.

—⟨2/2/2⟩—

Frank Nitto's horizon was not nearly as bright as Capone's, but by 1920, economically, the worst was behind him. Business and home life would be no easy matter, though. He and wife Rose likely remained in and about the Nineteenth Ward, as the location of his closest friends and business associates and especially demographics would suggest. Nitto's ongoing business confederacy with man about town

Greenberg notwithstanding, his most intimate friends remained there. Dr. Ronga and his family remained on McAllister Place, along with his practice. To the east of Ronga, the large Vicedomini contingent was rooted on the corner of South Bishop and Taylor streets, his theater and restaurant still in heart of the Italian quarter just down Taylor. Many of Nitto's possible barber acquaintances plied their trade on Taylor, while just to the south along Newberry Avenue in the Maxwell Street district, were Sidney Gottloeb and his wife. In particular, it appears that it was this German couple with whom the Nitto and his wife spent numerous evenings, perhaps sitting on the living room divan exchanging companionable chitchat.

While the homes might be cozy inside, their creature comforts greatly contrasted with the events unfolding and permeating the district outside their walls. By and large, the neighborhoods in the vicinity of Taylor and Halsted streets were not the most pleasant areas, and while life on the streets was always tough, peripheral events generated ever more remarkable peril. The mayhem materialized regularly enough for hacks to dub the ward "the Bloody Nineteenth." The trouble was, they weren't joking. Tough times for Nitto lay ahead.

4

THE BLOODY
NINETEENTH

T HE NINETEENTH WARD DURING NITTO'S stay, particularly during the years of his
     booze apprenticeship, was violent, literally explosive and often fatal—plainly
more hazardous than what he experienced in the Brooklyn Navy Yard area where he
was raised. Especially threatening for Nitto was the nature of his commerce and the
possibility of associating with those of both—opposing—interests, then getting
caught in the middle. In all probability, he had more to fear from everyday life in the
ward than he did any federal agent snooping about to enforce booze laws. All in all,
the dangers impacted Nitto favorably—a final bit of Chicago conditioning—fine-
tuning his occupational experience under fire while he observed the evolution of the
powers that be and possibly changing his course in Chicago.

The source of the tempestuousness in the Nineteenth was not business- or vice-
related. There were no mobsters in the Roaring Twenties sense. The bloodshed in
the ward occurred particularly when factions geared up for local elections, civic con-
tests of the most venomous type. The exceptionally calamitous periods began near
the late winter primaries and lasted through the spring to the final elections, while
out-of-season acts splattered on throughout the year anytime plotters saw fit. The
battles were fought by Italians against other Italians, their blood flowing now that
they comprised nearly 80 percent of the ward's population. When the wars raged,
stretches of Taylor Street and Blue Island Avenue where Nitto conducted business,
the epicenters of the Italian community, were the most embattled.

Most ominously for Nitto, political scraps eventually devolved into a battle for Italian supremacy. Bombs and bullets were common enough to bring reality to the newspaper headlines about World War I that were read only a couple of years ago. One occupant remarked at the height of the turmoil that "Conditions in the Nineteenth Ward are so terrible. Gunmen are patrolling the streets. I have received threats. . . . It is worse than the middle ages." Weapons popped off rounds, and the resulting shrieks echoed in the night too often. "If I got out of bed every time I heard a scream," said one woman drearily reconciled to the nightly circumstances there, "I never would get any sleep."

Using more sinister means to torment intended victims, the names of targeted persons might be tacked to a distinct tree, a notice board to the community—"Dead Man's Tree," as it became to be known. The sparse, scrawny poplar, a stick somehow growing in strained city soil on Loomis Street, stood in front of tenement number 725. Those whose names were posted for all to see became casualties.

The thudding resonance of an explosion here and there added a further touch of battlefield realism to the Nineteenth. Another denizen, observing the economic impact of those blasts, conceded: "Flats are vacant because the fear of bombs prevents anyone from moving. Houses cannot be mortgaged . . . because of the danger. And no one dares complain, or his life would be forfeited." This observer was almost certainly referring, albeit obliquely, to a man high on the ward's who's who list, Anthony D'Andrea.

By Prohibition, Anthony D'Andrea ranked as the Italian communal leader. Earlier, some recognized the highly-respected longtime resident Joseph Marzano as a key Italian in local affairs. Later, his protégé, Giuseppe "Diamond Joe" Esposito, became prominent, quietly manipulating the interests of the community. A jovial, orb-shaped character, "quaint and picturesque" yet "ninety percent bunk," Esposito abandoned a bakery to enter the more lucrative saloon business at 1048 Taylor Street. He also added the position of business agent for the International Hod Carriers, Building, and Construction Laborers of America to his résumé. Though these endeavors, he eventually controlled a block of votes and became a ward heeler who was prosperous enough to adorn himself with gems of his sobriquet. (A $5,000 ring and a $10,000 belt buckle with his initials radiating in diamonds were his regular gilding.) He was content with this small slice, but quite to the contrary, D'Andrea and an increasingly vocal portion of the ethnic majority Italians coveted exclusive political say in the region. They had no organized business to protect or advance as did Colosimo and Torrio; these voices simply wanted control. Even so, real district power had long resided with Irish Democratic alderman Johnny Powers. Therein lay the contentious issue.

After nearly twenty-five years, still overlord of the district, Powers was fully aware of his dwindling support from the Irish and German populations. Wisely, he began to construct a sizable and loyal Italian support base. Quite simply, in exchange for votes, the more unfortunate were given low-level district patronage jobs. Others played his political game for loftier employment. One eventually became a policeman and then used that track to be assigned less hazardous duty as a bailiff in a courtroom. He became a loyal Powers adherent and, later, a Powers precinct captain. In turn, these and other Powers supporters canvassed the ward scouting for other such go-getters. Just as he did years ago with the Irish, Powers tirelessly conducted himself throughout the ward's Italian neighborhoods as the refashioned and contemporary Italian benefactor. Posing as a humble, church-going servant of God, Powers gave presents at weddings and christenings, rallied round church bazaars, etc. He even paid funeral expenses for the most indigent cases. And naturally, when all else failed, bribery remained a remedy on Election Day. It worked well enough to garner sufficient Italian loyalty along the way and easily insure election victory time and time again.

D'Andrea and a number of Italians with long-standing residency, however, could not be hoodwinked by Powers's projections of concern. For them, Powers offerings were insufficient. In support of this opposition, the local Italian language newspaper *La Tribuna Italiana Transatlantica* derided Powers's Italian support as "disgraceful," even snidely referring to Powers as "Gianinni Pauli." They printed his unfulfilled campaign promises to fix the community. Consequently, the time was ripe for a change in the ward's political leadership, something Diamond Joe Esposito apparently declined. That's when D'Andrea stepped forward. He heaped upon himself the great responsibility of the Italian cause, an apparently righteous motive, but also one of potential self-serving autocracy—his cause. He was now the preeminent Italian of the Nineteenth Ward, some said in the whole of Chicago itself. Anyone who dared complain answered to him.

——⚬⚬⚬——

Born in Italy in 1872, Anthony D'Andrea attended the University of Palermo, possibly studying for the priesthood, before landing in Chicago about 1900. At first, he toughed it out as a laborer and hod carrier; after accumulating a little money, he utilized his educational experience in order to serve high society types as a linguist. With his serious, business-like manner and refinement, he very much behaved like an academic, with his suit, fedora, and round-rimmed spectacles providing the finishing scholarly touch. Eventually D'Andrea studied law, and in little time, he accrued a small fortune. As one of Chicago's most noted and popular Italian citizens, D'Andrea also became involved in many benevolent societies aiding his people such as the Italian-American Red Cross, the Italian Trinacria Benevolent Association, and the Italian Colonial Committee; he presided over these last two as their president.

Yet there was another version of D'Andrea shown mainly to his own people, and his sometimes sour facial expression hinted of his true demeanor, which one of his colleagues described as "so savage and so fierce . . . greatly feared in all the United States." Scholarly upbringing aside, D'Andrea could lay claim to being a local labor power for years. He served as business agent for the Sewer and Tunnel Miners Union, of whose members D'Andrea was suspected of extorting a certain percentage of wages in return for work assignments. Even so, he could later count on his résumé the presidency of both the International Hod Carriers and the Water Pipe Extension Laborers unions. In the sum of the three groups, he realized great power. They could allow him to wreak havoc among the construction industry, if he so desired. And as part of an earlier business venture, D'Andrea succeeded in imposing his jurisdiction on the Macaroni Manufacturers Union, a significant monopoly since pasta products were an Italian necessity.

Moreover, one local reporter recognized him as "a leader of certain elements of the ward." What he may have been referring to, and foremost among D'Andrea's affiliations, was his membership in the Unione Siciliana, one of the strongest foreign organizations in the country. The Chicago chapter was incorporated shortly before the turn of the century and soon became the city's largest, most influential Italian organization, with an estimated thirty neighborhood chapters. Originally benevolent in nature to its members, providing loans and insurance to new arrivals, the Unione eventually fell under the control of less scrupulous and empathetic individuals and was gradually perverted for use as a tool for personal gain and power. With the Unione as a pry bar, D'Andrea, who had elevated himself to the position of the organization's chief Chicago administrator, could now exact tribute from the poor community *pisan* in return for basic rights—something so small as the right to peddle fruit from a pushcart. It was simple extortion, just like the Black Hand, a New World imitation of the Old World Mafia tradition, though not necessarily the Mafia itself.

Regardless of whether the Unione had any connections with the Mafia, Nicola Gentile, D'Andrea's countryman and a prominent crime figure in the United States as well as a Chicago resident during D'Andrea's rise, recognized him as, in a sense, the city's *Capo Mafioso*. D'Andrea was described at the time as someone "who had long lorded it over a fear stricken ward, too afraid of his power to cross him." Anyone looking for Lord D'Andrea, Unione leader, labor boss, benevolent executive, might stop at his official office at 854 South Halsted, though he was more likely to be found at the Italian-American Educational Club at 1022 West Taylor. He counted the club presidency on his lengthy résumé, and here he hosted district businessmen as well as gun-toters.

With all his community attachments in hand, D'Andrea was set to make a run at Powers. Though he could not lay claim to twenty-plus years of public office as Powers could, D'Andrea was no political neophyte. Neither was he a "shining light of morality." Aroused to community activism in 1914, he campaigned unsuccessfully for county commissioner. During his run for election, an investigation into his past unveiled a criminal record for counterfeiting coins for which he served thirteen months. Further investigation revealed his unsavory history as a former authority in the old red light district, and he may have been a defrocked priest. "To make an accusation of this kind against a man," D'Andrea pleaded, "who has tried to outlive his past by an honest and honorable career, is worse than murder." The appeal was successful. Dirt notwithstanding, he gained enormous community sympathy.

Confident of his support as he perceived its growth, D'Andrea forged ahead with a campaign to dislodge Powers's crony, junior ward alderman James Bowler, in the 1916 primary election. The Powers machine was more than adequately oiled with money and patronage to maintain its position. The D'Andrea faction, though not as seasoned as Powers's, was not without great influence; for their side, guns spoke loudly. The most notable casualty, often regarded as the footing upon which all future violence would be heaped, was Powers advocate and ward heeler Frank Lombardi. At the height of the primary strife, on February 21, 1916, three men gunned down Lombardi in his saloon at 1120 Taylor Street in the very heart of the Italian quarter. Lombardi's daughter explained her father's dissension with D'Andrea and held his camp to be guilty, and newspaper accounts concurred with her estimate. In the end, the sides split the Italian vote with D'Andrea culling most of those district newcomers, the so-called "invaders." However, with all the votes counted and charges of vote fraud heard and denied, Irishman Bowler gained the party nomination and retained his city council seat.

Despite his ability to maintain his Nineteenth Ward position, Powers recognized in D'Andrea a determined adversary. In an attempt to alleviate the growing defiance he was able to defeat and respect but which he was unable to completely render impotent, Powers extended to D'Andrea what amounted to a peace treaty. Powers proffered D'Andrea his prize Democratic Committeeman post within the Nineteenth Ward in return for D'Andrea's support of Alderman Bowler in the 1920 elections. The position virtually ranked second in ward authority. In a speech full of munificence, Powers attributed his action to the need to empower Italian representation. Of course, the nomination represented a mere formality since Powers's candidates always won. D'Andrea ran unopposed. But the victory was short-lived. Only two months later, the Supreme Court of Illinois overruled the state's primary law under which the election was held, invalidating the outcome. As result, Powers retained his old post.

A loss of prominence, and perhaps smelling a double-cross in the latest encounter, soured D'Andrea and prompted more malicious endeavors. On September 28, 1920, barely two months after D'Andrea's defeat by the Illinois Supreme Court, a powder bomb detonated on the front porch of Powers's 1284 McAllister home. The midnight explosion broke several windows of Nitto friend Dr. Ronga's home down the street as well as windows six blocks away.

D'Andrea sent his notice and placed his cards on the table, with "no quarter asked and none given." That winter D'Andrea sidestepped the conventional primary campaign in favor of crusading as a non-partisan candidate in the general election, butting heads with Powers winner take all. Besides the usual threats of mayhem, bombs, and thuggery, D'Andrea cashed in his political debts to aid his battle. Though a Democrat by principle, in the previous mayoral election D'Andrea liberally donated to Republican Big Bill Thompson's re-election campaign. This action was thought to wrangle him enough say to select and dominate certain election clerks and judges in the ward. D'Andrea's strategy of outmaneuvering Powers on the inside and intimidating everyone else on the outside gave him one last run at victory and provided one last bloody confrontation. The election date was set for February 22, 1921.

As expected, the D'Andrea camp went on the offensive, continuously threatening Powers with mayhem at every campaign appearance. But Powers would not stand idly by either. He rallied his own troops to harass D'Andrea. In addition, he brought to bear real organizational strength on his opponent's relatively inexperienced coalition.

On February 11, a bomb exploded amidst three hundred D'Andrea supporters crowded into a meeting hall at 854 Blue Island Avenue. At least three were severely wounded. Four days prior to the election, another attempt was made against Powers's rivals, this time to take out or at least send a message to a pair of weighty D'Andrea associates with one blow. That bomb damaged the home of Joseph Spica, president of the Sewer and Tunnel Miners Union, the same union for which D'Andrea was business agent. Coincidentally, Spica's son-in-law, a D'Andrea lieutenant and the presumed target, lived there as well. That blast jarred the neighborhood in which the Nittos sometimes socialized; their friends the Gottloebs lived only two short blocks away. Still another explosive device detonated at D'Andrea's headquarters in the waning hours before the election. Powers, in mock solicitude, offered a $2,000 reward for the arrest of the culprits, but no one ever collected it. The number of blasts elicited a bit of wit and sharp black humor from the press: "If the system [of bombing] continues to grow in popularity, we may expect ward leaders to be chosen for the amount of TNT they can inject into a campaign."

In addition to knowing about the very public proceedings of the campaign, Nitto was probably well informed of the behind-the-scenes activities thanks to friend and business associate Dr. Ronga. The doctor was not only D'Andrea's physician but a staunch campaign supporter as well. Despite his perilous proximity to the recent bombing at the Powers's home, non-Sicilian Dr. Ronga contributed to the D'Andrea cause. He and other Italian community leaders headed the Nineteenth Ward Non-Partisan Organization, an organ of the D'Andrea machine. They deluged the district with anti-Powers literature focusing mainly on ward social issues, slinging mud only as the consummate exclamation point. One letter in particular, dated February 1, 1921, specified ward deficiencies in sanitation, streetlights, and streetcar service as well as inadequate schools and playground equipment.

To emphasize their point, disclosures were advantageously made of Powers's relationships with criminals, and it was suggested that he no longer resided in the Nineteenth Ward proper but rather in the Third Ward on Michigan Avenue. Nothing came of the residency issue, and Dr. Ronga was never harmed. Most importantly, through Ronga's activities, Nitto would come to understand what to expect if D'Andrea won, as well as learning D'Andrea's who's who list of Italian friends and enemies. Whether he participated in any campaign activities is not known, but he was surely better informed of the proceedings than the ordinary citizen and knew enough to safely guide himself for the duration of the debacle.

Sensing a climax of sorts in the battle on election day, the Board of Election Commissioners put as many precautions in place as possible. Extra poll watchers were assigned, and ballots were unavailable to polling stations until the morning of the election to prevent, in as much as possible, any irregularities. The city detailed a more potent force of 400 policemen for patrol duty in the ward that day. A special squad of twenty-five was sent to pick up loiterers and potential troublemakers;

some fifty suspects were arrested before noon, and a similar number were picked up as the day wore one. The polls closed without further incident. As the cold night wore on and the votes were counted, it became clear that, as author Humberto Nelli later wrote, "the only candidate who seriously threatened Powers's control over the ward failed because he could be pictured as even more corrupt and disreputable than Johnny De Pow himself." D'Andrea lost. The final tally gave Powers a plurality of 381votes (3,984 to 3,603), the closest contest of his career.

Of course, Anthony D'Andrea was not the acquiescent type.

<hr>

By 1921 Frank Nitto had settled down with his wife, Rose, into an apartment at 922 South Halsted, a short distance from Taylor. Taking a casual walk south to the busy corner the day after the election, he hardly could have missed the crude, hand-scrawled sign tied to a nearby telephone pole that read, "Move or die." The culprits addressed the threat to the owner and tenants of a three-story apartment building the next block up on Forquer Street. It was a sign of the times.

<hr>

With such a thin margin of victory and several precinct counts not in his favor, D'Andrea duly filed for a recount, charging fraud. Soon, he abruptly dropped the lawful challenge in favor of a self-directed and ultimately more disastrous strategy. D'Andrea may have lost the election, but as the local Italian power, he would teach those traitors of his own extraction a lesson. "Old accounts had to be settled," noted one contemporary.

There were whispers on the street of a post-election meeting between D'Andrea and his most loyal adherents, a gathering that most certainly included at least Angelo and Jim Genna of the notorious Genna family, a bundle of six scruffy brothers gradually assuming prominence in the affairs of Little Italy. Sons of Sicilian parents who perhaps died early and left the boys to fend for themselves in the hellhole community, the swarthy, dark-haired, dark-eyed brood may have started importing olives and other commodities to get by. Now hard-bitten and streetwise, they cast their lot with D'Andrea. Gunman and local cabaret owner Samuel Amatuna, usually known as "Samoots" or "Samuzzo," politician and saloon owner Frank "Don Chick" Gambino, and suspected murderer "Two-Gun Johnny" Gardino sat in on the conference as well. The meeting's rumored topic of discussion was a call for volunteers who might erase certain individuals from a list of names, with a reward of $500 for each name removed. Police think Gardino was responsible for importing gunmen for the feud. A little less than two weeks after the election, they began crossing off names.

The first Italian Powers adherent who made D'Andrea's hit list, though without a Nineteenth Ward political portfolio but with a foolish mouth that blabbered about his apparently minuscule contribution to Powers's election triumph, was one Gaetano Esposito. A dandy tough once charged with murder, he perhaps felt assured of his position after the election. But Esposito found out just how far his unsubstantiated, self-proclaimed clout would carry him. Early one evening, he was kidnapped, driven to the Columbus Extension Hospital at Lytle and Gilpin streets, shot twice and pitched out into the gutter. Just for good measure, one of the men leaned out the window and fired five more times into his body. No corpse pick-up was required—his so-called clout earned him a direct deposit at the hospital morgue.

Of more elevated community status and a Municipal Court deputy bailiff for many years, Paul Labriola—thirty-nine, married, and the father of two children—was another of those tagged for execution. He lived with his family on West Congress between Des Plaines and Halsted streets. Described as a "levelheaded, easygoing man . . . a fine type of Americanized Italian," he was also a loyal Powers supporter and precinct captain. During the aldermanic campaign, D'Andrea supporters, reportedly including gunmen Samoots Amatuna and Frank Gambino, attempted to sway his opinion. Labriola had none of their canvassing and explained he owed nothing to D'Andrea; he walked away despite their pleas, which now turned to threats. Unscathed through the election, Labriola secured top-billing on the death list by proficiently delivering his Seventh Precinct to Powers by a mind-boggling 230–9 margin. At approximately 9:10 a.m. on March 8, 1921, Labriola kissed his wife at the front door and proceeded west on Congress Street on his way to work. As he did, two men approached from the corner of Halsted. Labriola, ever the affable precinct man, nodded greetings to the two strangers as they neared, and in return they pumped two slugs into him, pitching him headfirst to the pavement. Another three rushed forward and may have contributed a couple of spiteful shots, then one of the assailants from the Halsted side straddled him and, with vengeful maliciousness, fired round after round into him as fast as he could repeatedly pull the trigger. Another name crossed off the list.

Four hours after Labriola's murder, another name was erased with blood. Harry Raimondi, one of D'Andrea's fellow alumni from the University of Palermo, followed the same path as D'Andrea to the West Side. From their time at the university, they considered themselves "blood brothers," a sacred bond not to be taken lightly. Both became labor leaders in Chicago early on, and later, Raimondi succeeded in carving out a business niche on the Near West Side selling olive oil and opening a cigar shop on Garibaldi Place between Polk and Taylor. During that time, though, he formed an association with the Powers organization, in due course becoming a precinct captain. Now as ward politics heated up, D'Andrea reminded Raimondi of their blood loyalty and perhaps of his community standing. Fully expecting blood to be thicker than politics, D'Andrea enlisted his support only to be rebuffed—so much for blood brotherhood.

At one o'clock in the afternoon on the day of the Labriola murder, four men approached Raimondi's cigar store on Garibaldi Place. Two passed by, then paused warily outside the old-fashioned little store whose narrow full-length windows announced the proprietor in gilded, arched fashion across each pane. The other two sauntered into the store. They stepped to the counter and purchased ten-cent cigars from Raimondi, lit them, and nonchalantly scrutinized the remainder of the interior. Satisfied at having established Raimondi's presence, the pair exited with a nod to the gunmen outside. Their accomplices entered to purchase the same cigars.

As Raimondi swiped their fifty-cent piece off the counter and fumbled in his pocket to make the necessary change, each man removed a gun from his coat and opened fire. Hit three times at point-blank range, one shot penetrating his head, Raimondi briefly sustained his stance, gasped as if to say something, then toppled over dead. The first and last lesson of violating of blood loyalty coolly administered, the men escaped. Soon the grieving widow appeared, fighting her way through a cordon of gawkers and sobbing the all-too-familiar district phrase, *Madre di Dio!* (Mother of God!) as she grieved over her husband's body.

The next day events continued to occur rapidly, not all of them lethal. A Powers follower reported a threat that was delivered in a slickly poignant and sinister manner. An elderly woman whose face was cloaked by a shawl entered his pharmacy near Powers's McAllister home to inform him that she had seen the death list and his name was on it: "You are on it and you will die. I warn you to get away from here." She then walked out. Though totally unhinged by the event, he survived unscathed. That night, another unfortunate did not—he was dumped from an auto against a back alley wall of a stable in the 1100 block of West Congress between Aberdeen and Racine. His body was discovered the next day by three laborers working in an abandoned saloon adjacent to the stable. Later, a gunfight ignited in a grocery store owned by a Powers advocate, once again only two blocks from the home of Nitto's friends the Gottloebs. This was followed by the murder of the presumed Powers associate Tony Marchese.

The murders alarmed the city enough for it to rush one hundred policemen to the ward with strict orders to maintain peace. Men were routinely patted down and searched for weapons, especially anyone meandering along Polk, Taylor, and Forquer streets. Word spread so quickly that the male denizens of the district seemed to evaporate from the streets. The rare man out, upon crossing paths with a policeman, would instinctively raise his hands in the air and say, "See, no gun." For a while, the police presence seemed to do the trick. The ward, one reporter announced after a visit, resembled nothing less than a ghost town under curfew. The once bustling Polk Street cafés and coffee houses were now deserted. Horse-drawn wagons clomped down the stone streets with a deafening echo, and people walked hurriedly with their eyes downcast.

⊰∘⁄∘⁄∘⊱

In the midst of the war in the Nineteenth Ward, Frank Nitto needed a moment of tranquility to attend to a piece of long overdue personal business. After nearly twenty-eight years in the country, Nitto was still an alien. Somehow, in all his time in Brooklyn and Chicago, the matter didn't seem to be very important to him until now. The fever pitch of ward violence may have induced him to act. Police swarmed the district, and if he were picked up by chance, he could be deported. His booze business added to his vulnerability, and friend/business associate Louis Greenberg may have been the catalyst for his actions.

Greenberg had learned his lesson the hard way. Back in May 1919, Greenberg, along with several others, was indicted for waylaying a load of whiskey. He wrangled out of the jam, supposedly by enlisting the aid of aldermen Kenna and Coughlin. Of course, it diminished his bankroll considerably to have the matter dropped, so much so that Greenberg grumbled incessantly about the price. The truth is that, at the time of his arrest, he was still an alien. Greenberg filed his Declaration of Intention on February 2, 1915, but had failed to follow through on it. The payoff amount may have been so excruciatingly high because he had to pay to make sure this detail was overlooked. By law, the declaration was valid for seven years from the date filed, and now in the spring 1921, with less than a year left to act, Greenberg was in the process of finalizing his naturalization papers at roughly the same time Nitto was beginning his citizenship proceedings.

The day after the Labriola and Raimondi murders, Nitto trundled over to the office of the deputy clerk of Superior Court of Cook County, Morris Marx, and filled out the brief document pledging to renounce King Victor Emmanuel III of Italy in favor of his present country. To the court Nitto declared his occupation as barber, his age as thirty-five, his marital status and wife's name (Rosa), and provided all the information regarding his entry into the country that he could remember. Then he duly signed the document as "Frank Ralph Nitto," received his copy of the triplicate form, and left. Inexplicably, the document remained in his possession gathering dust for a few more years before he would act on it again.

—⚬∕∿∕⚬—

The violence in the Nineteenth Ward flared up for a summer-long session, and this time, the momentum shifted inexorably against D'Andrea and his men. Abruptly, his bodyguard, Two-Gun Johnny Gardino, was shot and wounded in front of Giuseppe Nuzzo's poolroom at 934 Polk Street; thugs in a black auto shrouded with side curtains drove by and spewed out a volley from a sawed-off shotgun. With Gardino on the shelf, the opposition cut to the chase and went directly after D'Andrea himself. In the middle of a workday five men ambled into his office at 854 South Halsted and placed the muzzle of a gun against his windpipe, telling him, "You're going to take a big trip." Just as the posse was about to shuffle off with their prize, they panicked at the sight of a policeman and took flight without D'Andrea.

If the opposition couldn't kill him, they may have tipped off the police to a good time to raid his Italian-American Educational Club, and in April, the police did just that, hauling off several men, including Angelo Genna and Johnny Gardino, who were charged with disorderly conduct, gun-toting, and gambling. An annoyed D'Andrea was also taken in and booked for carrying a concealed weapon, but he was released in short order.

D'Andrea's foes remained steadfast. A brief time later, they sent an anonymous warning letter to the occupant of a first-floor apartment in D'Andrea's apartment building at 902 South Ashland. The occupant, Abraham Wolfson, showed the note to D'Andrea. In it, the culprits advised Wolfson, in the best interests of his health, to move his family and possessions out, for within fifteen days, they would "blow up the building and kill the whole D'Andrea family." Unfazed, D'Andrea paid no attention, thinking the Black Hand was behind it—about this triviality of ward life, he couldn't be bothered. Wolfson thought otherwise. He packed up his family and moved out. The next day, the family occupying the apartment above him did the same.

Nearly two weeks later on May 11, 1921, D'Andrea, Joe Lapisa, a building contractor who doubled as D'Andrea's bodyguard and chauffeur since the election violence, and Mike Iarussi, a local undertaker who would oversee some of the most prominent gangster funerals of the coming decade, were all playing cards upstairs at Amato's restaurant on South Halsted Street a block or so from D'Andrea's office. Shortly before 2 a.m., the game broke up. Iarussi, knowing of the threat against the D'Andrea home and still concerned for his friend's health, offered to escort D'Andrea home. "There's no danger," replied D'Andrea. Besides, Lapisa would be ushering him home. His confidence was clear to Lapisa during the short drive west to Ashland when he told his chauffeur, "This talk about blowing me up with dynamite is the bunk."

Earlier that evening, D'Andrea's next-door neighbor, George King, had been out for a stroll when he noticed lights in the vacant first-floor flat of the D'Andrea building. He didn't give it a great deal of thought, since decorators had busied themselves there for long hours the previous week preparing the rooms for the next renter. To King, the lights he saw through three windows in a half-hexagon-shaped architectural protrusion on the left side of the building, suggested that the workers were putting in another long day. The lights were later extinguished, and afterward a pair of men slithered into the building undetected through a basement window and tiptoed upstairs into the abandoned apartment, taking positions near the porch-side window. Veiled in darkness, they waited.

Lapisa curbed his vehicle in front of D'Andrea's residence, casually saw his boss out, and drove off south on Ashland. In the dim cascade of light from distant street lamps, D'Andrea traversed a fifteen-foot swath of turf and trees along Ashland before crossing the sidewalk to the concrete front steps of his building. He was perhaps on the second or third step when the assassins lurking in the former Wolfson apartment leveled a sawed-off shotgun through the slightly drawn window curtains and blasted him. D'Andrea tumbled to the sidewalk, hit in the abdomen and left arm by a dozen or more slugs.

Bleeding profusely, he pulled himself up, began to crawl, and drew a weapon. He might have heard the commotion of shuffling feet inside as the killers raced to escape to the rear. Weakly grasping his gun, D'Andrea aimed his fire where he perceived his enemies to be, the target now nothing but a black void. Three shots impacted near the top of the bay window, scattering grains of glass over the porch and steps; two grazed harmlessly off the decorative concrete pillar at the top of the stairs. Exhausted, anemic from his wounds, D'Andrea fell unconscious, face down on the lower step amidst some of the glass particles from the shattered window. Only the stillness of the late-night streets and the cascading glow of a nearby street lamp remained. Out back, the killers left or lost their hats. One contained a $20 bill and a penciled note that said "Flower for D'Andrea."

Gradually, neighborhood lights flicked on, including those in the third-floor D'Andrea apartment. His wife and daughters came downstairs to investigate the noises that had interrupted their late-night tranquility. There, they discovered D'Andrea among the detritus of violence. He was rushed to Jefferson Park Hospital, where surgeons operated without delay. Early the next morning, his physician, Dr. Gaetano Ronga, pronounced a slight improvement in his condition but warned that his chance of recovery was "one in a thousand." His wife and daughters kept vigil as he lingered, muttering incoherently. Shortly before noon, D'Andrea suffered a relapse of internal bleeding, and Ronga prepared for a last-ditch surgery to stop the hemorrhaging. However, after consulting with specialists, it was decided D'Andrea's body could not withstand another invasive procedure, and he was wheeled back to his room to await his fate. An hour later, cognizant to the end, he lovingly whispered "God bless you" to each member of his family, kissed each one, and then died.

⟶∘∕∘∕∘⟵

With D'Andrea dead and buried, the political score settled, it seemed the matter was ended, yet for the remainder of the year, the body count continued to rise, not decline. In addition, some of the bloodletting began to crop up *outside* the Nineteenth. Most of the attacks were easily traced back to the ward, the victims clearly recognizable as a Powers man or D'Andrea man—seemingly acts of political retribution played out back and forth. Toward the end of summer, the police were beginning to believe the motives had as much to do with "a new force attempting to solicit tribute" as much as with ward politics. Given that Prohibition and its potential illicit revenues were in their infancy, that estimation may have been very close to the truth, since with D'Andrea gone the tribute and domination of the ward's Italian population was at stake.

Within twelve days of D'Andrea's murder, assassins felled two other men in three attempts. Even before D'Andrea was buried, one of his reputed henchmen was fished out of the sanitary drainage canal near Summit, his body badly beaten and stuffed in a sack. Shortly after midnight on May 14, someone fired a shotgun through the front bedroom window of D'Andrea man Pasquale Tanzillo. He wasn't hurt, but nearly the entire 900 block of Vernon Park Place remained alert with fear and was brightly illuminated for the remainder of the night. Nineteenth Ward resident Michael Licari moved out of the ward south to 3021 Shields Avenue, believing himself to be a marked man. Word evidently was out that he was one of those arrested with D'Andrea and company back in April at the Italian-American Educational Club. His move perhaps took him too far if he was, in fact, the loyal D'Andrea gunman he was thought to be. In the early morning hours of May 26, scarcely ten days after his boss was buried, Licari was strolling along the 100 block of West Thirty-seventh Place near his business when he was gunned down from behind, five bullets fired into his back. Official police theory traced his murder back to the Nineteenth Ward.

Within another few weeks, the killings took a clear turn away from the tit-for-tat political feud theory when Joseph Lapisa, D'Andrea's chauffeur the night he was killed, was himself blown away on the afternoon of June 27. He had left his home near Dead Man's Tree on South Loomis in his touring car full of posters publicizing an Italian fundraising picnic intended to benefit the community's children. His altruistic business that day took him on a promotional expedition away from the Nineteenth Ward to the heart of Little Sicily on the north side of town. As he inched the car along Oak Street scouting for strategic positions for the placards in the car, two companions in the backseat leveled guns at the back of his head and fired. Lapisa slumped forward across the steering wheel, dead, as the pair dashed from the crawling vehicle and disappeared down a nearby alley. The Lapisa auto slowly rolled along Oak Street on its own for a half block before veering to the left side of the street, partially hopping the curb, and thumping to a standstill against a building near the corner of Cambridge Avenue.

Alarmed citizens soon crowded around the vehicle and observed, fittingly, the shadows of the magnificent spires and cross of the nearby Church of St. Phillip Benizi draped across Lapisa's body. Father Louis M. Gianbastiano appeared on the steps of the church and spoke to the crowd, saying, "If you know who the men were who have done this fearful crime, and if there is in you the least spirit of American-ism, you will go to the police and tell. You owe it to the good name of your race, which has been shamed on many an occasion by your silence. You owe it to our dear Lord. If you know these men, I implore you in the name of all good Americans and in the name of the Lord, to tell the police." The shamed community silence he referred to in his impromptu sermon was no doubt a reference to the many unsolved Black Hand extortion killings at nearby Death's Corner. Still, no one shed light on the Lapisa murder.

Some thought the motive for Lapisa's murder was a vow of vengeance he swore on D'Andrea's coffin, and on the surface Lapisa's death definitely appeared to be another tit-for-tat murder—except for one thing: the Maxwell Street police turned up information that Lapisa, prior to a fatal trip to Oak Street, had picked up his two passengers at the Italian-American Educational Club. Since D'Andrea's death, Angelo Genna and his brothers had been very active in the club, and young Angelo was regarded as being among D'Andrea's closest friends—so much so that on his deathbed D'Andrea was thought to have secured a promise from a powerful politi-cian to "take care of Genna." With this kind of political clout backing them, there is ample reason to pin this murder on the Gennas. It was they who aimed to step in as the local prime guns, and they weren't through.

Upon Joseph Lapisa's death, his foreman and the godfather to his children, Joseph Sinacola, took over the business with a promise to financially take care of Lapisa's widow and children. This he did loyally. Sinacola may have also gone one step further, uttering an oath of revenge at the time of his boss's death. This was an unwise move, especially when such outbursts could neither be taken back nor stay caged within the leaky, sieve-like walls of any Nineteenth Ward building for long. Apparently, though, it wasn't a pledge of violence; Sinacola had chosen the brave path of Americanism as laid out by Father Gianbastiano. Sinacola reported to police that he was ready to clear up all the mess in the Nineteenth Ward, to convey all he knew. Confident his intentions remained secret, he was sauntering down Blue Island Avenue on his way home from work one day, lunch bucket swaying in hand. An auto sneaked up alongside him, and hidden behind curtains, the occupants let loose with a shotgun volley and then sped off. Incredibly, poor aim saved his life. Only wounded, Sinacola was rushed to the hospital for treatment, and there he lay for a couple of days convalescing from his wounds.

Three weeks later, the Lapisa murder was played out again, this time on thirty-year-old Andrew Orlando, a barber, sometime bootlegger, and good friend of D'Andrea. One night, two men in Orlando's car shot him eleven times in the head and back.

Rumor had it that on D'Andrea's deathbed, he gave Two-Gun Johnny Gardino the name of his assailants to execute. This may have been enough to mark him for death by those in the opposing camp. Perhaps, though, Gardino was unproductive in tracing those individuals. Only four days after his boss was eliminated, police pinched Gardino again. Upon release, he disappeared, evidently not accomplishing much of anything. Somebody, though, had tailed him. Only two days after Orlando's murder, Gardino was felled only three doors from his home, outside Anton Basili's grocery store at 947 Polk Street. A lone assailant walked up to Gardino and two friends as they conversed on the street and discharged half of his six shots into Two-Gun Johnny. He then walked off, forever unidentified, ducking into a narrow alleyway between two buildings.

The Nineteenth Ward carnage climaxed on August 14 when Joseph Sinacola was gunned down in front of his wife and children. Sinacola was silenced forever, much to the dismay of the police, as he was really their only hope for breaking the code of silence surrounding the Nineteenth Ward bloodshed.

With Sinacola's elimination, the body count attributed to the Nineteenth Ward hostilities tapered off dramatically; only three other murders in the next three months might qualify for reckoning. On August 26, Dominic Guttillo, a retired grocer, age forty-four, who was identified as a former Powers man, was hacked down after he apparently moved to Little Sicily. On October 9, Joseph Marino, a D'Andrea henchman, was eliminated. Finally, on November 26, Nicola Adamo, another so-called Powers man, was dropped for good.

———⚬/⚬/⚬⚬———

When the dust settled, the bodies were buried, and the acrid smell of cordite cleared from the air, what did all the Nineteenth Ward hostilities amount to? The name Genna was the most prominent suspicious thread remaining in the Italian community. Angelo Genna, his brothers, and allies Samoots Amatuna and Frank Gambino remained unscathed throughout the battle. Amatuna and Gambino were fingered in the Labriola murder, then released after a mysterious witness identified Angelo Genna as the fanatical gunmen pumping bullets into the prone Powers associate. As for the corpses that piled up that summer, any one of them could account for a Genna attempt to eliminate suspected blabbermouths.

Quickly brought to trial, a judge found young Angelo not guilty of murdering Paul Labriola. During the trial, defense attorneys summoned a few local dignitaries to aid their case. Among them, Nitto associate Dr. Gaetano Ronga reliably testified to "the good reputation of Angelo Genna, but admitted he had never discussed that reputation with anybody." Genna was insulated from the law; D'Andrea saw to that as he lay on his deathbed.

After the trial, the Gennas inherited the local Italian-American Educational Club on Taylor as headquarters. It was here that Lapisa met and picked up his eventual murderers, and there was little doubt that Lapisa's friend Sinacola got it from the same source. Angelo may have rubbed out Raimondi as well—police suspected the same team that killed Labriola committed the Raimondi murder. Later, Mrs. Adamo quoted her husband as saying that if he were killed, "it will be the Gennas who will do it." Based on her statement, police arrested Angelo, Mike, and Jim Genna. That case quickly dissolved, and the men were released.

All told, the Gennas emerged from the scuffle with power radiating from two sources. First, Mike Merlo emerged as D'Andrea's successor as the leader of the Chicago Italian community and was the suspected head of the Unione. Contrasting greatly with his predecessor, Merlo conducted his affairs from the background in a quiet, business-like manner. He tolerated moneymaking lawlessness as long as the means of business did not include violence. Rather than fear him, locals on the street as well as community leaders looked to him to wisely arbitrate their disputes. The highly respected Merlo didn't delve directly into politics and apparently walked the line of neutrality during the Nineteenth Ward political scuffle even though the Gennas were close friends. They respected him greatly, and under Merlo's auspices, the Gennas were included among the Unione elite. His word was thought to be so valued throughout the community that even neighbors Torrio and Capone complied with his counsel.

Secondly, the Gennas' power came from the kind of weighty insurance that D'Andrea bequeathed them in the form of ward Republican go-getter Diamond Joe Esposito. The Gennas were now his "special pets." After several thriving years in the saloon game, Esposito opened the famous Bella Napoli Café at 850 South Halsted, just up the street from Frank Nitto and next door to his barber contact, Richard Russo. Here, simpletons and luminaries alike gathered for festive Italian cuisine or parties. The café's clientele was "a who's who of political Chicago," for if senators, mayors, judges, or even the governor wanted his votes, they came here to see him. During the café's run, it was often populated by hoodlums as well. Despite the Nineteenth Ward battles and Powers's ward rule, Esposito continued to extend his political clout by retaining his key block of Italian votes and leveraging connections extending beyond city hall all the way to the U.S. Senate. His opponents greatly respected him, and this, in turn, afforded him the ability to protect lawless associates.

───※⁂※───

Though Frank Nitto was never identified as a combatant, he emerged from the battles with a number of career-driving benefits. First, he survived the violence and as a bootlegger no less. Second, he certainly understood the Gennas to be the neighborhood authority and knew who their allied gunmen might be—vital intelligence, particularly in the ward's bootleg trade, which the Gennas would soon turn into their own. Third, he understood the underlying mechanics of power among many Chicago Italians, recognizing that Mike Merlo served as new head of the Unione and that local politics radiated from the Bella Napoli Café in the form of Joe Esposito. Fourth and finally, reinforcing his learning from Greenberg, he was likely more aware now than ever before of the value and necessity to suborn public officials rather than pompously ramming heads with them; they all had needs, be it votes, money, whatever. All this knowledge would serve him well.

At least one event outside the city may indicate that Nitto was at this time fairly advanced in the alcohol business. It is possible, but doubtful, that the Gennas were responsible for this. His alcohol business contact remained the expansive Louis Greenberg, who now networked great distances for a large amount of product. That event was Nitto's arrest in Galveston, Texas, early during Prohibition. The charge is unknown, but it is quite likely that it was alcohol-related.

Galveston lay at the water's edge on the Gulf of Mexico. Designated a port since 1837, it had recently experienced its greatest construction boom. Most importantly, Galveston was widely known as a notorious Wet town full of bawdy houses, gambling, and saloons—a Gomorrah by the sea to such an extent that one authority pronounced it as being "outside the United States." It was the ideal harbor to receive illegal booze shipments, and Italians were part of the port workforce; therefore, it would not seem odd for Nitto to be there. Nor was Nitto a stranger to Texas, having married in the state a short time back. Nitto's wedding in Dallas may have occurred while on just such a trip to the coast, the nuptials occurring little more than a month after legislation removed liquor from legal manufacture back in 1917. Further evidence that Nitto had indeed been to Galveston comes in the form of communications with two of the city's residents, one of whom was business contact Sam Maggeo, a most notorious character in that town during Prohibition.

Any such elevation of Nitto in the business could not have been the result of mere luck. While some of his good fortune was the result of accident—for example, meeting Louis Greenberg and subsequently entering the jewelry and liquor businesses through him—Nitto was mindful enough that should the door of opportunity open, he would walk through it and move up. No matter how small the step, he would be one rung above where he had stood on the economic ladder.

The one aspect of his personage that Greenberg knew about all along but that only became apparent to others much later, Nitto's cerebral focus on the business at hand, proved to be an exceptional plus at this time. This was particularly true in the money or accounting aspect of his business. To be sure, this focus was much overstated in later accounts that extolled his bookkeeping prowess, describing Nitto as being an "academic" or "almost alone in understanding business and accounting." Nitto really had no more erudition than many other hoodlums, but he applied himself so intensely to accounting because the skill was an essential ingredient of his everyday survival. This ability turned out to be his real asset and was the result of drive, not chance.

Among other fellows of his background, more often than not, manual tasks were the only route available to support a family, so few chose to pursue education or had reason or opportunity to exercise what education they had. To the more unlawful, regardless of ethnicity, education was scorned, thought to be beneath their dignity. It was easy and quite macho to carry a weapon and push your weight around, while bookkeeping probably appeared as a dreary, motionless, small-table task.

Of course, Nitto was no novice to the hooligan ways of the street either. As part of his Chicago ripening, he necessarily employed complimentary talents to solve business problems capably and efficiently. These abilities, combined with the nearly five years of the alcohol business he had under his belt and all his Nineteenth Ward experience, helped Frank Nitto evolve into an extremely valuable human resource for the height of Prohibition, something that would be in demand by the city gangs that were now forming to control the trade.

5

MR. NITTO, MEET MR. CAPONE

WHILE LOUIS GREENBERG JUMP-STARTED FRANK Nitto's career, the expansive Johnny Torrio unknowingly cemented his future.

The booze flow into Chicago during Prohibition was so extensive that the town was described as "the biggest alcohol clearing center of the world—Volstead or no Volstead." The supply, in part, came from the numerous opportunists who had jumped onto the bootleg bandwagon. Many nondescript rogue operators, some with an inkling of political pull (and many without), became small-time bootleggers and hit-and-miss retailers. In the main, most lacked Nitto's experience, yet, like Nitto, few possessed the wealth or position to become extensive speculators or permanent suppliers.

One of the best-known schemes of the early days of Prohibition was hatched by veteran First Ward panderer Michael "Mike de Pike" Heitler. Barely a year after the dry days were inaugurated, Heitler was arrested along with George Quinn, Nathaniel Pearlman, Frank McCann, William Trudell and others in what was then described as the biggest booze case of the time. As ringleader, Heitler slyly obtained $200,000 worth of whiskey directly from a Kentucky distiller using forged permits. When the rail car load arrived in Chicago, he attempted to double-cross the consignees at the rail yard but was caught. As Heitler's trial commenced, a chance raid on the Pioneer Bag and Metal Company on South Halsted netted another $150,000 worth of whiskey and the historically unremarkable personages of George and Abe Marco. Sundry loose cannon such as these might help alleviate the city's supply problems, but they lacked Torrio's orderliness and long-term business vision. The countless slipshod and greedy scoundrels might doom the bootleg trade to becoming a cutthroat free-for-all.

Amplifying the issue, gangs that were dominant within their indigenous regions of the city were evolving, generally set on satisfying the alcohol needs of local outlets. Their initial operations were rudimentary and consisted of obtaining product wherever it might be found. Some gangs were long-standing, like Ralph Sheldon's group, an outgrowth of the old Ragen's Colts gang on the South Side; others consisted mostly of career thugs, robbers, and burglars now turned booze entrepreneurs. For example, Terry Druggan and Frankie Lake came from "the Valley," a desolate section of the city south of Little Italy. Eventually they bought into five breweries and became so wealthy that the pair became the first Chicago gangster targets of the Treasury Department for income tax evasion.

The individuals who made up each gang were often of the same ethnicity, and booze sales could easily provide additional fuel for long-standing ethnic hostilities. Italians in the First (Torrio) and Nineteenth (Genna) wards faced the Irish, led by Dean O'Banion on the North Side, the O'Donnell brothers—William "Klondike," Bernard, and Myles on the Far West Side, and the unrelated O'Donnell brothers—Spike, Walter, Thomas, and Steven—on the far-south city limits. Near the stockyards to the southwest, a Pole, Joe Saltis, and his gang, including savage killer Frank McErlane, served the Slavic community. The gradual expansion of these gangs would leave little room for truly unaffiliated runners such as Nitto.

As an alcohol mover, influences upon Nitto would seem to have primarily tugged from two directions. Unquestionably most critical to Nitto's immediate business future were the Italians in his home borough. Though the commercial substance of Will Rogers's sage observation about Prohibition—"if you think this country ain't wet, just watch them drink"—was lost on D'Andrea in his quest for power, the Gennas got into the liquor business. They dabbled in the bootleg trade prior to the climax of the ward battle (James and Angelo were arrested for possession of miniscule amounts of alcohol), but the Gennas always seemed to be muddling carelessly in and out of other trouble. Old habits die hard, and Prohibition wealth did not come forthwith.

Angelo lengthened his rap sheet to include auto theft. He was also snagged red-handed with merchandise from a jewelry store robbery but escaped prosecution. Six months after dodging charges in both the Labriola and Adamo murders, Angelo was charged in the murder of local merchant John Notti, but in this case, too, he was absolved. Only a short time later, he was finally pinched for jail time in connection with a federal Mann Act case in which Angelo intervened on behalf of two acquaintances charged with mistreating a fifteen-year-old girl. To the girl's relatives, who had the guts to testify, Angelo gave a warning: "We've just killed three, and we'll add you people to the list." The threat earned him a one-year federal sentence.

The youngest of the Genna brothers was Mike, also known as "Little Mike" or "Il Diavolo" ("the Devil") for his fiery disposition, who was arrested in September 1921, along with two others at the Italian-American Educational Club. The group was charged with participating in an interstate auto-theft ring. Mike skipped bail, yet nothing came of the charges and he went free in time to be arrested and released along with Angelo in the Adamo murder.

James, the Genna clan's nominal leader, operated a speakeasy near Taylor and Halsted streets and was a murder suspect in the ward disputes. The other brothers seemed to steer clear of serious trouble but were no soft touches either. Sam acted as the political agent and sometime Black Hander of the group, while Pete operated a rough-edged saloon. Tony, the most even-keeled and dignified of the bunch, was thought to be "little given to disorder." Dubbed "the Aristocrat" for his more refined looks and genteel comportment, he never dirtied his hands in rough-and-tumble duty but acted more as the outfit's counselor, or *consigliere*. With half the family bouncing in and out of trouble, they would make little immediate headway to control or collect substantial bootleg profits, and thus Nitto's early commerce skated just outside their authority.

It was apparently only after they fully emerged as the power in the ward that the clan began in earnest to enter into wholesale alcohol production, which became their business forte, the foundation of their real power, and the basis for the Genna fortune—and the immediate menace to Nitto's own business. The Gennas, along with Samoots Amatuna, began an alcohol business by re-cooking commercial alcohol for use in bootlegging. Family friend and lawyer Henry Spingola was generally credited with expanding the Genna operation. He arrived at the rather simple but revolutionary idea of distilling alcohol en masse via simple home stills farmed out among their brethren. The Gennas supplied the locals with the copper stills, corn and sugar to start manufacture. The job, according to one contemporary reporter, "was a soft snap for the Sicilians. The man of the house had little to do save smoke his pipe, keep the still stoked, and scratch his back." In return, the *pisan* earned an average of $15 a day, a bonanza compared to honest earnings from sundry difficult, dirty street jobs. On schedule, Genna drivers collected the raw alcohol in five-gallon cans and paid the tenants. Gathered at their central warehouse on West Taylor, the liquid then became whatever bar stock they wished with colors, artificial flavorings, and labels added as required. It was an ingenious win-win situation so efficient that demand continually outstripped supplies.

Subsequently, the clan somehow gathered enough clout to obtain government permission to produce alcohol at a plant later identified by federal agents as the Allegheny Chemical and Products Company at 641 Orleans Street in the heart of Little Sicily. The federal permit allowed the legal withdrawal of 35,000 gallons of alcohol per month for sale to pharmaceutical supply houses and the like. Under the Gennas, a great deal of this was diverted to stills hidden in the Italian slums for refining. This rerouting was accomplished without difficulty since overtaxed enforcement officials seldom found time to visit the place.

To keep pace with demand, the brothers began to import families from their native Sicily to assist. They possibly organized the moves through their Marsala Club, a guild they founded to assist those from their parents' hometown in Sicily (for which the club was named). Of course, the monetary inducement easily swayed emigration. Spotless brother Tony, known on the surface as a benevolent contractor of homes for the poor, was generally credited with arranging flats for the newcomers and deciding when and who would cook alcohol. Family standouts Angelo, now "Bloody Angelo," and Mike, because of their fearless gunplay, enforced the Genna decree.

As a result of their activities, their operation was estimated to rake in $350,000 a month gross, $150,000 net. Overall assets reached $5 million. Overhead expenses necessary to maintain the cartel included payoffs to the Maxwell Street Police Station, only four blocks from their warehouse. Graft to police amounted to $6,500 or more a month, and as an extra carrot, any enterprising men in blue could purchase Genna alcohol at wholesale prices and become bootleggers themselves. The bribes gave the Gennas protection for their booze shipments and twenty-four-hour advance notice of any "show" raids the station might have to put on to demonstrate anti-alcohol activity to higher-ups.

Appearing in the spotlight of prosperity, the brothers revered their families and homes. All attended church regularly. All carried a rosary and crucifix, yet guns often accompanied them. Still, the mean, hard-bitten edge to the group remained. The community generally hated them, and the feeling was mutual. They respected few outside their intimate circle and maintained a shield of secrecy about themselves, huffily resenting any inquiries as to their business. They were described as possessing "heartless cruelty," and the best advice those who really knew them could offer to strangers was to stay clear of the brothers wherever they happened to land.

The brothers' intimate circle was composed chiefly of fellow Sicilian toughs. Of these, Samoots Amatuna was perhaps, at times, the looniest and most murderously erratic. A member of the musicians union, he tried to kill his business agent. Though unsuccessful in that venture, he achieved a more lethal level of success when a laundry delivery person returned his fine clothing in unsatisfactory condition. The pretentious Samoots killed not the driver but rather the horse pulling the wagon. Amatuna, as previously noted, abetted D'Andrea and Genna in the Nineteenth Ward vendetta war, yet when he attained a degree of wealth and flapped manifestly around the dingy streets of Little Italy in his habitually splashy wardrobe, it was Amatuna, rather than the Gennas, whom local citizens recognized as the most eagerly charitable to the district's needy.

The sleek Orazio Tropea, on the other hand, was an ill-tempered and utterly vicious gunman who, in most cases, needed only a gaze from his beady, obsidian eyes to obtain submission. Compounding Tropea's physical and temperamental intimidation was his belief that he was a sorcerer. As such, he could easily invoke fear in any superstitious immigrant, though for any holdouts, a firearm sufficed.

A more recent Genna recruit was Giuseppe Nerone, alias *Il Cavalieri*, also known as Anthony Spano. In Nerone, the Gennas had a far less eccentric character than either Amatuna or Tropea. Gaining a university education and teaching experience before drifting into crime in Sicily, he earned a reputation as a feared torpedo. The Gennas imported Nerone at the height of the D'Andrea-Powers war to act as a bodyguard and gunman. Recognizing the value of his education, they soon appointed him as a manager of sorts during their initial forays into the booze business and later elevated his status to some degree. All the while, he still maintained the slick sophistication and manners gleaned from his higher education, the source of his sobriquet.

Head and shoulders above all the Gennas hired thugs and cutthroats, however, stood the duo of John Scalise and Albert Anselmi. Imports from Sicily by way of the Marsala Club, they were most decorously pronounced later to be "the Mutt and Jeff of murder." Scalise, the taller of the two, had a powerful build, scruffy dark hair, and a lazy eye, while Anselmi was shorter and stocky. Neither possessed the least speck of moral conscious. Whether using point-blank pistol shots or the ripping spray of shotgun slugs or machine-gun-fire, to this pair, colder than any others in the Genna stable of executioners, murder was just a job—kill and collect the fee, all in a day's work. In this trade, they were quite valued for their unhesitating efficiency; their targets did not survive the date of execution. And if anyone came between them and their target, they mercilessly killed the interloper as well. Together, they would figure in several of the decade's headline murders.

Unfortunately for the Gennas, who enjoyed a rather high opinion of themselves, their followers suffered from the same bloated self-image. Combine this ego with the group's clannish nature and fierce vindictiveness, and the easily unhinged bunch was far from the business ideal. They were perfectly described as "allies to be handled as cautiously as scorpions." Nevertheless, the Gennas remained the biggest players in local alcohol production, and Nitto would increasingly have to consent to their gravity.

———

Another large player in the liquor business who might impact Nitto's share was Louis Greenberg's friend and financial client, Dean O'Banion. Excepting the Little Sicily conclave around Oak and Milton streets, he reigned as boss from the Chicago River north to Center Street and east of the river's north fork to the shore of Lake Michigan. Consisting of predominantly immigrant Irish, German, and Scandinavian populations as well as the high society Gold Coast, this area constituted the city's Forty-second and Forty-third wards. Gunplay and murder on a whim or well-planned were carried out with "sunny brutality" by O'Banion, who was never without a rosary. One police chief attributed twenty-five bodies to O'Banion's trigger finger.

A habitual roughneck from his early days, so he remained. With no organizational outlets such as Torrio had inherited from Big Jim, early Prohibition measures probably meant little to O'Banion other than a random hijack and sale—just another means in which to make a buck. This may explain why he whiled away much of the early bootleg period robbing and safecracking instead. A partial list of suspected activities for the year 1918, with approximate revenue of $9,919, reads:

January 29 The Western Dairy robbery: net about $2,000
September 3 The Schaeffer Theatre robbery; net about $1,400
November 5 The Prudential Life robbery: net $3,365
December 3 The Borden's Dairy Robbery: net roughly $1,154

Good money in 1918, but the risks were weighty and the amounts trifling compared to bootlegging potentials.

At what point the true promise of Prohibition and organization dawned upon O'Banion is questionable, but that it did is not. In part to seize the enormous beer supply potential among his own beer-drinking constituents, and probably in much larger part thanks to banker Louis Greenberg, O'Banion bought an interest in Torrio's gusher Manhattan brewery. Later, he added a percentage of the old Sieben Brewery, a colossus occupying 1454-78 North Larrabee, to his portfolio. Just as in Torrio's operation, liquor supplies for O'Banion's clients remained unsteady, so while he was astute enough to buy into the breweries and rake in easy profits, he continued to utilize prior skills to fill that void or just to fence. On March 14, 1921, he robbed a local business of twenty-two barrels of alcohol valued at $5,500. Gradually, his thieving ambitions grew more sophisticated in terms of both quantity and quality of merchandise, beginning with a $30,000 truckload of whiskey, followed by $100,000 worth of Canadian liquor, and reaching the summit with the snatching of $1,000,000 in pre-war, bonded Kentucky whiskey from a West Side warehouse.

By 1924, O'Banion's capital and organizational sense had accumulated to a point that, like the Gennas, he came to control a legitimate alcohol plant for bootleg use. But unlike the Gennas' Allegheny Chemical facility, O'Banion's Cragin Products, at 1833 Laramie on the West Side, held a permit for unlimited withdrawal of alcohol. O'Banion soon ranked among the city's top three bootleggers, with few willing to challenge his authority north of the river.

Success changed the Irishman's outward appearance from street ruffian to debonair gentleman. Finely yet modestly dressed, O'Banion wore no dazzling colors, garish linens or jewelry, and a sprig of some flower in his lapel sufficed to adorn his suits. He expected the same of his minions as well and "put gangsters into dinner clothes and full dress." The same elevated standard applied to the hoods' women—Parisian dresses were, without exception, to be worn at any lavish dining event in the chief's presence. O'Banion himself married a cultured young woman and settled into a residence on Pine Grove Avenue near the lake. His home was professionally and tastefully decorated floor to ceiling, with furniture, drapes, rugs and rich paintings all in congruence. Outside home, he extended his sophistication to his commercial holdings by obtaining a working interest in William F. Schofield's flower shop at 738 North State Street. The cultured enterprise served both as relaxing sanctuary and legitimate cover for his otherwise-illegal activities. The shop's upstairs served as his downtown headquarters. To police who came calling there regarding some local mischief, O'Banion simply demurred, "I am a florist."

Foremost among the North Siders and their cornerstone was the devout Hymie Weiss. "Always willing to turn a dishonest buck," he seldom missed an adventure with O'Banion, maturing with him from simple thief to safecracker to union slugger to bootlegger. Good with one gun or two, he was never successfully prosecuted for any of his unlawful endeavors. Indisputably the brightest of O'Banion's followers, if not smarter than the boss himself, Weiss supplemented his hoodlum know-how with clear, rational, and perceptive ambition. Described as "a mental hawk," it was he who was generally credited with steering the North Siders into bootlegging in the first place, and the ensuing windfall was the result of his hard work. He also invested in the Manhattan brewery and spent long hours hustling customers. Recognizing Weiss as even-keeled and a glib talker, the more impatient O'Banion usually sent most of his inter-organizational snafus and customer grumbles his way. "Call back later," O'Banion would advise complainants, "and ask for Eisen or Weiss. I'm not in that racket."

The mirror image of Frank Nitto, Weiss's devotion to business was absolute. Commerce was said to so occupy him that he spent little time chasing women, though when he desired, he had his way with them openly. Weiss was of average height, dressed flashily, and possessed slightly rough but handsome features—and when he schmoozed, the women fell hard. He strung along a number of them, but only during off-hours. One forlorn female called on him while he was working, wailing that they hadn't been together in what seemed like forever and that she was "dying by the inches" to see him. A busy Weiss couldn't be bothered with her complaints. "Well, die the last inch," he snapped, "and have it over with." Eventually, Weiss was hooked by a follies girl.

Though Weiss faithfully supported his mother, his brother once complained of having seen him only once in the past twenty years: "That was three years ago Christmas," he explained, "when he shot me." Weiss's hard-nosed nature carried over to his planning of counter-operations against competitors. To enemies he was ferocious, deliberate, and calculating—and, of course, he kept his rosary close at hand.

At the other end of the intelligence spectrum and by far the most colorful member of the group was Leland Deveraigne, better known as Leland Varain, alias Louis Alterie. He adopted the last and more enduring name from a boxing hero of his youth. Alterie said of himself, "I make no boast of being a tough man, but I am always ready to kill if necessary." Though unafraid of death and ready for a shootout, he was much too vain for pug-ugly activity. One reporter described Alterie as an "odd mixture of gangster, poppycock, playboy, bad man, and bad boy as ever swashbuckled through life."

Veteran Detective Captain John Stege was remarkably kinder to Alterie—quite out of character for the officer, given his numerous face-to-face confrontations with hoodlums and his extremely low tolerance for them. He thought Alterie presented himself with fine manners and without fluttering pretentiousness. "Louis dresses richly, but without hysterics," he pronounced. His taste in color ran toward the conservative end of the spectrum, favoring the dark blue hues, and never did he wear the same suit twice. His apparel was always of the finest expression, though not necessarily the finest; his markedly fine hats, for example, might be of the $10 sort, not the overdone $20 types. Alterie was sleek and meticulously groomed down to his sheik-slicked brunette hair and lush brows arching over his striking dark eyes. Politely warning women, Stege added, "If the face of the stranger to whom you are induced to speak is thus, and reminds you of Rudolph Valentino, then—lady, lady— it's Louis." Naturally, Stege alerted colleagues of Alterie's agreeable appearance: "If you went through the lobby of the Congress or any other leading hotel hunting a gunman, Louis would be the last you picked."

One of the older group members, Alterie in all probability was born in 1885 in California, the son of a French immigrant. He grew up on a ranch near the Mexican border and was said to have served a stint in the Venice, California, Police Department before heading east. Once in Chicago, Alterie didn't quite discarded his western proclivities and walked about town outfitted with two .38s slung in shoulder holsters and another lodged in a trouser pocket. Despite the three-gun habit, in Chicago he retained the westernesque nom de plume "Two-Gun Louie."

Fittingly, when Alterie managed to accumulate enough wealth, he bought the D Diamond V Ranch in Glenwood Springs, Colorado, to which he, along with his companions and their wives, might retire on furlough from time to time. At home in his environs, Alterie swaggered about in a beige ten-gallon hat, purple shirt, and doeskin chaps. Guests were often treated by their host to a professional rodeo in the Denver Stockyards arena, fully paid for by Alterie and frequently augmented by Two-Gun Louie injecting his own equestrian and rustling abilities. On one such trip, he and O'Banion even went so far as to take photographs and record over 1,000 feet of movie film as documentation for the Doubting Thomas city folks back in Chicago that Alterie was indeed a bona fide Westerner.

Back in Chicago, he promptly put the gun-slinging side of his western appetite to use. Initially, he teamed up with West Siders Nails Morton and Herschie Miller in local mischief. Then he went partners with Irishman Jerry O'Conner in gambling and dabbled with him in labor racketeering. Through these connections, in due course, Alterie joined O'Banion's outfit. Then the poppycock surfaced. As a suspect in a murder case, he retired to a hospital bed, feigning insanity. When his confederates "attended to" the potential prosecution witnesses to ensure his release from the charge, Alterie suddenly walked out of the hospital, amazingly cured. In yet another instance, he declared vengeance on a horse. When good pal Nails Morton died from injuries sustained in a riding accident—the horse had reared up, thrown him from the saddle, and kicked him—Alterie promptly tracked down the offending animal at a local stable and rented him for a ride. He then took the horse out to a remote spot on a trail in Lincoln Park and killed it.

His antics only got worse. While with the rest of the North Siders at a swanky political testimonial in a private dining room at the Webster Hotel—the Democrats were soliciting O'Banion's influence for an upcoming election—Alterie, in a bit of classic western theatrics, menaced a hotel waiter. Near the end of the evening, the unsuspecting employee made the mistake of approaching Alterie's table for the customary passing of the hat for the staff's gratuity. The ritual enraged Louis, who jumped to his feet, whipped out his guns, and remonstrated: "Hey, you, none of that racket stuff goes here!" He turned to the stunned audience and asked if he should kill the waiter on the spot. A thoroughly amused O'Banion, chuckling and snorting, intervened on the man's behalf, assuring Alterie that it was better to let the poor chap suffer on in life.

Yet when cleansed of the outlandish aspects of his western spirit and applied instead to the reality of metropolitan Chicago, Alterie could be exceptionally useful. He was without a doubt a bold and valued gunman. Much to his credit, he manipulated his early labor racketeering connections with O'Conner to further worm his way into the Theatrical and Building Janitors Union, a wise move given the increased number of houses accommodating the growing popularity of theater and motion picture shows. The enormous amount of union money represented a considerable source of racketeering income for years to come, one that many a crook envied with glowing eyes. Alterie maintained a dominating interest in the union for years, and his and Nitto's paths would cross later because of it.

George Moran, another follower, frequently ventured with O'Banion on his early safecracking sorties. Not wholly the unwieldy lunkhead he has been made out to be, he at least carried himself in fair fashion in 1920s courts. Other than a police record and immeasurable loyalty to O'Banion, his value to the gang lay in his fearlessness and unpredictable fury, which, combined with his size, often obtained the necessary submission from those who might challenge the gang. Early on, reporters, drawing on his physical size, referred to him as "Big George." Later, one police squad that came upon Moran and Weiss patrolling the Italian quarter noted his reckless courage. One of the officers asked, "What are you birds doin' here? Don't you think it's pretty hot over here for you?" Moran replied, "Hell no. I wish one of those 'wops' would show himself. I'm nuts to blow off some greaseball's head." Apparently Moran's reputation for unreasonableness grew so large that he became known as just plain "Bugs." The tag stuck.

The term *gorilla*, used to describe a tough gunman, was most appropriately applied to Frank and Pete Gusenberg. Hefty, thick-faced, and downright nasty brutes, violence just seemed innate to them, as if "they'd slap you around for nothing." Pete, the older of the pair, had served time in state and federal prisons for robbery; he would join the North Side group upon his release. Frank, on the other hand, generally had steered clear of prison, but he aroused police interest as a burglar, robber, and stick-up suspect. He apparently entered the gang's fold early in Prohibition as a gunman, and when united with Pete, they evolved as the gang's primary muscle.

The lone Italian in the gang was roughneck Vincent Di Ambrosio, alias Drucci. Older and with an imaginative and impractical intellect for helping plot gang operations, Drucci earned the sobriquet "Schemer." A nasty street tough with an extensive criminal background, he began his career by looting telephone coin boxes, then graduated to more serious crimes, with arrests for bank robbery and auto larceny before aiding O'Banion in liquor thefts. As aberrant as they were, the O'Banion group displayed diversity, cohesion, and intense loyalty to their leader rivaled by members of few other gangs.

———※※※———

While the array of gangs posed an obvious danger to booze fence Frank Nitto, Johnny Torrio saw in the potential rivals nothing but trouble if they weren't unified to some degree. His territory stretched from the Loop and the First Ward south along the lake to the Indiana border, and any belligerent bootleg fumbling might wreck his booze supply lines and his commercial interests as well. If, though, the gangs worked together, they stood to make millions. Torrio, thus, is generally regarded to have taken the initiative to bring the city's foremost groups to a mutual business understanding that would peacefully benefit all parties. By 1923, Torrio had finally coaxed most of the major players into a working consortium. Each interest would operate exclusively within its recognized territories, and sub-agreements with other participants were made regarding various commodities, such as additional or supplemental stores of beer and liquors.

For instance, the Gennas manufactured raw alcohol for their liquor suppliers. Thanks to Torrio's territorial proposition, which the brothers readily accepted, they received exclusive alcohol rights in their district. As a local source, the Gennas then filled part of Torrio's needs by providing cheap alcohol for his dives. The Gennas' production cost forty cents a gallon; Torrio bought it for $2-$3 and sold it retail for $6, a win-win situation for both interests. The Gennas, in turn, needed beer for their saloons. Torrio had specialized in beer all along and supplied their needs. For Torrio's classier clientele, he worked with O'Banion's group, who earned a reputation for importing quality liquor. Safe passage guarantees for each other's shipments was another issue covered by the agreement, as was the responsibility for protection pay-offs within each district. Under the agreement, gangs prospered and there was peace for the present.

——◆◆◆——

Ironically, in as much as the Torrio plan brought peace to the array of large ethnic bootleg gangs, in Nitto's case, it probably brought additional difficulty. Lines of jurisdiction created fiefdoms of considerable authority, and under the plan it was understood that independents operated by-and-large under the local paladin.

Few individuals could successfully walk the tightrope amidst the spheres of influence Torrio created and remain genuinely autonomous. Greenberg did, thanks to his already abundant wealth and the Roosevelt Finance Company, and he advanced as an underworld moneyman. As the bootleg industry itself grew, the Roosevelt Finance Company became the entity hoods were most likely to use to fund investments, some related to bootlegging. Both O'Banion and Weiss were shareholders in Torrio's Manhattan brewery, probably at Greenberg's urging, if not thanks to his direct financial aid. The extent of O'Banion's financial involvement would become clear a few years later when it was revealed that Greenberg had guaranteed notes in excess of $250,000 in the name of O'Banion's wife and father. Still later, he invested illegal profits in legitimate acquisitions such as real estate and theaters. They all grew fat in the process, and this, as one reporter noted, was Greenberg's "profound influence on the crime syndicate and its members." Greenberg thereby remained a true anomaly with strong connections apparently north and south.

Otherwise, few individuals could step out of bounds. Many relative unknowns tried and paid with their lives, leaving their historical footnotes among the tired tableau of Prohibition-related slayings: July 15, 1925—independents Sam Lavenuto and James Russo killed; August 28, 1925—bootleggers Irving Schlig and Harry Berman murdered; May 21, 1926—alky cooker Frank Cremaldi taken for a ride; etc.

A change in city politics served as the final straw in ending Frank Nitto's days as an independent booze fence. Ahead of the 1923 mayoral primaries, freewheeling Mayor Big Bill Thompson withdrew from contention. The political forecast for the incumbent was grim. Crime was even more of an issue now than when Thompson was originally elected; since 1921, city murders had increased dramatically. He had weathered this issue successfully before, but he couldn't distance himself from scandal, and State's Attorney Robert E. Crowe was investigating the misappropriation of nearly a million dollars of public school funds.

In a clear repudiation of any Republican stench left behind by Thompson, the electorate gave Democrat William E. Dever the mayor's office by a comfortable 105,000-vote margin. Sixty years old, a lawyer, alderman, and Cook County Superior Court judge, Dever was the Democratic machine's answer to the outcry of corruption—a political player but so squeaky clean that hardly a spot of venality could be found in his background. In great contrast to Thompson, Dever believed in strict law enforcement, even down to the Prohibition Act, which he disdained completely.

To a crowd of enthusiastically Wet Germans, he reiterated his law-and-order, work-for-change-within-the-system position: "I have said many times that I wish the good people of Chicago could have good, wholesome beer at moderate prices; but the poison that is being sold is not beer, and even the price is not moderate. . . . There is only one way to stop it; enforce the law to the limit. Then, when the city and country have been dried up, the people know the route to Washington, There they can find relief." Amazingly, the crowd was understanding and sympathetic.

As the new police chief who would carry out his proclamation, Dever selected the person some have called one of the best chiefs in the department's history, the bespectacled Morgan A. Collins. With the mayor's full backing, the incorruptible new chief immediately embarked on a cleanup campaign throughout the city, including enforcement of the nation's Prohibition law. Everyday raids on vice dens became the norm. The Four Deuces on Wabash was one of the first hit, and a hundred arrests were made on the West Side. Wider-ranging sweeps in the ensuing months netted as many as 400-500 booze violators at a time. The raids were a mere nuisance to most, as many were quickly released due to the letter of the law or sympathetic judges. But pain-in-the-neck Collins instilled extra precaution in bootlegger Frank Nitto, and the situation only got worse.

Dever's election and the change of administration disrupted the underworld agreement cherished by Torrio. With the old system of political protection gone, some gangs began boldly striking out on their own again regardless of Torrio's agreement. Spike O'Donnell was one of the daring. Laying his own supply lines and recruiting able gunmen, Spike opened saloons and his "drummers" or high-pressure salesmen swung into action. Tough brutes, usually with a gun protruding visibly from some pocket, they entered a saloon pinning fear on the owner with one line: "Who you buying your beer from?" A proprietor answering unfavorably was pummeled with gun butts and fists until he saw the light. Spike pushed into Joe Saltis's territory to the northwest and then advanced on Ralph Sheldon's territory. By late summer 1923, the beer war was on.

On September 7, 1923, members of the Saltis outfit caught up with and killed O'Donnell beer drummer and slugger Jerry O'Conner. The murder and its root causes enraged the usually even-keeled Mayor Dever, who was desperately trying to restore law enforcement. On September 12, the mayor announced more stringent alcohol interdiction measures. He reiterated his sympathetic stance for those who desired beer but made it clear that, until such time it became legal again, law and order must prevail. And since federal efforts were not sufficient in his estimation, the city would step up further. In an attempt to dry up supplies, he ordered Collins to raid the numerous illegal breweries and seize their production. A few shipments were seized, but rumor still had it that supplies could still be had easy enough.

Less than a week after his decree, the scoreboard tallied two more bodies. On September 17, 1923, O'Donnell sluggers George Meegan and George Bucher were murdered, compliments of the Saltis gang. This latest batch of killings completely unhinged the mayor. Dever now determined an all-out war in the name of Prohibition. His orders to Chief Morgan and his men were terse: not only would producers and distributors be stopped, but all retailers would be as well.

As promised, booze joints were immediately hit. First to go were the seemingly innocuous neighborhood soda parlors. During the early days of Prohibition, the 6,000 or so licensees served beer without police interference. Within the first two months of the mayor's edict, Dever's police closed hundreds of the parlors. To make sure they stayed closed, Dever revoked their licenses. When disgruntled proprietors protested to the courts for their recovery and succeeded with their pleas, Dever simply ordered Collins to ignore the court orders and close them again anyway. The police then moved on to closing suspect restaurants, private clubs, and drugstores. Dever's new enforcement edict ran just as harsh on the small guys, with individuals being hauled in as well. During the first five days of the new campaign, more than 800 people were arrested in the Loop alone. Chief Collins was said to go as far as to haul in the average-Joe consumer with as little as perhaps a pint of booze.

Apparently, through it all Frank Nitto escaped arrest. But clearly in 1923 his career had reached a pivotal point. Thanks to the gang alignments, the accompanying risks to the independent, and the added weight of Dever's all-encompassing crackdown, Nitto would have to join some group somewhere.

What about the Gennas? Nitto's relations with the Gennas, if any, are not known, yet by 1923, his attachment to that group was unlikely for any number of reasons. To be sure, they could utilize his talents, but the key personnel and inner circle of the Genna operation were all family or fellow Sicilians. At best, they might install him at the lower end of the pecking order—hardly a draw for the experienced Nitto.

Through Greenberg, Nitto might have become introduced into the North Side group. Like the Gennas, they were heavily into the alcohol business, but O'Banion's crew was also likely out of the question for Nitto. As late as 1923, they were still dabbling in blowing and robbing company vaults for cash—not the business ideal— and the demographics of O'Banion's showed Drucci as the lone Italian. Even with a Greenberg inducement, they were not a natural draw for the astute, old country

Neapolitan. More importantly for Nitto, by then Capone's name was recognizable on the street.

———⟫∘⟨∘⟩———

As Torrio reaped enormous benefits, Al Capone's position and wealth also increased greatly from his initial 1920 salary to a now-estimated $25,000 of the brothel business and 50 percent of the booze business. In 1922, the Internal Revenue thought him to be earning such a high income that they sent an agent to probe his finances. That year, a city paper first put his name and his declaration of clout in print when they reported an auto accident in the Loop in which he was at fault. Apparently after an all-night drinking binge, Capone rammed his auto into a parked taxicab on Randolph Street. To make matters worse, he pulled out a revolver, waving it about and threatening to shoot the injured cabbie slumped inside. Police arrived and relieved Capone of his weapon. Hauled into the station, he reportedly boasted, "I'll fix this thing so easy you won't know how it's done." Capone even threatened the arresting officer with discharge. Apparently there were no dismissals, but Capone made good on his promise to fix the case. It was expunged from the record without notice. He was not just another hood, but rather one crime pundits of the press recognized as being headquartered in the Four Deuces and possessing genuine clout.

Accordingly, as ranking number two, Capone continuously sought to surround himself with capable, trustworthy associates, and he excelled at this—his hired hands formed a more tightly knit group than any other in the city. New members included some of Capone's family. Older brother Ralph was the first family member to enter the fold. The tough, thick bully from Brooklyn tried his hand at honest labor, even attempting to enlist during the war (he was rejected for flat feet) before tending bar in New York. In Chicago, he went to work as a barkeep at the Four Deuces and graduated up the ranks by family virtue as Al assumed greater authority. Older brother Frank also joined. His dark, solid, typically Capone family features and banker-like manners masked a temper of "considerable savagery." The Fischetti brothers—Charlie, Rocco, and the lesser-known Joe—also came into the gang at Capone's urging. All roughneck gunmen, Charlie more than the others filled the dapper gangster stereotype. Understood to be cousins of the Capones, the Fischettis later formed part of his managerial corps.

It was most likely mid- to late 1923 as old Brooklyn acquaintance Capone blossomed in prestige when Frank Nitto entered their group. Just how did the paths of Francesco Raffele Nitto and Alphonse Capone cross and fuse? *Chicago Sun* reporter Dale Harrison painted the only picture of the historical gangland event, asserting that it was at a Colosimo-Capone brothel that Nitti is said to have met Al for the first time.

The rest is a matter of conjecture. The name of the bordello has never surfaced, though it might have been at the Four Deuces since a brothel was part of its composition. The club was still open despite Dever's attacks and was Capone's headquarters. Was the meeting purposeful or accidental? If anything fortuitous happened, it was certainly not vice-related—there is not even a faint historical suggestion that

Frank Nitto indulged in women outside his marriage (a contemporary later vouched for his apparent abstinence of company services and his apparent personal conduct as more business-like.) A chance business incident that precipitated a reunion rather than a person-to-person meeting is more likely. Given the overall conditions—Nitto's trade, ethnicity, proximity, and gang alignments—as well as Greenberg's connections to Torrio, Capone's status as Torrio's solid number two man, and the fact that the older Capone brothers were now in town—any number of scenarios may have played out to bring them together. It's even possible that Nitto simply overheard the Capone name somewhere in the Italian Quarter, recognized it, and inquired further.

Given the overall circumstances, a chance meeting seems less likely than a purposefully arranged encounter. As a contemporary said of the Torrio-Capone gang, it "was formed for the business administration of establishments of vice, gambling and booze." They were running a business, not a gang, as others were. By late 1923, a more intentional meeting seems likely, and the instrumental figure for setting this up might have been Louis Greenberg. Thanks to Torrio's group, his finances were growing, and around that time, Greenberg's share in the Manhattan brewery was increased to 25 percent. Greenberg later testified to their generosity, saying, "They never tried to hog it all for themselves." Anyone doing that much business with Torrio assuredly heard Capone's name or probably conducted business with him somewhere along the line.

Given Capone's importance and the need to surround him with a trusted team, Nitto's introduction may have been represented a bit of networking in that direction by Greenberg. While Greenberg never became a team member per se, should Torrio or Capone need a dependable man, he was in position to reference Nitto as a good Italian fellow working in the booze racket. He probably knew nothing of Nitto's past acquaintance with the Capone family; he was simply helping out his business colleagues Torrio and Capone and his friend Frank Nitto. At any rate, circumstances dictate too many real possibilities for these Brooklyn chums to be introduced due to common bootleg pursuits rather than through a purely coincidental meeting, and however they were reintroduced, Nitto went to work for Al in what then was known as "the Cicero Syndicate."

It is likely that Nitto's induction into the group lacked a ritual oath of fealty—the ritualistic prick-of-the-pin, die-by-the-gun Mafia stuff brought in much later by New York mob soldier Joseph Valachi. Valachi-type initiations appeared to be a ritual reserved for the strictly organized Italian gangs in the east where several Old Country elders still held sway. Torrio and Capone, on the other hand, were organizing and operating a moneymaking enterprise, not the Mafia—which was Sicilian in origin anyway, and most everyone in the Torrio-Capone gang was Neapolitan. Further, if such a bloodline oath had really been necessary, it's difficult to account for the high standing of non-Italian Jake Guzik (Jack Guzik in some accounts). Taking Nitto aboard was strictly a personnel decision in the purest business sense. The initiation was likely simple: "Here's your job, here're the rules, don't break them—or else."

Nitto was a natural fit, as he possessed useful Chicago bootleg and business skills, a coarse Brooklyn Navy Yard and a greater Chicago experience, and an Italian heritage. Capone could use him, plus Nitto was nearly old family to the Capones and could be trusted as much as or more than any other individual in their Chicago realm.

—⟨ɜ/ɜ/ɜ⟩—

Nitto's combination of trustworthiness, no-nonsense business acumen, and ruggedness impressed Capone, who brought Nitto into the gang at a high rung on the organizational ladder. That Capone appointed Nitto as one of his collectors, keeper of moneys, and tabulator of moneys due, probably under the auspices of overall gang bookkeeper Jake Guzik, demonstrates how highly Big Al valued his new man's talents. Later investigators placed Nitto's dealings at the time as "probably in the booze racket," a familiar job to which he was well-suited. He collected amounts due and maybe made some sales, returning the cash to Guzik for tabulation. In return for his vital abilities, even this early on, his salary may have been in the neighborhood of $250,000 annually.

To this end, it seems highly unlikely that Nitto rose through the Torrio-Capone ranks from that of "triggerman," a term reserved for those who carried and actively applied a gun for their pay. Nitto didn't have to kill anybody or run up a lengthy rap sheet to pay his dues or prove his worth; he was hired for his business skills. The only comparable talents in the organization belonged to the inoffensive Jake Guzik. Besides, gunmen were not relied upon to tabulate and collect receipts. Nitto may well have carried a gun through his early bootleg years as a concealed insurance policy, but he was never arrested with one in possession. When he brought a gun muzzle into the open, it was strictly a strategic move, such as on the occasion when, extremely upset with collections at a local gang-controlled firm, he entered the premises with a machine gun. Those in his field of fire knew he meant business, and the stunned crew complied instantaneously with Nitto's demands.

One high-ranking Treasury official later brushed aside Nitto's connections to Capone as basis for his elevation, saying of Nitto, "His worst enemy could never lay his success to hometown ties. Nitti had what it takes, and in very little time he was second to Al himself, charged with keeping discipline within the mob." As such, Nitto would soon enjoy an even larger share of the gang's profits.

6

BIG EVENTS
IN LITTLE CICERO

T HE JOINING OF FRANK NITTO with the Torrio-Capone Outfit could not have
been realized at a more opportune instant for both parties. The same citywide
cleanup campaign that may have ultimately brought Nitto into the Torrio-Capone
fold caused many vice operators, including Torrio, to seriously rethink their short-
term business strategy. An obviously pleased director of the Juvenile Protective
Association noted:

> "Nightly raids inaugurated by Chief Collins have played havoc with the
> vice ring and broken a majority of the most notorious resorts and driven
> others to cover. . . . His apparent desire to clean the town and keep it clean
> have reached the underworld, their ranks have been badly shattered."

Morgan Collins dampened not only Torrio's booze business but also a considerable amount of suspected prostitution.

Torrio found out just how serious Collins was when, through back channels, he
attempted to salvage what he could of his empire. With his usual guile, he inquired
as to whether Collins would accept $100,000 a month to overlook his activities and
received no response. The attacks continued. Would Collins accept $1,000 a day to
overlook the distribution of a mere 250 barrels of beer? Nothing doing. The leaders
of the gambling community also suffered. So extensive were the raids, one dismayed
habitué of Chicago's gambling action pronounced the business "absolutely dead,"

and added, "You'll find a 'cheater' here and there, but these fellows can't establish themselves in one place long enough to make it pay." While veteran Monte Tennes and his General News Bureau desperately held on to what they had left in the city, most of his cronies took their gambling interests to more friendly suburban areas.

Torrio understood that no administration could completely close the booze spigot any more than it could shutter all whoring and gambling establishments. But until matters in Chicago could be amended, he would have to find a haven outside the city proper for his enterprise, a new territory to make up for lost revenue. So, in October 1923, while Collins's sweeps were in high gear, Torrio logically planned to press his organization into the nearly untapped western suburbs, into locations that did not violate his own city agreement.

Frank Nitto accompanied the group west. The new and developing alcohol trade there corresponded precisely with his talents, and his gang role expanded. Then, a series of innocuous events in Cicero further extended his worth, and by the time the group re-entered Chicago for good, Nitto ranked as very nearly the second most powerful figure in the gang.

In late 1923, Cicero, the fifth largest city in Illinois, became the central objective for Torrio's organization. Five to six miles west-southwest of the Loop, approximately three miles long and half as wide, the suburb was a north-south oriented rectangle. Its eastern border touched the Chicago city limits at about the 4600 West block of city streets, and its western edge shouldered up against the neighboring suburb of Berwyn. To the south, Thirty-ninth Street acted as its city limit, while Roosevelt Road (1200 South) hemmed in its northern side. As one of Cicero's main throughways, Ogden Avenue bisected the lower third of the city and ran southwest to northeast into Chicago. After Torrio entered the city, the indisputable main artery for those really in the know was Twenty-second Street (now Cermak Road), where Torrio set up shop. Very near the commercial district, Twenty-second Street also bee-lined straight back to within a block of the gang's Chicago headquarters, the Four Deuces. Better still, Cicero fell under county jurisdiction, and Torrio had the sheriff in his pocket.

Cicero had a natural commercial attraction. Though it possessed a rowdy reputation of sorts extending back to the mid-1800s, now many of its solid middle-European citizens, primarily gritty Bohemian Czechs, worked hard at one of five large manufacturing plants near the commercial district of Twenty-second Street. Average, orderly citizens in this community setting thought nothing of delightfully downing a beer or two after work. Here, no law would impede cultural tradition.

Not surprisingly, saloons liberally dotted the town. The contents of many of these beer mugs and shot glasses were supplied by whomever the owner desired to purchase stocks from. The West Side O'Donnells, who rightfully claimed booze distribution in the parts of Chicago adjacent to the north edge of Cicero, had only recently expanded into the Roosevelt Road area. Outside of their section, pug-ugly ex-boxer and popular local bartender Eddie Tancl commanded considerable local pull. He had long owned the enormous fort-like Hawthorne Park Bar and Cabaret at 4801 Ogden, but he and his fellow tapsters were not affiliated with any group.7 Thus, as per agreement, Cicero largely remained unclaimed for prime booze distribution—the perfect target for Torrio's lost city supplies.

Torrio claimed the prize peacefully through connivance with Edward D. Vogel, the acknowledged owner of Cicero government, a man with whom both Tancl and the O'Donnells necessarily associated. Vogel hardly looked like one who commanded much pull—of average height at about five feet, seven inches and slightly weighty at around 170 pounds. Vogel's oval Bohemian face lacked any distinguishing lines and was simply placid. However, he has been described as "the first to discern the lucrative possibilities in corrupting suburban officials and police," and if he was not, he and Torrio came up with the possibility at around the same time. Born in 1895 in Chicago proper, Vogel moved to Cicero during the war. Once there, he chummed his way into Cicero's political sphere and set up so many close relationships that his ex-wife at the time reminisced that the many fine people in Cicero in those days "were all politicians."

Maintaining that rapport was a lifelong preoccupation for Vogel because he commanded the most pervasive gambling action in Cicero in the form of slot machines that were easily installed and maintained and highly profitable. One-armed bandits were conveniently placed in any saloon, soda parlor, or store where they received heavy play from locals, who generally accepted the machines as a harmless but convenient vice. Greatly enriched, Vogel liberally dispersed funds to elect city officials and select police most understanding toward his operations.

Backed by so much power, Vogel could afford to deal with incidental difficulties in a peaceful manner. He personally eschewed the use of violence in any form; like Torrio, he reached the pinnacle of his success without personally firing a shot. Print depictions of him as a "common, ordinary, cheap thug," seemed to genuinely upset him, and the only real run-in with the law seems to have come in 1926 when federal agents raided his wedding party and charged him with liquor violations.

Vogel preferred to maintain the business through conspiracy. For example, when a business in which he maintained several slot machines decided to opt out of their agreement and install their own machines, thereby excluding him from gambling proceeds, Vogel simply called on friendly police officials. They arrived to inform the renegade owner that he operated contrary both to fair trade laws and to Vogel. The owner got the message and reinstated Vogel's 40 percent of the take, no exceptions—and no guns or violence were necessary. Vogel even reimbursed the owner $1,800 for the new machines, and everyone profited. High on influence, Vogel was a reasonable man to deal with.

By October 1923, Torrio entered into an agreement with Vogel and the O'Donnells. Torrio was awarded beer rights in Cicero outside of the recognized O'Donnell sphere of influence and gambling rights on Twenty-second Street, exclusive of Vogel's slot machines. The O'Donnells retained their exclusive lordship over the Roosevelt Road sector on the town's north edge, and Vogel retained his exclusive right to slot machines—and with Torrio's county backing, that enterprise not only thrived in Cicero but later sprouted up over the whole county, where few machines that didn't bear his distinctive upside-down V were allowed to operate. Both the O'Donnells and Vogel were now firmly on Torrio's side, and Torrio prepared to ship off to Italy for vacation, confident his protégé Capone, now interim leader of the gang, could handle matters.

⸺◦/◦/◦⸺

Cicero became Capone's priority. Not that he neglected the remainder of their Chicago holdings, for the Four Deuces remained their city headquarters. As Torrio's emissary, Capone established their nerve center for suburban operations in Cicero's Hawthorne Hotel at 4823 Twenty-second Street, near the center of the block. This was only one block west of Cicero Avenue, a main north-south artery situated only two blocks outside the Chicago city limits. The group took up nearly an entire floor of the three-story brick building, and the small size of the hotel no doubt afforded them complete ability to protect Capone.

Sandwiched between the nearly identical Anton's Hotel and the Hawthorne Restaurant, the hotel's front entrance opened into a long, narrow corridor that led to a lobby in which all furniture—including the clerk's desk and even the switch-board—faced incoming visitors. With several guards always posted throughout, no one could get through for a direct shot at the boss. Even a drive-by shot might be difficult, for the portion of Twenty-second Street fronting the hotel was not a run-of-the-mill city street. Estimated to be one hundred feet wide, twice the normal width, the street featured an extra-wide sidewalk and angled parking almost perpendicular to the walk. This layout put considerable distance between the traffic flow on the street and the hotel, but bulletproof blinds on the windows added the final touch of impregnability.

With Vogel, Cicero City Hall, and the county sheriff as backing, Capone embarked on implementing Torrio's gain, bringing the necessary work force, including Frank Nitto, into the new headquarters. Beer and liquor were a priority, as was organizing saloon operators into a consortium of vendors. Trusted brothers Frank and Ralph, whom many believed to head up beer distribution, probably acted as point men or chief convincers. The message was simple: purchase products from Torrio and his allies or you're out. With menacing, thick-bodied brute Ralph and other equally intimidating assistants staring them down from across the bar, many readily or unenthusiastically bought their stocks. The only objection came from saloon owner Eddie Tancl, and his blatant pigheadedness exasperated the new combine and finally necessitated the regrettable use of force. With aid from the West Side O'Donnells, Tancl was goaded into a gunfight outside his café and killed. The Tancl incident represented the only serious gunplay Capone or the O'Donnells needed to consolidate Prohibition supplies in Cicero.

Frank Nitto followed up behind the sales brutes, probably collecting and reporting booze trade receipts either directly to Capone or to chief gang bookkeeper Jake Guzik. He may have also lined up new liquor accounts while maintaining the original and now more difficult endeavors in Dever's Chicago city limits. Expanded Cicero operations opened the door for Frank Nitto's success as well as his reputation.

Capable and dependable, backed by a powerful organization, Nitto rounded up accounts in a firm, businesslike manner, with no bullish physical methods necessary on first call. As one associate later said of him, perhaps admiringly, "He was very frank and to the point. He never went into long, lengthy conversation." His terseness, backed up by gang firepower, instilled sufficient dread in many to readily pay their bills on a timely basis.

Those foolish enough to be tardy found Nitto's collection methods unequivocally efficient. "If a debt went unpaid," said one observer, "he first sent a warning. If the account was still in the red, he turned the item over to a collection squad." Though he was certainly personally capable of violence, no murders were linked to his fingerprints. The collection squad, a group of gunmen put at his disposal by Capone, made the second visit, which usually settled the matter. Balances due on alcohol accounts were secured, income receipts were matched to outgoing sales slips, and everything was tabulated with management. Nitto "got things done in a hurry," and he may have earned an enforcer-type reputation among his customers.

Through Nitto's efforts, cash poured into the gang's coffers. A moneymaking job well done, his loyalty toward boss Al, and mutual trust from all parties cemented his position in the organization and accounted for the "rapid" rise later ascribed to him by the press. Two events in Cicero particularly showed Capone how important Nitto was to him.

Not long after Capone developed the Cicero booze operations, the threat that had sparked the move to Cicero now loomed in their new base. Cicero's town president, Republican Joseph Z. Klenha, had run Cicero for three terms since 1917, and now the Democrats who had swept Dever into office as mayor of Chicago were threatening to run a slate of candidates in Cicero. Through local power Eddie Vogel, a political intermediary asked Capone if he would support Klenha in the April 1924 election in return for certain favors. Capone accepted the proposition as a necessary part of doing business.

In order to safeguard their newfound command center as well as cement their recent business gains, Capone mobilized the troops for the April elections. Besides their growing roster of gunmen on active duty, the West Side O'Donnells contributed their force, and even North Sider O'Banion was thought to have loaned the Torrio combine some of his finest troops. Naturally, there would be some opposition; the Democratic slate rallied a force of vigilantes and hoods, the latter anxious to capitalize gains at the expense of the Torrio faction in the event of a favorable outcome. On election day at least twelve touring cars of thugs patrolled the Cicero streets, guns in hand, and the air of terror kept many voters from the polls. Ballot watchers were beaten and replaced with hoods instructing voters on how to mark the ballots correctly for their candidates. Strategic points of resistance were plotted, and those citizens who might vote "incorrectly" were kidnapped until the election was over. One patrolman foolish enough to attempt to enforce the law at a polling station was beaten.

The situation declined to such a state that someone turned in a riot call. A force of deputies, perhaps numbering a hundred, began assembling at Chicago's Lawndale police station just east of the Cicero city limits and eventually made their way to Cicero in the late afternoon. As part of that force, Detective Sergeant William Cusack and his patrol of four crossed the city limits into the hotbed toward sunset. As the squad approached the polling place at Twenty-second Street and Cicero Avenue, three characters loitering on the corner outside the station aroused their suspicions. The detectives instincts were correct, though they probably didn't know the men were Frank Capone, Charlie Fischetti, and David Hedlin.

Piling out of the unmarked squad car in plain clothes, the lawmen rushed across the street. Since the detectives displayed no identification, the men on the corner might have mistaken the oncoming group for rival hoods. As the squad crossed the street, gunfire erupted. Who fired first is uncertain, though the detectives testified that Frank Capone squeezed off three rounds from his gun, retreating from the oncoming lawmen in the process. Fischetti and Hedlin also took off, Fischetti firing as he ran. Fortunately for the detectives, neither Fischetti nor Frank Capone hit their marks, but the detectives' shots did. Capone fell to the ground, while Hedlin was wounded and disappeared under cover of darkness. Fischetti ran into an open field and later surrendered unscathed.

After the gun smoke abated and the votes were tallied, the final count gave the Klenha slate of candidates an overwhelming victory. Thanks to the results, Torrio's Cicero operation could run virtually unimpeded. But the final score of the election also showed the loss of Nitto's early roustabout Brooklyn friend, Frank Capone.

The fusillade that dropped Frank Capone on election day killed him instantly. It isn't known where Nitto was at this time, but the mutual regard between him and the Capone family no doubt dictated his subsequent actions. The following Saturday, thousands crowded the Capone family home at 7244 South Prairie Avenue, packing the streets for two blocks all around the two-story brick home. As an increasingly important player in gang operations and a close family friend, Frank Nitto was probably close at hand during the proceedings and contributed handsomely to the procession.

Frank Nitto may have lost an old friend, but Al lost an older sibling and, more significantly, a business associate. Frank's death left brother Ralph as the only ranking related member in the business. This in itself was not significant until it was coupled with events a few months down the road that caused concern for discerning gang administrator Al Capone. And business was business.

———◁•∂/∂/∂|▷———

The Cicero election, partly bought at such a high price with Frank Capone's death, cemented Torrio's organization in Cicero. Neither Klenha, his police chief, the county sheriff, nor State's Attorney Crowe seriously bothered operations there. Federal authorities were rarely effective; somehow, the targets of their raids were always alerted. Yet one person continued as a petty, noisome irritant—young Cicero newspaper owner and editor Robert St. John. Unlike the *Cicero Life*, St. John's reform-minded *Cicero Tribune* attacked the activities of the Capone Outfit from the start, going so far as to investigate and print lurid details concerning one of their suburban brothels. Town officials received no quarter from St. John either as he lay bare their alliance with gang leaders. Capone and the Cicero government acted. First, they tried pulling the plug on the *Tribune*'s finances by persuading advertisers to yank their ads. A sudden rash of "No Parking" signs in front of the building inconvenienced the paper's patrons. City inspectors always seemed to find some violation of building codes. All these things cost St. John money, but his *Tribune* managed to keep the presses running, printing yet more muckrake. All the while, behind the scenes, Capone negotiated to buy controlling interest in the *Tribune* from St. John's two corporate partners and thus end the matter peacefully.

Capone was still working on a buyout when the whole thing finally blew up. Another St. John exposé irritated the gang, and Ralph Capone in particular took exception, sending a warning to the editor to lay off. St. John sent back a message of defiance. Perhaps not used to such stubborn resistance from an ordinary citizen, Ralph and his crew puffed up with hostility, but Al refused to resort to violence to resolve the matter. He repeatedly warned them, "Let the kid alone." True, St. John was a thorn in their britches, but Al reconciled himself to the true value of such media attention to turn a negative into a positive—St. John was providing them with free advertising for illegal activities! And with city hall in his pocket, did Capone really have much to fear?

The lesson was obviously lost on brother Ralph. Still sore at the editor for holding out in the face of such force, bully Ralph was chafed interminably. One morning, his raw temper inflamed further by an all-night drinking binge, Ralph and three companions cruising Cicero spotted the editor crossing the street to the *Tribune* office. Immediately, they halted their vehicle and crossed the street after St. John, Ralph barking orders to the other three. They beat St. John unmercifully with gun butts and the simple time-tested but lethal weapon of a cake of soap in a sock. St. John curled on the pavement, absorbing blow after blow until one hit the crucial mark and knocked him unconscious. The brutes left the battered editor on the street, while a policeman nearby casually ambled along his beat, scarcely paying any attention to the matter.

Of course, brother Al was responsible for Cicero was left to mend the situation, quietly paying. St. John's hospital bills. Upon recovery, St. John insisted on prosecution. Capone arranged a meeting. He wished to amicably compensate St. John for time lost, for damage, and for whatever else he might be ultimately responsible. Instead of accepting an offer reputed to be in the thousands of dollars, St. John stormed out, slamming the door on the gang leader. Unbeknownst to St. John, however, as he stomped out of the room, Capone had acquired control of the paper, obtaining a controlling 51 percent of the stock in the paper and thereby ensuring a more judicious treatment of Capone's activities. His man Louis Cowen was now in charge, and when he discovered this, St. John left both the paper and town for good.

St. John was finessed out of the picture, but Ralph had acted foolishly. Not only did he let his temper get the best of him, but he was liquored up as well—two strikes in Al's business eyes. The gravity of Capone's feelings on the matter was made clear to Robert St. John when the gang leader attempted to explain the incident: "I tell 'em, 'We sell the stuff, we don't drink it.' . . . They made a mistake and now I gotta straighten it out. Always I gotta fix up their mistakes. Christ, how I hate people that ain't smart!" Surely this was an example of "do as I say, not as I do," since Al drank and often over-indulged on his own time. Stories of such excesses are abundant. But business manager Al under Torrio's tutelage clearly grew to know the importance of separating his partying and recovery hours from his business hours. He might even have been amused by Ralph's brutality, but it then dawned on Cicero manager Al that brother Ralph, though usually well-dressed and loyal, was in fact incorrigible.

Capone sensed that Frank Nitto projected a more Torrio-like image than anyone else in his circle. The meticulously dressed Nitto carried himself strictly in a businesslike manner. He made money for the gang, just like Ralph, but he was a purebred workaholic with one mission—running accounts efficiently and profitably. "Banker-like" is the most oft-used description of Nitto, and according to one photographer, "He appeared very intelligent."

Nitto mostly kept to himself in public, a reticent, retiring sort who didn't look for publicity. Even Capone lodged a woman at various times in his headquarters for pleasure, but Nitto apparently did not indulge in company vices. One gang member recalled Nitto's habits as plainly dreary compared to some of his more colorful associates, especially given the temptations of their products. A self-admitted "moderate drinker," another associate thought Nitto to be repulsed by the products of his particular trade, noting that outside of a shot of wine now and then, "You couldn't pay him to take a drink." Not surprisingly, according to one who was privy to several Capone parties, Nitto was absent from every party this man attended. Further, nothing has surfaced regarding any unfaithfulness to wife Rosie; on those occasions when he was out until the wee hours of the morning, it is suspected that he was still out conducting business before coming back home.

From all these sources, the picture of Nitto that develops is that of a devoted company man, absorbed in his business, smoking incessantly as he pored over paperwork scattered about the desktop, retiring home to his wife long after the time-clock employees have punched out for the day. Clearly, Nitto wouldn't cause his boss any great headaches.

―――⟐⟐⟐―――

The real potential windfall in Cicero for Torrio and Capone lay outside of booze distribution in the ancillary gambling privileges. By the fall of 1923, gambling of all types operated openly in Cicero in establishments large and small with games running the gamut from dice to roulette to cards. Under agreement with Vogel and the O'Donnells, the Torrio outfit had to limit their operations to the area about Twenty-second Street, but even so, gaming outside of Vogel's slots was more or less open for development. Most advantageously, Mayor Dever's vice crackdown in Chicago shuttered many longtime centralized gambling concerns in the Loop and sent city crowds seeking action into the suburbs. Torrio and Capone were in place to capitalize.

Just as with the saloon operators, Capone's group first moved to corral the few existing gaming houses into their central authority. One such gaming joints in their neighborhood was run by a tall, chubby-faced, beady-eyed character named Pete Penovich. His partner was the James Cagney look-alike Frankie Pope. The son of a gambler, Pope peddled newspapers as a kid and managed to strike it rich via his father's profession, hence his nickname the "millionaire newsie."

Another major independent operation was oddly named The Ship. Veteran gambling agents Louis and Joseph La Cava, Jimmy Mondi, and Jimmy Murphy owned this lucrative business. All presumably emigrated from the West Madison Street gambling crowd in the Loop to Cicero upon Dever's citywide crackdown before Torrio's move into the gambling arena. They were doing fabulously in Cicero until Torrio and Capone moved in. Taking them over was simple because Torrio's crowd owned city hall—his investment in the city's 1924 elections now paid off. This valued commodity, his trump card for non-violent takeovers, consisted of year-round guaranteed protection from local authorities in return for which they were granted 25-50 percent of the house take.

As with the saloon owners, the door-to-door sales pitch was clear: if you didn't pay, you didn't operate. Pete Penovich recalled years later that, after the Cicero elections, brutish Ralph arrived to announce a takeover of the joint. Ralph was succinct; making a case for his authority, he informed Penovich that if he put in with them he "would not be molested." The burly yet pliable owner, questioning his future, was reassured by Ralph: "You go along and I will take care of you." In return, Pete's percentage of ownership was sliced from fifty to twenty-five. Capone inaugurated their flagship gambling venture, the Hawthorne Smoke Shop, immediately next door to his Hawthorne Hotel headquarters on Twenty-second Street.

Jimmy Mondi and his investors in The Ship found their treatment differed very little. Mondi privately confided to a house cashier the futility of his situation in 1924: "Al Capone and his bunch have horned in and are going to take charge." That, in cold fact, is exactly what the combine did. They absorbed The Ship and reduced Mondi in rank, just as they had Penovich. After the inevitable submission, a Torrio-Capone agent was posted on location to ensure an accurate accounting of the take. The combine became such an instant and dominating success that few places retained their unique ownership. With the original proprietors thoroughly cowed, Torrio and Capone could count a majority of those places as their inventory.

Next came the Subway Casino. A stroll east down the block from the Smoke Shop and across lively Twenty-second Street took one to the casino's ground floor, though sometimes the action was moved to the second floor to avoid the staged police raids that occurred periodically. The Subway provided additional secure space for the gang, serving as a central bank room and accounting nest of sorts. Smoke Shop profits were often hauled there for storage in the huge strongbox. If one of the staged raids closed the casino, its operations were simply relocated nearby on a temporary basis to a place like the Radio Inn at 4726 W. Twenty-second Street. The operation migrated among a half-dozen or more sites and under as many different names in case of raids, and all were, like the Subway, near the Hawthorne Smoke Shop and Hotel headquarters.

The major success for Torrio and Capone, however, was Mondi's original creation, The Ship. Located at 2131 South Cicero, it occupied part of a square, two-story, brick structure that dwarfed the small frame buildings on either side. Facing the building from the wide street, a storefront occupied the right side on the ground floor, while on the left side, large windows extended nearly to the second floor on either side of a central door. The windows were draped completely so as to obscure the view of the interior. Affixed to the brickwork just below the windows of the second floor and directly above the entrance was a feeble sign scrawled in thin lettering that said "The Ship." Nothing on the sign or building indicated what took place within. It was the perfect cover.

The profits were due in part to its keen placement. It was situated on a major auto thoroughfare, and it was strategically located near the elevated train terminal. Commuting patrons from the Chicago simply stepped down from the platform and ambled over to gamble. "Ropers" worked the pavement outside the entrance, enticing additional passersby through the drab storefront. As a result, the roulette wheels and betting tables ran day and night. The atmosphere inside exuded nothing less than a vivacious "composite of Monte Carlo . . . and Barbary Coast." This one gaming joint, according to federal agents, generated estimated revenue of $500,000 a year.

For the Cicero gambling operations, Jake Guzik headed collections. The increasingly cumbersome new amounts of Cicero revenue, combined with the revenue from the remaining city operations, likely created more bookkeeping volume than Guzik could handle. Frank Nitto was a familiar and capable Italian, and this, coupled with an incident to be related shortly, illustrate that Capone quickly expanded Nitto's responsibilities. The endorsement consisted of at least some direct accounting on the Cicero gambling books. A gang spot auditor or fill-in for Guzik, Nitto did not appear to handle money on a day-to-day basis at this early stage but rather checked to make sure the cash collected tabulated with the books. Yet this was no trivial advancement in the ranks, for one of the operations he was entrusted was none other than the immensely profitable hot spot, The Ship.

The bookkeeping scheme of The Ship, like that in many of the Torrio-Capone Cicero gambling conquests, ran along the following line. Former owner Jimmy Mondi managed the place on a daily basis, overseeing the action and hiring employees. A head cashier tallied the cash turned over from each of the tellers for the various activities—poker, 21, wheels, etc.—and promptly entered the numbers for each in a general ledger. An amount was set aside for direct expenses such as employee pay, approximately $12,000 in cash was retained for the following day's operating bank, and the remainder was tallied as the day's profit or loss. Earnings were then stashed away in a safe for weekly distribution to the owners.

Cashiers claimed the place never lost a dime, and to ensure it stayed just that way—or at least to make sure the gang's full percentage of the profits was granted—Guzik or a pre-approved Capone agent double-checked the amount and often made the final transfer. In the event Guzik was unavailable, Nitto filled in to make sure the books reconciled. Sending in an Italian close to Capone and Torrio also probably evoked a great deal of incentive on the part of the gambling managers to stay on an honest accounting path. With collections proceeding smoothly, Nitto's position rapidly advanced to chief auditor-collector with Guzik. Few, if any, outside the gang's business habitat recognized this early acceleration of Nitto's career; he was still an unknown to the press corps, though the Capone epoch was gathering full steam.

—◁◦/◦/◦▷—

Back home, Nitto was celebrating nearly eight years of marriage, though the extent of the commitment was undetermined. Given surface conditions, there is no reason to suspect any great difficulties between husband and wife, and Rose at least had financial security—she may not have known the source, but she surely knew her husband's income had greatly increased in a very short period of time. In just a few short months, the thirty-eight-year-old Frank Nitto had vaulted from a booze fence to high-rated gang collector with an income likely in the many thousands. Despite his pay increase, Rose could not complain about her husband's excessive spending; unlike most colleagues who spent their cash on the easy-come, easy-go extravagances of booze, women, and gambling, Nitto apparently modeled extreme thrift. (Boss Al gambled excessively and regularly, his brother Ralph was buying into racehorses.) The worst she might complain about might be his increasingly extended hours away from her.

Whether they desired a family is unknown, but the couple continued to be active socially with their longtime Little Italy friends as well as with the Gottloebs. In 1924 and 1925, the Nitto household appeared hopscotch among rentals on the Near West Side near Roosevelt Road, all conveniently located so that Nitto might access that artery or take Ogden to Twenty-second Street and drive directly into Cicero. However, each location was also near city headquarters at the Four Deuces so that Nitto could conduct business there with equal ease. Nitto apparently owned no property in the city and seems to have been quite content piling up cash with Greenberg for some future occasion.

In June 1924, Nitto tended to the processing of his legal naturalization. The first document had been gathering dust since 1921, but now he was in a more vulnerable position than he had been in before. Nitto again gathered theater owner Joseph Vicedomini and plumber Paul Carmosino to witness the new document, a Petition for Naturalization, and he again employed the humble profession of barber as his occupational alias, listing his address as 800 South Oakley—which was, coincidentally and curiously, the home address for Italian ward power broker Diamond Joe Esposito.

—◁◦/◦/◦▷—

Circumstances beyond Cicero—specifically gang warfare—also inflated Nitto's value to Capone in 1924 and 1925. Unlike much of the gang warfare later attributed to beer sales, the combustion of the 1924 hostilities ignited with the alcohol trade. By early 1924, the Gennas and their ingenious in-house production methods, in conjunction with their Allegheny Chemical plant, were competing directly with

O'Banion and his Cragin factory. Besides going head-to-head on local output, O'Banion's crowd began importing shipments of quality liquor from Canada. His customers among the Gold Coast crowd demanded quality, and they paid more. Wholesale prices of his local stuff commanded $6-$9 per gallon.

The problem for the Gennas was their enormous production volume. No matter how much they distributed to others per the Torrio agreement, they continually found stock to dispose of. To make matters touchier, the Genna factory, located in Little Sicily, was a great deal closer to the market area than O'Banion's Allegheny facility three miles or so west on Laramie Street. The Gennas were upset that nominal beer man O'Banion had entered the alcohol business in the first place, and they began edging over the agreed-upon boundaries to the east and north, probably from Little Sicily, into O'Banion territory. Further, their production volume and lower quality rotgut enabled them to reduce their wholesale price by at least 50 percent.

This incursion naturally infuriated O'Banion, who asked Torrio to intercede and talk to his countrymen. Torrio may have reasoned with the Irishman that intrusions of such poor quality liquor in fact hurt O'Banion very little, appealing as it did to an entirely different market than O'Banion desired. But O'Banion seethed at the invasions nonetheless—rotgut or not, territorial lines were to be obeyed. Minor scuffles occurred as the Gennas did little to restrain the flow of their product into surrounding territories. O'Banion, apparently not satisfied with Torrio's efforts to curb the Sicilian bunch, took matters into his own hands, deciding he would teach the Gennas a lesson—he hijacked a $30,000 truckload of their whiskey. The clannish Sicilian bunch fumed at the crime, but Unione Siciliana chief Mike Merlo restrained them from retaliating.

O'Banion struck at Torrio, too. Out of the blue, O'Banion came to Torrio and Capone in early May and announced he was looking to retire to a ranch in Colorado that he and Louis Alterie had purchased. However, there was the matter of their brewery partnerships, in particular the giant Sieben Brewery on North Larabee Street in O'Banion's domain. Any deal concluded with O'Banion now promised a double bonus for Torrio and Capone, as it would not only vastly increase their holdings north of Madison Street but would also rid them—and everyone else, for that matter—of a vexatious northern competitor and reduce the chances for an all-out brawl.

O'Banion appraised his share of the brewery at a half-million dollars. Torrio accepted without hesitation. Unfortunately, though, the massive Sieben Brewery was within the still-unfriendly confines of Mayor Dever's jurisdiction. That it was shipping out consignments of the real brew was evidently no secret, for just prior to the closing of the deal, someone leaked information about its continued operations to Police Chief Morgan Collins. A leak back to O'Banion concerning the exact time and date of the raid allowed him to close the Torrio deal and set the meeting date accordingly. O'Banion might be snared in the raid, but to see the urbane Torrio tossed in jail was much too gratifying an opportunity to pass up—and besides, he thought, Torrio deserved such a fate for not taming the Gennas more efficiently. Frivolous stupidity ruled. When Collins raided the brewery as scheduled, Torrio as well as O'Banion and his crew, including Weiss, were hauled in. Perhaps O'Banion had known all along that a second conviction under Prohibition statutes would net a mandatory jail term for Torrio—further gratification from O'Banion's point of view.

O'Banion spent most of the remainder of the year avoiding contact with the police while vacationing in Colorado with gunman Louis Alterie and campaigning for select candidates in Chicago's upcoming elections. O'Banion still had business interests in Chicago, and since some of them—including the Manhattan brewery—involved Torrio, exchanges with unavoidable. Torrio awarded the Irishman points in the highly profitable Ship, either as a reward for his help in the Cicero elections the previous April, or as a later account has it, in response to demands by O'Banion and Weiss for compensation for the Gennas' growing alcohol invasion. The latter account notes that Angelo Genna regularly dropped bundles while gambling at The Ship, and this would allow O'Banion to recoup his liquor losses without firing a shot. Despite the Sieben perfidy, Torrio still honored the agreements; deals were deals. But that didn't necessarily mean things were on the mend between the two. Amazingly, with the Sword of Damocles hanging over his head, O'Banion could still take his hotheaded foolishness to new extremes—enough finally to bring the blade down.

In early November, O'Banion stopped by The Ship for his cut of the profits and met with Torrio and club manager James Mondi. The Italians declared the week a bust, saying there were several large markers for cash that had not yet been collected—including one for $30,000 from the fiery Angelo Genna, the result of a string of dippy horse bets. Mondi told O'Banion Genna was expressing a lack of enthusiasm for paying the debt and suggested they simply write it off and leave it at that. O'Banion jumped up, full of rage at the Sicilian anyway, and snappishly demanded payment. Torrio, perhaps already content with a hidden agenda, agreed with Mondi that if O'Banion wanted his share, he should collect it himself from Genna. O'Banion stormed out of the club determined to get what he was owed.

Frank Nitto may have witnessed O'Banion's recklessness firsthand. One account places him at the meeting as the bookkeeping agent in charge and also notes that Capone, Weiss, and others were also present. If Nitto wasn't at the meeting, he certainly heard about it through the organization.

O'Banion immediately and doggedly pursued Genna for recompense. He was either unaware or unimpressed that Mike Merlo, his savior after his first ruckus with the Gennas, lay dying of cancer and was not expected to survive the week. He died on Saturday, November 8.

Preparations for Merlo's funeral offered the perfect vehicle for retaliation against the Irisher. Merlo's send-off promised to be an enormously lavish affair, rivaling that of Big Jim Colosimo. As usual, hoodlum orders for flowers ran into the thousands of dollars. Torrio placed an order for $10,000, and Capone ordered nearly that much. The total tribute was thought to be in the neighborhood of $100,000. Many of the extravagant and gaudy floral tributes of orchids, carnations, and the like were ordered from the flower shop of O'Banion's partner, William F. Schofield, on the

Near North Side. His shop occupied the first floor of a two-story brick building prominently jutting toward State Street from a block-long row of otherwise taller stone and brick residential edifices hugging the west side of State Street. A fanciful cloth awning protected the face of the shop, and just above it, attached to the building, an ornate sign pronounced the establishment Schofield Co. Above the second floor windows, a ten-foot-long sign simply described the business within: FLOWERS. Inside, with Merlo's death having occurred the day before, floral designers and arrangers worked at a breakneck pace that Sunday to fill the crush of orders. The pace was to be expected to be the same Monday, with O'Banion himself handling at least part of the gangland orders, constantly busying himself about the shop snipping stems and creating arrangements. Regardless of whose funeral or his past behavior, a truce was normally observed during funerals, and O'Banion could expect nominal enemies to drop by for enormous orders—a fact that would aid conspirators

On Monday morning, O'Banion and four employees were tending to the deluge of orders. At approximately 11:30, three men entered the shop, and O'Banion, who had been in the back area filling orders, moved forward through the swinging doors that divided the work area and the front displays to tend to them. The other workers carried on as usual. The Irishman affably greeted the men, whom he may or may not have known, and they told him they were there for Merlo's flowers. One, a tall man in the center, suddenly grasped his arm, and the two men on either side drew guns. The next morning, the newspapers delivered the headline: "O'BANION KILLED BY GANGSTERS." The Gennas and Torrio had expunged an unpredictable and noisome neighbor.

The remainder of O'Banion's gang conjured up a list of suspects. Feuds with the Gennas naturally put the members of that family at the top of their list, and the Gennas' murderous associates John Scalise and Albert Anselmi also ranked high. Torrio and Capone were equally suspect. Moved by intense loyalty to his fallen leader, the impulsive gunslinger Louis Alterie stepped forward with a solution: "If I knew who killed Dean, I would shoot it out with the whole gang at State and Madison. If they got me, I'd die with a smile because I'd wipe out two or three of them before they got me."

O'Banion's successor, however, was the more calculating Hymie Weiss. Like many of his gang, Weiss raged with revenge, but he didn't aim for just any gunmen: he would wait, biding his time, planning the perfect hit. The targets of his revenge would be those he suspected most strongly.

———

With Torrio on vacation, Capone offered Weiss's guns their first target at vengeance. Early on the morning of January 14, a touring car with curtains drawn curbed a Capone sedan near Fifty-fifth and State streets. Inside the touring car, Weiss, Moran, and Drucci manned the guns. Assuming Capone was among the occupants, they raked it with fire from as little as three feet away. Shotgun slugs and bullets penetrated the vehicle, but amazingly only one of the three occupants,

Capone's chauffeur Sylvester Barton, was wounded when a slug passed through his coat and grazed his back. Capone was not there.

Shortly after the incident, Torrio returned from his travels and walked into the court of Judge Adam C. Cliff on January 17 to answer the Sieben Brewery charges. Rather than fight the charges, he pleaded guilty, drawing a nine-month jail sentence and a pitiful $5,000 fine, the stiffest penalty metered out to any of the defendants. Judge Cliff allowed Torrio ten days to settle his affairs before reporting for incarceration. He might celebrate his birthday on January 20 and possibly plot with Capone any strategy for the impending months to come, perhaps even hatch a plan to deal with Weiss.

Four days after his birthday, Torrio tended to business downtown in the Loop. When he arrived home late that afternoon, neither Torrio, his wife nor chauffeur Robert Barton noticed the three North Siders in the ominous vehicle around the corner. At the wheel was Schemer Drucci. Emerging from the vehicle were Weiss with a shotgun and Moran, armed with a .45-caliber automatic. Both approached Torrio's Lincoln, Weiss moved to the rear of the vehicle, while Moran lumbered toward the front. Both fired simultaneously at their victims in the car. The first burst shattered the Lincoln's windows, spraying glass all about Torrio and Barton. The fusillade caught Barton in the right knee, while an unscathed Torrio started for the entrance of the apartment.

Weiss and Moran zeroed in on him, and their crossfire felled him on the sidewalk. A bullet hit Torrio's left arm, spinning him around, and buckshot from Weiss's gun caught Torrio full front, shattering his jaw and ripping through his neck and torso. Mrs. Torrio watched from the doorway in horror as her husband lay sprawled on the ground helpless. Moran reached to put a last shot in him, but the automatic clicked empty. As he fumbled to reload, a laundry delivery truck approached the corner. Drucci signaled by tapping the waiting car's horn, and the gunmen quickly departed the scene, more than likely satisfied that the bloody heap they left on the walk could not survive. Barton, wounded severely in the leg, pulled himself into the Lincoln and drove off, stopping at a drugstore long enough to phone Capone before seeking medical attention for himself.

The badly wounded Torrio was rushed to nearby Jackson Park Hospital, where, amazingly, he recovered rapidly. In perhaps as little as six days, he felt well enough to check himself out, though against medical advice. Capone arranged for his still-bandaged boss to exit through a fire escape early one morning to confound any hostile lurkers.

The repercussions of the actions initiated by the Genna-O'Banion feud finished Torrio as a direct leader in Chicago crime. Upon his departure from Jackson Park Hospital, Torrio's lawyers successfully convinced Judge Cliff to allow Torrio to serve his time at the jail in Waukegan (Lake County) because it offered more accessible medical treatment, necessary due to their client's severe wounds. With time to recuperate and contemplate Chicago's gangland future, Torrio concluded that the city-wide combine he strove so hard to build and maintain would inevitably disintegrate. Gunplay and violence would follow, but not for him. Therefore, probably sometime in March 1925, Torrio convened a meeting with his lawyers and Capone and declared he wanted nothing more to do with Chicago. For an undetermined sum, Torrio turned everything—brothels, gaming joints, and beer and liquor distribution—over to Capone. He would, however, stay in touch and act as a consultant, if necessary.

At twenty-six years of age, with five years of field experience, Capone now commanded the entire operation started by Colosimo and expanded by Torrio. He made all the business decisions and his word was final, just as Colosimo had dictated to chief lieutenant Torrio and Torrio later had dictated to Capone. Scarface Al's strategic planning paid off. The organization remained intact with no notable upheavals. He possessed a loyal and dedicated band, all of whom continued to perform magnificently. Gang strategy would remain the same: hold onto and advance business while molding a true, structured enterprise operation.

Thanks considerably to the bullets spent on Torrio, Frank Nitto now became more important to Capone than ever before. Of those in his diverse group at the time, who ranked more highly? Not Al's brother Ralph, who, though important in his own brutish way, demonstrated a lack of polished business sense. The feds later speculated that Ralph was "never much of a power in the gang," with one official pronouncing his financial conduct as plain "stupid." As for the trusted and efficient Jake Guzik, his inoffensive nature proved a minus in such a nasty business environment. Capone's cousins, the Fischettis, still acted as mere gunmen and key aides. Although there was no official number two in the organization, the de facto runner-up was unquestionably Frank Nitto.

7

VALIDATION IN THE CITY

FRANK NITTO'S METAMORPHOSIS INCLUDED A more personal, yet superficial, attribute in early 1925, the timing of which the reserved hood might look upon as providence as events unfolded in his gangland career. As Torrio contemplated his decision to retire from the Chicago stage while in Lake County Jail, the Superior Court of Cook County granted Francesco Raffele Nitto citizenship. On that same day, February 25, 1925, affidavits and papers filed officially Americanized his name simply to Frank Nitto. He, however, used the Americanized Ralph or the simple initial "R" instead of Raffele in some official papers, even resorting to Ralph as a first-name alias on some occasions. At last, four and a half years after he filed a declaration, final insulation from deportation as a result of arrest was in place—just in time.

Early 1925 found Frank Nitto scurrying back and forth between his apartment on South Marshfield Avenue in Cicero, and the gang's harassed city interests on the near South Side. There, in the city's First Ward, the gang had lost the use of its Four Deuces headquarters on South Wabash, but Chief Collins and Mayor Dever could not possibly shutter gang operations entirely. So while Capone maintained his Cicero headquarters, he sought to establish a conveniently located ancillary city office for business, at least until such time as he could safely reestablish his main base there. Secretively, gang members, probably led by Jake Guzik, established a subsidiary operation a block north and east from the old Four Deuces on the corner of Twenty-second Street and South Michigan Avenue. The area was dotted with medium and small hotels, restaurants, and shops. Across the street was the ten-floor Lexington Hotel, whose columnar second-floor portico opened over Michigan Avenue facing the gang's new headquarters. Down the block sat the Metropole Hotel, and the much smaller New Wabash and Carleon hotels stood nearby. Any offered a temporary haven in which to conduct business in relative obscurity within walking distance of the new nerve center.

The building at 2146 Michigan Avenue, unlike the long-notorious Four Deuces, seemed benign enough. The two-story, dark brick expanse blended with the construction of every other structure in the area. It extended approximately one hundred feet west along Twenty-second Street from the corner and perhaps fifty feet north along Michigan Avenue. Smart shops shaded by cloth awnings occupied the street level, including a quaint oyster bar on the West Twenty-second Street side. Passersby window shopped in comfort, perhaps picking up a paper at the newsstand on the corner. On the top floor, a series of large paned windows in sections three feet long and two feet high, each spaced perhaps six feet apart, illuminated the various offices within.

Capone's staff—Guzik, Nitto, and Johnny Patton—organized their operations in a suite of rooms upstairs superficially disguised as a physician's office. Contrary to what most previous accounts of the office report, the nameplate attached to the front door did not name "A. Brown, M.D." as the occupant, "A. Brown" being one of Capone's many aliases. Rather, "Dr. Ryan" or "Dr. Frank Ryan" was listed as the occupant. Opening Dr. Ryan's front office door revealed a small waiting room with an array of shelves lined with seemingly medicinal glass apothecary in the form of half-pints, pints, and quarts of various shapes. Beyond the waiting room lay other rooms "surrounded by towering barricades of file cabinets." Typewriters echoed within, clerks scurried about filing this or that document, and ledger books of many types lay here or there—just another seemingly efficient office setting.

The medical office disguise was a simple yet ingenious spin-off of the common "speakeasy hidden in a drugstore" disguise of the time that offered no obvious, ready-to-raid street-front address—just an apparently common, ordinary workplace tucked away in a large, nondescript building filled with other ordinary workplaces. Furthermore, none of the nearby tenants would give a thought to the numerous comings and goings during the day since many people needed to see doctors. Even a casual peek through the opened door would pique no great interest thanks to the clever apothecary disguise. No one else would be around to notice traffic during the evening, as most of the offices were closed.

The reverberation of typewriters, however, produced not doctor's orders or records but sophisticated hoodlum memoranda: buyers and payoff lists, addresses, and phone numbers. The gang's network extended to the ports of New York, New Orleans, and Miami, possibly guaranteeing quality import merchandise. Records were maintained for at least four breweries. Personnel accounted for sales and shipments of booze in blue and black leather-bound books. One possibly privileged reporter later reproduced a page said to have come from the booze ledger. In part it read:

Week ending April 4, 1925
Jack, 16-10-$970.
Ralph, 89-46-$3,584.
Hei, 3615-$1,522.
Hei, 7-7-$315.
Sam, 11-$385.
Fus, 19-$665.
Sal, 5-$200.
Wallace, 1-$30.
Total, $7,671.50.

Authorities surmised the first two numbers were probably sales of units of some type—perhaps cases of gallons—followed by amounts in either collections or commissions. Other notations, they guessed, represented locations—for instance, "Cic" probably stood for Cicero. Still other records may have reflected inventories by types of booze—"A" perhaps indicating alcohol, while "B" may have implied bourbon. "On hand: 21d's, 69 gals., 8 cases" suggested inventories, "d" representing drums of product. At the end, meager expenses listed rents and labor, tallying all of $107! A typed final copy probably served as official correspondence.

In addition to alcohol registers, account books for several bordellos were maintained. The records were so detailed that one who viewed them labeled them "disgustingly accurate." In all, the Michigan Avenue office was doing the accounting for an estimated minimum of $25,000-$40,000 a month in gang profits.

Nitto in all likelihood enjoyed what was probably his daily routine, conducting his alcohol business in the city then commuting to Cicero to collect liquor accounts, balance the books at The Ship, and conduct his personal banking there. Monday, April 6, 1925, played out no differently, except that Nitto and company returned to the Michigan Avenue office late that night to finish up additional business. With Nitto were Capone's Burnham caretaker John Patton, beer and liquor authority Joe Fusco, gunman Robert McCullough, and four other minor hoods. Each carried a minimum of $500 cash. They attended to business as usual, delivering collected checks, checking liquor orders, arranging deliveries, and checking the payoff lists. Considering the illegality of such operations, they were apparently emboldened by the confidence of their cover, leaving ledgers and records spread about in open view.

The efficient gang setup, however, was no longer a secret from the city's detective bureau. Acting on an anonymous tip, virtuous Lieutenant Edward Birmingham led his detective bureau squad 1-A to Dr. Ryan's office and burst in the door. The incredulous looks on the detectives' faces certainly matched those worn by Nitto and company inside. Surprise was total and complete, a rare coup for law enforcement in those days. Run-of-the-mill Prohibition-raid items such as liquor samples and a small quantity of ammunition, including shotgun shells, were taken from the front section of the office. It was when the squad proceeded into the rear rooms and found a few clerks still typing away that the enormity of what their foray had uncovered became apparent to the invaders. Among the filing cabinets were books, ledgers, and notebooks tracking liquor sales and brothel accounts that covered, if not the gang's entire operation, a very significant part of that business, including county sources. Closer examination of other papers revealed phone records that the raiders guessed might be part of a nationwide alky trafficking network. Among the reams of paper was a noteworthy bill for bottled water: the delivery address was, of all places, the Lake County Jail; the customer was thought to be ally Johnny Torrio, who was currently serving time there for the Sieben Brewery affair. Persistent reporting claimed many other prominent names of citizens and businesses were among those who purchased alcohol from the gang.

The calamitous nature of the raid sent Patton, the only immediately recognized big shot of the bunch, into immediate action. Would Birmingham accept $5,000 cash to forget about the matter? The guileless lieutenant, who would cause more headaches for the gang in the years to follow, turned Patton down flat. Flushed, the ex-mayor of Burnham upped the ante, possibly to $15,000, but still no dice. Nitto's expertise was not subornation of public servants but rather selling, collecting, and moving booze. All Patton and associates got for that not-so feeble effort was a ride to the detective bureau corral for questioning.

There, none of the gang offered much of value to the inquiring officers outside of the standard information—age, address, and occupation—required to fill out the arrest card. Barely a month after finally becoming an official U.S. citizen, Nitto's first known arrest was duly recorded:

> Name: Frank Nitto
> Address: 833 South Marshfield Avenue
> Age: 38 Nativity: American Married
> Charge: 2655 (Disorderly Conduct) Date Arrested: 4 / 6 / 25

As to his occupation Nitto provided interviewers with the appropriate answer: business manager. To no one's surprise, he refused to elaborate upon further questioning. Police already knew Patton as the former mayor of Burnham, and he gave his age as forty-five. The imposing Robert McCullough gave his age as thirty-five. Both he and Patton gave South Halsted home addresses that were probably fake. The men and their cohorts spent the night in lockup before they were arraigned by Municipal Judge Howard Hayes and extricated by lawyers posting bonds Monday afternoon. Their next appearance in the matter was set for April 23.

The press, much to the reserved Nitto's probable chagrin, reported the incident in bold front-page headlines. Excitedly, the papers pronounced the event as a law enforcement coup of epic proportions: "SUPERTRUST BARED!" There was little doubt this was a major operation, yet no one attached any significance to Nitto's claim of being a manager in the Torrio-Capone Outfit. Seemingly disappointed, the *Chicago Tribune* pronounced the group to be "minor heads of the Syndicate," while the *Daily News* announced John Patton was the only headliner of the group. In both papers, Nitto, whose name they published as "Frank Nitta," rated as a nominal third runner-up for top billing. Only a *Herald and Examiner* reporter, with perhaps remarkably keen insights into Capone's administration or simply no particular concern for ranking the names, put Frank Nitto, name correctly spelled, in the top spot.

The whirlwind excitement of the incident swept up city, county, and federal law enforcement officials more than it did the arrested. Eager at first, authorities reported patron names were attached to the records, and soon a few blushed that payoff lists to local police and federal agents were alleged to be contained within. Then the speculation reduced the detailed entries to simple phone numbers, maybe only initials not names, and names for booze dealers only. The Bureau of Investigation (later known as the Federal Bureau of Investigation, or FBI) was interested in the interstate transportation of any stolen merchandise the case may have revealed. The local collector for Internal Revenue wanted an immediate audit to determine any tax fraud. Chief Prohibition Agent Charles Vursell, in charge of the district, was curious as to the alleged bribery of Prohibition agents.

For the gang, the loss of equipment and headquarters obviously paled in comparison to the loss of the records. Now with three federal agencies looking to get involved, Capone's organization was threatened with one of its greatest crises to date.

Miraculously, a ray of hope shone the next day as Lieutenant Birmingham was served with a summons demanding that all records seized in the raid be placed in the court's custody, whereupon Judge Hayes impounded the records. His motives are not known, but he set the next hearing on the matter for April 28. To the gang's relief, the records were now away from probing federal eyes.

Exactly what happened next, if anything, behind the scenes is uncertain. U.S. District Attorney Olson complained that Judge Hayes acted without giving notice of his immediate intention. The next day, in an unscheduled hearing with gang lawyers, Hayes returned the records to the custody of the arrested men. In making his decision, the judge explained, "The law forced me to do it." He noted the defendants were charged only with disorderly conduct. "There were no federal cases against the men arrested," thus law enforcement had no right to take the records—this was a case of illegal search and seizure. In that, assuming there were no search warrants, Hayes may have legally been correct.

But it was apparent Hayes's underhanded action—not so much the act of turning the files back over to gang representatives, but rather providing no notice to federal attorneys of the hearing or the intent to return the files—that infuriated U.S. District Attorney Olson. In his view, Hayes's actions illustrated "a direct refusal to cooperate with federal authorities." Police officials also noted that Hayes's actions effectively "knocked the bottom out of the case." Reasonably, Olson noted that the decision rested solely with Hayes, as the raid had occurred within his jurisdiction, but for the record Olson described his decision as a "peculiar procedure." In any event, Hayes's action settled matters. All that remained was the original disorderly conduct charge, and on the scheduled court date in late April, Judge Hayes dismissed the remaining charge against Nitto as well as the rest of the company.

Emboldened by the April triumphs, and perhaps coupled with the fact that Mayor Dever's valiant efforts to enforce the dry laws and hold gang members behind bars were futile, Capone's next administrative action was to begin shifting his forces back into the city's Near South Side. Nitto's boss chose a site near the original Four Deuces headquarters only a block and a half south of the near disaster at 2146 South Michigan. The address was 2300 South Michigan, the seven-story Metropole Hotel. As to why he selected the Metropole, Capone, obviously fearing little from the authorities, made no bones about it: "my interests have expanded and I required a central headquarters."

Capone entrenched himself into a suite of two fourth-floor Metropole rooms overlooking Michigan Avenue. Altogether, the gang initially booked eight or nine rooms spread over three floors for their activities. The hotel was also convenient to Nitto's apartment. Perhaps still wary of harassment by Mayor Dever, who still had two years remaining in his term, the movement of headquarters from the Hawthorne Hotel in Cicero back into the city would apparently occur in phases.

Nonetheless, the Metropole served as a beehive of the gang's activities for at least the next three years. According to one who frequented the hotel during the time, "Prominent criminal lawyers and high officials of the police department, along with politicians and dive keepers waited their turn to consult with the Big Shot. Policemen in uniform streamed in and out." With so much activity, the gang found it necessary to rent as many as fifty rooms at times. They operated a private elevator. For security, Capone's personal guards constantly patrolled gang floors and the hotel lobby. The gang operated private bars, gambling ran wide-open twenty-four hours a day, women were brought in as desired, and meals from favored local Italian eateries were delivered. For Nitto, though, it was simply another business location.

Sometime during his climb up the gang ladder, Nitto accomplished arguably one of the most important human resource actions for the gang since his own employment. Trekking in and out of the Metropole Hotel conducting business, Nitto's elevated stature required that he secure people for the operations for which he was responsible, building a second echelon of underlings who would serve as trustworthy assistants and help him function efficiently. A meeting that would prove important was said to be the result of Nitto going out for lunch or dinner.

Nitto and others in the Metropole stepped out to various Italian restaurants to take a meal from time to time, many prepared from genuine Old Country recipes. The more understanding proprietors allowed their valued patrons to discuss business in private booths or rooms, a common practice at the time. A couple of doors north from the scene of Nitto's arrest on Michigan stood the Little Florence Italian Grill. Noting the frequency of visits by Capone's men, one critic wrote of that quaint restaurant, "You are as safe in the Little Florence as you are in a church." He also rated the spaghetti as first rate.

Gang members also traveled to the heart of Little Italy, where establishments enticed passersby with the tantalizing aroma of their food. At Amato's restaurant at 914 South Halsted, maître d' Amato Maglialuzzo served original Italian spaghetti "in its true native state." Another favorite, a block down the street, was

John Citro's Café, at one time thought to be owned silently by Genna gunman Samoots Amatuna. Just up Halsted, at least until the end of 1923, Capone's men regularly dropped into Diamond Joe Esposito's Bella Napoli Café. Diamond Joe's, more than any of the other restaurants, resembled a syndicate "meeting hall" and was, at the time, the ward's nerve center for business. However by 1925, Esposito had sold the place to Louis Coscioni, and the restaurant was no longer called the Bella Napoli.

It was during one such lunch or dinner at one of these establishments that a particularly intelligent waiter was said to have caught Nitto's attention. Quiet, respectful, and well mannered—cast from the Torrio blueprint—the waiter had told Nitto that he worked tables locally and that he had ushered dusty peasants to their bench seats in the Dante Theatre around the corner. Nitto knew the place well, as he had performed the same service years earlier and was still good friends with the owner. The twenty-something Italian waiter stood barely over five feet, seven inches tall and was of medium build, weighing about 160 pounds. Rugged, virile, yet urbane, the server possessed dark features, dark chestnut hair parted on the left, heavy dark brows, and sleepy, hazel eyes which somehow portended a hint of foreboding. The waiter's name was Felice DeLucia, more notably Paul Ricca.

Ricca had followed the same course to the United States as many of his brethren, only much later. Born probably around 1898 in Italy, Ricca immigrated to New York in the late summer of 1920, perhaps as a murder fugitive, under the alias Paul Maglio. After a month's stay in New York, Ricca moved to Chicago. Speaking little or no English, he naturally gravitated to Little Italy on the West Side. Curiously like Nitto, his first employment was for Dante Theatre owner Joseph Vicedomini, and he quite possibly became an assistant manager before moving on to a position with ward power Diamond Joe Esposito at his famous café around 1923. After possibly serving as a manager at Diamond Joe's place, Ricca may have struck out on his own and acquired his own restaurant at South Halsted and Taylor streets, followed by yet another, The Falstaff at 543 South Wabash. Either as a result of his time in the restaurant business or from a witness to his naturalization years later who vouched for him as a good restaurant server, Ricca's nickname was "the Waiter." Nitto installed Ricca as an aide in Camp Capone.

⸻

While shifting his command post back to the city, Capone's most compelling concern was once again the city's sagging inter-gang relationships. Everyone on the South Side seemed to be gunning for each other. Spike O'Donnell lashed out toward neighbor Saltis once again, retaliations ensued, and then Ralph Sheldon and his agent Dan Stanton jumped into the fray. On the North Side, the vengeful remnants of the O'Banion gang still lay coiled. Unsuccessful in eliminating Torrio, they figured sending him packing was just as good. They had targeted Capone once already, and he had every reason to believe another strike would come soon. For the same reason they assaulted Torrio, the Weiss crowd might assail the Genna clan, totally dissolving what little peace remained.

Unfortunately, Capone's putative allies in Little Italy, the Gennas, perceived just as great a perceived threat from his organizational plans. The Gennas' wealth had grown to the millions, enabling them to become the social, industrial, and political leaders in the West Side Little Italy enclave, and they were a cantankerous and arrogant bunch. Using the cottage alcohol industry and district allies, ill-tempered Angelo Genna brazenly set himself up as Mike Merlo's successor of the Unione Siciliana as a means to guarantee his family's dominance in the region and to possibly expand. However, it was thought Capone, who as a non-Sicilian may not have qualified for membership in the Unione, wished to place his own local ally, widely respected Sicilian importer and wholesaler Antonio "Tony" Lombardo, in charge of the Unione Siciliana.

At age thirty-three, Lombardo did not qualify as a hoodlum in the regular sense. He had built up a thriving wholesale grocery house on West Randolph, partly by his popular standing in the community, but also through strong-arm methods—for the lowly *pisan*, it was in the interest of one's good health to buy from him. Lombardo was also widely respected and wealthy, in part from Prohibition. He didn't deal directly with booze but had grown financially stout along with partner Giuseppe "Joseph" Aiello, in part by supplying distilling ingredients such as sugar and yeast to a significant portion of the Genna operation. In addition to being Sicilian, the fact that he was a "level-headed man of remarkable calmness and poise" made Lombardo the perfect Capone delegate to run Little Italy as well as the northern Sicilian enclave.

Nitto's boss knew that whoever became Unione president would wield great influence over the community and its cottage alky-cooking industry, worth an estimated $10 million a year to Unione coffers. They could stabilize, or agitate, the West Side Italian community, if so desired. A firm ally would act as an insurance policy for Capone's current alcohol holdings as well as help expand them. And if Capone were eventually to battle other gangs of the city, he would naturally have to line up his own people first. Who represented the greater threat, the North Siders who were openly hostile or the oily Genna pack, his own kind, who exemplified surreptitious treachery?

⟞◦◦◦⟝

The North Siders under Hymie Weiss may have jumped the gun on Capone to get the Gennas. The morning of May 25, 1925, dawned bright and sunny in Chicago, and newlywed Angelo Genna started off down Ogden Avenue from his fashionable $400 a month suite in the Belmont Hotel overlooking Lake Michigan on the North Side. Carrying a down payment for a house his bride desired in Oak Park, he drove leisurely in his shiny roadster southwest down Ogden toward Cicero. He was set to pick up the remainder of the intended purchase amount from his brother-in-law lawyer Henry Spingola on the West Side and maybe inspect a Genna alky plant on the way.

No more than a few short blocks from his starting point, a curtained touring car carrying four men pulled off a side street and began to quickly make up ground on

Genna. Approaching the Hudson Avenue intersection, the hunters overtook the hunted and let loose a barrage of gunfire. Despite horrific wounds, Angelo remained conscious long enough to fumble for his weapon before losing control of his roadster and smacking into a lamppost on Hudson. Genna was carted off to a nearby hospital and expired without giving police a clue as to the identity of the killers. After several hours of investigation, though, Chief of Detectives William Schoemaker concluded that Angelo's murder was carried out not by Italians but rather by the same group who had made the attempt on Torrio's life in January and was simply an attempt to exact revenge on the other party thought to be responsible for the O'Banion murder and a continuation of their earlier alky feud. Names of suspects were bandied about: Moran, Drucci, and Weiss. If they were in fact the killers, while they may have satisfied a thirst for revenge and nipped the Genna alcohol incursions, they also performed a remarkable service for Capone.

Less than three weeks later, Mike Genna and the Sicilian killing team John Scalise and Albert Anselmi were cruising south on Western Avenue. An hour earlier that morning, they and other members of the Genna combine had released a torrent of lead upon a sedan occupied by George Moran and Vincent Drucci on the northern edge of Little Italy. (Both men escaped slightly wounded with the car worse for wear—the barrage obliterated the car's top, and there were more than sixty bullet holes elsewhere.) As the Genna trio raced south away from the scene in their Cadillac, a detective bureau squad of four detectives passed them in an unmarked car going the opposite direction. Recognizing the swarthy gents in the southbound vehicle as possible hoodlums, the squad commander ordered his driver to whip their car around in hot pursuit. They may not have heard about the morning gunplay, but within the last week, police comrades had fallen to criminal gunfire, and this crew was on the lookout for any hoodlums on which to exact some inconvenience. The car speeding off toward the southwest rail yards showed promise, perhaps headed for an alcohol transaction the detectives might break up and put these guys off the street.

Ringing the police gong only caused the Genna car to accelerate and swerve through traffic, dodging streetcars along the way. The chase that began at Forty-seventh Street ended twelve blocks further south when a truck swerved into the path of the Genna vehicle. Slamming on the brakes, Genna's car skidded nearly 360 degrees, the rear coming to rest against a light pole. When the police approached the wrecked vehicle, a gun battle erupted. Just who fired the first shot is in question, but a blast from Scalise's shotgun mortally toppled one of the detectives as he approached their vehicle. Another discharge of slugs sent another officer to the pavement, dead. A blast from Anselmi's gun wounded one more. Genna, Scalise and Anselmi then broke away. Outnumbered three to one, the lone detective gathered up the weapons from his fallen comrades and valiantly gave chase.

As they ran across a vacant lot, Genna wheeled about to fire a round from his shotgun, but the hammer clicked on an empty chamber. The lone detective shot Genna in the left thigh eight inches above the knee. Ordinarily, this was an incapacitating but not fatal shot, but in this case the slug apparently opened up Genna's femoral artery, the enormous gateway artery that feeds blood from the heart to the leg. Blood gushed as Genna hobbled an amazingly strong retreat, finally finding refuge in a residential basement after smashing through a ground-level window. His reprieve was short-lived; following the trail of blood, the detective closed in on his location. With the aid of another policeman, he entered the house and crashed the basement door only to find a very weakened, blood-splattered Il Diavolo lying on the floor amongst fragments of glass. Mike the Devil died on an ambulance gurney before reaching a hospital. Scalise and Anselmi were netted a short distance away as they scrambled for a trolley.

Police gunfire notwithstanding, underworld talk had it that Mike was a dead man that day regardless. He was himself was being taken for ride at the time the police chase occurred, for the murderous Scalise and Anselmi were now working for Capone, not the Gennas, as Mike thought. Having probably enticed the pair to his side (indeed, Capone was arrested with Scalise in an April incident), their double duty that day was to be a bonus for Capone: Scalise and Anselmi would help kill sworn enemies Moran and Drucci that morning then dispatch the lethal Mike Genna afterwards.

A month later, on a rather pleasant July day, Tony Genna received a call from a friend to meet him at Cutilla's grocery store. Cutilla's was located in a mostly two-story, brick residential neighborhood near the corner of Grand Avenue and Curtis Street close to where Ogden Avenue slants across Grand. Tony arrived at the rendezvous point before his caller; waiting patiently, he engaged owner Vito Cutilla in casual palaver about the weather as the grocer arranged fresh produce on his counter.

Overwhelmed by such an agreeable, fine summer day, Tony stepped outside to enjoy the sunshine while he waited. A moment later, a car pulled over to the curb on the opposite side of Curtis Street. His caller finally arrived. The man started across the street to greet Genna, full of cordiality, and just off the storefront curb, Tony received the gentleman in a line manner, stretching out his hand in greeting. The fact that Tony was never the crude, brutish, violent type like his brothers, that he acted more like a community benefactor, did not insulate him from the violence. He sat in on all family councils, and that was all that mattered to somebody. A repeat of the O'Banion murder played out as the man grasped Tony's hand in welcome but held on hard. Two other men sprang from concealment nearby and pumped five shots into Tony before scampering off.

With half the Genna clan shot down in forty-two days, their power base was broken. Police raids instigated shortly after Mike's death helped finish them off. Armed with Chief of Detectives William Schoemaker's mandate—"It's war. And in wartime you shoot first and talk second"—police wrecked Genna headquarters in the Italian-American Club at 1022 Taylor Street. An unremitting series of raids on other installations within the hub of the Genna province netted 15,000 gallons of alcohol, 7,500 barrels of fermenting mash, four and a half tons of sugar, and a half-ton of yeast. With the business now in shambles, older brother and head of the clan Jim Genna, in their native Sicily at the time of Mike's death, wisely opted for an extended stay. Brothers Pete and Sam laid low and kept out of trouble. Eventually they would surface again, wisely shying away from the booze business and confining their activities to their original olive oil and cheese importing commerce.

As to who killed Tony Genna, the police could only point suspicious fingers. The North Siders again ranked high, the possible motive viewed as retaliation for the failed ambush attempt on Moran and Drucci the day Mike died. The initial police web was cast for both these men. They expanded the net to include Italians when, on his deathbed, Tony repeated to his brother Sam in faint whisper "Cavallero," similar to the *Il Cavalieri* alias for associate Anthony Spano. What's more, police noted the parallel to the handshake in the O'Banion killing and also a suspected Italian job. A couple of days later, a brave soul who witnessed the murder came forward and declared the assassins looked "Italian."

Surely, the North Siders possessed motive to kill Tony and probably rejoiced at the battlefront news, but as in many gangland activities, motive can be traced rather simply: who in the end would benefit the most from someone's downfall? The void left behind in the Taylor Street district of Little Italy could only be adequately managed and rebuilt by a preeminent, organized Italian operation such as the one that belonged to Frank Nitto's boss. In addition to acquiring booze territory, Al now employed the Gennas' two best gunmen, Scalise and Anselmi. He would even support them over the next two years in their legal battles resulting from the murder of the two detectives in the Mike Genna affair. That hectic affair, the Defense Fund drive, would begin in the fall.

———

Elimination of the Gennas, however, did not bring immediate rewards in terms of additional alcohol territory; much consolidation remained to be carried out. Three men described as independent alky dealers who failed to recognize Capone's new authority were killed on July 15. Both Sam Lavenuto and James Russo got it during the day, while that night a drive-by fusillade claimed ex-con Tony Campagna and wounded cohort Sam Ciminello, alias Joseph Novello. Both were ex-Genna men reportedly working for a commission merchant, possibly in variance of Tony Lombardo.

Those with foolish delusions of ascending the Gennas' vacated throne continued to make attempts for the remainder of 1925. After the elimination of the Gennas, their territory, as well as the vacancy for president of the Unione Siciliana, once again fell open. Brazenly loyal Genna gunmen and onetime musician Samoots Amatuna envisioned himself as the Gennas' heir apparent over the West Side alky enclave. Samoots had grown fairly prosperous from various dealings allied with the Gennas. He had long been engaged to Mike Merlo's sister-in-law, and by virtue of this relation, he now claimed the Unione position through a self-proclaimed right of succession. He had bowed out earlier when the young and more powerful Angelo desired the seat, but now Samoots and two longtime West Side henchmen would run the show. However, Nitto's boss hadn't finished off the Gennas to allow this dapper fellow to set up shop for long.

Regardless, at least for the time being, Amatuna indirectly served Capone's best interest by taking charge of collecting a community defense fund for cop killers

Scalise and Anselmi. He was probably the most recognized and best-suited person in Little Italy to carry out such an activity. Perhaps Samoots was not aware of the shift of allegiance and thought the two charged Sicilians were still his cronies. Rumor had it that he spent in excess of $20,000 of his own fortune to secure their release. With State's Attorney Robert Crowe promising the gallows for the pair, a large monetary reserve might insure at least a more vigorous defense than would otherwise be obtained from a public defender for two men with thick accents.

Amatuna, long regarded as the real benefactor in the community, appealed to poor and wealthy Italians alike, imploring them to contribute since nothing less than the good name of the Italian community was at stake. If the sermon failed to open the pockets of the poor, they were effectively relieved of their coin by more potent means. Sizable donations came from the more prosperous. Capone gave generously, requiring gambling operators and vicemongers in his domain to ante up . . . or else. Over the course of late summer and autumn, as much as $100,000 was collected to pay for a top-notch defense team. The trial for the murder of one of the detectives started that October. Armed with two capable attorneys, the defense fund efforts paid off early in November with a verdict of guilty—but not of murder, only manslaughter. The judge pronounced a sentence of fourteen years in prison. Gleeful they beat the more serious charge of murder, Scalise and Anselmi were sent to holding where they would await their trial next spring for the killing of the second detective. In the meantime, the pair of killers could count on another fundraising effort to bolster their cause. (Eventually, they would go free.)

As the first trial coursed to its end that fall season, so perhaps did Amatuna's usefulness to Capone. On the evening of November 10, two days before the jury rendered their verdict in the Scalise and Anselmi trial, Amatuna hopped off a trolley into Isadore Paul's barbershop on the corner of West Roosevelt Road and Halsted, near the heart of the Italian community, for a shave to tidy up a bit in anticipation of *Aida*, for an opera date beckoned that night. Shortly after situating himself in the barber's chair, two armed men walked in and disturbed his serenity. Their first four shots all missed the mark, and as Samoots ducked behind the barber's chair, four shots found him, one through his neck. Carted off by taxi to Jefferson Park Hospital clinging to life, it was Nitto acquaintance Dr. Gaetano Ronga who gave Amatuna's prognosis: though the bullet to his neck had somehow miraculously missed the vital carotid artery, it shattered his spine. Even if Amatuna survived, paralysis would ensure his hoodlum days were over. Ultimately, though, after three days of apparent progress toward recovery, he died.

Within a twenty-day period following the elimination of Samoots, his loyal henchmen Eddie Zion and Abraham "Bummy" Goldstein, an alky distributor on the West Side, were also cut down for good measure; Zion got it after paying his final respects at Samoots's funeral. Initial police speculation pegged Amatuna's murderers as members of the North Side Gang and the West Side O'Donnells. Neither would have cried over the final pruning of a pesky, perennial Genna weed, but again, in the end, who most directly stood to gain from Samoots's demise? Nitto's boss, of course. When witnesses finally came forward, they pronounced Amatuna's killers as "dark of skin," a sketch hardly fitting any North Sider outside Vincent Drucci. With the removal of Amatuna, the amalgamation of lucrative home stills on the Near West Side into the Capone fold could finally begin. Al's ally, the thick, suave Antonio Lombardo, became president of the Unione in Chicago.

Was Frank Nitto himself in on planning the elimination of the Gennas and their allies? There is no record of this, but who in the Capone ranks was best suited to assist Lombardo in active liquor management? With Lombardo's authority in the Unione in its infancy, the gang mission did not end with the elimination of the Gennas—they would face resistance. Within the Capone group, who had long known the area, the residents, as well as the liquor business best? Who amongst the Italian portion of the gang possessed the most appropriate business persona and the brains to boot? Who was abrupt enough to force gang will? Frank Nitto, the man who got things done in a hurry.

Federal agents provided confirmation of Nitto's role, noting that he derived much of his lofty and traceable six-figure income that year by organizing the alky business in Cicero, Little Italy (the old Genna territory), and the western suburbs. One of those suburbs was Melrose Park, just northwest of Cicero. Nominally "open"—that is, not assigned to any city gang—Chicago's fringes offered refuge for many a bootlegger harassed by Dever's city police. Diamond Joe Esposito reportedly made a fortune selling sugar to the suburban bootleg operations headed by main alky dealer and Genna operative Aniello Taddeo. When the Genna operations took a hit that summer, reports had Amatuna moving more stills out to Melrose Park, inducing local residents to maintain 100-gallon setups at a rate of $25 per week. Coincidentally, on September 27, only a month and a half before Amatuna got his, alky chief Aniello Taddeo was shot dead in front of his restaurant. The bloodletting ceased when Taddeo friend and self-appointed seeker of vengeance, James Campanille, was gunned down near the same spot. In Taddeo's place came ex-Genna man and now Capone ally Joe Montana, a friend of Tony Lombardo. From this point forward, federal agents believed Nitto was sent into neighboring Bellwood and beyond with successful results.

Other events, however, confounded Nitto's task. While Capone's group was trying to bring the alky industry in line, a second, apparently unofficial, defense fund collection effort in the name of Scalise and Anselmi was in the works that winter. While Capone was out of town on family matters, leftover Genna gunman, the capricious mystical wizard Orazio Tropea, stepped forward as lead executive for the charity. Finding donors not so willing to ante up a second time, Tropea and his bottom rung of thugs resorted to murder. Apparently those rich and easy sources who had hitherto gained much from the cottage alky industry, the commodity suppliers, were at the top of the visitation list. With or without Capone's blessing, Tropea and his men may have temporarily served Capone's interests in more ways than just gathering defense contributions.

Henry Spingola, wealthy lawyer and brother-in-law of Angelo Genna, contributed $10,000 to the defense fund on the first go-around but ponied up a mere $2,000 for the encore solicitation. On January 10, 1926, after a rich dinner and several hands of cards in Amato's restaurant on South Halsted, he emerged from the restaurant and climbed into his car. Four men immediately ran across the street, withdrew revolvers, and pumped nine or more shots into him. The spotter, maybe Tropea himself, evidently was one of those sitting in the card game. He alerted those waiting down below. Capone or Lombardo were at best indifferent to Spingola's demise.

The millionaire Morici brothers, Agostino and Antonio, were another matter. They thrived as prosperous wholesale grocers and macaroni manufacturers, with offices just north of the Italian quarter at 662 West Washington Boulevard. Much like Tony Lombardo, though, they had supplied ingredients for the Genna alky operation for the past couple of years. Not long ago, Agostino aided young Angelo Genna when the latter was tried for the Labriola murder by testifying to Angelo's good character and reputation. Recently, the brothers had purchased Jim Genna's large Lakeside Place residence shortly before the latter fled to Italy. But they, too, brushed aside another plea for the defense fund. Charity was one thing, but this was dipping into the well once too often for them. Besides, the brothers were no softies, having refused to knuckle under to Black Hand threats as far back as 1919. Now they were even larger community figures, and under no circumstances would they contribute any further, even to a cause some considered communal altruism.

Two weeks after Spingola died, a light snow began falling on Chicago with minor accumulations. By 7 p.m., the temperature dipped to near 15 degrees. The Moricis were driving warily through the powder on Ogden Avenue north to their new Lakeside residence in the classy new automobile they had recently purchased. Prudence made them easy prey. Preoccupied, they did not notice an auto pulling along broadside, sawed-off shotguns protruding and about to be fired. The severely wounded Agostino lost control of his vehicle, veering over the nearby curb and smashing through a metal signboard before crunching into a building. Morici blood splattered over the three-inch carpet of snowflakes, and both men died. As a premium, importer Tony Lombardo might assume their business within the old Genna operation.

Following this series of retaliations, the pace of contributions was said to have picked up. However, during the next four weeks the fundraisers themselves perished. Perhaps it was payback by prominent community spirits, relatives of the businessmen slain the month before. The press speculated this might be the case but could not discern who in the community could muster the power take on "the Scourge," Tropea. Tropea's withholding of the donations—it was suspected that he had already deposited $20,000 in his own coffers, an affront to Capone's interests—probably had more to do with it. And gang guns did not fear him.

About 9:10 p.m. on February 15, Tropea hopped off an eastbound Taylor Street trolley and ambled across snow-sloshed Halsted Street near the intersection at Taylor. When he was almost across, an auto with curtains concealing the occupants nearly ran him down. The apparent insolence of the careless driver enraged tough man Tropea, and without considering that anybody would dare retaliate against him, Tropea angrily cursed the driver: "Why the hell don't you blow your horn?" A load of buckshot answered him. As he lay bleeding, face down in the cold, snowy slush, perhaps mustering his last reserve of life, "the Scourge," age forty-something, recently on top of the old Genna realm, was finished off by a second discharge of lead.

In quick succession, two Tropea aides were dropped. Booze peddler in the Genna ward and opera devotee Vito Bascone was abducted and battered. At some point during his torment, his captors drilled a single shot through his forehead and then insolently dumped his body in a ditch in the southwest suburb of Summit. Two days later on the numbingly cold night of February 23, two watchmen passing through a dark alley behind a factory near Austin Avenue and Curtis Street found the body of Eddie "the Eagle" Bardella sprawled on an ash heap. The Eagle, a chauffeur for Tropea, had been beaten hideously, shot twice through the head and once in the heart. The lack of blood at the scene and the wheel marks of an auto in the soot nearby indicated his tormentors preformed the gruesome service elsewhere before disposing of him.

Barely two weeks later Joseph Calabrese and three other men were riding as passengers in an auto driven by Ralph Cavalerri. Police had known all men to be minor upstart traders in the alcohol game allied with Orazio Tropea. They were headed west on Twenty-second Street to Cicero, presumably to pay a restaurant bill. As their Cadillac neared Keeler Avenue about a half-mile from the Cicero border, one of the men cried out, "They've got us, get down." Sawed-off shotguns protruding from a rapidly passing vehicle exploded. Calabrese took a salvo of pellets to the head and died instantly, and two others were wounded. The last man eventually vaulted from the car and escaped unscathed. Their auto, as it turned out, belonged to Tropea aide Phillip Gnolfo. Police believe he was the intended target and that the assassins mistakenly assumed he was in the car. Gnolfo fared no better when, in May 1930, gunmen in an auto squeezed his machine and raked him with gunfire. As a result of these murders, Genna territory became Capone territory.

The year ended with Frank Nitto tallying up a spectacularly lush income that certainly was not that of an obscure gunman or mid-level employee. His pay came from sweeping alcohol deals that measured in the thousands of dollars. Still, despite the succulent earnings, no evidence of extravagance surfaced. He and his wife still occupied apartment rooms close to both the convenient east-west Roosevelt Road artery and the Little Italy quarter (probably on Marshfield or Throop Street). They lived at least comfortably but owned no detectable property in the city or elsewhere. Nitto likely invested and tucked the majority of his funds away with Greenberg's finance corporation. He may have sent money back to Brooklyn to aid his sister's family of fourteen, perhaps even to help purchase a graystone at 104 Garfield Place a year earlier. In the Torrio mold, Nitto laid low with no phone or city directory listings referring to him. He was simply the astute businessman, effectively attending to gang enterprises—behavior that was especially unusual during the freewheeling Roaring Twenties.

8

MEMBER OF THE BOARD

I N 1925 OR PERHAPS 1926, with the gang's empire growing and a city-wide booze war flaring on more than one front, survival increasingly began to occupy Capone's priorities as he reigned from his suite at the Metropole. He was the boss: he planned strategy and called all the important shots. His proven leadership and immense force of personality carried the organization, but he still could not realistically oversee all details around the clock. What would become of the gang if something happened to him, as it had to Torrio? Hymie Weiss was still on the loose. However, since Capone's elevation to boss, he remained without a succession mechanism.

As George Murray noted, Capone already had "found and surrounded himself with men needed to head great—if illegal—business enterprises." Capone maintained Torrio's vision of a highly organized, tightly knit crime administration. One insider thought Big Al's idea was similar to a corporate setup, "something like General Electric or the Ford Motor Corporation." In the event of Capone's absence, the enterprise "would be carried on at least to the point where it could be left to the direction of less skillful hands" than his own, thus ensuring continuity and survival. What he established was not a true board, in the sense of making appointments or electing officers, but something more like a corporate board composed of the leaders in their fields who would carry out the day-to-day administration of their respective areas and report the results to the boss, while Capone himself would retain the ultimate authority to make strategic decisions.

Once firmly established, the board would come to enjoy a lion's share of the gang's profits: one-sixth of the profit went to each of the four key leaders, with the remaining one-third of revenues set aside in a general revenue fund reserved for paying regular employees, chauffeurs, bodyguards, and the like. According to one of their suburban gambling cashiers, the "Big Four" were, besides Capone, Al's brother Ralph, who spearheaded beer distribution, longtime money man Jake Guzik, responsible for gambling collections and the distribution of most payoffs, and, in charge of collections in the alcohol racket, Frank Nitto.

Of course, their respective duties evolved as the corporation changed, and they also ran small concerns independent of their own specialty. For instance, Nitto, like Ralph and Guzik, was given portions of gambling collection, just as these two collected on large booze ventures. In the event of Capone's absence, he could receive information from and relay orders to any of the three, who provided for the board a mixture of longtime immeasurable trust, wide-ranging experience and the brains to implement directions.

Paul Ricca remained at Nitto's side, as did Louis Schiavone. Another of the quiet business types brought on board by Nitto as well as a gunman who rarely flaunted wealth, he assisted Nitto's alcohol deals through his Midwest Drug and Chemical Company. He also helped maintain discipline in Little Italy and lost an eye in the process. Scalise and Anselmi joined him after they were released.

The Fischettis, meanwhile, remained close at hand on the managerial level, and Capone added a dwarfish Cicero newsstand attendant Louis Cowen to the roster as an integral part of the Cicero operation. Cowen had come to worship Capone, and in return Capone entrusted him with thousands of dollars of real estate to function as, among other things, the gang bail bondsman. In the rare event of an arrest, they could call on Cowen to extricate them. Also at the ready was a retinue of utility gunmen. All of these men were junior to Nitto in age and rank, but each was a key component to the functionality of the organization, and all were familiar to Nitto as he shuttled in and out of the Metropole headquarters.

Already in the group was the suave Frank Rio. Of average size and about the same age as Capone, he was thoroughly practiced in the art of street violence. He had scrabbled about on the opposite side of the law extensively, perpetrating such things as mail robbery, extortion, and labor slugging. Recruited early in Al's tenure, he performed odd jobs for Torrio's group, possibly running whores between houses. His toughness and exceptional loyalty elevated him to a position perhaps as chief among Capone's bodyguard. Another gunman brought aboard was Frank Maritote, alias Diamond. Full-faced with heavy, dark eyebrows stretching nearly uninterrupted across his brow, his deep, menacing look was asset enough. He was a thick brute of average height and unpredictable conduct which even his cohorts found difficult to handle at times. When armed with a weapon, he was extremely dangerous. Robert McCullough entered the fold early on. An agile, menacing brute nearly six feet tall, he qualified for employment via the traditional arm's-length résumé of robbery and burglary arrests as a teenager. Tony "Mops" Volpe came on as a close Capone bodyguard. Thought to be an unfailing gunman, Volpe was picked up around Diamond

Joe Esposito's restaurant, where he worked sometimes as a manager while procuring the star of a deputy sheriff from the glittery owner.

Another familiar face to Nitto was that of Vincenzo Gibaldi, alias "Machine Gun" Jack McGurn. In top physical form, handsome, and finely tailored, this sleek Valentino figure combined oozing machismo that withered the ladies with unfailing gunslinging bravado on the streets. His "professed value," noted one Cook County coroner, "was top because of his invincible nerve. There was no likelihood that he would ever collapse under the strain." Born in Italy and reared in Brooklyn, he became a boxer in his youth, and it is thought that a ring manager gave him the more fanciful and pronounceable label, Jack McGurn). Transplanted to Chicago, he returned to New York at age nineteen to kill two men in connection with the murder of his father. Shortly thereafter, when his stepfather was murdered in an alcohol feud in the Gennas' Little Italy, he killed those men too—a gutsy feat given the easily ignitable Genna temperament. McGurn was a perfect addition to Capone's gang, especially with killers Scalise and Anselmi temporarily on the shelf for murder.

Gunman Philip Louis D'Andrea may have been associated with Capone's Outfit earlier than most. Born in Buffalo, New York, in 1891, he was brought to Chicago at age eleven. A high school graduate with possibly two years invested at the Hamilton Law School in Chicago by the time of the Great War, D'Andrea (no relation to Anthony D'Andrea) pursued trucking and transport interests with other family as early as 1919. With Prohibition on the horizon, transporting illegal booze would be much more profitable yet more dangerous than hauling, say, produce. This mix of legal and illegal was unusual for the gang, and the usually well-tailored, educated D'Andrea, a small man bedecked in suit, tie, and horn-rimmed glasses, looked more like a perched owl than a cartage tough.

He may have been running booze and involved with Capone and Torrio as early as 1921 and was thought to be good friends of the Fischettis. By 1925, D'Andrea had racked up arrests for receiving stolen property, assault with a deadly weapon, and carrying concealed weapons. He was discharged in all instances. He continued with his family's trucking concern, perhaps owning another outright through the twenties, and made a considerable fortune, according to federal authorities, as a result of Prohibition transport. Thanks to his occupation, D'Andrea honed his skills with a gun to the point that he achieved marksman status. To Capone, in a business in which many were consumed with greed and irrationality, D'Andrea's intelligence combined with his marksmanship made him invaluable as a key bodyguard.

Gunman Louis Campagna arrived on the scene about 1926. The stubby (five feet, five inches) yet unyielding Campagna earned his badge of toughness and his place in the gang after gunslinging a couple of robberies before he was twenty. Some said that Capone "imported" Campagna from New York as a gunman-killer, but in truth, he had been in the Chicago area most of his adult life. True, Campagna was born in Brooklyn; however, he left New York for good at age fifteen.

He landed in Chicago before Prohibition in the area around Taylor and Halsted streets waiting restaurant tables, maybe working as a laborer and hanging around pool halls for entertainment. Soon, Campagna turned to criminality as a preferred means of support. On October 1, 1917, he and a companion, armed with revolvers, allegedly robbed a passerby of $257. Nearly a year later, he was a co-defendant with four others on a complaint filed in the matter of an Argo, Illinois, bank robbery. According to the indictment, the group allegedly netted $57,000 in cash, government bonds, and War Savings stamps. Campagna exchanged a plea of guilty to a lesser charge for a one- to fourteen-year sentence at the State Reformatory at Pontiac, Illinois. Paroled, he kept clean and was officially discharged from the sentence in 1925. Still, in Chicago, he latched on to the Capone Outfit as a key bodyguard and gunman.

Another gunman, Nick Circella, was born in Italy about the turn of the century and was yet another product of Chicago's Little Italy who entered the Capone fold. As a teen, in December 1915 he pleaded guilty to robbery and was placed on probation. Not long afterward, he was back in court pleading guilty to assault with attempt to commit murder in a saloon holdup. After a short stint in prison, he was alleged to have been involved with Frank Rio in everything from stealing cars to mail robbery. Eventually, he tied up with Capone as a bodyguard and later acted as a business agent for the newsboys union.

———

Well-documented mid-twenties gang events, while making made extraordinary fodder for the Capone epoch, also played out favorably for Frank Nitto's stealth development in the higher echelon. While working his alky end of the business, Nitto, along with the rest of the board, was called upon more often by Capone to operate the business on a day-to-day basis. As early as 1926, Capone's increased stature became a lightning rod for authorities looking to pin blame on someone. One prosecutor, declaring that he knew who was behind a particularly high-profile murder, implicated Nitto's boss, but fully aware of the legal conundrums of the time, smartly opined, "I want to know it legally and be able to present it conclusively." Nevertheless, Capone found himself necessarily darting away from the battle to avoid the inevitable police roundups and subpoenas. Wealth and status also primed him to long for tranquil getaways from Chicago, and he eventually headed to Wisconsin and Florida for downtime. Capone's absences became more frequent, and each greatly seasoned the board and Frank Nitto.

When the Gennas were killed, the police rightly suspected the vengeful North Siders, almost ignoring Capone. But from here on out, almost anytime a major hood action occurred, Capone's name would surface as the target of law enforcement. Most importantly, Capone disappeared in the summer of 1926 as a result of the accidental murder of State's Attorney William H. McSwiggin. When the West Side O'Donnells thought they saw a chance to move against Capone's western interests, he retaliated with a machine-gun attack on ace O'Donnell gunman James "Fur" Sammons. Regrettably, the Capone gang's next attack killed gunmen James Dougherty and Red Duffy and also took the life of the their drinking buddy McSwiggin. The murder of a couple of hoods might not draw much public wrath and condemnation; their corpses would be mere footnotes in the list of perhaps sixty-four gang murders that year (of which only three were prosecuted, and all three prosecutions were unsuccessful). But a dead public official was different.

This was not a favorable circumstance under which to be a board member. Predictably, State's Attorney Robert Crowe declared, "It will be a war to the hilt against these gangsters." All Nitto and company could do was hunker down and absorb the blows as best they could. Gang business was quickly brutalized and heavily published for the public's benefit. Agents reportedly smashed about 275 of Nitto's alcohol stills (the twenty largest were in the city of Chicago) that were responsible for an estimated 1.25 million gallons of alcohol production. Law enforcement officials directed by Crowe hit the suburb saloons and gambling joints in such a tempest they never again opened with quite the audacity of the good ole days. Capone's Stickney headquarters, the Stockade, complete with slot machines, was wrecked.

Of course Cicero received special police attention. The flagship gambling houses, The Ship and the Hawthorne Smoke Shop, were knocked out. In one instance, the $80,000 bank of one den had to be dashed out to avoid confiscation; the cashier, along with Frankie Pope, brought the wad to Nitto and Guzik, who were holed up in a downtown hotel to avoid police sweeps. The harmless Guzik had grown an overabundance of whiskers to avoid detection. The physical damage to the overall organization in terms of trucks, stills, and the like was nearly a million dollars.

The board now faced a more serious crisis—the repercussion. A federal grand jury was called to investigate Prohibition violations in the wake of the Cicero raids. The gang sent out immediate warning to all saloon owners in Cicero: "There is going to be a big investigation. Don't tell anybody anything." Cicero policemen were directed to collect samples from bar owners as insurance. These were stored in Cicero City Hall for safety's sake. The warning continued: "If you open your faces, these samples go to the Prohibition Office, and your prosecution under federal statutes is certain." The feds found the samples, however, and through further inquiry, they indicted Al, Ralph, Charlie Fischetti, the O'Donnells and several others. (Two years later they were still pending an outcome.)

Through the remainder of the spring and summer, Nitto and the board relayed intelligence on the city gang proceedings to Capone, some of it simmering of a Weiss-Saltis-O'Donnell conspiracy:

The West Side Report
Since the Capone attempt to kill O'Donnell gunman Fur Sammons and the murder of two gunmen in the McSwiggin affair that spring, the West Side was mostly quiet. Papers report that part of Sammons's bond for his arrest in the McSwiggin affair was put up by the mother of Hymie Weiss. Klondike O'Donnell and Fur Sammons were arrested for attempting to purloin 1,000 gallons of whiskey from a government warehouse; they will be sidelined to some extent.

July 14: Nominal Capone operative Jules Portuguese killed, a possible victim of Weiss-O'Donnell perfidy. Myles O'Donnell is sought by police.

The South Side Report
Frank McErlane, a key Saltis gunman, still in jail on murder charges (since April).

July 20: Ralph Sheldon and Capone allies counterattack the Saltis gang, attempting to kill Vincent McErlane (brother of Frank). That spring, the Saltis crowd killed or wounded four Sheldon men.

July 23: Sheldon men kill Frank Conlon while attempting to kill McErlane again.

The North Side Report
May 21: Frank Cremaldi, ex-Genna alky cooker and Detroit booze peddler, was killed; Weiss is a suspect.

Otherwise, the North Side is uneventful, placid nearly all summer—foreboding.

Sometime in early to mid-July, a report was dispatched to Capone informing him that one of his young drivers, Tommy Cuiringione, alias Rossi, had vanished without a trace. While the gang wasn't sure this was cause for alarm, they suspected the most competent and notable of their enemies, Weiss and crew. On August 3, after Capone returned to the city, their suspicions were confirmed: Rossi's badly beaten and burned body, weighted down by bricks, hands wired together, was pulled from a cistern south of the city. His tormentors had ended the session with gunshots to the head.

Clearly, someone had tortured him, presumably in an attempt to force him to divulge secrets about Capone's comings and goings. Nobody wanted Capone more than the police except Hymie Weiss. With this information about Capone, Weiss's gang could then set up a long-anticipated ambush in retaliation for O'Banion's death nearly eighteen months earlier. Capone had every reason to believe Weiss would strike soon. Nitto's chief knew war was inevitable on the north; all he needed was a reason to declare it. Tommy Rossi was that reason, and so Capone wisely preempted the North Sider and started the war himself.

A week after Rossi's body was hauled from the water, the gang took an ambitious poke at the North Siders. Schemer Drucci kept a room at the Congress Hotel. The morning of August 10 beamed sunny and bright. Both Drucci and Weiss had business in the Standard Oil Building down the street at the corner of Michigan Avenue and Ninth Street. The pair was spotted as they leisurely strolled the short distance from the Congress to their destination among the usual daily pedestrian and auto traffic. As they crossed Ninth Street, a car homed in on them and pistols protruding from the open windows opened up. Amazingly, in light of the thirty-plus bullets flying about, only one casualty was sustained, a passerby who was wounded in the leg. It was an extremely sloppy job, and the attempt to take out the leader and co-leader of the North Side Gang was lost.

Utilizing information likely extracted from Rossi, Weiss and company finally returned a masterstroke of gunfire on September 20. That afternoon, Capone and his indefatigable bodyguard Frank Rio enjoyed a coffee at the Hawthorne Restaurant in his Twenty-second Street stronghold in Cicero. The day was bright and nice. Hawthorne Park Racetrack opened for the season that day, and the street and restaurant teemed with the usual track crowd. Capone and Rio sat at the last of the fifteen tables along the west wall of the restaurant, toward the rear. The clattering of a machine gun suddenly disturbed the day. Patrons ducked for cover, and instinctively, Rio dragged Capone to the floor.

Strangely, there was no broken glass or splintering of furniture, dishes or the like—absolutely no damage was incurred. Just as the hefty gang boss rose to investigate, Rio, suspecting a ruse, pulled him down again. Instantly, real gunfire poured into the building. From the west came seven more cars, one at the rear to ward off any pursuit while the six lined up ahead casually spewed a savage blizzard of slugs into the restaurant, the nearby Anton Hotel, and Capone's Cicero headquarters, the Hawthorne Hotel. Flying debris, particularly a multitude of glass shards, exploded through the restaurant, nearby shops, and parked autos. An occupant of one of the last cars calmly stepped to the street, knelt at the restaurant door with a Thompson machine gun, and emptied his hundred-round drum of .45-caliber slugs into the restaurant. The salute lasted no more than ten seconds, but experts later estimated the total number of rounds fired by the cavalcade to be at least a thousand. Miraculously, Capone, Rio, and most of the crowd were unscathed. Capone paid for all the damage incurred by the nearby shops.

Capone left Chicago once again, not out of fear but in search of a solution to the problem. Leaving Nitto and board members behind to care for matters, he may have huddled with Torrio in Florida. The question was what to do next? Since both sides had taken their fair shot, Torrio advised peace as usual. Capone, too, wanted peace—it was the only real solution to the business of making money.

Returning to Chicago, he commissioned Tony Lombardo, his good friend and head of the Unione, to arrange a meeting in a downtown hotel in early October. Lombardo, representing Capone's interests, met with Weiss, who was interested in peace as well. But the price of peace, according to Weiss, was the forfeiture of gunmen Mops Volpe and Frank Clementi, perhaps gunners in the recent Standard Oil Building shootout. This would be a solid show of faith. Lombardo was said to have phoned Capone about the conditions for peace. Capone would have none of it. He was much too loyal to his men for that; betrayal would only weaken gang cohesion. Weiss stormed out in disgust. Prepared for the expected tantrum, this time Capone would get him for good.

Successful organizations plan strategically, and board member Frank Nitto was believed to be part of the proceedings. He wasn't the killer type, and no one ever directly attributed a murder to his fingerprints. "What had Nitti ever done," an acquaintance said later, "except push a few punks around and shoot some guys in the back." But his job required murder as a prerequisite last resort for conducting business. Nitto didn't kill because he didn't have to—he managed, controlled, and directed others to do so as part of his business. The man who got things done in a hurry in Cicero and Little Italy was succinct, efficient—and successful.

Now that hoods had horribly botched the Weiss-Drucci hit—thirty slugs and nothing to show for it—no low-level concoctions would suffice for Capone this time. Hit men would have a devil of a time getting that close to Weiss or catching him in the open again. To ensure incontestable results, the situation demanded precision planning, something few gangsters were truly capable. One reporter observed that "lots of the gangsters are just plain alley rats in tuxedo suits," and he further criticized many as having more cement between their ears than brains. Certainly this did not apply to Nitto. "It was Nitti," a policeman later maintained, "who originated the second-floor-front type of ambush." Maybe. The technique would remain the *modus operandi* for key executions until nearly the mid-thirties, and if it was indeed invented by Nitto, it bolstered his reputation as an enforcer. Just a week after the dissolution of the peace talks, the gang employed the method to deal with Weiss in what one writer of the period would later term "gangland's most perfect execution" and "perfection in the art," unmatched even by the later St. Valentine's Day Massacre.

Weiss still used the second-floor rooms above Schofield's flower shop on North State Street as his downtown headquarters. Next door, on the north side of the shop at 740 North State, sat an immense stone rooming house. Though it sat slightly back from the shop front, it afforded an excellent view of the comings and goings at the Schofield's. Prior to the peace conference, a stranger of fair complexion had rented a second-floor room at the rear of the building, telling the landlord that if a room overlooking the street came available, he would want it. On October 5, the renter moved into a forward-facing room, but he soon left, turning it over to two dark-skinned strangers.

Superior Street intersects North State a short distance south of the shop. Around the corner, on the same side as Schofield's and across the street at 1 West Superior, a woman rented a third-floor room that conveniently had a commanding view of Superior below and also overlooked the alley at the rear of Schofield's. This room, too, was given over to strangers shortly after it was rented. Neither the woman on Superior nor the gentleman renting on State was ever identified. Those who occupied the premises after the renters left lay in wait.

On October 11, 1926, the waiting ended. Weiss and his companions curbed their cars on Superior Street at the south border of Holy Name Cathedral and across the street from Schofield's. From information gathered later, Weiss and company were returning from a day in Criminal Court. Weiss was in the lead with another fellow, while another companion tailed slightly behind and the last pair brought up the rear as they crossed State to the flower shop. The two men in the room at 740 State had waited days for this opportunity—a simple frame bed was pulled close to the window and cigarette butts littered the wood floor at their feet as they peered out from behind the nearly opaque curtains.

As Weiss came into range, a shotgun and a machine gun fitted with a hundred-round ammunition drum simultaneously opened fire from the second-floor window.

The twenty-eight-year-old Weiss fell mortally wounded to the chipped pavement. His partner was hit seven times and died instantly. The other three men, struck randomly by the spray at a greater distance, retreated for cover. The last pair frantically retraced their steps toward the cover of the cathedral's south side. Machine-gun fire tailed them, hammering the pavement behind them and spraying concrete fragments in their wake. The fusillade was so heavy that it obliterated most of the inscription on the southwest cornerstone of the grand cathedral as the wounded men rounded that corner. Somehow, they survived the assault.

The gunmen inside number 740 vaulted down the back stairs of the rooming house, scrambled to the alley, dropped their weapons, and easily lost themselves on the city streets. The auxiliary gun nest on Superior Street was not needed—Weiss was dead, and those observers evacuated the post at their leisure. The plan was a devastating, sure-fire hit.

⸺◈◈◈⸺

Through more or less neutral gangland intermediaries, peace talks once again resumed. And once again Capone man Tony Lombardo was called in from his Unione office to broker an agreement. The principals of the groups attending agreed the war had to stop; the profits of peace surely would bring them riches beyond even their own dreams of greed. After one or more tête-à-têtes, a simple accommodation to their problems was arrived at—all citywide gang interests would observe the original 1923 territorial agreement hammered out by Torrio.

Saltis could safely operate in his previous 200-odd saloon assignment among the Slavic population in the Back of the Yards. Sheldon remained north and east of the Yard and also was apparently awarded Spike O'Donnell's territory, leaving Spike out, although Capone reportedly provided for him. Out on the West Side, the O'Donnells resumed business as usual within their previous Cicero strongholds as well as their previous chunk of Chicago north of Cicero's city limits. Eddie Vogel allied himself with Capone. North Siders Drucci and Moran held sway in O'Banion's old domain north of Madison Street and east of the river. Casino kingpins Billy Skidmore and Christian "Barney" Bertsche leaned toward an alliance with prominent West Side pimp Jack Zuta and his aid Frank Foster. Zuta, in turn, tended to favor the Drucci and Moran crowd. They could operate their concessions as before, provided they caused no trouble. This left the Capone Outfit with booze rights in most of the Loop, the Near South Side, the Near West Side, and, with Ralph Sheldon in his pocket, a greater part of south Chicago all the way to the Indiana state line.

In the winter and spring of 1927, Capone's holdings increased without any further bloodshed. Both Klondike O'Donnell and gunman Fur Sammons headed to jail on booze charges, greatly weakening the O'Donnell hold on the West Side. The McSwiggin affair had "put a quietus" on their operations, and now with no firm successor in place, Capone's Outfit filled most of the openings there without major altercations. In early March, South Side beer baron Joe Saltis lost two more prized gunmen to gunfire. With his guns and muscle nearly exhausted, he increasingly traveled to the wooded north Wisconsin countryside he loved. He liked the scenery so much that he purchased a 238-acre estate on Barker Lake eight miles north of Winter, Wisconsin. An avid angler, fishing in a serene woodland setting seemed much preferable to the hostile drudgery of maintaining his beer business, and he spent so much time there that his South Side domain drifted into the hands of Capone and Sheldon's allies.

9

NITTO: THE MAILED FIST

COINCIDING WITH CAPONE'S FRESH CITY and county territorial acquisitions, Big Bill Thompson busied himself with taking another run at the mayor's office. Prospects for election were sweet. To a large extent, the public had grown weary of Dever and decency, especially his sincere effort to enforce Prohibition laws. Thompson's unmistakable promise of a wide-open town was too tempting for most of gangland to pass on. His election promised to enlarge gangland coffers whose growth had been stalled by honest law enforcement. Most gang leaders, regardless of past antipathies toward each other, now made common political cause—Capone men, North Sider Vincent Drucci, West Side pimp Jack Zuta, and others were seen shuffling in and out of Thompson's campaign headquarters. The hoods donated large funds to his campaign; for example, Capone was thought to have contributed at least $100,000, while Zuta claimed a $50,000 donation. Capone's organization also canvassed allied saloon owners to demonstrate similar beneficence to the Thompson ticket. In Cicero, a donation of $40 was demanded from saloons without slot machines, while those with slots that wanted to stay in business were obliged to pay $50.

Backed by an immense war chest that was enhanced by gangland efforts, Thompson gained the Republican nomination by a record 180,000 votes. Against Dever, Thompson won by a landslide and emerged as mayor for a third time. As expected, Thompson immediately swept out tough police chief Morgan Collins in favor of submissive ally Michael Hughes, who generally caused the gangs no great discomfort.

Of the new mayor's appointees, one illustrated the inroads Capone made into city administration. For the office of city sealer, Thompson repaid the Capone crowd for their support in the mayoral elections by designating up-and-coming First Ward Italian politician and Capone ally Daniel Serritella. Ostensibly, the office of the city sealer inspected scales of various merchants to ensure consumer protection against weight fraud, but with Thompson's see-no-evil, know-nothing administration, Serritella was free to corrupt the office for Capone's gain. By the end of Thompson's term, he and his associate Harry Hochstein, also on the periphery of gangdom, were both accused of short-changing consumers of nearly half a million dollars that went into their own pockets. For Capone, Serritella acted as his errand boy back and forth to city hall.

This same election provided Nitto's boss with a convenient dividend. Just prior to the election, Vincent Drucci and two companions were rounded up in a police sweep. On the way to the station, perhaps perturbed by his apprehension as well as the guard, the fiery Italian turned abusive. Police said he reached for an officer's gun. In the scuffle, the officer's weapon discharged four shots, killing Drucci. Thus, a dangerous Capone adversary fell without the gang having to expend a single bullet. That left George Moran as leader of the North Siders.

With the changed political landscape, Capone comfortably lounged in his desk chair at the Metropole knowing that now, at only twenty-eight years of age, he was nearly on top. Few, if any, could challenge Capone's power, and the gang could comfortably solidify and expand their city alcohol and beer business. Budding Capone ally Martin Guilfoyle built up a $2 million alcohol racket in his northwestern sliver of the city, centered on his headquarters at Kedzie and Chicago avenues. Just to the east, across the river from Aiello territory, Capone operated with onetime St. Louisian Claude Maddox and his beer runners at the Circus Café on North Avenue. Minus the North Side and certain smaller concessions, his personal gang or allies controlled much of the booze business from the city out to the western suburbs and south to Chicago Heights, as well as in a few adjoining suburbs. For the time being, peace reigned. Bugs Moran was behaving himself, and the newly emerging Aiello brothers kept to their Little Sicily confines cradled within Moran's territory.

Nitto's alcohol collection and enforcing responsibilities now extended with the empire to include supplying 20,000 speakeasies, and he managed stills and collections in Cicero, Little Italy, the Valley, Stickney, Burnham, and Melrose Park. His duties may have included dealings with Marty Guilfoyle as well allies to the southeast in Chicago Heights near the Indiana border. He worked closely with the Unione and Lombardo to ensure ample supplies and price. He also might work with out-of-town suppliers arranged for by Capone; these tentacles of supply reached the East Coast, the Gulf Coast, and the Canadian border to make sure supply met demand. In all, it was an enormous territory to maintain.

Violence was a part of business, and the gang's leaders knew that discipline and "law and order of the Capone variety must be maintained." Dangers included everything from informants, invasion of territory, questioning Capone's authority, the price of sugar for the still, to a saloonkeeper seeking an alternate source. If necessary, a crew of thugs was brought in to help the offender "see the light with a crash of a gun butt on his head."

Murder, when necessary, was also a part of business, as some found out. At dawn's early light on March 14, 1927, ex-Genna hand Alphonse Fiori was found dumped in an alley off Taylor Street, perforated with bullets. Earlier in the year, Cicero saloon-keeper John Costenaro may have tried to run his business independent of gang authority. Further, it may have leaked out that he and Santo Celebron were thought to be potential witnesses in an alcohol case the feds had been trying to build against Capone since the McSwiggin incident the previous spring. In January, Costenaro went missing, and on May 13, authorities excavated his body—a rope around his neck—from the floor of a Cicero garage. Celebron had been murdered a month earlier, so the government case evaporated. On July 27, authorities discovered the body of Frank Hitchcock, a saloonkeeper and distiller who ran afoul of someone in gangland's business as usual.

⸺◦/◦/◦⸺

By virtue of his status, Nitto's income and activities were not wholly confined to his labyrinthine alcohol obligations. According to federal agents, "Nitto got his bread by acting as a silent partner of sorts in the gang's gambling operations"—in particular, immensely profitable Cicero operations the Subway Casino and The Ship. The gambling operation was more sophisticated at this time than when Nitto had audited the books three years earlier. This sophistication was, as one hood explained, carried out in order to avoid becoming "mixed up with the revenue agents." They employed capable and trusting cashiers to work the joints, and both Ralph Capone and Jake Guzik dropped in occasionally to check on business.

The day began with the cashier holding an operating bankroll of $10,000 (at the Hawthorne Smoke Shop the daily bankroll was $12,000). After a day's action, usually the next morning about eleven o'clock, the cashier would go to the nearby Pinkert State Bank with the winnings—the amount above the original $10,000—to purchase cashier's checks made payable to the fictitious J. C. Dunbar. The checks were turned over to a Guzik representative, usually his driver Robert Barton (Capone's previous chauffeur), and Guzik then accounted for and distributed the profits. The net earnings from the Cicero house amounted to $25,000-$50,000 per month. A cashier was asked later whether there was ever a month in which a loss was sustained and replied, "I would say not."

The same prosperity could be forecast in the city now that Thompson was back in office—his wide-open mindset promised a return of unmolested gambling concessions. Combined with gangland peace, Capone and other bootleggers fat with Prohibition wealth now looked forward to additional wealth from city gambling. For Nitto's boss, the business strategy to rule a share of gambling privileges proved necessary as well as supplementary—since the political change in Chicago, their Cicero gambling houses were straining to match previous year's revenues. As one potential Chicago gambler put it, "Who's going to go out there when I can find anything I want right here in the city?"

The trouble for Capone was that, although the gang and allies enjoyed majority control of beer and alky interests in the city, the same was not true for gambling. The gang did hold considerable interests within their First Ward stronghold, taking in much of the desirable and heavily traversed Loop district, and Lawrence Mangano managed a few other places for them. However, longtime pimp Jack Zuta joined with Barney Bertsche and bond bailsman Billy Skidmore to manage a portion of the vice on the West Side that was nominally viewed as Capone territory otherwise. William "Big Bill" Johnson, with William Skidmore, had long managed a significant portion of gambling under the aegis of affable county politicians. In addition, aging chief Monte Tennes and underling Jack Lynch monopolized the essential and highly lucrative wire service necessary for disseminating horse racing information to betting parlors, and all parties paid these two for that service. In addition, everybody paid local politicians for the privilege to operate.

Still, Nitto's boss wielded considerable high influence in city hall, with Dan Serritella and other representatives now roaming the corridors freely. Capone settled Jake Guzik and Jimmy Mondi into their new city gambling headquarters on Clark Street, a short distance from the municipal nerve center. Capone's move aimed to relieve community politicians of the power to dictate gambling conditions and collect fees—the same method by which he'd obtained the Loop privileges. First Ward aldermen Coughlin and Kenna were called in to see the crime czar. Coughlin sweated out the meeting, learning that he would continue to get the vote only as long as he toed the line. Upon leaving, he told political partner Kenna and everybody else: "My God, what could I say? S'pose he had said he was goin' to take over the organization! What could we do then? We're lucky to get as good a break as we did." Jimmy Mondi went forth brandishing the same heavy stick. He dictated gang policy to gambling operators south of Madison Street: "We'll get up to forty percent of what you guys take in. For that we'll keep the cops off you. You take it or else." They took it, for the time being.

<hr />

Nitto, meanwhile, was not simply a party to but, with Johnny Patton, seemed to be leading the march toward a new gambling sphere that would prove to be of long-term importance to the gang. During the twenties, dog racing caught the fancy of the freewheeling public, first in California and whipping cross-country to the east coast. The key component to nearly every dog track was the mechanical rabbit that cruised along the inside rail and drew the hounds to give chase. The device was the invention of Owen P. Smith, who lacked the monetary resources and the brain trust to organize races on his own. To that end, Smith took on Martin Hyland, a self-starting commission man, sporting event bankroller, and "huckster" promoter. They successfully introduced the rabbit to Hialeah Kennel Club in Miami, Florida, while back home in the St. Louis area, they opened the Madison County Kennel Club across the Mississippi in Collinsville, Illinois. The track was described as "one of the largest money-making enterprises in the history of greyhound racing in this country," and Hyland served as track president.

Early in his term, Hyland introduced a young, ruggedly handsome, tough-minded St. Louis lawyer, Edward J. O'Hare, into the fold to overlook the track's growing legal details. The son of "Paddy" O'Hare and owner of a well-known restaurant in downtown St. Louis, O'Hare was a mix of refined culture and hearty athleticism. He almost never swore or used coarse slang, and those around him professed to seldom ever see him drink liquor. He always dressed very well. Robust in build, O'Hare went horseback riding and golfed regularly, and he loved to take turns in the boxing ring, sparring a few rounds to maintain his edge. He attended St. Louis University where he studied law and was accepted into the bar shortly after graduation. As a lawyer who many believed possessed a brilliant legal mind, great things were predicted for him. After a brief stop in politics, he resumed his law career. Successful as his practice was, many of his clients were thought to be bootleggers and even members of St. Louis's preeminent gang, Egan's Rats. While maintaining his practice in downtown St. Louis, O'Hare entered into a bootleg scheme himself. It was then, at Hyland's insistence, the lawyer hooked up with the dog track business.

Seizing on the monopoly potential for Smith's invention, the tough, business-minded O'Hare immediately incorporated a company to control distribution and use of the mechanical rabbit. The aggressive lawyer was then thought to have sold the rabbit's use on a state-by-state basis to individuals who, in turn, dictated who could operate tracks. Operators then paid royalties, usually a percentage of the take, to the corporation. The corporation, meanwhile, maintained rights to build tracks wherever they pleased. The quarter- to half-mile oval tracks could be graded and constructed in short time and at low expense and soon sprouted up all around Missouri, Illinois, Ohio, Florida and elsewhere—most using Smith's invention to egg the animals on.

The trio strengthened their stranglehold on the trade by forming the International Greyhound Racing Association, which they corralled many racing dog owners to join. The association could manipulate the supply of hounds to tracks, and any rogue operators who utilized a device infringing on Owen's rabbit patent faced not only legal action but also a potential shortage of racing dogs. The corporation thrived, prospering even when, in 1927, Owen P. Smith died. O'Hare took charge of matters for the widow, who became "commissioner" of the International Greyhound Racing Association and continued to collect moneys from her late husband's patent.

O'Hare and company still faced major obstacles, though. Dog racing was illegal in most states, including Illinois, as was the real windfall driving the animal racing industry, pari-mutuel betting. The basis of pari-mutuel betting lay in the fact that betting winners share a percentage of the overall betting stake with track management, a system viewed with some suspicion by many at the time—so much so that pari-mutuel betting was not allowed in the fledgling and legal horse racing industry. Several thoroughbred tracks dotted the states north and south, operating on a very limited race and betting schedule, but those in the animal racing industry knew pari-mutuel was coming soon. Once pari-mutuel betting was legalized in June 1927, O'Hare and his partners expanded the number of racing dates to a hundred or more for the eager crowds who nightly packed his Madison track.

Unfortunately for O'Hare and company, just as pari-mutuel legislation promised riches, the attitudes of Southern Illinois business leaders toward the Madison County Kennel Club changed. Since dog racing was still illegal, there were no governing regulations or overseers, so, unlike thoroughbred racing (the Fairmont Park track was nearby) which was governed by strict state regulations on the number of racing dates, O'Hare's kennel club could run an unlimited number of race dates. Local merchants soon complained of shriveling commerce as result of people gambling away their income at the nightly races. Additionally, dog races in general were viewed with suspicion; "doctored" dogs, who were either overfed or run through exhausting workouts in secret prior to race time, ensured a handsome fleecing of the gullible public. When efforts to reach an accommodation with the Madison track failed, it was raided and closed. This was, however, only a temporary setback for O'Hare and company. While he continued the fight to reopen, he had set up shop elsewhere in Illinois—in Chicago, to be precise.

According to his original legal contact, O'Hare favored a West Side site close to an elevated commuter track for his new venture. The transportation line, he reasoned, provided easy access for the droves of race fans he anticipated. However, the site lay within Capone territory, and O'Hare found the option blocked. Taking matters into his own hands, the savvy St. Louis lawyer ironed this wrinkle out—apparently bypassing the Capone interests by contacting a lawyer, who contacted a politician, who contacted a judge—and paved the way for Cook County dog racing. Instead of opening on the site he originally preferred, he opened first in Thornton, an outlying town south of Chicago, near Chicago Heights and the Indiana border. Power broker Homer Ellis of Chicago Heights owned this diminutive speck on the map, which was near Burnham, the domain of Nitto business ally Johnny Patton.

In short order, O'Hare got a West Side dog track, the Lawndale Kennel Club, a quarter-mile track in southwest Chicago near Cicero's border. Once again, this move did not involve Capone interests. Instead, West Side gambling power William "Big Bill" Johnson and partners put up an initial $150,000 investment to create the club in 1926. Johnson possessed plenty of political pull, enough to allow him to open and operate throughout the following year.

O'Hare then found out just why he had been turned away from the West Side earlier: when Capone's Outfit saw the immense profits generated from the dog racing hysteria in Thornton, they wanted in. Without O'Hare's approval, they opened the Hawthorne Kennel Club just up the road from the Lawndale Kennel Club. No matter how frenzied the crowds might be over the sport, two tracks so close together over-saturated the market. In addition, the gang, in flexing its muscle, apparently disregarded the legal entanglements surrounding the use of the rabbit.

Not to be defrauded or intimidated, the gutsy O 'Hare notified the gang of his position: his corporation owned the rabbit and could force legal action and could reduce the supply of hounds to the hood track. The lawyer himself put the matter very straightforwardly: "If I can't operate in Chicago, then nobody can." Capone the shrewd businessman saw no point in starting a conflict he could easily win through muscle but would ultimately be a lose-lose situation. Instead, if he made a deal with the trackman, who had an association with the Egan's Rats gang in St. Louis, then Capone could strengthen his St. Louis booze network as well as gain a track. The two western tracks merged, and Johnson and his partners in the Lawndale club were allowed to recoup their original investment through monthly payments from Hawthorne's 1928 season. After that, Johnson and company were told they were out.

Nitto handled the transaction. First, he hired a local accountant to dispense new track stock. Then, Nitto took a total of $33,500 in cashier's checks made out to the non-existent Charles Grosscourth to a local bank in order to purchase more checks. Of the converted checks, $28,500 went toward stock purchase in the new Laramie Kennel Club (named for nearby Laramie Avenue, it would later be called the Hawthorne Kennel Club again). In name, O'Hare owned much of this new venture, but authorities also suspected Capone had a piece of it, with Johnny Patton managing the operation up front, Nitto keeping an eye on finances, and tough gunman Robert McCullough upholding the peace. Chauffeur Robert Barton daily escorted the deposits in the name of the Laramie Kennel Club to a large Cicero bank where, that year, Frank Nitto cashed in $31,000 in Laramie Club cashier's checks.

Johnson and his partners weren't the only ones to feel the monopolizing pinch from the hoods. There still were as many as six or seven dog tracks (many apparently unlicensed by O'Hare) in the greater Chicago area. Gradually, gangster guns forced competitors out of business, leaving only three: Capone's Hawthorne Kennel Club, the Thornton track, and a constant nuisance for Nitto's crowd, the unlicensed Fairview Kennel Club on Lawrence Avenue and Manheim Road under the direction of Bugs Moran.

⸺◦◊◦⸺

In 1927, the organization's take ballooned magnificently. Capone's receipts tallied as much as $105 million from all sources. Perhaps $50 million came from beer. Gambling produced an estimated $25 million with income from the roadhouses and whores generating an estimated $10 million. An equal amount came from Frank Nitto's alcohol department, and even the relatively fledgling gang endeavor of racketeering added another $10 million. "A racket," noted one late-1920s study, "is any scheme by which human parasites graft themselves upon and live by the industry of others." The gang already possessed the tools necessary for racketeering—muscle for intimidation, and for good measure, gunfire or the occasional bomb.

Two methods of racketeering had long existed in Chicago. One method was the "trade association." Originally conceived as a group of like businesses banded together for commercial profitability, in predatory hands such organizations suffered dearly. Enough goons and guns could take over an existing coalition, or the charter for an innocent-sounding association could be drawn up and violence used to organize shops. The association charged a membership fee, and if the amount was not forthcoming, the headstrong shop owner faced strikes or more devastating "or else" options. For example, Jewish butchers who failed to join the Kosher Meat Peddlers Association, run by the rapacious Maxie Eisen, were slugged or found their stocks splattered with poison or their storefront windows broken. Another alliance, the Master Cleaners and Dyers Association, charged fees and dictated laundry prices. Those who resisted found racks of customers' clothes ruined by acid or stink bombs.

Within Chicago, at least fifty similar rackets were flourishing by 1927. A year later the number doubled. To enforce their rule, association hoods exploded at least 157 bombs in businesses during a fifteen-month span from 1927 to 1928. In a short time, few products or services in Chicago were left unaffected; there were associations for rubbish haulers, garage owners, restaurant workers, florists, druggists, beauticians, bootblacks, milk dealers, and workers in the meat, poultry, and fish industries, to name a a few. The president of the Chicago Association of Commerce was forced to admit, "There is scarcely a commodity exposed for sale today that does not cost more because of the racket."

Labor unions offered another attractive means to wealth. Members were often victims of corrupted leadership imposing "special assessments" for some purpose other than unionism. In some cases, racketeers might randomly call on members to donate as much as $25-$100 for a phony benefit drive, often offering the advice, "The more you give, the better you'll feel." Mostly, however, unions offered gangs dual income from both skimming union treasuries and providing leverage through threats of strikes against business owners to obtain extra graft. The latter was particularly effective when used against the city government. For example, Mike Carrozzo was long dictator over the unions of the street workers, all those men who swept, paved, patched, or shoveled snow from the city's thoroughfares. If the city did not bow to his demands, the streets fell into disrepair.

Capone realized the benefits of racketeering with the installation of the Thompson administration when he settled former Sheldon tough guy Dan Stanton in city hall as head of the City Hall Clerks Union. Soon, Capone organized the employees of the board of education and the park districts and doubled the monthly dues and initiation fees. So entrenched was the boss, he was credited with the vision to install a henchman as head of the plumbers union in anticipation of the enormous pipe work required for the planned World's Fair. Like Carrozzo, he could now dictate to the city, "suggesting" new ordinances or selecting which contractors would be awarded work in an area.

Further, Capone was thought to have reached an agreement with West Side gunman George "Red" Barker and his sidekicks—a balding 210-pound, six-foot-tall gunman named William "Three-Fingered Jack" White and fearless, Welsh-blood hoodlum Murray Humphreys—for a 25 percent slice of their activities. When not serving one of their frequent stints in jail, Barker and White moved in on the teamsters, particularly the valuable Coal Wagon Drivers Union. When an arresting police officer asked White his position with the teamsters, the hoodlum replied "superintendent of transportation." The officer then wisecracked, "What kind of transportation, taking people for rides?" Humphreys assisted and later moved in on the laundry associations, something he held onto for at least the next two decades. His advice about entering the racketeering game was simple: "If you want tribute from the mugs driving the wagons, a pair of brass knuckles and a blackjack will get it." By 1929, the

Chicago Crime Commission estimated the cost of racketeering in the city at $136 million a year, a bright means of generating future gang "unearned income" that was not lost on Frank Nitto.

⟞◦⁄◦⁄◦⟝

The gang peace achieved after Weiss's murder dissolved, thanks primarily to Joe Aiello, who had severed all ties with Tony Lombardo when his old friend and partner, and not he, was named head of the Unione. Aiello and his numerous brothers and cousins directed the alky business in Little Sicily, and the family also owned a large bakery, so none of the Aiellos could complain of penury. Ego, however, was another matter. Lombardo's control of the Unione via Capone rubbed Aiello raw, and Aiello expected to take a backseat to no one, especially Lombardo. Nineteen twenty-seven promised to be "a banner year" for attempts on Capone and intrigue against his Unione alky business. When gang war broke out that year, with control of the Unione hanging in the balance, the responsibility for the survival of both Capone and his alky empire predictably fell on the shoulders of chief administrator Frank Nitto. Charged with enforcing and maintaining Capone's decrees, Nitto, "the mailed fist which crushes the opposition," as a *Daily News* reporter later described him, again displayed his true value to Big Al and the organization.

In the spring of 1927, Aiello commissioned assassination attempts on Capone. However, the vast network of those loyal to Big Al picked up the chatter, and an alerted Nitto sent out the Capone gunners, led by Jack McGurn. When Scalise and Anselmi were finally cleared of the 1925 cop murders in early June, they also became available as gang gunmen. The bodies began to pile up, and McGurn was hauled in to police headquarters on at least four occasions.

On May 25, New Yorker Antonio Torchio was found shot at the corner of Des Plaines and DeKoven, just east of Little Italy. He was identified as a "professional killer," and his intended target, police thought, was Capone. Next, Aiello attempted to kill Capone by more surreptitious means, offering the chef of a restaurant frequented by Capone $35,000 to poison Capone and Lombardo, a double strike. Luckily for the pair, the chef wavered and spilled the plot to the intended victims. Capone gunners responded quickly by demolishing the Aiello store on West Division Street with machine-gun fire. During June and July, whether through intrigue with Nitto's alky business or complicity with Aiello's campaign to eliminate Capone, six men recognized as old Genna hands were exterminated; the last, Dominick Cinderello, was slain, trussed up in a bag, and dumped in a canal. This hit was specifically chalked up to McGurn, who was arrested but later released.

Aiello then turned for aid in his attempt to snuff Capone to two small-time alky cookers, Anthony Russo and Vincent Spicuzza, who were originally from St. Louis but now lived in his Little Sicily domain. They were supposedly offered $25,000 each for the murders of Capone and Lombardo, but it was their lifeless forms that were found peppered with lead and discarded in Melrose Park on August 11. In September, bootlegger Sam Valenti may have tried to kill Capone; he was found on a Stickney farm with an ax buried in his head. Aiello then was thought to have upped

135

the bounty to $50,000 per man if Capone's South Side ally Ralph Sheldon performed the lethal services. Nitto's intelligence network vacuumed up that piece of data, and soon enough they shot Sheldon in front of a West Side hotel. Sheldon survived; Aiello did not.

To promote his personal vendetta, Aiello had made common cause with Capone's North Side enemies under the leadership of Bugs Moran. Still reorganizing after the deaths of Weiss and Drucci, they would at least be able to offer Aiello moral support. Also hitching to the alliance were those chaffing from the restrictions agreed to under the 1926 peace treaty and the more recent restructuring of gambling rights, the terms of which were dictated by Capone. In this category were gambling magnates Billy Skidmore and Barney Bertsche. They had long operated pretty much anywhere they wished under political protection for a flat fee of 25 percent, but Capone agents under Jimmy Mondi had visited the joints they ran south of Madison Street and required Skidmore to pay double for the same service. West Side vicemonger Jack Zuta also joined the Aiello alliance for the same reason. With Aiello's greed and ego fueling them, they thought it might be possible to throw off Capone's yoke and all gain in the process more—Aiello would cut in on the alky business, Moran the beer business, and Skidmore and company the gambling business.

By mid-November, the anti-Capone interests were poised to strike. Aiello gunners placed a machine gun ambush across the street from Tony Lombardo's home at 4442 West Washington Boulevard. Another gun nest was ensconced in the Atlantic Hotel on South Clark Street opposite and overlooking a frequent Capone stop—the political nerve center of the First Ward, Mike Kenna's saloon. But before either site could be exploited, an anonymous tip led police to raid an apartment in Joe Aiello's territory. Clues found there scene prompted a second police raid on a North Side hotel, where they seized a cache of weapons and ammunition along with Milwaukee gunman Angelo La Mantio and four Aiello kinsmen. In La Mantio's pockets, police found rent receipts for the room on West Washington and a key to Room 302 in the Atlantic Hotel, where weapons were trained on the entrance to Kenna's saloon. Soon, police rounded up Joe Aiello and placed him in a cell at the detective bureau with his friends.

It was time for the Capone organization to cut off the head of the Aiello alliance. In an uncharacteristic move, they sent six carloads of gunmen to the detective bureau at 625 South Clark Street, ostensibly to remove Aiello and his conspirators and save law enforcement the trouble. Perhaps twenty men, Jack McGurn among them, surrounded the building, setting up a perimeter on surrounding street corners and guarding all approaches. Then three tough gunmen—Capone bodyguard Louis Campagna, ex-convict Frank Perry, and Sam Marcus—made for the entrance, but before they could enter, anxious police quickly pulled together a posse to meet the intruders. The trio was arrested and disarmed, and their compatriots scattered back into their cars and raced away.

It was in an adjoining cell at the bureau that a policeman who understood Italian listened in as a terrified and now de-fanged Aiello recognized Campagna and company as Capone agents. Aiello pleaded for mercy, saying he would gather his family and possessions and leave Chicago for good. Campagna sneered, "You have broken faith with us twice. Now that you have started this, we are going to finish it." When finally released, Aiello obtained a police escort.

When Aiello's case was called in court on November 22, his attorney stepped forward with a doctor's certificate claiming his client was suffering from a nervous breakdown and was unable to appear. Police reconnaissance of the Aiello bakery and spaghetti factory on West Division revealed drawn blinds and inactivity—Aiello had stolen away to New Jersey with part of the clan, fatefully leaving his brother Dominick in Chicago to attend to family matters. Away from Chicago, a determined Joe Aiello remained upbeat about toppling Capone and Lombardo.

Capone, too, was optimistic, and he could well afford to be with an army anchored by the likes of manager Frank Nitto and gunmen McGurn, Scalise, Anselmi, Campagna, Frank Rio, Frank Diamond, and the seldom-mentioned Jack Heinan, an ex-boxer and the only man of the corps reputed to be tougher than McGurn. Capone gathered the faithful at Lawrence Mangano's Minerva Athletic Club on South Halsted and announced: "I'm the boss. I'm going to continue to run things. They've been putting the roscoe (revolver) on me now for a good many years and I'm still healthy and happy. Don't let anybody kid you into thinking I can be run out of town. I haven't run yet and I'm not going to. When we get through with this mob there won't be any opposition and I'll still be doing business."

With Aiello apparently out of the picture and the alcohol business intact, gang business turned to dealing with Aiello's allies and enforcing Capone's gambling rights. Capone and a phalanx of hardcore troops visited the Skidmore-Bertsche-Zuta headquarters on North Dearborn Street to make sure they understood the danger of their association with Aiello. Skidmore, the only member of the group present, stalled, arguing the Aiellos were an independent entity beyond his control. Nitto's boss apparently left unsatisfied.

Skidmore's resistance disturbed Capone on yet another front. According to the 1926 underworld treaty, everything below Madison Street was recognized as Capone's territory for gambling, meaning that operators there should pay him for the privilege of conducting their business. And payments from this area were long overdue. For example, it was common knowledge that the Skidmore combine operated in Capone territory at 823 West Adams, and observers had counted as many as fifty to seventy patrons an hour coming and going from the place recently. But Skidmore and a number of gaming veterans had, instead, paid pols for the privilege, feeling that, treaty notwithstanding, this was enough.

Skidmore and Bertsche may have banked on their political pull, rightly knowing that, regardless of underworld agreements, the "upper world" still had the real power. However, what they underestimated was the true extent of Capone's political capital in this upper world. His men freely roamed city hall, confronting politicians on important matters; a few city aldermen were so thoroughly cowed they refused to discuss matters with the press. "Don't quote me," said one fearful public servant, "I'd get a pineapple or a bullet." Of Capone's power at the time was so great that one pundit later declared him to be "Mayor of Crook County."

For the past month or so, Nitto and company had enforced Capone's decree by bombing the minor gambling players of their realm into submission. A move against Skidmore and his bunch might be risky, but Capone banked on his influence to break further resistance and wanted to end their complicity with Aiello and any danger of further defiance. Orders went out to his crews that anyone who wasn't toeing the line should receive a forceful visit. The next day, James "King of the Bombers" Belcastro's pineapple (street slang for bomb) squad was called into action, and a blast partially destroyed a Skidmore-Bertsche gambling house on West Adams as a warning.

The political landscape, however, was about to change again. Capone and company might push their way around individual lower-pole politicians, but political adversity was soon to come from the top.

—⟨ɷ/ɷ⟩—

When Republican Calvin Coolidge announced he would not seek another term as president of the United States, Thompson, backed by his Illinois allies, saw a chance for the high office. At the outset of the mayor's new term, freshly appointed Chief of Police Michael Hughes announced he would drive all the crooks out of Chicago in ninety days. He did not, and gangsters, in fact, appeared to be having their way in Thompson's town more than ever before, creating a liability for the aspiring politician.

With the brazen attempt by gangsters to lay siege to the detective bureau, an Aiello-Capone war, and a war for gambling privileges brewing, Hughes ordered Chief of Detectives William O'Conner to send squads to the West Side to haul in known gangsters. On one such raid, Sergeant Thomas Lynch and his command of Squad 21-A Detectives Harry Lang, George Maher, Charles Wetter, and F. T. Barnes were nearing Lombardo's home on West Washington when they noticed a green sedan nearby and two dark strangers within. As the police approached, the sedan took off. Barnes mounted the passenger-side running board, while Lynch, in the front passenger seat, directed driver Lang to give chase. Speeds raced to nearly seventy miles per hour, with the detective car nearly tipping as it made turns, while gunshots were exchanged between the two vehicles. As the cars rounded the corner at Western and Lake streets, Barnes took aim at the suspects, but the detectives' car lurched unexpectedly, causing Barnes's gun to accidentally discharge and send a bullet into Lynch's head. The suspects got away, and twenty-four hours later Lynch died of his wounds.

Although the hoodlums did not inflict the casualty, their actions had prompted the patrol, and the furious police deemed that they would suffer. That night, Wednesday, November 23, police rounded up fifty gangsters and raided the Metropole Hotel looking for Capone's men. After searching the place thoroughly, they arrested bomber James Belcastro and an associate on their way out. Capone ally James Genaro was taken at his Whip Café. On the Near West Side, they raided the Terminus Café and snagged a scruffy Peter Genna. Though long removed from power, he was made the headline sensation. To the north, police took up to twenty men associated with gambling there. Chief O'Conner proudly announced, "We have the gang situation in hand now, and the first move toward further violence is going to be regretted by somebody."

Lost to the press the next day in the litany of action was the capture of ranking Capone board member Frank Nitto. The specifics of the arrest are lost except for a single *Daily News* snapshot of the original police lineup. Nitto appeared before the camera emotionless and well-groomed, with his hair slicked back and parted just left of center. He was dressed in a clean, neatly pressed white shirt, diagonally patterned tie, dark vest and coat of heavy material, the coat collar of black velour. On what was probably for him just another business day, he was apprehended with associate Joseph Coscioni. Still relatively unknown, neither the press nor the police grasped the import of Nitto's seizure, and both Nitto and Coscioni were released without announcement.

Determined to make Chicago unwelcome to thugs, two nights after Nitto's arrest, Chief O'Conner bagged a flock of high-quality Chicago hoodlums. Knowing many hoods to be boxing enthusiasts, he raided the Coliseum during the evening's main event, the Walker-Berienbach fight. The crowd in attendance viewed a double thrill: in addition to the fight, the police swooped down ringside and hauled away Capone agent Jake Guzik, Saltis gunner Frank McErlane, South Side hulk Danny Stanton, and Melrose Park alky agent Joseph Montana. Around forty others were escorted to patrol wagons, some snatched while still standing in line with their tickets. Joe Aiello's brother Nunzio was nabbed earlier in the day.

Due to the prominence of the men taken, there was a political stir to gain their freedom. The men thought they held sway with city hall, but politicos were referred to Chief O'Conner for action. Denying requests for freedom, O'Conner savored the coup by announcing, "Under lock and key they are and under lock and key they stay." O'Conner's men repeated their prize fight performance a couple of nights later, this time snagging only one big name, West Side Frankie Pope, from among a crowd of 3,000. Most all of those taken in the raids, however, gained freedom after only a day in holding.

Chief of Police Michael Hughes expanded the campaign further, announcing the closing of gambling resorts in the city. Not since Dever's crackdown three years earlier had gamblers experienced such a blackout. While a few operations managed to keep their doors open, the estimated total loss to gangland coffers was $300,000 a day. Capone's group was hardest hit, although the police efforts didn't completely scuttle the gang's finances; their suburban operations ran wide-open, picking up the slack. Extra roulette wheels and gaming tables were hauled into their Cicero resort, the Subway, and customers trekked in from the city by the busload—so much so that many latecomers were turned away.

Back in the city, Capone continued what amounted to a one-sided war of gambling enforcement, which, audaciously, now included community officials. He dictated terms to First Ward Alderman Coughlin and Committeeman Kenna, which they accepted. Others, however, did not see the light. Nitto may have directed the detonation of a large black powder bomb that wrecked the home of Peter Spingola and family a few blocks north of Cicero. In-laws of the Genna clan, the Spingolas were prominent figures in Italian politics and part of Thompson's successful campaign. Police figured the bombing could be traced to their unwillingness to go along with Capone's desires. Not persuaded by the first bomb, a second bomb the next day targeted Spingola at the home of his brother-in-law and blew off the house's front porch. Three other bombs exploded, all at noncompliant gaming establishments, making five explosions in five days.

Overall, enforcement via the bombs only hurt business further. Attendance dwindled. Who would risk patronizing any joint? Still, there was cause for hope, as the manager of one noted of the crackdown: "It won't be for long. There's too much money in the gambling racket. They might have meant well . . . but I'll bet a hat they'll give the boys an opportunity to make some Christmas money for themselves before Santa Claus gets here."

In an attempt to settle the gambling matter, Capone gathered his key aides, certain politicos, and police officials to a location just outside Cook County's border. Capone's group wanted their 25-40 percent share, as did the politicians. Why the police crackdown? Officials explained the raids came in response to complaints from local merchants. More money, they said, was being spent on dice, cards, and races than on ordinary needs and holiday shopping. Talk filtering out of the meetings hinted at progress: for example, Capone's agent Jimmy Mondi appeared to be out as a collector, but there was still no rock-solid agreement. Capone left, gathering an armed troupe and heading to the north woods for eight days of hunting. Chief O'Conner announced, "Brown and his men had better stay away from Chicago if they don't like our cells." Capone's absence left Frank Nitto as perhaps the most capable member in town to direct activities.

The day Capone departed, John Remus's restaurant on the North Side was blown up. Remus, a former Illinois state representative and brother of notorious lawyer and bootlegger George Remus, said three Italians had visited him earlier and warned him to buy their alcohol. He had refused. That same day, two gambling resorts of the Skidmore-Bertsche-Zuta regime were bombed, including the previously hit West Adams location. The next day, bombs nine and ten exploded in gambling joints.

Carmen Ferraro, wealthy and respected owner of Ferraro Equipment Company, which for years manufactured wire auto parts, was murdered and dumped in Bensenville in Du Page County. Ferraro's other more covert business life involved alcohol distribution from a 1,000-gallon still he operated with several others. The feds broke this racket up earlier in May, arresting Ferraro and his crew. As the federal court case developed, two of Ferraro's associates were murdered, then Ferraro himself. Whether these murders were committed to eliminate potential loose tongues or rogues operating in defiance of Capone, no one knows.

10

GANG STALWART: MR. NITTI

T HANKS IN PART TO A forceful Frank Nitto, Capone's organization was strong enough to repulse almost any attempt by external gang forces to weaken it. Weiss was dead, Aiello was on the run, and George Moran was huddled in the north. Nitto's boss could afford more downtime than a simple hunting trek. Capone built a combination fieldstone-frame lodge overlooking Cranberry Lake near the tranquil town of Courderay, Wisconsin, that doubled as a relaxing summer getaway and private meeting place for the gang. In 1927, Capone began exploring Florida as a winter haven, leasing a Miami Beach home that fall for six months under the alias Mr. Brown. The sunshine so agreed with him that he decided to buy there, settling on an estate located on Palm Island, a man-made sliver of land located between the mainland and the beach.

For the first three months of 1928, Capone spent many days away from Chicago, closing his real estate deal and enjoying the warm rays. He could afford to. Frank Nitto had emerged as Capone's key operations manager, directing activities from the Metropole Hotel and had even stepped into Jake Guzik's shoes for a spell that winter when the latter fell ill. By that summer, the press also finally recognized him as a key player in the organization.

⸻

Crucially for Nitto and his associates, underworld success overlapped with upper world efforts to exploit a bright municipal and commercial idea. Among the civic agendas inherited by the new Thompson regime was a proposal for a Chicago World's Fair to celebrate 100 years of the city's existence in 1937. Fair committees began enthusiastically exploring the possibility with Dever's blessing in 1925. Thompson, however, was not so moved, though eventually the idea grew upon on him, and he lent verbal support for the project. But backing by word of mouth alone was far from enough. Business leaders recognized crime and the city's growing gangster stigma to be a liability and knew that more lawful order was needed to successfully change Chicago's image worldwide for such an extravaganza. Mayor Dever at least tried to enforce the law (and eventually denied the problem as serious). Now it fell upon Thompson to work on the issue.

Yet alliances between vice and politicians combined with Thompson's open town policy to foster quite the opposite situation. Unofficial tallies of gang murders for the two years prior to 1928 numbered about 130, all of which remained to be solved. In 1927 alone, bombings numbered roughly 108. Window smashings plagued business owners who did not bend to racketeer demands to join "protective associations." Spring 1928 found Chicago's unruliness worse than ever before. When would it end? "The rulers of the city," according to Virgil Peterson, later operating director of the Chicago Crime Commission, "were actually the gangsters who had become so powerful they had no hesitancy in resorting to violence against leading officials."

Without playing any favorites, hoodlums stepped up attacks against politicians. For example, when opposition arose from within Thompson's own party in the person of Senator Charles Deneen, who controlled federal patronage in Illinois and threatened to spoil the momentum from Big Bill's victory in the spring mayoral primary, Thompson could count on money and troops from Nitto's boss. In January, however, months before the primary, bombs exploded at the homes of two Thompson cabinet members as a result of the gambling fracas.

Two days later, Capone's troops proved their political worth when they murdered Diamond Joe Esposito's brother-in-law. Diamond Joe was a known Deneen supporter and committeeman. Running against him, apparently with mob support, was Joseph P. Savage. In early March, it was thought Lawrence Mangano paid Esposito a visit, warning him to step aside and save Savage the expense of a tough campaign. Esposito affirmed his loyalty to longtime friend Deneen, declaring, "I can't cross them." Their final warning to Esposito was "get out of politics in the Twenty-fifth Ward or ———." Esposito, pillar of the Italian West Side community, remained firm.

On March 21 at approximately 9:30 p.m., fifty-six-year-old Diamond Joe Esposito was walking home from the National Republican Club in his ward, only a few blocks from his home at 800 South Oakley. A pair of bodyguards, brothers Ralph and Joe Varchetti, accompanied him. They were less than a block from his home, strolling under the light of a street lamp, when Esposito was blasted by gunfire. The portly Italian fell dead, punctured fifty-eight times. Amazingly, his bodyguards emerged unscathed—and suspect, though eventually they were released.

Five nights later, bombs shook the homes of Senator Deneen and Judge Swanson, who narrowly escaped the intended blast. Campaign mudslinging on both sides came to include the name of Nitto's boss as being responsible for the bombings. There were so many bombings that pundits dubbed the election the "Pineapple Primary." One cynic further ragged:

> *The rockets' red glare the bombs bursting in air*
> *Gave proof to the world that Chicago's still there*

Election day, April 10, proved no less vicious in the Capone-dominated Twentieth, Twenty-seventh, and Twenty-eighth wards. Roving carloads of gunmen shot two men, a gang stole Deneen ballots from a poll worker, and a corrupt policemen chased away voters in the Twentieth. Kidnappings were recounted in the Twentieth as well as the Second wards. Two lawyers for the Chicago Bar Association watching polls in the Twentieth were kidnapped and slugged. Reports of ballot box stuffing prevailed. The violence climaxed in the ward shortly near the end of the day when a carload of goons chased down and murdered Octavus Granady, a black candidate opposing Thompson team player Morris Eller for committeeman.

This was not the direction in which the civic planners had hoped to steer the city for the Fair. It also turned out to be too much for the electorate who, only a year ago, elected Thompson and his Wet plank. Now public indignation washed away Thompson's slate with a tidal wave of disgust, leaving the mayor's local influence greatly diminished of local influence. To a degree, the gang was also diminished in the public's eye. Though the gang success to which Nitto contributed remained at full zenith, the Fair and Chicago's reputation supplied a core motive for compelling external pressure to extinguish them.

The war with Aiello was renewed where the primary violence left off. Determined to rid themselves of Tony Lombardo, Aiello's group tried to blow him and his place of business up in April. In retaliation, the bodies of Aiello men started piling up in the morgue soon thereafter: May 14 found, Giuseppe Cavarretta, age forty-five, gunned down in an alley at 816 Milton; while June 19 saw John Oliveri, forty-five, and Joseph Salomone, thirty, shotgunned in their car at 503 West Oak Street.

Perhaps Aiello's courage perked up when he enticed the backing of Capone's old friend back in Brooklyn, Frankie Yale. The Brooklynite evolved into a mob boss and had assisted Capone in networking booze from the East. Of late, some of those consignments had begun disappearing along the way, a form of double-cross from the earliest Prohibition days that had the stench of Aiello about it. When Capone asked an old Brooklyn friend to check the source of the hijackings, the friend was killed, but not before he confirmed Capone's suspicions.

On July 1, Yale was called from his saloon on a supposed emergency. As he drove toward home, a Nash touring car full of men trailed him. When they caught up to him, a barrage of shotgun, pistol, and machine-gun fire raked Yale's vehicle, causing it to thump to a rest against a homeowner's front stoop. The Nash pulled alongside, and one of the occupants emerged and shot an already mortally perforated Yale in the head for good measure. Suspicions leaned toward McGurn, Scalise and Anselmi as the killers.

Capone's faction wasn't finished. Because Joe Aiello evidently could not be located, on July 19, fifty-six-year-old Dominick Aiello was cut down in front of the family store at 928 Milton. A few days later, Aiello lieutenant Sam Canale was shot-gunned to death in his auto.

⚬ⱷⱷ⚬

Notoriety forced a change of headquarter locations. Police (and enemies) had long recognized the Metropole as Capone's nerve center, so in mid-summer, Nitto's boss moved operations up the street to the Lexington Hotel at 2200 South Michigan Avenue. There, he reserved part of the third floor and all of the fourth floor for his entourage of gunmen and assistants. Management allowed one room adjoining Capone's suite to be torn out to accommodate a private kitchen. One reporter allowed in later marveled at the remodeling, describing its quality as the equivalent of that found in "the better housekeeping magazines."

It was the move to the Lexington that sparked the first genuine recognition of Frank Nitto among the press—and the incorrect spelling of his last name that remained forever fastened upon him. An observer reported that, among those attending meetings, was stalwart "Frank Nitti," who had "lately risen to an important place in the Capone scheme of things." None of his surviving contemporaries could say for sure whether the exchange of the *o* for an *i* was a simple press gaffe or a Nitto contrivance designed to throw authorities off track. The press later quoted many of his fellow hoods as referring to him as Nitti as well, but on almost all legal documents, he used his actual name, not an alias. The rare instances of disguise occurred much later and involved complete changes of name—such as Ralph Nitto, Frank Raddo, or Frank Sasso—and not simple letter alterations. In any event, the public always identified him as Nitti.

Though Nitto surely conducted key business at the Lexington, for some time he ran street-level operations from 901 South Halsted. Sometimes referred to as Nitto's "speakeasy," it was really the Naples Restaurant. Nitto owned at least half of it, though on the record, the place was owned by Louis Coscioni, father of Joseph, one of Nitto's aides. Nitto's influence there, however, weighed heavily. On one occasion, a young porter robbed the safe of a small amount of cash and valuables. A short time later, he returned with a change of heart and made full restitution—no doubt after he found out just with whom he was dealing. According to law enforcement officials, Nitto stopped in every evening between 5 and 6 p.m. for dinner.

In due course, Nitto acquired a hotel suite for business at the Congress Hotel, 500 South Michigan. Guzik and Capone sometimes called upon him here, though for other top-level meetings, Nitto traveled to see the boss. Ralph later admitted that the three would conclave at the Capone home in Mercer, Wisconsin. One resident also recalled Nitto in the north woods on a rare vacation. Another longtime resident who Nitto assigned to get booze for the group remembered his generosity: "He always paid me well—four dollars an hour. And every time I bought booze, say it was four bottles, he'd pay me for eight."

Nitto's alky dealings with Greenberg had become a mere side interest compared to his gang interests. Back in 1925, Nitto's income, traced to a single Cicero bank, was no less than $426,000—almost half a million dollars in income in a year when thirty-seven cents bought a dozen eggs, twenty-one cents bought a dozen fresh doughnuts, thirty-five cents bought a pound of fresh lobster, and twenty-seven cents purchased a pound of salmon. Nitto could outfit himself in a fine suit for as little as $55. He may have been making big money a year or two prior to that, but by 1926 his income tallied only about $170,000, and a year later it was less than half that amount. Why was his income dwindling when his prestige had yet to peak? He had, quite purposefully, reduced the visible amount himself.

Federal agents had been prying into Ralph Capone's income since 1924. At that time, an agent caught up with him and, in a friendly way, implored him to pay his taxes like any good citizen. Ralph agreed and supplied the agent with income numbers (on the low side, of course). The agent then filled out the forms and supplied them to Ralph with the note that he owed approximately $4,065 in taxes—sign the form, supply the funds, and that would be that. Instead, Ralph let it go, and when the agents inquired about his tardiness, he pleaded poverty. The agents then began an investigation into Ralph's affairs, starting a cat-and-mouse game that went on for the next couple of years. Late 1927, the feds assumed a no-nonsense tone.

Word of agents nosing around for income undoubtedly reached other high-level gang members. Ralph's experience presumably alarmed board member Jake Guzik. The squat little bookkeeper decided to file forms and pay taxes, thinking the feds might leave him alone. But like Ralph, he seriously downplayed his income, and before long they probed his returns.

Frank Nitto may have tried to fill out the tax forms but instead settled on an intricate form of evasion. Nitto had cashed checks for alcohol purchases at the Schiff Trust and Savings Bank in Cicero. From gambling proceeds, board members received cashier's checks made out to the fictitious J. C. Dunbar. Agreements at banks allowed the members to sign the checks and receive cash. In light of Ralph's experience, Nitto approached bank President Bruno Schiff to set up a special arrangement. Normally, cashed checks were recorded on the daily ledger accumulated from the bank teller activities, but these detailed transactions were subject to investigation by bank examiners. Schiff allowed Nitto to present checks directly to him. The checks were credited to a "collection payable account," and Nitto received a receipt for the total due him. When the checks cleared, the bank president delivered the cash, and Nitto would then sign a receipt on the general ledger debit ticket for the collection payable account. These transactions showed up only on the general bank ledger, and Nitto's name appeared only on the receipt, not on any account. The arrangement was not illegal, but certainly was not normal practice. With the transactions buried in the general ledger, the only risk might be if some myopic examiner found the bank totals elsewhere in disagreement and began a detailed search, which for any reasonably managed bank was a long shot.

Nitto also diversified, investing more with Greenberg and even going so far as to by stocks, something Capone generally ridiculed as "a sucker's game." The forward-thinking Nitto bought into Yellow Cab, a perfect choice when the only real competitor was Checker, and in any cab war, Nitto could call on an army of thugs to tilt business his way.

———

Nitto's power and stature now appeared to be second only to Capone's. George Meyer said he was hired as a chauffeur and all-around tough guy on one of Nitto's crews. He first met Capone when Nitto called for the car to pick up Capone, Rio, and himself for a trip to the Hawthorne racetrack, where Nitto and Capone sometimes conducted meetings in offices above the track. It appeared to Meyer that Nitto ran the Outfit in Capone's absence. Nitto was responsible, he said, for finding and awarding moneymaking enterprises such as handbooks or saloons to deserving troops above and beyond any salary paid. Miffed because he was turned down on one occasion, Meyer recalls Nitto telling him, "With three hundred of you bastards laying around here, I can't give everyone a fat ticket." Still later, Meyer was thunderstruck when, in a hotel elevator with Nitto, Capone, and others, Nitto, discussing some difficulty, told Capone, "I'll handle it, you just keep out of it."

Despite his success, the long hours away from home did not play so well on the Nitto home front. Since January 1928 Nitto had lived apart from wife Rose. Alleged physical abuse in late 1927 sent Rose seeking shelter among friends, and this wasn't the first time such abuse had happened. She cited several previous events during their marriage, but things had gotten worse: sometimes Nitto would rap her in front of friends, and once he struck her while they were guests in another home. In July, she filed for divorce. A week later, the summons was served on Nitto while he was attending dinner at the Naples Restaurant. In court, Nitto at first demurred, then settled, giving Rose an undetermined sum of money plus $5,000 to be paid within the next six months. Nitto was officially divorced the same day his name first hit the press as a major hood.

Bachelor Frank Nitto, age forty-two, did not stay unwed for long. In the spring of 1927, the daughter of Dr. Gaetano Ronga filed for divorce. Anna Ronga, the doctor's oldest child, was nearly twenty-five. She had been working as a clerk and typist in 1920 when she met and married an up-and-coming neighborhood physician. After nearly seven years, their marriage had dissolved in much the same manner as had Nitto's, and Anna was living on North Austin Avenue when she met her father's acquaintance, Frank Nitto.

———

Tony Lombardo's success had always chafed Joe Aiello. On September 7, Tony Lombardo, accompanied by two bodyguards, emerged from the offices of the Unione Siciliana (recently renamed the Italo-American National Union) in the Hartford Building just north of Madison and Dearborn streets. It was 4:30 in the afternoon, and the street was crowded with people finishing the workday. Two assassins emerged from the shadows of a nearby doorway, ran up behind Lombardo, and shot him in the back of the head. They plugged one of the bodyguards as well before melting away into the alarmed crowd. Police theories as to those responsible led to New York avengers of Frankie Yale and to Aiello and Moran; either way, the taint of Aiello was on the bullets.

With Lombardo's death, the Unione presidency fell open, and Aiello wanted to elevate Peter Rizzito. Rizzito was a powerful figure in Aiello's Little Sicily domain, governing a local Unione chapter (Number 13). However, before Rizzito became head of the Unione, he was blasted by sawed-off shotguns in front of his Milton Avenue home.

A *Daily News* reporter later reflected that the Unione mess was ultimately responsible for prompting the celebratory rise of Frank Nitto, noting it was "Frank Nitti who has taken the place of the slain Tony Lombardo in the Syndicate's affairs." In truth, Nitto was no more a member of the Unione than Lombardo had belonged to the gang, though 1928 did mark Nitto's ascendancy. The man who succeeded to the Unione throne and eventually worked with Nitto was Lombardo associate Pasqualino "Patsy" Lolordo.

Aiello, though, was not through . . . yet.

11

ENTER THE FEDS

L ITTLE KNOWN BY HISTORY, WILLIAM Dawes rode off with Paul Revere on the latter's famous journey from Charlestown to Lexington in 1775 to warn of the
British arrival. Dawes's great-great-grandson Charles rarely receives much historical
notice either, but it was Dawes who sparked federal intervention in saving Chicago
from gangland. Dawes practiced law in Chicago, and both he and his brother Rufus
had been respected in the city's financial world as far back as 1902, when Charles
organized the Central Trust Company of Illinois, for which he served as president
and, later, chairman of the board. He had served President McKinley as comptrol-
ler of currency, but in 1924 he rose to a much higher office, vice president of the
United States, as Calvin Coolidge's running mate.

In the early 1920s, Dawes recognized the abject corruption of Mayor Thompson's administration as a menace to Chicago's economic well-being. As a first step,
through local campaigning, he sought to elect honest judges. When Dever ascended
to the mayor's office and essentially failed in his noble effort to cleanse the city, it
was Dawes as vice president who lobbied higher authorities to investigate the gangland crisis. First, he went before a Senate subcommittee and detailed the alliance of
politicians and bootlegging gunmen as well as the ineffective state's attorney and
corrupt county sheriff. His efforts were rebuffed when the subcommittee told him
this was not a federal matter, but Dawes didn't give up and quietly worked other
Washington sectors to get aid.

149

Meanwhile he and brother Rufus were key planners for a Chicago's World's Fair—so much so that Rufus eventually became the World's Fair Corporation president. In February 1927, Dawes pushed for the appointment of George E. Q. Johnson as district attorney for the Northern District of Illinois, which included Chicago and Cook County. Johnson's pristine reputation and twenty-six years of legal experience eventually proved to be the correct remedy for the gang problem. As an assistant for Johnson, Washington sent rock-solid, former Internal Revenue lawyer Dwight H. Green, who worked in all phases of tax evasion cases, including writing opinions on tax questions for the Board of Tax Appeals. Dawes could at least count on these men to be morally upright as they dealt with Chicago.

While Dawes worked in Washington, concerned civic leaders in the Chicago Association of Commerce—including such luminaries as Sewell R. Avery, president of U.S. Gypsum; Julius Rosenwald of Sears, Roebuck and Co.; and Frederick R. Scott of Carson, Pirie, Scott and Co.—planned a war on crime through revision of the state's antiquated criminal codes. The Chicago Crime Commission was established in 1919 as a non-profit organization dedicated to tracing and recording crimes in the city crime (all crime, not just bootleg gangsters) as well as the principle characters responsible. Sparked by his love of the city and his outrage over the impact of gangsters on the city, Frank Loesch, a man then in his seventies, resigned from a lucrative law practice in 1928 to lead the commission and mount a public awareness campaign.

The new Thompson regime provided glaring examples of a worsening crisis: continuing gang murders, Capone's siege of the detective bureau over Aiello, a bombing war over gambling, the Pineapple Primary, and the Capone-Aiello war. The violence exasperated Chicago's anxious business community, and Loesch appealed to Dawes in Washington directly A new weapon against the gangs was needed. Liquor laws were hardly enforceable, the penalties not worth the effort in most cases, and so law enforcement could hardly expect to make any headway against the Prohibition gangs.

That new weapon came when, barely a month before the next national election, Dawes lobbied Coolidge, who on October 18, 1928, signed an order to target the biggest gangland hood, Nitto's boss Capone. The agency and the legal weapon to be used were relatively innovative: the U.S. Bureau of Internal Revenue (later the IRS) would lead an investigation to rid the city of Capone and his ilk. The weapon: income tax evasion. Penalties to evade and defeat income tax laws, the government figured, carried much weightier consequences than the bootleg laws and were viewed in a much different social context than booze.

As a wide-ranging, organized crime-busting technique, the tax angle was indeed innovative. Although income taxes had been part of Americana since 1913 and evading them had always been a crime, building a tax evasion case was not always straightforward since income, not simply wealth, had to be proven. If someone earned legitimate income and did not pay, this was easy enough to demonstrate. But gangsters who earned illegal moneys and cloaked them presented more serious challenges. Agents might proceed in two ways: 1) the "net worth" method that compared a person's expenditures to any declared income with the difference being the amount evaded; or 2) the "net expenditure" method in which a person's expenditures were tracked to illustrate some reasonable suspicion of income earned.

For some time, though, federal agents had faced another difficulty. In 1921, a small-time Carolina bootlegger named Manley Sullivan was arrested for income tax evasion. Rather than pay, he argued that honest Uncle Sam was not entitled to collect taxes on his perfidious bootleg income because the government had caused him to violate his Fifth Amendment right to avoid self-incrimination when they forced him to admit his illegal activities, much less the income they brought him. His lawyers carried the case up the judicial ladder, and it was only in 1927 that the U.S. Supreme Court upheld the government's original position that all income was indeed taxable.

Until then, Treasury agents and Assistant U.S. Attorney Green proceeded cautiously. Agents began keeping books on the mob big shots. According to Green, "They made a practice of clipping newspaper paragraphs about these people on occasions when they made a display of money." Journalists frequently wrote about this hoodlum with an overstuffed wardrobe or that hoodlum losing a bundle at the track—and neither hoodlum had a visible means of support.

When Herbert Hoover succeeded Coolidge as president, *Daily News* Publisher Frank Knox escorted a delegation of Chicago citizens to inquire about the status of federal help. Frank Loesch visited Hoover after Knox and asked the same questions. To each, Hoover upheld the pledge initiated by Coolidge to rid the city of Capone.

Ultimately, the unit assigned to investigate Nitto's boss was the Special Intelligence Unit of the Treasury Department, headed by Elmer Irey. For this group, taxpayer fraud cases were as new as the concept of using the crime as a means to send gangsters to prison. The group was originally created to investigate corruption within the Treasury Department. During World War I, profiteers and increased tax rates provided opportunities for collusion between taxpayers and agents to avoid paying taxes. Not until the 1920s did the SIU's focus shift to the outside world to investigate non-payers for prosecution.

Agents selected for the SIU were necessarily incorruptible. The agent in charge of the Chicago bureau was Arthur P. Madden. Assisting him were key men Archie Martin and Nels Tessem. Imported from Baltimore specifically for the Capone case was agent Frank Wilson. Clarence Converse arrived from Hollywood after investigating those in the movie industry, whose million-dollar contracts sparked concern, and nabbing stars Tom Mix and Charlie Chaplin, among others. Following up on their newspaper clipping collections, they checked files for returns. Whenever they found none, a case warranted further investigation.

Madden and his agents had been interested in Ralph Capone for some time. "Ralph was stupid," one agent observed, for when they gave him a chance to settle, he stalled and pled poverty despite the fact that he was known to be financially flush. Irey later remembered Ralph's tactics as providence: "If Ralph had not been such an inveterate chiseler he would have paid it, and neither he nor a long and distinguished group of hoodlums including brother Alphonse would have gone to jail when they did, if at all." Still, Ralph almost weaseled out of it. When the feds signaled their intention to seize property in 1927, he offered $1,000 as a complete settlement—but not without bemoaning the fact he would have to borrow the amount to do so.

The local Internal Revenue collector recommended acceptance and forwarded the agreement to his Washington superiors for approval, reasoning that something was better than nothing. However, his superiors refused unless Ralph could provide some substantiation of his indigence. Madden sent an agent to investigate. By the summer of 1928, he had learned that Ralph owned four horses at the Hawthorne track. Distressed by the agent's discovery, Ralph upped his offer to roughly half the amount due, then to the full amount of $4,065, but he steadfastly refused to pay an extra $1,000 in penalties and interest. There the matter stood when Coolidge authorized the Treasury to get Ralph's brother.

———⟨⟨⟨⟩⟩⟩———

Almost as soon as the SIU received the green light to get Al Capone, providence dropped in their lap from Chicago Heights, a town southeast of the city near the Indiana border long known as a sanctuary for hoods. Capone's Italian allies there ran bootlegging operations with as bloody a hand as anyone in Chicago. One tabloid in fact dubbed the Heights the "center of lawlessness."

In December 1928, after the police chief of South Chicago Heights dared to molest bootleggers, he was shotgunned to death in his home. Less than a week later, when Frank Basile was to testify in the case, he too was killed. Federal agents noted that several people who had been slated to testify against the local gang had been murdered. It was at this point that Charles Dawes's efforts began to bear fruit.

U.S. Attorney George Johnson determined to rein in the lawlessness of the Heights. Before daylight on a frosty Sunday morning, January 6, 1929, agents from the Prohibition Bureau and the U.S. marshal's office gathered in south Chicago. Meeting them there were over one hundred Chicago detectives, police, and men from the state's attorney's office. These men knew nothing of their impending task; in order to ensure surprise, federal agents saved discussion of the raid and the nature of the warrants for the ride to the Heights.

It was the coldest morning of the year to that point, eleven degrees and falling, as the raiders swooped into Chicago Heights sometime after five a.m. They took control of city hall and held the police. Raiding known hotspots, they confiscated arsenals of weapons and ammunition, seized gaming machines, and rounded up hoodlums. The real windfall came, however, when raiders hit the estate of Oliver Ellis. Ellis was known to be the local payoff man and to run gambling in the area, while his brother Homer ran the nearby Thornton dog track. Crashing down the iron-gated entrance to his country estate, the raiders proceeded to a rear building that disgorged nearly 400 slot machines, fifty gallons of alcohol, and several cases of Canadian whiskey and beer. The most important find was the gambling records and hundreds of cancelled checks showing a split of gambling profits and pointing to Ralph Capone, Jake Guzik, and Frank Nitto.

Enter the Feds

Two days after the feds raided Chicago Heights, the war with Aiello and the North Siders flared again. The head of the Unione Siciliana, Patsy Lolordo, liked to represent himself as a wealthy olive oil importer and grocer. He and his wife occupied an ornately decorated flat at 1921 West North Avenue, only a block from his business. He was only four months into his reign as Unione chief when, on the afternoon of January 8, he and Mrs. Lolordo returned home from a trip downtown. At 2:30 p.m., two men called on Patsy regarding business. His wife made lunch for the men, as she had seen them before—her husband often entertained at their home.

After the pair left, three other men arrived, full of joviality. They sat in velvet-cushioned chairs in the living room, in the center of which was a small, ornately carved octagonal table. Drinks were served from a tray with two liquor bottles, and the men conversed with Patsy. From the kitchen where she was attending to domestic chores, Mrs. Lolordo heard the men clink glasses in jaunty toasts for an hour. At approximately 4 p.m., gunshots broke up the meeting. As Mrs. Lolordo frantically ran out to investigate, one of the killers brushed her aside. Their drinks sat half-finished on the tray, while her husband lay on the area rug, shot eleven times in the head and back. Mrs. Lolordo could identify no one for police, but many suspected Aiello. He was the only person who stood to gain from Lolordo's death, which eliminated a Capone ally and left the Unione open for takeover once again.

One newspaper headline for January 10, 1929, declared: "FORECAST FOR CHICAGO: MORE GANG MURDERS." Frank Nitto surely knew that forecast was correct. Capone was, after all, down south in the Miami sun, and Nitto's contemporaries all agreed that he was too important not to know what was coming. He did not plan the up-coming operation, nor did he fire a gun, but as perhaps the most capable board member in Chicago with Al gone, he was likely most responsible for seeing that gang functions were successfully carried out.

Gangland suspected Bugs Moran and his men were complicit in the Lolordo hit since Aiello lacked the firepower to mount such an operation. Without a fix on Aiello's position, taking out Moran and his North Siders was the next best thing since they had been just as pesky recently. Moran, with his Fairview Kennel Club on Mannheim Road, attempted to run head-to-head against Capone in the dog racing business. Perhaps even more annoying was that Moran was thought to be using the mechanical rabbit without permission from its patented owner and Capone ally, Eddie O'Hare. With his Fairview track lagging far behind in terms of attendance, Moran was thought to have taken his frustration out against the Hawthorne Kennel Club with a bombing and later with arson. Also, early in 1928, his goons, probably Pete and Frank Gusenberg, raked gunfire at Capone's prized gunner Jack McGurn. After discovering they only wounded him, Moran's men made another attempt a month later while McGurn sat in a taxicab; this time missing altogether. Lolordo's murder now gave the Capone mob an incentive to implement a plan some suspect they began hatching in the fall of 1928 to rid themselves of Moran once and for all.

A vehicle disguised as a police flivver pulled up in front of CMC Cartage Company at 2122 North Clark Street. Two uniformed men entered then lined up and disarmed the occupants. Next, two plainclothes men entered and, together with the fake policemen, mowed down and blasted seven men into a bloody mess. The *Daily News*'s headline for February 14, 1929, said it all: "MASSACRE 7 OF MORAN GANG." While the plan failed to hit the intended target, Moran, it eradicated the core of his gang. Key among the dead were annoying gunmen Pete and Frank Gusenberg, Moran racketeer Albert Weinshank, Moran's partner in dog racing Adam Heyer, gunman and killer Albert Kachellek, and two acquaintances of little or no gang value.

Afterward, Moran and a couple of survivors scurried out of town for cover. One associate, however, chose another course—gunman Ted Newberry, who had overlooked Moran's booze business, defected to the Capone ranks, earning him a diamond belt buckle which Capone now awarded those he valued most. Along with him went Frank Foster. Neither was said to be happy with their split of northern gang proceeds.

The authorities' lengthy list of suspects in the St. Valentine's Day Massacre did not include Frank Nitto. Either just before or immediately after the slaughter, Nitto shuttled off to St. Louis, Missouri, a safe place for Capone hoodlums thanks to connections with lawyer Eddie O'Hare and that city's preeminent gang, Egan's Rats. On February 16, Frank Nitto and Anna Ronga rushed to St. Louis City Hall, applied to clerk Frank S. Meyer for a marriage license, and married in a civil ceremony. Their honeymoon destination was unknown, but they would be away long enough for the heat to die down before resuming business as usual. However, when his boss returned in March, newlywed Nitto would have to deal with an internal threat. It was only after that episode that the public truly discovered Frank Nitto's importance.

—◦◦◦—

After Lolordo's murder, the Capone group was able to elevate Joseph Guinta to head of the Unione. Like those before him, Guinta cloaked his unlawful activities in innocence, proclaiming himself to be a humble furniture and cigar store proprietor. However, at his side enforcing his power were the ever-dangerous duo of John Scalise and Albert Anselmi. Three weeks after the St. Valentine's Day Massacre, Guinta was hauled into jail with prime suspect Scalise. With Moran now out of the picture, this potent triumvirate could easily dissuade Aiello from further aspirations to Unione office. Unfortunately for Capone, the group apparently held higher aspirations— either through connivance with Aiello to eliminate Capone or through blinding narcissism.

Word filtered out of the Unione office that Guinta and company, bloated with self-importance, had declared that they were the real bosses in Chicago now. These high self-opinions reached Capone at the Lexington Hotel, and Nitto's boss could not risk allowing such beliefs to mature into treacherous action against his person or the organization. Elimination of the trio, according to alleged gang chauffeur George Meyer, "was Nitti's idea." He conceived a huge banquet to honor the trio at a large gang place. Capone and the core of the gang would be there, and guns would be checked at the door. The three guests would be sated with mounds of food and rivers of drink. When the guests relaxed, Capone's men would pounce and administer gang justice.

The party was held at the Plantation, a gang roadhouse and casino over the state border in Hammond, Indiana. In a private room, the jollity echoed until Capone rose and personally beat all three to a pulp with a baseball bat. Meyer later recalled: "They said Capone got so worked up they thought he had a heart attack." The traitors were then served fatal gunshots. The bodies of the three who thought they might be kings were loaded into the rear of an awaiting vehicle and driven away for disposal. Before the corpses cooled, they were discovered when a patrolman, investigating the oddly parked car on a lonely stretch of road near a Pennsylvania Railroad line, shown a light in the dark interior and saw Scalise and Anselmi a bloody heap in the back. Further searching turned up Guinta, tossed seventy-five feet away near the railroad tracks.

Immediately afterward, Nitto, along with Capone bodyguard Frank Rio and fellow board member Jake Guzik, accompanied Capone to Atlantic City. They checked into the President Hotel, where a hoodlum conference of epic proportions was being held for nearly all the Midwest and East Coast gangs. Besides Capone, Moran was said to be there, and other competitors such as the Aiello and Saltis-McErlane factions were supposedly represented by proxy. Though retired to New York, Johnny Torrio was there. One press report had him in Chicago recently trying to mediate between Capone and his enemies Moran and Aiello.

According to one source, the men discussed arrangements to govern the peaceful distribution of booze, Nitto's key responsibility. For example, Capone's bootleg interests extended to imports through New York; Frankie Yale was thought to have handled this traffic, but now that Capone had had him killed, who would handle it now? Others reported that the recent St Valentine's Day Massacre and peace in Chicago were key topics of discussion. After about a week's worth of negotiations, Nitto's boss claimed they all "signed on the dotted line," so to speak, to end the violence.

Business concluded, Capone and Rio left by car for Philadelphia to hop a train. Nitto and Guzik left separately. Two days later, Nitto was headed back east: both Capone and Rio, while in Philadelphia on the return trip, were nabbed carrying concealed weapons. This was ordinarily a petty nuisance crime, but within sixteen hours, both men were tried and sentenced to the extraordinary maximum term of one year in prison. With time off for good behavior, the boss expected to be absent from Chicago for at least ten months. Nitto went to Philadelphia to confer with Capone about the status of further legal assistance from Chicago and to obtain directives to run Chicago in his absence.

Immediately, writers filled reams of newsprint with the plight of the gang boss. It was in this instant that Nitto's true value finally radiated to the outside world. Speculation keyed on who Capone's intermediate in Chicago might be. On May 18, one paper announced, "TORRIO COMING BACK TO SEIZE CAPONE POWER." Nearly four months later, the same paper still pronounced Torrio as "Racket King." One report from the street had Ralph in charge, conferring with attorneys in Nitto's immediate absence. An earlier report had Guzik as the new "field marshal" of Capone's troops, with Ralph supervising Cicero activities from his "new and brilliant" suburban Cotton Club. Later federal wiretaps of Ralph's Montmartre Café and nightclub indicated a heavy traffic of subordinates (at least in Cicero) in his direction.

Tom Pettey of the *Tribune*, however, may have picked up more correct data. According to him, Capone henchmen regarded "Frank Nitti as "the business manager of the Capone organization." He continued: "Nitti, although he has remained in the background in Chicago gang dealings, has long been known as one of the best 'brains' in the Capone band of hoodlums."

There is one piece of solid evidence that Nitto assumed charge during Capone's absence. Sometime after Johnson and the tax men arrived in Chicago, Washington sent a young, honest Prohibition agent named Eliot Ness to organize a crew and take the federal fight to Capone's alcohol stocks. With Capone gone, they began to smash breweries, distilleries, and supply lines, and when Capone's staff attempted the usual bribes, they found Ness's men as incorruptible as their boss, earning the bunch the nickname the "Untouchables."

Through a tip, Ness learned that Nitto called a meeting of several important gang members, including Ralph Capone, Jake Guzik, Mops Volpe, Phil D'Andrea, and others. The group was set to discuss what to do about the feds. Killing federal agents was out of the question; it could only bring more serious harm to the organization. They decided to get word to Al and ask him. But that Nitto reportedly called the meeting and thereby exercised respect and power at least implies the authority that only a number two could pull.

In Capone's absence, Nitto and the gang faced few external gang threats. The North Side was relatively quiet. Contrary to popular belief and despite the massacre of his men, Bugs Moran did not abandon the area altogether. Contemporary reports had him in Evanston, just north of the Chicago. Gunman and torpedo Willie Marks stayed on. Eccentric gunman Louis Alterie hung around to take control of the theatrical janitors union, and indications were that Jack Zuta and Barnie Berstche remained in his corner. Aiello was hiding locally. It's possible that the gang, with Torrio's help, was ironing out further peace details with Moran and Aiello. Nitto backed gang diplomacy with his typical ruthless stick. In September, when minor North Sider Charles Brown stepped out of bounds, he was taken for a ride and dumped in a ditch on the South Side. Two months later another North Side member was hacked to death, bound with wire, and thrown in the Chicago River.

South Side ally Ralph Sheldon had retired due to tuberculosis, and the most forceful of his men, hulking Danny Stanton, fought to retain control and was wounded at least once by allies and remnants of the Saltis-McErlane mob. Retaliation claimed the lives of the supposed gunmen George Clifford and Michael Reilly, killers for the McErlane outfit. Stanton proved victorious early the following year when a third conspirator died and the powder keg of the Saltis-McErlane gang, Frank McErlane, was wounded and put on the shelf. Saltis, with most of his gunslingers lost, was thought to have made peace with Capone, and the South Side stabilized.

With booze and gambling operations in hand, the primary concern during 1929 for Nitto and the organization boiled down to Ness and his raiders. True, their efforts never came close to closing the spigot of the organization's alcohol output, but Ness and his men did inflict considerable physical damage to the Capone booze empire through time, money, and investments lost. For Nitto, though, the strategy was simply dodging and attempting to ward off the band of raiders—even as his role in the gang was becoming more unmistakable to the tax men as well as to Ness.

12

TARGET: NITTO
"THE ENFORCER"

FOR ALMOST A YEAR, SIU agents dissected the records and cancelled checks seized in the January 1929 Chicago Heights raid. One agent flipping through a pile of checks found a single cashier's check for $1,000—endorsed by Frank Nitto. This was an eye opener; the amount represented nearly half an agent's yearly salary in those days. Nitto might be somebody big, though to that time, he had hardly looked like a primary target. And to date, Wilson and agents had unearthed only a few dreary scraps on main target Al Capone. The Big Guy kept no books or accounts, remaining two or three times removed from his operation.

The Nitto amount, however, looked like a promising trail. Evidence on Jake Guzik surfaced, and they already had Ralph on the hook. Ultimately, as U.S. Attorney Johnson later recalled, "This process of breaking down these partners was a plan to reach Capone." Target Nitto.

—◁◈◈◈▷—

That Nitto got "careless," according to agent Frank Wilson, didn't make for an open and shut case. Like Ralph Capone, beer barons Terry Druggan and Frankie Lake were under surveillance since 1926 when the feds quizzed them over an estimated $15 million in income. A difficult net-expenditure case, they thought they might prove $3 million, but to be sure of even this amount required additional inquiries. With "stupid" Ralph, the feds built both a net-expenditure case based on his generally known and lavish purchases and a net-worth case based on his underreported tax forms. But these cases dragged on until investigators could unearth hard evidence.

They finally nailed Ralph when a single check from the Heights raid drew the attention of investigators. Worth $3,200, it was drawn off an account owned by Oliver Ellis, the man from whose home the checks were seized and who authorities suspected as a conspirator in illegal gambling operations operations. The signature on the check belonged to James Carroll. When SIU agents Archie Martin and Nels Tessem investigated Carroll's account, they found it had previously been started with the exact sum of a closed account that had belonged to a James Carter. No one in the bank professed to know either man. Doggedly flipping through countless bank accounts, the agents found the amount initiating the Carter account matched the amount that had been in one closed by a James Costello Jr. The thread of names and balances weaved back to October 27, 1925, when the original bank account was opened by Ralph Capone. In all, just over $1,750,000 passed through the accounts under Ralph's aliases. The investigation also revealed that, at the time Ralph pleaded poverty and promised to borrow $1,000 to cover his full tax liability, the James Carter account held a balance of over $25,000.

To verify that Ralph Capone and the persons named on the accounts were indeed one and the same, an agent pored over Ralph's arrest records. The agent noted that, in May 1926, when police had wanted Ralph for questioning about a high-profile murder, the nameplate on his Forty-ninth Street apartment had read "James Carroll"—matching the name on the bank account at the same time. On October 8, 1929, agents arrested Ralph just as he was settling into a front-row seat at Chicago Stadium for a prizefight. He was held overnight on $50,000 bond, but that was later reduced to $35,000.

Agent Nels Tessem was assigned the Nitto case. But even with Nitto's name attached to a check, the case proved even immensely difficult. Because Nitto carried himself in such *sub rosa* fashion, few outside the gang knew of his affairs, and, consequently, there was little newsprint for Tessem to digest. Secondly, Nitto's investments with Greenberg and apparent frugality presented no sparkling trail for a net-expenditure case. Additionally, Nitto apparently took early alarm over the revenue agents snooping into Ralph's affairs and moved to conceal his financial transactions more effectively. Further, even though the feds kept the investigation under wraps, Nitto, maybe as the result of a leak or perhaps sensing trouble after Ralph's indictment, moved to ensure his existence remained shadowy.

On January 11, 1930, Nitto, accompanied by a lawyer, marched into police headquarters armed with a court order demanding the destruction of Nitto's fingerprint records and photos from the 1927 arrest. Their case was argued before some friendly judge, and the Frank Nitto file documents were consigned to history.

Tessem worked on the single check, tracing it to the Schiff Trust and Savings Bank in Cicero. His initial combing of the records revealed no accounts, checks, or deposit slips in Nitto's name. Laboriously, he checked reams of teller sheets for a $1,000 transaction, but none occurred. He plodded through the records again, this time keeping a set of his own books, which, when examined, showed a discrepancy somewhere of exactly $1,000—the amount of the Nitto check. Schiff claimed to know nothing. Tessem then demanded the general bank ledger and there unearthed Nitto's cryptic banking methods thanks to a long list of checks credited to Nitto. Schiff admitted an arrangement with Nitto to clear his checks and return cash at a later date. However, doing so required Nitto to sign a receipt for the amount due him, and this he did, fatally, true to his name. The amounts matched a significant number of checks cleared in this manner. Double-checking signatures on receipts versus signature cards at the bank verified Nitto's handwriting. Curiously, Nitto claimed on the cards to be "retired" or a "salesman."

Scanning through the Nitto checks, agents determined an initial aggregate income for the years 1925-27 to be $671,160.37. This might not have been his entire income, but the amount was big enough to start a major prosecution. The agents had confirmed Nitto as one of "the higher-ups" in the Capone organization.

The agents still had a long road ahead. When the evidence was presented to U.S. Attorney Johnson and his assistant Dwight Green, the latter, because of previous tax case experience, noted the amount represented "gross income" only, since the cost of running his business could not be determined. What the government needed for both criminal and civil cases were witnesses to corroborate his transactions.

Tessem went to work questioning bank employees about the transactions, but his line of inquiry proved ineffective. Next, investigators began tracking writers of the checks as potential witnesses. Many of the checks were written on dummy accounts attached to untraceable aliases. Those that gave the largest aggregate moneys—a nameless ordinary businessman turned bootlegger, gunman Louis Schiavone, and Capone gambling superintendent James Mondi—disappeared. Two Nitto bootleg dealers were hauled in, however. When interrogated by agents, the makers of the checks were "evasive in their answers, and others frankly admitted that they could not give the agents information." Somehow, the word was out.

Tessem wasn't the only agent experiencing frustration. Having been specifically assigned the Al Capone investigation, SIU agent Frank Wilson had accumulated very little evidence by the winter of 1930. Witnesses clammed up all over Chicago and the suburbs. Wilson remembered one potential gang observer scoffing at his inquiry: "Why, if I open my mouth and tell you about any deal I had with Capone, he'll have me bumped off." In the late winter of 1930, such people had ample reason to be fearful.

On the morning of February 1, Julius Rosenheim left his home on Dickens Avenue on the Northwest Side. He was not far down the block, plodding over the snow-covered sidewalk, when a car pulled to the curb from behind. Two men jumped out and gunned him down in front of at least two witnesses before clambering back into the vehicle and escaping. Information soon came to light that Rosenheim was an underworld informer. Of course, the Capone mob was suspect; within three weeks, police hauled in Jack McGurn and his protégé Tony Accardo, but to no avail.

Among the revelations to make print that supposedly came from Rosenheim was the extent of vice in the Loop, despite the fact that boss Al Capone was still in a Philadelphia prison with Rio. This hardly seems an eye-opener; everybody knew the

Loop to be open. Rosenheim, however, had recently been spotted near the Lexington Hotel, and his undercover dealings touched more sensitive nerves—particularly in the Ralph Capone and Frank Nitto tax matters.

Two days after Rosenheim was gunned down, Frank Nitto's sobriquet was born in the *Daily News*:

Nitti Directs Outrages

At his post in the Lexington Hotel . . . Nitti, known as "the Enforcer," decides what unfortunates will feel the weight of the Syndicate's educational committee and to what extent.

The "Enforcer" tag stuck. A couple of days later, a reporter reaffirmed what Eliot Ness already heard. Reports had Nitto holding daily team meetings at the Lexington in which business was discussed, problems were presented, and solutions were dictated by "Capone's Dispenser of Justice":

Not a "pineapple" can be tossed at a recalcitrant saloonkeeper, not a blackjack nor pistol butt can go klunk on a foe's head, not a "nosey" or "hungry" policeman can be transferred, not a rival beer truck hijacked, nor an enemy of the Syndicate be sent on a one-way ride until Nitti has given the word.

By February 6, gangland mortality numbers for the month reached nine. Nitto's "beauty squads," as some in the game facetiously liked to label the cleanup gunmen, probably contributed to two additional deaths. Other minor gang squabbles, union racketeers, and labor disputes accounted for the rest. Outraged, as Charles Dawes had been years before, a member of the Chicago Association of Commerce pronounced conditions in the city "terrible." He continued: "Chicago must do something about it. Not only is the situation terrible in relation to crime, but also to municipal finances." If nothing is done, he said, "the time is not far off when gangland kings will virtually rule the city." Commerce President Robert Isham Randolph agreed, and the committee offered a $1,000 reward for information leading to the arrest of the killers in one of the labor-related murders.

As a result of the February outrages, Randolph formed and led a committee of six highly placed financial figures called the Secret Six (Randolph was the only self-admitted member.) They shared the Dawes-CAC view of Chicago's financial demise if gangland was not put out of action. The aim of the group was to assist law enforcement, particularly the feds, by expediting the apprehension and prosecution of gangland members, including Nitto.

Recently, the group had assisted SIU agent Frank Wilson. Unable to make much progress in his efforts against Al Capone, Wilson decided on an undercover mission. An agent who could pass for an Italian would be planted as close to the Capone group as possible to perhaps infiltrate the Lexington Hotel and feed the feds information to break open the case. Financing such an operation—for example, the agent had to be tailored in gangland style—normally entailed going through time-wasting bureaucratic channels. The Secret Six instead provided funds to turn agent Mike Malone (the best undercover agent ever, according to Wilson) into a hoodlum, on-the-run "Mike Lepito." By 1930, Malone successfully gained the confidence of those in the gang's lower echelon, becoming a fixture around the Lexington Hotel lobby, his radar ears and eyes picking up tidbits later transmitted to Wilson. During the course of his spying, he also assisted in the Nitto case.

—◦⁄◦◦⁄◦—

The growing Chicago gangland problem pressured the feds to get results. The key was Al Capone. President Hoover remained adamant about making progress. The Attorney General and Treasury offices continually kept him abreast of developments. As of yet, Ralph was the only one hooked. Ralph's lawyers attempted a plea bargain—two years in exchange for a guilty plea. Perhaps in need of an example, at least certainly not prepared to deal with a proven liar and cheat, U.S. Attorney Johnson refused: "Nope. Bottles goes to trial." The trial date was set for late spring.

Meanwhile, further digging into the Chicago Heights material provided a gold mine of incriminating evidence for a net-worth case concerning Nitto associate Jake Guzik. The material detailed over a million dollars passing through his accounts, though he previously inked tax returns for far below that amount. His prosecution appeared to be a cinch, according to the feds. The attorney general reported to Hoover, "Considering the amount of crime at that point, the results are meager, but in proportion to our responsibilities we have done much more than the State authorities in making a dent in gangster racketeering and corruption."

The Nitto matter, though, remained a thorn in the feds' side. In comparison to his associates, what they could dig up on him was paltry. Moreover, unlike recent evidence collected on Guzik, Nitto's visible income beyond 1927 proved minuscule. The best bet for prosecution appeared to be the 1925-27 period. Therein lay extra concern for Johnson and his staff. Though the Manley Sullivan decision made it clear the government could collect taxes on illegal income, the legal question regarding the construction of the tax evasion statute as a misdemeanor or a felony was still open. Various appeals courts were divided. The statute of limitations for a misdemeanor was of shorter duration than that for a felony, and if tax evasion was ruled a misdemeanor, Johnson risked losing the surest and most damning part of the Nitto case, years 1925 and 1926.

The March 15 deadline for filing taxes was rapidly approaching, and still the Johnson team could locate only two of Nitto's check makers—both substantial dealers, but neither willing to appear before a grand jury. Adding to Johnson's dilemma was a letter from Commissioner of Internal Revenue Robert H. Lucas to Assistant Attorney General G. Aaron Youngquist, dated March 8, 1930, regarding Frank Nitto:

> The short time remaining, and the attitude of the witnesses when examined by the field agents, make it appear necessary that the case be presented directly to the Grand Jury, if prosecution is to be instituted. . . . It

is therefore recommended that, under the peculiar circumstances of this case, The United States Attorney at Chicago be authorized to present the matter directly to the Grand Jury . . . charging willful failure to file income tax returns for 1926 and 1927, and willful attempt to defeat and evade income taxes for 1925, 1926, and 1927.

Luck then dropped in Johnson's lap. He was approached by an attorney who was representing a pair of men in another federal case before Johnson and also happened to be the attorney for one of the key men in the Nitto case. If Johnson would drop the charges against his client, the attorney would induce the key Nitto witness to talk. Johnson immediately agreed. The witness, described by Johnson as "unreliable" and of "poor character," was nonetheless hustled before the grand jury in great secrecy. Fearing for his life, he shakily outlined the checks as purchases of alcohol from Nitto, and additional evidence added to the severity of the 1927 case.

On March 14, 1930, formal tax evasion charges were filed against the Enforcer; his gross income was tabulated to have been $742,887, with a tax of $158,823.21 due. Hoping to catch the shadowy Nitto unaware and perhaps give agent Mike Malone a chance to draw a bead on his location, the indictment was kept under wraps for a week. "The secret indictment," Irey later recalled, "was evidently no secret to the Enforcer," who had likely caught word of it from the federal building and absconded. By remaining free, Nitto, a key cog in the organization, could meet with Capone and the others to plan a strategy to meet the federal threat. But with Ralph's trial set for mid-April, Nitto under indictment, Guzik under investigation, and the boss himself certain to be targeted next, how could they fight this thing?

With Nitto untraceable, the feds issued a warrant for his arrest. It was only then that the press got wind of the story, describing Nitto in such somewhat overblown terms as "banker" and "brains," as in this March 23 headline: "CAPONE 'BANKER' INDICTED BY U.S. FOR TAX FRAUD." Despite diligent searching, federal agents were unable to locate him. The *Daily News* suggested Nitto was a regular at the Lexington Hotel. Johnson approached the Chicago police for assistance, and acting on a tip, detectives raided a residential mansion five blocks south of the Lexington. They didn't find Nitto, but they did haul in nine associates and $10,000 worth of liquor.

The heat was on. In connection with the Nitto case, warrants were issued for brothers Charlie and Rocco Fischetti and for two bootleggers of importance, but none of these men was found. The Chicago police issued orders to arrest all hoodlums on sight. When Capone hit town, he voluntarily walked into police headquarters. They ran him through perfunctory procedures, and he left without being arrested.

Serious about settling his own tax affairs, Capone retained tax attorney Lawrence Mattingly. Neither realized that the federal priority was not a civil settlement, which wouldn't remove the big guy from Chicago; the feds anxiously desired a criminal prosecution. In April, Capone and Mattingly initiated a conference, but this sparring match with the agents amounted to nothing. After the conference, having complained after his prison release, "I haven't been down at my Miami home for ten months," Capone left for the Florida sunshine—and so, apparently, did Nitto as well as associates Jack McGurn, Cicero bondsman Louis Cowen, and bodyguard Nick Circella.

On March 31, the feds issued warrants for Nitto's arrest in another jurisdiction, as he was thought to be a guest at the Capone home on Palm Island. While lounging in the sun, Nitto reportedly whiled away the hours swinging his clubs on the links of the Illinois Golf Association near Miami. If so, he performed his usual stealthy job of escaping the wrath of Florida officials, who, like the feds, were bent on aggravating Capone and his men. They nabbed McGurn on a golf outing, and everyone else was pinched at least once. Capone himself was inconvenienced at least four times.

In April 1930, the Chicago Crime Commission added to the heat. It published its first list of proclaimed "public enemies," as President Frank Loesch liked to call them—the most notorious individuals plaguing the city. Capone received top billing, and other notorious characters included Jack McGurn and Joe Aiello. Has-beens Bugs Moran and Joe Saltis were named, and several lower-rung gang members and gunmen from all over the city made it as well. Of Capone's board, brother Ralph and Jake Guzik appeared, but Nitto's innocuous behavior and low-key professionalism, despite his recent "Enforcer" tag, allowed him to remain invisible. But not to the *Daily News*, which published its own version of the list. Despite classifying Nitto as an "arch killer," they ranked him a mere twenty-seventh out of fifty-seven criminals.

—≡∘/∘/∘≡—

Though in Florida, Nitto and Capone no doubt kept abreast of events in Chicago. This was the initial test run for both feds and hoodlums, and the feds were, according to Elmer Irey, in "somewhat uncertain legal territory." They documented Ralph's clumsy attempt to dodge tax liability and built a net expenditure case based on his lavish spending on jewelry, racehorses, rents, and the like. But as in the Nitto case, the prosecution lacked a hard witness for the bank transactions, and the net-expenditure evidence, as described by SIU chief A. P. Madden, appeared "remote from the defendant." The prosecution was unsure whether it would be accepted in a trial by either a judge or jury. Johnson's assistant assessed the difficulties: "It is one thing to argue a technical point of law with lawyers—quite another to bring the same point home to a jury of laymen."

The U.S. attorney's office spent weeks preparing for every contingency. Ralph's trial started on April 18. Irey described it as a "tiresome" fifteen-day affair. A. P. Madden was also there. Despite Ralph's blunders, Madden rated his lawyers' handling of the case as first-rate: "I don't see how a better defense could have been made. . . . The defendant's attorneys made extended arguments and demurrers. . . . Mr. Kelleher's objections, almost without exception, were based upon sound reasoning. The prosecution had to be well fortified and alert all of the time."

Madden praised the prosecution as well, saying, "I do not believe that I have ever been familiar with a case in which the United States attorney was better prepared." Even the judge, he noted, exercised extreme caution about evidence presented. The jury found Ralph guilty, and in June he received a sentence of three years in prison and a $10,000 fine. Now that they understood the ramifications of the feds' intentions, Nitto's case moved to the forefront for determining mob strategy to deal with the impending prosecutions.

Years later, it was George Murray who suggested that, in the spring of 1930, Capone sought to bribe or "fix" high officials to favorably manipulate Nitto's pending case. Bribery was the standard gang remedy for problems with local officials; they may have figured it was worth a try with the feds. The first attempt was through Italian lawyer William "Billy" Parrillo. Described by Chicago Crime Commission President Frank Loesch as "a known partisan of Capone's," the lawyer had earlier been appointed assistant U.S. attorney in Johnson's office. According to Murray, the plan was for Parrillo to approach Dwight Green about a fix. Green, in his memoirs, does not relate such an incident, but Parrillo may have aided Capone's group in more ways than one.

Parrillo's primary duty was handling cases related to, of all things, the Prohibition Act. Nels Tessem later remarked to a colleague that, during the Capone investigation, they became "suspicious" of Parrillo. His office adjoined the grand jury room, and they suspected him of feeding inside information to the Capone interests. Though they could not prove perfidy without a shadow of doubt, Tessem noted that authorities moved Parrillo's office to another part of the building, just in case. At the very least, Tessem's suspicion would go a long way toward explaining how Nitto was able to avoid the secret indictment handed down in March.

From the margins, Nitto conducted his customary business. The Loop remained wide open for booze and gambling, so much so that local police hardly bothered them—it was impossible to close all the joints, and to pick on one or two seemed unfair. Despite nuisance raids by Eliot Ness, the Outfit's alcohol supply remained plentiful, though prices edged up. Entering the 1930s, the cost of protection for moving a single case of booze rose to $35.

Nitto, the "chief of Capone's murder squad" and "arch killer," was repeatedly seen around the Lexington, and the squads remained bloodily active. On May 30, alleged stool pigeon and thief Dominick Costa was found beaten and shot nine times. When Joe Aiello dared to rise again, Nitto's squads hit hard. A day after the Costa murder, Aiello organizer and collector Pete Plescia was gunned down in an alley. A few hours later, Aiello men Samuel Monistero and Joseph Ferrari were killed. The same day, for the benefit of the Capone mob, old Genna hand Phillip Gnolfo was murdered in his auto at Peoria and Eighteenth streets.

The next day at Fox Lake north of the city, men armed with machine guns wiped out minor adversaries Sam Pellar, a tough who escaped bullets in the Hymie Weiss massacre in 1927; Joseph Bertsche, the brother of gambling thorn Barney Bertsche; and gunman Michael Quirk. General suspicion laid the murders at the feet of the Capone gang. Jack McGurn and his protégé Charles Gioe, along with Frank Diamond and Frank Foster, a recent North Side defector (with Newberry) to the Capone camp, were all hauled in but released.

On June 9, the spectacular murder of *Tribune* reporter Jake Lingle pushed Nitto and company out of the papers. On that day Lingle was crossing below Michigan Avenue in a pedestrian underpass when someone dropped him with a .38-caliber gunshot to the back of his head. Media and citizens' outrage filled columns of newsprint and sparked offers of reward for information about the reporter's death.

However, Lingle's heavy involvement with the city's gambling interests gradually came to light. These put him in touch with underworld characters on opposites sides of the gangland war: Jack Zuta, formerly aligned with Moran on the North Side, and Al Capone. It was also revealed that he acted as a go-between for corrupt police officials and hoodlum interests, exacting hefty fees in return. Evidence eventually traced his death to vice chief Zuta, who had been on the receiving end of a Lingle double-cross when Zuta allies attempted to open a new gambling joint on the North Side. Another source cited Zuta's recent attempt to oust defector and Capone's new North Side ally Ted Newberry from his gambling interests. Either way, Zuta stepped over the line with Capone.

Barely a month later, police picked up Zuta for questioning. Fearful for his life if released, he received a police escort. In the Loop, a car of hoods pursued and exchanged gunfire with police while attempting to kill Zuta; one of the gunmen was identified as Ted Newberry. Zuta fled, but not far enough. On August 1, Capone men, led by South Side power and ally Dan Stanton, quietly stepped into a resort near Delafield, Wisconsin, approached a man feeding nickels into the jukebox, and blasted him dead with gunfire. The man was Jack Zuta.

As for Lingle's killer, witnesses identified Frank Foster. Nitto's strange involvement in the case spanned the remainder of the year. Unable to find Foster, authorities pressed Capone about the murder, and the circumstances demanded that the police apply extraordinary heat to hurt Capone's business citywide. To ease the situation, Capone offered to help find the killer. The name of St. Louis gunman Leo Brothers cropped up, and in December 1930 he was arrested and charged with Lingle's murder.

According to two separate sources, it was Nitto who arranged for Brothers, who matched the killer's description, to be taken. Brothers was wanted for murder in St. Louis, but the mob could fix his case in Chicago for a lighter sentence than he could possibly get in St. Louis while at the same time protecting Capone's employees and interests. If Foster was the killer, he could remain free. Police also received a tip early in the investigation that North Sider James "Red" Forsythe was the killer; he did not completely match the description but was a well-known underworld character and gunman. This tip may have originated with Capone's interests. In any event, Capone's agents remained free.

⚜

By the summer, SIU agents were no closer to finding Frank Nitto than they had been in March. Again they issued warrants for the Fischettis and for known Nitto alcohol check makers, and again, the warrants were returned unexecuted.

On July 21, Nitto's squads eliminated another piece of Aiello's network when they killed Peter "Ash Can Pete" Inserra. A week later, the feds reissued Nitto's arrest warrant. The big picture of gang finances had come into much sharper focus for the

SIU agents. After eighteen months of digging, Frank Wilson barely had a net-expenditure case against Scarface Al.

One evening, after a particularly trying and desperate day's work, Wilson stumbled onto a dusty, brown-paper-wrapped package in an old filing cabinet. Curiosity turned to destiny when, upon opening the package, Wilson discovered a financial ledger from Capone's Hawthorne Smoke Shop casino taken in a raid in 1926 and long dismissed as inconsequential by the state's attorney. To Wilson, however, this was pay dirt. Figures linked to names demonstrated a division of profits directly to Capone and his associates. All the feds needed was for the maker of the books to verify the receivers, and the case could be made. From collected handwriting samples, they quickly identified Leslie Shumway as the maker of the ledgers.

While the search for Shumway was on, Wilson and the SIU looked to hone the case against Jake Guzik. Noting J. C. Dunbar as the maker of many of the cashier's checks attributed to Guzik, they cast yet another dragnet. Checking the Cicero bank where the checks originated, only one of the current tellers professed knowledge of Dunbar. From the mid-1920s, he remembered Dunbar as Fred, a fussy cashier from The Ship casino who always requested crisp, new bills. He provided Wilson with a physical description.

With a tip from O'Hare and a little digging, Wilson and company discovered that Dunbar was Fred Ries. From a separate lead, Wilson learned that Ries was in St. Louis working as an accountant for a local gambler, presumably at the behest of the Chicago mob to hide him from prying SIU eyes. In late August 1930, Wilson and Nels Tessem left for St. Louis, where they monitored mail delivery to the rooming house where Ries lived. Sure of their target, they moved in and detained him as a material witness—just in time, as it turned out, for he had just received a letter from a Guzik relative warning him to travel farther west.

Though the search for Ries originated with the Guzik case, its result touched Frank Nitto first. Initially uncooperative, after several days of languishing in a remote Danville, Illinois, jail cell, Ries admitted his position at The Ship and named the "Big Four" who split proceeds there: Al and Ralph Capone, Jake Guzik, and Frank Nitto. On August 29, the cashier agreed to testify in the Nitto case first.

Finally with a reliable witness, all U.S. Attorney Johnson needed was to track down Nitto. With the murder of Inserra, the Aiello nastiness in a lull, and Chicago authorities still hopping mad about the Lingle case, Nitto left for Florida, staying at the Capone home on Palm Island. Capone was there off and on throughout the summer, and the two laid low and perhaps discussed legal strategy. Through intermediaries, they surely heard of the Ries affair and knew the net was closing. Nonetheless, daily jaunts to the Illinois Golf Association grounds were part of the Enforcer's sunny routine.

———

When the SIU got word that Nitto had decamped to Florida, U.S. Attorney Johnson turned to the Bureau of Investigation (later the FBI). Johnson knew the request would be no easy maneuver. His boss in Washington, Assistant Attorney General

Youngquist, spent days haggling with bureau chief J. Edgar Hoover to provide protection for very apprehensive star witness Fred Ries before Hoover relented. Hoover
equally resisted Johnson's telegram for assistance in apprehending Nitto, arguing
that "this was not a matter coming within the investigative jurisdiction of this
bureau." True enough, since the bureau at the time only covered matters that did not
fall within the jurisdiction of other agencies—issues such as white slavery, motor
vehicle theft violations, Bank Act violations, and anti-trust matters.

Johnson, however, implored the bureau chief, arguing that the Nitto case overshadowed the usual type of investigation carried out to locate fugitives in cases of
lesser importance. Receiving no answer, Johnson went to boss Youngquist. In early
October, the FBI agent in charge in Chicago received the 1927 photo of Frank Nitto
and was instructed to apprehend him.

Johnson's assistant Dwight Green outlined the case for the FBI. One of the first
stops for bureau agents was a check for fingerprints, but as Nitto had long anticipated this, they found none. The agents fanned out, questioning Nitto's local relations and obtaining a photo of Frank and wife Anna for the records. From there, they
traced Nitto's lineage to New York and his sister, Anna Vollaro. Working the tidbit
that Nitto had decamped to Florida, the Chicago office forwarded Frank and Anna's
photo to the Jacksonville field office, which would direct the investigation in that
state. Agents staked out the sleazy Roamer Inn in Michigan City, Indiana, for days
after they discovered it was a likely mob meeting place. Everywhere the agents
looked, they found no sign of Nitto.

With the Lingle affair still running hot, Nitto's evasion turned the fervor of local
law against the Chicago mob up a notch. Joining the crusade in mid-September,
Municipal Court Judge John Lyle employed a unique stratagem to deal with local
hoods. A long-faced fellow, a "defender of faith" and "savior," Lyle was one of the few
who practiced true war against organized crime. Possessing "independence and
vigor"—and sometimes going so far as to ignore basic rights—Lyle, in his six years
on the bench, frequently demanded excessively high bonds for crooks on even
minor charges. For lawyers he proved equally difficult. On one occasion he admonished an attorney presenting his client's case: "Don't interrupt me. I'm not going to
be pushed around by lawyers who . . . have been known for years as representing the
underworld in court." Not surprisingly the Chicago Bar refused to endorse him for
re-election, viewing him as lacking "judicial temperament."

Nonetheless, Lyle gained enormous press coverage and popularity through his
new vagrancy warrant campaign. No doubt utilizing the *Daily News* and Chicago
Crime Commission lists of notorious characters, he issued vagrancy warrants in
those names, demanding high bond, usually $10,000. If the crook paid, he would
then be forced to explain his income—which was, of course, illegal, thereby allowing authorities to press more charges. If the detainee could not make bond, he withered in jail, at least off the streets.

Armed with the new vagrancy warrants, detectives, accompanied by U.S. marshals, surrounded and stormed the Lexington Hotel, targeting Frank Nitto. After
sweeping several floors, the posse was informed by the hotel manager that Nitto had

not been around for months. A couple of days later, acting on a tip that Nitto was back in town, SIU agent Clarence Converse led federal men and city detectives into the Carleon Hotel, a block from the Lexington on Wabash Avenue. They found a bevy of scantily dressed women roaming the halls. Only a few men were taken, including Charlie Fischetti, and Tony Tagenti, a supposed Capone gang bondsman. Particularly disturbing to the law enforcement officers was a supposedly secret, complete list of hoodlums for whom vagrancy warrants had been issued that was found in Tagenti's room. The list identically matched the one possessed by the detective bureau. Converse remained convinced of Nitto's recent presence and concluded that he escaped the hotel raids through some "subterranean passage."

Continuing to press Nitto's underworld associates from all sides, Converse and agents raided a speakeasy up the street from the Carleon Hotel. There, they arrested Jake Guzik's brothers Sam and Harry, both minor cogs in the gang machinery. Only days before, the Treasury Department authorized criminal proceedings against Jack for income tax evasion. Outside the speakeasy in a waiting car, they arrested Robert Barton, Jake Guzik's sometime chauffeur, whom authorities suspected at least knew of Guzik's transactions. On September 30 the SIU arrested Guzik himself.

—⚞⚟—

With two of the gang's big four caught, SIU chief Irey remembered, perhaps with a trace of frustration, "if we could catch him [Nitto] the decks would be cleared for the major soiree, a joust with the Big Guy himself." But "desultory" is how the *Daily News* summed up the search for Nitto in mid-September.

Rumor floated to federal authorities that Nitto might be angling to flee the country; otherwise, the FBI had been able to develop little else on his whereabouts. Aided by a $1,000 reward put up by a committee within the Chicago Association of Commerce for information leading to the arrest of Frank Nitto, the Treasury Department began a nation-wide sweep for the fugitive hoodlum, distributing 150,000 wanted posters (10,000 around the Chicago area). Alarmed, Nitto made the next move. Through back channels, he slipped word to the local FBI office that he might surrender if the original bond of $50,000 were reduced by half. This information was relayed to Assistant U.S. Attorney Green, who refused as a matter of policy. His office, he said, was "reluctant" to negotiate with gangsters. Further, as Green noted, Ralph Capone's bond was held at $35,000, and the feds considered Nitto a more desperate character.

In Chicago, U.S. Attorney Johnson turned to Capone and Guzik tracker Frank Wilson for help in the hopes that his undercover man Malone might find some trace to follow. Malone reported that he spotted Nitto at or near "Camp Capone" on two occasions. Once, while in the Lexington Hotel, he was invited upstairs to Capone's fourth-floor suite for a birthday party for Capone's enforcer, Frank Nitto. The second encounter, apparently more recent, had taken place on the second floor of the Little Florence Italian Grill across Michigan Avenue from the Lexington. Al decided to throw a large gala dinner to celebrate Guzik's release on bond. Afterward, Malone was able to phone Wilson with a report: Nitto had changed his appearance slightly by growing a thick, neatly trimmed mustache (which one reporter thought "softened the hard lines about his mouth") and had perhaps dyed his hair darker. Not much of a disguise, but for Nitto it was enough, since law enforcement possessed few photos of him. And of course his a physical description—a short, swarthy Italian with dark hair—matched a great many members of the Italian community.

On the inside of Capone's organization, Wilson had someone he saw rarely but with whom, through a mutual acquaintance, he maintained in constant contact. This man, dog-track mogul Eddie O'Hare, was, according to Wilson, "the most important single factor resulting in the conviction of Al Capone," but he was tied to Nitto's business as well. Wilson said O'Hare came forward voluntarily through St. Louis newspaper man John Rogers. O'Hare's reasons for doing so remain ambiguous. Explaining his desire to Wilson one day over lunch, O'Hare claimed he was coerced into accepting his role with the gang, and now he wanted to break away so he could send his son to the U.S. Naval Academy in Annapolis, Maryland. This, he believed, was impossible as long as Capone was connected in any way to his name, so O'Hare began feeding Wilson tidbits about the gang.

SIU agents for some time had been suspicious of Louis Greenberg. At least some of the cashier's checks found during the Nitto investigation suggested a connection between profits from the Hawthorne Kennel Club and Louis Greenberg's Roosevelt Finance Company. The investigators suspected a connection to Capone. "As a matter of fact," observed SIU agent A. P. Madden, "there is fairly convincing proof that substantial sums were paid to Frank Nitto." They monitored his phone calls, several of which were to Capone, and when SIU agents dropped by Roosevelt Finance to snoop, Greenberg, they noted, became nervous and evasive of their inquiries. Though lacking the manpower to press him full time, agents tailed him and noted the addresses he visited.

What happened next has been told with many variations over the years by those involved. Certainly, all accounts have some foundation of truth, and no single version is absolute—rather, a series of events led to Nitto's arrest.

Wilson's undercover man, according to Irey, was the most responsible. While hanging around the Lexington Hotel, Malone learned that many gangsters chose to live away from the city in the quiet, tree-lined western suburbs. "Don't look for him in the Loop," Malone's source, a newspaper reporter, whispered. "Watch Cicero, Burnham, Berwyn, Stickney, and adjoining towns." From the same source, Malone also learned that Nitto owned two vehicles, one of which was a black Ford sedan with Wisconsin license plates to divert attention. The reporter also gave him the plate number of the sedan.

A check of the plate registration revealed, not surprisingly, a phony name. Malone, temporarily off duty from his Lexington Hotel beat, began checking with local postmasters for clues. One late-October day in Berwyn, the next town west of Cicero, Malone spotted the Nitto car. Armed with a photo of Nitto and his wife provided by Wilson, he recognized the "very pretty woman" at the wheel as Anna Nitto. Malone swiftly hailed a passing truck. Flashing his badge, he ordered the driver (a mechanic taking a client vehicle for test drive) to follow the black Ford.

It turned out to be a long day for the driver. For hours they followed Anna, at one point momentarily losing her in Cicero traffic before catching sight of her again as she headed off to the grocery store and a three-hour session at a local beauty parlor. Probably warned to be cautious by her husband, she took a round-about route through the country before returning to their Berwyn apartment building on South Clinton Avenue. Malone followed at a distance. When she stopped, agents recognized the address as one of the same ones to which they had tailed Greenberg previously. They watched Mrs. Nitto cart groceries inside and saw her open a front window.

The SIU felt fairly certain Nitto was now within their grasp. Wilson reported to SIU chief Irey: "We have been devoting considerable time in an attempt to locate Mr. Frank Nitti and believe that he will be apprehended within a few days, unless something unexpected happens."

Immediately, Malone and Nels Tessem, the man who originally cracked the paper trail, staked out the building. They gained permission to use a church belfry kitty-corner from the Nitto apartment building as a vantage point. After three long, cold October nights with no sign of Nitto, the pair was able to rent an apartment directly across the street. Careful not to tip their hand lest someone there warn Nitto, they told the landlady they were watching a certain mailbox so that she would think they were postal inspectors. Sure they had the right target, but absent the gangster, investigators decided to snoop further for verification. Again sensitive to disturbing someone who might tip off the couple, they thought they could not enter the Nittos' apartment building directly, so Malone came up with a novel alternative: they pushed the Nitto sedan in front of a fire hydrant and called in an alarm. From the firemen who asked the astonished Anna to move her vehicle, Malone and Tessem learned that she was Mrs. Ralph Belmont as well as the "Belmont" apartment number.

Soon after, agents observed Greenberg at the apartment building. Suspecting that something might be about to occur, the agents saw a man with a mustache they thought was Nitto entering the South Clinton building just after midnight on October 31. Using field glasses, they peered through blinds carelessly left open and saw Nitto helping himself to a late night snack. Confident,Confident their prey was comfortably settling in for a stay, about 2 a.m. Malone and Tessem called Pat Roche, an ex-federal agent who was now chief investigator for the state's attorney's office.

Just the sound of the phone at that hour agitated Roche: "Now what the hell at this time of morning?" Roche's attitude changed, however, when he realized it was the feds. Roche had already had a busy night: when the phone rang, he had just hauled in O'Donnell gunner James "Fur" Sammons, who was wanted for questioning in the shooting of a policeman. Roche nabbed him no more than a few blocks from the Nitto stakeout. With word from Tessem, he and a detail of detectives were headed right back out on a tip that Nitto was finally cornered.

With Malone remaining in the shadows across the street so as not to compromise his identity—he was still on the Capone case—Tessem and Roche led the detective squad into Nitto's building. Two men covered the exits, while the remainder jimmied

172

the apartment building door open. Stealthily, they made their way up to the "Belmont" apartment. A detective knocked on the door.

A male voice answered: "Who's there?"

"The police. Open the door."

"Who are you looking for?"

"Who are you," responded the detective.

"My name's Belmont."

"Which Belmont?"

"The well-known Belmont, you son of a bitch," a perturbed Nitto replied. "Come on in."

The detectives entered and surveyed an apartment richly furnished with fancy rugs and a few pieces of ornate furniture, though some crates remained unpacked. Obviously, the couple had arrived recently. As the nervous young wife stood nearby, her husband, in pajamas, continued his ruse. Dwarfed by the detectives, Nitto protested the intrusion and claimed to be a respectable businessman, perhaps offering a business card as proof. The detectives challenged his identity. The standoff continued at the door. Then Pat Roche entered. At that moment, Nitto knew the game was over.

⟞∘⟨∘⟩∘⟝

When Nitto was apprehended, a last piece of gang business for the feds was concluded; for Capone, there would be few, if any, external agitations with the Enforcer detained. Since Patsy Lolordo's murder in January 1929, gaining control of the Unione Siciliana seemed impossible for Nitto's boss. The St. Valentine's Day Massacre and resulting heat kept the gang off balance. While Capone was in jail for a year, pest Joe Aiello probably emerged to gain control of the Unione. Reports had it that he was attempting to wrestle away the Melrose Park and Chicago Heights booze business. Worse yet, his travels may have included the northern suburbs and points as far away as Minnesota to see Bugs Moran, who fled Chicago after the massacre. Capone learned this from Moran defector Ted Newberry. The Capone gang decided on the decisive and proper cure to this annoyance.

Locating Aiello, however, had always proven difficult at best for Nitto's boss. In the past, the gang was often left meting out retaliation against the Aiello family business on Division Street while the head always survived to agitate another day. Resurgent once again despite his 1927 eviction notice, Joe Aiello treaded Chicago's streets gingerly. After his bodyguard Anthony Spano was killed in September, he set up residence concealed within the Prestigiacomo (Presto to most) household at 205 North Kolmar on the Far West Side.

Sandwiched on a stretch of Kolmar between Maypole Avenue to the north and West End Avenue to the south, the location was a cramped, post-World War I apartment building of tan brick. The family occupied a front-facing first-floor section furnished to suit a successful businessmen's family: a rich $1,000 davenport rested against the front wall, a $500 Morris chair kept it company, while an ornate $1,000 radio cabinet rested nearby. The head of the household could afford such

173

luxuries, for he partnered with Aiello in his importing business. Comfortable within, an apparently angst-ridden Aiello hadn't stirred much from the Presto family residence. Once in a while, Aiello's wife and child visited him there—a possibly fatal mistake. The Capone organization no doubt followed the movements of those connected to Aiello and had already staked out similar locations in an attempt to locate him.

The Presto windows faced west; across the street was number 202 Kolmar, a three-story building of efficiency apartments. About the time Aiello moved into his hideaway, a "good-looking young man" who gave his name as Morris Friend approached landlord Mrs. Harriet Lasson about a room. She showed him a second-floor room overlooking the front of number 205. He liked it and paid his rent in advance. Soon, another man moved in. They were well liked by the neighbors— courteous and pleasant, they seemed nice enough, and though few saw them much, they were stationed at the front window, watching and waiting.

Days later, after confirming the location of Aiello, a fine-looking fellow named Henry Jacobson approached the owners of the apartment building at 4518 West End Avenue and rented a third-floor room. His rear kitchen windows looked in a northerly direction over a sliver of a courtyard below separating the West End building from the Presto residence beyond. One, maybe two men waited here, with Mr. Jacobson on watch. Just as in the Weiss ambush, the crosshairs were in place.

On the evening of October 23, Aiello left the Presto home. In his possession was a train ticket to St. Louis along with an address in Brownsville, Texas—possibly a layover on his way to Mexico. After supper with his business partner, he directed one of the women to call for a cab.

Driver James Ruane of the Yellow Cab Company received the call and arrived ten minutes later. No fare appeared, but through the Presto front window, the cabbie saw figures moving about. He waited a minute, and then, double-checking the address, Ruane left the cab to have a try inside. In the vestibule, he could hear conversation and stirring within the Presto apartment, but he still received no response. Perhaps sensing a false alarm, Ruane returned to his cab as Aiello, his hat low and his coat collar turned up, emerged from the building.

With Aiello still at the doorway, Ruane opened the passenger-side door when a burst of machine gun fire whizzed over his head toward the Sicilian. Ruane crouched behind his vehicle as another burst flared. Aiello groaned loudly as he twisted and pitched from the impacts. He frantically fidgeted for his weapon and staggered toward the rear of the West End building, seeking refuge in its shadows. When he did, Ruane recalled seeing "sharp brilliant flashes" from the West End apartment. The firing angle was so steep from above that machine-gun slugs actually tore through the top of Aiello's hat. It was the end of the line for Joe Aiello, age forty, who was filled, as one policeman at the scene described, with "a ton of lead." The fifty-plus .45-caliber slugs embedded in his body surpassed any individual count from the St. Valentine's Day Massacre.

Though one press story pitched the Moran gang as the responsible party, detectives observed that the precision machine gun ambush was a typical Capone trademark. In the Kolmar nest, they found the usual litter of cigarette stubs and cartridge shells along with one ironic touch: one of the killers was reading Rudyard Kipling's *Soldiers Three*. He never finished; when he pulled the trigger on his target, the book lay open at the next chapter, "His Chance in Life."

The day after Aiello's murder, Malone spotted Mrs. Nitto, and Nitto's days were numbered.

13

DESTINATION: "THE BIG TOP"

AS MUCH AS NITTO'S CAPTURE was a coup for the tax men, locals thought it a boon too. They could parade a "public enemy" wanted for questioning in the Lingle and Zuta murders and now the machine-gun murder of Joe Aiello. After a few hours in Roche's office and the detective bureau, U.S. marshals whisked Nitto to the Federal Building where he was officially arrested on tax charges. Local SIU Chief A. P. Madden and Assistant U.S. Attorney Green grilled him; the tax men were soon joined in interrogating Nitto by the immigration service. Only the next day did the world receive the first real biographic pieces information on the Enforcer.

Authorities set Nitto's bond at $50,000 and whisked him off to Cook County Jail for holding. When the almighty Enforcer, remained all weekend in lockup, the press quickly capitalized on the public's fascination with gangland, running headlines such as "NITTI, CAPONE AIDE, FAILS TO GIVE BOND AND STAYS IN JAIL." After all, the press noted, Ralph Capone and Jake Guzik posted bonds and walked free. Even when Jake's much lesser-known brother Sam was hauled in on tax charges, he walked as well. The *Herald and Examiner* noted that Nitto was "the first of his lieutenants whom Capone has allowed to see the inside of a jail cell when it was possible to keep him out."

That boss Capone failed to bail out his valued Enforcer signaled to some a rift between the two men, a theory reinforced by a story about a month earlier that had Capone urging Nitto to give himself up because of the police crackdowns. It was said that Capone would kill him if he didn't. Another view held that the gang's finances had been strained trying to keep up with all the arrests. Certainly many of Capone's allies were falling to Lyle's vagrancy warrant campaign. A few days after Nitto's arrest, police raided his old Naples Restaurant hangout, where they nabbed big-shot Frank Rio, Nitto aide Paul Ricca, gunman Murray Humphreys and his apprentice sidekick Ralph Pierce, and two Capone-sponsored politicians, Alderman and state Representative Al Prignano and state Representative Roland Libonati.

On the other hand, some saw this refusal to make bond as a shrewd move on Nitto's part. Why peel off cash wads to gain freedom when, in fact, one is faced with tax evasion charges? A show of wealth was incredibly poor judgment in view of any defense to made in the future. Instead, Nitto let lawyer Benjamin Epstein argue for a reduction in bond. Nitto appeared in court with his attorney on November 1, a silent, but dapper figure. A press spectator commented:

> Nitti stood in court, a velvet glove over an iron hand. . . . There was about him no suggestion of the grim name—the Enforcer—he won in the Capone organization.

Federal Appeals Court judge Even A. Evans's denial of the request showed the soundness of this strategy when he noted that the Nitto motion "did not show what property is owned by Nitti or what amount of bail could be posted by him."

Nitto's strategy for making bond now turned to locating friendly property owners for donations and raising the difference through a surety company, making certain there was nothing in his name—he would not duplicate the mistakes of Ralph Capone and Jake Guzik. Nitto also knew that as soon as he left federal custody, Chicago police were sure to slap him with one of Judge Lyle's vagrancy warrants. That would require another $10,000 bond. Colonel Henry Barrett Chamberlain of the Chicago Crime Commission also thought it a good move on Nitto's part, but from an entirely different perspective. If Nitto bailed out on the federal charge and could not make bail on the vagrancy warrant, he might just end up spending the weekend in detective lockup downtown with a bunch of riffraff—Cook County Jail seemed a much preferable place to stay.

On November 7, Nitto obtained release through bonds posted by the Grand Central Surety Company of New York. This maneuver caused yet another flap for Chicago and later Nitto. Surety companies were a relatively new business. Cloaked from view of the law, a defendant could put up unseen collateral with a surety company which would, in turn, produce the bond. When the defendant walked out of court, if he ran from the law, he forfeited the collateral to the surety company. There was no risk on company's the part, whereas, at least with a bondsman, if the defendant ran, he personally stood to lose.

For a moment, the city forgot about Capone. The previously indiscernible Nitto was now ranked by one paper as "great a menace to society as exists in Chicago." As Nitto stepped from the Federal Building, as expected, a pair of detectives met him on the steps. Nitto greeted sergeants Frank Kehoe and Edward McVeagh with the word, "All right, now you boys take me," and they did just that, arresting him on

Lyle's vagrancy charge. Nitto produced the bond and expected to walk free, but the name on the bond, "Nitti," did not match the name on the warrant, "Nitto," his actual name. A legal technicality, but the gaffe cost him a few more hours in jail.

Nobody could argue that Judge John Lyle lacked nerve in the fight on crime, least of all Frank Nitto, who remained free for all of three days. When the flap over the surety bond practices reached New York, Grand Central Surety's president called in all bonds on notorious Chicago hoodlums. Nitto and Frank Rio both were ordered back to court to confront Judge Lyle. Nitto arrived in a three-piece suit, still sporting his moustache. Prepared, he and his lawyer presented a bond financed by a Good Samaritan's property. Lyle scrutinized the document and discovered a technicality, rejecting the bond as Nitto stood in amazement. Lyle explained, the bond lacked a returnable date—that is, the date on which Nitto was due back in court. Additionally, the cantankerous, crusading judge ruled that the property set forth had not been investigated for encumbrances so there was no way of knowing what it was really worth. In court, Lyle verbally shoved Nitto around, declaring, "I will extend no courtesy to this gangster. Meanwhile, have this man taken down to the Bureau of Identification. Have him photographed and fingerprinted like any criminal."

Press photographer Tony Berardi, famous for his camera work throughout Chicago's 1920s gangland period, remembered the scene. As Detective John Grace inked Nitto's prints, Berardi arrived to snap a picture. Loathing the publicity, Nitto refused to pose. Berardi remembered Lyle admonishing the gangster, "Hey you, pose!" Nitto didn't growl or get angry like some hoods, Berardi recalled sixty-five years later, but "you could tell he didn't like it." Berardi then snapped perhaps the first candid Nitto picture for the world to see.

After a few hours, Nitto's lawyers raced back into court with yet another property bond, this time after Lyle's session was finished. A different judge released their client by dinnertime. He could read the evening paper, knowing Jake Guzik's tax evasion trial had started that day.

A week after gaining his freedom, a nattily dressed Nitto with hair slicked back appeared before Lyle on the vagrancy charge. His lawyer immediately petitioned for a change in venue. A surprised Lyle asked, "Is this man out on bond?" When Lyle reviewed the previous bond (approved by another judge), he ruled that it also was not entirely free of encumbrances and ordered Nitto back to jail. Protesting Lyle's blistering action, Nitto attorney Michael Goldberg, who had anticipated such a Lyle outburst, presented a backup bond which he said was free and clear and had been approved by the bond court earlier. Lyle's temper detonated: "That doesn't mean anything to me. Get a new bond here and submit it to . . . the prosecutor's bond department." When Goldberg protested on behalf of his client, Lyle exploded further: "The character of this man is such he should not be allowed out on anything. . . . A man who is head of a band of murderers should be shown no consideration whatsoever." Lyle's obstinacy produced the outcome he had desired all along, namely, forcing Nitto to pay his $10,000 bond in cash.

No doubt, Nitto's eyes focused on the outcome of the Guzik tax matter. According to presiding federal Judge Charles E. Woodward, the Capone Outfit made a roundabout attempt to fix the matter for Guzik at the federal level sometime in October, which ultimately could have swayed the legal action against Nitto as well. Shortly before the November elections in Illinois, an individual with such high political influence that he could appoint cronies to the Prohibition service approached Woodward with a scheme. If he Woodward would put the Guzik case off until February 1931, the individual would deliver a substantial number of votes that otherwise might go to the Republican Party. When Woodward refused, the individual assumed a rather threatening tone, as if he might be able to bring about some unfavorable political action. The topic, Woodward later heard, was relayed and discussed at a "Capone meeting." The reason became clear to Woodward when he read in the newspaper in February 1931 that the intermediary who had offered the deal was to be appointed collector of internal revenue for the First District of Illinois, which included Chicago. Woodward remembered thinking that if such an impending disaster happened, "that is the end of income tax prosecutions of gangsters in this locality." When Woodward notified higher authorities, the appointment was withdrawn in April 1931.

Guzik's trial proceeded grimly, for Nitto as well as for Guzik. On November 14, the prosecution's star witness, Fred Ries, testified about the role of the Big Four in Cicero gambling. When the details of cash transfers were exposed, Guzik's defense counsel countered with witnesses who testified about Guzik's heavy gambling losses, saying they thought Guzik was a sap for regularly betting upwards of $1,000 per race on the wrong horse. That, however, wouldn't absolve him, and it took a jury just a few hours to find him guilty on three counts of tax evasion. On December 5, Guzik received the harshest tax-related penalty to date when Woodward sentenced him to five years and a day in prison coupled with a fine of $17,500. As Ralph Capone had done, Guzik filed appealed the decision.

=≈≈=

Nitto attorney Benjamin Epstein approached George Johnson with an offer that his client would plead guilty in exchange for one year in prison. Johnson refused on the grounds that the precedent in similar cases was a minimum term of eighteen months. Johnson did, however, relay the enticing offer of at least getting the Enforcer behind bars to agents of the SIU, and together they formulated a compromise offer. Johnson offered eighteen months but with special consideration for parole after one year if:

1) Nitto promised to aid in full settlement of his tax liability,
2) agreed to pay a $10,000 fine,
3) and promised to leave Chicago and his gangland career to pursue a "useful life."

The feds considered the offer a reasonable one for several reasons. First, the federal workload was increasing because of an increasing "number of indictments against men of the same occupation, or similar, and of similar character," including several corrupt Chicago politicians and contractors. Both Ralph and Guzik had elected to battle through the appeals process, and Johnson recognized the risk of losing at least part of the convictions given the unsolved question of whether tax evasion was a misdemeanor or a felony. Further, in Nitto's case, while the government had Ries as a witness, he could only testify about the income Nitto derived from gambling operations. The bulk of his income, on the other hand, came from alcohol, and Johnson was afraid that the lone grand jury witness for that would likely not hold up in court. That left the prosecutors much less than they had hoped for.

Five days before Christmas, Nitto appeared in federal court with attorney Epstein. One reporter pronounced his appearance as that of an "opera singer." He was clean-shaven and wore a brown suit of expensive material, a green tie, and shiny shoes topped by spats. In his hand he carried a gray fedora. Nitto and Epstein waited an hour or so before Judge Woodward called the case.

"I wish to withdraw the demurrer to the indictment," Epstein announced, "and present my client for a plea in arraignment."

Woodward granted the motion and asked how the defendant how he would plead.

"Guilty," Nitto responded.

As Johnson's assistants outlined the case before Woodward, citing Nitto's income as more than $700,000, Epstein wisely objected: "We do not admit guilt as to the to-wit account. We do as to failure to file. Those boxcar figures are always a matter of controversy. I am making this statement because of the possibility of clearing the civil liability." He did not, he said, wish to forfeit any rights in civil proceedings.

The deal was ambiguous and open to legal question. The defense apparently never specified to what they were pleading guilty, whether it was the tax evasion or failure to file charges. Complicating matters greatly, in announcing the proposed sentence for Nitto as eighteen months, neither prosecuting attorneys nor defense attorney Epstein apparently informed the court of the Johnson deal. Woodward accepted the eighteen-month recommendation and it was entered into the record as is—an omission of far-reaching consequence for Frank Nitto. Prosecutors said that "while the sentence may not be adequate for the crime charges, I believe it will satisfy the ends of justice." The judge allowed the defense motion to postpone execution of sentence until January 10, 1931.

Nitto was much more expansive outside court than prosecution. In a speech in which he appeared to be an "educated man"—though the words were at least partially contrived by his lawyers—Nitto announced:

> I talked with a half a dozen attorneys and they didn't know any more than I did. In 1926 the Circuit Court of Appeals held that income from illicit sources could not be taxed. The next year the Supreme Court ruled differently. I have never committed a crime of moral turpitude. I have never done anything that is condemned by society as morally wrong. I didn't pay income taxes because the laws were not clear. But if society demands a penalty from me, I am glad to pay it.

Another source quoted him as wanting to "get it over with." Months of uncertainty did not appeal to the Enforcer. One press tabloid hailed the court proceedings, saying, "Frank Nitti, 'brains' of the Capone gang, used his celebrated wits today in a 'bargain' with the government." However, the press knew nothing of the Johnson deal, and so as far as anyone knew, Nitto's Chicago gang days were finished.

⟨⟨⟩⟩

Was there something more to Nitto's adroit maneuver? He was certainly brainy enough, after having viewed the government's success in both the Ralph Capone and Jake Guzik trials, to know that his was also lost. Some press jabberwocky still played the Capone-Nitto feud. Nitto, the story goes, jailed himself to save his life. At the very least, his meek showing in jail, they thought, signaled he was taking the rap at Capone's insistence to take the heat off. This implies Capone sacrificed him, but for whom—Guzik or his not-so-bright brother? Not likely, but there may have been some Capone-friendly component to Nitto's making a deal.

Capone knew that he was now the primary target and was searching for a way out or, at the very least, a way to draw minimum time behind bars and attempt to keep the Big Four more or less intact as the most viable gang leaders. Nitto's maneuver at least proved the feds were open to negotiation. In the meantime, the appeals by Jack and Ralph might open some new tack in fighting the tax laws. And Capone in February 1931, as far as he knew, might still be able to work on a more "understanding" man as collector of local revenue and effect a possible fed fix.

That month also might prove significant in another matter: U.S. District Attorney George E. Q. Johnson would be up for re-appointment. From the gang's view, it was quite possible that if for some reason Johnson's endorsement fell short—combined with their efforts to put a fix in on the revenue collector position—they might all catch a break and Nitto might return to Chicago. If all failed, Nitto would do his shortened stint, and Capone still might not see the inevitable indictment and trial for months. Even then, if he were found guilty and sentenced to jail, stalling on appeals could potentially add a few more weeks of freedom, invaluable time that would allow the leadership of the gang to transition more efficiently and more than enough time for veteran Nitto to complete his proposed sentence.

George Murray, in his *Legacy of Al Capone*, concluded as much. Capone, he said, wanted to delay any entry into prison so that Nitto could be released and take over the gang. Was this part of a long-range plan? In late 1930, did Nitto hope to retain great influence over the gang in some fashion after the tax mess cleared? No one knows the sincerity of Nitto's pledge to stay away from Chicago or knows for sure whether the feds had the ability to enforce the decree. But with the Big Four along with Sam Guzik and Tony "Mops" Volpe under federal pressure, a *Daily News* reporter noted Charlie Fischetti, Frank Rio, and Frank Diamond as the most capable lieutenants left to run the empire.

After spending the holidays with family, Nitto, accompanied by lawyer Benjamin Epstein, reported to the office of the U.S. marshal on the afternoon of January 10. As usual, Nitto attired himself richly, even carrying an expensive clothes grip for the trip. It was Deputy Marshal Joseph Spizzeri who escorted Nitto to Union Station to catch the Burlington to the United States Penitentiary in Leavenworth, Kansas. A couple of reporters met them near the track. Nitto was affable, saying, "Well, boys, here I am." They shook hands all around and chitchatted, and then came the cutting question: "Do you think Leo Brothers is the man who killed Jake Lingle?"

Nitto scowled, "Do you think I'm nuts?"

End of interview.

Spizzeri cuffed Nitto to his travel companion, a minor drug peddler destined for a five-year term who was a stark contrast with Nitto in both appearance and prestige. But Nitto had earned the distinction as being the first major Chicago hoodlum to go to prison for income tax evasion.

———◆◆◆———

By an Act of Congress, the Bureau of Prisons became a federal agency to centralize prison management only seven short months prior to Nitto's conviction. Though there were eleven prisons coming under its auspices, the customary course for Frank Nitto or anyone else convicted of a federal crime in Chicago at the time was the most convenient, leading them to one of the mainstays of the system: nestled high upon the western bluffs of the Missouri River and surveying the initial great, westward stretches of the Midwest plain, was the federal penitentiary at Leavenworth, Kansas.

Until 1891, few federal laws existed to be broken, and most of those involved military service. Thus, many "federal prisoners" at the time were soldiers who were housed in military institutions; the few outside the military realm were housed in state prisons, their upkeep paid for by the federal government. Unfortunately, a great deal of corruption permeated the state level. For example, wardens appointed by state governors were known at times to lease prisoners to local businesses as cheap labor. Congress stepped in, enacting legislation to establish the basis for a federally run prison system. Establishing a trio of prisons to serve three geographic regions—East, Midwest, and West—was more than ample at the time. The proposed Midwest site was very near the place where, almost seventy years before, Colonel Henry Leavenworth and 188 men of the Third Infantry Regiment had established a protective enclave along the Oregon and Santa Fe trails that was named after the colonel: Fort Leavenworth.

In 1895, Congress transferred the military prison there to the control of the Department of Justice and a year later authorized construction of a replacement facility. St. Louis architect William S. Eames designed "a marvel of custodial architecture." The enormous administrative building would look much like a state capitol building when finished and was so unique at the time that it would be a tourist hotspot throughout its first decade. From the center of its great length, two five-story cellblocks accommodating 1,200 prisoners stretched to the rear at forty-five-degree angles. The walls were thirty-five feet high and extended far below ground, enclosing sixteen acres. The prison was designed to be self-sufficient, with a power plant, hospital, and—a first in penal history—a school inside the walls. Outside the walls, a prison farm produced food.

Shortly after the first prisoners occupied the space in 1903, Leavenworth added yet another mark of distinction to its résumé. When confusion arose as to the identity of prisoner—for instance, when his name and Bertillon (physical) description were identical to those of another prisoner—the warden's son and prison record clerk studied and introduced fingerprinting as a means of identification. Leavenworth became the first prison to identify all its inmates by this method, and because various arms of law enforcement queried those records, it soon became "the Identification Center of the United States."

At the time of Nitto's stay, nearly thirty years after its inception, many parts of the prison were still fairly new. The cellblocks weren't fully completed until 1919, and many of the craft shops were only completed in the late 1920s. The crowning glory to Eames's original blueprint was set only in 1926—the enormous gleaming dome over the central rotunda for which the prison has always been known as the "Big Top."

When Deputy U.S. Marshal Joseph Spizzeri delivered Nitto to the marble-stepped entrance at Leavenworth's doors on January 11, 1931, living conditions there had changed for both better and worse since the prison opened. Nitto traded in his stylish suit for blue cotton prison garb, not erstwhile stripes. Original rules such as "no smoking" and "no talking" had been taken out of force. Cropped haircuts were not necessary. Recreation was allowed, and the prison even had its own baseball team. A prison newspaper circulated, though radio was still prohibited. News from outside the penitentiary walls, if any, reached the men via letters and visitors, and the only real restriction on these avenues of communication came in obtaining clearance for all visitors except family members from Warden Thomas B. White. Otherwise, a prisoner could send letters as long as he maintained a sufficient stamp account, and letters from the outside could be received freely. The food, though far from the big city extravagance to which Nitto was accustomed, was decent.

On the downside, when Nitto entered the prison in 1931, its population had reached the bursting point. For the first two decades of its operation, the prison population hovered slightly above its capacity. Then came Prohibition. Now, nearly 3,000 prisoners crammed the cellblocks and makeshift cells in basements and attics. The prison demographics also shifted toward city dwellers, to whom the rural officials were mostly unaccustomed. Chicagoan Big Tim Murphy served a stretch there for mail robbery, and panderer Mike Heitler did a stint as well. Nevertheless, on the whole, discipline was remarkably relaxed. For example, it was here that convicted killer Robert Stroud was first allowed to keep and study birds, earning him his title "the Birdman." (He was still at Leavenworth when Nitto arrived.) Big Top prison life wasn't all agonizing, as Nitto found out.

On his first day, Nitto was processed. He became prisoner L-38021 and spent the day going through a litany of procedures. He stepped before the camera for identification photos, full frontal and profile, showing a dreary-eyed Nitto sans mustache and clearly reconciled to his new environment. Next, he was fingerprinted and given a medical exam which revealed him to be in good shape. Finally, he was assigned a temporary cell. His strategy upon settling in was simply to play out the system. He possessed a deal with the U.S. attorney for early release, and anyway, by federal law, he was due a parole hearing after doing one-third of his official eighteen-month sentence. If he could keep out of trouble for the next six months, he could get out as soon as possible.

Nitto immediately busied himself with external communications, apparently without censors. He depleted and replenished his stamp fund frequently throughout his stay, particularly during the first six months. The overwhelming majority of his outgoing letters were dispatched to four key individuals, three of whom were above suspicion: 1) wife Anna; 2) father-in-law Gaetano Ronga; 3) lawyer Benjamin Epstein; and 4) the mysterious William Nitto. Occasionally, he sent letters to the older of his Vollaro nephews; Italian friends in Chicago who were not gang members, such as old pal Joseph Vicedomini; Italians in nearby Kansas City whose mob status was unknown; and to an acquaintance in faraway Galveston, Texas, who received an update or two. In return, he received an endless string of correspondence from all points. Seldom did he go two or three days without opening mail from someone, and sometimes he received as many as three or four letters in a single day. The bulk of the letters came from family, with wife Anna sending the vast majority. The Vollaros in New York wrote him regularly, mainly through Nancy Vollaro, the wife of one of the nephews. Nephews Louis in New York and James in Kansas City also wrote.

The primary recipients of Nitto's correspondence also became his vital personal contacts. Claiming to be his brother, William Nitto became his first visitor on January 22. When prison officials discovered that Frank actually had no brothers, they barred William Nitto from future visits, but incoming and outgoing letters bearing the name of the mysterious stranger continued unabated. From the address given, he may have been a member of the Coscioni family who lived at that location, or perhaps someone using that family's address as a mailing point. Joseph Coscioni was a Nitto associate, and among his kinfolk was one William Coscioni. Nitto's wife and lawyer separately trekked to Leavenworth once a month, with Anna usually arriving around the first and Ben Epstein visiting about the middle of the month.

Though much of Nitto's communications are no longer available to determine their substance, it's clear through the remaining record that these key individuals assisted in easing Nitto's current situation and apparently apprised him (as much as possible) of events in Chicago (the latter information probably funneled in through the shadowy William Nitto). However, the main priority for the outsiders by pen or conversation was to get the high and mighty Nitto some breathing space in Leavenworth. Testimony as to the big city hoodlum's early gain of privilege—or at least to lax prison discipline—can be found in the fact that, on two occasions, Anna visited in both the morning and the afternoon. Subsequently, visitors numbered five per month. Then Nitto began receiving his lawyer visits in the warden's office, and most of his other "business" appointments were similarly arranged. Contacts eventually allowed for well-to-do Chicago Italians such as undertaker Joseph Marzano and

high-standing sanitary district trustee and businessman Paul Colianni to pen reference letters on his behalf.

As result of all this lobbying, Nitto landed a plum job away from the jam-packed
interior of the prison as a trusty (a prisoner cleared for less supervision) working outside the prison gates. His spotless record for the first three months doubtless also
helped. A mere week after starting his job, Nitto advanced his trustyship position via
his appointment as personal chauffeur and laundry man for the superintendent of the
prison farm. Dutifully working the next three months in this capacity allowed for the
necessary high praise to favorably gloss a parole report.

If officials at Leavenworth didn't make life unpleasant enough for Nitto, other agencies would at least try. In August 1930, the Chicago Crime Commission under
Henry Barrett Chamberlain had suggested deportation of fugitive Frank Nitto, once
caught, as an appropriate course of legal action. After a review of Nitto's naturalization file, officials in Washington D.C. found that everything checked out okay.
They sent Chamberlain their conclusion: "In view of the above, no deportation proceedings can be instituted against Frank Nitti."

The Naturalization Service retained the transcript of their perfunctory interview
with Nitto after his arrest on tax matters, however, and on November 25, 1930, the
feds revisited the idea of ridding Chicago and the U.S. of any possible Nitto return
to the general population. He could be deported for good if it could be proven that:
1) within the last five years, he left the country and returned combined with a previous conviction; 2) he had racked up more than one conviction since his citizenship; or 3) he had falsified some detail on his papers. An initial search of local police
records produced nothing sensational.

The move was part of an extensive end-of-year sweep of aliens, especially
criminals. The day Nitto boarded the Burlington line to Kansas, a federal train
arrived from Seattle to collect a record load of 125 persons, compliments of the
Chicago District director of naturalization. They were headed for the East Coast
and the nearest outbound ship. The feds decided they might as well use the measure as yet another weapon in their arsenal to help clean out the Capone gang.
Perhaps the first to feel the sting was Mops Volpe, Public Enemy Number Two.
He received his deportation papers, but actual deportation was stalled through
legal action.

In March 1931, the feds more aggressively sought documentation to do the same
to Nitto. A letter date March 7, 1931, from the district director of naturalization in
Kansas City to the director in Washington, D.C., contained the following:

> If the Bureau has not already done so, I believe the suggestion of the Dis-
> trict Director of Immigration (Chicago) . . . that finger print records in the
> Bureau of Investigation be consulted to determine whether Nitti had con-
> tact with law enforcement officers within the five years immediately pre-
> ceding his naturalization, is a good one.

Nitto doubtless received a heads-up on the matter through visitation whispers, for the move was no secret and had been all over the Chicago papers days earlier with headlines such as: "U.S. TO DEPORT NITTI WHEN HE LEAVES PRISON."

Officials could dredge up only the recent 1930 arrests, but this was not good enough. With two avenues of deportation apparently closed, the feds had only the application slip-up angle to pursue. Curiously, though, the department remained nearly motionless on the matter until June.

═══◦/◦/◦═══

While Nitto perfected model prison behavior, Chicago, not unexpectedly, welcomed a new city leader on April 6. In Mayor Thompson's latest term, he assuredly transformed the skyline of Chicago, but citizens at the outset of the Depression had grown weary of his administration's bungling and corruption and the overall crime conditions. By 1931, Cook County Board Chairman Anton "Tony" Cermak sensed the time was ripe to become Chicago's mayor. Everyone who had ever know him knew the Bohemian Democrat was ambitious, but the road up was never easy. As a teenager, he came to the city after working the coal mines of Braidwood, Illinois, a community sixty or so miles southwest of Chicago. Settling in the Bohemian Pilsen district, the physically tough young man worked as a railroad brakeman and later drove a team of horses pulling the Blue Island Avenue street-car. At the same time he joined a gang of young Czech men who staked out their favorite saloon, spending their after hours drinking and brawling (habits he had acquired in Braidwood).

Marriage helped rid him of his rowdy ways, and the young couple moved to the Bohemian community of Lawndale on the Far West Side. Instead of working for someone else, Cermak decided to buy the horse he had driven for the streetcar company and run his own hauling and wood business. Crafting contacts along the way, he became the budding community's spokesman, and as precinct committeeman, he fought for basic improvement such as sidewalks, pavement, and sewers, giving the Czech society its only real say in politics at the time. When he was voted to the state legislature in 1902 and took office as city alderman in 1909 as a Democrat, he owed no debt to any outside political power.

Despite an acknowledged lack of education and social refinement that effectively gilded public office seekers, Cermak continued to be re-elected time and again. "I believe," he analyzed later, "I understood the people better and had much common sense." Another observed of him, "He didn't want to seem other than a rough, ordinary guy, speaking for the man on the street."He campaigned vigorously each election, taking nothing for granted and was also able to buck the political shifts that periodically cost many incumbents their jobs. For example, when Teddy Roosevelt's overwhelming Republican landslide swept in, Cermak was the only Democrat from his district to survive.

Locally, Cermak shrewdly balanced among all sides of the Democratic Party. In 1911, he supported Harrison for mayor, though the candidate had long split from Illinois Democratic power boss Sullivan. In 1912, he ran for Municipal Court bailiff, opposing Sullivan's candidate in the primary, and won the position while still supporting the Democratic Party as a whole. By this time, he was recognized as running one of the best Democratic wards in the city. In the 1915 mayoral election, he backed neither Democrat candidate Sweitzer nor the Republican, Thompson. He was powerful enough to take on winner Thompson's political maneuvering to enforce the Dry laws, and he won again. In 1918, he ran for Cook County sheriff on Sullivan's ticket against a candidate pushed by his previous ally Harrison, losing to the Republican candidate in the general election by just over 3,000 votes (out of nearly 250,000 cast). That and a narrow escape from graft and corruption charges were his only real career setbacks.

In 1922 Cermak was solidly entrenched in the traditional Sullivan-Brennan Democratic camp. They nominated him for president of the county board and chairman of their party committee. He was also the Democratic leader on the city council. His election as head of the county board illustrated that he had learned well the shrewd and crafty game of politics. At the time Republicans, riding Thompson's power, held an eight to seven advantage on the board; yet, Cermak seeing a split amongst the Republicans for leadership was able to coax a lone Republican vote and enable his election. As "Mayor of Cook County," he expanded his offices to include the presidency of the Board of Forest Preserve Commissioners, and thereby gave himself the opportunity to give out many more jobs for favors. He dished these out fairly, attempting to make Democrats out of nominal Republicans.

After two terms of flagrant abuses in the Thompson administration, the Democrats sought the mayor's chair in 1923. Cermak sought the nomination but was rebuffed by party elders, who felt that the winner of the race would be someone who did not appear to be a professional politician and whose nationality would be well recognized by the voting populace. They thought a Bohemian stood little chance of winning among the heavily Irish, German, and Scandinavian majorities. Despite getting the cold shoulder, Cermak supported Dever and the Democrat was elected with heavy pluralities in the Lawndale district. Though the Democrats gained the mayor's office, a year later, they lost nearly across the board in state and county elections.

Cermak continually promoted his Wet campaign, even going so far to criticize fellow Democrat Dever and his cleanup efforts for nearly always picking on the little guy. Cermak agreed with the prevailing thought that gangsters and the Prohibition crime wave were linked, but he blamed the Volstead Act rather than police and corrupt politicians. His fervent Wet stance, says his biographer Alex Gottfried, along with his high position in the county, led many to the belief that Cermak ran the county outside the city, particularly the wide-open suburbs of Cicero and Stickney, in league with Prohibition gangsters. While Cermak did not have control over law enforcement in these areas, he could have wielded considerable influence upon the state's attorney and sheriff to clean out the burgs. That he did not exercise this influence suggests his complicity with the gangs, but he likely was not working with them—in fact, the suggested collusion that would haunt his legacy was said to have troubled him considerably.

Nonetheless, in 1927 he made the Wet plank and "personal liberty" his primary Democratic election issue when the mayor's chair was again up for grabs. When Dever again got the Democratic nod, Cermak's support was "conspicuously" absent. Dever won the heavily Democratic Cermak ward by slim margins, but this was not enough to overtake Thompson, who won a third term.

After Democratic boss Brennan's death the next year, Cermak maneuvered to take control of the state's Democratic Party with a remarkable piece of political choreography. He faced off against the traditional Irish heirs to the party who had been close to Brennan and held key and powerful city positions. He accomplished his victory through welding together Democratic allies throughout the city.

First, Cermak made peace with the remnants of the anti-establishment Democratic factions he once deserted in the old Harrison clique. On the North Side, he wooed Germans through state Senator Charles Weber. The Poles and dissident Irish such as Pat Nash came to his side, while on the West Side, leaders such as Moe Rosenberg and Jacob Arvey grew increasingly powerful. To nail down the party boss position, Cermak played his trump card: only he could lay claim to having the longest uninterrupted tenure of party service and to being a tested political winner, having only lost two elections in thirty years (compared to other Democrats who had lost several recent elections).

Cermak's rise coincided with Thompson's fall. Approaching the 1928 Republican state and county primaries, Thompson's regime faced increasing sharp barbs after a series of high-profile murders and bombings in the city. "It costs two hundred forty-three million dollars to run Chicago," one Republican opponent observed, "and what are we getting?" His crowd replied, "Bombs! Pineapples!" The electorate overwhelmingly repudiated the mayor's ticket, and the wrecked Thompson scurried for cover, leaving the mayor's office to be run by his corporate counsel.

Meantime, Cermak pushed the Democratic slate to victory in the 1929 judicial elections, and in the next city, county, and state elections, his choices led the Democrats to an overwhelming victory. Cermak also wrestled control of patronage platforms, taking, for instance, the rich sanitary district away from his last Irish opponents. Those who chose to make peace with him did so; the rest were vanquished. He now had a model political machine ready to change the Chicago political landscape for good.

As the 1931 mayoral primaries approached, Thompson recovered sufficiently from his lethargy to throw in for another run at the mayor's chair. Of his misery, rumored illness, and withdrawal from politics, Thompson bellowed to a flock of supporters that January: "I'm not dead yet, and I'm not sick anymore! I'm not withdrawing yesterday, today, or tomorrow, no matter how many lies you'll hear about me! I have 250,000 loyal friends in Chicago! Dead or alive, they'll vote for me!" He supported the workingman, he assured them, while his rivals were tools of the rich establishment, harnessed by the guild high brows at the *Tribune* and *Daily News*. In the primary, Capone's mob threw in their support to Thompson, who beat his nearest rival, Municipal Judge John Lyle, by 70,000 votes.

Revived, Thompson charged out to spar with Cermak. Only Big Bill the Builder was fit to be the World's Fair mayor, he claimed. Employing the same strategy he used to vanquish Lyle, he cast himself as a supporter of the unemployed in these hard Depression times, while Cermak, he said, had the support of the city's millionaires. As he had since World War I, Thompson the isolationist made the King of England an issue for Chicago. To connect the dots for the electorate, Thompson presented Cermak's pedigree: Cermak was born in Europe, a natural and automatic ally of King George, he pronounced. If Cermak were elected, the millionaires would then become a tool of the King, leaving ordinary Chicagoans high and dry. Then he sank to name-calling, asking the electorate, "You want a Bohunk for mayor?" His campaign ditty was equally slinky:

> Tony, Tony, where's your pushcart at?
> Can you picture a World's Fair mayor
> With a name like that?
> What a job you're holding!
> And now you're trying for two.
> Better start thinking of one for me
> Instead of two for you!

"I won't take a back seat from that Bohunk—Chairmock, Chermack or whatever his name is," Thompson croaked. He also reminded his audience, "Tony is the biggest crook that ever ran for mayor!" Commenting on Cermak's personal fortune, Big Bill slung as much mud as he could: "Saving Tony . . . saving six millions out of a ten thousand-dollar salary. . . . [Cermak] built the county jail without a boiler . . . [and took] grafts on coal and paving. . . . [The] *Chicago Tribune* called him a horse thief, now they say elect a thief." On the political side, Thompson wooed the discontented Irish Democrats. The façade of Thompson's spirit exuded the positive. "I expect to win," he crowed, "by the greatest majority I have ever received." His declaration was either an enormously flawed hope or a dishonest forecast covering up much gloomier political weather.

Cermak was forged from much harder steel than Thompson's primary opponents. As much as Cermak seethed at Thompson's harangues, rather than engaging him (as Lyle, who dubbed Thompson a "hippopotamus" and "blubbering charlatan," had done), he stayed the course and campaigned on the issues that marked Thompson's irresponsible buffoonery. Reckless spending combined with the Depression to force the city government to institute higher taxes to make up the revenue difference. Chicago was one of the hardest hit by unemployment, and what did Thompson propose to do about it? Cermak also reminded people that crime and graft dominated Thompson's regime. As if to prove it, a week before the election, the state's attorney prompted police to raid the city sealer's office, arresting Thompson's appointee and Capone stooge Dan Serritella and his sidekick Harry Hochstein on charges of shortchanging the good citizens of Chicago nearly $54 million.

In terms of organization, Cermak's patronage force now outnumbered Thompson's. Around town, Cermak enjoyed overwhelming support amongst the ethnics he had long wooed; the Poles, Germans, and Scandinavians went with him. Significant numbers of Italians also crossed over. The Irish were certainly split, but as the election drew close, dissident Republicans, fed up with Thompson, crossed over in droves. Civic and business organizations supported Cermak wholeheartedly as well. One member of that community remarked of Thompson's regime: "Your own common sense will tell you that Chicago is in the grip of gangs and racketeers." Nitto's boss ruled the underworld, and they stood accused of killing McSwiggin and reporter Jake Lingle. Thanks to the bombings of the 1928 election primaries, gangsters and hoodlums were a key issue to the mercantile community; they viewed Cermak as the best chance for "salvaging Chicago's reputation" and successfully attracting the crowds for the planned World's Fair—and thus protecting their investments. To be sure, Cermak enjoyed some support from criminal elements, but these were the less rapacious, less renowned hoodlums outside of Capone's grip.

As the election neared, it became obvious that all Thompson possessed was the meager backing of a portion of his own Republican Party, his black stronghold wards, a small majority of the Italian Near West Side, and the endorsement of William Randolph Hearst's two papers, the *American* and the *Herald and Examiner*—and Capone. Nitto's boss no doubt viewed Cermak's proposed crime cleanup plank suspiciously. Though Thompson had long ballyhooed cleaning up crime, he generally did nothing. Cermak, on the other hand, owed the Outfit nothing and, as an unknown, was seen as a possible threat.

As in 1928, whatever the mob could muster in gunplay and muscle eventually failed in the face of the public's irresistible desire for change. Two days before the voting, a political pundit forecast that "Cermak's plurality will be the largest, numerically, ever given a candidate for mayor of Chicago." He was correct.

On April 7, an enormous 82 percent of the electorate turned out to cast votes. Upon seeing the first election returns an hour or so after the polls closed, Thompson sulked, a cigar hanging loosely from mouth, for tallies showed his "Bohunk" opponent up by 150,000 votes. In the end, Cermak trounced him by over 190,000 votes, a record plurality. In doing so, he carried a humiliating forty-five of fifty wards. Of the five lost, three black wards went for Thompson as expected; the other two, the Twenty-Eighth and the Bloody Twentieth, where mob influence might have been at its heaviest, Cermak lost by 1,000 votes or less.

Reaction to Cermak's election was mixed. The *Tribune*, which had called for Chicagoans to get rid of the Thompson "skunk," applauded the results the next day. Civic leaders viewed Thompson's defeat as a "red letter day" in Chicago history, marking the "political, economic, and spiritual" revival of the city. On the other hand, another leader warily noted Cermak's ties to the old, corrupt Democratic machine and said Chicagoans may have opened the city's gates to Cermak's "wooden horse." Cermak had built a political machine similar to the one with which New Yorkers were familiar—the old Tammany Hall machine, which was corrupt to the core—which was noted by the *New York Nation* less than twenty-four hours after the election as the paper pointed out that, despite Cermak's millionaire status, he had, suspiciously, never held a job paying more than $12,000 annually. And in fact, the Cermak administration would catalyze greater synergy between the city of Chicago and the Capone gang than ever before.

The low profile Nitto had maintained during Chicago's roaring Prohibition days aided him in prison. No bumpkin convicts were drawn to try to knock off a famous big city hoodlum, because none really knew him as such (unlike later with Capone). The calendar on the prison wall flipped forward according to plan, with no incidents or reprimands for L-38021.

14

No Early Discharge

T HE VAST MAJORITY OF NITTO'S prison visitors, other than his wife, first arrived in the busy spring of 1931. At least three of these visitors were quite peculiar, and their visits almost certainly pertained to events outside Leavenworth's walls. And as always, the meetings with these visitors were held in the security of the warden's office.

On March 8, Nitto received "Mr. Rogers" and "Mr. O'Hare" from St. Louis, both of whom logged in the penitentiary record that they were visiting on "business." Rogers most certainly was John T. Rogers, a writer for the *St. Louis Post-Dispatch*, and O'Hare was, in all likelihood, Edward J. O'Hare, Nitto's St. Louis and dog-track connection, and the man who may have helped finger his location the previous October. What the men discussed is not recorded, but the visit's timing and irony of the visitors raises a few interesting questions.

Both men, to some degree, aided Treasury agents in the campaign against the Capone gang, and O'Hare, probably still unbeknownst to Nitto, was still working for the government. Just a month before the visit, O'Hare divulged fugitive Cicero bookkeeper Leslie Shumway's location to the feds to aid in the case against Capone. Thanks in part to his knowledge of gang gambling operations in Cicero during the mid-1920s, the Treasury Department was able obtain "secret" grand jury indictments for tax evasion against Capone before the fifteenth of the month. Was the pair hoping to somehow obtain from Nitto some useful pieces of information for the feds' case against Capone? Or were they double-dealing, serving as messengers to inform Nitto of Capone's difficulties? Or were they there on racetrack business? The answer to all these questions could be "yes."

Another visitor arrived on the seventh of April: "Frank Patton of Bunhaer, Illinois" had trekked west for a chat. He was, most certainly, Nitto's close associate and racetrack partner John Patton of Burnham, Illinois. Also there for "business," Patton could very easily have informed Nitto about any current events regarding his boss.

Both visits point to the notion that Nitto, more than anyone else in the gang, was the key to the gang's dog racing interests—especially after the bad news for Capone had been revealed to the gang. The status of dog tracks remained uncertain in Illinois, where they had been closed by the courts until further legislation determined the sport's legal status. The interested parties might have been consulting with Nitto as to what might be in the gang's best interest. Patton and O'Hare might confer with the gangster should they suppose, as Nitto did, that he would be out on parole by July. Late that summer, gang stooge, city sealer, and state Senator Dan Serritella was rumored to be waving $100,000 around the Illinois state capital hoping to buy enough votes to legalize the canine sport.

On May 5, both Frank J. Wilson and Nels E. Tessem, agents of the Treasury Department working the Capone case, dropped by Leavenworth to engage Nitto in conversation about his gang business. The Italian admitted to conducting business in liquor and gambling but apparently nothing more. The purpose of his visit may have been to settle Nitto's unresolved civil liability, which the prisoner had promised to iron out as part of his plea agreement, but it seems unlikely that they pursued such a legal matter without Nitto's lawyer. The timing of the visit, instead, suggests a probe for more clues about the gang's business structure for the current work on the Capone case. In any event, the agents left disappointed, and two days later, officialdom appears to have determined that an example be made of Nitto. After a two-month pause, copies of fingerprints taken from prisoner L-38021 were sent to the Chicago District director of naturalization for use in the deportation effort against Frank Nitto. And that was just the beginning. . . .

⟐

Department of Justice Form 7-1926, dated March 23, 1931, was received in Leavenworth. It stated:

> I have the honor to inform you that the Board of Parole for the United States Penitentiary Leavenworth, Kansas, under the provisions of the Act of Congress to parole United States prisoners and for other purposes, approved June 25, 1910, will be called upon to consider the application for the release on parole of Frank R. Nitto, No. 38021 (alias Frank Nitto; Frank Nitti). . . . The Board of Parole desires . . . a report regarding this

> prisoner's offense, his history, such information . . . during, or subsequent
> to the trial, which, in your opinion, would be material in hearing the pris-
> oner's application for parole.
>
> (Signed) H. C. Heckman
> Executive Secretary, Board of Parole

It was an old form, the transition of bureaucracy from the state to the federal level not fully complete. Along with the centralization of the prison system in 1930, Congress also created the U.S. Parole Board, a panel of three individuals appointed by and answering to the U.S. attorney general. They would review the Nitto case in Washington; his case would not be reviewed by a board of local prison officials as would have been done before the federal board's creation. In Nitto's case, a local board might have been a real help as it might well have been a soft panel whose members were not necessarily in tune with outside events.

On Friday, June 5, a federal grand jury in Chicago indicted Al Capone on twenty-two felony counts of violating income tax laws—thereby cheating the government out of slightly over $200,000 in taxes—and two misdemeanors for failing to file tax returns. A week later, Eliot Ness's highly visible investigation of the Capone gang's liquor trafficking culminated when the jury handed down an additional indictment charging Capone and sixty-eight henchmen with conspiracy to violate the Prohibition statutes ranging over a ten-year period. The agents estimated Capone's booze revenue at $70 million per year, and to illustrate the enormity of this charge, consider that a single year of Capone's income in 1930 would have covered most of the expenditures of all three branches of federal government or paid the entire federal budget for law enforcement with $25 million to spare or paid income taxes for the entire Chicago metropolitan population in 1929—twice.

The Justice Department, having already garnered convictions of gang board members Nitto, Guzik, and Ralph Capone, now wanted the boss put away for good—and for Chicago's sake—as soon as possible. The pressure put on the department, particularly on U.S. Attorney George E. Q. Johnson, was tremendous. Together, these circumstances greatly diminished Nitto's parole chances, regardless of his meager criminal record, good conduct, and outside support. Nitto's parole hearing was set for July 3.

As required in preparation for the hearing, Leavenworth record clerk Carl F. Zarter dutifully called upon the Chicago Chief of Detectives and the local U.S. marshal for records on Nitto. He received no more than the Naturalization Service had months before—a record of two arrests in the current case. The prison also obtained the Bureau of Investigation file on Nitto showing the same information. Zarter sent the information to Arthur D. Wood, chairman of the parole board in Washington.

The U.S. Board of Parole reply, dated June 22, 1931, to Leavenworth contained a veiled hint of an unfavorable determination in the upcoming Nitto matter:

> I have shown your letter to Mr. Wood, Chairman of the Parole Board, and
> he requests that I communicate with you for the purpose of ascertaining

whether all of the avenues of inquiry have been exhausted to ascertain this inmate's past criminal history. If this has not been done it is requested that the matter be pursued further.

It is also requested that you forward to this office copies of all of your outgoing and incoming communications pertaining to this investigation made at the request of Judge Wood.

(Signed) H. C. Heckman
Executive Secretary, Board of Parole

Again, Zarter complied. Promptly.

Anna Nitto and contacts on the outside worked the community, lining up fine points for the parole board. Through acquaintances in Kansas City, she got work for her husband there, away from Chicago, as they had promised U.S. Attorney Johnson. The owner of Forest Dairy wrote the board to say he could use a man like Nitto as a "Route Foreman or Solicitor." The wage of $150 a week was offered, he said, "as long as he attends to business and his services are satisfactory." In anticipation, he added: "It will be appreciated if the board will advise at your earliest convenience the action taken in Nitto's case, so we will know when we are to have his services."

As a last-minute touch for good measure, tributes by two prominent Chicago citizens were forwarded. Joseph Dire of Colianni and Dire Railroad Contractors wrote he had known Nitto for the past ten years. He added:

> In all my dealings with the public, both in commercial and social way, I have never met a man, whom I consider more trustworthy and honorable than Mr. Frank Nitto. He has been, at all times a liberal giver to all deserving charities. In other ways he has at all times been a good neighbor and a credit to the community in which he lived.
>
> It is the earnest plea of the writer that you grant this man's application for parole, send him back to his family. He will do nothing to cause you to regret your action.

Joseph Marzano, a mortician and longtime Italian community spirit, reminisced about family relations. He saw Nitto and his wife almost daily. Of the couple and Anna's family, he said, "None better live any where." He continued:

> As far as the crime for which Nitto is now serving sentence, I know nothing about it or the circumstances. . . . During the past ten years or so that I have been acquainted with Frank, I have learned to know him as honest trustworthy citizen, a man of his word at all times. He has always been one of the first and largest givers to all deserving charity campaigns.

On June 29, Nitto's young wife penned a three-page plea for her husband's release as soon as possible. In clear, graceful handwriting, Anna wrote:

> Frank and I have been married for three years and this is the first time he has been away from me. We were the closest of companions. If he wanted to have a little diversion from the daily routine, we would have some of our intimate associates out to our house, or to one of the better class hotels where we would dine and dance.

That was the kind of man he really was, she gushed. She mapped out their future in Kansas City—a normal job, a nice house and family—adding that she would "keep him on the straight and narrow path in the future."

> Won't you please grant my prayer and send my husband back to me at the earliest date possible. I will be anxiously awaiting the good news. Don't disappoint me.
> Thanking you in advance for the consideration I am sure you will show my husband, I am
>
> Yours very truly
> (Signed) Mrs. A. Nitto

The picture painted by Nitto in the Big Top was equally rosy. Farm superintendent W. J. Ryan, for whom Nitto performed his trustyship at Leavenworth, sent the board his report. Nitto's overall work ratings were consistently "Excellent." How would he classify Nitto's performance? "Excellent." How would you classify his character? Please circle five of nineteen adjectives ranging from "Hot-Headed" and "Stubborn" at the low end to "Boastful" and "Tricky" near the center to "Trustworthy" and "Friendly" on the high end. In Ryan's opinion, Nitto merited the top five adjectives, which included "Faithful," "Pleasant," and "Energetic," along with two aforementioned descriptors. Under "Remarks," Ryan wrote: "I have observed Frank Nitto for the past 2½ months he has worked at our residence; he is quiet, mannerly and faithful with his work and does not discuss his case."

Parole board member Irwin B. Tucker dropped into Leavenworth on July 3. The three board members, responsible for the entire U.S. caseload, conducted prisoner interviews that were sharp, to the point, and over within a matter of minutes. Parole applicant Frank Nitto was called in. Tucker asked the perfunctory background questions and then quickly found he was not questioning any ordinary jailbird. He probed Nitto about the case that had landed him in prison.

"How much did you owe the government in income tax?"

Planning to contest the matter in civil proceedings later, Nitto shrewdly parried with ignorance: "Well, sir, I don't know. We never did come to that point at all."

Tucker asked a couple of more simple background questions, then aimed for a second time: "Did you pay any income tax?"

"No sir."

"You never have paid any?"

"No sir."

Again, Tucker tried to pin down the total: "Well how much should you have paid?"

Nitto, nimble as a mountain goat, replied, "Well, what the government claims is something like $200,000, according to what the newspapers had it."

"Well," fumed Tucker, "they had to say something when you were in court there. They read a bill to you or something stating how much you should have paid."

"Well, it runs around those figures."

When asked how he made his money, Nitto gave what turned out to be the standard Capone board member answer (Guzik and Ralph used the same): he just deposited receipts for the gang and took a portion as a salary. Nitto admitted gambling and racetrack interests, and, yes, he made some money on booze too. Again, Tucker pressed for his total income, asking whether he had made the amount the government claimed or not.

"Why of course not."

"Well, how much income did you have?"

Tucker kept playing the same tune, and Nitto kept dancing the same step: "Well, I never kept books or anything. . . . I just done all this banking. . . . I would draw a salary. . . ."

"You have a pretty good idea about what your part was?"

"Well, I made some money."

Tucker prodded for the high edge, "$100,000, or $200,000, or how much?"

Finally Nitto owned up, but only to the lowly amount of "about $80,000 or $90,000."

As to why he didn't pay, Nitto explained that the laws were too vague and the forms too complicated. Again, his attorneys didn't even know how to go about solving the matter. Then came the one stumble in his interview: Nitto awkwardly claimed, as Ralph Capone had, that when he wanted to pay up and clear the record, he didn't have the money. "After it was over," Nitto dolorously chimed, "I held the bag, that is the way the story turned out."

While they were on the subject, Nitto took the opportunity to tell Tucker of the deal made in the courtroom between him and U.S. Attorney Johnson: "There was an agreement I would plead guilty and would get some consideration for parole." Self-servingly, he polished his case further to Tucker: "There were some of those cases, they had taken appeals and no one had been sent down here yet. I thought I would have it over with and come down here and in return I would get some consideration for parole. . . ."

Tucker glanced through his file. "There is nothing in the file from the district attorney at all that I can find."

"Well, I am just stating what they said."

The board member looked again, and found nothing, telling Nitto that "if there was an understanding like that, there is no evidence of its having existed so far as the court record is concerned."

"I can't understand that. It was promised to me."

"Well, that is a matter you can take up with your attorney or somebody else."

Of the outstanding $10,000 fine, Nitto could arrange to have that paid through his wife. Nitto's last declaration was that he wanted nothing more than to leave Chicago to get away from the whole embarrassing mess and make an honest living. He ended with, "That is all I can say, and the facts I stated about the district attorney and my lawyer and myself are facts."

Prisoner L-38021 was excused, and Tucker's on-the-spot conclusion was transmitted to the stenographer: applicant serving time for failure to return income taxes; admitted amount around $90,000; excuse not to file—insufficient ability; income derived from questionable sources. The last, noted Tucker, possibly "had more to do with his failure to give in the tax than the complicated return blanks." Tucker admitted to having neither the paperwork from the district attorney's office regarding the details of Nitto's case nor the agreement Nitto claimed to have obtained. Tucker didn't need it, nor was there any need for the other board members to mull the decision. Government intentions from higher ups had earlier dictated the outcome, as implied in Tucker's next words:

> [F]raudulent conduct which deprives the government of the income tax on income of this size is no small offense in itself. . . . Defendant hasn't a bad court record and has maintained a good institutional record, *but the need for an example to be set for others who thus defraud the Government of its revenue is so important as to make the parole of this prisoner under the present facts and circumstances incompatible with public interests*, and his application is denied.

"Circumstances incompatible with public interests" meant Chicago hoodlums, particularly Capone. Word percolated around Chicago that Capone was ready to cut a deal with Johnson and the Treasury Department, as Nitto had. Jake Guzik and Ralph Capone were still pursuing legal recourse, as were Frankie Lake and Terry Druggan. Sam Guzik, Jake's brother, pleaded guilty in April and joined Nitto in Leavenworth, but no other high-profile gangsters were behind bars. Regardless of Nitto's plea deal, and even if he paid his fine as part of that requirement, the current state of affairs dictated that no leniency be shown to any hood once inside a prison to keep them away from Chicago as long as possible. News of Nitto's parole denial did not make the papers—Capone was the mouth-watering headline—but certainly the gang heard about it. And surely the gang understood the government message.

As if to underline the point, two weeks later and for no apparent reason, Nitto's trustyship privileges were revoked, and he was reassigned to slop duty in the prison hospital kitchen. Word for the change may well have come right from the top. The Chicago Crime Commission's Frank Loesch, who also served on the National Commission on Law Observance and Enforcement, wrote President Herbert Hoover of the featured Capone news just five days before Nitto's unsuccessful parole hearing:

> [A] very distinct undertone of dissatisfaction, which had been expressed to me a good many times, that there has some sort of arrangement been

made by reason of which he [Capone] will be allowed to get off with a sentence of two and one-half years.

On the other hand, Loesch continued, a great many people expressed relief that, at any rate, the law will surely get Capone before gangster guns do:

> I hope that some day you will allow me to tell the public how much you had to do with it and how much of the impetus was personally given by you.

President Hoover kindly replied in part on July 1:

> Some time when the gentleman you mention is safely tucked away and engaged in very hard labor, you can tell all about it.

In late July, Judge James H. Wilkerson, in hearing the Capone case, refused to accept what turned out to be true: Johnson, the Internal Revenue agency, and the attorney general had signed off on a pact with Capone's defense team. In exchange for a guilty plea, they recommended a sentence of two and one-half years. In the Capone case, the feds accrued far less hard evidence than in the cases against his minions, and their net-worth strategy, using the amount of his expenditures to prove income, seemed risky—and authorities did not want this bird to fly free. The deal, therefore, seemed a sure avenue to route Capone to prison and was not out of the ordinary. However, Wilkerson lectured the defendant:

> The court will listen as I said this morning, to the recommendation of the district attorney. The court will listen to the recommendation of the attorney general. . . . But the one thing the defendant cannot think, must not think that in the end the recommendation of the attorney general and secretary of the treasury, all considered, the court is bound to enter judgment according to those recommendations.

Wilkerson allowed Capone to withdraw his guilty plea. He then scheduled a trial for October.

⟨•⟩

Despite momentous legal distractions, the gang continued to function. In Nitto's absence, his protégé Paul Ricca gained increasing importance to Capone. The value of trusted Capone bodyguards and gunmen Frank Rio and Louis Campagna blossomed fully. Jack McGurn had perhaps lost some luster after he and his wife were convicted on dubious Mann Act charges in July, though they remained free on appeal. Gunman Sam "Golf Bag" Hunt gained value as a gang go-to troubleshooter. Capone had bestowed command of the recently conquered North Side booze interests on former enemy Ted Newberry.

The gang had also performed some internal pruning. Panderer Mike Heitler, for instance, was gradually being pushed aside. Resentful, the sagging, circular Austrian was thought to have dictated a cloak-and-dagger letter to the state's attorney outlining gang operations—but if the gang could unwrap the feds' hush-hush indictment of Capone, then nothing was secret in Chicago. On April 29, 1931, Heitler slummed away the evening in a card game with Lawrence Mangano, Frankie Pope, and two others, then he drove the group to a Loop restaurant. That was the last anyone saw of him until the next day when a witness reported a small fire in an estate icehouse in Barrington Township, thirty miles to the northwest of the city. When officials extinguished the blaze, they found inside a severely charred corpse with an apparent gunshot wound to the chest. Through dental bridgework work they were able identify Heitler, dead at age fifty-four. Five months later, the tell-all letter he dictated and supposedly sent to authorities surfaced in newsprint. In it, he fingered members of the Capone group, including "Frank Needy," for the Zuta and Lingle murders. But the letter caused hardly a ripple in the underworld or among government officials.

———

The only recourse for a prisoner refused parole was to petition for a new hearing from the very board that had turned him down. Because no record of the apparent deal with U.S. Attorney George Johnson appeared before the parole board, Nitto immediately appealed the decision. Then he worked the inside track, appealing his case to Leavenworth parole officer. N. R. Timmons, who, in turn, wrote to both Johnson and the board in Washington on Nitto's behalf. Nitto's communications to the outside at this time were almost exclusively with his wife Anna and his lawyer Ben Epstein, both of whom also appealed directly to Johnson. Anna came to visit him occasionally.

In mid-September, Johnson wired telegrams on Nitto's behalf to parole officials in both Leavenworth and Washington. He also forwarded Form 792, the Parole Report by the U.S. attorney, the key item omitted before. The form required the convicting attorney to provide the details of the case to parole officials. In the form, Johnson attested that he had extracted certain promises from the Italian hoodlum in exchange for the one-year deal. Johnson added, "To that he [Nitto] agreed personally." He explained that Internal Revenue agents also exacted a promise from Nitto to actively work to resolve the issue of his back taxes, and these agents had also approved the special stipulation. However, he explained, the term of the sentence allowed for time off for good behavior—but not for parole.

Under the guidelines of the Johnson deal, Nitto was required to serve at least until October 26, the nine months and sixteen days minimum length of a one year and one day sentence with time off for good behavior only. The legal gray area, the "no parole" stipulation, was undoubtedly inserted by Johnson to prevent an even earlier Nitto release. Under the one-third statute for parole hearings, Nitto would have been entitled to a hearing after four months under the Johnson deal rather than six months stipulated in the official sentence. By law, Nitto received his official hearing at six months and was denied. Nonetheless, the principled U.S. attorney owned up to the July paperwork gaffe:

I have a responsibility for this in that I did not send in the report. The mistake and reason for this was that I did not think the report should go in until the prisoner was eligible for consideration, and I thought that would be at the present session at Leavenworth which had just been concluded.

Writing on Nitto's behalf on Form 792, Johnson said, "If his conduct, while he has been in the penitentiary, has been such that he is entitled to his good behavior time, in view of the promise that was made to him on his plea of guilty and the statement of the facts as I have herein set forth, I feel that in justice to him parole should be granted him, to become effective only as stated above."

On the twentieth of September, Nitto formally petitioned the chairman of the U.S. Board of Parole, Arthur D. Wood, for a rehearing. On the matter of Johnson's promise, he wrote:

> My Attorney has advised me the United States Attorney at Chicago has forwarded his report in my case and in this report recommended me for parole. . . .
>
> It is my understanding there was no report of my case at the time my application was heard, and denied. . . . For this reason I believe my application was denied.
>
> Trusting you will reopen and reconsider my case, I am,
>
> Respectfully,
> (signed) Frank Nitto
> #38021
> Leavenworth, Kas.

In the meantime, Nitto's $10,000 fine remained unpaid. Addressing this issue with his possible October release date fast approaching, Nitto appealed to Wood once again on the fifteenth. Clumsily, he called attention to the financial penalty:

> If I could obtain my release at this time, I would make every effort to secure money to liquidate the fine, and I believe I could raise the money. However, in four or five months many changes can occur, and it is very doubtful if I could gather together sufficient funds with which to pay a fine of such amount.

He reaffirmed his promise to take up residence in Kansas City and start anew. He had served the term desired by Johnson in an upright manner. In self-serving, fatalistic fashion, he concluded:

> A reply letting me know if the above is sufficient new evidence to justify a reconsideration, so I can reconcile myself to my fate, will be appreciated.

In his relatively short term as chairman of the parole board, Wood had wearily perused a multitude of similar vows from anxious and desperate prisoners. Five days later, Nitto received acknowledgement of his communication from Wood. He read the droning, bureaucratic reply: "Should a change be made in the previous action you will be advised through the regular channels."

―◦/◦/◦―

Absent a deal, Nitto's boss made the usual attempts to avoid jail. Bribery attempts started in Washington. Unsuccessful there, Capone and company worked through backdoor channels, angling to bribe the jury pool, the list for which they had somehow obtained. Once again, Ed O'Hare covertly tipped off the feds, showing SIU agent Frank Wilson ten names on the panel scheduled for the Capone case that he had somehow obtained from gang hands. When authorities checked this list against the one in the federal building, they matched. Notified of this, Judge Wilkerson avoided any intrigue by switching jury panels with another judge the day the trial opened. Capone would receive a fair trial by unblemished jurors.

On October 7, 1931, prosecutors paraded witnesses to the stand. An IRS agent testified the agency had received no tax returns from the defendant; parties to the 1925 Cicero gambling raids attested to Capone's confessed ownership of one place; bookkeepers Shumway and Ries did the same while supplying approximate earnings. Then came the damning Mattingly report—the pivotal confessed starting point in the net-worth strategy. A procession of contractors and store managers attested to the vast expenditures of the defendant, which, given the current economic plight, might enrage the mostly impoverished jury. When prime-grade meat ran as high as thirty-three cents per pound and elaborate three-layer cakes went for thirty-eight cents apiece, Capone's meat bill totalled $200-$250 a week and his bakery bills about $21 a week. The extravagances ran deeper. A highlight list included more than $6,000 for fine suits in 1925, individual parties in 1926 that cost as much as $4,925, landscaping in 1928 that cost $2,100, floor furnishings that tallied $859 in 1928, and his outrageous phone bill in 1929 which amounted to $3,100.

Defense counsel attempted to argue that there was a simple lack of hard proof in the case. They asserted that the government failed to take into account Capone's gambling losses when arriving at his supposed income; this might have been effective in a civil contest but not in the criminal case that was being tried. Finally, they attempted to salve any wounds made by Capone's pompous behavior by noting their client's many generous charitable contributions.

George E. Q. Johnson then delivered a final rousing call to the jury before they adjourned for deliberation. Appealing to the jurors about the great responsibility that lay before them—he told them they would decide the continuing evolution of mankind, which teetered on their decision—he announced:

> If the revenue laws cannot be enforced, then government will fall; the army and navy will be swept aside; our courts and all our institutions will fall, and our civilization will revert to the chaos of the Middle Ages.

Johnson continued:

> Who is this man who has become such a glamorous figure? He has been
> called a Robin Hood by his counsel. Robin Hood took from the strong to
> feed the weak.
>
> Did this Robin Hood buy $3,000 worth of belt buckles for the unem-
> ployed? Was his $6,000 meat bill in a few weeks for the hungry? Did he
> buy $27 shirts for the shivering men who sleep under Wacker Drive?
>
> The United States attorney was never more sincere or determined in
> the five years that he had been in office than he is in this case in which
> the facts cry out a violation of law.

On the seventeenth, the jury found Capone guilty of three felony counts of tax
evasion and two misdemeanor counts of failing to file tax returns. A week later, he
was sentenced to a total of eleven years in jail plus six months due on a previous contempt charge. His fines amounted to $50,000 plus court costs of just over $7,600.
Refused bail, Capone went to Cook County lockup pending appeal. Despite strict
instructions from U.S. Marshal H. C. W. Laubenheimer, jail superintendent David T.
Moneypenny was believed corruptible enough to allow Capone, to some extent, to
run his organization from his new home.

Since 1930, Nitto's boss had attempted to leverage his way into the northwest
county territory of competitor Roger Touhy and his large, brawny, yet affable partner Matt Kolb. At first, the gang tried a businesslike approach by establishing a certain amount of beer business with him. Then they desired to expand their relationship to include gambling and girlie joints. Rebuffed on this account, according to
Touhy, Nitto tried to lure him to a Cicero meeting, ostensibly to discuss matters.
Touhy thought that if it was the Enforcer calling, the meeting was more likely to be
a deadly ambush. However, Touhy's tactics changed when Kolb was kidnapped and
ransomed for $50,000; he paid the money for his partner to the supposed interme-
diary in the deal, Capone.

When Capone's Outfit moved again in the summer of 1931 to expand northwest,
they tersely warned Touhy and Kolb to go along or else. The two refused, but this
time, the outcome was different. Very early in the morning on the day after Capone's
conviction, two well-dressed men walked into Matt Kolb's Club Morton roadhouse
in Morton Grove and asked for the amiable, doughboy owner. Kolb shook hands
with the men and engaged them in chitchat. Then, in a move reminiscent of the
Dean O'Banion slaying, one of the men retained a grip on Kolb, while his partner
pulled a gun and shot Kolb six times in the head. On the way out, the gunman
turned around, walked back, and pumped another slug into the forty-year-old Kolb,
just to make sure he was dead. One down, one to go.

Unbeknownst to Nitto, his parole efforts had forces beyond Johnson's parole report batting in his favor: the very persons who put him away now agreed to his release, and they let this be known to the powers in Washington. Nitto's parole officer in Leavenworth, N. R. Timmons, wrote a final and favorable report to U.S. Attorney Johnson in mid-October. Johnson, in turn, wrote directly to the United States Board of Parole on October 21 that he again was enclosing copies of his files and report outlining the agreement made with Nitto. In regard to Frank R. Nitto, No. 38021, he wrote:

> My purpose in writing you is that I have a moral responsibility of seeing
> to it that a promise made by the United States Attorney is discharged.

Elmer Irey, Chief of the Intelligence Unit of the Treasury Department, phoned parole board secretary H. C. Heckman on the twenty-ninth, noting that he felt Nitto "should be paroled" as well. He would personally come to see chairman Arthur Wood on the matter in a couple of days. But that would be too late: in regard to Johnson's appeals, a message came to the parole board office on October 24 from "T" and initialed "IBT"—no doubt from parole board member Irwin B. Tucker—relaying the sender's opinion: "I am doubtful about following the D.A.'s request in case."

A few days later, Nitto read about the decision to reopen his case. About the missing Johnson file, Chairman Wood wrote, "I am impelled to believe that had it been in the file at the time your case was heard that it would not have tended to change the final disposition." Regarding the $10,000 fine, he continued, "the fine is a condition of sentence. . . . Thus far, according to the record, there has been no gesture on your part to meet this obligation." Wood hammered the final, although erroneous nail, by stating that Nitto could only be paroled after serving one year and a day, noting the earliest possible release date was January 11, 1932. "After a review of the file," he continued, "I am impelled to the opinion that the previous action should not be disturbed."

The sincerity of Nitto's Kansas City intentions is unknown. Whether he planned to humbly retire there, possibly work for his Kansas City allies, or use time there as a temporary means to extricate himself from federal suspicion before returning to Chicago, no one can be sure. What is clear is that, with Capone heading into long-term federal lockup, even out west, Nitto would be in a position to freely assist his associates in Chicago—and the sooner the better. Guzik's case was with the Court of Appeals, while on November 3, Ralph Capone lost his case in the U.S. Supreme Court and entered Leavenworth on the seventh.

On November 20, Charles M. Bates, clerk of the U.S. District Court in Chicago, received from Anna Nitto the sum of $10,000 due in the case of #21246, *United States vs. Frank R. Nitto*. Anna appealed to the parole board once again on November 23 in a four-page letter accompanied by a copy of the receipt for the paid fine. She delicately wrote to Wood:

I know Mr. Wood that you and the other members of the Board only want
to do what you consider fair to all persons . . . and I am sure Mr. Wood
you will pardon me when I call attention to the fact the recommendation
was not that my husband was to serve a year and a day, but that he was to
serve nine months and sixteen days which would be the time that he
would have served if his sentence had been a year and a day.

Despite Nitto's past, she implored Wood to note that:

My husband notwithstanding all that might be said against him, acted in
good faith with the government and in the future he will conduct himself
as we promised. . . . I am sure that my husband in view of all that has happened in Chicago has learned his lesson.

Pledging to standing beside her husband always, she assured Wood further:

I know that I shall have no occasion to feel ashamed of anything that he
will do in the future.
    May I plead with you . . . that my husband gets the consideration due
him in accordance with the recommendation that was to be made in his
case . . .that this may be done so that on the coming holidays we may start
life anew.
    Hoping that you will see the justice of our position. . . .
                                        (Signed) Mrs. Anna Nitto

Per procedure, and perhaps to lend weight to the matter, U.S. Attorney George
Johnson also wrote the board advising that the fine had been paid.

On December 2, Nitto learned directly from Warden Thomas B. White exactly
how much the holiday spirit had infected the parole board. His case had been
reopened three days earlier, and this time parole was denied without comment.
(Leavenworth prisoners batted zero-for-three that day.) With time off for good
behavior, the most favorable forecast for release would be in the third week of
March 1932.

Nitto remained upright, continually earning high marks for his conduct and
work in the prison. With the holidays, mail communications from his wife and
family flooded into the prison—perhaps because, strangely, December marked
the only month of his stay in which Nitto received no visitors. Occasionally,
William Nitto or William Coscioni sent a message from the notorious gang
address 901 South Halsted. A lawyer might drop a note once a month or so. Periodically, others from Kansas City chimed in, perhaps preparing for his supposed
March release date. Correspondence from the seemingly unlikely source of Miss
Annette Caravetta also began to arrive for Nitto. The oldest of five children born
to a wealthy Oak Park family, the twenty-eight-year-old worked as the chief secretary for Nitto associate and trackman Edward J. O'Hare. She almost certainly

acted as a business conduit, though whether for track strategy or for gang matters is uncertain.

Anna Nitto visited Johnson again on the parole matter in January. This time, the U.S. attorney promised her he would take more direct action. He called upon Elmer Irey, who concurred with his assessment, and Irey agreed to take his three assistants and visit the parole board personally on Johnson's behalf. Face to face with Wood, Tucker, and the third member of the board, Dr. Amy Stannard, they conveyed Johnson's strong feelings, including the fact that the board was making him look bad—his word appeared to be worthless. The board, however, held firm and finally imparted the real reason for their disapproval: Nitto's "connections with the Capone gang" made any premature release impossible.

Had the parole board perhaps been stalling for some other agency all along? The Naturalization Service had also pressed to keep Nitto off the streets. For months they scrutinized his records for the smallest of slip-ups. U.S. Naturalization Examiner Michael McCaul popped into Leavenworth to question Nitto on November 24, 1931, hoping for some useful slip of the tongue about illicit relationship or the exact details of his shadowy marriage to Rose Levitt. It was a suitable tactic since all they had to go on about the marriage was his lie that he married in Brooklyn.

Nitto answered few of McCaul's questions about the marriage outright, explaining he had been through this same grilling by an examiner in the Cook County Jail after his arrest and was not about to participate again. He did, however, admit to one discrepancy—that Rose was born in Russia, not Italy. But this was of little use to the Service. Pressed as to the location and legal certification of the nuptials, McCaul asked if he had obtained a license to marry. Nitto snapped, "Yes. There is no other way to be lawfully married, is there?" Nitto waved aside further inquiry on the grounds that "he was afraid he might make some statement that would contradict a prior statement of record." If they wanted further statements, Nitto said, he expected to be out in a couple of weeks; then he would drop by the naturalization office in Kansas City and give them everything. The examiner advised his superiors to concentrate on locating Rose Levitt in New York and obtaining records relating to the couple in hopes of finding a slip there or perhaps some testimony of perhaps illegal activities.

Chicago District Director of Naturalization Fred J. Schlotfeldt agreed. On January 4, 1932, he wrote: "It is believed that he [Nitto] now senses the fact that this service is trying to find some fraud in his naturalization through which his certification can be cancelled." With little more than two months until Nitto's potential release on the original eighteen-month sentence, Schlotfeldt urged his New York counterpart to speed the investigation of Levitt:

> Nitto is rated as one of the so-called "public enemies" and every effort is being made to bring about cancellation of his certificate of naturalization. It is therefore requested that your office make every effort to ascertain whether or not Nitto was, in fact, married to Rose Levy or Levitt in Brooklyn. . . . There is urgency in this matter.

Amazingly, it was almost two weeks later before some bureaucratic slow-wit hit upon the idea of checking the Nitto-Levitt divorce records in Chicago. Only then did the service track his legal Dallas marriage.

On March 17, Nitto sent his last letter to his wife Anna from Leavenworth. Four days later, he forwarded notes to associates William Coscioni and Annette Caravetta. On the twenty-fourth, Nitto received his personal clothes. For Deputy Warden F. L. Morrison, he signed a ticket acknowledging receipt of $12.50 in discharge money due every prisoner upon release, $2.80 in personal money registered upon arrival, and four cents from his postal account. Private transportation met him outside the prison walls and whisked him away, his immediate destination unknown. One thing was certain: because the government's word wasn't worth diddly, he would head back to Chicago, and there was nothing they could do to prevent that. Even though the Naturalization Service investigated for over a year, when it finally closed his file in December 1933, all it could prove was that when Nitto claimed to be a barber, he was in fact violating liquor laws and making enormous sums of money—not nearly enough to instigate deportation proceedings.

The next day, Friday, March 25, a *Chicago Post* reporter thought Nitto was back in the city. The gang update he received upon his arrival informed him that if Capone's appeal to the U.S. Supreme Court was unsuccessful, his boss might be held in Cook County for another six weeks at the most. With Nitto back in town, the boys might now schedule a meeting to determine new Syndicate management.

15

DAYS OF GANG MONARCHS OVER?

WITHOUT THE VOLSTEAD ACT, HE could not have existed," an editor wrote of Capone at the time of his downfall. "With it, he was the predetermined product. For anyone who could see, he was the flower of the Noble Experiment. . . . The conditions which made him remain [are now gone], and no one knows what they will make next." Guesswork about the gang's survival and leadership began almost immediately after Capone's conviction. On October 25, 1931, the *Tribune's* headline read: "DAYS OF GANG MONARCHS ARE OVER, U.S. AGENTS BELIEVE." Federal agents believed that Capone really was no more powerful than any one member of his board, that he served as the "front man" and lightning rod for legal action against the gang. Surely, they thought now, "no other Al Capone will be pushed forward as titular head," and that by "profiting by Capone's example, no man will aspire to dictatorship."

In case they were wrong, they scanned the gang roster for a prospective replacement. Agents did not believe Johnny Torrio was a candidate; he claimed to be retired to New York City, and they believed him. Of the previous board members, Jake Guzik was still appealing his five-year sentence for tax evasion. Should he lose (and he did), the squat bookkeeper would be sent away for at least three years. Ralph Capone, they reckoned, didn't fit the bill. He lacked the strength of leadership and, like Guzik, was appealing a lengthy sentence for dodging taxes. Their opinion of Nitto, though, was different: "If a straw boss of the gang is needed to fill Capone's place, there is Frank Nitti, former treasurer of the Syndicate who will be getting out of Leavenworth penitentiary in the spring." Unquestionably, the feds had an edge with their information.

The local press corps had a much more difficult time. They helped create the Capone icon, and the affable crime boss was so accessible, the media habitually filled columns of newsprint with all things Capone. Now, however, they had to learn to live without. On the bright side, Capone's departure might cause a gang war. As to the Capone gang's new leader, the press focused on whoever was most familiar or visible to them, and speculation for over a year ran rampant—and wrong. It at least continued to sell papers in the Depression era while the Big Guy was away.

The day after Capone's arrival at the federal penitentiary in Atlanta, the *Daily News* wondered, "WHO'LL WEAR CAPONE'S SHOES AS GANG CHIEF?" The article beneath supposed that leaderless vice lord Dennis "Duke" Cooney was coming apart at the seams. Gang loyalties all over town were uncertain. Red Barker's strength appeared resurgent. Would Hymie Levin, Murray Humphreys, Jack White, and/or Ted Newberry go their own ways as well? Loyal Capone bodyguard Frank Rio seemed to stand out as the chief candidate to locals, as far as anyone could tell. Nitto's name was absent from the discussion.

The *Herald and Examiner* headline for May 9, 1932, declared, "GANGLAND LEADERS OIL GUNS FOR WAR." The article below proclaimed that "the king is dead!" and for whoever dons the crown, "the forecast for the Chicago gang situation does not include fair weather." A few days earlier, the *Daily News* had wisecracked that Coroner Frank J. Walsh should seek additional funds for juries and supplies. The Italians, marshaled by Frank Rio, appeared to be on a collision course with the perceived insurgents of Barker, White, Humphreys, and non-Italians in the labor field. Another notion was that Barker and Humphreys were uniting to drive the Italians out. In the whole scheme of gangland, the press ranked Frank Nitto simply as chief fixer of politicians and police.

Presenting the mob's organizational chart on May 22, a *Herald and Examiner* writer doubted the identity of the top man but firmly believed Red Barker and Gus Winkler were closest to the top. The chart designated Frank Rio simply as a supervisor. The "Board of Strategy," as laid out, included Nitto, along with the much more obscure figures of Mops Volpe, Dennis Cooney, and George Howlett.

Another source suggested the New York mob would have a say in who would lead their western allies. Chicago and New York gangs had long-established business relationships in the Prohibition trade. And just as Capone was thought to have taken sides in the New York Castellammarese War of 1930-31, the reverse was said to have occurred in Chicago. Lucky Luciano had recently emerged as head of the New York commission, the leaders of the five Mafia families in that city. He and top financial aide Meyer Lansky arrived in Chicago early April 1932 to meet with their counterparts about mob affairs in the Windy City. It has been speculated that a series of meetings was held to determine a new Chicago mob boss. According to this theory, Lansky considered Paul Ricca and Jake Guzik to be the real thinkers behind Capone, and Guzik was Lansky's choice, but his prison term scuttled that idea. The Fischettis' names cropped up—after all, they were Capone's cousins, but Nitto protégé Paul

Ricca seemed to be the person New Yorkers could trust most. He had been one of Capone's emissaries to the East Coast when his leader was in county lockup. The disappointed New Yorkers supposedly left town after a belligerent Nitto argued his right to the top title, but Nitto didn't need to argue anything.

Actually, the New Yorkers were in town April 1932, but their presence probably more realistically represented a social visit—a call in which the new leaders of New York could meet Chicago's new regime. Perhaps they were able to communicate to Capone one last time and reaffirm business arrangements, but it is highly doubtful New York would have much say-so in Chicago affairs at this point. It is quite possible that the East Coast crowd worried that a violent turnover might occur in Chicago as had happened recently in their town.

But the New Yorkers needn't lose sleep: federal agents recognized that Capone had set his organization up to thrive long before Luciano and his New Yorkers settled down and became organized in 1931. Informed agents estimated the Chicago Syndicate was "so well organized that it will take care of itself." No true member need aspire to leadership in this business-like gang; control transitioned in a natural progression to ensure survival.

Of the previous board members, the feds accurately forecast the exclusion of Jake Guzik and Ralph Capone by virtue of lengthy prison sentences. Their estimation of Ralph's abilities was also correct. Guzik, though a vital numbers man, lacked the Italian pedigree and toughness. Nitto protégé Paul Ricca certainly rose in importance during Capone's jail stay and in Nitto's absence. Ricca was quiet, smooth, businesslike, and forceful; however, at the time, he ranked far too junior to other key men, especially his mentor and board member Frank Nitto, to be allowed to jump so high.

Other analyses justifiably centered on veteran gang member and key Capone bodyguard, Frank Rio. Longtime devoted gunman Rio performed a key role, doing Capone's bidding while the boss was in the Cook County lockup. As chief bodyguard, he also knew his boss's business as well as anyone. With the knowledge that Nitto, as part of his deal for leniency, promised not to return to Chicago (though his true intentions were undetermined), Rio did represent the most logical successor to Capone and was probably groomed to take the lead role during 1931.

When word reached town that the federal deal with Nitto was off and that he would return, plans apparently changed. Nitto certainly possessed more nuts-and-bolts business experience and vision than did gunman Rio. Writing shortly after Capone's departure, Hal Andrews, professed author of *X Marks the Spot*, a 1930 chronicle of the gang bloodbath in Chicago during Prohibition, expressed his thoughts on the matter in a follow-up by showing a pre-tax-trial picture of a mustachioed Nitto under the headline "THE PRESENT HEAD OF CAPONE CRIME, INC.," and a legend beneath stating: "Frank Nitti, the Enforcer"

Nearly everyone else overlooked the diminutive, sleepy-eyed gangster. But hard-nosed board member Frank Nitto stood alone as the natural successor, possessing the combined business experience and foresight to financially transition the mob from Prohibition. His sensible yet sharp dictate to preserve group cohesiveness and eliminate any internal and external foes while was carried out while working in discreet fashion so as to make all of the above 1931-32 press gossip possible. He need not profit by Capone's brassy example; he had lived *sub rosa* all along. Nitto was exactly the right medicine for the mob, at exactly the right time, at exactly the right place.

Still, one *Daily News* pressman pessimistically evaluated their chances, writing that the booze syndicate seems "about to fall to pieces." Repeal of Prohibition appeared to be a sure bet, and with such a great loss of income, what would the gang do then? One local editor hoped "the band of criminals of which he was master should follow its master into enforced oblivion." In Nitto's step up to top command, he faced many internal and external organizational difficulties similar to those Capone had faced in 1925. However, Frank Nitto in 1932 faced fewer violent external threats—the Touhys on the Northwest were the last remaining united obstacle to the gang's total control—but much more uncertainty on the vital political front with antagonist Cermak in as mayor.

Successful vice and gambling revenues were dependent on political cooperation. As in the past, a change of administration might upset that applecart, and the mob had no reason to believe in Cermak's cooperation. Doing battle with top politicians could not involve wholesale gunplay, the typical "solution." This sort of fight required Nitto to strategically apply "muscle" and kill only when necessary.

With the repeal, the army of Prohibition-era gunmen employed for such services found themselves idle, and future gang economics looked grim. Prohibition revenues that raked in millions for gang coffers would eventually evaporate, creating hardships on membership paid through gang funds. Even for those members who owned franchise gambling joints, speakeasies, nightclubs, breweries, and the like, the Depression dwindled their take. In this way, Nitto faced a financial and unemployment crisis within his own ranks. He had to find these men new income and invigorate old sources of wealth. The organization needed to adapt. It was, as federal agents certainly knew, strained but far from extinguished—ramrod Frank Nitto would take care of that.

To Johnny Torrio's credit, he subscribed years ago to an American principle of success: diversity. Capone applied it, as did Nitto. The Nitto organization lined up a heterogeneous bunch of select experts from the old city gangs under Italian direction with Capone's departmental structure—some crossover interests were allowed, like before, though—from the twenties more or less intact. With Nitto as board president, the highest placed mob principals likely consisted of Frank Rio, Paul Ricca, and Louis Campagna.

Through his financial agent, Louis Greenberg, Nitto had acquired the Manhattan brewery, and with booze agent Joe Fusco, probably dictated that end of the business. After his release from prison, Ralph Capone handled the ancillary tavern water and soft drink business. The Fischetti brothers, along with Nick Circella, remained key aides, perhaps lining up nightclubs while engaged in gambling interests. Eddie Vogel dominated slot machines throughout the county, while John Patton fronted efforts in racetracks nationwide; at times, Nitto held interests in both these endeavors. In gambling, Nitto's mob dominated the lucrative downtown Loop district, from which many of the gang profited. Jake Guzik, when he returned from prison, accounted for those moneys and political payoffs with Hymie Levin, who later became prominent in the mob's efforts to gain the handbook wire service. Beyond the Loop, mob handbooks and casinos eventually ran in agreement, as Nitto developed a working relationship with foes Billy Skidmore and Big Bill Johnson in gambling. They were not in the gang but still retained considerable political pull and in time acted as the conduit for political payoffs while Nitto's mob oversaw most street-level operations outside the black South Side.

During the thirties, individuals aspiring to a place of their own needed a political sponsor and then permission from both Skidmore and the mob. To secure this, they sought Skidmore at his humble junkyard headquarters on South Kedzie Avenue. If cleared, the new owner would, once a month, join the flock of operators who descended on Skidmore's with a percentage of their profits as payoffs. Skidmore then divided the booty three ways: himself, politicians, and the Nitto gang. Leading mob agents in city and suburban gambling appeared to be old gang allies Lawrence Mangano, Marty Guilfoyle, Willie Heeney in Cicero, and Rocco DeGrazia in the Melrose Park area. Prominent in local labor racketeering efforts were Klondike O'Donnell, along with Red Barker, Jack White, and Murray Humphreys.

When the mob moved to dominate nationwide labor organizations, the pilots were ranking Italians: Nitto and the board, along with gunmen Phil D'Andrea and Frank Diamond. Claude Maddox graduated from the Near Northwest Side to labor racketeering and gambling in Cicero; in his place, emerged gunman Tough Tony Capezio. Dan Stanton had previously entered the labor game under Capone and emerged dominant as such on the South Side while commanding some gambling interests as well. Capone had previously awarded Ted Newberry, the Moran gang defector, booze and nightclub concessions on the Near North Side. In some circles, his assistant was thought to be August "Gus" Winkler, a St. Louis-born gunman and St. Valentine's Day Massacre suspect.

An entourage of toughs enforced mob rule. Jack McGurn led key aides Tony Accardo, Charlie Gioe, and Sam Giancana. Sam Hunt, known as "Golf Bag" for his penchant of hiding his weapons in a golf bag, evolved as another favored go-to gunman. A youthful Ralph Pierce advanced as a favorite, with both Humphreys and Hunt as tutors. To dissolve resistance without gunplay, the group put James "King of the Bombers" Belcastro in charge of the bombing squad. Key allies running Chicago Heights near the Indiana border included Frank LaPorte and Jimmy Emory. Stooge politicians William Pacelli and Dan Serritella assisted the mob locally, while at the state capital, they had state Senator James Leonardo and state Representatives Al Prignano and Roland Libonati working their interests.

Not everyone absorbed into the gang was content with the setup, however. The newspapers weren't completely off the mark in some of their prognostications. Nitto's group faced a number of calculating, egotistical characters anxious to take advantage of Capone's downfall. Either politically connected or seriously underestimating the mob's cohesion, they sought to make their own fortunes with complete disregard for or at the expense of Nitto's Outfit. The mob apparently recognized the threat. Paul Ricca was said to have commented to a New Yorker on a visit: "There's just too many independent bastards out here. We'll be lucky to keep the peace here." There were, though, no gushing bloodbaths as in the twenties gang wars, just some selective pruning.

Curiously, in May 1932, barely a month after Nitto assumed command, North Sider Ted Newberry announced his retirement. In an exclusive two-hour interview with a *Daily News* reporter, the always-jaunty gunman declared gang life was just too dangerous. Most of his friends were dead or in prison, so he was going into the egg business. Nitto's mob let him go. Always a troublesome area, the Nitto group would have to keep a close eye on the North Side—and perhaps on Newberry himself.

At least one of the men rumored to be Capone's successor didn't live to see much of the summer of '32. Robber-gunman George "Red" Barker was a forceful, ambitious character and a rebel. This red-haired, fleshy Irishman might be credited with the real "gangster" invasion of labor unions during the late twenties, subverting the teamsters union by hauling heating coal while most of the major gangs concentrated their efforts on booze. Eventually operating under the Capone flag with Klondike O'Donnell, Jack White, and Murray Humphreys, Barker expanded his Teamster empire and came to rule stealing as much as $25,000 a year from some of them.

The revolutionary Barker was never really a rock-solid gang conformist; moreover, he spent a considerable portion of time revolving in and out of the Pontiac Reformatory on parole violations. He paid his legal bills by spending sums of union money ranging from $5,000-$11,000. In his latest tenure behind bars, the state's attorney forced him to relinquish control of the Coal Teamsters Union. While Nitto was doing time in Leavenworth, Barker was out and ready to take a stab at the teamsters again. This time, he set out to organize all truckers, city and county, under his umbrella group, the Trucking and Exchange Teamsters (TNT, as it was known). In this way, Barker and company extorted from businesses needing goods and from unions alike. They even assisted Capone's unlikely entry into the milk business, Meadowmoor Dairy, by roughing up union deliverymen to gain lower labor costs. In the county, however, the group ran afoul of the Touhy gang, who professed to be protectors of the legitimate union guys but collected large sums while doing so. Gun battles erupted. Men fell on both sides, with Barker more or less confining his activities to the city. Then rumors flew about his union activities and his soured relations with Michael Galvin, ally and leader of the outlaw members of the Chicago Teamsters.

Then Nitto stepped in as chief officer of the gang. The general understanding at the time among crime beat reporters was that Barker owned or aimed for a piece of the gambling proceeds run by Klondike O'Donnell and Marty Guilfoyle. Tidbits from Prohibition agents suggested he was also now into beer distribution in Cicero. To police, prosecutors, and other officials in the know, Barker appeared to be setting himself up as Capone's successor. Chief of Detectives Schoemaker understood Barker desired recognition among his colleagues as a powerful "ruler of illegitimate enterprises as well as legitimate unions and business." In all events, Barker misjudged the new regime. Nitto and the Italians called the shots, and at this critical time of power transfer, it would appear that Nitto determined to set an example. No Irish rogue—or anyone else, for that matter—would impose on his Outfit.

Barker kept a room in the small Norford Hotel out on the Northwest Side at 1512 North Crawford (now Pulaski). Marty Guilfoyle also roomed there, perhaps using it as a headquarters for his gambling joints only a stone's throw away. In early June 1932, a well-dressed couple in their twenties checked into the small apartment house hugging the street at 1502 Crawford, a couple of doors south of the hotel. To owner Martin J. Foley they claimed to be honeymooners named "Nolan." The couple wanted a second-floor room, preferably overlooking Crawford. They paid for the room from a wad full of cash, and Foley thought they must be quite wealthy. The happy pair moved in on June 6, and later, in an odd twist for a honeymoon, were joined by the woman's "brother."

The pleasant summer evening of June 16 found Barker not far from the Norford enjoying a card of local prizefights at an outdoor sports venue on Kostner Avenue. Also attending the boxing matches that evening from Nitto's group were Claude Maddox, Jack White, and the powerful mass of Tony Capezio. Whether the two parties met up is not known. After the final bout, Barker headed toward home with three unknown companions, two men and a woman.

It was shortly past midnight when Barker curbed his vehicle a block south of the Norford Hotel, and the group proceeded to walk to their rooms—his friends discreetly putting some distance between themselves and the Irishman. As Barker passed by 1502 Crawford, a machine gun opened up on him at close range from the "Nolan" apartment. Pierced by thirty-six slugs, Barker crumpled instantly to the walk. His friends, not even scratched, hurriedly dragged Barker's limp body into the lobby of the Norford. Seeing the bloody heap, the night clerk frantically called upon the strangers to "get him out of here!" Just then, a dining room waiter who had known Barker for some time, arrived to load him into a car and deliver him to nearby Keystone Hospital, where he was dead on arrival at age thirty-six.

Authorities investigating the murder had little to go on. Barker's companions had fled, their identities never known. Sifting through the Nolan apartment, police turned up shells from the machine gun, but nothing else of value. A search out back turned up the machine gun and an automatic rifle, obviously dropped in the killer's flight through the yard next to the hotel. The Nolans and her brother never reappeared. From descriptions given by owner Foley, the men were described as about thirty years old, of light complexion and medium height.

Some speculation as to the culprits was aimed partly at the Touhys. They were the primary adversaries of Nitto's group in the labor field and therefore had every reason to kill Barker. The night before his murder, they were thought to have killed Fred Giovanni at the Dells roadhouse, a Capone club in the Touhys' territory. Those who fingered the Touhys for the murder suggested Barker may have been victim number two of their offensive. Maybe, but police did not put the dragnet out for Touhy men. Police and newsmen instead recognized the "Second Floor Front" ambush method as a Nitto killing routine when he was Capone's Enforcer.

On June 17, 1932, the *Daily News* declared, "RACKET CHIEF SHOT DOWN BY MACHINE GUNNERS; NITTI HUNTED." Also on the pick up list were three fair skinned fellows: Three-Fingered Jack White, Murray Humphreys, and Sam Hunt. A few days later, the Nitto gang's involvement seemed like a sure bet: despite the owner's attempt to obliterate it, the serial number of the machine gun was raised. When cross-checked through a "machine guns sold" list created at the time of the St. Valentine's Day Massacre, police discovered the gun was purchased in January 1928 at the Haber Die and Tool Works at 854 West North Avenue—right down the road from Claude Maddox's former headquarters, the notorious Circus Café. The Nitto bunch at the prizefight were thought to have been tracking Barker's movements, with possibly White and another man as the two men accompanying Barker home. Perhaps they served as a signal to alert the gunners, aiming through the dark, to their target.

The police department's best guess as to the identity of the killers was "the Sicilian element." Chief of Detectives Schoemaker reasoned that "Barker died of too much ambition." Further, he was expendable, for Nitto possessed in Jack White and Murray Humphreys two more-than-capable, trustworthy thugs for the labor field. After all, they had apprenticed with Barker and had more or less kept operations functioning earlier during Barker's many stints in jail.

"The great problem of Chicago," as someone later observed in considering the city's long history, "is this invisible alliance between the rulers of the Upper and the Under World." Mayor Cermak, however, was determined to change this. Yet even as mayor and leader of a political faction poised to take control of the entire state of Illinois, he greatly overestimated his position.

The Depression hit Chicago as hard as any city, if not harder. By 1932, nearly three-quarters of a million souls were out of work (nearly 10 percent of the nation's total), and the tremendous strain of relief to maintain them cost $1.5 million weekly. Commerce fared just as badly. Business rents declined 50 percent from their mid-twenties level. One estimate had the number of banks in the city down from 231 to fifty-one. The city itself faced considerable shortcomings. City employees often went unpaid for great stretches of the calendar, and delinquent taxes contributing to the problem: nearly 20 percent of taxes for 1928 went uncollected, as were 40 percent of the total for 1929 and 50 percent for 1930. Anton Cermak, elected as the "World's Fair Mayor," knew he had to deliver prosperity to both his party and the people. He was just the man for both the place and the time.

With complete control over the party and city patronage, Cermak employed the weight of his office and prestige to hammer the city back into shape. Away from his office, he hounded bankers and the financial elite for funds to keep the wheels of city government turning. The "fifth floor" (on which the mayor's office was located in city hall) became the nerve center for every decision made concerning city operations. "No Chicago mayor," said his biographer Alex Gottfried, "surpassed him in detailed knowledge of the intricacies of administration. A Cermak contemporary pronounced upon him "a master of detail." He understood everybody's role in city government from cabinet member to department head to the ordinary beat cop or clerical employee.

A high-level employee noted in Cermak "a considerable shrewdness in judging men. He made few mistakes in his appointments; and when he did make a mistake, he proceeded to rectify his error without sentimentality." Thus, deviation from orders emanating from the fifth floor, a frequent problem for many administrations, was nearly nonexistent in his. Fear ruled the lower echelons. If asked to do other than bidden would prompt the common protest: "The s.o.b. would crucify me!" To enforce his will, Cermak employed surveillance in the form of stool pigeons, wiretaps, and letter openings. In this way, he stayed up on the identity of enemies as well as the strengths and weaknesses of his minions.

On the first day of his reign, Cermak observed both fiscal responsibility and political loyalty, letting his hatchet fall upon 2,000 temporary employees of the previous administration. They were partially replaced, at least for a while, with loyal Democrats. In four months, nearly 1,100 additional employees, mainly Thompson leftovers, were axed. For any of the remainder to be promoted, the question, "Who is his sponsor?" had to be answered appropriately.

Of particular interest to Cermak was cleaning up crime—his way. First, he revamped the police force. Sensibly, he cleaned out the dead weight and put more men on the street where everybody could see them. Occasionally, the mayor dropped by precinct stations to inspect things and make it known that they were going to work vigorously on crime. The police were to do what he said and, if necessary, forget about "the niceties of due process." Thus programmed, they went to work.

Fresh from victory, Cermak moved to shape his slate of candidates for the upcoming 1932 elections, aiming to relieve the Republicans of any county and state positions left in their hands. However, his foe Thompson was not completely vanquished; he hoped to weld the Republicans together for a comeback with ex-governor Len Small in front. Then, "four years from now," Thompson prophesied, "we got Tony Cermak back on his pushcart." He noisily campaigned in his usual crude manner, branding Cermak as "Tony Baloney" and "Anton the First, Emperor of Cook County." Agitating for crossover votes, he snarled of the new administration; "Yah, Cermak to Szymczak to Zintak—the Irish are out!"

Cermak determined to extinguish this irritation once and for all. He understood Thompson's chief support was among the South Side black community and adjusted his demographic support accordingly. As an earlier tip-off of things to come, many of the city employees previously laid off by Cermak as Thompson supporters were from the black community or "Bronzeville," as Chicago's black South Side was known at the time.

Then Cermak initiated his citywide crime drive in the black wards. They had much to lose: for years, a thriving "policy" racket or numbers lottery business had operated in the community. The numerous lottery "wheels" (so-called for the rotating steel drum used to mix numbers for the daily drawing) operating under various names were a popular means for poor residents to change a nickel or dime into a relative fortune, no matter how remote the odds. In the process, operators of the wheels made hundreds of thousands of dollars and pulled considerable political favor.

New Mayor Cermak warned them that if conditions did not improve, he would shake things up. In the fall of 1931, Cermak's police drove hard into the area, disrupting the games and other forms of popular gambling and hauling to jail as many as 200 people a day. They went so far as to raid homes for small games, even stopping cars routinely just to check for gambling evidence. Community newspapers there soon complained of "political persecution" and came to reference Cermak's men as "Cossacks." With the games endlessly busted up, the policy chiefs clamored to the mayor for relief, asking him, "What do you want?" Cermak replied, "More Democrats in your wards."

The 1932 elections proved to be the ultimate repudiation of Thompson. His usual black support evaporated. The Democratic tidal wave that carried Franklin D. Roosevelt to the presidency washed away Thompson's last real political hopes. His man for governor, Len Small, lost to Cermak's choice, Henry Horner, by over 500,000 votes; the entire bevy of state offices also went to Democrats. Locally, Cermak man, state senator, and legal neophyte Thomas Courtney won the key state's attorney's office, giving him a man to assist his bidding in law enforcement. The Democrats swept the entire county, minus two judgeships. Cermak, not Thompson, now bossed the state.

After insuring electoral victory, Cermak rolled up his sleeves and ruthlessly refocused on "vice and gambling suppression." His priority was to clean up the rest of the town ahead of the Fair, ridding it of a certain group of individuals. As in the past, nobody really thought an absolute clearing possible. The problem lately, though, was that the enormous wealth and power achieved by the Prohibition gangs under Thompson allowed a decided shift of power in certain gambling and vice business from the politicos to the gangsters—namely those controlled by Nitto's Outfit in the Loop district. Cermak's pledge to clean these places out and bring them back into the sphere of city hall signified a change in the old arrangement. With the all-powerful Capone gone, city administration would dictate business—and to whom they desired.

Again, Cermak took personal command of the drive. Outside of the city police force, he organized his own investigators and undercover men to search out vice and gambling joints. They reported back, then special squads instituted by the mayor closed the places the mayor wished to see closed—not all owners were on the list for closure. Cermak did have certain political allies in the business. On the West Side, Cermak, as president of the county board, had set up old bail bondsman and gambler Billy Skidmore in the scrap iron business with lucrative county contracts. Skidmore's buddy, William "Big Bill" Johnson, had long operated gambling enterprises with impunity from a vast complex of houses in Cermak's territory. The pair seemed to always be at odds with Capone during the 1920s. On the North Side, "retired" gangster Ted Newberry was thought to be in line for privileges—so much for the egg business. In the northwest part of both the city and the county, Roger Touhy was said to be in the mayor's good graces. On the outs were Marty Guilfoyle to the northwest and Nitto's group in the Loop and Near West Side. Though both groups ran wide open under Cermak's county watch, both had supported Thompson and his Republican regime in the mayoral election.

To explain away any vice joints left visible thanks to this double standard, Cermak reverted to the old Thompson technique, denial, claiming, "There ain't no crime in Chicago," or if there is, it's no worse than any other city. At the same time, he could point to plenty of perceptible evidence of his anti-crime crusade: gangster roundups were commonplace—and, curiously, most the victims belonged Nitto's group. Informed of his general intentions a year back, friend Judge John Lyle privately warned Cermak that it was an extremely dangerous game he intended to play.

⟨⟨⟨ ⟩⟩⟩

On November 2, 1932, the *Herald and Examiner* blared: "ARREST TEN CAPONE GANG HEADS IN LOOP OFFICE RAID." William "Three-Fingered Jack" White, William "Klondike" O'Donnell, Charlie Fischetti, Murray Humphreys, and several others were arrested in a Loop office at 1 North LaSalle on a tip. When asked by detectives what he was doing there, White replied, "Me? I'm just a visitor." "Well," said the detective after relieving three of the known hoodlums of guns and eyeing the office, including a nearby photo of racketeer Red Barker, "you look pretty much at home." For Humphreys, it was déjà vu: the previous March, he had been picked up outside gang headquarters at the New Southern Hotel at Thirteenth and Michigan.

That same day, the *Daily News* headline told of yet another raid: "POLICE ROUND UP MORE OF CAPONE'S 'BIG SHOTS'; NAB RIO IN LOOP HOTEL." Police had burst into a fourth-floor room at the Planters Hotel in the Loop and arrested Frank Rio, Paul Ricca, Phil D'Andrea, and Michael Costello. No damning gang evidence was found, though. Rio offered the explanation: "Well, we expected to be nabbed, but we didn't expect it here. We just rented this room yesterday."

Another raid on Republican headquarters at 954 Harrison netted gunmen Sam Hunt and Tony Accardo, along with Melrose Park racketeer Rocco DeGrazia. This marked yet another arrest for Hunt, who had been picked up earlier in the year with his brother on gun charges.

Cermak's intelligence appeared extremely accurate and reliable, and the *Herald and Examiner* headline for November 3, 1932, reported: "GANGSTERS FLEEING CITY BEFORE RAIDERS." The story continued, "Forces of the law landed more body blows on gangdom yesterday as the greatest criminal roundup the city has seen in years" began pushing around Capone's aces. Eight of the big shots taken, including Rio, remained in police lockup. Squads raided the West Side, taking another fifteen hoodlums. James "King of the Bombers" Belcastro tosser Joseph Caduta was picked up and imprisoned after a police chase. Rio and D'Andrea professed the police "heat" so bad in Chicago that November that they were planning a trip to the "cooler" climate of Florida.

Three days after the 1932 general election, Cermak's police nabbed more hoods, and the *Herald and Examiner* declared, "CRIME, INCORPORATED IS FIGHTING FOR ITS LIFE." Detectives arrested Nitto's Near West Side hoodlum allies Lawrence Mangano,

219

James Adducci, and William Bioff as suspects in the local kidnapping of a family member close to a Democratic official. One well-informed detective thought it was part of a campaign of intimidation in the mob's fight against Cermak. He recognized the trio as a force in running the Twenty-seventh Ward. Mangano, speaking for the trio, said this was nonsense and that he was only a bookie. Officials, however, recognized him as the longtime owner of the Minerva Club gambling joint, while they knew Bioff from an arrest in April on suspicion of murder. More recently, Adducci and Bioff were thought to have muscled for local mob candidates and to have raked a police squad car with machine-gun fire. By a week before Christmas, nearly all of the major Capone associates had been picked up and jailed for a time—all except Frank Nitto.

16

DECEMBER 1932

MAJOR SURGERY PREVENTED POLICE OFFICER Chris Callahan from participating in much of Cermak's 1932 crusade against the Nitto mob. After a long recovery period, he returned to the force on December 19. His first day back implanted his name permanently in the Nitto record.

Named for the confluence of the two streets that intersect where it stands, the LaSalle-Wacker Building was one of the latest high-rises to appear on the Chicago skyline. The sleek, gray stone structure at 221 North LaSalle stood perhaps forty floors above the north edge of the Loop, with the Chicago River flowing close by.

The location seemed ideal to accountant William Brandtman, who rented several offices and suites, some of which he had recently subleased. A few weeks earlier, an unmemorable character named Fred Smith wanted to lease a three-room suite, Room 554. Soon after, the Quality Flour Company moved in. The company, with offices also on West Randolph, bought supplies of flour, sugar, and corn, the bulk of which it acquired in southern Illinois, and then ostensibly resold the items to local grocers.

Room 554 was perfect for the company's office. The large reception room immediately inside the hall door contained a large table, a number of chairs, and a glass-topped desk positioned off to one side. Farthest from the door were two smaller interior rooms, private offices replete with luxurious, red divans and chairs and large glass-topped desks. Quality Flour journals and ledgers, in addition to adding machines and sundry office supplies, completed the masquerade. A slight break in the charade was that one of the inner offices contained three telephones and a radio capable of monitoring police calls. Since the previous spring, other tenants in the building had recalled seeing a number of gangster types around the office.

This was not surprising since Nitto's group used the office as one of their many quiet holes-in-the-wall to conduct gang business. Capital disbursements from activities to Syndicate members were usually paid out on the first or last day of the month, the transactions dutifully logged in a ledger. One of the lesser lights may have taken bets there. Primarily, though, the office appeared to act as an alcohol business center for the Near North Side, with samples of alcohol and a map of the city's Forty-second Ward part of the decor. Police speculated that much of Quality Flour's dry products ended up in alcohol production, a speculation confirmed when the raiders found a cache of red stickers that reading "Do Not Drop" and "Leaking packages must be removed to a safe place."

About 11 a.m. on the nineteenth, Nitto dropped by Quality Flour for a meeting. Six of his associates were there, four in the large reception office and two others with Nitto in the right rear office. Nitto sat at a large wooden desk covered with ledgers, papers, a phone, and sundry official clutter.

Detective Sergeants Harry Lang and Harry Miller were fleshy, oval-faced, tough characters. Veterans, both worked the wild Prohibition years. Lang had been at the bureau for eight years, while Miller, brother of West Side Jewish gambler Herschie Miller, claimed sixteen years of service. A contemporary remembered Miller as "crooked as they come, but didn't talk tall." His partner Lang proved at least equally underhanded. The pair's December day was planned. The two were assigned to the mayor's office as part of Cermak's special detail and had previously participated in the crackdown on the Nitto mob, reporting results to the mayor personally.

About noon, Lang and Miller met downtown at the Sherman House to plan yet another raid. For days, Miller had worked to collect information on the Quality Flour office on a tip he said came from the mayor. A half hour or so later, Miller put in a call to the detective bureau requesting assistance: could he be given Al Hahn's squad as backup? They were out, so he asked about George Maher's force, but that squad was also engaged. By default, and crucially for Lang, police officer Chris Callahan and his partner Mike Shannon were assigned to the raiding party.

The four met in front of the LaSalle-Wacker Building shortly after noon. When they burst through the door of Quality Flour's office on the fifth floor, they surprised four hoodlums in the large reception room. Miller and Shannon rounded the group up to be searched. Nitto, in the right inner office, heard the commotion, stepped to the doorway to investigate only to be greeted by Lang and Callahan. The detectives flushed Nitto's two compatriots from the office as well. While Callahan searched the mob boss, Miller and Shannon herded everyone but Nitto into one of the inner offices. Just then, Nitto slipped a scrap of paper into his mouth.

Callahan saw it and grabbed the mob leader by the back of his collar, saying, "Spit it out." Nitto refused. As the detective wrestled Nitto along the wall, they came to rest against a chair and an office drinking fountain near one of the room's corners. Callahan searched him again. Just then Lang walked up and asked Nitto, "What's your name?" Nitto refused to answer.

While Callahan locked Nitto's wrists from behind, preparing him for handcuffs, Lang fired point-blank at Nitto, the trajectory of the projectile tracing through the fleshy portion of the right side of Nitto's neck just below the jaw. In an instant, Calla-han fell away, stunned. Nitto twisted around, and Lang fired two more slugs into his torso, one penetrating below the shoulder and nicking his lung, while the other punc-tured a kidney before lodging near his spine. As the gangster fell into the chair and slid to floor, Lang turned and popped off another round, this one aimed toward his own left arm, leaving a grazing gash. Grasping his wound, he announced to the detectives in the other room that Nitto had shot him and he was leaving to seek medical atten-tion. On the way out, he claimed to have picked up Nitto's gun.

The headline of the *Herald and Examiner* on December 20, 1932, announced the results of the raid: "SHOOT NITTI IN POLICE RAID: GUNMAN FELLED BY WOUNDED DETECTIVE AT GANGLAND OFFICE." The story continued:

> Frank Nitti, who as the feared "enforcer" of the Capone gang, is reputed to have ordered the execution of hundreds of men, had his personal record balanced yesterday.

Lang described marching Nitto to one of the rooms to be searched when Nitto swallowed a piece of paper and drew a gun from a shoulder holster. Nitto fired a shot that hit Lang in the arm. Lang returned fire, taking down the gang leader. The oth-ers retrieved the paper Nitto tried to swallow, while Lang found the gun.

Accustomed to the general lawlessness of 1920s Prohibition and the terrible toll inflicted upon the police force, another daily rag offered its salutation to the detec-tive force:

> Chicago police representatives displayed the sort of spirit which was con-spicuously needed, and which in the past was curiously lacking in police circles.

Lang and Miller were awarded "meritorious service" bonuses of $300, and it looked as if the coup provided Mayor Cermak with something major to buttress his anti-crime plank. By evening, the news had Nitto dying with little chance of recov-ery. The morning prognosis noted Nitto was "growing weaker."

Nitto was indeed on the brink: he was still bleeding internally, his color turning a sallow olive due to loss of blood and possible infection. Immediately after the shooting, procedures dictated that a prisoner charged with a crime be transported by police not to the nearest hospital but straight to the house of corrections known as the Bridewell. The Bridewell included a medical facility that had been staffed for the past seven years by physician and experienced surgeon Dr. Charles J. Besta (who treated Nitto), but accommodations were primitive and bleak. A heavily bandaged Nitto lay in a simple tube-metal frame bed; the only other furnishings in the room were a rudimentary wood-plank bedside table with a wash basin on top.

In the face of Nitto's critical state, Chief of Detectives Schoemaker, State's Attor-ney Chief Investigator Dan Gilbert, and Assistant State's Attorney Charles Dougherty all questioned Nitto at his bedside, but to no avail. A press photographer snapped a couple of pictures before the annoyed mob leader finally erupted in a fit of rage. The cameraman retreated as the patient dodged one last flash. Finally, officials permitted Nitto's father-in-law, Dr. Gaetano Ronga, to enter. As chief of staff at nearby Jackson Park Hospital, he called for two of the city's best surgeons to operate. Their diagnosis, together with Besta's, dictated otherwise: because of the location of the bullets (two were still lodged in his torso) and the loss of blood, they dared not even recommend x-rays. In the days before antibiotics, the best medical advice was bed rest to stop the internal bleeding and preventing any additional excitement from causing further—possibly fatal—hemorrhaging.

While news hawks actively paced nearby, Nitto's wife Anna rushed in, only to be rebuffed by prison officials. Overcome by grief, Nitto's ailing young wife returned to her father's residence on McAllister to await updates while Dr. Ronga maintained vigil. In a private moment, Nitto confided to him his version of events. Ronga relayed it to the press corps: "Frank, who is probably dying, told me at the hospital, 'It's a lie; I never had a gun.' Whatever happens, I shall stand by my own and protest against this shooting." The press now had the other side of the story, but because Nitto was Ronga's son-in-law and a gangster to boot, it received scant consideration.

Nitto's health improved slightly the next day; nonetheless, attending physicians expected the twentieth and twenty-first to be the critical days for Nitto. The patient balked at such urgent prognosis and defiantly declared, "I'm going to get well. I feel fine. I'm determined to live, and I won't see anyone because I want to have quiet." Physicians concurred. They upped his survival chances to fifty-fifty.

Throughout the day, Ronga tended to Nitto's legal troubles, bringing in attorney friend Rocco de Stefano to represent him. The lawyer recommended that they fight in court to have any charge against Nitto made a bailable offense so that Ronga might post bond and transfer his son-in-law from the relatively primordial conditions of the Bridewell to Ronga's own, cozier Jefferson Park facility. To the judge, he argued that it was "a matter of life or death." With Lang's condition far from serious, the state's attorney's office agreed to charge Nitto with assault with intent to murder and set bond at $25,000. Ronga quickly organized the necessary funds and that night arranged for an ambulance to quietly ferry Nitto, still in critical condition, from the Bridewell to Jefferson Park.

—————

About the organization's ability to carry on while he was recovering, Nitto had few worries. His six associates that day—Louis Campagna, Louis Schiavone (alias Massessa), John Yario (alias Pope), Charles McGee, Martin Sanders, and Joseph Parrillo—offered police no useful information. Treasury agent Clarence Converse and Eliot Ness of the Prohibition Bureau took their turns with the six, unsuccessfully. Only McGee cracked, spilling his role as Mrs. Nitto's (probably actually Frank's) chauffeur; otherwise Louis Campagna set the example by going so far as to refuse to attach his signature to any reports on the matter. Booked on vagrancy and disorderly conduct charges, their bail was set at $1,100 apiece. All paid and walked out the same day Nitto was transferred to Jefferson Park.

As part of the mob's senior staff, Campagna almost certainly relayed the particulars of the event to Paul Ricca and Frank Rio. Popular accounts had the bulk of the Syndicate hierarchy frantically meeting at Nitto's bedside in Jefferson Park for a series of strategy sessions, which was certainly possible given Nitto's new location away from police supervision. The plausible topic of discussion was what to do about the business in the face of all the heat the police were applying.

Newspapers plainly reported hints of Cermak's determination to exterminate the gangsters. As if to emphasize the mayor's crime crusade, two days after the Nitto shooting, detective Harry Miller gunned down a know-nothing robber in a hotel room. Other squads followed up by killing two black robbers and a bandit. The squads hit Nitto's mob hard: Martin Sanders was brought in again, and a few days later, Miller was in on the arrest of mob middlemen Sylvester Agoglia and Michael Costello. Then Miller's squad (minus Lang) knocked out a gambling office owned by Lawrence Mangano.

Per Cermak's orders, squads hit all "disorderly" places, speakeasies, and beer flats, the latter in preparation for what most understood was Cermak's plan for an obedient transition and licensing for the places with the end of Prohibition now in the forecast. Under the Cermak plan, no licenses were to be granted to places occupied or owned by hoodlums or disreputable characters—a plan that created a further dent in mob revenues. Whispers, however unlikely in the Syndicate playbook, reported mob threats against police unless they let up. Cermak's men allegedly picked up the street chatter, and the mayor answered back in no uncertain terms.

The *Herald and Examiner* headline on December 22, 1932, relayed the mayor's determination: "CERMAK VOWS WAR TO FINISH ON GANGS THREATENING POLICE." The article below it illuminated the mayor's state of mind.

> The threats against police who are doing their duty is nothing short of a declaration of war. If that is what the gangsters want, then that it shall be, for the Chicago police can fight when called upon to do so. . . . The gauntlet is down, and the challenge of the underworld will be met with fearlessness.

His New Year's Day message was more acerbic: "I hope, if there are any more shootings, they will be by policemen and the victims [will be] gangsters." He advised police to shoot first and make it count, then ask questions. If necessary, he threatened, federal men would be called in to assist. Cermak then departed Chicago with ally and Illinois Governor-elect Henry Horner to enjoy some post-election Florida sunshine.

Nitto and his command, however, had experienced the dynamics of shifting political fortunes before. As the city's dominant gang, they saw that the recent and most visible police raids had been aimed exclusively against them—little or nothing had been aimed at the Touhys in the city's northwest section or at the major players of the gambling world. The raids reeked of Cermak's desire to either bend their organization to his will or replace their dominant underworld regime with one more favorable to his influence. He had coerced the black South Side into line, and it was fairly common knowledge that he had persuaded West Side gambling magnates Bill Johnson and Billy Skidmore to join his camp. Were there others?

The gunning down, without provocation, of mob leader Nitto by police smacked of assassination, and retaliation against the shooter, Detective Lang, seemed obvious. By now, Lang was well protected, and killing law enforcement personnel had been deemed bad business since Prohibition. However, Lang might have pulled the trigger for someone who lacked the firepower to take on the Nitto Syndicate directly. That someone knew the Quality Flour location for what it was, that it likely supplied alcohol for the recently added North Side locations, and that Nitto went there on certain days suggested an associate who dwelled in the city's northern environs.

By Christmas, doctors thought that Nitto, despite the two slugs still lodged in his body, would survive. They anxiously monitored his condition, waiting for him to build sufficient resistance and strength to allow surgery. As he convalesced, his gang set out to even the score.

A couple of months earlier, veteran North Sider Ted Newberry returned from his professed retirement as his usual affable self, spending money freely at his old North Side nightspots. When at least a portion of his booze import business was broken up by the feds a couple of years earlier, he entered the gambling trade—something he could not have hoped to do without political connivance. He went in as part owner of a newly renovated, high-class gambling spot at 225 East Superior, appropriately named the 225 Club. Some suspected Newberry's other North Side interests extended to the Sky High Club, a gaming joint atop the fashionable Lincoln Park Arms Hotel, as well as possible expansion into the highly lucrative handbook business. Given the mob's current transition from illicit alcohol into other rackets, particularly the profitable gambling sector, informants heard the local mob warning to the supposedly retired hood, "to get out and stay out."

The connection between illegal gambling and Chicago politics was long established, and the only reasonable way for a persistent Newberry to trump the mob was to play the political card. How far he may have pursued the issue is unknown. With Cermak's licensing plan, raids on Nitto's speakeasies, and the raid on Quality Flour, a possible alcohol command center for North Side, it may have appeared that the current group of Italian hoods were to be phased out of the booze business. After Nitto's shooting by detectives attached to the mayor's office, Newberry was suspect. Further, Newberry harbored no love for Nitto. All of a sudden, after the Nitto shooting, Newberry's acquaintances lost sight of him and figured he was, for some reason, lying low.

The reason for his disappearance was revealed late on Friday night, January 6, when Newberry was called away from one his North Side haunts. His companions that night never saw him again. The next morning, Porter County, Indiana, officials were called to a lonely gravel road near Chesterton, eleven miles west of Michigan City. There lay the dapper Ted Newberry in his usual designer suit, the diamond encrusted belt buckle from Al Capone still adorning his waist, shot through the back of the head. The amiable gangster, most likely in his early thirties, had taken a one-way ride—nearby tread marks indicated a vehicle had approached from the west, then the occupants pitching his body out, wheeled around, and darted off toward the Illinois state line. Questioned about his death, one police officer voiced a familiar Chicago line: "[H]e must have done something. They don't kill you for nothing." Months would pass before investigators could connect the dots.

—⁊/⁊/⁊—

Shortly afterward Newberry's death, surgeons successfully removed the slugs that had been lodged in Nitto since the shooting. While Nitto recuperated, Chief of Detectives William Schoemaker placed him on the city's new 1933 Public Enemy List. His ranking of fifth was possibly the highest position he reached on anybody's list at anytime, perhaps a dismal showing for a mob boss. But what this really illustrated was how little officials understood the hierarchy of the mob and also how successful the mob's top level strove to become imperceptible. The *Tribune* published the list under the headline, "39 HOODLUMS ON NEW PUBLIC ENEMY ROSTER."

1. Murray Humphreys—labor racketeer
2. William "Three-Fingered Jack" White—labor racketeer
3. William "Klondike" O'Donnell—beer runner, labor racketeer
4. Machine Gun Jack McGurn—gunman
5. Frank Nitti—principal Capone man of business and boss

Notably, "Paul Ricco" (Ricca) merited a remote number twenty-six, while Frank Rio and Louis Campagna were absent altogether.

Within two weeks, Public Enemy Number 5 slipped out of Jefferson Park unnoticed and retired to his residence at 36 North Menard near Oak Park to convalesce. The case of *The People of the State of Illinois versus Frank Nitto* inched forward without the gangster, attorney de Stefano handling legal matters, which at the moment consisted only of cancelled bail bonds arguments. In other legal matters, Nitto triumphed decisively. On January 24, the Bureau of Internal Revenue announced that, in accordance with a ruling by the Tax Court of Appeals, Nitto had been granted an abatement on the $285,723 bill from the income tax charges levied in 1930. The U.S. government, the court ruled, could not determine gross versus net income, so they threw out the "boxcar" figures altogether, and Nitto settled the entire bill for 1925-27 for a mere $15,000. His legal team's strategy not to admit civil liability had paid off.

When, on January 27, Assistant State's Attorney William Rittenhouse asked the court for a continuance of Nitto's assault case due to other pressing litigation, Nitto's attorney de Stefano asked permission for his client to recuperate in Florida. With the bonds issue still unresolved in entirety, Rittenhouse protested, "If Nitti is able to go to Florida, he is able to come to court."

De Stefano responded, "Surely, I'll bring him here in an hour."

"You wouldn't make that offer," snapped Rittenhouse, "if the state were ready for trial."

The judge set a bond hearing in Criminal Court for February 3.

When Nitto appeared in court, he cut a delicate, sorrowful-looking figure, hobbling in on a cane between attorney de Stefano and medical attendant Dr. Ronga. De Stefano presented the gang leader as ready for trial and posted a scheduled bond of $10,000 for his client. The property for the bond was conveniently located at 1206 McAllister Place, next door to Dr. Ronga, and the owner listed as Grace D'Allesio, whom Nitto claimed as an aunt. It was at this address where he was served a summons by Sheriff William Meyering on the ninth to appear in court the next day. Nitto answered the door without either a cane or a doctor, but he nonetheless was a pathetic, wan, hunched over figure, his overcoat enveloping him like a shawl. In court on the tenth, he heard Chief Justice of the Criminal Court John Prystalski fix the definitive date for the trial as March 17. Unmoved, he returned to McAllister Place.

⎯⎯·§·§·⎯⎯

Business was still business. A World's Fair was only months from opening, and the mob maneuvered to take advantage of the crowds. Incapacitated or not, Nitto directed the men accordingly. With Newberry dead and Cermak away, police pressure on the mob let up a bit in January, and it appeared their gambling, booze, and racketeering interests might survive the threat after all. mob strategy for 1933 centered on gambling: much of the lucrative gambling business remained free of mob shackles, but to conquer the politically linked business required both diplomacy and time.

Of the other enterprises, the mob was still well entrenched in its Prohibition mainstay, booze. Nitto and Louis Greenberg prepared to make the old Malt Maid Brewery legit since President-elect Franklin D. Roosevelt had promised to lift the ban on 3.2 percent beer after his March inauguration. In April, they renamed the operation the Manhattan Brewing Company. As president, the pair installed Chicagoan and former U.S. Postmaster Arthur Lueder, who claimed he knew nothing of the brewery's gangster connections. Nitto called upon New York associate Joe Adonis to send in an experienced colleague, an anonymous face in Chicago, to line up Manhattan's out-of-state beer sales. However, Nitto's group still stood to lose considerable beer sales once local competitors and the national industry giants reentered the market. To ensure consistent flow of mob-owned beer, they reverted to a tactic they had successfully used against gang competitors in the 1920s—muscle.

This coincided in February 1933 with perhaps the most pressing aspect of mob enterprises and the easiest means for Nitto to ensure that money kept rolling in for his men: racketeering. Three-Fingered Jack White, Murray Humphreys, and Klondike O'Donnell emerged after Red Barker's death to lead efforts into the expanding field. Their supporting cast included bully Frank Diamond and untamed Klondike aide, Fur Sammons. The chief prize to be won was control over the men who delivered the city's supplies: coal for heating, food, building supplies, even beer and ice. They all wanted the local Teamster unions, and as usual, the Roger Touhy mob were the fiercest competitors.

Possibly sensing that the mob regime was destabilized with Nitto wounded and/or that Cermak's crusade had weakened the position of Nitto's group, the Touhys went on the offensive. On February 2 a car full of Touhy men, thought to be led by Roger's brother Tom, lay in wait on the Far West Side at the intersection of Harlem and North. They recognized an approaching care and readied machine guns. When Fur Sammons and the two men in the other car—which had armor plating—came within range of the guns, Touhy's men raked it with gunfire. A pair in the Sammons car returned fire from a rear drop window, wounding Tommy Touhy before escaping unscathed. Unsuccessful this time, the Touhy mob kept after Nitto's extortionists.

Apparently unable to deal straight away with the well-insulated Touhy threat, the mob's extortion department sent terse warning to those who might similarly miscalculate their potency. When henchmen and criminal allies reported that certain collections and demands were not met forthwith, a mending Nitto was said to have growled gruff orders to one luckless crony: "Make the collections or I'll shoot you in the head." The war continued on the Teamster/racketeering front as well. Racketeers smashed storefront windows by slinging hails of brass marbles from speeding cars; this method of "persuasion" alone had cost store owners an estimated $1 million in 1932 and helped many see the mob's light. For the more obstinate, James Belcastro's bombing unit was called in, and for the next eighty days, his crews blasted at least twenty-five businesses, not destroying them completely but inflicting enough damage to cause grief. All were affiliated with groups that had previously been targeted by racketeers: meat and fish markets, poultry associations, construction sites and businesses dependent on Teamster work, and cleaning and dyeing establishments— Humphreys's future specialty—were victimized by several bombs. The blasts apparently had the desired effect and also kept Touhy's head down for a period.

The same level of success was achieved in the booze department. First, Nitto's "brewery agents" visited several outlets that previously had sold bootleg products. Those who thought they might sell beer from quality competitors when it became available were told bluntly by a menacing figure, "You'll take beer from us or your place will be blown up." The goon squads then made the rounds of other potential outlets, such as hotel bars, restaurants, and the like. They heard the same sales pitch. "Buy our beer or get pineapples," they were told. A few refused, and those addresses were added to Belcastro's list.

When President Roosevelt signed into law legislation allowing 3.2 percent beer sales to begin at 12:01 a.m. Friday, April 7, the mob targeted local breweries as well. Seven breweries had thus far received licenses for production, and advance orders for product were enormous. The Atlas Brewery received calls for 100,000 cases; Prima Brewing Company orders, a week before legalization, stood at 200,000 cases and were growing. Whether by bombs or muscle, the mob would make sure their teamsters unions would deliver the product and possibly even supply leverage for some revenue from the sales.

After conferring with aids in Warm Springs, Georgia, President-elect Franklin Roosevelt spent nearly two weeks in early February cruising the warm waters off the east coast of Florida in Vincent Astor's yacht, the *Nourmahal*. The voyage served to relax Roosevelt after months of strenuous campaigning. On the evening of the fifteenth, the yacht anchored at the Miami Municipal Pier on the north edge of Bayfront Park. A welcoming rally was planned in the park for Roosevelt; then he would depart for New York and finish plans for his March inauguration. Two hours after docking, a motorcade carted Roosevelt down expansive Biscayne Boulevard to the south edge of the park, where dignitaries awaited his arrival at the Moorish-style amphitheater. Palm trees and well-wishers lined the boulevard as the cars passed by; another 25,000 people or so, the largest crowd to assemble in the city's history to date, waited to welcome the next president of the United States in the park. Among the privileged group seated under the amphitheater's canopy was Chicago Mayor Anton Cermak.

Cermak was there to see the president on business. At the top of his list was funding for city schools, and also key to Cermak's absolute rule over the state of Illinois was the entitlement to appoint federal patronage jobs. For the latter, he had been passed over in favor of Illinois Senator James Hamilton Lewis because Cermak had persistently directed his political machine to back declared Wet candidate Al Smith, rather than Roosevelt, at the Democratic presidential nominating convention. He threw the Illinois group to Roosevelt only after the delegates had given the New Yorker the nomination. Now, Cermak was worried about his Illinois hegemony and prepared to make peace.

At about 9 p.m., Roosevelt's open car pushed through the throngs and approached the amphitheater. Cermak stepped forward, hoping to shake hands and have a few words with the president-elect. When the car stopped in front of the ornate theater, someone hoisted a microphone to the car. Roosevelt spoke a few words, and the crowds cheered. Red, white, and blue floodlights lit the stage area, skimming the palm trees above. Cermak, escorted by Chicago Alderman James Bowler and Miami City Manager L. Lee, stepped forward to greet the president. The mayor and the president spoke briefly; Cermak wanted to talk business, but Roosevelt replied they would do so on the train ride home. Satisfied, the mayor withdrew toward the rear of the car when five loud pops were heard. A commotion ensued about twenty-five feet away, where spectators subdued someone with a gun. At the bottom of the pile they held a scruffy, dwarfish, unemployed Italian named Giuseppe Zangara, whose five shots had all found human marks. None of the shots were immediately fatal, and none of them hit Roosevelt, Zangara's apparent intended target. One bullet, however, struck Mayor Cermak in the right ribcage area, the bullet lodging near his spine.

The mayor was taken to Jackson Memorial Hospital. To doctors, the sixty-year-old Cermak seemed fit enough, and his vital signs were quite sound—he was given a better than even chance for recovery. A week later, the doctors pronounced an eighty-twenty chance for recovery, despite a suspicious rise in Cermak's temperature and increased intestinal pain. But when Cermak's family was called to the hospital on Sunday, March 5, the news was grim. Peritonitis had set in, and colitis also weakened the mayor. Worse, tests revealed gangrene in the lung. At 10 p.m., doctors held out slim hope, and four hours later it became obvious the mayor would not live long. He slipped away that morning at 6:57.

Authorities hurriedly charged Zangara with first-degree murder. The gnome-like Italian couldn't have cared less. Earlier, he had received four consecutive twenty-year terms in the state penitentiary on four counts of attempted murder. His only response at the sentencing was to taunt the judge in his imperfect English: "Oh, judge, don't be stingy. Give me a hundred years!" It wouldn't matter to him, he explained, because pains in his stomach had bothered him for years and he expected to survive perhaps two years at most.

Zangara's recorded ramblings never made much sense. When examined by a psychiatrist, the diminutive Italian was found to be psychopathic and anti-social. The superintendent of the state prison to which he was remanded found Zangara to be no mystery. In his unofficial estimation, "Zangara was merely a crack-brained product of socialism in its extreme form." Regardless of his mental state, a jury swiftly found Zangara guilty of murder, and a sentence of death was pronounced. On Monday, March 20, two weeks to the day after Cermak died, Zangara became the fortieth inmate to be executed in the state's electric chair. As he sat in the chair with a hood over his head, he eagerly egged officials on, saying, "Pusha da button! Go ahead, pusha da button!" They did.

The Chicago City Council appointed an acting mayor to succeed Cermak until party high-hats had selected a candidate for a permanent successor. State law allowed, at the earliest, an election in June. Until then, the council grappled with the city's fiscal problems. Cermak's death on March 6 wasn't the only bad news they faced. That same day, President Roosevelt invoked extreme measures to deal with the country's economic troubles: he closed all banks, declaring a four-day holiday. The Chicago and New York stock exchanges were closed until further notice.

⟨•/•/•⟩

On March 17 Frank Nitto and attorney Ben Short arrived in court as scheduled, and the defense went on the offensive. Short entered a motion to suppress based on the absence of a warrant to search the Quality Flour premises. The petition, signed by Nitto, also listed a number of missing personal items to be returned and also included a bombshell—Ronga's earlier-ignored claim that Nitto was shot without provocation. Still, the press gave it little notice. Who would believe a gangster? The following Monday, in stark contrast with his prior appearance, a confident Nitto arrived in court dressed in a fine-cut suit and sporting a gray fedora. He was amiable to the press and even smiled for photographers. When the hearing was continued until April, Nitto departed for Florida with Charlie Fischetti.

A couple of weeks' respite allowed the gang leader to recover away from the Chicago cold. By now, he had a rental home in the Miami area, conveniently close to Capone's Palm Island residence. While resting, Nitto, Fischetti, and others were thought to have entertained fellow mobsters from the East Coast. Meyer Lansky was making inroads into gambling there. New Yorker Frank Erickson, with whom Nitto would later partner in Florida racetracks, may have come along with others. The talk was probably casual, centering on Nitto's health and the situation in Chicago. Business talk was likely Florida-related, and booze might have been on the agenda since legal beer would be available in a matter of days.

Nitto returned to court in Chicago on Monday, April 3. Well-tanned and relaxed, he lounged comfortably in the fine leather courtroom chair, chatting confidently with attorneys de Stefano and Short. In what must have been a bonanza for press photographers, the previously almost unrecordable Nitto, in a finely cut dark suit with spats topping his highly glossed shoes, smiled jauntily as cameras homed in on him. Jury selection took two days. On Wednesday, Detective Lang took the stand. Assistant State's Attorney Dougherty opened the questioning. As Lang's testimony approached the point of entering Quality Flour, Nitto's attorneys pressed a motion to exclude the evidence based on the lack of search warrants. Trial Judge Rudolph Desort excused the jury to hear arguments. Dougherty continued with Lang to establish cause for the raid but did not inquire about the shooting. When Nitto's attorney Ben Short cross-examined Lang, he asked the detective about warrants. Lang said there were no warrants.

"Who shot you?" Short asked.

Lang answered, "I don't know who shot me."

Startled, the two prosecutors jumped from their chairs. Police officials attached to the state's attorney's office also scrambled forward as Short continued, "Would you say under oath that it was the defendant Nitti who shot you?

"No," Lang replied softly and calmly. "I wouldn't say he did."

Steamed at the testimony, Dougherty jumped forward, waving his finger at the detective and practically shouting, "Do you see the man in this courtroom who shot you?"

"No," came the response.

Dougherty read Lang his grand jury testimony. Defense counsel jumped forward, arguing that the prosecution could not impeach its own witness. Attorney Daniel Covelli suddenly hurtled out of his seat in the gallery, advising the court, through the wrangle at the bench, that he was counsel for the witness. He advised Lang not to answer any more questions. Pandemonium ensued. When order was finally restored, Dougherty gave the detective a second chance to recant. Lang only admitted that "because of the shock" after his wounding, he couldn't remember things as clearly then as he could now. At one end of the courtroom Nitto grinned a Cheshire Cat smile, while Lang remained on the stand stone-faced and calm. Dougherty asked for a recess. On the way out, he professed to have known for some time that "all was not well" with the case. He was suspicious of Callahan's refusal to testify before the grand jury in the first place. A priest, he said, had called on the officer's behalf back then. Harry Miller raged, suspecting Lang had buckled because he feared the hoodlums, even though he was supposed to be a tough cop.

After the recess, Desort dismissed the jury for the day. Dougherty then presented a perjury warrant for Lang. Judge Desort released the detective on $2,000 bond, reasoning that the amount was plenty for a policeman. Dougherty sarcastically cracked, "You mean [he] *was* a policeman."

The next morning, Lang was recalled to the stand. He refused to answer the questions put forth by Dougherty for fear of incriminating himself. Dougherty once again read Lang's grand jury testimony and asked him whether he had made those statements. Covelli, now accompanied by attorney Abe Marovitz, again advised Lang not to answer.

Chris Callahan followed Lang to the stand. Unfortunately for Lang, this policeman was more scrupulous than either he or Miller. Quizzed by the assistant state's attorney, he related the entire incident as he witnessed it, starting with marching Nitto out of the inner office, followed by his scuffle with Nitto in trying to retrieve the note, and finally recounting Lang firing three shots into the mob boss. The prosecutor continued:

"Did you see Nitti shoot?"

"No."

"Did Nitti have a gun?"

"I found none."

"How was Lang shot?"

"There was only one gun and he must have shot himself."

Shannon was next, but could add little since he was in the adjoining room when Nitto was shot. Finally, Miller took the stand. He followed Lang's original story, saying that he found Nitto's gun in the room and subsequently showed it to officer Callahan. Upon cross-examination, Nitto's attorney Ben Short peeled Miller's story apart. Short began by asking, "Why was Nitti put in that room before he was shot?" Miller froze and gave no answer. Short continued, "Was it for the purpose of killing him?" Miller remained nervously silent.

Short forced Miller to admit the gun was found outside the presence of the other men. Miller, in fact, did not go directly to the bureau to file a report of the incident but went instead to the mayor's office for the remainder of the afternoon. Then Short delivered the obvious and most potentially combustible question: "With whom did you talk there?"

Dougherty's objection was sustained. The public would never know for sure.

Again, Miller claimed he showed the Nitto weapon to Callahan. Short recalled that officer to the stand and asked, "Did Miller show you that gun?"

"Not to my knowledge," the witness replied, "I never saw that gun until it was turned in at the detective bureau."

The prosecution rested its case, half-apologizing to the jury for the testimony. Dougherty assured the citizens the matter would be cleared in front of a grand jury. Desort then granted Nitto a directed verdict of "not guilty."

The day was far from over for Nitto, though. Before the verdict was announced, the police served grand jury summons upon the gang leader, Miller, Shannon, and Callahan. Leaks from Miller's testimony suggested an answer to the Newberry murder question. The detective was thought to have said he heard rumors of a $15,000 offer from Newberry to Lang if he'd kill Nitto. Confronting Lang prior to the raid about the rumored bounty, Miller said his partner denied it. Miller claimed he did the legwork investigating Quality Flour, but that it was Lang who called for the raid's timing—after he had received a call from Newberry five minutes earlier. Nitto then spent a reluctant twenty-five minutes on the stand. Queried about Newberry, the mob boss stated he had not seen Newberry for some time and that he knew of no Newberry connection with his business. Pressed further, Nitto drearily explained that "he would just as leave drop the whole thing and go some place to recover his health."

State's Attorney Thomas Courtney would not allow for such a simple solution and determined a full investigation into the matter. The investigation really had more to do with the goings-on in the police department than with Nitto. Why hadn't Miller reported the Newberry rumor to authorities? What about the inconsistencies in his and Lang's account of the events, particularly the "Nitto" gun? Based on Nitto's grand jury testimony, speculation was that Nitto would not press charges for assault, which would leave a simple perjury charge against Lang, for which the gang leader would not have to appear in court. Nitto could then get on with gang business. However, Courtney determined, if Nitto did not choose to prosecute, the state would.

On April 7, 1933, the *Tribune* ran a headline noting the unexpected turn of events: "POLICE RAIDER IS INDICTED FOR SHOOTING NITTI." For Lang, not only were formal indictments handed down charging him with assault with intent to commit murder, but Police Commissioner James Allman suspended the detective from the force as well. (One week later, Miller was also suspended.) Pondering the alleged $15,000 bounty, Courtney wondered how it is that a policeman, who has not been paid for some time (due to the city's budget crisis), could pay the fee to a bonding company for his release and afford two former assistant prosecutors as defense counsel. Hard-pressed by Courtney's resolve, Lang determined not to be the scapegoat of the boiling hullabaloo. A defiant Lang openly drew the line in the sand, announcing that if the authorities insisted on shoving him, he would tell the whole "truth" and "wreck the Democratic Party."

Lang's noises only incensed Courtney to instruct Dougherty to press onward. After serving Nitto with a summons and announcing that another hearing would be held the next week, Dougherty, dizzied by the events, wearily finished his business by opining, "This undoubtedly is the most astounding situation I have ever encountered in my many years as a prosecutor." A judge ruled that Lang would have his opportunity to trash city politicos in September when he faced trial for assaulting Frank Nitto.

—◆◆◆—

Nitto probably thought little about the political implications. He and his mob resumed more important business. Courtney's decision to allow Dougherty to prosecute such a high-profile case may have been due to earlier repeated complaints of hoodlum threats against the new and upcoming beer trade. Courtney invited the leaders of several Chicago business associations into his office for a strategy session and declared, "We will drive the gangsters out if they attempt to enter this new legitimate business." The state's attorney continued, "They must not and shall not be permitted to make sales by spreading fear." The *Tribune* reported an uneventful first day of beer sales under the headline, "ALL'S QUIET AS BEER ARRIVES."

The peace was shattered the next morning, though, when the Prima Brewing Company was bombed, resulting in approximately $1,500 in damage to the bottling works and storage house. Company officials professed no knowledge of hoodlum threats and suspected instead a "small jobber" who was disgruntled because his order was not timely delivered. The bomb, described as a "time machine," seemed much too sophisticated for a small jobber. Later, a nitroglycerin bomb was defused before detonating in the engine room of Nitto's Manhattan brewery. For once, Nitto might have agreed with Courtney: the other gangsters would have to be eliminated.

The bombings may very well have been the work of the Touhy mob. With some Florida (vacation and prison) time behind him, Roger Touhy apparently readied for another go at the Nitto mob racketeering corps. On Friday, April 27, a pack of Touhy men armed with machine guns, shotguns and automatic pistols invaded the Chicago Teamsters Hall on South Ashland. Inside were about thirty or forty union members meeting with Fred Sass, the business agent for the Ash Wagon Drivers, and Morris Goldberg, a clerk for the Moving Van Drivers. Both were led away at gunpoint in front of a stunned membership. Most important to the Touhy mob, Goldberg was the brother-in-law of Klondike O'Donnell. No ransom was asked for the hostages; instead, the kidnappers spent the weekend interrogating the pair. Where could they corner O'Donnell, White, or Humphreys? The kidnappers planned to blast their way toward taking over the union, and Goldberg was told to tell his friends O'Donnell, et al., "to leave town or we'll kill them." They advised Sass and Goldberg to do the same, then they released the pair.

The Nitto mob pineapple corps went on the offensive to support their teamsters. In the dark, early hours of May 1, five bombs exploded downtown within minutes of each other, causing approximately $65,000 in damage. All the bombings were aimed at defiant businesses and Teamster labor leaders. Among the victims were Illinois Bell Telephone and a Marshall Field's cap factory on South Wells. Collateral casualties included the Bismarck Hotel, which lost several windows to a nearby blast. One night later, bombers blasted the home of an opposing Teamster official. Two more bombs later that week, numbers forty-one and forty-two for the year, tore apart a restaurant and milk plant, both suspected of using transportation unions not within the mob fold.

Next, White and Humphreys sought to strangle the city via Red Barker's old TNT agency. On May 8, at the tail end of the heating season, they strategically shut down over half of the city's 200 coal yards with strikes. To reopen, employers simply had to sign a trucking contract with the mob's outlaw Teamster organization, which put a $2 per truck monthly fee into the pockets of Nitto's racketeers. The next day, the racketeering force received a boost when, after six weeks of trial, seven TNT comrades were found innocent of earlier racketeering.

The offensive into the labor field was well-timed: thanks to the Depression, Chicago was one of the most financially strapped cities in the country, and Cermak's death had left relative political chaos in town. State's Attorney Courtney blabbered on about rooting out racketeers, but accomplished little.

Rather than waiting until June to elect a new mayor as Illinois law provided, Democrats pushed legislation through the state house to allow the city council to select the mayor. To some surprise, on April 14, the council selected fifty-seven-year-old Ed Kelly as mayor. His name had been tossed into the ring almost as an afterthought. As former chief engineer of the sanitary district and head of the South Park Board, the Irishman lacked the typical political *vitae* for higher rank. Kelly, however, was younger than some of the more obvious candidates and had few political enemies. He also had the backing of most of the city's Democratic powers.

From the start, things were less than pleasant for Chicago's new mayor and soon-to-be World's Fair host. To accommodate President Roosevelt's schedule so that he might attend the event's inauguration, fair officials moved the opening date from June 1 to May 27. The new mayor initially wrote off the adverse conditions, as Thompson had written off crime years before, by saying such things were normal in the course of any city's existence.

But the racketeering problem remained at the "acute stage." The number of bombings promised to outpace the even more violent 1929 mark of eighty-eight bombings. In early May, the chief of detectives reported the theft of 1,000 sticks of dynamite, now "probably in the hands of Chicago gangsters for use." The May 4 edition of the *Daily News* ridiculed law enforcement efforts in a caricature: entitled "All in a Bomb King's Racket." Bomber Belcastro's picture appeared at top center, surrounded by sketches of civic ineptitude. The most stinging figure by far was the comical, stick-like fellow who stood before a storefront holding a fuse connected to a powder bomb. Turning to a nearby duffer of a policeman clodhopping by, the bomber asks the oblivious cop, "Gotta match, mister?"

The end of the most overt portion of the labor racketeering war came not through the actions of local authorities but rather thanks to the announcement that the federal cavalry was riding in once again. The *Daily News* headline on May 4, 1933, trumpeted an "OPEN INQUIRY ON INCOME TAX OF HOODLUMS," while one of the paper's headlines the next day reported, "U.S. PUSHES FIGHT ON CHICAGO RACKETS." Officials from the local office of the Treasury Department announced that SIU agents were targeting Murray Humphreys, Klondike O'Donnell, Jack White, and other gangsters for income tax violations. Records from the local Teamsters were seized for scrutiny. Days later, forced to change his tune, Mayor Kelly immediately broke the TNT strike threat by ordering all private trucking concerns hauling for the city to be laid off. Only those clear of association with the hoodlum TNT were called back to work.

The fact that Nitto's hoods were out didn't end the battle with Touhy. The latter still targeted Humphreys, O'Donnell, and White. Nitto's group took a couple of potshots at a Touhy labor ally a couple of weeks before the fair, but for now, Nitto would concentrate on income from the fair. He would deal with Touhy once his fair activities settled smoothly.

17

1933: CONQUER AND CONSOLIDATE

T HE IDEA FOR A CHICAGO World's Fair struck as early as 1925. "We desire," the
fair committee wrote, "to present, as the central theme, the progress of civi-
lization during the hundred years of Chicago's existence." Originally christened the
Chicago World's Fair Centennial Celebration, the fair's title was later economized
simply to "A Century of Progress." During the eight-year struggle to bring it to
fruition, Mayor Dever advanced it, Mayor Thompson at first opposed it, Cook
County Board chairman and later Mayor Cermak helped push it along, President of
the South Park Board Ed Kelly helped develop it, and now *Mayor* Kelly opened it on
Saturday, May 27, 1933.

An exhibit of technological advances, everything about the event flaunted mag-
nificence; it was all brilliant and larger than life. The fair occupied 427 acres of
lakeshore parkland (Burnham Park) extending from Twelfth Street on the north edge
three miles south to about Thirty-ninth Street. An eighty-six-acre lagoon separated
the main shore from a large outer island lined with fashionable exhibit buildings and
an accessible beach on the north edge. To reach the exhibits, one could walk across
one of three bridges or make the journey 200 feet above the water in the Tower Sky
Ride. By far the fair's highlight, its twin suspension towers on either shore rose nearly
600 feet; the suspension cables were strung with lights and the towers were illuminated to make a brilliant display in the evening. There was a Ferris wheel comparable to the 1893 Columbian Exposition mammoth, and a 200-foot thermometer,

whose individual numerals measured ten feet tall, greeted visitors near the Twenty-third Street entrance. The fair glowed from the world's largest collection of colored lights operated by exciting gas in sealed tubes—the novel neon.

Light illuminated the fresh, art deco designs of the exhibits. The science and art displays dwarfed anything previously seen. The Hall of Sciences and its huge dioramas gave visitors a glance into the dinosaur age, while the nearby Art Institute displayed over $75 million in art pieces donated for exhibition. The fair's ultramodern landscape was flavored with new and traditional foreign pavilions from all corners of the globe. A visitor could stroll through Italian, Belgian, and Japanese villages or visit the Old Heidelberg Inn, a replica of the German original that boasted some of the best food in the world over and could seat 2,500 patrons at a time. Chicago constructed its own piece of history by recreating Fort Dearborn near Twenty-sixth Street. Scattered in between the exhibits and pavilions were refreshment stands, rides, amusements, and vending machines. On the fair's first weekend, one that was graced with cool weather, over 130,000 pushed through the turnstiles for the spectacular gala. On six weekends that summer, attendance topped the one million mark and peaked on September 3 at 1.4 million. The extravaganza garnered revenue from admissions, rental space, and concessions totaling nearly $16 million for the cash-starved city.

The timing was perfect. As much as it served to retrieve Chicago from the doldrums of the Depression, the fair also provided a measure of at least temporary relief for the mob as they were preparing to exit the Prohibition era. However, that the Nitto mob "had the whole place sewed up" that year, as Charlie Fischetti supposedly claimed, was probably an overstatement. To be sure, they did claim their piece of the tourist trade both inside and outside the exposition. Inside the fairgrounds, Nitto's brewery agents pushed their brands of beer. Ricca was thought to have a significant investment in the San Carlo Italian Village where Joe Fusco's Gold Seal Liquors distributorship cornered the market. Humphreys was thought to have lined up the popcorn purveyors and to have a hand in a couple of well-patronized rides, while primitive games of chance swindled others. Assisting everyone was Louis Greenberg. Undoubtedly, the gang managed subsurface interests as well.

Outside the fairgrounds, Nitto's group was well placed. Fair visitors who desired a taste of wide-open Chicago stepped out to the gang's old domain, the city's First Ward. James Mondi managed the lucrative gambling interests, which seldom allowed a winner to leave the premises, and mob saloons served fair patrons off-site. Striptease shows and women were available, some of whom also worked inside the exposition under the guise of various stage acts. And Cicero remained wide open.

A month after the fair opened, Nitto lost a key member of his racketeering department when federal authorities indicted Murray Humphreys for thinking too little about his taxes for the years 1930-32. Compared to what Nitto had been indicted for, the amount was trivial—just over $22,000—but after putting away Nitto, Capone, and the rest of the upper echelon, the government was determined to get all the other gangsters as well. Of particular interest were the troublesome racketeering types, for putting them away would also rid Chicago of some notorious "public enemies." The feds had eyed Barker before he was killed, and Jack White and Klondike O'Donnell also were thought to be targets. Humphreys, however, did not learn the earlier lesson of Nitto and Capone. He filed no returns before 1930 and only filed that year's form more than a year later when he learned he was under investigation. For the preceding years, the government alleged, he grossly understated his tax liability. Rather than face the charges, he was thought to have absconded to Mexico for a time. Humphreys was absent until October 1934, when he finally surrendered and accepted an eighteen-month sentence and a $5,000 fine.

———⊲◦◦⊳———

Chicago attracted far more than hearty fairgoers that summer. Bank robbery and kidnapping became the recurrent solutions to net easy money for many a Depression-drained gunman in the early 1930s. Plucking a millionaire off the street, for example, might earn tens of thousands of dollars. Unfortunately, the scourge of kidnappings inked many a press headline. The tragedy of the infamous Lindbergh kidnapping a year earlier only inflamed law enforcement's resolve to eliminate the deeds. Rather than run in the open, many a captor sought to blend in with the near-anonymous crowds of a large city. Cities also provided the crook with avenues to launder kidnapping money and spend it lavishly. The frontier and World's Fair city of Chicago fit the criminal's bill.

Capone is said to have had a soft spot for the outlaws. In some cases, the more skilled gunmen might be hired by the mob—Fred "Killer" Burke, August Winkler, Fred Goetz, and Byron Bolton were all thought to have performed occasional heavy work. After all, many of the mob's regular guns started out as wild and daring desperados too. Winkler stayed on as a valued gun and was now enjoying several North Side concessions after being a suspect in the Ted Newberry case. Others outlaws circled in and out of Chicago's revolving door. Last winter, ex-O'Banion hand Louis Alterie was sought in the snatching of Denver tycoon Charles Boettcher II, but his actual abductors were eventually nabbed by the FBI—in Chicago. Verne Miller, a friend of Winkler's, escaped to the city after participating in the June 1933 Kansas City Massacre. Machine Gun Kelly and his wife also fled to Chicago after involvement in the kidnapping of Oklahoma City oilman Charles Urschel. Authorities this summer sought Fred Goetz, Arthur "Dock" and Fred Barker, and Alvin "Creepy" Karpis in the kidnapping of wealthy Minnesota brewer William Hamm. That cadre of kidnappers hunkered down in a Chicago suburb before obtaining the ransom and releasing their victim.

Chicago was becoming a little too madcap for Nitto and a mob in transition aiming to conduct affairs on Nitto's straightforward, businesslike, *sub rosa* terms. Nitto did not necessarily welcome the desperados with the kindness that Capone had tendered earlier—particularly when they tried to dabble in business in which the mob was interested or when they hired themselves out to the mob's last major opponent, the Touhy gang. One man who knew Nitto and the mob, Alvin Karpis, remembered being called to a downtown office where Nitto grilled him about his associations with the Touhy gang and told him that he suspected Verne Miller of being with the

239

Touhys. Karpis later said he sweated out the meeting, wishing he were someplace else. These "independent bastards," as Ricca noted, posed a problem for the Nitto Outfit. Near year's end, Miller was slain in Detroit and his body dumped in a ditch. Authorities in both cities looked for four Chicago gunmen whom they suspected of following Miller there before killing him.

The mob, however, did not necessarily spurn kidnapping as a tool. As early as 1931, the hardened guns of the racketeering department utilized the method as a strategic twofold means to union takeover riches. A crew would march into a union office, and if the stubborn officials failed to bow to their demands, the racketeers snatched a high union officer as a warning and then exacted perhaps as much as $50,000 for his freedom. When they paid, the money often came from union coffers. It wasn't a long-term solution, but one way or another, the gangsters tapped into the union treasury. In 1931, they snatched Milk Wagon Drivers business agent Ritchie for $50,000, while in 1933, they snatched James Petrillo, long time leader of the musicians union, and gained another cool $50,000. Regardless of the recent Lindbergh case, kidnapping union officials was less risky than kidnapping others because these men often had unsavory backgrounds themselves—which discouraged any thought of seeking aid from the law. In July, some suspect they implemented the brigand method to purge a competitor.

The Northwest Side Touhy gang dabbled in the action with the same union goal. Some witnesses claimed they were connected to the Hamm case in June. Then came the summer's bolt from the blue: on July 1, 1933, the *Chicago American*'s headline blared, "KIDNAP FACTOR, ASK BIG RANSOM." A posse of men had snatched John "Jake the Barber" Factor as he left the boisterous Dells roadhouse near Morton Grove, Illinois, in the northwest part of Cook County. This was the same Jake Factor who was thought to have barbered with Nitto for a spell so many years before. Continuing along his unscrupulous, clipping ways, the Barber had become a millionaire stock promoter—and, hence, a desirable target.

At first, the erratic reports coming in placed the ransom demands in the $100,000-$200,000 range. The next day, son Jerome Factor received a demand for $75,000 in small bills. Astonishingly, this was the second kidnapping to befall the family; back in April, Jerome was grabbed and held eight days. With Factor family transactions shrouded in ambiguity, both affairs left the public with a real sense of mystery. The lawyer for the family claimed they made no payment for Jerome's release, but others reported a $50,000 fee was paid through the intercession of Murray Humphreys and Sam Hunt.

The Dells was a Nitto Syndicate casino franchise as result of the Capone invasion of the Northwest Side a couple of years earlier. Some saw Factor's kidnapping as an attempt by the Touhys to muscle easy money now that Humphreys was on the lam. Law enforcement focused on the big picture, however: fully aware that Morton Grove long lay in Touhy territory, police immediately focused their efforts in that direction. The state's attorney's office commenced raids on all known Touhy hideouts. Touhy, though, in an interview with a leading Chicago newspaper, denied involvement, claiming that he and his wife were visiting a couple of sick friends in the Oak Park hospital when Factor was taken. The police raids were unsuccessful as Touhy, by his own account, shrugged off the episode and departed to the Wisconsin woods for a few days of fishing. Twelve days passed before an unshaven, somewhat bedraggled-looking Factor was dumped by the side of the road in the western suburb of La Grange, released after his family allegedly paid kidnappers.

Allegedly is the operative word. The murkiness of the case never seemed to clear and promised to provide the Century of Progress public yet another suspenseful feature to follow in the papers (second perhaps to the ongoing, volatile ruckus of the Nitto shooting). First, Factor said $50,000 in $10 and $20 bills was paid for his release. Other reports suggested a $75,000 ransom. Aldermanic powerhouse and friend Jacob Arvey, who aided the family, claimed "not one penny of ransom was paid to the abductors," though he says he wasn't involved in the final negotiations. Factor also eventually recanted his prior statement about the ransom amount. In an interview with the *Chicago American*, he said he could not identify the kidnappers and could not determine where he was held because he was blindfolded nearly all the time. They treated him well, but at times roughed him up, poking him with machine guns. Sometimes his tormentors asked about the stock market. Other times they talked about getting $500,000 for him, but otherwise didn't talk about a ransom. Factor also claimed, with a touch of bravado, that he steadfastly refused to pen any ransom notes. Of his abductors, Factor thought there might have been seven or eight men involved, then suggested as many as twenty.

"Do you intend to prosecute?" asked reporters.

"What can I do? I never saw any of the kidnappers. I couldn't recognize them," he replied.

The day after his release, two curious newspaper reporters noted Factor's "conscious, cautious effort to avoid remarks that might afford a clue to the identity of his captors." There remained a curious lack of consistency in his chronicle. How might a blindfolded man identify machine guns? The patrolman who found Factor in La Grange noted a few peculiarities. Factor, he observed, appeared far from an unraveled inmate of a twelve-day ordeal; his light Palm Beach-style suit, though slightly wrinkled, was tidy. Factor's shirt collars were pressed neatly, his shoes were clean, and his hands and nails were "perfectly clean, cleaner than mine," the policeman said. Most amazingly, the handkerchief in his pocket was still neatly pressed and folded. For someone who hadn't bathed or been out of his clothes as he said, Factor appeared remarkably unsoiled except for his matted hair and beard. The officer did not comment on any pungent scent resulting from Factor's supposed lack of bathing for such a long period. The whole thing smelled of fabrication, and the *Tribune*'s headline on July 8 crowed, "FACTOR CASE BRANDED A HOAX."

Federal authorities, led by Chicago FBI agent Melvin Purvis, entered the case early on. They were involved not because of the crime itself (the recently adopted Lindbergh law allowed federal jurisdiction when kidnappers crossed state lines) but rather at the behest of the British government. A couple of years earlier, Factor promoted a stock venture that collected nearly $7 million from investors of the island nation. He then skipped to the United States with the entire sum, leaving investors high and dry. Since then, Britain had sought his extradition to face charges for the alleged theft.

Factor lost the first round of the fight when, in 1931, he was ordered extradited. He appealed to the U.S. District Court and won a reversal but lost again when the U.S. Court of Appeals overturned the lower court. Now, counsel for the British Crown suspected Factor of attempting to delay his extradition by staging a phony kidnapping. They thought this may also have been the reason for his son's timely disappearance: at an earlier hearing for the British swindle, Factor posted a $50,000 bond, and a new hearing was scheduled before the U.S. Supreme Court on April 15—remarkably, the same day the younger Factor disappeared, and surely no one would expect a father to forsake a son in a time of need. In May, U.S. authorities gained another hearing for October, but then, as tough luck would have it, the senior Factor was kidnapped.

Investigators were still working the Touhy angle when the call to arrest direct or indirect suspects hauled in Carl Fontana and Charles O'Leary of the old Fontana gang from the Valley district. Closer to Nitto's gang, police wanted Lawrence Mangano. (Louis Alterie was also sought.) Police guarded at least forty prominent Chicagoans from the latest scourge with orders from the top to "shoot to kill" any kidnappers.

A few days later, Touhy, suspected murderer Willie Sharkey, labor slugger Eddie McFadden, and St. Paul, Minnesota, stick-up man Gustave "Gloomy Gus" Schafer were returning from a fishing trip in Wisconsin. Six miles north of Elkhorn, they skidded off a rain-soaked road into a wooden utility pole, snapping it off at the base. Touhy drove off in the seven-passenger Chrysler sedan with only a dented fender. Fatefully for the group, a local good Samaritan witnessed the incident and, judging that the property owner deserved reimbursement, called authorities. Elkhorn police caught up with the crew, who then put in an appearance at the station and gladly paid the $22 and change for the broken pole. They did not continue their journey, however. Suspicious of the group, police searched Touhy's vehicle and found seven pistols, a German rifle, cotton rope, and cloth bandages that might be used as blindfolds. Touhy and his clan were put in the local backwoods pokey, and by morning the FBI and officials in the Cook County state's attorney's office were there to greet them. Purvis announced, to the astonishment of Touhy, his intention to indict them for the Hamm kidnapping, and there was also talk of an indictment in the Factor case.

The first harbinger of ill fortune came the day after Touhy's arrest in Elkhorn. Factor and his son were on hand for a lineup. It took only a few minutes, and they were gone without a word. Even the police could not be sure of the outcome. State's Attorney Courtney, on the other hand, was not as guarded: "We know positively the men that kidnapped Factor. If certain men will stand up, we will get a conviction. If the $1,700 found on the gang isn't payoff money, I don't know what payoff money is."

Had Touhy heard Courtney's harangue, he might not have been so optimistic, but at the time, Touhy thought nothing of his dilemma. He always maintained his group was nowhere near Minnesota on the day of Hamm's abduction, and he believed such an outstanding public figure as Hamm would never risk perjuring himself to send them up. The Factor case hardly seemed a bother since, as he understood it, Factor failed to identify him in the police lineup. Besides, he rationalized further, why would the state's attorney allow him to be extradited to Minnesota, if they deemed such an airtight case against him in Illinois?

On the opening day of the Hamm trial, Touhy and his cohorts in the defense docks were informed of the indictment against them in the Factor case. As the Hamm case progressed that autumn, Factor, accompanied by Chief Investigator Dan Gilbert, materialized in the courtroom. Their presence alarmed Touhy, for he knew the two to be boyhood chums from the old Valley district, and neither was relevant to the Minnesota case. What they were doing, he could only speculate. Were they there as celebrity presences to invoke sympathy for the prosecution efforts? Perhaps they were reminders to the jurors that Touhy was wanted in a similar case in Chicago. Or perhaps Factor was building a public relations scam of sorts—hoping he would be perceived as an unfortunate, wealthy stock promoter (not swindler), who, like upstanding public figures Hamm and Urschel, had been abused by kidnappers and was there to see justice served.

As Touhy predicted, the jury found him and his associates innocent in the Hamm case when none of the witnesses could place them at the scene. He was shipped off to Chicago to await a hearing in the Factor case, which by now he knew was not going well for him. While in Minnesota, Factor gave a press interview. The man who once could hardly fathom being able to prosecute anyone because he hadn't seen his abductors now seethed outside the court. "I wouldn't hurt a fly," he said, "but I could take that guy's [Roger Touhy's] throat and twist it until the blood came out. And I could drink the blood, the way they tortured me."

In December, the United States Supreme Court ordered John Factor extradited to England. State's Attorney Courtney, along with Special Assistant Attorney General Keenan, however, petitioned Washington to keep Factor in the states as a material witness in the kidnapping case until it was settled. The British Embassy was informed they would have to wait for their man.

The trial was set for January 1934. The prosecution called for the death penalty. Touhy's defense opened with a statement to the jury charging a Factor frame-up tied to the Capone mob. On the stand, Factor altered his tune from July. He now claimed to have identified Touhy in the police lineup by recognizing his voice as belonging to one of the kidnappers; he also said he had been allowed to drop his blindfold and write a ransom note after all. The defense countered with the La Grange policeman's testimony and numerous witnesses, including an Indiana priest who swore that Touhy was nowhere near the incident. The clergyman said he was with Touhy in Indiana the day of the Hamm kidnapping and that he spent time with Touhy at least one day while Factor was still being held. The first trial ended a hung jury.

When the second trial began in February, both prosecution and defense transformed—to Touhy's disadvantage. Factor amended his previous testimony again, and then before the prosecution rested its case, they called two surprise witnesses: Isaac

Costner, a habitual criminal from Tennessee wanted for a mail theft in North Carolina, and Basil Banghart. Both "recognized Touhy men" were apprehended within days of each other on outstanding warrants. Chief Investigator Gilbert brought Costner to Illinois from Baltimore. Factor identified both men as captors. At first, the pair steadfastly refused the claim, but then Costner broke. Banghart followed somewhat reluctantly. On the stand, Costner announced his part in the kidnap plot and identified Touhy and his henchmen as the guilty parties. Why did he only now confess? He wanted to make amends for his sins, he said. In fact, he was attempting to make a deal on the federal mail charge against him (despite his testimony, he didn't get a deal). Touhy's counsel this time around lacked perhaps the most believable witness, the priest, who found himself constrained by church administrators from testifying on Touhy's behalf. Doomed, Touhy was found guilty and received a sentence of ninety-nine years in the state penitentiary.

Touhy spent the next twenty-five years clamoring for his freedom, claiming Factor had pulled the "swindle of his life." Factor, he said, hornswoggled the feds and Cook County officials along with a boob judge and twelve dimwitted jurors. In need of some scheme to beat the feds, Touhy theorized that Factor, through his friends Humphreys and Hunt, went to the Nitto mob for assistance, offering to pay them for the service. Arrangements for the "kidnapping" were made at the lower echelon, remote from the bigwigs, but the owners of the Dells were thought to be in on it.

Did the Nitto mob engineer the whole episode? If not, it was a remarkable blunder on Touhy's part. Touhy's labor unions were left unprotected, and the Northwest Side gambling and beer concessions were now open to a mob invasion. Would he have risked so much in order to perform this kidnapping? Possibly. Touhy faced the same fiscal crunch in the beer trade as the Nitto mob and was looking for new sources of income. But given Factor's track record at the time and his familiarity with certain men in the mob, a frame-up is quite plausible. English officials certainly suspected a phony kidnapping to avoid extradition and thought him capable of such. Humphreys was suspected in engineering the phony Jerome Factor kidnap for just that purpose. Did they do it again?

One signal from the underworld relayed to the FBI claimed that Nitto paid to have Touhy and his crew accused of the Hamm kidnapping. Another tip suggested the whole affair was contrived by the Nitto mob to entice a Factor investment in a brewery. In one master stroke, the gang could neatly corner another brewery with Prohibition nearly at end, Touhy could be framed and run out of the picture, and Factor could avoid extradition. After a full review of the case, Federal Judge John P. Barnes in 1954 concurred that there had been some sort of conspiracy:

> The court finds that John Factor was not kidnapped for ransom, or otherwise, on the night of June 30 or July 1, 1933, though he was taken as a result of his own connivance. . . . The court is of the opinion that the incident of June 30 and July 1, 1933, was a hoax planned by, and executed under the direction of, John Factor in order to avoid extradition to England.

Barnes further found that Roger Touhy did not participate or have knowledge of the plot. Courtney was responsible for keeping Factor in the states and Gilbert for suppressing evidence favorable to Touhy's defense; as such, the two were "apprised at all times" of Factor's windy kidnapping story yet still proceeded to pursue the matter, indulging "numerous stratagems and artifices" designed to bring about a conviction—and thereby violating Touhy's Fourteenth Amendment right of due process. Gilbert's relationship with Factor was "far more than the ordinary relationship between prosecuting witness and prosecutor." The judge held that the kidnappings of both Factor family members were an attempt to gain sympathy for the victim in a time full of kidnapping awareness.

It seemed unlikely to Barnes that Factor, so soon after the kidnapping of his son, would risk visiting a roadhouse "known to be run by members of the so-called Capone Syndicate, located outside the city of Chicago . . . along a lonely road. . . . To put it mildly, Roger Touhy was not an acceptable person to Captain Gilbert. Touhy and the opposition with which he was identified was an obstacle in the drive of the politico-criminal Capone Syndicate to control and dominate the labor unions. . . . That criminal Syndicate could not operate without the approval of the prosecutor's office. . . . They did continue to operate and thrive without interference from Courtney or Gilbert."

No doubt, the chief beneficiary of the whole scenario was the Nitto mob, which took over the Northwest Side and adjoining Cook County. Factor also accomplished his goal, for after the episode, he successfully delayed his overdue trip to England indefinitely; authorities, for unknown reasons, allowed the extradition warrant to lapse. When Factor applied to the Federal Alcohol Commission in 1940 for a permit to run a distillery, Dan Gilbert appeared as a character witness on his behalf. The commission was far from impressed, opining in their decision that "John Factor is an individual who cannot be believed under oath." Three years later, he was convicted of mail fraud in connection with a bogus whiskey deal and sentenced to ten years in the federal penitentiary system, where he served nearly five years. During that trial, his unsavory past that included leasing Arkansas oil properties, dealing in Florida real estate, and settling with the Internal Revenue Service for $120,000 were all brought to light. Years later, he was found to be wheeling and dealing stocks with Murray Humphreys.

—◈—

Frank Nitto wasn't completely removed from the Factor affair. A week after Factor's release, Nitto was tending to business in the Loop when Detective Sergeant William Drury spotted him outside the LaSalle Hotel. Always willing to inconvenience gangsters, and with the Factor kidnapping mystery fresh, Drury followed Nitto with the aim of hauling him in for routine questioning. Alerted to the detective's presence after glancing over his shoulder, Nitto ducked into the Metropolitan Building and made it to a nearby elevator. Drury gave chase, then, knowing the second floor crossed over to the Bismarck Hotel, he decided to stake out the hotel entrances and wait. When Nitto emerged two hours later, Drury gave him a ride to the detective bureau.

Along the way, Drury asked his captive why he ran off. Nitto's arrogant reply was: "Me? I'm not running away from anybody. Look, Drury, the mayor doesn't want me, the chief doesn't want to see me, and the state's attorney's office doesn't want to see me. Why don't you wise up?" Nitto prophesied in a rage that the chief of detectives would be "kicking pebbles off the sidewalk at city parks." He answered nothing more, and the enraged detective charged him with disorderly conduct (the charge was later dismissed). As an extra present, he tendered Nitto a subpoena to appear in the Lang trial scheduled to begin in September. Remarkably, the detective and his chief were, as Nitto predicted, in Drury's words, "farmed out," which was police vernacular for being transferred to remote stations where they could do no harm.

On the twenty-fifth, jury selection for the Lang trial began. Of particular concern to attorneys was the political affiliation of the jury members given Lang's threat to "wreck the Democratic Party." Empanelling the jury took most the day, but Nitto wasn't there on day one. For a month, the state's attorney's office had a vagrancy warrant out for his arrest. Given his previous run-in with Judge Lyle and his exorbitant bonds on such matters, Nitto lay low, preferring to have attorney Ben Short handle the matter. The law agreed to drop the warrant.

The next day gang leader Nitto finally appeared, tanned, wearing a finely cut olive suit, relaxed, and ready, albeit reluctant, to testify. How ironic, one newspaper reporter noted, that the state's attorney was prosecuting *for* hoodlum Nitto while attorneys Rittenhouse and Marovitz, normally counsel for hoodlums, were defending the police force. After waiting five months, Lang blustered nothing sensational. Defense counsel Rittenhouse outlined the surprise defense in his opening statement: they would show that the late Mayor Cermak lived "in constant fear of assassination at the hands of hired killers" because of the mayor's war on crime. State's Attorney Thomas Courtney and the two detectives in the raid had joined the mayor in that war, he continued. "They had been told," he said, "to watch Nitti and the gang of alleged gunmen. . . . When they entered the room the detectives drew their revolvers because they knew they faced desperate characters."

Detective Harry Miller was the first to take the stand, testifying that "Mayor Cermak told me that he had found out through his undercover agents that the Syndicate was determined to get him and had imported a killer, Louis Campagna, from New York to do the job." He continued, "The mayor told me he was to be killed because he was trying to drive the hoodlums out of town before the World's Fair opened." The Saturday before the shooting, he claimed Cermak pulled him and Lang aside and gave them the address of Nitto's headquarters, suggesting Monday as a good day for the raid. Miller said the mayor wanted to "talk" to Nitto about the Syndicate since he was understood to be the boss. They made the raid, he said, but when the shooting erupted, he was in another room. Curiously, the prosecution did not bring to light Miller's key grand jury testimony concerning Ted Newberry; his alleged bounty may have shown better than any other evidence the malice which they were trying to prove.

"Desperate character" and main prosecution witness Frank Nitto took the stand, annoyed to be there in the first place. In a low, disinterested voice, the swarthy mobster testified that he lived at 1208 McAllister, that he was in the Quality Flour office placing bets, and that he was led out of the inner office, crumpled a piece of paper and put it in his mouth, and then was shot. Assistant State's Attorney Dougherty continued:

Q: "Did Lang or any other officer show you a warrant for your arrest?"

A: "No."

Lang's counsel cross-examined:

Q: "How many times had you been to that office before December?"

A: "Several times."

Q: "You say this was Palumbo's office. What was his business?"

A: "Oh, he took bets on horses."

Q: "What business have you ever had?"

A: "I was in the restaurant business at 901 South Halsted Street."

Q: "When was the last time you were in a legitimate business?"

A: "I am in a legitimate business right now, in the restaurant business at 5829 Madison Street."

He admitted he had served a stretch in prison for income tax evasion. Marovitz asked him if he had ever seen Lang prior to the shooting? No, Nitto said, and claimed he bore him no ill will now. That was the end of his testimony, and Nitto lolled away the remainder of the day with Ben Short at his elbow.

Chris Callahan followed, relating his same upright story that Lang had shot Nitto and that Lang must have shot himself because Nitto didn't have a gun. No, he confirmed, they had no warrants. His partner, Mike Shannon, offered his tidbits, and the prosecution rested its case.

The defense put Lang on the stand to have his say. They asked him if the mayor had told him where to make the raid; he responded in the affirmative. He saw Nitto and Callahan scuffle, though it was "pretty dark in the room" and he couldn't see who had the gun. In doubt, he ran over and shot Nitto to protect Callahan. He thought Nitto lunged at him, so he fired twice more. He didn't know it was the gang leader until later. Then Lang said he discovered a wound on his arm but didn't know how it happened. His counsel then asked:

Q: "Prior to December 19 did you know Frank Nitti by sight?"

A: "I did not."

Q: "Did you know him by reputation?"

A: "I did."

Q: "What was that reputation?"

A: "Bad."

[later]

Q: "Did you intend to kill Nitti?"

A: "Yes."

Q: "Would you have shot Nitti if there had been no struggle?"

A: "No. I would not."

Regarding his defense that Cermak had told him about "import" assassin Campagna, the state's attorney asked Lang:

Q: "Do you know that 'Little New York' lived in Chicago all his life and could not have been imported?"

A: "I did not."

Q: "Did you know he served time in Joliet?"

A: "No."

To bolster the case by demonstrating Cermak's fear, the defense brought in other witnesses. A manufacturer of bulletproof vests testified that Mayor Cermak had placed an order for one with his company. Chief of Detectives William Schoemaker and Colonel Henry Barrett Chamberlian, operating director of the Chicago Crime Commission, testified about Nitto's bad reputation, among other things. Nitto simply wore a wan smile and was clearly disinterested.

Prosecutor Erwin Closene closed for the state's attorney. To the jury he announced: "Police as well as hoodlums must observe the law. Nitti did nothing to warrant Lang's shooting him. . . . The defense has laid its whole case on a dead man—the late Mayor Cermak—who cannot come into court to refute their testimony. . . . Lang went to that room with the express purpose of killing Nitti, and his self-inflicted wound is proof of that." Further, the defense case was built upon "falsehoods." Louis Campagna was not imported to kill the mayor; Campagna had been a citizen of Chicago for over ten years, even spending time in Joliet for robbery. Lang was a liar, as proven by Callahan's observations. Curiously absent from the prosecution's case were the assertions that Ted Newberry paid the detective to shoot Nitto.

"Sergeant Lang," countered defense counsel Rittenhouse, "should have a medal for shooting this gangster." Attorney Marovitz cleverly continued on Lang's behalf, "We, the defense, stand on the side of law and order and in the name of 6,000 policemen. If you find Harry Lang guilty, you will receive an invitation to one of the biggest dinners ever given in Chicago; a dinner given by Frank Nitti to the city's hoodlums, to celebrate a triumph over the forces of law and order."

Faced by what one reporter deemed "a case as strange as any in the history of Chicago crime," the jury brought in a compromise verdict a few hours later: Lang, they said, was guilty of assault with a deadly weapon—a misdemeanor, not the felony sought by the prosecution. Instead of facing a possible sentence of one to fourteen years in jail, the misdemeanor verdict meant he could receive one day to one year and/or a fine. A relieved Lang commented, "That ain't so bad." Marovitz immediately appealed the decision.

In November, a police trial board discharged Lang from the force. He received a late consolation Christmas present when Judge Thomas Lynch granted Lang a new trial in the shooting. Lynch had a more sympathetic view of the case and asserted that all those in the room at the time of the shooting were hoodlums and that police "used good judgment" in their actions. Upon pronouncement of the good news, Lang stepped forward to the bench to thank Lynch, who said, "Don't thank me. Thank your good record as a police officer." Besides, he said, the evidence didn't prove his guilt beyond a reasonable doubt.

Nitto dodged all further summonses in the matter, and after a half-dozen postponements, the state's attorney finally agreed to strike the case off the docket. Still, lingering suspicion fueled speculation that Nitto, after his wounding, settled the debt by murdering both Newberry and Cermak. Prior to the September trial, two monthly magazines, *Real America* and *True Detective Mysteries*, chimed in on Cermak and the shooting. The article in the latter—authored by "XXX," a purported personal undercover agent for the late mayor—perhaps gave rise to the more colorful accounts of the Cermak conspiracy. He says that Cermak told his force he wanted all the hoods chased out, all the beer flats and gambling places closed up, urging them to "go to it!" The author also claimed that Ted Newberry confided in the mayor the location of the Quality Flour office. Frantic conferences at Nitto's bedside, with dialogue such as, "Tony can't do this to me!" and "Tony is on the spot; his number is up," peppered the story. Another Nitto higher-up was said to have whispered, "Tony will come back in a coffin." XXX makes a great deal out of White and McGurn being in possession of train tickets to Miami when arrested and claims that Zangara, who was to be paid $1,500 for the job, did the shooting as "an out" after double-crossing some alky representatives in Florida. The agent reported that his underworld source told him they would hit him, but not in Chicago.

The four-part piece on the political career of Cermak written by Lester Freeman for *Real America* magazine was less sensational. He exposed the mayor's sleazy political side. Everyone understood that his crime drive against the gang, Freeman said, was not to drive out the gambling and speakeasies—impossible even in Chicago's most lawful periods—but rather to bring them under the sphere of city hall. All that law and order talk was simply Tony's baloney, he said; Cermak was interested in power. The Nitti shooting "fiasco" concerned the mayor, to be sure, and put him "on the run." Freeman judged assassination by the mob to be a likely probability, but he stopped short accusing the Nitto mob directly. He offered no more specifics than to suggest the mayor knew it was the gang who shot him.

Those Chicagoans familiar with the inner workings of the city's political and organized crime circles officially remained mum on the subject for years. When they did finally talk, the verdict was generally thought to be a mob assassination. The first discussion appeared in 1944. The day after the former operating director of the Chicago Crime Commission, Frank Loesch, passed away at ninety-two, the Daily Times printed an item relating his belief that the mob manipulated Zangara's "tortured mind," playing on the assassin's declarations to kill all leaders, including mayors. Four years later, police Captain Tom Connelly and Lieutenant Bill Drury penned a *Herald-American* story claiming, in part, that "militant" Mayor Cermak was a victim of gang guns. Explaining further, the officers said Nitto "gambled that the crime crusade would blow up if he got rid of Mayor Cermak." They found proof of their contention in the fact that, for the next decade, gangland observed its "greatest period of prosperity and immunity from arrest."

Cermak friend Judge John Lyle firmly believed the Mafia to be behind the mayor's death, as he told the *Tribune* a few years later. In the article, the judge, who threw his Republican support behind Democrat Cermak in 1931, told of personal meetings with Cermak in which the mayoral candidate outlined his plans. "John," Cermak is reported to have said, "I am against this Mafia business. . . . I won't tell them now. If I am elected mayor in April tho, that is the time to speak up. . . . I will have special policemen with instructions to waste no time with those people. . . . I am going to call in the leaders—and I know who they are—I will tell them to fold up their tents." When Lyle expressed concern over such a dangerous mission, Cermak told him he had over 8,000 policemen at his call. Still, Lyle warned him, the mob could get him anywhere outside of the city, even at the prizefights Cermak enjoyed so much. The clincher for Lyle was that when Cermak was shot, the guilty character turned out to be an Italian with an alleged rifle marksmanship background in the Italian army; further, that Zangara died with his lips sealed seemed significant to the judge.

Three years later, Lyle penned a book stating the case once more with further detail. Following Miller's explanation, Lyle claimed the "imported" Louis Campagna was assigned the job of killing Cermak, but his cover was blown with his arrest in the office where Nitto was shot. Afterwards, so the story goes, a call was sent out for someone else who could do the job, the Nitto mob ending up with anti-social, authority hater Zangara. Lyle also noted that his opinion coincided with that of Frank J. Loesch, who was thought to have obtained information that the Philadelphia mob assisted the Chicago crowd in the endeavor by locating assassin Zangara.

Chicago Sun-Times writer Jack McPhaul wrote with a piece entitled "The Shot that Shaped Chicago Politics" relating Lyle's assertions but pointing no finger himself. He did, however, note Roger Touhy's claim that a Syndicate gunman was also in Miami that day. The mob plan was to allow Zangara to take potshots at Roosevelt, while in the confusion, a mob marksman would hit Cermak.

Several naysayers argued convincingly against the rumored conspiracy. Cermak biographer Alex Gottfried reasoned that though the press had long observed Cermak to be a micromanager of his regime, the "Nitti affair was not the type of thing in which Cermak would characteristically have been willing to entangle himself." One might question his moral scruples at time, he says, but his caution and "shrewd calculations of risks" versus possible gain were greatly pronounced. Former Mayor Carter Harrison agreed, noting of Cermak, "He was too conservative to get mixed up in murder." Not only is Gottfried's contention based on the personality of the mayor, but it is based on the assassin's personality as well, noting his paranoid nature and his resistance to conforming to others and arguing that he would, therefore, not be a suitable candidate to perform the function for the Nitto mob. Further, he noted the observation of yet another mayor who said the mob did not operate in such a "haphazard way."

Based on Zangara's personality, Blaisé Picchi, who penned the assassin's side of the episode based on original federal and State of Florida documents, also says "no" to a mob conspiracy. His investigation records information from those in close proximity to Zangara, particularly Leonard F. Chapman Sr., Superintendent of the Florida State Prison at Raiford where Zangara was held during his last ten days. Chapman, who talked to the prisoner every day until the end, called Zangara an uneducated "lone wolf" and "utterly unassimilated" being, saying there were no accomplices, no connections. Zangara, he noted, never mentioned Cermak by name (he apparently did not even know the Chicago mayor), only Roosevelt.

Picchi also notes that Secret Service and FBI investigations laid to rest many popular public accounts relating to the incident. For example, the story of the woman who saved the president by deflecting Zangara's aim at the last minute is doubtful, as is the story told by the hotel manager who claimed Zangara approached her for a room just for a few hours before the shooting—she guessed afterward that he wanted to "load his gun," but Zangara was elsewhere at the time. The most apocryphal story, and perhaps Loesch's source for the Philadelphia mob theory, was that of Zangara's supposed membership in a group of Pennsylvania anarchists which in December 1931 blew up a post office there, killing three. The same group killed two others with a bomb in January 1933. An informant, a bricklayer, thought he identified Zangara as a missing member of his work group and the bomb culprit. A couple of other masons agreed, but all, however, eventually recanted, admitting to the FBI they were mistaken. The mysterious man they assumed to be Zangara showed up for work as usual soon after.

Just as Picchi convincingly laid to rest the conspiracy theory and many of the tales attributed to the affair, Robert Schoenberg, author of *Mr. Capone: The Real—and Complete—Story of Al Capone*, argues simply, as had Gottfried, that Nitto and the mob would hardly be inclined to use a crackpot like Zangara for so delicate a chore. The bottom line is that evidence of conspiracy has never been established. Of the Touhy claim, there is no evidence that other marksmen, mob men or otherwise, fired a shot during the confusion. Regarding the claim that White and McGurn were caught with train tickets for Miami, this was not that unusual since the Capones still owned a home there and Nitto rented a home there, as others in the mob apparently did for frequent meetings away from the Chicago cold. Certainly, Cermak's autocratic management style and the bulletproof-vest story leave him open to suspicion regarding whether he knew of Lang's intentions. The whole issue of Cermak surfaced only when Lang threatened to blow the lid off Chicago politics.

That a member of the mayor's personal detachment shot Nitto and was caught in a lie, to be sure, proved awkward to the powers that be, whether the mayor was in on it or not. The mortification was enhanced by news of the alleged $15,000 offer by Newberry, especially after Nitto lived. Because Newberry was killed shortly after word of the offer surfaced, a hoodlum-detective conspiracy of some sort looks credible, but whether this is because of the bounty or simply because of Newberry's hatred of Nitto and his uncooperative nature in North Side gambling matters, the truth about such a conspiracy remains unknown. The story of the $15,000 prize remains nothing more than a whisper from the grand jury room, never brought into legal proceedings.

Perhaps that is why the state's attorney never brought the issue before the court. The involved legal parties, perhaps, concocted a suitable course for Lang to explain away his dastardly actions. To have had Miller testify to the Newberry plot would open him and Lang to potentially embarrassing examination as to the actual connection, if any, between Newberry and Cermak—why was a mayor's detective, painted as a stalwart soldier in the war on crime, involved with hoodlums, and during a crime drive no less? The fact remains that the mayor proved inhospitable toward the Nitto mob at the very time they were fighting for survival, and that undeniably proved motive for the group to do away with him. To say, though, that the mob targeted the mayor in Miami is tantamount to searching the Kennedy "grassy knoll" three decades ahead of time with even less data on which to proceed.

Had Nitto died, the police story would likely have held up, and he would have been counted as a high-profile victory in the war on crime. The friction between the mob and politicians heated up for an unspecified length of time, and the title of McPhaul's *Sun-Times* piece might have easily been "The Shots that Shaped Chicago Organized Crime." The bullets Lang fired December 19, 1932, ended any specula-tion as to who was the genuine leader of the mob. The death of Cermak, coinciden-tal or otherwise, cemented the Nitto mob as the major player in Cook County organized crime for the next quarter-century. As Judge Barnes later adjudged the Cermak situation and the elimination of Touhy from the scene, there would be no more major interference from local executive or judicial government.

⌐◦/◦/◦⌐

As Nitto emerged from the Lang fiasco, the World's Fair was winding to a close. Those who had missed the extravaganza needn't worry: long before shuttering the gates on the spectacular success that November, organizers promised to reopen again for the summer of 1934. The Nitto mob would be there in force. On Nitto's remaining agenda that fall, Red Barker's dream of dominating the Teamsters wrapped up without a real mob victory—even with Touhy out of the way, the sit-uation was simply too hot to handle. The Touhy gang didn't win with the Team-sters either. Their remnants attempted one last attack on outlaw union headquarters in September, but they were repulsed, and one attacker was killed. Ten days later, a union ally was wounded in an attack. After that, a special election resulted in over 18,000 outlaw members rejoining the international union. Of the forty-six locals in Chicago, only three chose to stay with Galvin's outlaw organization. Renegade leader and mob ally Michael Galvin took the white flag to State's Attorney Court-ney, saying, "We've had enough."

Other outstanding business taking precedence that fall involved the gang's inter-nal gambling fraternity. Chiefly troublesome was the North Side and the ugly left-over affairs of Ted Newberry. After Newberry was murdered, Gus Winkler inherited the interest in Newberry's 225 and Sky High clubs as well as Newberry's partner, a debonair, well-to-do war veteran named Edgar Lebensberger. Particularly disturbing to Nitto, no doubt, was that the gang dealings of all three predated Nitto's leader-ship and were products of Capone's generosity. Lebensberger and Newberry were credited with opening the swank 225 Club. When the Capone group muscled in for a percentage of the profits, they retained Lebensberger for his classy connections. Only prim society dared enter the "severe sophistication" behind those doors. A grandiose dinner might be served on the main floor, and afterward, high-hat gentle-men withdrew to the third floor for roulette, dice, and cards, tended to by waiters delivering complimentary drinks. The place was a money machine, with police protection disbursements estimated at about $3,000 monthly. This all seemed to be slipping away when Cermak entered the mayor's office.

Another player in the North Side gambling problem was onetime politician John J. "Boss" McLaughlin. The Boss was well past his high-ranking prime, but with a new gambling alignment taking hold after Cermak's election, McLaughlin was thought to be branching his activities into the North Side, while old friend and Cermak stalwart William Johnson gained favor along with a previous Capone and Nitto antagonist, Billy Skidmore. As far as the mob was concerned, this would not do. The North Side group may have even daringly decided to short-change the mob on its share, possibly eyeing adding another club on Walton Place independently.

Further, Winkler was not necessarily the Nitto ideal. Though his newfound wealth had made him more urbane, as a former loose cannon, he still maintained contacts with outlaws and kidnappers. As recently as 1931, Capone had bailed him out of trouble for conspiracy in a high-profile Nebraska bank robbery. Nitto, however, was no Capone. In October 1933, Winkler was still dabbling in small-time nonsense. On the fifth, the feds prepared to indict twenty-seven individuals for complicity in a daring December 1932 Loop mail theft in which the robbers made off with nearly $500,000 in government bonds and securities. Among those named were Winkler, Lebensberger, and McLaughlin, who were suspected of disposing of at least $50,000 of the hot loot in return for as much as 10 percent in handling fees. For a Nitto mob trying to run a tight ship through tough financial times, these antics were out of bounds. Worse yet, reports also surfaced of McLaughlin's previous dealings with Eddie McFadden, a Touhy co-defendant and, thus, a Nitto enemy.

On the day the indictments were handed down, one element of Nitto's problems effortlessly evaporated when Lebensberger committed suicide in his swank, three-story home on Lake Shore Drive. Despite the prim glitz of their dwelling, his young widow claimed that Lebensberger had recently been indigent and suffered "financial embarrassment," which may account for his involvement in laundering bonds. The indictment was also a disgrace. Darker rumors at the time included a forceful Nitto visit in which the mob leader was said to have outlined Lebensberger's options: suicide, the more dignified answer to prison, or violent death. One paper even reported a kangaroo court in front of mob men.

Winkler surrendered earlier in the day and posted a $10,000 bond; his case was continued to December 13. McLaughlin, unable to pay, was held on $50,000 bond. The Nitto mob saved the government the trouble of holding a trial for Winkler. The decision to kill him probably was made as far back as August, when Albert Bregar, a Newberry aide turned Winkler sidekick, left the Lincoln Park Arms Hotel for a haircut and was never seen again. When his wife reported him missing, a bondsman checked police headquarters to no avail. "If the police haven't got him," he resigned himself, "then he's gone bye-bye."

October 9 looked to be a fair Chicago day, with high temperatures forecast to reach the lower fifties. Because of the weather, fifteen-year-old Paul Geirsbach and his younger brother, Willard, were tasked by their parents to paint the stovepipe protruding on the open back porch. The family lived in a second-floor apartment at 3258 Southport Avenue, just to the south of Roscoe Street. Their rear terrace overlooked the far side of Roscoe, about seventy-five feet away. Located there was the office of Charles H. Weber Distributing Company, dispensers of keg and bottled beer and owned by County Commissioner Weber himself. The boys lollygagged along, stirring the bucket and slopping paint while periodically peering down to the street below.

Suddenly, a new, two-door Ford whisked to a stop across the street in front of the distributing warehouse; the car was facing the opposite direction of the traffic flow. A tall man in a fine-cut, green suit emerged and crossed the street to enter the Weber building. A small, green-paneled delivery truck sidled up very close. The boys then witnessed a scene they excitedly described as being "just like the machine guns in the gangster movies." According to one of the youths:

> He [Winkler] stepped up on the sidewalk and was just reaching out to open the door at the warehouse when the second car came along from the east, just like it had been following him. . . . All at once there was a burst of shots . . . and the fellow across the street in front of Weber's sorta turned around, kinda slow, and began to fall. They must have fired a hundred shots.

The juveniles' perception may have been skewed by Hollywood films, but even so, the assassins unleashed a barrage of shotgun fire from the rear window of the truck, felling Winkler at the door stoop. The truck sped off to the west, then turned south and disappeared. Winkler lay in a bloody heap, pierced by 111 slugs—a new gang record surpassing the fifty-something bullets retrieved from Joe Aiello's body, the papers noted. Most struck Winkler in the chest and legs; some sliced his polished shoes. Edward Conrad, a clerk inside, heard the blasts and went to investigate only to find Winkler facedown on the pavement, begging, "Turn me over on my back so I can breathe."

Police removed the hood to a nearby hospital, where the ghastly sight of his wounds made even the surgical team blanch as they frantically cut away his apparel and attempted to save him. The diamond and emerald belt buckle given to him by Capone lay nearby as the hood groaned in agony and asked first for a glass of water and then for a priest. "I'm going to die. I know I'm going to die," he chanted, the litany fading as Winkler began reciting the Lord's prayer. The words after "Our Father . . ." tailed softly away as Gus Winkler expired at the age of thirty-five.

Two young Italian men were hauled in as suspects in the murder but were eventually released. Detectives trawled up the names of Three-Fingered Jack White, Klondike O'Donnell, and Tony Capezio as the culpable figures, but none could be located. The coroner's inquest into the death of August Winkler proved just as futile and brought about more embarrassment for some than the real investigation. The inquest brought up questions about the presence of a hoodlum like Winkler on the premises of a company owned by the county commissioner, wondering if they were in business together. Weber swore he never knew Winkler, while others said the gangster financed and dominated the beer plant. One source claimed Winkler and Louis Alterie as frequent visitors to the address, which would have been all the more reason for the mob to eliminate Winkler for double-dealing with the likes of Alterie. Further, Weber's business cornered the beer business at the Streets of Paris exposition at the fair.

Then there were Winkler's connections in city gambling. The jury called in known principals from the gambling world such as Billy Skidmore, who claimed he was "in the scrap iron business" and knew nothing about gambling. Eventually, one newspaper investigation implicated Weber, his partner in the distributing business Charles Conrad, Winkler, and others with managing over 300 slot machines on the Near North Side, raking in 60 percent of the gross. The coroner's jury continued their investigation by visiting some of the city's gambling dens, much to the flushing chagrin of police officials who professed no knowledge of the joints. The October 30, 1933, headline of the *American* reported the inquest jury's findings: "CHICAGO HONEYCOMBED WITH BOOKMAKERS, JURY REPORT SAYS." The *Tribune's* headline the next day read: "STOP GAMBLING OR LICENSE IT, JURY TELLS CITY."

In the end, the opinion of the press pointed to Winkler's gambling rivalries or friction as what did him in. He simply wasn't a Nitto team player. One reporter wrote of the "speed and accuracy" of the assassination, reminding readers of the peculiar efficiency when Nitto sent men out for a kill. The jury wished to question Frank Nitto as a "representative of the Capone gambling Syndicate," but police were unable serve the subpoena. They located a supposed relative who said that he was "out of town." He may well have been out of town, for good reason: with the Near North Side straightened out, Nitto now sought to iron out a small matter in Cicero.

As the Winkler jury wound toward a close, Nitto's mob eliminated onetime gang bail bondsman, the diminutive Louis Cowen. A millionaire in boom times, "Diamond" Louis as he was sometimes known, had lost a bit of his luster by the 1930s. Under investigation for failed income tax reporting, in 1931 he reconciled with the Internal Revenue Service for just over $50,000 to avoid criminal prosecution. The Depression also devalued him: he lost several properties and a considerable portion of stocks, his fortune sagging to mere "wealthy" status. He still owned the *Cicero Tribune* from the old days, and in mob circles, he owned interest in Sportsman's Park.

After Al Capone went to prison on income tax charges, it was thought Cowen assumed greater importance in the Cicero gambling world, exerting considerable influence while exacting his share of the proceeds. Rumor also had Cowen investing in a new dog track across the state line in Indiana with unknown parties. Cicero citizenry suspected that the Nitto mob had recently suggested to Cowen a new split in the proceeds to benefit more rank and file members distressed by the Depression and the coming transition out of Prohibition. Cowen rebuffed them, and both the public and police theorized that a change in the management of gambling concessions to put in place a more amenable associate was now due.

On the afternoon of October 27, after a lunch in downtown Chicago, Cowen dropped by Sportsman's Park racetrack. Finished with business, he traveled to

Cicero's north side to pick up his bodyguard, Joseph Corngold. He curbed his pricey, oversized Lincoln automobile in front of 5935 Roosevelt Road, the Clifford Theater. Next door was one of the gang's hot gambling joints. As Corngold approached the car, a small coupe drove up from the west. Shotguns barked, the first and second salvos punching neat holes through the Lincoln's windows, the buckshot smashing into Cowen's head and neck. A third blast, fired as the car sped off, only managed to clip Corngold in the legs and shred a movie poster pasted near the theater's marquee. Quickly, the bodyguard retrieved Cowen's now rolling car and sped off to a nearby hospital, where the little editor was pronounced DOA—complete with his diamond-studded belt buckle, compliments of Al Capone, and a mere $2.25 in his pockets. Inheritors of at least some part of his Cicero concessions were thought to be Willie Heeney, Claude Maddox, Louis Campagna, and Joseph Corngold. Ownership of the *Cicero Tribune* passed to race-track mogul Edward J. O'Hare.

⸻⸻

On December 5, just 288 days after Congress sent the proposed Twenty-first Amendment to the state legislatures for ratification, Pennsylvania and Ohio cast their votes in favor, leaving the amendment one vote short of the thirty-six necessary for passage. The Utah legislature decided to hold its vote ahead of schedule "to give [the] U.S. a break." It did, and by early evening Chicago time, booze was back for good. Chicago crowds were expected in the saloons and nightclubs that night, a Tuesday, though the official Repeal parties were set for Saturday. All of the conference, dining, and bar rooms of Chicago's finest hotels—the Palmer House, Sherman, Drake, Morrison, and LaSalle—were fully booked. At least two hoteliers expected the bash to be "bigger than New Year's Eve and 'beer eve' combined," partly because women, banned from bars prior to Prohibition, would now be able to take part.

On the other side of the mahogany, bartenders fretted over the expected avalanche. The public, after ten years of learning to drink simple things, one bartender complained, will want to go back to mixed drinks. "Only this morning," he said, "a guy comes in and wants an old-fashioned cocktail. Whoever heard of that?" Reading down the latest mixed drink menu disturbed the bartender further: "Here's a thing called a pousse café with twenty-seven different things in it besides the spoon, and all I got to make it with so far is two kinds of bourbon and, of course, some gin." "Just order a shot of whiskey" seemed to be the plea of most bartenders. For those who had been to the bar before the dry spell, the advice extended to expect cash register-shock as well: the price of drinks was now two to three times higher than in speakeasy days. For example, bourbon that had sold for fifteen cents a shot or two for a quarter now cost half a buck. High-grade blended whiskey went for the same amount, though the cheap grade cost twenty-five cents a shot.

Supply was not necessarily the issue for the Nitto mob. Their problem was how to cash in by pushing their local products over the national brands. In due time, they would solve their dilemma by going right to the tapster.

Since about the time of the Winkler murder, Three-Fingered Jack White had lazed away in an Oak Park apartment on Wesley Drive as ordinary "contractor" Henry J. Cerny. White enjoyed his books and flowers, spending most of his hours at home and venturing out only when huddled well below his upturned coat collar. His wife, the former Nancy Kelly, claimed a heavenly wedded life during that time. They had been married only a few months earlier after a meeting at the Club Royale on South Wabash, where she worked as a club-favorite entertainer. Smitten with the red-haired beauty, White and his bride-to-be eloped to Crown Point, Indiana, for a quickie wedding. They honeymooned on the Florida sands before making sightseeing stops in Washington, D.C., and New York before retiring to Chicago's western suburbs.

Once in a while, Mrs. White's brother, a former actor, and a girlfriend dropped by for a visit. No one professed to know White's real business, though club employees suspected and had serious misgivings for the young woman when she took flight with White. Newlywed Mrs. White had no idea why her husband preferred to spend his days so close to home.

Racketeer and gunman Mr. White had been on the lam for months, wanted for conspiracy in connection with the TNT affair. That trial was due to open shortly, and while local authorities failed to put a finger on his whereabouts, the FBI had recognized his location. They visited him to question him on matters still not clearly understood. On the afternoon of January 23, 1934, an agent dropped by again, along with an officer from the state highway patrol. Soon they left, and Mrs. White's brother and girlfriend dropped in. They planned a shopping trip, and as they departed, two dark-complected men whom Mrs. White recognized as business associates "Joe" and "Bill" entered and sat down to talk business with her husband. White, slumming comfortably without a shirt, offered the men drinks. They downed a few beers and emptied a couple of whiskey bottles before preparing to depart. At the door, one of the guests whipped out a pistol and took a shot at White but missed, the projectile embedding harmlessly in the living room wall. White struggled away, frantically overturning the furniture in his path, and escaped down the hall to the bedroom. Just as he reached into a dresser drawer for a hidden gun, the pair blasted him twice, leaving White slumped over the clothes cabinet, dead in his early forties.

The laundry list of motives for the murder ranged from squealing to the feds about someone or something to double-crossing Fur Sammons to White's previous union antagonisms with the Touhy mob. The last motive received considerable newsprint based on talk from White that he had lived in constant fear of Touhy since last November; "That outfit's looking to kill me," Melvin Purvis quoted him as saying. However, why would a gun-toting gorilla like White fear the Touhys at this point? With Touhy and a number of associates under indictment for the Factor kidnapping and the trial already under way, the real threat, the brain trust of that outfit, was out of action. They were no longer a major threat to Nitto and his mob, including White. Further, why would White open the door for anyone he remotely suspected of aiding the Touhy gang?

White's killing, in fact, hinted more of another house cleaning operation by Nitto. Mrs. White identified the killers as dark-skinned, a characteristic more common to members of the Nitto mob members than to any of Touhy's gang. When residents of the apartment complex, alarmed by the gunfire, saw the getaway men, they insisted they were Humphreys and Klondike O'Donnell. Neither fit the "dark" description, but both scenarios point to a Nitto mob hit. Authorities shrugged off the Humphreys identification because he was on the lam, but they pursued Klondike to no avail.

Later information turned up a White quarrel with fellow labor goons Claude Maddox and Marcus Looney. They had supposedly disagreed over planned activities that ran contrary to mob desires in light of the heat that would be generated by another upcoming TNT conspiracy trial. These disagreements or simply having a valued gunman on the lam for months hiding out from the Touhys likely caused the mob to terminate White's association—he was no longer useful, no longer needed, and was, therefore, a liability.

After being pushed out of his management position in Cicero gambling by the Capone interests, ex-millionaire newsie Frankie Pope descended to dabbling in dope peddling, for which he was sentenced to four months in a local lockup. He was equally unsuccessful pushing alcohol in 1929 when the feds busted him and a family member for various Prohibition violations. In November 1933, Pope was released from Leavenworth after serving a year for the old Prohibition violation. Since then, he had occupied a third-floor room in the old Vernon Hotel at 758 West Jackson. Indications were that Pope was still dabbling in narcotics and slumming with riffraff criminals and parolees from his jail days. These days, one detective remarked, "There was nothing too low for Pope."

At about 3 a.m. on March 7, 1934, two men inquired at the hotel desk for Pope. He was not in; the men said they were friends and would try back later. When they returned shortly before 8 a.m., the desk clerk gave them Pope's room number. They knocked on the door, and Pope, though evidently entertaining a lady friend, let them in. The two men whipped out guns and mutilated Pope in a crossfire of bullets as the down-and-outer lunged for a weapon beneath his corner bed. They left him there a bloody ruin, hunched over and haloed by bullet holes torn in the wall behind. None of the hotel staff professed to see their escape or the disappearance of Pope's woman friend. Whether by design or mere coincidence, the old hand was scratched from the scorecard.

Nearly two weeks later, Winkler's old pal J. George Ziegler, alias Fred Goetz, was walking along the 4800 block of Cermak Road in Cicero late at night when a large automobile filled with several men passed by. The occupants unleashed four shotgun blasts at Goetz; one missed, obliterating a nearby saloon window behind him and narrowly missing the bartender and patrons, but the others struck Goetz in the head and killed him instantly. The college graduate was dead in his late thirties. No one witnessed the shooting, though some bystanders did see the vehicle carrying the shooters race off to the east toward Chicago's city limits. From the papers in his pockets, police determined that Goetz was either hiding out (probably from the Hamm kidnapping case) or was a drifter. He maintained no permanent address and received his mail at an Oak Park gas station where the attendant said he was only obliging a regular customer. The police were stretched to determine a motive, but recognized the shotgun slaughter as being carried out in "approved Capone fashion."

18

"IF IT ISN'T BOOZE, IT'S SOMETHING ELSE . . ."

T HE TITLE QUIP FROM A *Collier's* writer in 1932 summarized mob strategy not only in Chicago but in other cities as well: they were interested in diversifying beyond bootlegging, and by 1934 they were ready to make good on it. Generally, old Chicago boss and now New York resident Johnny Torrio received credit for the idea of a national syndicate to accommodate business expansion of the various mobs. After New York Mayor Fiorello LaGuardia threatened destruction of mob businesses and arrests of major hoodlums, they looked to more friendly out-of-state locales to which to move some of their businesses. For example, Frank Costello looked to move a large portion of his slot-machine empire to Louisiana, now under the notorious regime of Huey Long. The sunny climate of Florida had long looked promising to both Chicago and New York gambling interests. The concern, though, was how to expand without stepping on one another's toes and risking war.

To that end, a series of meetings was held in 1934 that included all parties from around the country and looked to lay the groundwork for peaceful expansion. The first, groundbreaking meeting appeared to have taken place in New York, with a follow up in the central location of Kansas City, Missouri, where Nitto allies under John Lazia ran the city. Nitto's protégé Paul Ricca represented Nitto in New York and Nitto and Charlie Fischetti attended the Midwest get-together to wrap up the details. The general agreement was to create a commission to set territories of local authority, divide open cities or states along industry lines, and set a means to resolve disputes should they arise.

Nitto had looked to diversify his mob beyond Chicago and booze probably in much greater fashion before the idea occurred to his New York brethren. With Ed O'Hare in his pocket from the old days, he retained exclusive control of the dog racing industry throughout the country. Though ruled illegal in Illinois, Nitto, with associate Johnny Patton out front, built tracks in Florida, Ohio, and Massachusetts. The Hawthorne Kennel Club in Cicero transitioned into horse racing, another pari-mutuel moneymaker, and Nitto and Patton had a piece of it. Likewise, they moved into tracks in Florida along with their New York brethren. These moves allowed opportunities for hard-pressed lower-echelon gang members as well: notorious Chicago gunmen received the parking concessions or worked as security.

Nitto aimed for natural horizontal expansion from the racetracks via a major entity that existed right in his own back yard, the General News Bureau. In 1934 he laid the foundation for his plans. Formerly owned by veteran Chicago gambling magnate Monte Tennes, General News disseminated vital horseracing data to gambling houses and handbook parlors all over the country, usually via phone cables. Of course, there was a subscription fee, and with an estimated 7,500 handbooks in Chicago alone, General News was worth millions of dollars. In 1934, their prevalence was such that patrons freely threw losing tickets out on the sidewalk even across from city hall without fear.

When Tennes retired in the midst of the 1927 gambling war, he sold 50 percent of General News to Moe Annenberg. He later sold the remainder to James Lynch, but Annenberg stayed in command and turned the business into a gold mine. He brought in as general manager the shrewd, rough-and-tumble ex-newspaper circulation manager James Ragen. Forceful subscriptions garnered General News a million dollar profit by 1933. In 1934, that profit jumped another 50 percent, with greater possibilities beckoning. It was then that the two partners began falling out, with Lynch accusing Annenberg of swindling him out of profits.

The more aggressive Annenberg decided to force his partner out. Still owning half interest in General News, Annenberg created a competing service named Nationwide News Service. He transferred a portion of the General News staff and began going after General News customers even though he still controlled the General News board and General Manager James Ragen. Annenberg was in the money; he "merely had to decide which side would win." Lynch retaliated by filing suit in court.

When news spread of the falling out, Nitto saw an opportunity to move in. Would Lynch be interested in helping to fight Annenberg? If so, the price would be half his shares, to be turned over to Nitto's mob. A message then went out to general manager James Ragen to meet Nitto at the Auditorium Hotel on business. Nitto outlined the specifics to Ragen and claimed that all the major law enforcement officials were on the mob's payroll. Nitto could influence these people to force all handbooks to take General News subscriptions or face closure. Nitto continued, telling Ragen that the mob had been following Annenberg and knew he resided in the Congress Hotel. If Ragen decided to go along, the mob would kill Annenberg within twenty-four hours, and Ragen could then have whatever percentage he wanted. Ragen, an original Annenberg pick, naturally reported this to Moe, who then sent Ragen to Nitto with a counter-offer: Annenberg would pay the Nitto mob $100,000 if they helped him prevail over Lynch. What happened next is not clear, but Chicago Crime Commission Operating Director Virgil Peterson thought Nitto's role in matters had been "forceful and convincing." Lynch saved his life by selling Annenberg the remaining interest in General News for $750,000.

Annenberg then incorporated a new company that included Nationwide News and several necessary printed publications for the business. One such publication was the run-down sheet, which gave a handbook operator and his customers the run-down of the day's races, the horses, and the jockeys at each track. Another was the scratch sheet, a large, single sheet issued at the betting parlor that announced all entries scratched from the day's races as well as the track conditions and betting odds. From the account of the new corporation, Annenberg wrote a check for cash and entered it as part of the purchase price of General News, listed at $850,000. The very day Lynch cashed in, Ragen met Nitto at the Auditorium Hotel and turned over to the Enforcer the difference in the buyout price, $100,000, in $100 bills. What Annenberg may have not discerned was that on the day he plunked down cash for Nitto's services, he made a pact with the devil.

A pundit once said of an underhanded labor character and his wealthy victims that "some men has plenty of money and no brains, and some men has plenty of brains and no money. Surely them as has plenty of money and no brains is made for them as has plenty of brains and no money." This same quote easily could have applied to Nitto and his group. It was the Depression, and his men needed money. The key to their finances, with unionism growing, was organized labor and various "associations."

Up until now, most corrupt coalitions were based solely on the strength of the scoundrels at their head, many of whom associated or allied themselves with one of the Prohibition gangs. When Capone emerged as the dominant gang force, they generally operated with his blessing. Red Barker and White worked on the Teamsters via the old O'Donnell gang, and Murray Humphreys cornered the cleaning and dyeing associations with Capone's blessing. Danny Stanton weaseled his way into control of the municipal office workers during Thompson's administration, while Mike Carrozzo ruled the hod carriers union, thanks to Capone. Louis Alterie had the theatrical janitors union. Others preyed on the Master Bakers Association, the Master Beauty Shop Owners and Employers Association, the Hebrew Butchers Association, Tool and Die Makers Union Local 113, Athletic and Public Events Venders Local 78, etc. All operated under gang influence with nearly all aspects of the groups affected. Costs to the Chicago public by 1932 were estimated at $165 million a year. Those not in the direct sphere of Nitto's organization paid a percentage to the group.

This was good, local money for gang staff, but Nitto's vision was bigger. Instead of a cornucopia of small moneymakers, he envisioned exerting control over a wider area, which might benefit existing mob investments. Even when random opportunities fell in his lap, he looked to run with them to the top.

⸺◦◦◦⸺

By 1934, Nitto had moved his primary headquarters from the Naples Restaurant at 901 South Halsted to the Capri Restaurant at 123 North Clark Street—nearly across the street from city hall. Some of the mob's favorite chefs ran the place, including Amato Maglialuzzo from the old Nineteenth Ward on Halsted. At the Capri, the mob ran a highly profitable and well-attended handbook, always attributed to Nitto's ownership. On the third floor, one racketeer said, "There was an empty loft . . . . [and] a long table" around which Nitto usually held court with key men such as Rio, Ricca, Campagna, D'Andrea, Fischetti, and Frank Diamond. A private elevator provided the only access. As a labor leader called to a meeting there remembered, "You couldn't get in unless the elevator operator recognized you."

In April, Nitto and board entertained New Yorkers to discuss their first major and mutually beneficial venture into the labor field. The target was the Building Service Employees International Union. The BSEIU originated and was headquartered in the Windy City. A natural racketeering attraction, the BSEIU's membership consisted of elevator operators, janitors, maintenance crews, engineers, and like staff that kept many of the public buildings in cities functioning. They also extended to the private sector of large apartment complexes. The union's services were vital, and any strike could disrupt an entire community, preventing individuals from reaching offices on, say, the twentieth floor or perhaps leaving residents or workers in the dark due to a lack of maintenance staff.

It was suspected that, a few years earlier, Capone had installed a couple of hoodlums to pull strings on current BSEIU president and head of the local Janitors Flat Union, Jerry Horan. Still, the Nitto crowd appeared unable to fully exploit the international union—they lacked the means to organize in other cities and to enlarge union coffers for plunder. The largely undeveloped East Coast beckoned, particularly New York City where the BSEIU had little membership. The New Yorkers brought with them a start in that direction.

When the international representative for the East Coast announced his departure, Brooklyn racketeer and Luciano crime family lieutenant Anthony Carfano, alias Augie Pisano, proposed a local labor hoodlum to fill the position. George Scalise, born in Italy and transplanted to Brooklyn, was a dark, robust, thirty-eight-year-old minor associate of the crime world. At age seventeen he was arrested on Mann Act charges and served nearly four years at the Atlanta federal penitentiary. Through the 1920s he worked at various jobs, always around unions, until he had recently become vice president of the garage washers union in Brooklyn. With the Depression, however, they went bust. He followed up by working in the window cleaners union and in various organizing efforts but brought home little to sustain a wife and daughter.

Eventually, his labor dealings put him touch with underworld character Carfano, Joe Adonis, and the bigger name of Lepke Buchalter, chief racketeer among the Luciano crowd. When the vacancy came open at the BSEIU, an associate suggested he try for it. Scalise then contacted Carfano about the job. Carfano, in turn, arranged a meeting with the Nitto mob, which was held in the Capri Restaurant. Nitto put his stamp of approval on Scalise as East Coast representative, with the understanding that all new labor dues would be split fifty-fifty between the New York and Chicago groups. Scalise and Carfano would split their end equally. Scalise was as happy with the prestige as with the money, and the mob had a true racketeer in higher office and began to derive real financial benefit from the international union.

Scalise did not disappoint, returning to New York City and beginning a new organizing campaign. In December, he shut down public buildings until a contract was signed with his unions; the city capitulated, and he added about 20,000 new members to the BSEIU. Thrilled at the success, Scalise optimistically remarked to an associate, "This looks like a good thing, we ought to make a lot of money out of it." There was a future for George Scalise.

—◈◈◈—

Nitto and associate Paul Ricca both briefly worked in movie houses when they were younger. Movies with sound had fueled the public's passion for cinema since 1927, and the movies' appeal as an escape from the Depression prompted the hoods to realize the potential of theaters as they sprang up across Chicagoland. Louis Greenberg, the moneyman, provided the lead, including the increasingly and highly profitable theater sector in his, and apparently Nitto's, investment portfolio. Lawndale Enterprises incorporated on February 14, 1929, and included as its flagship enterprise the Lawndale Theater. Among Nitto's holdings, though not in his name, by the early 1930s was the Symphony Theater near Oak Park. Ricca also held an interest in the market, serving as vice president of the World Amusement Corporation. Established just in time to entertain the Century of Progress crowds, the corporation operated the World Playhouse, located at 410 South Michigan Avenue.

One theater-related union presented far more enormous opportunity than the average union. Owning a theater necessarily involved employing skilled personnel. Before sound film, musicians played in the pit and "faders," working audio, coordinated with projectionists, who labored to swap cumbersome reels of films on large machines. When technology put sound on film, the projector men became the key, and such a skilled position had long been a union trade. In Chicago, projectionists organized as the Moving Picture Operators Union, Local 110. Since at least 1920, the union's business agent had been veteran projectionist and active unionist Tommy Maloy. Fortunately for Nitto's crowd, the wiry Maloy was a racketeer of the finest cast.

Though he stood no more than five feet, five inches tall, Maloy was a natural and experienced tough who literally crowned himself king of the local. His qualifications were earned, as he tirelessly reminded the rank and file, telling them about the time he disarmed and knocked out the teeth of two hoods who invaded his projection booth; what he failed to mention, however, was that he was running a gambling operation above the theater. When the previous BA announced he was leaving for greener pastures, Maloy stepped up. When one uninformed unfortunate stepped forward to challenge him, Maloy hinted at the tenor of his future rule by tossing his challenger out into the street.

Barely a year later, during a theater-building boom, his name surfaced in a racketeering investigation in which unions associated with theater operations were charged with extorting up to $2 a seat for new theater construction with non-union labor. Maloy also closed Local 110's membership rolls, despite high demand to join brought on by the popularity of films. Outwardly, he may have represented the move as a wage-boosting measure (he did in fact raise wages about one-third), but the real boost went into Maloy's pockets, and in the end the membership suffered.

Instead of adding new dues-paying members to the rolls, Maloy milked the "permit system," which allowed non-union men to work as projectionists as long as they held a permit. The precondition for anyone seeking this employment was to return 10 percent of his wages back to Maloy. (Top wages in 1924 ranged from $55-$112 a week.) With work rules mandating a two-man booth, Maloy soon filled up to half the theaters in Chicago with these "permit projectionists." To pad his pocket further, he also saw to it that permit men received the highest-paying theater jobs, and he allowed friends to retain "ghost jobs" in the union for which they didn't have to report but just collected a check. Of course, Maloy charged a hefty fee. Any projection jobs assigned to them were left vacant leaving a one-man booth or given to a permit man, thereby doubling Maloy's money on the job.

Theaters often challenged Maloy's rule, but with little success. By the late 1920s, he backed his position with plenty of muscle. To help maintain his reign, he picked handsome Irish thug and experienced labor hang-about Ralph O'Hara as chief organizer, and he also picked up gangsters along the way. At first, he teamed up with Dapper Dan McCarthy, a North Side tough allied with Dean O'Banion. Together, they lured the business agent of the theatrical janitors union to a nightclub to be murdered so that O'Banion gunman Louis Alterie could take over. Well after O'Banion's death, when film operator Henry Gusenberg desired to run against Maloy for BA, Henry brought in his ferocious brothers Frank and Pete of North Side (and St. Valentine's Day) fame. Cagey, Maloy sidestepped any battle by tendering Henry a financially fat union position. After the Massacre, with Capone at his peak and his gang diversifying, Maloy found himself with new partners. Capone ally Danny Stanton frequented Maloy's office, and Maloy gave Stanton and other Capone gang members ghost jobs on the payroll; in return, he could count on their support.

When movie houses protested Maloy's extortions, they received stench bombs as warnings. A second visit to a theater brought the real thing and considerable physical damage. One particularly long dispute resulted in at least fifteen bombings. In one instance, police nabbed the suspects, both of whom were members of Capone's bombing squad headed by James Belcastro. The theaters eventually all reopened after losing over a million dollars in property damage and proceeds while gaining very little against the union. When any among the rank and file dared to agitate against Maloy, they first were given a beating severe enough to lay them up for a few weeks, keeping them out of work and without a paycheck as a reminder to toe the line. The most obnoxious agitators were shot, fatally only when necessary. The June 20, 1931, murder of rebel operator Jacob Kaufman serves as an example. Kaufman was shot five times by a gunman, and police sought Danny Stanton in connection with his murder.

Of course, Maloy was not all brawn. Strikes against the Exhibitors Association (representing theater owners) were sometimes settled with cash, and Maloy's circle collected one payment as high as $65,000. When hard financial times hit small theater owners, they begged off the two-man booth rule. Overtly, he stood firm, but behind the scenes, Maloy pocketed payments of $1,060 per man to reduce his own union workforce. He frequently walked picket lines in sympathy with other theater-related unions such as James Petrillo's musicians union and George Browne's Local 2 stagehands.

Maloy wisely expanded his power base by worming into the electric sign business, a natural sideline that gave him additional leverage on theater owners. Any uncooperative owner might suddenly find his business with smashed, irreparable marquees as well as no projectionist. Maloy's power was such that he could force film distributors to deny film deliveries to theaters of his choosing. Contributing handsomely to Mayor Cermak's campaign, he placed his brother Joe Maloy in city hall as chief in charge of licensing motion picture operators. His union thought so highly of his efforts that they gave him a $5,000 European vacation, raised his salary $8,000, and gave him $4,000 to refurbish a home bathroom and $5,000 to build a bar in his basement—all at a time when a common street sight was a veteran selling apples on the corner for a nickel just to get by.

Having allied with Maloy for some time, Nitto and Greenberg's joints thrived. And now after Capone, this plum union looked too good to resist.

———✦✦✦———

In the theater business, two contrastingly dodgy characters opened the door for Nitto and his organization on the international level. George E. Browne began his working career as did many a citizen born into the nineteenth century: as a youth forced from school. His parents pulled him out of fifth grade to work as an errand boy and Western Union messenger. When he reached his teen years, he took a job as a stagehand in the property department of a local theater setting and moving stage props and sometimes performing light carpentry work building sets. He never looked for another job.

At the outbreak of Prohibition, Browne was moving up the union ladder, having been appointed to secretary pro tem of the local. It was a non-salaried position, but it led to him being appointed to fill the remainder of the term of a resigning business agent. When the former agent angled to get his job back on a permanent basis, he lost the union election to the increasingly popular George Browne. The burly stagehand possessed thick facial features that might as readily transmit a tough, scowling union front as a warm, jovial Santa Claus façade before changing to a well-groomed business and family man. Thereafter, Browne campaigned for the business agent position and won election every two years without opposition, except in 1934, when his brother-in-law ran against him and lost.

Browne's position naturally put him in contact with other union leaders. The most closely allied to his own Local 2 were the movie projectionists Local 110 and its agent, Thomas E. Maloy, and James Petrillo, head of the musicians union, whose members supplied the orchestrations for theatrical plays. A labor dispute between an owner and any one of the locals would find the owner without the services of the other two. In such matters, Browne unhesitatingly upheld his position regardless of the consequences, admitting later to having been arrested on numerous occasions. One event in 1924 involved Browne and Petrillo's BA at the time, labor tough Ralph O'Hara. The pair, armed with guns, roughed up an unfortunate and later were booked by police. A year later, Browne was shot and wounded in action. O'Hara, in the meantime, also took a high-paying job with Maloy as a special representative.

Increasingly, Browne's activities also put him in touch with some of Chicago's murkier characters. Through his association with O'Hara, he made the acquaintance of Big Tim Murphy, a labor racketeer with whom O'Hara also dabbled in countless organizing schemes. Playing his labor card, Browne found squeezing theater owners on the side quite profitable; he collected kickbacks, usually in the neighborhood of $150 per week, to guarantee the owners of existing theaters that no new competing theaters would receive better labor contracts for their stagehands. (This was especially important for the very competitive burlesque theaters.)

Browne did well enough with the union and soon jumped into the speakeasy business, becoming a money partner in a couple of joints. Browne helped bring in customers and soon became, as he described, the joints' "best customer, always paying for what he drank." His businesses, all located in the Loop district, also put Browne in touch with beer runners from the Capone Outfit.

Browne's ascent continued beyond Chicago's Local 2 when, in the late 1920s, he was elected the sixth national vice president of the International Alliance of Theatrical Stage Employees. During his tenure, pay for rank and file members rose nearly fourfold, but then his luck soured. First, a partner in one of his saloons was arrested for Prohibition violations and used Browne's name at the booking; Browne paid the $50 fine. Then, when the worst of the Depression knocked the wind out of the free-wheeling spending public, the local theater business died. By his estimation, only three of the fifteen major show theaters remained open during this time. Disillusioned, Browne declined to run for re-election in the 1930 international election. The ranks of Local 2 dwindled, and members voted a 25 percent pay cut and, later, two days off to help other members. As business agent for Local 2, Browne accepted a 40 percent pay cut, and his salary was paid only when the union treasury could afford to do so. Because so many of the burlesque houses remained dark, his on-the-side kickbacks dwindled to the point where they came from only one theater, Nathaniel Barger's Star and Garter.

With little or no income coming in, Browne began fishing around for other revenue. Fellow stagehand and union member Harold Huchberger suggested the poultry business: the poultry dealers at the Fulton Street Market, he said, had an association to manage prices but couldn't get together on anything. If Browne were interested in trying his management skills at lining up the dealers, the pair would split any income. The venture provided no solution for alleviating Browne's financial condition, however; after eleven months on the job, the dealers were still bickering over details and going nowhere, leaving Browne with little in his pocket.

During his work at the market, however, Browne became acquainted with a fellow who jump-started his work career most profoundly. Huchberger introduced Browne to the head of the Kosher Jewish Butchers Association, William Bioff, alias Willie Berger. The butchers union was doing much the same work as Browne and Huchberger, and at times the three worked together to boycott certain merchants and factories to maintain prices.

Perhaps six years Browne's junior, William Morris Bioff was a compact, muscular character (five feet, six inches tall and 195 pounds), thick and fleshy all the way to the tips of his fingers. His oval face was marked by thin, piercing eyes, which were capped by heavy eyelids that gave him a perpetual sneering look. His pudgy jowls very nearly produced a double chin, obscuring a thick, heavy neck—in all, he looked like the stereotypical bully. Unbeknownst to Browne, Bioff had previously performed odd jobs for the Chicago Outfit under Capone and now Nitto. Growing up in the Back of the Yards district, in his early twenties, he was a bodyguard and driver for Teamster official Michael Galvin and picked up dues and collections for the union. Along the way, early in Prohibition, he met up with Frank Diamond and Phil D'Andrea. Thanks to these two as well as to his Teamster experience and connections to Galvin, he was able to land a job within the Torrio organization as a beer truck driver. His initial assignment was hauling brew in Hillside Township in the western suburbs for Phil D'Andrea, Frank Rio, and Nick Circella. As a trusted tough, they gave him sundry heavy assignments within mob gambling houses.

In 1922, he found himself working as a bartender, general thug, and low-level collector for whoremaster Jack Zuta. When police raided an establishment in which he was present, they charged Bioff with pandering; apparently left unprotected by the higher-ups, he received a six-month sentence and a $300 fine. Zuta and Michael Galvin, though, interceded directly and somehow made arrangements for Bioff to walk free on appeal after serving only eight days in the clink. A few months later his appeal was lost, but he never went back to serve the time, nor were his bonds forfeited (something that would come back to haunt him). Once out, he resumed his work, sometimes with Galvin, sometimes selling beer and working gambling houses, mainly within the Capone clique. At the same time, Bioff dabbled in miscellaneous larceny, primarily with Rio and Circella—anything to make a buck. Three times in 1924 and 1925, the trio were suspects with others in attempted or actual robberies. While Bioff's two chums later moved up in the Capone sphere, his career remained status quo. When the Depression hit and Nitto assumed command of the mob, Bioff found himself tagging along with the West Side crowd of Lawrence Mangano as a utility thug scratching out any income possible. For that reason, he found himself an organizer at the Fulton Street Market.

In those tough times, Bioff did much better than Browne in the market business, primarily through the force of his personality. Someone once asked Bioff how he survived after being tossed out by his parents. He replied that he got pretty good at stealing hams from the Swift warehouse nearby: "Some weeks I wouldn't have anything but ham to eat, except maybe apples that I would sneeze from peddlers' carts on South Halsted Street."

"Didn't eating ham conflict with your religious principles?" the interviewer asked the Jewish Bioff.

"An empty belly ain't got no religion," he retorted.

In addition to hoping for some market gain, sage character Browne threw his hat in the ring as a candidate for president of the IATSE in the upcoming union election. In order to strengthen his position, and with 60 percent of his 400-member local out of work, Browne took over a hard-luck greasy spoon in the Loop, paying the overdue rent and equipment bills, and opened a soup kitchen, the Stagehands Club, to feed his unemployed brethren. Meals were doled out via coupons usually paid for by working members, fellows of high standing in the community, and politicians. The benevolent effort was far from enough for Browne to win a national election, and in June 1932 his comeback failed miserably as he lost by a two-to-one margin.

Refocusing on local union matters, Browne knew the upcoming Century of Progress fair promised to bring more stagehand jobs. He also recognized the potential for jurisdictional headaches since international stage shows on the fairgrounds were not necessarily constrained by agreements governing local theater chains. That's when he thought of Bioff, a "rather nimble-witted, aggressive fellow" he could use to delegate authority. They established a deal under which they would split Browne's $300 per week income.

With the first year of the fair a success, Browne and Bioff began looking higher. Browne received word from friends in the IATSE that the union's current president was in a political quagmire due to a disastrous California strike which led to the loss of a great many jobs. Both men looked favorably upon Browne's election chances at the June 1934 convention. But to first build support, the men went to local theater chain owners with a proposal to reinstate the voluntary 25 percent pay taken during hard times.

Perhaps the largest theater owner, if not the most influential, was Barney Balaban, head of the Balaban and Katz chain. As part of the Paramount Corporation, they owned movie houses throughout Illinois. Browne met Balaban in Gibby's Ogden Grill on North Clark Street, an establishment patronized by many of the theater crowd. It was there that Browne laid out his plan: the theater owners were now recovering, and the union's rank and file wanted full restoration of their pay. Balaban wanted to take care of Browne—if he would drop the pay-raise issue. Browne remained adamant. After one or more tête-à-têtes, the idea arose of resolving the pay issue through donations to the soup kitchen, perhaps $150 a week.

When Browne reported this to Bioff, his small-time partner turned major racketeer said: "Well, if he is in that frame of mind, I will go see him myself." Bioff figured $150 a week translated to $7,500 per year, but the fleshy racketeer immediately pounced on Balaban with a demand of $50,000. When Balaban balked, the trio met in the office of local attorney Leo Spitz. Bioff later recalled the Spitz proposal: "Now, fellows, we got to get together here. Barney is too low. You guys are too high. . . . How about $20,000?" The money was paid via check through Benjamin Feldman, an attorney connected to the law office of suspected mob attorney William Parrillo. The attorney presented Balaban with a phony bill for services and cashed the check. Bioff allowed the attorney a small fee and enough to cover his taxes, while he and Browne split the rest, something like $19,000.

Flush with cash when most everyone else was suffering through days of hardship, the two racketeers could hardly resist an expensive celebration, their first mistake—it made them stand out. Their second slip-up—probably thanks to Bioff's inherent desire to impress upon the world his new importance—was their choice of clubs; they selected the 100 Club, owned by previous Capone bodyguard and minor labor persona Nick Circella. Bioff knew Circella from the old days, when both were mere gunmen. After a gala night of food and drink, including some rounds on the new guys, they paid a "very substantial" bill of nearly $500. Browne noticed through his barrage of highballs that Bioff knew Circella. They whispered out of earshot of Browne, and then, Browne recalled, Bioff came over and introduced Circella. The club owner engaged them in casual chat, then asked their business. They were partners, Bioff explained. Without tipping the nature of his true inquiry, Circella asked them the whereabouts of the soup kitchen, saying he would like to drop by some time.

A couple of days later, Circella stopped in and took a look around. He asked Bioff, who happened to be there, why, if their organization was doing so poorly, he and Browne had so much money. Bioff just snickered in reply.

A day or two later, Bioff reported to Browne a phone call telling them that they were to meet "some people" and assuring Browne that "they are all right." The meeting was to be held in a saloon across the street from the Carleon Hotel on South Wabash. When they arrived, McGurn aide and handbook operator Charlie Gioe met them. He escorted Bioff to a mob meeting room in the Carleon to wait, while Sam Hunt protégé Ralph Pierce drove Browne to Jackson Park.

They were waiting alongside a deserted stretch of the Outer Drive when another vehicle pulled alongside. Out stepped Frank Rio. Placing one foot on the running board, the gangster leaned in the window and appeared to Browne to be "quite angry." Rio wanted to know if Bioff was muscling him. Browne vindicated Bioff, telling Rio he was working for Browne downtown. Rio pressed further, telling him the Outfit wouldn't tolerate any of their men muscling friends. The gunman explained "friends" in relation to Browne. They knew him from their dealings with Maloy but had left him alone. Browne maintained Bioff's innocence, and apparently satisfied, Rio left, wishing him well. Browne later maintained to Bioff that he did not spill the source of their sudden wealth, but then, he didn't have to, for two nominal labor men flaunting affluence spoke volumes to a mob looking for revenue.

The next visitor to the soup kitchen was Frank Nitto. He sat down with the pair, exchanged casual talk, and surveyed their joint before leaving. Bioff soon received another phone call, this time from Frank Rio himself telling him to come to the Carleon Hotel. Bioff did as directed and recognized the suite as the same one where he had waited for Browne. Rio's presentation was to the point: "We want fifty percent or else."

When Bioff next saw Browne, he reported the message. Browne abhorred the thought of gangsters in his Local 2, but his pudgy associate knew full well the consequences of refusing to comply. He'd quit, he told Browne, if he didn't go along, because "you couldn't lock horns with these guys."

The Nitto group was in for 50 percent.

Seven-year-old Frank Nitto traveled to New York from Naples aboard the Werra (above). • When Nitto came to Chicago in 1913, he likely settled in the Nineteenth Ward's Little Italy section (above right). • Detour to Dallas, in 1917: Nitto's marriage certificate (below).

In the Beginning

The Genna family dominated the alcohol business in Little Italy in the early twenties. Three brothers, including Angelo (right, with sister-in-law), were killed in gang wars; three, including Pete (below right), survived but retired from bootlegging.

A typical slaying in the "Bloody Nineteenth" (above), likely the result of Black Hand extortionists or intense political feuding.

First Ward gang leader Johnny Torrio (top left) brought Nitto associate Louis Greenberg into the Manhattan brewery at the outset of Prohibition. • Al Capone (above left), almost certainly a contact from Nitto's Brooklyn youth, came to Chicago circa 1919 and became Torrio's chief aide. • According to one account, Nitto met up with Scarface Al and joined the Torrio and Capone gang at the mob's Four Deuces club, 2222 South Wabash (above right), in 1923.

By 1924 the gang had moved to the suburb of Cicero, making their headquarters in the Hawthorne Hotel (above). Their gambling hotspot, the Hawthorne Smoke Shop, is just beyond the canopy at right. • Ralph Capone (above left) was gang chief in Cicero during the later Prohibition years; Eddie Vogel (left) was the city's slot-machine boss and later a Nitto business associate.

PROHIBITION COMPETITORS

The death of North Side Gang leader Dean O'Banion (above left) sparked a series of events that chased Torrio from Chicago and left Nitto's pal Al Capone boss of the South Side Gang. • O'Banion devotee Two-Gun Louis Alterie (above center) gravitated to labor racketeering and ran the theatrical janitors union until 1935, when Nitto's mob eliminated him.

Earl "Hymie" Weiss (top right) succeeded O'Banion as North Side Gang leader until he was gunned down on October 11, 1926, in front of O'Banion's old headquarters (above) by Capone operatives. Some credit Frank Nitto with originating the second-floor ambush to kill an enemy.

Joe Aiello (second from left) and part of his Sicilian gang: Mike Bizarro (left), Joe Rubinelli (center), Jack Manzello, and Joe Russo (right). This photo was after their arrest in late November 1927 following police discovery of an Aiello plot to kill Capone.

Nitto (above) was arrested in a police dragnet for gangsters on November 24, 1927. Still relatively unknown, his pick-up slipped by the city press corps. His "Enforcer" tag did not surface in the press until 1930. • Joe Aiello (far right) during one of his many arrests.

The February 14, 1929, St. Valentine's Day Massacre achieved the desired effect on the remnants of O'Banion's North Side Gang, although leader George Moran escaped the carnage.

The marriage license (above) from Frank Nitto and Anna Ronga's 1929 St. Louis wedding shows that Anna was sixteen years Nitto's junior. • Bootlegging gang chief Roger Touhy (above right) was removed from the Chicago scene in 1934 when he was sentenced for kidnapping Jake Factor (right), a charge many contend was a phony rap.

When Joe Aiello exited the first-floor apartment (above at left) on Kolmar Avenue on the night of October 23, 1930, machine-gunners opened fire on him from this vantage point. As he staggered for cover between the buildings, another machine-gunner blazed away at him from the third-floor apartment at right rear. Some accounts say Aiello was struck by as many as fifty-five .45-caliber slugs—a classic ambush.

Nitto was indicted for tax evasion in March 1930 but eluded capture. The wanted poster at right, issued September 27, 1930, by the Treasury Department and published here for the first time, features Nitto's 1927 arrest photo.

HARD TIMES

Arrested on October 31, 1930, one week after the mob wiped out Joe Aiello, the diminutive Nitto—who stood just five feet six, at best—was photographed surrounded by (below from left) Chief Investigator for the State's Attorney Pat Roche and Detective Sergeants J. D. Greer, Julius Siegen, and David Levin.

FRANK R. NITTO
WANTED
$1,000 REWARD

September 27, 1930

A Reward of $1,000 will be paid by the *Citizens' Committee for Prevention and Punishment of Crime* of the Chicago Association of Commerce for information leading to the arrest of FRANK R. NITTO, alias FRANK NITTO, alias FRANK NITTI, Capone gangster and fugitive from Justice, for the arrest of whom warrant is in the hands of the United State Marshal for the Northern District of Illinois.

The information with reference to this man should be communicated to A. P. Madden, head of the United States Intelligence Unit, Room 587 Federal Building, Chicago, Illinois. Tel. Harrison 4700, Extension 392.

DESCRIPTION

Age	35 to 40
Height	5 ft. 4½ in.
Weight	About 145 lbs.
Complexion	Swarthy
Eyes	Dark
Hair	Dark, fairly heavy, usually combed smooth and parted on right side
Italian	Usually well dressed

FINGER PRINTS
31 M M 14

Nitto altered his appearance slightly (above left) and moved to a quiet suburban Berwyn neighborhood to evade police. • According to the record, Chicago police booked Nitto as prisoner C-25924 on "general principles." His mug shot (above right) is the earliest such photo of Nitto obtained by the Chicago Police Department known to exist and was only recently rediscovered. • Nitto's Cook County jail card (below).

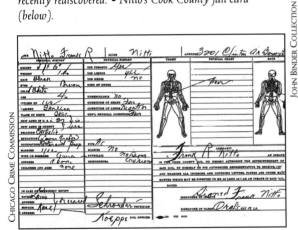

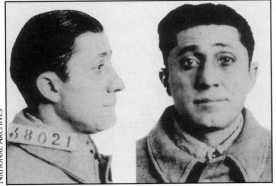

U.S. Attorney George E. Q. Johnson (above at right) obtained convictions of Ralph Capone and Jake Guzik for tax evasion. While they appealed, he accepted Nitto's plea for the same offense in exchange for an eighteen-month sentence. Johnson assured the gangster that, if he met certain conditions, he could be released in just ten months. • On January 11, 1931, Nitto entered the federal penitentiary at Leavenworth, Kansas, as prisoner No. 38021. His mug shot (left) is published here for the first time. Also revealed for the first time, Nitto served the full term of his original sentence, despite his agreement with Johnson, because the parole board refused to accept the deal.

Nitto's boss, Al Capone (above at center), in the custody of U.S. marshals, was sent to the federal penitentiary at Atlanta in May 1932; Nitto had been released on March 24.

BACK ON THE OUTSIDE

When detectives raided a gang office in the LaSalle-Wacker Building (above) in December 1932, one of the lawmen shot new gang boss Frank Nitto three times, falsely claiming that Nitto had pulled a gun first. Nitto, who was shot in the far-left back room of the office (left), survived, and the incident set off a firestorm of controversy and intrigue that has lasted to this day.

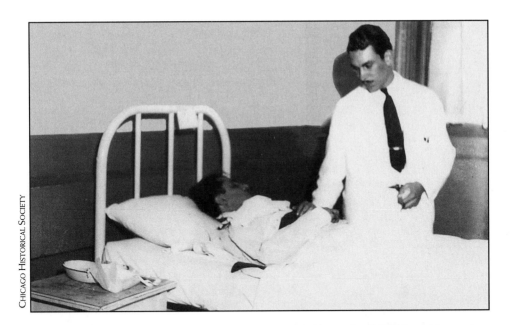

A wounded Nitto (above) with Dr. Testa in the city's prison hospital. • Chicago Mayor Anton Cermak (below at center) was shot in the abdomen in February 1933 at Bayfront Park in Miami while attending a rally for President-elect Franklin D. Roosevelt. He died three weeks later. Many believe that Giuseppe Zangara (right) was not aiming at FDR but at Cermak, and was sent by the Chicago mob as retaliation for the shooting of Nitto. • Ed Kelly (below right) succeeded Cermak as Chicago mayor. He retained the office until 1947 and posed no serious threat to Nitto's operation.

Bearing scars where one of Detective Harry Lang's bullets passed through his neck, Nitto (above) appeared in court on February 9, 1933, charged with assault in connection with the December 1932 incident. Other photos show the gang leader in court during March and April, when he was exonerated and Lang was charged with assault, although the case was later abandoned.

NITTO'S ORGANIZATION

Key members of the Nitto mob included (above from left) Felice DeLucia, alias Paul "the Waiter" Ricca, Nitto's protégé and likely No. 2 man; Louis "Little New York" Campagna, a former Capone bodyguard; and Frank Rio, perhaps Capone's most loyal bodyguard and his designated successor before Nitto proved more capable; gunman Charlie Fischetti (left); and (bottom from left) labor racketeers and gunmen Frank Maritote, alias Diamond, and Phil D'Andrea; and Jake Guzik, the mob's money and payoff man.

Ralph Pierce (above left) served Nitto as a gunman and was a suspected hitman, while Danny Stanton (above right), seen in a rare and youthful photo, was a South Side racketeer and gambling ally.
• Machine Gun Jack McGurn (near right) and his half-brother Anthony Demory are shown after police hauled them away from a golf course in the early 1930s. During Nitto's reign, wholesale killings were no longer necessary; thus, McGurn's antiquated talents could no longer support the lifestyle to which he had become accustomed. Perhaps because he was a bother to a gang evolving in a more sophisticated business sense, he was eliminated (below).

Labor unions were a major source of income for the Nitto gang during the 1930s. Among key figures were Tom Maloy (left), longtime boss of projectionists union Local 110; George McLane (center), boss of bartenders union Local 278; and George Scalise (right), whose rise to presidency of the Building Service Employees International Union was engineered by Frank Nitto.

INTO THE UNIONS

Louis Romano (left) was Nitto's appointee to take over McLane's Local 278. • George E. Browne (center) was boss of Local 2 in Chicago before Nitto helped elect him president of the International Alliance of Theatrical Stage Employees. • William Bioff (right) was a minor mob thug before he met Browne and began extorting cash from Chicago theaters. When Browne became IATSE president, Bioff was appointed an IATSE representative and the two headed for Hollywood to orchestrate the mob's extortion operation targeting the motion picture industry.

DECLINE

Key figures in the Hollywood extortion case included (above from left) Nick Circella, shown in a rare photograph; John Rosselli, the mob's West Coast representative; and Charlie Gioe. • Chicago labor racketeer Murray Humphreys (left) figured prominently in Local 278 of the bartenders union.

The death of Nick Circella's para-mour Estelle Carey (above), who was savagely killed in her Chicago apartment (right) in 1943, was thought by many to be a warning to the imprisoned Circella not to tell prosecutors what he knew about the Hollywood extortion case.

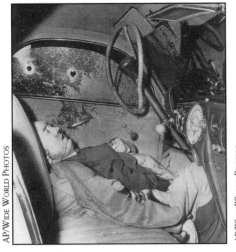

By 1939, racetrack mogul Edward J. O'Hare had outlived his usefulness (left) and was eliminated.
• Edward H. "Butch" O'Hare and Annette Caravetta attended the inquest into his father's death in 1939.
She became the third Mrs. Nitto in 1942 and retained the name until her death in 1981. Chicago's largest
airport was named for the younger O'Hare, an ace pilot and World War II hero.

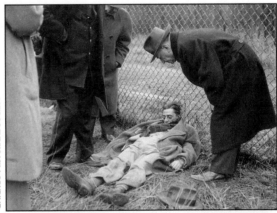

During the McLane fiasco in October 1940,
Nitto (above) waved off the press . • On Friday afternoon, March 19, 1943, shortly
after indictments were handed down in the
Hollywood extortion case, Nitto left his Selbourne Avenue home, took a walk along the
nearby Illinois Central Railroad spur in
North Riverside, and committed suicide
(above right). His body was carried from the
scene at dusk (right).

William Bioff (right) and George E. Browne (far right) both testified against Louis Campagna et al. in the 1943 Hollywood extortion case. All of Nitto's indicted associates, with the exception of Ralph Pierce, were convicted. Browne and Bioff were released from prison early, given new identities, and secretly relocated. Browne lived out the remainder of his life in anonymity, but Bioff was killed in Arizona in 1955 by a bomb attached to the starter of his truck. His body (below right) lies just to the left of the small tree.

EPILOGUE

Paul Ricca (far left) is shown with Louis Campagna after their parole. They and four others of the Chicago mob were sentenced to ten years in federal prison, but four managed parole after serving just one-third of their sentences, sparking a major scandal and a congressional investigation. • An extraordinary photo (below left) of city officials viewing Frank Nitto's body in the Cook County Morgue. • Nitto's headstone (below) at Mt. Carmel Cemetery reads, "There is no life except by death. There is no vision but by faith."

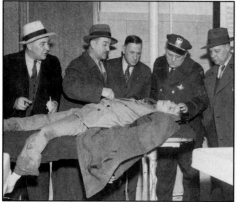

19

SHOW TIME

Aᴛ FTER HE WAS BOOTED OUT of his city sealer's position in 1931, Capone crony Daniel Serritella, with mob backing, rose high in local politics, eventually becoming an Illinois state senator. His deputy in city hall, Harry Hochstein, became an errand boy for Frank Nitto and Frank Rio. In the early 1930s, Hochstein, alias Harry Weisman, rented a small house in the western suburb of Riverside. It was at this house in about mid-April 1934 that Willie Bioff and George Browne first met the cream Nitto's mob.

Nick Circella drove Bioff and Browne to the Hochstein bungalow. Inside, Hochstein acted as host, leading them into a living room. Bioff later recalled, "It was a small living room-very small . . . maybe ten foot wide by twelve—maybe ten by twelve. . . . There were little tables around the chairs, little end tables or whatever you call them."

Neither man knew exactly why the meeting was called, and the intimacy of the setting added to their trepidation. Bioff and Browne were seated on a sofa, while standing or sitting close at hand were Frank Nitto, Frank Rio, Paul Ricca, Louis Campagna, and Nick Circella.

The two labor men remembered Nitto and Rio assuming the lead speaking roles. First, Nitto laid out rules of loyalty: they were partners fifty-fifty; it would be "no good" if they did wrong. Nitto and Rio then inquired about Browne's failure to become IATSE president in 1932, and Browne noted that delegations from New York City, New Jersey, Cleveland, and St. Louis had been prime movers against his

273

candidacy. Browne did not wish to run again and lose—he wanted a certain win. Nitto explained that would be no problem, as they could use a man with a clean background. "We will take care of Jersey and New York," said Nitto. "[W]e will take care of Jersey through Longie Zwillman." Nitto went on to explain they would contact Lucky Luciano and Lepke Buchalter in New York, Al Paliese in Cleveland, and Johnnie Doherty in St. Louis, all of whom would tell their respective projectionist locals to vote for Browne at the upcoming IATSE convention in June in Louisville, Kentucky. Another in the bunch chimed in reassurance, telling Browne they had made Jerry Horan president of the Building Service Employees International Union and Mike Carrozzo head of the street laborers and hod carrier unions, so they could certainly make Browne president of the IATSE.

In May, key New York labor racketeer Lepke Buchalter traveled west to meet the Chicago mob. His first stop was Maloy's Local 110 office. Maloy was in on the Browne campaign and introduced Lepke to Browne as a fellow who knew people back east. They ironed out some union squabbles before Charlie Fischetti drove Browne, Bioff, and Lepke to the Hochstein house.

Bioff and Browne met the same Nitto group, but with the addition of Fischetti. Drinks were served as they settled in, and again Nitto and Rio assumed the lead. Nitto inquired as to the time and place of the convention and then turned to ask Lepke about IATSE's largest local, New York's Local 306: "Well, now, will it be necessary for me to see Lucky, or will you see him, or how will we do it?"

"I don't have to see Lucky on that, Frank," Lepke replied, "I'll handle that myself; I will take care of it. I will also see Kaufman of Jersey (Louis Kaufman of Local 224 in Newark). I will see Longie and see to it that Longie delivers Kaufman."

With Nitto and company assured of East Coast support, Lepke and Fischetti left. The conversation then turned to money strategies, a topic that exhilarated small-time ruffian Bioff, who blurted, "There will be money—there will be a million dollars. We will make two million dollars." Rio cut him off: "We won't worry about the money now; we will wait until after the fellow is elected, and then we will worry about ways and means of getting money."

Nitto and Rio instructed Browne that he would have some company at the convention for insurance. Rio then named veteran associates Nick Circella, Robert McCullough, and Frank Diamond as well as McGurn sidekick Tony Accardo and budding labor goon Louis Romano. All would stay at the Brown Hotel, and expenses for all would be paid out of Local 2's coffers. The date of the convention was June 8-9.

⸻

Nitto's *sub rosa* means of conducting business paid off. While Nitto's gang was manipulating the BSEIU and IATSE, local authorities lost track of Nitto. The state's attorney continued the old Harry Lang case seven times, mostly based on pleas from Nitto representatives that he was "too ill to show." Frankly, Assistant State's Attorney Dougherty admitted, he had no idea where prosecution witness Nitto was. One rumor had him in an Arkansas hospital; another held that a doctor was hiding him closer to home in an Oak Park infirmary. This last may have been possible. Talk persisted for years of complications from the wounds inflicted by Detective Lang. However, Nitto never had any intention to press Lang. That matter for him was closed—he said so back in 1933—and he had nothing to gain from reopened it. Somehow, prosecutors believed otherwise, but on May 31, they gave up and entered a nolle prosequi. Case over.

⚜

The editor of the *Louisville Courier-Journal* thought the IATSE convention was a great story for his paper, but he found union members unwilling to talk. The editor thought this was strange, since conventioneers were usually anxious to court public-ity, and he sent a reporter to the Brown Hotel to check things out anyway. When the reporter discovered hotel doors sealed to outsiders, he shrugged the story off. Louisville would read about something else.

The union had good reason to keep its business behind closed doors. Nitto's "del-egates"—McCullough, Diamond, Accardo, and company—swarmed through the place, concentrating in the lobby, their sinister presence known to all. They occu-pied suites next door to Bioff and Browne. Circella shadowed Browne, while Lepke stalked Harry Sherman of New York and Louis Kaufman of New Jersey. Even Tommy Maloy and his entourage from Local 110 were there. Bioff's role as Browne's assistant was to meet and familiarize himself with many of Browne's peers. As Nitto promised, the delegates delivered Browne the vote with no opposition. Only one hitch to the otherwise smooth election of George Browne developed when ape-like Frank Diamond beat a delegate who was trying to gain access to Browne in his suite. It turned out the union member was a close friend coming to wish Browne well.

The IATSE conspiracy ripened upon their return to Chicago following another meeting at the Hochstein home. At first, the meeting was celebratory. Hochstein poured drinks, and congratulations were heartily exchanged among Bioff, Browne, and the customary Nitto group of higher-ups. Gradually, the tone changed as the mob men got down to business. Nitto and others ordered Bioff and Browne to go out, get organized, and "start getting some dough." The deal was for a fifty-fifty split. The mob then made Browne's first human resource decision for him: Nitto and Rio put Nick Circella on the payroll as Browne's personal representative, a position sim-ilar to Bioff's. Under no circumstances were Browne and Bioff to meet an exhibitor or a producer or discuss any business outside of Circella's presence. When Browne insisted on formal union procedures to approve the appointment at an upcoming meeting, Nitto reprimanded him and told him that he would have to pay Circella out of his own salary ($20,000 a year plus expenses) until formal approval was granted. Meeting over.

⚜

Only ten days after the IATSE convention and the blossoming of Nitto's grandiose nationwide racketeering plans, a new federal statute, the Anti-Racketeering Act, became law. The legislation made it a federal crime to obtain money or interfere with interstate trade and commerce by violence or threats of violence, and provided penalties of up to ten years in prison and fines of up to $10,000 upon conviction.

———※※※———

IATSE business necessitated frequent trips to the union's New York headquarters. President Browne felt that one of his first tasks was to recover the jobs lost in Hollywood through financial tough times during 1932. The craftsmen, carpenters, painters, and various set people all belonged to unions, and Browne wanted to bring the people and their dues back under IATSE jurisdiction. To do so, Browne had to negotiate with Pat Casey, the lead negotiator for the Hollywood producers, who was also in New York. Shortly after they arrived, Browne and Bioff met with Casey for an informal introductory meeting—but without Circella. The chubby hood lay in bed late that morning, hung over from an all-night binge. When the pair returned from the meeting, Circella exploded, asking what did they not understand about his orders never to meet with anyone outside his presence. The hood quickly dressed and dragged Bioff and Browne to the Medical Arts Hospital on Fifty-seventh Street at Sixth Avenue, leading them to a fine-looking man convalescing in bed. Circella made the introduction: "This is our man Johnnie."

"Johnnie" was John Rosselli, a mob man allied with Capone, Nitto, and Ricca back in the 1920s. Originally from the East Coast, he had moved to Chicago and hooked up with the gang. Capone took an immediate liking to the kid, but when the severity of Chicago's cold climate affected Rosselli's delicate health, Capone sent him to Los Angeles. Polished and smooth, not a coarse, cheap thug, he eventually entered labor circles and gained a paying position on Casey's staff. From bed, Rosselli related previous Hollywood labor events. To Browne, "It seemed Rosselli knew a great deal about it and Casey's business concerning it." The next day, Rosselli and Casey meet with the labor leaders, and Casey agreed that Browne's people were handled poorly and he would try to help him.

———※※※———

With the gang's foot in the IATSE door, the mob slowly poked Browne for more. Shortly after his election, Browne was called to the Capri Restaurant to meet Frank Nitto. Over dinner, the Enforcer explained the difficulty of his position as boss. His people needed money, he said. For instance, Jack McGurn needs $150 a week, and there were many others. Nitto continued, "When I can't find places to put these fellows, to earn money, we have to take care of ourselves, and I feel that you should put in one-half of your salary to help the good work, so to speak."

Browne refused, noting that Circella's expense was already coming out of his pocket. Nitto waved it off: "Well, all right, okay, no point one way or the other; I just thought you might like to do it." What Browne failed to realize was that this was a voluntary call to contribute more; at the next meeting, he would have no choice.

———※※※———

In the summer of 1931, the state's attorney in Chicago was deep into an investigation of Maloy's sleazy panjandrum, estimated to be raking in about $750,000 a year. Rumor had rebel operator Jacob Kaufman (no relation to Louis on the East Coast) scheduled to testify on June 23, 1931. On the twentieth, someone murdered him, and the investigation fizzled out. Maloy and the mob undoubtedly thought the matter put to rest with Kaufman, but for industry bigwigs, the Maloy outrage played on long enough for the following postal telegraph to be sent from Atlantic City, New Jersey, on June 20, 1931:

> Hon. William D. Mitchell—Attorney General
>
> Representatives of Illinois Motion Picture Theater Owners meeting here have requested me to invite your attention to investigation being made by State's Attorney in Chicago of Thomas E. Maloy and others connected with Motion Picture Operators Union on charges of racketeering with view to federal action for failure to report and pay income taxes . . . Maloy has been selling operators permits in violation of state law for large sums . . . also said to have extorted large sums from theaters . . . prompt action is thought necessary.
>
> Abram F. Myers

"The department appreciates having this situation called to its attention," U.S. Assistant Attorney General G. A. Youngquist assured Myers that same day. "You are advised that the department has taken this matter up with the United States attorney at Chicago."

It took little time for the attorney general's office to verify Maloy as "a racketeer of the worst type." SIU agents were sent to probe theater records for payments, especially any miscellaneous expenses divisible by $1,060, Maloy's annual rate for dropping a projectionist. Initially, they unearthed more than $150,000 in payments from 1929 to 1932. One theater chain's books revealed an "M. T. Expense," which the investigators assumed were Maloy's initials backward. Money was handled by Maloy himself at annual contract negotiations or at various times by his organizers Ralph O'Hara and Elmer D. Miller, representative of the exhibitors association. For over two years, SIU agents unwound the thread of Maloy's dealings. On March 8, 1934, U.S. Attorney Dwight H. Green was authorized to broaden the Maloy investigation to include "individuals, partnerships, or corporations connected with the activities of Maloy. . . . This authority is with a view to obtaining indictments."

Nitto's mob reasonably feared that any federal investigation of Local 110 might lead back to the hoods whom Maloy had placated for years with union proceeds. It would be even worse if the inquiry spilled over to their newly acquired parent organization, IATSE. Newspapers relayed suspicions of a Maloy income tax investigation that fall and reported federal contempt citations against Elmer Miller for refusing to explain $85,000 "in gifts" to Maloy. Ralph O'Hara was called before the grand jury in December. He protected boss Maloy, being evasive and utterly uncooperative. When he remained in the same frame of mind in January, the feds slapped him with a perjury charge.

Not long before, Frank Korte, a member of Local 110 and a "business and social" acquaintance of Paul Ricca, came to the hood and dropped the hint he would like to become business agent. Ricca informed him, "I will see what I can do about it." But that was Maloy's local, and he had been on top for fifteen years. Korte was obviously well informed about who wielded the real power in IATSE, parent of Maloy's Local 110. He even may have understood the mob intentions.

The Nitto mob, since the departure of the Touhys, their last real opposition, had had little reason to employ murder except to settle the most difficult internal matters or as the last resort to obtain what they desired. Their next hit typified this strategy.

Maloy was forty-two, though he appeared older, and had played both sides for years. Recently, his two-story, tile-roof summer home in Long Beach, Indiana, had been invaded by five men who cleaned out an estimated $50,000 in cash and $13,000 worth of his wife's jewelry. The robbery was performed, no doubt, by someone who knew the union leader and his business well, someone who did not necessarily fear him. For months, a friend had warned him of a whispered mob threat against his life, and Maloy considered this might be true. Possibly to mollify the mob, he threw a $30,000 fundraising banquet in a downtown hotel for mob-connected union officials.

By January 1935, Maloy's usually unruffled demeanor changed. Neighbors noticed that he doubled the usual guard on his South Side apartment building. Anxious to put the rumor of an investigation to rest, Maloy played the political card. The U.S. attorney general's office received a letter from an unnamed Illinois congressman demanding some conclusion, one way or the other, to the Maloy investigation. The matter, he said, was "causing severe and undue difficulties" for the union man. Informed of the communication, U.S. Attorney Dwight H. Green obliged the racketeer, indicting Maloy on January 25 on four counts of tax evasion for the years 1929-32. Maloy had filed income tax forms for those years but for grossly low amounts—never more than $33,000 a year. The feds thought they could prove that his income exceeded the admitted annual total by at least a quarter-million dollars.

Maloy posted $20,000 bail and on February 2 entered a plea of not guilty on all four counts. He then went about his regular business, usually with Dr. Emmett Quinn, a dentist turned union shop steward for Maloy. Lately, Quinn had driven for Maloy, and as a precaution he and Maloy had contrived a method to minimize Maloy's vulnerability. The racketeer's expensive new Packard was stored in a distant garage, and when Maloy wanted to venture out, Quinn would phone a third party to have the car delivered to him, and then he would collect Maloy.

For some reason, on February 4, Maloy altered the precautionary routine and decided to take the wheel for the drive to his Loop office. From his South Side apartment, he and passenger Quinn proceeded north along Leif Erickson Drive (now Lake Shore Drive). At about Thirty-fifth Street, they noticed a dark Ford coupe following behind. Near the Twenty-third Street viaduct and opposite the old Century of Progress Colonial Village display, the coupe pulled nearly even with Maloy's Packard. The union man glanced over at the vehicle with no particular interest and saw two men with their coat collars turned up and hats pulled low against the blustery, thirty-three-degree winter weather.

Quinn then heard blasts and what he thought "sounded like bricks hitting the side of the car." The men in the other car had discharged a barrage of automatic and shotgun fire. Splinters of glass sprayed, and when Quinn looked over at Maloy, he saw the man was slumped against the car door, his green fedora resting against the steering wheel. The uninjured steward reached over and took control of the car, bringing it to a stop. Among the first motorists to stop and assist Quinn, ironically, was Joseph P. O'Connell. He had never seen Maloy before, but the incident saved his office considerable work. As special assistant to the U.S. attorney general, O'Connell had presented some of the Maloy evidence to the grand jury, but he now could take the case off his docket. The union czar was dead.

Maloy's sudden death paved the way for a complete Nitto takeover of Local 110. The union's membership had no say. As president of IATSE, Local 110's parent organization, it was up to figurehead George Browne to administer affairs. He assured the state's attorney's office that he would assist in ending racketeering, but instead, the future of the local was decided in a series of meetings attended by Nitto, Rio, Ricca, Campagna, Circella, and Bioff. Browne confirmed later that the question of who was to run the local was decided at that meeting: "As I understood, he [Circella] was to run the affairs of the local."

Circella met with Browne to discuss union formalities. The opening mob strategy was to have Browne declare an emergency decree to take over the union, force all current officers to resign, and replace them with mob friends. In return, the grateful new officers would be required to kick back 50 percent of their salaries to the mob. When Browne balked at terminating union men he had known for years, Circella reprimanded him, "Well, that is what we want done, and that is the orders from my people and what you better do. . . . Willie, you better go with him and see he does it." Browne then suggested that the best approach was to have their men placed officially so that they could at least be above the reproach of any disgruntled bunch. This would also ensure their placement regardless of any change of union leadership. Nitto's group, though, had that covered too.

The mob's nomination to fill Maloy's vacant business agent position was made at a meeting at Frank Rio's home. Paul Ricca, Nick Circella, and Frank Korte were there when it was agreed that Korte was to be the new BA for Local 110, but that final approval was needed by Frank Nitto. Korte went to see Nitto, who was laid up in a nearby hospital. From his bed Nitto approved but with conditions. "It is all right," he said, adding, "you will have to carry two men on the payroll with you." Nitto also decreed that their pay was to come out of Korte's salary.

The second order of business was to work on the permit system. Nitto ordered Bioff to eliminate the permits so that mob family members and friends could be given work. The people, he said, that currently held those jobs, "would have to seek employment elsewhere." Furthermore, the new employees would have to kick back a portion of their salaries. Nitto arranged for former union slugger Ralph O'Hara to be part of the ghost payroll. He then arranged for sidekick Joseph Coscioni to get a job, while Ricca, Campagna, Diamond, and D'Andrea all loaded family into the local. Even after kicking back half of their salaries, these mob men and friends of the mob still took home $45 or more a week, not bad for those days.

—◆/◆/◆—

Mob higher-up Frank Rio saw little if any of the money that resulted from the scheme to which he had greatly contributed. On February 23, just as the new arrangements began bearing fruit, Rio quietly died of heart disease in his Oak Park home. He was thirty-five.

The funeral service was a muted yet tasteful affair at the popular gangland undertaking establishment, Rago Brothers. Large floral tributes decorated the walls, but the scene was not excessively splashy. When a reporter noticed the tribute cards were missing from the displays, the undertakers explained it as "mere routine." Mourners, however, whispered. No police bothered the proceedings. Nitto led gangland followers Louis Campagna, Claude Maddox, and Joe Fusco to the graveside. Ralph Capone, recently released from prison, and brother John were there. Notable absentees included Jake Guzik and Murray Humphreys—both in prison on tax charges—and Nitto's Melrose Park overseer, Rocco DeGrazia, who also recently had been sent up on tax fraud. Reporters did not recognize Paul Ricca, Phil D'Andrea, or Frank Diamond among the crowd.

Neither Bioff nor Browne were there—there was no time off from looting unions. Before the funeral, Nitto sent the pair to New York and instructed them to bring back money. He knew IATSE maintained an expense fund of $35,000, and now he wanted at least part of it. The pair raked off $20,000 and returned to Chicago, where Nitto and Campagna met them for the split.

Before Rio's demise, Nitto, Rio, Circella, and Bioff had met to discuss imposing Maloy's one-man booth extortion scheme to their advantage. Since Cermak's 1931 one-man booth agreement, some theaters had enjoyed a rebound in profits. With the worst of economic times behind and Cermak gone, Nitto decided the mob deserved a share of those profits. Through Maloy's theater contact, Elmer Miller, they directed Bioff to demand the major theater circuits put an additional man back in the booth. However, Bioff noted to Miller, they could avoid additional labor costs for a $100,000 payment. Miller thought the pudgy punk was joking and said if they put another man back in, they would go broke. In no uncertain terms, Bioff brusquely replied; "My answer to that is what it takes to kill grandma, grandma is going to die."

Just to make sure the message got through, Bioff and Browne called a meeting with James Costen, representing the Warner Brothers chain, and Barney Balaban, whose chain was a Paramount subsidiary. They met at the union office, where the theater men were informed of the demand. Balaban tried to reason with Bioff without success. If they wanted to operate, said Bioff, suddenly bloated with self-importance, they would have to deal with him. With the average salary of a projectionist at just over $5,000, the demands were in fact a bargain, and the alternatives were ruinous strikes, if not bombings, stench bombs, and other assorted vandalism. The theater owners surrendered. From the major exhibitors, the mob collected $60,000 from Paramount, $30,000 from Warner, and $10,000 from the lesser S&S circuit. The Allied Theater Association, representing smaller independent owners, would pay a monthly rate based on seating capacity. Bioff and Circella arranged payments through local lawyers who presented phony bills for legal services. The two then collected the cash for the fifty-fifty split.

In January, after several meetings, the IATSE board decided to move the union's headquarters from New York to Washington, D.C., in order to be closer to legislation affecting labor laws. Browne, however, had already forgotten who really ran things. Word of the proposed move percolated back to Nitto in Chicago via loyal shadow Circella. He and Rio immediately left for New York, where they met with Browne and Bioff at the Warwicke Hotel. After a sociable drink and "how's everything going" palaver, Nitto got to the point: "What is this I hear about moving headquarters from here to Washington? Did you talk to anybody about it?"

"No, I didn't talk to anybody," Browne replied.

"Well, you know you are supposed to," Nitto reminded him, his suspicion and temper ratcheting up a notch, along with his voice. "Is this one of these moves that you guys are trying to get away from us? What is this?" Before Browne could reply, Nitto barged on: "If you have any thought that you are going to sneak off on us that way, you have got another thing coming. You are not going to get away with it. If it is because you think you have connections in Washington, you are crazy. What is your reason for wanting to get out of New York?"

Browne explained he thought he could make simple decisions about his office on his own authority. The move was based on a desire to influence legislative matters, and he added that they needed to clear out of New York City while prosecutor Thomas Dewey was busting up gangs and racketeering. Jokingly, he asked Nitto, "What's the matter, do you think I am going to run out on you?"

The humorless Nitto responded to Browne's mistake by barking, "Yes, and we're here to see that you don't." He reminded Browne of the oath of loyalty he had taken in Riverside and noted that breaking it would not be good. Browne could consider this a reminder that he was to consult Circella on all matters, period.

With Local 110 in hand, Nitto turned stagehands Local 2 into a more efficient money-collection mechanism. Setting props and sets for live shows in the city included the rebounding and very lucrative burlesque market (and some burlesque houses also showed films). Browne had leveraged $150 a week from key show-house operator Nathaniel Barger for some time in exchange for suppressing union wages, and his Star and Garter and Rialto houses profited handsomely. Bioff reported back to Nitto on Barger's prosperity as well as the reason for it. Nitto immediately demanded 50 percent of the profits. Barger received the news in the usual mob fashion: he was told to meet Browne and Circella at Gibby's Ogden Grill just up the street from the Capri. The Italian thug informed Barger of the mob's decree, saying, "I have got instructions from my people to tell you they want a fifty percent interest in your theater." When an outraged Barger jumped up from the table, Circella said calmly, "Jack, that is the story. That is what my people want, and you will have to give it to them."

Shortly after his meeting Barger received a visitor, Beau Brummel Willie Bioff, who marched in and callously announced, "Hello, partner" before demanding his share of the week's profits. Barger again protested the 50 percent demand. Bioff snickered and announced he would like to have half of him any day. It was either pay the percentage, recalled Barger, or go out of business, so he went along. From Barger alone, the mob sucked $14,000 in 1935 and a further $32,000 in 1936. That was far from the end. Upon learning that Barger had decided to sell off the Star and Garter's theater equipment, Bioff marched in and collected the mob split of $3,500 from the sale.

Bioff soon discovered that Barger was pocketing $200 a week in salary and reported the news to the Nitto group at the Capri Restaurant. Nitto, at the head of the table, wouldn't stand for it. "Well, I am going to put a man in there to get two hundred dollars, too," he said. When Bioff protested that the entire amount might be a bit much, considering that he was already handing over 50 percent, Nitto growled, "We're not going to let him get away with two hundred dollars a week." He instructed Circella to inform Barger to put Frank Diamond on the payroll, or else. Of course, Diamond performed no work; all he had to do was show up on payday. Barger's dilemma did not end when the flaky Diamond suddenly and with no explanation gave up the free money and was replaced by gunman Phil D'Andrea. Soon D'Andrea brought in additional weight when he installed his sister as Barger's bookkeeper. When, after a few years, they bled Barger to the point of near insolvency, the Nitto mob backed off and allowed him to pay mob men at a reduced rate.

One morning, Browne was on his way to the union offices for work with Bioff when Willie turned to him and announced a mandatory mob meeting that day at the Bismarck Hotel. "They want a revision of profits, so to speak," Bioff said. At a suite of rooms in the Bismarck, Bioff and Browne met Nitto, Ricca, Campagna, and Circella. Nitto announced the apportionment of money was hardly fair, given the size of his organization, and that Browne and Bioff collected salaries in addition to their split. Nitto's group, he reminded them, was responsible for Browne's election in the first place. Ominous figures Ricca and Campagna chipped in support for their boss, then Nitto decreed, "We should get two-thirds and you fellows one-third."

Browne may have foolishly resisted, as he had at the Capri Restaurant when Nitto plugged for a voluntary contribution. This time Nitto erupted, "All right, let us forget about it. We will forget the deal altogether." Bioff, attuned to the way the mob had of eventually getting its way, usually by untimely deaths, begged for a moment with union boss Browne. In a separate room, Bioff quietly explained to Browne that they were in no position to argue, that the mobsters would get what they wanted. When the pair emerged, a new deal was set, and from then on, Bioff and Browne would share one-third of the proceeds.

After the newly agreed-upon split, Nitto and his mob parasites found a new, effortless method to milk IATSE members nationwide. A measure passed at the June executive board meeting, with Browne present, allowed the international union to deduct a 2 percent tax from each member's paycheck, under the pretense of building a reserve 1) for IATSE promotion and protection, 2) to combat the rival Congress of Industrialized Organizations labor organization, and 3) to advance legitimate IATSE issues. With the membership at 40,000, this was no small-time local racketeering feat, as the mob figured the amount generated might run a million dollars a year. Pressed through as part of the plan, the executive board delegated the account's management to President Browne and required no answerability. He could do as he wished with the money.

To track the balance and develop a surreptitious means to extract the cash for the mob, Nitto ordered Circella and Browne to put a trusted mob accountant on the payroll. When Browne questioned this, Nitto came up with a human resource maneuver that gave the appointment a touch of legitimacy: he instructed Browne to run a classified ad for the position, then cut out copies as proof, reject everybody, and hire his man. It was at the stagehand's Chicago office that Circella marched in and introduced Nitto's accountant from the Manhattan brewery, Isadore "Izzy" Zevin, to Browne and Bioff. Other so-called 2% Fund "representatives" would be hired at $194 a week, their salaries a part of the account expense. Reps were allowed enough for taxes on their salary plus perhaps $10 for spending; the rest went into the Browne account. Zevin arranged for checks to be sent to himself via registered mail; he then cashed them and gave the money to Circella for dispersal to Nitto and company.

Nitto's mob extended their claims to New York. Local 306 was the largest projectionists union in the country. The opening came when, after a round of rank-and-file grumbling about the local's officers, Browne stepped in and declared an emergency decree for new elections. The move was also necessary in order to negotiate a new contract with local exhibitors, primarily Loews and RKO. When theater executives cried poverty and deemed a cut in pay necessary for survival, Local 306 agents called for a strike.

According to union rules, however, a strike had to be authorized by the international organization first. As part of the scheme, Browne refused to authorize the strike and then sent Bioff to New York. Bioff told union agents to demand even more from the theater people, and again, the executives balked. Bioff called Loews officials and informed them that if Local 306 wanted a strike, he would authorize it—unless they were prepared to pay $150,000. Loews and RKO phoned Browne for help. The burly labor president offered no pity: "Well, that is not my business. You can talk to Bioff about that. Whatever he does in the matter is okay with me."

The headstrong owners resisted, arguing they couldn't come up with that amount. The Local did not flex its muscle with a strike; rather, it employed a different type of leverage, catching owners off guard. Anxious crowds filed into theaters for the hot new comedy *Broadway Gondoliers*, starring Dick Powell and Joan Blondell. In one theater, comfortably seated customers suddenly became irritable when the characters appeared onscreen—with no sound. In other theaters, there was sound, but no picture; another had both sound and picture, but the picture was upside-down. A stench bomb ruined one movie house before the film even unwound. Calls from angry customers besieged Loews and RKO.

Theater executives gave in to Bioff's demand, signing a new contract with Local 306 and agreeing to pay the $150,000. Bioff gloated over having put the theater big shots of New York in their place, but he did not bleed his newfound serfs dry all at once as negotiations allowed for timely payments. Not long after the issue was settled, Browne obtained the first installment for division with Nitto and his crowd.

————

A one-third split for Willie Bioff was a gold rush compared to anything else he had achieved in his criminal escapades, and now he and his wife could live rather comfortably. For Willie, though, it was as much about ego. The IATSE affair inflated his importance among the upper-tier hoodlums and provided a means for him to push around legit businessmen, which must have caused him great pleasure in light of his meager background. He became so greedy that Nitto even had to reprimand him on one occasion.

For stout union man George E. Browne, the money was a side benefit that, according to his account, he lost track of at times. On one occasion, when Bioff handed him his split of $5,000, he professed not to know what the money was for; Bioff had to remind him of their deal with the mob. He admitted that he handled little money. The money served him well nonetheless: he bought a farm west of Chicago, where he raised a family, though union matters gave them little time together. Before all this mob conspiracy when he was a rough-and-tumble labor official, all he had wanted was higher stature. Now he had his higher stature, thanks to a pact with the devil; Browne's hardened union enamel was no match for Nitto and his cohorts. Browne admitted later that, after his first few meetings with Nitto and his bunch, he turned from a man with average drinking abilities to a "very hard drinker." Legend hung upon him a 100 bottle of beer a day habit.

The influx of new revenue served principal mob higher-ups well. Gunmen D'Andrea and Diamond collected a few thousand dollars from local theater extortion in addition to income from other gang activities—not bad for the 1930s. From his Browne and Bioff shadowing duties, Circella lived high, eventually running casino nightclubs on the Near North Side. Dominant figures Paul Ricca and Louis Campagna bought large farms away from the city, though they still resided and raised families in the west suburbs. They were not above extravagance. When they saw a lawn in California with automated sprinklers, they insisted that the union pay for a large number of them for themselves, even after they were told the sprinklers wouldn't operate properly in Chicago because they would freeze in winter. Ricca's and Campagna's lawns were watered automatically.

Extortion money, according to Bioff, was sometimes pooled together and divided. On one occasion during the conspiracy, Bioff remembered turning over to Nitto a direct payment for $12,000. The racketeer recalled with a snicker, "This was chicken feed, though, in comparison to the money coming in those days." For Nitto, union dividends embodied a miracle of relief. Not that Nitto indulged in any extravagance for himself; he was much too conservative and businesslike to squander finances. Other than some undetectable Chicago residence, he maintained homes in

Hot Springs, Arkansas, and Miami, Florida—all likely rentals for leisure and business. The source of any money problems was young wife Anna.

For some time, marriage number two teetered near break up. Talk had young Anna burning through cash nearly as fast as Nitto could rake it in. While Nitto worked critical gang matters, she tripped to where the couple maintained homes. In these resort towns, living the fast lane nightlife with friends was her natural activity. Near each of these places were casinos and racetracks where, regrettably for Nitto, Anna whooped it up, frequently dumping money into dice, cards, and roulette. The horses suckered her for bets as often as they did any big hood, seldom finishing in the money. Conservative and business-like Nitto raged about divorce. Friends of his intervened to save the nuptials, suggesting the couple adopt a baby and start a family life. In April 1934, in between strategy sessions to get Browne elected IATSE president, Nitto and wife Anna traveled to Hot Springs and adopted a six-month-old Italian boy who had been left in a nearby convent by migrant worker parents. They named the boy Joseph Ralph Nitto.

The immediate impact of parenting on wife Anna is uncertain, though indications are that she still indulged in nightlife. On the other hand, concerned mob leader Frank Nitto, after obtaining a $100,000 payment from James Ragen to clear out James Lynch in the General News affair, turned over to mentor and financial advisor Louis Greenberg a payment for the same exact amount early in 1935 toward a trust fund for the adopted boy.

20

BACK TO BASICS: THE BARTENDERS UNION

TWO EVENTS IN 1935 SEEMED to indemnify Nitto's absolute rule over Chicago, perhaps even giving him as firm a hold on the town as Capone had enjoyed during the late 1920s. The first of these occurred only a few weeks after Tom Maloy's violent death. Elected as part of the Cermak machine two years earlier, thirty-nine-year-old Cook County State's Attorney Thomas Courtney was a politically ambitious fellow. With Cermak gone and Mayor Kelly up for re-election in 1935, Courtney's support for the mayor was far from wholehearted. Not that the state's attorney bolted from his party, but the mayor's chair was one he would eventually seek for himself—and crime would be an issue. Before the election, Courtney undermined Kelly as if he were a candidate, noting that the mayor had hardly concerned himself with Nitto's mob.

Meanwhile, Courtney trumpeted his own crime-busting résumé, never failing to remind constituents that it was he who had continued Cermak's war against the gangsters. In reality, though, of Courtney's estimated 4,000 convictions since his election, none were mob figures. He could, however, boast of breaking up several arson and auto-theft rings. His top trophy, he claimed, was the breakup of the so-called Touhy kidnapping gang. Otherwise, the closest he came to molesting a mob-related entity was the breakup of Red Barker's TNT organization. Recently, Courtney had continued that particular crusade, aiming for Michael Galvin's outlaw and likely mob-controlled Teamster organization.

Underlying his war on labor racketeers, was Courtney's desire for an investigation into the recent death of Tom Maloy and his Local 110, which may have come too close to Nitto's group. After killing Maloy to gain his union and head off a federal investigation, it appeared that the mob wasn't about to let a state's attorney muck up their plans—legally or politically.

During the very early and dark hours of Sunday, March 24, two detectives drove Courtney and Eighteenth Ward Alderman Harry E. Perry through the South Side on Normal Boulevard. Both were to be delivered home after a long political meeting. Just south of Seventieth Street, a car began to overtake them. Gunmen leaned out and squeezed off eight shots, five of which hit Courtney's car, before their vehicle sped off. Except for cuts from shattered flying glass, no one in the car was hurt.

The *Tribune's* headline the next day reported on the state's attorney's investigation: "COURTNEY HUNTS GANG FOES." Pressed to account for the shooting, Courtney surmised, "It was members of 'the mob' that fired the shots." Just whom "the mob" referred to, he would not specify, but one reporter took it to mean the old Capone Outfit. When the reporter pressed Courtney further, he noted the official's evasiveness about the Nitto gang, especially when asked about his campaign against certain unions. "Labor racketeers in Cook County," as far as Courtney knew, "are on the run." When asked whether the gambling rackets might have been behind the assassination attempt, Courtney said, "It wasn't gambling and it wasn't any petty larceny group that sought my life. . . . It was the mob. You can figure it out for yourselves as I'm going to say no more about it."

Mayor Kelly backed Courtney, declaring again a war "to the finish on gangland," invoking that worn-out cliché from the 1920s." Police dragnets on hoodlums snared only old South Side Prohibition figure Spike O'Donnell, who happened to be slumming at the intersection of Dearborn and Randolph streets. Everyone else evaporated. Three days later, a $5,000 reward was posted for the arrest and conviction of those responsible for the shooting, but no one collected it. The same day, Courtney backtracked on his original dismissal of "petty larceny" suspects, announcing the search for suspected auto thieves.

It might have been a mob attempt, but it certainly was a sloppy job for an organization usually marked by efficiency in such matters. More to the point, killing a state's attorney was out of the question and bad for business, as Nitto well knew from the 1926 McSwiggin affair. With several of the shots only impacting carelessly off the rear of the vehicle and without the more efficient use of shotguns (machine guns were no longer easily obtainable due to new federal regulations), it may very well have been meant as a warning. Such an attempt on a highly placed target by anybody else probably could not have been possible without mob sanction. In any case, further investigation by Courtney's office of local labor racketeering completely dissolved, as did any remote prospect of uncovering Nitto's stranglehold on Locals 2 and 110 as well as the IATSE and the BSEIU. Courtney caused the mob no major headaches; his zero-conviction score would remain intact.

The second factor that ensured that the mob would keep running with near impunity was the April 2 re-election of Mayor Kelly. Nitto's group was part of the re-election effort, though their help may not have been necessary since the Republicans were still reeling from the 1931-32 Democratic landslides. Facing Kelly in the mayoral contest was relatively unknown Emil Wetten. Kelly won by a scandalous mark of 798,150 votes to Wetten's 166,571, carrying the heavily mob-influenced First Ward by an obscene margin of 14,674 to 486 and the "Bloody Twentieth" Ward by 17,465 to 862. (The former "Bloody Nineteenth" Ward in 1923 was divided into the Twentieth, Twenty-fifth, and Twenty-seventh wards; since the Twentieth comprised most of the old Nineteenth, it retained the "bloody" moniker.) Charges of voter fraud went nowhere, and pundits figured it wouldn't have mattered anyway. When frustrated civic groups tried to push state legislation to curb voter fraud, they were successfully contested by the Kelly regime.

As with many of the local elections during the Nitto reign, stolen votes however represented a payoff that cemented crime to politics, and Kelly's regime did not disappoint. Nitto's agents fixed local juries when necessary, and when exposed, the investigations into the matters usually went nowhere. Increasingly business leaders complained of outright extortion by unions stage-managed by the Nitto mob. His men went so far as to dictate to certain ward committeemen and defy city police outright in running nightclubs and gambling operations. Kelly men in the Illinois capital of Springfield even pushed for legalization of handbooks. The key to this movement was state Representative John Bolton, an owner of handbooks on the West Side. The move served both political and criminal elements: Kelly might consolidate power through increased patronage, licenses fees, and leverage, while underworld interests could run their operations uninterrupted and rake in vast amounts of cash. This also dovetailed with Annenberg's wire service business, on which Nitto kept an anxious eye. Wiser heads in the state capital prevailed to defeat the measure.

———

Because the Bioff-Browne affair came about so casually and immediately fell into their laps, it wasn't until late spring 1935 that Nitto could decisively act on marketing and inflating the gang's old Prohibition monopoly booze business. The key to the mob's plan rested with neighborhood bartenders, who were represented in Chicago by Local 278 of the Bartenders and Beverage Dispensers Union. For most of the past twenty-five years, the key man for the white apron barkeeps had been business agent George B. McLane. A "regular guy" as one colleague described him, McLane had a droopy, elliptical shape of medium height and 200 pounds. He had an ordinary, affable face, a ski-slope nose, and slicked-back graying hair, although he was only in his early forties.

Behind the average appearance, however, lurked the soul of a bartender—boisterous and crude yet possessing an astute character that was more than capable of quickly sizing up any situation. On the flip side, he was thought to indulge in the products of the tap, and his harshest critic labeled him a "habitual drunkard" and a "habitual violator of the laws of the state of Illinois and the United States." This last may have been a bit too much, as only one instance suggests a police record when, in 1920, he was charged with robbery and attempted murder but was acquitted. Otherwise, as a youthful bartender, he could be found in the old Levee district around Twentieth Street and Armour Avenue. One story had him earning extra cash by hiring himself out as a professional escort for ladies who wished to patronize the nightclub circuit at a time when the general public and law enforcement frowned on single women habituating drinking establishments. Otherwise, all that could be really pinned on him were disorderly conduct and assault charges from later union work.

In 1920, business agent McLane faced the unenviable circumstance of keeping alive a labor union whose products of trade were illegal. (There were other locals in Chicago, but his was most dominant.) One curious news hawk decided to investigate the bartenders situation for himself in 1923:

> [F]rom the jovial, florid countenance of the obese, bald-faced Santa Clauses that jostle in and out of their humpty-dumpty headquarters at 123 N. Clark St., you'd think the jolly barkeeps of yesteryear had already won a decision from the United States Supreme Court.

Yes, McLane told the reporter in smug defiance of the law, "Our business is bubbling right along." Thirty new members had joined in the past week, upping the total membership to more than 800, and his association, the Bartenders Benevolent and Protective Association, Local 89, had accumulated a $25,000 nest egg toward pushing out the Dry Law.

Other Locals were not so fortunate. Saloons, now illegal speakeasies, no longer felt constrained to hire union men, and the union was at a loss: they could hardly force an owner to hire a union man via the conventional picket or boycott. To bolster locals hit by sagging membership (waiters and waitress unions as well as bartenders), some went into the speakeasy business themselves. In order to operate, they were forced to buy bootleg beer from one of the city's Prohibition gangs, which allowed gangs such as Capone's to dominate affairs. In no time, instead of guarding the tender flame of unionism, the headquarters for barkeepers and their allies housed gambling in addition to dispensing illegal liquor. For McLane, this was an additional boon. He was thought to be running a handbook and dice game from which he was thought to be profiting at least a $1,000 a month.

When word of the blatant corruption of the Chicago locals filtered back to their parent organizations, the Hotel and Restaurant Employees International Alliance and Bartenders International League of America, three vice presidents came to Chicago to investigate. They disbanded one local, as an example perhaps, then left, leaving McLane's intact. By 1930, when federal laws stiffened penalties for Prohibition violations, pressure also forced a change in the local's name to drop any hint of alcohol, and it became the Beverage and Soda Dispensers Union, retaining about 500 or so members.

When Roosevelt lifted the sanction on beer in March 1933 and pressed toward Repeal, McLane's local looked to expand its membership; the union was swamped by more than 500 hungry applicants for jobs that paid about $35 a week. Few were judged to be qualified to serve across the mahogany, so local President Thad Wittwer announced the creation of a bartenders school to train the men. After all, he noted, anyone can follow a recipe and put together a mixed drink, but drawing a beer is not a "hash-slinger" job. "Drawing a glass of beer looks simple," he said, "but it's an art." The angle of the glass under the tap is the key to leaving just the exact amount of desirable froth without wastage. However, Wittwer would no doubt come to regret his position and the end of Prohibition.

McLane's desire to expand union membership collided head-on with Nitto's plan for horizontal expansion of mob Prohibition products. After the Century of Progress, Nitto looked to expand the Manhattan Brewing Company, and accomplice Joe Fusco also sought to expand Gold Seal Liquors. From the outset, they easily developed their client base out of state. Customers poured Manhattan products almost everywhere in the Midwest. Kansas City mobster Tony Gizzo was allied to distribute product in that city. Nitto placed sales agents in Iowa, and through their Manhattan outfit, they obtained a brewery in Wisconsin. Certain brands were shipped to the Deep South. Nitto extended distribution to Miami, Florida, where he pushed beer, liquor, and bar water from the F. R. Nitto Beverage Company. Wines came from the Roma Wine Company.

At the Manhattan brewery, old Capone booze hands Nick and Frank Juffa supervised activity in the brewery yard. After his stint in prison for tax evasion, racketeer Murray Humphreys dropped in often, possibly lining up sales locally and finding the strong-arm tactics from the old days still effective. Nitto, despite his extensive administration activities, was not above managing accounts himself. On one occasion, word came down that one wholesale beer distributor had decided to drop Manhattan products; worse yet, they still owed Manhattan money. Nitto and Greenberg paid the owner a visit, the Enforcer bullying him before leaving. No word of any further action surfaced: the owner no doubt realized the value of his Manhattan subscription.

Competing in the venerable brewing town necessitated horizontal expansion, and the Nitto Outfit looked, via Greenberg, to obtain a number of rival hometown breweries. As outlets for their products, they converted their speakeasies to saloons and opened or gobbled up others, including nightclubs as natural mob-allied ventures. In due course, they owned or controlled an estimated 17 percent of the retail booze outlets in Chicago. But this did not in itself guarantee patrons would readily accept mob-owned products when previous and long-recognized nationwide brands scrambled back into the post-Prohibition market. Mainstream giants invested enormous sums to improve quality and advertise for name recognition, something the mob could not or would not do. One Manhattan employee remembered the beer produced there as just plain "lousy" as a result of mob pressure to reduce costs and increase profits. Such a review made Manhattan increasingly a hard sell.

The situation implied that the best way, other than muscle, to overcome the competition's advertising dollars and ensure steady sales for mob brands was to control the tapsters behind the bars. The strategy was simple: customers, who in those days had yet to be comprehensively programmed by advertising, frequently bellied up to the bar and called for a beer without specifying a brand; a mob-controlled bartender could slide them a glass of Manhattan beer. Should the customer demand a specific brand, the bartender could easily claim he was out of stock out and recommend "another just as good" to introduce the mob product. Of course, the same held true with distilled products. In addition, the union collected nearly $150,000 a year in dues from its members. With the union in mob hands, the gang could ransack the union treasury while simultaneously cutting labor costs at their businesses—a racketeering trifecta potentially worth millions.

Business agent George McLane was looking to increase union membership, but his unionists had no idea which outlets were mob-owned. "Our first trouble with the gang," recalled McLane, "came when we tried to organize bartenders working in taverns or night clubs owned by the Nitti Outfit. Our employees were beaten and threatened with death. If we picketed a place owned by the gang, our pickets were assaulted." The tapsters, however, were a hardcore bunch, maintaining the lines through the assaults.

In the spring of 1935, the mob decided to move in behind Nitto's choice, massive South Side ally Danny Stanton. He was the most suitable mob employee available for the job. In addition to alcohol and gambling concessions in the South Halsted district, he had cornered many of the restaurant and food service employees unions. These were quite profitable and numerous given that many neighborhood dime stores and grocers possessed lunch counters for customers. Allied with him in running the associated black unions was long time crook J. Livert "St. Louis" Kelly. Most of these local unions belonged to the same umbrella group as McLane's bartenders, the Hotel and Restaurant Employees International Alliance and Bartenders International League of America (now known as the Hotel Employees and Restaurant Employees International Union).

Stanton's approach to McLane was indirect but blunt: he phoned union headquarters out of the blue wanting $500 in union funds to go to the Kentucky Derby on May 4 and said two men would be over to collect it. McLane argued he had no such authority to turn over union funds to strangers. Nonetheless, a half-hour later, two men arrived for the money, and again McLane turned them down. Perhaps, they said, McLane would like to explain it again to Stanton. One of the hoods dialed up the racketeer and put McLane on the line. Goon diplomacy over, Stanton's voice roared through McLane's receiver, "You son of a ——, we'll get the money and take the union over." Stanton had sent his warning, but McLane held firm and never heard from Stanton again. Perhaps McLane saved his union and Stanton money by missing the derby. Betting favorite Nellie Flag finished out of the money, while Omaha, ultimately a Triple Crown winner, outpaced eighteen starters by a length and a half on a drizzle-soaked track.

Two or three weeks later, having heard from Stanton about the first nudge to get Local 278, Nitto sent an emissary to McLane with a communiqué summoning him to the LaSalle Hotel, where McLane met the Italian hood one on one. Nitto asked him about the Stanton demand, and McLane retraced the event, also complaining about the sluggings endured by some of his group's members. The mob boss then laid out his true intentions, saying he and his associates were interested in the liquor business and that a certain man as business agent would be useful. If he went along, everything would be all right. As for the assaults on McLane's men, Nitto told him, "The only way to overcome this is to put one of our men in as an officer." Given union rules, this would be impossible, McLane explained, but Nitto wasn't interested in union bylaws. Recognizing the union man as neither cooperative nor ambitious, Nitto employed more forceful rhetoric reminiscent of his Enforcer days: "We've taken over other unions. You'll put a man in or get shot in the head."

McLane went to the board, but they shrugged off the threat, falsely believing in their own muscle, as perhaps many at the outset of the Cermak administration believed that the mob without Capone was through. No gangsters would dare push into their union, they believed.

Hearing no word, Nitto commanded his thugs to continue the onslaught of picketing union men. Not long after, he ordered McLane to a meeting at Nitto headquarters above the Capri Restaurant. The barman nervously sat down at the long table in center, while around him were the forceful mob personalities Nitto, Paul Ricca, Louis Campagna, and their spearhead in the liquor industry, old Capone beer distributor Joe Fusco. As an added touch of terror decor, McLane noticed three guns lying on the tabletop. Nitto again demanded that one of his men be placed in the union as an officer to supervise Syndicate liquor distribution. Unless he did so, Nitto told McLane, he would find himself "dumped in an alley."

McLane whined that he couldn't do this alone even if he wanted to, blathering such union technicalities as membership prerequisites and executive board approval. With the nucleus of his mob present, Nitto raged, "Give us the names of any who oppose. We'll take care of them. We want no more playing around. If you don't do as we say, you'll get a shot in the head. How would your wife look in black?" Terrified to the point of mindlessness, McLane replied, "No. She has never worn black." Nitto assured the bartender, "You either put them to work or she will be in black."

McLane relayed the threat to the executive board, telling its members they must understand it was not only his life on the line but their lives as well. Foolishly, they turned down the proposal.

McLane faced the mob at the Capri Restaurant again in early July. Nitto and Campagna were there as well as a new face, Fred Evans, who had worked with Nitto and Guzik in the booze trade during Prohibition. A street tough but a good numbers man, he may have been partially filling Guzik's role with the gang after the latter was shipped off to prison on a tax evasion charge. As McLane situated himself, Nitto growled, "What are you stalling for? The slugging of your pickets and intimidations of your business agents will stop if you put our man to work. I'll give you a man without a police record. The places that are Syndicate owned will join the union. There will be no pickets and no bother."

McLane informed him that the board still refused to go along. Nitto heatedly demanded the names of board members, but McLane refused to divulge any. His obstinacy didn't matter. "We'll take care of that," Nitto haughtily assured him. "This is your last chance. This is the only way we'll stand for anything. Put in our man or wind up in an alley." As McLane rose from his seat to leave, Nitto reminded him, "No more ifs or ands. You put a man on at $75 a week or we'll blow your head off."

Finally, the Local 278 board agreed, and a meeting was arranged for McLane at the Capri. In the presence of Ricca and Campagna, Nitto introduced McLane to his new union officer, mob man Louis Romano, one of the Nitto goons who had accompanied Browne and Bioff to the convention in Cincinnati. "Here's your man. He has no police record," Nitto lied. Romano's rap sheet stretched back a dozen years and listed arrests for assault and murder. "He'll go along with you as an organizer and assistant," Nitto continued. "His salary will be $75 a week. Provisions must be made to raise it later. He'll adjust trouble on the picket lines and see that all the places join the union." McLane took Romano to the union offices and introduced him around. On July 8, just a month after hijacking the IATSE, Louis Romano officially became the mob's union organizer in the bartenders union. And, whether he realized it or not, McLane, still none too eager to help, became a mob stooge.

Greenberg, at the front of the mob's booze financial interests, called a meeting on Nitto's behalf at the Auditorium Hotel, where he and Nitto gave McLane his orders: the bartenders are to push mob brands—Manhattan and Great Lakes draft beer, Badger and Cream Top bottled beer, liquors produced by Joe Fusco's Gold Seal Liquors Inc. (including Fort Dearborn whiskey), and any products from Capitol Wine and Liquor. McLane argued that he might get in trouble with federal laws governing fair trade. And that, he believed, was risky business, especially given the recent enactment of the Anti-Racketeering Act. Nitto immediately brushed his worries aside, saying, "See that your men do this, and let us worry about fair trade."

As Nitto had promised, bartenders of mob-owned joints enrolled in the union. With their foot in the union door, they moved to organize those places outside the city limits, particularly the countless taverns and restaurants in mob-occupied Cicero. Nitto directed local power Claude Maddox and new union man Romano to organize bartenders there, and in August 1935, they applied to the international union for a charter. McLane was the signature organizer of Local 450. Of the twelve names on the application, one belonged to the relatively unknown mob newcomer and future mob boss Joseph Auippa.

Amazingly, McLane furtively resisted Nitto's order to pitch mob brands, but it wasn't long before spies and sales reports reflected below-par sales. Nitto had Romano bring the union agent to Nitto's room at the Bismarck Hotel. Johnny Patton, Nitto's connection to the Sportsman's Park racetrack, was there, and the topic of discussion was liquor and beer sales at the track, where the bartenders were not pushing mob brands as expected. McLane attempted to vindicate his bartenders, arguing that it was one thing to slide a patron a Syndicate beer if he sidles up to the bar and asks for a beer without specifying a brand, but when the customer requests a national brand and refuses the Syndicate substitute—well, there's not much a barkeep can say. Sensing the usual stall, Nitto roared, "If the bartenders don't push it, they'll get their legs broken." At least one additional admonishment by Nitto was necessary before the mob boss was satisfied, but there were no reports of broken legs.

Having subjugated the bartenders, Nitto aimed for the mob to control other saloon-related commerce as well, which would further extend the operation's grip on the city. Through Louis Greenberg, the mob controlled an equipment company that supplied tavern fixtures to many saloons. Through Humphreys and Stanton's efforts in the cleaning and dyeing industry, they controlled the supply of tavern linens, as well as linen service to other area businesses, such as hotels and service stations, through the Chicago Linen Supply Association. When Ralph Capone emerged from his stint in federal prison, the mob gave him control of the bottled water business through W. W. Inc. (Waukesha Water, 99.44% pure), which also serviced water coolers throughout city buildings. Nitto assigned John Capone control of the Havana Beverage Company on Lake Street, which produced soda pop and carbonated water. Tavern water alone used as mixers for drinks and "chasers" represented nearly a million dollars annually in Chicago. One tavern owner remarked about the lack of muscle employed by the water purveyors but added that it was a "good idea to have a bottle of hoodlum water on hand in case some of the boys drop in."

Coin-operated cigarette machines and the booming jukebox business in the county belonged firmly to slot-machine king Eddie Vogel and his Apex Cigarette Services, while accounts in the city were maintained by longtime First Ward fixture Dennis Cooney and his Century Music Company. Operators outside their sphere were forced to join the shady Associated Phonograph Operators Association, in which annual dues amounted to $45,000. Apex and Century tied in with friendly police, politicians, and inspectors who would suddenly find a flurry of violations in any dissenting tavern or restaurant. Once installed, the machines could only be serviced by members of the mob-friendly electricians union run by Michael "Umbrella Mike" Boyle. Failure to comply, as one restaurateur discovered, was a visit from a mob affiliate who asked, "How would you like a picket in front of your place? No milk, no bread, no deliveries."

⚜

That summer, Congress ratified the National Labor Relations Act, called the Wagner Act after its main sponsor, which enabled the majority of employees in an industry to elect the manner in which they wished to deal with employers on the issues of wages, work hours, and conditions—a landmark event for workers' rights. In a way, the Wagner Act fit hand in glove with mob intentions, for if there were more unions, the mob would have more opportunities to take them over and profit from them. That's the way one razor-sharp reporter forecast it, worrying that:

> A shrewd gangster like Frank Nitti, the present Capone leader who always was the business "brains" of the criminal organization, is considered quite capable of realizing that the Wagner-Connery measure practically guarantees to union heads the domination not only of union members, but also of employers.

Apparently, nobody took note of the reporter's concerns. Willie Bioff more brashly explained later: "We let no Wagner Act or any other act stand in our way. We confronted our problems as they came along. . . . As long as we got the dough, that was the important thing."

A last bit of local theater-related union business cropped up in mid-1935. Since the mid-1920s, leftover O'Banionite Two-Gun Louis Alterie had directed the

Chicago Theater and Amusement Building Janitors Union Local 25. He administered union dues as he wished since he had allowed no elections during his tenure. More recently, he had hijacked the Associated Ash Haulers union and had claimed membership in the Hotel Clerks Union Local 202. With the mob sidetracked by consolidating gambling, IATSE, and bartender interests, Alterie thrived, doing well enough to maintain a pleasant studio apartment, registered under the alias Varain, on Eastwood Avenue opposite Lincoln Park on the North Side for him and his wife. The couple frequently traveled west to Alterie's home region but not to his favorite state, Colorado, which had banished him for a wild shootout a few years earlier. Trips to Florida also were not uncommon.

Alterie's union activities finally attracted mob attention. His Local 25 belonged to the BSEIU, and as such, he had represented the union at the American Federation of Labor convention in San Francisco the previous year. BSEIU officials had long known that Alterie refused to pay the local's per capita tax and probably pocketed the amount himself. What Alterie didn't comprehend was the scope of Nitto's influence over the BSEIU now. Thanks to the mob, in May 1935 George Scalise, the international union's East Coast rep, was elevated to fifth international vice president, with fellow racketeer Izzy Schwartz put in his old position. Chicagoan Thomas Burke, suspected of being under mob influence, served as first international vice president. Moreover, the Nitto mob understood how Local 25 worked nicely in tandem with their locals during theater strikes. The union was a natural fit for them, and there was no need for it to be in such unpredictable and obstinate hands. If Alterie were gone, his union and its funds would fall under control of Thomas Burke.

Dapper "gentleman cowboy" Alterie and his wife spent the first week of July in Valparaiso, Florida, where the gangster purchased a nightclub. After arranging for the club's management in his absence, he returned to his Eastwood Avenue apartment on July 8. The standard mob setup was put in place the day after he arrived in Chicago with, as one reporter noted, "all the loving care and attention to detail which Frank 'the Enforcer' Nitti was wont to use." A man who gave the name Sullivan but looked Italian rented a first-floor apartment in the graystone directly across the street from Alterie's building. The room was ideal. Just above a garden apartment, it gave a sufficient view of the entrance to the building across the street, which was partially obscured by a stylish cloth awning that extended over the walk. After paying $4.50 in rent, Sullivan announced he would occupy the room at night while two friends would be there during the day.

Two "model roomers," according to the landlord, the "friends" removed the screen panel from the middle window of the three that faced front. The pair settled in behind cracked curtains waiting; one with a shotgun and the other with a .351 high-powered rifle with telescopic sight. The equipment matched the need for this particular job: some thought Alterie donned a bulletproof steel vest as an occupational precaution, but more to the point, Alterie seldom left the apartment without his wife. Getting him necessitated the precision offered by the rifle. The shotgun was employed as insurance in case he came out in the open.

Just after 10 a.m. on July 18, the wait ended. Alterie and his wife exited their sixth-floor studio apartment for a trip downtown. The couple planned to leave the next day for Wyoming and the Frontier Round-Up rodeo of which Alterie was so fond. On the way out, Mrs. Alterie stopped in the lobby for a moment to speak to the desk clerk about some parcel delivery. Louis emerged from the building alone, standing just out of the shadow of the entranceway canopy at curbside, waiting to take command of his large blue sedan. The rifle across the street popped, then the shotgun exploded, followed by three rapid cracks of the rifle. The last volley was unnecessary; the first two blasts dropped the dapper Alterie facedown on the pavement with slugs to the head. When his wife rushed forward in a grievous panic to help him, she could only hear his fading voice: "I'm sorry, but I'm going. . . . I can't help it. I'm going." Rushed to nearby Lakeview Hospital, the cowboy gangster died at age forty-nine without going down in the blaze of dueling glory he so preferred back in the O'Banion days. A search of his person revealed none of the instruments that carved his marquee sobriquet.

Neither Frank Nitto nor Willie Bioff was available for police questioning, though both ranked at the top of their wanted list. Three days later, investigators surmised that Alterie's death was "due to efforts of the Caponites to seize his union or another [Local 110]." Tom Burke, who would give Nitto's group no particular headaches, was named to replace Alterie.

On the night of the twenty-first, Alterie's widow packed her husband's body off on the Rock Island train to Los Angeles for burial. Alterie's sisters remained in his birth state of California and had recently settled in Burbank. He would be home with the family again. Nitto's mob and IATSE were headed west too.

⚬⚬⚬

The making of a Hollywood movie involved many diverse talents. Electricians, painters, plumbers, plasterers, and carpenters, to name just a few, built sets; musicians contributed audio atmosphere; sound technicians and camera people guided recording equipment during filming; makeup and hair stylists dolled up and primped actors and actresses; and of course, there were the players themselves. In the filmmaking beehive, approximately 12,000 men and women belonged to at least one of nearly two dozen unions or guilds. This meant studio executives exhausted more time negotiating separate contracts than governing movie productions.

Rather than negotiate annually with each entity, the major studio producers formed a labor relations committee within the Motion Picture Producers Association to hammer out what became known as the Basic Agreement, which covered wages and conditions throughout the studio lots. Studio magnates made their job easier by preferring to negotiate only with representatives of parent labor organizations, the international unions. They could make such demands in the pre-Wagner Act days. In turn, it was advantageous for various local unions to function under the jurisdiction of some parent organization; remaining autonomous risked obtaining a lesser deal than their brethren. Though some remained independent, at the time of the first Basic Agreement, in 1925, most local organizations were represented by one of five international unions.

Historically, a majority of the set-building craft unions belonged to the IATSE, totalling several thousand members. However, during the strike fiasco of 1932-33 in which the IATSE attempted to recover lost wages and obtain a closed shop, many ranks were broken by Depression-strained producers, leaving IATSE's roster at a mere 158 persons and, once again, a number of self-governing locals. One promise left unfulfilled from George Browne's electioneering for IATSE president was regaining jurisdiction over those Hollywood craft jobs. Initial dialogue with the MPPA over the matter went nowhere, and by fall 1935, he was ready to take more direct measures. Though Nitto and the mob's name is not attached to this incident, they almost certainly sanctioned the moves since this gave them the pry bar to a bigger hoard of cash than any Chicago local could provide them.

Late in 1935, Paramount prepared to film *Thirteen Hours By Air*, a drama-in-the-sky story starring Fred MacMurray and Joan Bennett that would be shot on location in New Jersey and New York. In preparation, Paramount demanded that two cameramen resign from IATSE jurisdiction and join the International Brotherhood of Electrical Workers, which had absorbed IATSE operators and electricians during the IATSE strike earlier. Veteran labor man Browne did not panic. Instead, he immediately recognized the current act as the opening he and Bioff needed to instigate a crusade to regain jurisdiction in the studios.

Browne called upon IATSE representative Fred Raoul, who knew Paramount and Hollywood executives best, to negotiate with company executives in New York. In the meantime, Browne anticipated a strike. He used connections to the IBEW to make certain they would honor it and not attempt to gain new jurisdiction for themselves. As Raoul parried with movie execs in New York, Browne and Bioff approached Barney Balaban in Chicago and asked if he, as a member of the Paramount chain of exhibitors, would use his influence in the matter. Having paid through the nose to these extortionists earlier, it's doubtful he helped. After a few weeks of dithering with executives in New York, Bioff and Browne recognized the stall and decided to act. In addition to Local 110, the pair would use projectionists from all over to their advantage against the big producers.

The union men understood the entire Hollywood machine: the studios made movies, distributed their own films, and owned theaters in their name. Monolithic and vulnerable, the income from one end kept the whole industry running. They realized they might not have jurisdiction over production, but they did have the projectionists. They also knew that Paramount officials would be in Chicago for a scheduled a conference at the Drake Hotel on Monday, December 3. Paramount had the largest theater circuit in Chicago, Warner Brothers had a few houses, RKO had maybe one, and Loews, which operated mainly in the east, had none. Still, Browne and Bioff decided on a show of force for all the producers. It was set for Friday night, a big movie-going night for the public.

All over the country, the projectionists waited until patrons settled in their seats. In Elgin, Illinois, at 6:30 p.m. the projectionists walked out. Shortly thereafter, the plug was pulled in Joliet, Aurora, Evanston, then south in Peoria and the state capital of Springfield. St. Louis went dark next, followed by San Francisco, New York,

Indianapolis, Philadelphia, and Boston. Chicago men were called out late, and in the middle of their respective showings, the screens went dark in forty-six Balaban and Katz theaters. The disruption was brief, just long enough to run off a reel of film, but it was sufficient to ruin the night's pleasure.

Bioff accepted an impromptu invitation to join the Paramount brass at the Drake, where Bioff, with Circella alongside, reveled in his importance as he told the producers they could not hope to profit if the projectionists were on strike. Barney Balaban remembered that the Paramount executives decided to save their company from "financial collapse." Bioff pushed further, asking for a Hollywood agreement for IATSE and a closed shop for the craft unions. A couple of days later, George Browne and staff in New York met with all the major producers and completed a verbal agreement with Pat Casey, chairman of the MPPA Labor Committee, for a closed-shop article in the next Basic Agreement. The IATSE instantly gained jurisdiction over some 5,000-6,000 union members. In return, the studio heads once again secured relief from the annual headache of laboriously negotiating with each individual craft union. Now they needed only to negotiate with the union's designated president or representative—a mistake with characters like Browne and Bioff, who would seek to pull the rest of Hollywood's workforce into the IATSE.

Nitto's local organization evolved into a more finely tuned, more powerful unit than ever. In December 1935, Jake Guzik returned from a three-year stint in prison. Ever valuable, he retained his importance as mob bookkeeper and payoff man, primarily for the mob's main revenue source, gambling. His position, though, was slightly diminished from his Capone days, with Nitto, Ricca, and Campagna at the gang's top. These last two, Browne and Bioff remembered later, handled most of the extortion payouts for the Nitto group. When, in late 1935, Browne scheduled Local 110 elections to replace the officers dismissed after the Maloy murder, the slate of candidates was chosen by the mob. It was at Campagna's home that the two union men were informed of the mob choice for secretary-treasurer. Campagna's candidate, Bioff was informed, would do whatever the mob wanted. To Browne, Campagna said, "He is all right. He is my man." The mob slate was elected, and the mob put Nick Circella's sister in to check up on everybody in the office.

In January 1936, Murray Humphreys regained freedom. He resumed his local racketeering activities in the cleaning and dyeing industry, eventually assisting Nitto in managing the bartenders union. Like Guzik, he would evolve into a master fixer, serving as the connection between the mob and the politicians in the labor field.

An organizational clipping was deemed necessary in December over the issue of gambling rights. Joe Genaro, a onetime "public enemy" associate of bomber James Belcastro, reduced now to "public nuisance" by Repeal, was seated near the front window of a bar on East Sixty-third Street. A sedan drove up, and a passenger with a shotgun leaned out the window and discharged two loads of buckshot through the plate glass, striking Genaro in the head. Police were at a loss for a solid motive, except that Genaro may have tried to pry his way back into the gambling world either on the West Side or in Calumet City, both of which were off limits. His old buddy James Belcastro was wanted for questioning.

Even before Nitto wielded the reins of the Chicago Outfit, Machine Gun Jack McGurn's value as a gunner was essentially outdated. With no more gang wars to be fought, killings under Nitto became a last resort "means to an end" or, rarely, necessary discipline. McGurn's position, and his salary from such, essentially evaporated. Generally, Nitto, like Capone in the past, found men other work to make a living, especially in hard-pressed Depression times; they ran Outfit handbooks, gambling joints, speakeasies, and the like. If they applied themselves, gunmen like Frank Diamond, Phil D'Andrea, and Louis Campagna transitioned to new and bigger mob arenas, such as labor racketeering—*if they applied themselves.*

In the early thirties, McGurn and his wife, the former Louise Rolfe, had fought a running battle with the feds on an old Mann Act (white slavery) charge. The case was flimsy, probably meant to remove him and his reputation from Chicago's streets, and he beat it. Still, the press followed him. He was a most enthralling and dashing underworld icon. Now with his doting champion Capone gone, McGurn dabbled in gambling for income but seemed more dedicated to leisurely golf activities; he became well-tanned and nearly attained tournament caliber. According to his younger half-brother Anthony Demory, McGurn established himself as golf professional at the Maywood Country Club in the suburbs. Media hawks flashed pictures of the handsome McGurn and glamorous Louise on the links, on the beach, and in court. However, golf wasn't gang work, and crime beat correspondents duly noted his celebrity absence from gang circles wondering where the suave, gun-wielding gunman from the old days had gone and McGurn wasn't doing anything. Mob boss Nitto may have wondered too. Rumors quickly spread that he was murdered on a golf course and his body had been spirited away by Touhy gangsters. The story wasn't true, but his urbane routine gradually soured.

In 1933, police did haul him off the links a couple of times on warrants that amounted to nothing. He once was brought in while competing at nearby Olympia Fields in the Western Open golf tournament. On one occasion, when a reporter asked him afterward what was up, the bronzed gunman replied, "All that I did was play golf." He then offered a view of his set of spoons as proof.

Next, the reporter asked the obvious: "Why hasn't the great Jack McGurn been in trouble lately?"

"How can I get in trouble when I've got no dough?" McGurn retorted.

In June 1934, Jack was ready to score as half owner of Edgar Lebensberger's old 225 Club on East Superior. He and his partners were prepared to make a lucrative new run, complete with expensive new gaming equipment on the third floor. On June 20, the club opened, and such underworld headliners as Sam Hunt, Frank Foster, and Ralph Pierce were whispered to be in attendance. McGurn's younger half-brother Anthony Demory was there. Before the party got cranked up, though, police got wind of the gala and raided the joint but seized only Demory. Two days later,

Captain Andrew Barry of the Chicago Avenue station padlocked the club, pronouncing it a "resort for hoodlums" that would stay closed.

At about the same time, McGurn and Louise lost their Oak Park home to foreclosure. A year later, someone nosing around a handbook in Melrose Park recognized McGurn there taking fifty-cent bets. The bartender confided McGurn's role and his routine: he still plays golf in the mornings, attends this joint in the afternoon, but as for the bar, he never drinks alcohol, only root beer. Rumor had it he had sold off his expensive jewelry for much needed cash. He was no longer among the mob's elite. They moved on to bigger and better endeavors, while he slummed in his celebrity lifestyle. Now he would have to settle for what Nitto's management group allotted him, and that evidently was not enough to sustain his image.

Late in 1935, suspicions evolved that McGurn sought aid from Albert J. Prignano, state representative of the Seventeenth District, Twentieth Ward Democratic committeeman, and a powerful ally of Mayor Kelly. It was natural move for McGurn to sidestep Nitto, for Prignano was an old pal of Capone. They had grown chummy in the late 1920s and were pictured together attending a Notre Dame-Northwestern football game in October 1931. It was an unwise move for McGurn, since Prignano was not a Nitto favorite either. It was no secret that the Nitto favored Republican Alderman William V. Pacelli as ward boss over Prignano, who was also running for state representative and enjoyed the support of the Municipal Voters League as well as the local merchants. That support may have come from word of Prignano's whispered to a local cop that the bloodshed from which the ward obtained its epithet sickened him. "The boys," meaning Nitto's mob, he claimed, "are going too far."

In the fall 1934 local elections, someone tried to dissuade Prignano's candidacy. On one occasion, he was called to a popular Italian restaurant on the Near West Side and drugged into unconsciousness, more than likely a failed attempt on his life because only a short time later he was fired upon near the intersection of Cermak Road and Wentworth Avenue. Having survived both drugs and guns, Prignano called for police protection and swept to victory with other Kelly Democrats. To the further annoyance of the Nitto crowd, Prignano had recently quarreled with Nitto lieutenant Lawrence Mangano about protecting some West Side gambling dives.

Nitto's group was going national, but this ugly local affair had to be settled. Rumor had the Outfit selecting ex-city sealer and popular figure Carmen Vacco as their candidate for the Democratic Committeeman to replace the stubborn Prignano in that seat. Further Prignano resistance offered the mob a means to employ an innovative method of assassination—the faux robbery, which would at least throw another possible motive into the equation to divert suspicion.

Prignano spent the entire day of December 29 at his brother-in-law's with his wife's family, his wife and their eight-year-old son. Back home, their maid, Harriet Stubbs, received two phone calls inquiring as to when the Prignano's might return, but she really couldn't say. The mysterious callers hung up. Late that afternoon, a car containing three men was stationed in front of 731 Bunker Street, directly across the street from Prignano's office and home above at number 722.

The Prignano family gathering broke up shortly after 10 p.m. The night air was a frosty twenty-three degrees, and the temperature was dropping quickly. Prignano's chauffeur, Victor Galanti, drove the politician, his wife, their son, and her mother home. As Galanti curbed the vehicle in front of the street-level home's door, he noticed two men exit a car across the street. The women sallied forth with holiday packages in hand, leading the boy to the door as the third man exited the car. On either side of the Prignano vehicle, the trio announced a holdup. Mrs. Prignano told her husband to just give in and let it go at that. The would-be robbers directed the women and child to go inside, and Prignano, saying he would handle the situation, directed his chauffeur to do the same. As the driver disappeared between the gangways and Mrs. Prignano reached the first step on the stairs, shots rang out. The first slug hit Prignano in the head; the second missed. His wife ran down just in time to see one of the men lean over and pump four more shots into the politician. The three then fled across the street to their car, which refused to start in the cold. Abandoning the vehicle and a weapon, the killers disappeared into an alley near Halsted and Twelfth streets.

McGurn had expected the worst as far back as October, and now he had every reason to believe the threat was no delusion. Lieutenant Harry Wilson of the Oak Park police remembered an incident the previous fall when McGurn called lawmen to his home only to find him barricaded inside. Wilson recalled that the pleas for help had been repeated at least a dozen times since then.

After spending the morning of February 14, 1936, at the funeral of a friend, McGurn snoozed the afternoon away. Waking at about 11 p.m., he slipped into his usual fine duds—a fine gray suit, a fine-cut shirt with a red tie, and gray spats—and bid his wife Louise goodnight before stepping out for a round of bowling. After picking up two companions along the way, he finally dropped by the Avenue Recreation Parlor at 805 Milwaukee Avenue. It was a familiar place; the owner was chummy with McGurn and had run a handbook there until late last year. The bowling lanes were on the second floor. If so inclined, patrons could loaf around billiard tables and a nearby cigar counter instead. Fifteen regulars filled the place.

At about 12:50 a.m., McGurn shed his overcoat and derby, laying them on a nearby bench, rolled up his shirt sleeves, and took to alley number two, about twenty or so feet from the door. He may have completed one game and was in the midst of another, selecting a ball for a toss, when three men calmly walked in, weapons drawn, and said, "Stick em up, everybody." Before McGurn could react, they opened up on him with perhaps as many as fifteen gunshots, striking him in the head just above the nape of his neck. Another slug hit him behind the right ear and back. McGurn fell face up, the blood from his wounds snaking across the polished maple flooring. Finished, the assassins departed as they entered—in a deliberate, orderly fashion.

When police arrived, few patrons professed to having seen anything, and those who did, gave fragmented and jumbled accounts. Investigating the scene further, police found an envelope addressed to McGurn eight feet from the body. How it got there is a mystery as no one saw the killers toss anything. It may have been left with the establishment's owner for McGurn, a regular patron, and after receiving it,

McGurn may have tossed it aside. Inside, was a comic greeting card that, while thoroughly contemptible, quite accurately embodied McGurn's state of affairs. Portrayed was a twiggy couple fraught with sagging fortunes, their house for sale nearby. The card read:

> *You've lost your job, you've lost your dough.*
> *Your jewels and cars and costly houses.*
> *But things could be worse, you know.*
> *At least you haven't lost your trousas!*

McGurn, a holdover from the old Prohibition days and the perfect mob anachronism, was dead at thirty-two or thirty-three. Few doubted the Nitto crowd was culpable.

On March 2, a similar hit was carried out in Little Italy after three men entered Santa Cutia's dusty poolroom at 1003 Polk Street. One positioned himself at the door, while the other two, their hat rims carefully folded down to protect their identity, calmly moved to a back room where a group of three men were seated around a simple wooden table playing cards. The two strangers whipped out pistols and announced a stick up. The player with his back to the front door quickly scooted his chair, stood up, and turned. As he did, the guns barked. A bullet broke his watch, and others embedded in his left jaw, left shoulder, and chest. The killers retraced their footsteps to the door, entered an awaiting vehicle, and left. Within a block they tossed aside a .38 revolver and a .45 automatic pistol. Patrons at Cutia's carried the severely wounded man to nearby Mother Cabrini Hospital, where he soon died. The victim was twenty-four-year-old Anthony Demory, whose grieving mother bore a heavy load with two husbands and now two sons killed. Police suspected the mob knew the death of McGurn might very well inflame the younger man, perhaps a bodyguard to his older half-brother, to revenge. Given the well-proven temperament of McGurn, the Nitto mob took no chances.

Differences over gambling turned mob guns on yet another politician in July 1936. Friend of Prohibition beer runners and now state representative of the Second District John Bolton was thought to be running a gambling joint or two on the West Side near Paulina and Madison. Bolton had recently sponsored a bill in Springfield to legalize handbooks, which was passed by the legislature before being vetoed by the governor. Whether the move was mob-sanctioned or was Bolton's attempt to buck the mob has never been fully revealed, but before the veto, he had incorporated the Handbook Employees Union and the Handbook Operators Association as surefire moneymakers—and a means to give him great control over mob hirelings. Talk had him opening additional handbooks without Nitto's authorization.

Driving home west on Harrison Street just after midnight July 9, Bolton noticed the bright lights of a car following far behind. As he accelerated, so did the pursuer. Bolton sped up to sixty miles per hour on the city street, dodging autos for blocks, but the hunter closed the gap. As he passed under a railroad viaduct near Washtenaw Avenue on the West Side, the chase vehicle drew alongside. Bolton desperately fought them off, but they gradually forced his vehicle toward the curb. As they made the Washtenaw intersection, a shotgun slid through the window of the pursuing car, now only four to five feet away. Two blasts punched through Bolton's window and took off part of his head. Their job done, the killers raced away to the south as Bolton's car veered north, slamming into a nearby light post. Police were at a loss for a motive other than his gambling activities, or perhaps the mob had quarreled over his political position, as had been the case with Prignano. Bolton and his brother Joseph "Red" Bolton had been allies of Capone's in the 1920s, but with the mob under Nitto, that had clearly changed.

The moves were not undertaken so much for Nitto personally but rather for the mob workforce. The mob owned the handbook business, and a few were even attributed to Nitto's name. They had already paid for Annenberg and Ragen's wire service; they were not about to let some unreliable politician dictate to them, much less through unions or associations. They still held the political reins of state representatives James Adducci, a West Side thug, and Dan Serritella of the First Ward. Also rising in prominence on the West Side was a hoodlum and McGurn associate about whom he once bragged to a policeman following a pick up in 1930, "This guy is not a punk. He's a solid kid named Tony Accardo and he's going places."

——————

The murderers of McGurn, one paper pronounced, were Nitti and his "miserably lessened Capone model" gang. However, after two state representatives were murdered, local pleas for relief to the FBI poured in, declaring the Nitto gang to be "more powerful than the Capone mob." Another put the Capone gang under Nitto as "bigger, more powerful than at any time in its history." State's Attorney Courtney wanted the public to think that it was only "a skeleton of its former self," but the organization was run with an "'iron hand' by Frank Nitti." The passing of Capone and all the jabber about his weakened remnants was "hooey;" the gang was "1000 percent stronger now than it ever was." Director Hoover would have none of it, however.

No one really stood in the way of Nitto and his mob now. Personally, Nitto had expanded his personal wealth beyond racketeering to include gambling holdings. In 1936, he entered into the lucrative slot-machine racket by buying in as 50 percent partner with slot king Ed Vogel. Vogel was so thoroughly a county fixture that few if any machines operated without the distinct upside-down "V" trademark sticker attached. Through Johnny Patton, Nitto gained 15 percent of Sportsman's Park racetrack, the old Hawthorne Kennel Club that had turned to horse racing since the state outlawed dog racing. Patton also gained for him an 8 percent holding in Tropical Park when East Coast mobsters Meyer Lansky and Frank Erickson moved in. Nitto wasn't completely out of the doghouse either. Outside the boundaries of Illinois, he had acquired interests in Ed O'Hare's sport in the New Kensington and Steubenville kennel clubs, and in Miami, he gained income from the Miami Beach Kennel Club, where he sometimes conducted business. Nearby, he rented a beachfront home or used the Capone home for business meetings. The next meeting there would outline the charge to Hollywood.

21

HIGH TIDE: HOLLYWOOD, THE BSEIU, AND THE BARTENDERS

HE IATSE CONSTITUTION MANDATED THAT the union's executive board meet twice a year, mostly to discuss regional conditions, strategy, and membership appeals. Winter weekend sessions were mostly conducted under the semi-tropical sun of Miami. In 1936, the board gathered at the Fleetwood Hotel, and Nitto's Chicago Outfit congregated nearby to retain control. Frank Nitto, recalled Browne, was there every year. After union meetings, Bioff and Browne would meet Nitto's men at the Capone house on Palm Island, with Ralph as host, or at Nitto's rented home.

Mob strategy turned to the administration of the Hollywood locals. Officially, the IATSE executive board voted to send Bioff west to take charge. Afterward, when Bioff met with Nitto and his guest Johnny Rosselli, Nitto informed Bioff to put Rosselli on the payroll, saying that he was the mob's man out west, he knew the producers previously, and he's in charge. Bioff protested—probably as much about the reduction of his newfound leadership role as anything else—that Rosselli's name on the payroll would "stick out like a sore thumb" and cause them nothing but trouble. Additionally, there were union rules and payroll. Nitto then unleashed a verbal lashing familiar to McLane. "I don't care what payroll you put him on," Nitto barked. "I want you to put him on. That is your problem." Rosselli received $194 a week as an IATSE ghost employee.

After the meeting adjourned, Rosselli and Browne left for Hollywood; Bioff hopped on a cruise ship with his wife and met them there several days later. The mission for the trio was to scout the studios and plan strategy. Since 1925 and the institution of the annual Basic Agreement, Hollywood wages rose and conditions improved. At the depth of the Depression, however, studio heads were able to obtain significant concessions on worker's pay. Unions that elected to strike were most often broken, and some craft unions elected to switch international alliances. For example, IATSE operators and electricians of Grips and Crafts Local 37 elected to join the International Brotherhood of Electrical Workers. The Brotherhood of Painters, Paper Hangers, and Decorators of America elected to bolt the Basic Agreement altogether in 1933 because it failed to include a closed-shop clause. Carpenters attached to the BPPHDA then hooked up with IATSE Local 37. When that local, perhaps the largest single IATSE union in Hollywood, struck against the studios for better wages, it was broken down to a mere sixty-five members.

The triumvirate heading west understood this. They also knew April to be the month that major studios and the international unions were to sit down and hammer out a Basic Agreement, and they wanted to make sure the pact was established per their accord the previous December. For leverage, they understood the most militant Hollywood craft unions wanted to reinstate their pre-Depression pay scale, which would amount to raises of between 33 and 100 percent. Conspirators Browne and Bioff had trumped local, untrustworthy IATSE Local 37 officers by revoking the district IATSE charter in favor of direct control from the international office. In their pocket, as an example during the parley if needed, was the projectionists walkout staged the previous December. They went to work, knowing, as Bioff recalled later, "that as Nicholas Schenck [of Loews] goes, the industry goes."

Browne softened up Schenck in New York with the usual pre-negotiation grumbles about previous poor treatment of workers. Two days before the first Basic Agreement meeting, Browne brought Bioff into Schenck's office on Broadway. Straight away, bully Bioff talked tough and laid it out to the head of Loews. The producers had profited from low union wages long enough, and the international organization and its members had lost an estimated $1 million to $2 million in wages and dues. Now they wanted restitution, Bioff demanding it point-blank. Schenck immediately threw up his arms and protested, "You are crazy. Where are we going to get two million dollars to give you?" Bioff had no pity, telling him, "That's what we have to have." Bioff further advised Schenck to get together with the rest of the producers and reach an understanding before the meeting. If they didn't, just like December 1935 with Paramount, at a snap, Bioff and Browne would close down every theater in the country. Further, Schenck shouldn't forget that they could call a strike on the production end in Hollywood. "By the time we get through with you," warned Bioff, his jowls flapping, "you'll be lucky if you can get a job peddling newspapers." The two turned and walked out on the stunned executive.

The next afternoon, Schenck and Sidney Kent, head of Twentieth Century Fox, met with Browne over lunch. Hoping Bioff's bluster was only a bluff, they reasonably appealed their position to Browne. The labor leader waved them off, saying Bioff was his personal representative in those matters: "Well, that is not my department; you will have to talk to him about it." Browne explained he negotiated only wages and hours for the union, adding, "Any business you have with Bioff, as I told you before, will be okay with me."

It was in Pat Casey's office in New York City on April 16 that the heads of the eight major studios—Loews, Paramount, Twentieth Century Fox, Warner Brothers, RKO Pictures, Columbia Pictures, Universal, and United Artists—with Schenck, Kent, and Major Albert Warner of Warner Brothers in the lead, squared off against Bioff and Browne. Bioff handled the shakedown price tag. Of his negotiating skills, Bioff crowed, "You got to be tough in this den of hyenas. . . . I've found out that dickering with these picture producers goes about the same all the time . . . they start hollering about how they're bein' held up and robbed. That goes on and on . . . I always go to sleep when the roaring starts. After a while it dies down and the quiet wakes me up. And I say, 'All right, gentlemen, do we get the money?'" On the side, Browne supervised the legitimate union issues, occasionally tossing in reassurance in support of Bioff's threats. "You don't want to be bothered with troubles on location," he said. "We can ease your paths in many ways. You wouldn't want theaters pulled."

The producers knew they had been backed into a corner. RKO and Twentieth Century Fox had only recently emerged from receivership triggered by the Depression, and most of the studios had suffered greatly and were only now beginning to rebounding. A large Paramount theater, remembered one executive, could now expect to make $30,000-$40,000 a week. With 1,200 theaters across the country, he didn't expect Paramount to remain solvent for more than a week or two during a projectionists strike since the money lost could never be recouped. Strikes notwithstanding, experience had taught them that any average incident—poor weather, a sick actor, faulty props—might cost a studio thousands of dollars in lost production time. Exploring their options since the December 1935 projectionists walkout, Paramount officials conferred with high-brass lawyers about an injunction. Officials at Twentieth Century Fox also surveyed alternatives, raising a $100,000 defense fund to find a legal maneuver to avoid the union. Both, however, were told the new labor laws forbade them from interfering with employees' right to strike. As Sydney Kent remembered, the situation was "hopeless," so the producers agreed to take the best deal they could get. With mob representative Nick Circella close at hand, after two or three days, Bioff remembered later, "We all got together and sold out [the union]."

The upshot was that the Hollywood producers would pay the union $1 million to guarantee labor peace. Due to legal fears of showing large, unexplainable payments on their books, Bioff accepted an installment plan, with payments due at the time of the annual Basic Agreement negotiations until the amount was paid in full. Further wrangling over the sum to be paid was settled when producers huddled together and agreed to a prorated fee for each studio: for the large producers—Paramount, Loews, Twentieth Century Fox, and Warner Brothers—the sum was fixed at $50,000 per annum, while smaller producers such as RKO and Columbia Pictures, the makers of the Three Stooges comedy shorts, were to pay $25,000. In exchange, the producers received guaranteed labor peace with pay raises to union members limited to 10 percent and virtually no changes in working conditions.

Given a few months to discreetly gather the funds, studio heads began to shell out the tribute, usually in New York, parading over to Browne and Bioff in their extravagant Waldorf-Astoria or Warwicke hotel suites. Nick Schenck and Sydney Kent recalled making the first trip together, carrying briefcases containing $50,000 and $25,000 respectively. The two dropped the cases on the bed and turned away to gaze out a nearby window as bully Bioff thumbed the count. After Bioff approved the tally, the pair of executives left without a word. Major Warner came in with only $10,000, complaining that they didn't "have any such large sums lying around." Bioff then agreed on installments. Warner payments were collected, usually stuffed into a simple envelope and left with Warner's secretary so that the producer could avoid the racketeer. Paramount officials claimed the same circumstances, and Bioff sneered but approved similar payments, warning that he would visit them to collect the money. A Paramount official was later asked: "What did Bioff say, indicate, where the money was going that you were paying?" The official answered that "He didn't. It was for his people, his union [he thought]. They had done—it was 'they.' That was the expression." When the same question was put to Albert Warner, he recalled: "It is possible, but I wouldn't recall. It is possible that some of the conversation went that he had to pay this money to other people."

Bioff shuffled back to Chicago with two-thirds of the loot for Nitto, Ricca, and Campagna. That year, they split nearly a quarter of a million dollars from the producers, while the 2 percent tax raked in a nearly a million dollars. In addition, the international treasury presented a nice pie from which to slice, collecting $3 monthly from each union member as dues. The new Hollywood additions boosted the annual take by nearly another quarter-million dollars.

Organizational efforts also served to promote Browne's re-election as IATSE president in the summer of 1936. Just to make sure the rank and file voted unanimously, Nitto personally led a menacing mob delegation to the site, the Auditorium Hotel in Kansas City. At his side were newly installed bartender and labor thug Louis Romano and the relatively new face, Charlie Gioe. For Nitto, the trip served a dual purpose: in Browne's suite, the mob introduced Nitto's Kansas City allies Tony Gizzo and Charlie Corrallo to Browne and Bioff as contacts, and Gizzo and Corrallo met Nitto's new bartenders union man Romano, possibly to line up more business for Manhattan Brewing. As expected, the membership elected Browne unanimously, and Nitto directed him to announce the official appointment of Bioff as international representative in charge of the West Coast.

Nitto's extortionist Bioff set himself up with a rich home in Westwood, California, near Hollywood. He continued to squeeze money for Nitto's mob, but he also didn't hesitate to graft under the table for himself free and clear of them either. When RKO fell behind on its share of the extortion payments, Bioff gave them a conditional pass. Mr. and Mrs. Bioff hadn't quite gotten around to furnishing their new home with draperies, glassware, and the like, so he approached RKO head Leo Spitz: "I would like for your company to make it possible for me to buy these things wholesale through your purchasing department." Of course, Willie said he had no intention of paying the bill anyway, and Spitz recognized the wrath he might incur if he tried to collect the debt, so he let it be. The amount was over $4,000 free and clear of the mob and Bioff's partner George Browne. Bioff even charged $1,300 in Oriental carpets to IATSE. From Westwood, Bioff's routine settled into trips to Chicago, usually stopping at the Blackstone Hotel for a meeting with Nitto's group and the division of cash, and then on to New York or Washington to meet Browne.

In spring 1937, the ever-shrewd Bioff found the IATSE in a position of great advantage. Because of the Basic Agreement, approximately twelve diverse and independent Hollywood unions, representing roughly 6,000 painters, hair stylists, makeup artists, grips, draftsman, and other special crafts that predated IATSE in Hollywood, remained locked out of bargaining for lack of a parent organization. In particular, members of Local 724, the International Hod Carriers, Building, and Common Laborers Union (Studio Utility Employees), sought sole bargaining rights for studio workers in direct competition with IATSE. Worse yet, some of those craft members' support leaned away from the AFL and toward the rival CIO labor organization.

Observing the IATSE's success at the bargaining table, the activist trades banded together into a loose bargaining organization christened the Federated Motion Picture Crafts. Led by Herb Sorrell and Charles Lessing of Local 644 of the Studio Painters Union, the FMPC demanded 20 percent increases for its members. Pat Casey, who had just agreed to the usual 10 percent raise for IATSE members, turned them down cold, knowing he could count on Bioff and Browne per their extortion agreement. On April 30, Lessing called for a FMPC strike and asked Bioff, in the interests of labor unionism, for IATSE support, but Bioff declined. The walkout, however, promised to hold up production and force IATSE members out of work regardless.

Consummate racketeer Bioff worked all the angles. First, he approached Sorrell with a financial proposition: he, Bioff, might be able to obtain $75,000 or so from the industry to be turned over to Sorrell, which Sorrell could use to pay his members the lesser 10 percent raise retroactive for about thirty days and then keep the rest—maybe $25,000-$35,000—for himself if he went along. When Sorrell declined, Bioff began isolating IATSE enemies. He created a new class of IATSE membership to accommodate those trades now on strike. Next, he began strategically raiding FMPC unions, winning over union members who were ill at ease about a walkout. Analyzing the situation, Bioff incisively assessed the makeup artists union Local 731 as the linchpin in the whole matter—no makeup and the players would be out of work, and with no actors or actresses, there would be no production, and everybody would be shut out. This was a chance to promote himself as a benefactor to the producers and increase IATSE membership rolls at the same time.

At the outbreak of the strike, Nitto summoned Bioff back to Chicago for a report on the situation. One evening, the pair listened to the live strike action over the radio. A phone call was put through to Johnny Rosselli, and Nitto directed strikebreakers to be sent from Chicago with Rosselli in charge. Reporter Florabel Muir, in the thick of the Hollywood action, recalled the clash: "I saw these fellows in action. They all drove Zephyrs and obtained gun permits from the administration then governing Los Angeles." She continued, "I also saw a platoon of swarthy gents identified as the Chicago mopper-uppers swagger into a gun store directly across the street FMPC headquarters. Word came they were at target practice." On the other side, boss Lessing recruited nearby CIO longshoreman as reinforcements. Roaming pitched battles exploded outside studio gates. Cars were overturned. One young actress living near one studio recalled hearing the racket and the torrent of screams, saying, "You'd go out in the street, and you'd see men lying there with blood running down their faces."

While Rosselli managed the battle, Bioff approached the makeup artists union. They wanted raises of at least 10 percent, but Bioff asked if they would go along with IATSE if he obtained a 10 percent raise and a closed shop guarantee. They said yes. Bioff pushed a deal through Pat Casey and issued IATSE cards to the makeup people. He then announced to the industry press that striking unions could only get an agreement through IATSE, but only if their members carried a union card. Most of the other unions, except Lessing's painters, followed one by one, with Bioff issuing IATSE cards and weeding out the malcontents. In one swoop, Nitto's Hollywood team doubled IATSE membership on the studio lots, meaning more money for union coffers, and broke a strike for the producers, who now owed Bioff a favor. Bioff admitted later the reason to break the strike while keeping IATSE strong was "to accomplish the end we were seeking in our [IATSE] selfish way."

Shortly afterward, according to Bioff, a grateful Louis B. Mayer, head of the producers association, called and profusely thanked Bioff for his work, telling him "that the door was open to him and his organization." Schenck was equally appreciative and enthusiastically told Bioff that "if an opportunity showed where he, Schenck, could do anything for him, Schenck would bend backward." Further effusing, Schenck said, "You see, we had a strike at the studio—Mr. Bioff was damned decent about it. . . . I like the man."

During the mayhem, the Screen Actors Guild, representing the players—an entity outside IATSE domination—voted to cross picket lines. These people, Bioff recognized, made the real big money in Hollywood. He kept a greedy eye toward getting the ones he contemptuously labeled "them actors."

⟨⟨∘⟩⟩

Back in Chicago, the press hardly noticed Nitto's mob. A rare exception was the day after Representative Bolton's murder in July 1936, when the *Tribune*'s headline read, "CAPONE'S GANG RISES AGAIN IN VOTES AND VICE." Police put Nitto, with friends Campagna and state Representative Adducci, under watch as they suspected a revival of the *Camorra*, or Mafia, to take control of gambling, booze, and vice. After a few weeks, however, they could find no sign of Nitto in town. With Nitto's usual *sub rosa* demeanor and the international scope of his business, few headlines containing his name surfaced during the 1930s, and some other gang member usually was erroneously pronounced as the new gang leader—someone like Jake Guzik or his assistant Hymie Levin, Murray Humphreys, or whoever happened to be most noticeable in Nitto's absence.

On August 11, police detectives arrested Nitto and Louis Campagna in the Loop on a standard pickup for questioning in the Bolton murder and about the state of mob affairs. Nitto managed a rascally smile for a photographer at the detective bureau but had nothing much to say. To detectives he only divulged a recent trip to Florida for recuperation and treatment for his old wounds.

In addition, he and Anna were there to scout properties for a home to call their own. They finally settled on Di Lido Island, a sliver of man-made land less than a mile north of Capone's Palm Island home. Both islands served as midway points for causeways that crossed Biscayne Bay to Miami Beach. Nitto bought four property lots, concealing the new assets under his wife's maiden name, Anna Ronga (for the home), and the alias Frank S. Nitto (for the other three lots). At 714 West Di Lido Drive sat a newly constructed, two-story white concrete block home with a tiled roof shaded by towering palms along 300 feet of ocean frontage. Spacious at seventy by eighty-four feet, the home contained four bedrooms, three complete baths, and even two rooms that served as maid's quarters. Off the back was a large patio, and a pool was added later. Around the property ran a high wall hugged by a thick cover of tropical plants for privacy. Just down the road was another mobster, the East Coast sponsor of George Scalise, Anthony "Augie" Carfano.

Anna spent considerable time slumming at the new house, frequently hitting the Miami Beach nightclub circuit, while son Joseph was thought to attend school there. Despite his wealth from his enormous interests in local handbooks, slot machines, nationwide racetracks, and labor racketeering, the Florida house was the Nitto family's only detectable property during the 1930s. Stays in Chicago were apparently in various outlying rentals and higher-class downtown hotel rooms.

The rest of the mob extortionists prospered as well. Louis Campagna, Ralph Pierce, and their wives enjoyed a few weeks' stay in Malilbu Beach at a house complete with attendants, a chauffeur-driven auto, and food paid for through IATSE accounts. It was there Louis caught the idea of a fancy lawn irrigation system for himself and Paul Ricca. Bioff looked to move to a large California ranch.

Bioff in particular seemed overcome by greed. Of the many thousands of dollars passing into the hands of Nitto's gang, Bioff once became upset over a single $15,000 payment to Louis Kaufman of Local 244 in New Jersey that Kaufman had bullied out of Warner Brothers during a contract dispute. When Bioff learned of the transaction, he protested to Nitto that the money derived from *their* extortion idea and that they, therefore, deserved a share. Nitto dismissed Bioff's claim, saying,"No, don't bother Louis. He is Longie's man." The reference was to ally and associate Abner "Longie" Zwillman, mob boss of New Jersey. A worried Bioff countered, "We can't afford to leave such conditions go on, because the thing will get out of hand if we allow every Tom, Dick, and Harry to dig into it, that we will be the fall guys." Nitto again told him to forget about it. He was promoting mobster goodwill.

In April 1937, Nitto's group gained absolute control of their second international union. Word reached mob associate and BSEIU officer George Scalise that BSEIU President Jerry Horan lay in a hospital dying and was not expected to last more than a few days. Scalise thought that as a vice president and director of the East Coast locals, the majority of the BSEIU, he might become the new president and immediately called Anthony Carfano about the opportunity. He arranged a meeting the next day with Nitto's mob over dinner at the Capri Restaurant. Taking the lead for Nitto were Frank Diamond and Charlie Fischetti. The problem for Scalise was that two more-senior Chicago men, First Vice President William McFetridge and Third Vice President Thomas Burke, stood to move up as well. Burke, known to be cooperative with the mob, appeared to be their initial choice, but Scalise was Italian, a valuable organizer, and a mob guy.

After a series of subsequent meetings, Nitto's group agreed to Scalise as the new president, but he would have to kick back 50 percent of his new salary to Chicago. The two mobs planned the division of spoils as well. Prior agreement dictated a 50 percent split only of new union dues, but Chicago now authorized complete plundering. Scalise and Carfano were allotted the territory east of Cincinnati, while the rest belonged to Nitto's group. Nitto's conditions also required Scalise to report to Chicago at least once a month. With mob business settled, there was still the matter of formal union approval.

In any vote by the BSEIU executive board, however, the mob knew neither McFetridge nor David Paul, a BSEIU officer from the East Coast, would support their choice. Scalise was told to sell himself to McFetridge as an honest union official, a representative of a large part of the BSEIU who wanted to run and then get McFetridge to drop out, which the veteran did. For the eastern votes like Paul's, the group turned to Willie Bioff, who happened into town. In his hotel suite, Bioff was ordered to head east and wise up Paul and anybody else there to the virtues of Scalise's candidacy. As a result, Scalise was unanimously elected president.

As with IATSE, the fringe benefits included both union plunder and vacations. For one trip, Scalise, Burke, Carfano, and Charlie Fischetti decided on a lavish Cuba jaunt. Their fun in the sun included staying at Havana's fabulous Hotel Nacional. All expenses for their top of the line suites, chauffeur-driven vehicles, and long-distance calls to the U.S. were paid compliments of the BSEIU President Scalise.

———

With the union precedents set, Frank Nitto possessed grand designs for puppet George McLane. The mob dropped him a hint when Louis Romano contacted Mrs. McLane and suggested that her husband run for higher union office. A short while later, Nitto called McLane to a meeting at the Bismarck Hotel to make his plan official. Present besides Nitto were Louis Romano, Nick Circella, Willie Bioff, and IATSE President George Browne. Discussion centered on the presidency of McLane's parent union, the Hotel and Restaurant Employees International Alliance and Bartenders International League of America. President Edward Flore, a hard-nosed union man from the east who had run the international organization for a quarter-century, was up for reelection in August 1938, and Nitto desired a change.

The gang leader ordered McLane to run for president. "We will make you," explained Nitto, "all we want you to do is be loyal." McLane balked, as usual, and Nitto assured him one term would be long enough: "All we want is two years' control of the union. That'll give us the money we want. Then we'll give the union back to the members." McLane nitpicked the wisdom of going up against such an established organization. Nitto assured him this would be no problem, for during the intervening months, the mob would groom him for the presidency. "Willie Bioff will get you all the support you need on the West Coast, and George Browne will take care of it in the East," Nitto said. The gang leader declared they had made Carrozzo, Browne, and Scalise union leaders—and they could make him one, too. The alternative, Nitto reminded him, was ending up in "an alley."

Of course, Nitto did not divulge his entire agenda. With a president at his command, he could exercise more control for favorable nationwide distribution of mob beer and liquor products. Then, if he could elevate a local like McLane to a position on the AFL executive board, the mob might gain control of the entire Chicago Federation of Labor. President McLane would be told to disengage 600-700 tavern owners from the Illinois Tavern Association and charter a new association controlled by Frank Nitto that would allow the mob to exercise a complete stranglehold over Chicago product output. Nitto even dreamed up an idea to create an association and union slush fund that would be used to bribe police captains to allow certain taverns to remain open after hours and increase profits.

According to McLane's later account of events, he campaigned privately within the international union to oppose his nomination, but to others, McLane appeared to have seriously warmed up to the idea of becoming international president—or at least he acted like a serious candidate. Jay Rubin and M. J. Obermeier, both high-ranking international officers from the east, remembered that McLane had begun to modestly push his candidacy in 1937. With the support of General Secretary-Treasurer Robert Hesketh, who controlled the international's domestic journal, unofficial candidate McLane began receiving preferential print space to air his views on union matters over other vice presidents.

At the international union's 1937 general executive board meeting in Cleveland, he and Hesketh aimed to fill a new board vacancy with someone helpful to his campaign. McLane understood Flore turned down one aspiring official from the east, and they approached this man with a proposition: McLane and Hesketh would get him elected over Flore's objection; in return, he must support McLane's drive to oust Flore. After a successful campaign, the conspirators assured him that they would "see that you're taken care of." When the man surprisingly showed true union loyalty instead, McLane pushed his barrel frame close and turned a more threatening voice on him, telling him he had "better reconsider it." Instead, the individual divulged the incident to President Flore. Rubin remembered that Flore understood he "faced the strongest opposition he had ever encountered."

With his run no longer a secret, McLane campaigned hard around the country, proclaiming the leadership of Ed Flore as soft and antiquated. He intended to put "guts" back into the international union. As promised by Nitto, his men, including Browne and Bioff, hit the campaign trail as well. Stiff resistance welcomed McLane and Browne in the east where Flore enjoyed the advantage, especially after prosecutor Tom Dewey had cleaned out local crooks from the affiliated unions in New York. Bioff, however, enjoyed considerably more success out west. With the international convention scheduled for San Francisco, the enormous sums of money spent along the West Coast by "mysterious, unidentified persons" on McLane's behalf were especially noteworthy. As the convention date neared, the mob engaged in pure showmanship and camaraderie to swoon arriving delegates. McLane banners draped commandingly over the hotel lobby, and a highly visible McLane-sponsored bar was established where delegates were encouraged to "drink on the house." Upstairs, grandiose suites were reserved for more subtle but still convivial diplomacy.

As expected, Nitto directed geniality to be mixed with the old standby, mob muscle. Nitto's reinforcements arrived at convention time and kept an eye open for pro-Flore delegates throughout the hotel. Those unwise enough to display such loyalties were tugged to one side by the shirtsleeve and admonished by a hoodlum through a side-of-the-mouth warning. When it appeared that Flore's ticket still ran strong after the nomination of a New Yorker for vice president on his ticket, Chicago thugs followed the nominee from the hotel one night and, in front of his family, beat him to the pavement. That act miscarried on the McLane effort, and from then on, San Francisco police manned the convention hall and deprived the Chicago force of all weapons.

On the last day of the convention, Flore's name was placed into nomination and seconded. Then Delegate Staggenburg of Local 278 rose and announced: "I carried my first card in 1892. . . . I am no racketeer and don't associate with them, and I think it is cowardly, dastardly, and malicious infamy to make those remarks in an attempt to break down a man's character. We come in here with clean hands, we come in here to propose a candidate, a real man . . . George B. McLane." The seconding speech by Ben Parker of Local 25 proved perhaps to be the clincher even for the most unperceptive delegate, who might now join with many of his colleagues in suspecting McLane's true sponsor:

> I have worked in every millionaire's house in Chicago; I have worked in every silk stocking club in Chicago, and every political club. . . . I worked with a caterer that used to cater in Cicero—in Cicero, when they built a great community house there for the underprivileged people of Cicero.

Parker continued, "And while I worked there I came into contact with a wonderful character by the name of Al Brown, afterwards hung on him the name Al Capone. And what crime did he commit?" He was wonderful, proclaimed Parker, a generous man, a victim of the establishment. Before he could finish the homily, however, Chairman Hugo Ernst interrupted: "The gentleman who is now addressing the convention is evidently seconding the nomination of Al Capone." Chuckles from the Flore crowd echoed, and the two traded a few stinging barbs before Parker proceeded: "I am talking about a man we intend to make president of the international union. . . . I take great pleasure now, after having been disturbed both by insane people and those who want to stop progress, in seconding the nomination of George McLane."

McLane's nomination represented perhaps the absolute high-water mark for the Nitto mob's racketeering efforts as a whole. The roll call vote returned 1,095 votes for Flore to 611 votes for McLane. Not only did the membership repudiate McLane's candidacy, he lost election as international vice president as well (officers were elected every two years), leaving Nitto with control only of Local 278 in Chicago.

Back home, Nitto drew up Plan B for McLane and ordered McLane to a meeting in his Congress Hotel suite. Louis Romano escorted him there, and the gang leader immediately raked the business agent over hot coals. He had heard McLane's drinking was getting out of hand, so Nitto told him "to get on the wagon and quit drinking." His Outfit, he barked, didn't tolerate drunks; they might get careless and shoot off their mouths and get everybody in trouble. Besides, Nitto explained, McLane still retained some value to the mob: they wanted him to front efforts to grab district labor councils, local umbrella groups for unions. When the familiar "alley" option was presented, McLane obeyed.

In what remained of McLane's union career, he mimicked a punching bag. His value resurfaced within a month of the Nitto meeting when the president of Local 278, Robert Stanchi, died. Nitto sent an emissary to the wake to inform McLane he was to meet Murray Humphreys and Fred Evans at the Capri Restaurant the next day. Humphreys suggested Louis Romano as a fine replacement for Local 278 president. The union constitution, explained McLane, dictated that any nominee must be a bartender to qualify, and Romano was no bartender. Humphreys couldn't care less about the constitution. Under threat, McLane was to see to it that Romano was nominated and elected president at the next union meeting. Two weeks later it was done.

One of the groups taken by the mob was the Chicago Joint Council of McLane's parent international union composed of fourteen locals representing 30,000 workers in allied employment such as waitresses, waiters, checkroom attendants, liquor salesmen, and cooks. Each member paid a monthly ten-cent maintenance tax to the council, though there were no expenses except cheap stationary and the occasional $5 for a secretary to record meetings. When he asked what had happened to the monthly $3,000, McLane was told that "Romano took that money out to Cicero."

For nearly a year McLane retained his position but was no active organizer for mob interests. Nitto's agents noticed and might have even detected some discontent. One summer day while McLane attended to business in his union office, Romano and attorney Harold Levy stepped in. Behind them came Humphreys and Evans. President Romano stated his point directly: "I'm taking over." Noticing that McLane stood very near an open desk drawer and suspecting perhaps a hidden gun, Humphreys and Romano drew guns and ordered McLane to step aside.

Romano continued the menacing lecture: "We're taking over. You will receive your pay. What goes on around here that's not right—well just shut your eyes." The business agent may have stalled, but Romano continued the verbal assault. "Listen you son-of-a-bitch, you're through! You've been in long enough and haven't been able to make any money. We're in for the money. You better call up the executive board and tell 'em you're sick and then take a trip."

McLane turned a gaze toward legal counsel Levy as if for relief. The bespectacled attorney's advice was, "Turn it over to them." Humphreys chimed in, asking, "Why don't you have some sense? You have been in the labor game all your life, you ain't got a quarter, you have a home and a mortgage on it."

"I can go to sleep at night," McLane professed, "and put my heart on a pillow, I don't have to smoke a pipe to go to sleep, and I ain't going to push nobody around for you or anybody else."

"That is the trouble," replied Humphreys, "we call it business and you call it pushing people around. You ain't going to push them around and I ain't either." Humphreys warned him to do nothing except take orders from Romano, assuring McLane, "There's no use getting excited; you stay here, draw your salary and your job will not be bothered and anything you see that ain't right, close your eyes and you will draw your pay and never be bothered." Later, after sensing further obstinacy, the Syndicate sent a hoodlum over to visit McLane. He slipped him a live bullet with the prescription "to go south for his health." McLane packed his bags and left town as advised.

The union rank and file immediately suffered under Romano's dictatorship, as he directed that union funds be used to bail out gang members. He also weeded out McLane men, as Don Seeger, former business agent and McLane ally, discovered firsthand. One day, Romano directed some of his boys to grab Seeger. At the union office Seeger protested, but the chisel-faced Romano said, "If you want the muscle, we'll show it to you." He then directed his men to "take this so-and-so out and make him resign"— which Seeger did.

Nitto influenced formation of the quasi-official Trades and Crafts Council that pulled together several mob-dominated trade unions, including McLane's bartenders and Humphreys's laundry workers. In tandem with the BSEIU they could thus command a greater percentage of the service labor in the city's buildings. The council also could wring additional moneys from those unions. Organizations were charged a $100 initiation fee and $25-$75 a month in dues for "maintenance." Whatever happened to those funds is not known. Nitto installed McLane as a figurehead president, with Romano apparently calling the shots. McLane didn't shy away from council activities, however. Several nasty organizing strikes ensued, and during one at the Del Prado Hotel, a non-union laundry driver was beaten death with a baseball bat. When authorities dispersed pickets there, McLane surrendered for questioning and afterward directed that a new picket line be set up.

On the neighborhood level, besides the aforementioned internationals and locals, Nitto's gang dominated fifteen South Side waiter, waitress, and bartending locals under the direction of Dan Stanton, including black locals under Livert Kelly. Stanton was suspected of attempting a grab of the painters union in which at least a half-dozen leaders had been murdered recently. Thanks to the Nitto mob, longtime labor leader—or "gangster," as one local paper described him—Mike Carrozzo increased his stranglehold on the city's vast army of street laborers he claimed as head of the International Hod Carriers, Building, and Construction Laborers of America. He dominated six Chicago unions representing 4,000 workers, including asphalt and concrete workers, who repaired city streets. Investigators found that those unions seldom held elections for officers under Carrozzo, who also was able to dictate terms to the mayor's office on road construction projects, costing the city millions. He led strikes against the use of labor-saving asphalt-laying machines and "ready-mix" concrete on city projects—and won.

Carrozzo also selected which construction and trucking companies received city work. If the company of his choice did not receive the contract for a new city project, he called a strike or, at the very least, had the unions supply the city with the most incompetent and inefficient works crews in town. He once blocked efforts to clear city streets of snow, completely stifling commerce downtown. The refuse his street sweepers and garbage men collected went to landfills owned by his friends that usually charged a higher price than others. If the trash didn't go to his friends, his men went on strike and allowed the Loop to fill with rancid rubbish—which happened on at least one occasion.

Beyond the streets, Carrozzo dominated a local hod carriers council consisting of nineteen locals and 11,000 workers who labored on concrete projects of all types. If the city or private interests didn't deal with Carrozzo, there was no construction. Altogether, outside his official salaries, Carrozzo was able to obtain nearly $680,000 in "secret income" during Nitto's reign, much of which was suspected to have come from his nefarious union activities. The amount siphoned by Nitto's mob was subject to guess. By contrast, the average Carrozzo worker at the time was lucky to earn $1,200 a year and rarely collected union benefits because of technicalities.

Perhaps the most underrated Nitto labor vandal was Max Caldwell, business agent for Local 1248, the Retail Clerks International Protective Association. A hefty, balding hoodlum, Caldwell was arrested on a Prohibition charge in Indiana before tying up with the Capone Outfit. During Nitto's reign, he slugged for Local 25 of the waiters union and was arrested on three occasions for labor terror, including once with bartender George McLane at a particularly violent strike at a local nightclub. From there, he may have served Nitto locally on behalf of IATSE by organizing approximately 800 of the city's café entertainers. They heard a familiar threat: join and pay monthly dues or "get your legs broken."

In 1937, he emerged as an organizer and then the business agent of Local 1248, which represented roughly 12,000 area grocery clerks and workers. Caldwell organized several food service companies on his initial $125-a-week salary. According to some workers, his methods also involved deceit. As a spokesman for employees of the Hillman store chain recalled, Caldwell once summoned the store's 600 employ-ees to a meeting to inform them of their new union status. They joined and paid dues, then later they found out no union contract existed. Reports of Caldwell's extravagant living surfaced—homes in Miami, weekly airline trips there billed to the union, Chicago real estate, expensive cars, and jewelry. Union dues increased from $1.50 to $2 per month, initiation fees went from $15 to $25. Members paid $2 a month toward a hospitalization plan, which in the end never was proved to exist.

A Chicago judicial luminary claimed, "Whenever crime and politics are united, the illegal gambling enterprise is the link that binds them." Another observed just before Capone went to jail that "gambling and its agencies are one of the greatest auxiliaries of vice which spurs racketeer and gangster to crime and murder." This was just as true during Nitto's reign, for despite the riches of labor racketeering, gambling remained the staple of mob income, earning the gang untold millions of dollars.

After the upheaval of the late 1920s and Cermak's abortive attempt to reel con-trol back to the politicians or at least to hoodlums favorable to him, it was generally understood that a win-win agreement had been reached between the Nitto's under-world and politicians to allow gambling to run wide open. Investigators during the thirties often found the joints honeycombed throughout the city. One reported unabashedly: "How many of these there are, no one can say, save the gambling syn-dicates and the police. Naturally the good mayor [Kelly] knows nothing of them. These are evil things, and he sees no evil, hears no evil, and speaks no evil."

Continuing, he summed up operations: "As the number of these places is very great. The amount of money involved is enormous, running into the millions. And, even if proof were absent, any man in his senses would know that these elaborate establishments could not run without protection from the city authorities." Nitto's group did rule a magnificent portion of the gambling pie.

To open a handbook or gambling joint, one contacted a local politician, perhaps an alderman who then contacted various individuals to connect to the Nitto mob and police protection. A site was selected, and the initial fix of about $200 or more was paid, with one-third to one-half the profits going to the Syndicate. The mob provided insurance against the rare interloper, provided legal services, and paid off the politicians. Of course, from then on one was obliged to purchase linen and laun-dry service, booze, and bottled waters from the Syndicate.

Capone's old group operated the highly profitable Loop district, where as much as $10,000 could be wagered on a single race. Jake Guzik and Hymie Levin acted as collectors and payoff men. The Near West Side was perhaps overseen by Lawrence Mangano, while characters like Louis Campagna, Willie Heeney, and Claude Maddox operated in Cicero. The system allowed many old adversaries to operate as long as the mob got a cut. Billy Skidmore, thirty-year veteran of the gambling world and "political fixer," evolved into perhaps the most powerful figure in gambling outside mob rule. He was thought to dominate gambling in the old Moran territory, the Forty-second and Forty-third Wards, and was the go-between for gamblers and public officials outside of the mob realm. Associate William Johnson, tall and quiet, "with that tranquil dignity of the Monte Carlo croupier," ran twenty-six or more casino-type places. His payoffs all went through Skidmore. Approximately 900 handbooks paid an average of $100 a week to stay open. Black policy-wheel king Ely Kelly on the South Side paid up to $250 a week on each of his twenty-eight wheels.

Business was conducted from the Skidmore junkyard at 2840 South Kedzie, an unlikely place for both Skidmore, described as the well-tailored "country squire" type, as well as public officials. Later surveillance indicated a constant parade of owners and public officials in and out of the junkyard. Between the first and the tenth of each month, payouts were made. The split was thought to run four ways: Skidmore kept a percentage, the Nitto mob took a slice, part went to police, and the remainder went to city politicians.

By 1937, Nitto thought it high time to collect an old favor for his organization after he put Moe Annenberg and his manager, James Ragen, in a favorable position by forcing out James Lynch. Annenberg's Nationwide News wire service now supplied horseracing data to an estimated 80 percent of the handbooks in the United States. Nationwide also supplied information to various independent scratch sheets across the country, and even owned the companies that printed them.

Nitto wanted in on the scratch sheet business. A necessity for every handbook, the scratch sheet provided current information regarding horses and jockeys at various tracks. Race changes or "scratches"—i.e., those horses dropped from a race for whatever reason—gave the sheets their name. Annenberg had his own sheet, the *National Scratch Sheet*, but failed to compete locally against the longstanding *Chicago Turf Bulletin* or *Red Sheet* (named for the color of paper on which it was printed to distinguish it from competitors) owned by the Flannigan brothers. Moe didn't like losing to anybody and acted to spite the Flannigans, but Nitto's strategy was simply applied and far-reaching: he wanted to acquire a local scratch sheet and drive out the competition, thus enabling him to exert more influence over existing gambling and perhaps even muscle Annenberg to discount or eliminate his fees for mob handbooks.

When Nitto approached him, Annenberg appeased the gangster by closing his local sheet in favor of the new mob-controlled *Green Sheet*. Nitto named Jake Guzik to run the new sheet, with state Senator Dan Serritella officially the frontman. As expected, the mob presence behind the publication forced others out of business. The last one standing—and perhaps the oldest, in business since the 1920s—was the Flannigan *Red Sheet*. Annenberg gladly aided in its decline by discounting his wire service fee to Nitto's sheet while charging the Flannigans full price. The Syndicate issued the usual death threats, recruited some Flannigan employees, and in a matter of months saw *Red Sheet* subscriptions dwindle from an estimated 500,000 to just 600.

The true nature of Nitto's strategic planning dawned on James Ragen months later when the feds indicted his boss, Annenberg, for tax evasion. Nitto agent Dan Serritella walked into Ragen's office one day with a proposition from Nitto, explaining that, with Annenberg on the way out, the Outfit wanted to get into the news wire business. The plan was on a national scale, the aim being for the mob to take over gambling wherever they could, especially in Las Vegas and Reno where gaming was legal and not yet subject to underworld interference. (Bugsy Siegel fabulous Flamingo casino was still a few years away.)

Serritella explained further that the mob recognized race betting as a come-on for other forms of gambling, such as dice and roulette, that returned perhaps ten times the profits. With a wire service in his hands, Nitto planned to withhold wire information and wreck the resort betting parlors, if necessary, until they gave in to mob demands. The Nitto mob thought their initial take would be at least $10 million a year. In return for his help, they would give Ragen $100,000 a year plus a percentage of the business. Ragen sensibly saw that letting Nitto gain a foothold in the business was an eventual threat to his well-being. The mob would keep him long enough to have him set up and teach them the business, and then, as Ragen testified later, he figured would wind up "in an alley and somebody else will have the job."

22

THE FIRST ORGANIZATIONAL CRACKS

NITTO'S MOB BUSINESS IN EARLY 1939 unavoidably turned to local politics. The halcyon days of Mayor Ed Kelly's 1935 reelection seemed far behind as the party that stood to slaughter the Republicans fractured under Kelly's autocracy. A member of his own party, State's Attorney Thomas Courtney, aspired to the mayor's chair. As a Cermak appointee, he owed nothing to the current Democratic Party leader or the mayor. Neither the mayor nor Courtney necessarily liked each other, a fact that became glaringly visible in 1935 when Courtney escaped assassination and the mayor suggested the state's attorney had engineered the attack to arouse political sympathy. In subsequent elections Courtney neither supported nor opposed Kelly nominations for political office. Rumors circulated that the Kelly party machine would dump Courtney from the ticket. When dissident Democrats searched for a candidate to oppose Kelly, they selected Courtney as the obvious and strongest nominee.

The nuisance for the Nitto mob appeared far ahead of the primary election. At a December 1937 luncheon, speaker Courtney announced: "Syndicate-controlled and -organized gambling, dominated and operated by such characters as Nitti, Campagna, Stanton, Skidmore, and 'Dutch' Vogel, is not going to be permitted." Nitto's mob had run the gambling syndicate since Courtney first came to office, but now a politically charged "Fighting Tom" needed to authenticate his appearance by doing something. Courtney attacked gambling dens and handbooks all over the city. The press documented his forays lavishly and daily, and a scorecard of smashed joints regularly appeared in one paper. He even went after the policy wheels. It suddenly appeared as though the city was infested with crime, and Courtney quickly lambasted Kelly as "part and parcel of the syndicate which controls gambling. No syndicate," he said, "could operate here under the eyes of the mayor if he wanted it stopped. . . . The fix is in at the top." Of course, few political pundits actually believed the sincerity of the drive, chalking it up to political opportunism, pure and simple. The mob, on the other hand, believed, since most of the joints, particularly in the Loop, were theirs.

Only days from the primary, the *Daily News* offered an exposé entitled "OLD CAPONE MOB PROSPERS AGAIN." Marking the tenth anniversary of the St. Valentine's Day Massacre, the writer noted Nitto's men were back on top: "In right with the Kelly-Nash machine, reputedly through organization of gambling privileges . . . the old Capone guard is celebrating Valentine's Day as the best of good times. . . . The Capone gang has reorganized and widened its field. Concessions granted by the Kelly-Nash machine in return for support of Mayor Kelly at the polls on primary day." The writer pronounced the big shots "immune from interference . . . they are as well hidden as they would be if conducting their rackets from the superintendent's office of some graveyard."

This, of course, was exactly as Nitto intended. The author did, however, mention Nitto's name (erroneously identifying him as Capone's cousin), along with that of Paul Ricca for perhaps the first time. He openly announced Campagna as important in collecting gambling revenue from gambling joints, Guzik back in form overseeing gambling, and Ed Vogel as slot king. Humphreys was portrayed as a top aide in the cleaning industry and chief salesman of bottled water for taverns, along with Ralph Capone. Phil D'Andrea was marked as a chief "trouble shooter," with Lawrence Mangano as the mob enforcer for nightclubs.

Relaxing in Miami, Nitto received word of the story. Rumor says he exploded. He called a meeting of available men at his Di Lido Island home and ordered them to get back to Chicago and "support Kelly one hundred percent." On primary day, Kelly, backed by a well-oiled political machine and, undoubtedly, by the mob, trounced Courtney by a margin (nearly two to one) many thought would be slimmer.

One hurdle overcome, the mayor now looked to face a significant challenge from the Republicans. As their candidate for mayor, the Republicans selected dynamic and popular attorney Dwight Green, a far more acute threat to the mob than Courtney. Nitto's bunch knew Green all too well as one of the men who had prosecuted the federal tax cases back in 1930. In the primary, Green routed aging political phoenix Big Bill Thompson for the nomination, and he carried out an informed and direct attack on corruption under Kelly. For instance, Green wondered why Kelly and his cohorts spent $2.5 million on the primary to retain the mayor's $18,000-a-year job. (They would spend at least an equal sum on the general election, according to Green.) What was the source of their money? Green alleged that at least a part of the sum came from Nitto's crews, who, he said, after being broken apart by tax trials, now enjoyed vast new power thanks to Kelly's nonchalance.

To meet the threat, buzz had the Nitto mob contributing approximately $50,000 to the Kelly campaign. Union membership under their thumb apparently received the call to mobilize with an "or else" reminder. One anonymous dispatch to Elevator Operators and Starters Union members that was later made public read in part:

> This letter is sent to urge you to put forth all your efforts and energy to work for the re-election of Mayor Kelly and Alderman Mulcahy. If we hear of any of our members going out and working for the Republican ticket, regardless of who they are, we will be obliged to call them in.

The editor wondered what "call them in" meant.

On election day, an energized electorate turned out in record numbers. The results indicated Nitto's mob performed superbly. Though Green carried an amazing fifteen wards and garnered more votes than any Republican office seeker in a decade, he lost in what was considered a tight race, falling short by 183,000 votes. The entire difference came from the inner city and river wards, the usual wards where Nitto's group held considerable sway—the First, the Bloody Twentieth, the Twenty-seventh.

A few weeks later, *Daily News* reporters surveying the city discovered Syndicate gambling was back to normal—no panic, no alarm, no more state's attorney's men crashing through doors. Part of the reason, they heard, was the need to replenish Kelly's coffers after the election, and a 50 percent post-election levy on each joint was in effect. Nitto's Outfit, they noted, ran twenty-seven handbooks and gambling dens within blocks of city hall, one of them directly across the street above the Capri Restaurant.

One reporter gained an intimate glimpse of what he considered their "best patronized" place, entering the restaurant and passing a street-side lookout without difficulty. Walking straight through to the back, he climbed the stairs to the den. Several of Nitto's men guarded the approach and maintained order in the "jam-packed" place. The den itself was pandemonium: loudspeakers blared race calls— "They're off!" and "They're down the stretch!"—which mixed with patrons boisterously exhorting their race picks in a room that was approximately sixty-five feet by twenty-five feet. The room was standing room only, except for a single row of miserably hard seats. The reason for the bleak décor, he found out, was the mob's commercial strategy of "getting 'em in, getting their dough, and getting 'em out." Most of the estimated 3,000 patrons that day went home having had their dough "gotten," he noted.

The gambling boom proved fleeting, however, thanks to the feds once again. On the afternoon of June 1, 1939, the U.S. attorney in Chicago issued the first grand jury subpoenas for witnesses in the Moe Annenberg and William Skidmore investigations. Both had been under the government's eyes for income tax charges for some time. Annenberg's Nationwide News wire service and its ancillary activities, the feds suspected, bordered on violating racketeering and monopoly laws—besides supporting an illegal business in the first place.

Fearful the investigation might reveal the extent of mob gambling activities, including the links to politicians, and that they might be called to testify—along with bookies and their subpoenaed records and gambling associates—hoodlums, including Nitto, scurried for cover. Business holed up in alternate locations waiting for things to cool down. When one regular patron approached a place at Fifty-fourth Street and Lake Park Avenue, a capper for the joint steered him in the right direction, telling him, "We're shut tight, but we're running at Ninety-seventh and Western Avenue." He announced a car would be along soon to taxi him there.

This trouble came in addition to an ongoing civil suit in federal court against Annenberg and Nitto ally state Senator Dan Serritella filed by owners of the *Red Sheet*. When Nitto received his subpoena, he dropped from sight but remained in or near Chicago to iron out matters with the Flannigans, whose suit threatened to wreck everything. Nitto offered to sell them the *Green Sheet*, ostensibly in return for dropping their federal litigation. The Flannigans warmed to the offer; they wanted to stay in the business. They sent Nitto a proposal for $1 million, payable with $200,000 down and the rest in installments. Nitto agreed, and the next day he sent Dan Serritella over to Ragen to announce the gang's intentions.

Ragen was outraged. He and Annenberg had given up their scratch sheet for Nitto, and now he was willing to sell out to their original competitors. Ragen met Nitto in a secluded tailor shop on LaSalle Street about the matter. Nitto told him he was taking the deal, whereupon Ragen smartly informed him he smelled the usual mob double-cross. He told Nitto, "You are probably telling Flannigan they are having the exclusive"—that is, the scratch sheet monopoly—when, in fact, Ragen said, he suspected Nitto already had plans to start a new competitor once he got his money. Ragen's suspicions were accurate, but premature. The sale of the *Green Sheet* did not progress immediately, and the Flannigans lost in court, clearing the way for the mob sheet.

However, the scratch sheet business and gambling in Chicago became infinitely more difficult to handle by the end of summer, and eventually the *Green Sheet* crashed. The ongoing federal probe culminated with the largest single tax evasion indictment to date: Moe Annenberg was indicted on five counts of tax evasion amounting to $3,258,809. from 1932 through 1936 and five counts of filing false and fraudulent returns. A series of indictments followed, naming his associates in various attached corporations for running illegal interstate gambling and tax evasion. James Ragen was snared for dodging just over $410,000 in taxes from 1933 through 1936. A day later, gambling kingpin Billy Skidmore was indicted for evading $210,118 in taxes. On March 1, 1940, William Johnson was indicted for what became the second largest case ever—nearly $1.4 million in taxes. Related to the investigation, the feds also indicted policy kings the Jones brothers—Edward, McKissack, and George—for evading just over a million dollars in taxes. In July 1940, Judge James Wilkerson, the same judge who had sentenced Capone to an eleven-year stint, decreed a three-year term for Annenberg after the publisher agreed to settle back taxes by paying a $1 million down and allowing the feds to take mortgages on his properties.

As October waned into November, Nitto planned a lengthy stay in the Ozark resort town of Hot Springs, Arkansas, to play a little golf, enjoy the mineral baths for which the town was named, discuss business, but mainly get out of town. Back in Chicago, on Saturday, November 4, 1939, Sportsman's Park on the edge of Cicero had just ended one of its most profitable racing seasons. Established on the site of the old Laramie Kennel Club, Sportsman's Park converted to horse racing in the early 1930s when Illinois courts ruled dog racing illegal. Nitto, in Patton's name, silently owned a fair piece of the track since then. The other prime mover at the track was the man who, back in 1930 and 1931 during the tax investigations of Nitto and Capone, aided the government, if only in a relatively minor way, greyhound racing mogul Edward O'Hare.

The 1930s treated Edward O'Hare very well. Apparently Nitto and his associates never discovered O'Hare's complicity for his dealings with the mob hardly wavered. He was somehow convinced, in his own words, that one "can make money thru business associations with them and you will run no risk if you don't associate with them personally." Outside of horses at Sportsman's Park, O'Hare's interest in dog tracks blossomed in Miami, Tampa, and Jacksonville, Florida; West Memphis, Arkansas; Steubenville, Ohio; New Kensington, Pennsylvania; and Taunton, Massachusetts. One inside source claimed Nitto associate Johnny Patton was active in all the above tracks. Of these, according to Nitto's tax returns, the gang boss definitely had interest in the Steubenville, New Kensington, and Miami Kennel Club operations. For cover, much was held in Patton's name. All seemed to run well. O'Hare emerged from the Depression years worth millions. He enjoyed an enormous colonial-style home in Glencoe near Chicago and split time between there and Florida.

His private life steadily improved. Although divorced from his first wife since 1932, their relationship remained amiable. Son Edward H., a sturdy man twenty-six years of age, was away undergoing naval air training. Teenage daughter Marilyn stayed with her mother in St. Louis, perhaps seeing him occasionally. Patricia, age twenty, enjoyed the lifestyle O'Hare could provide, often staying at his Glencoe home and even traveling with him, especially to Florida. She accompanied him frequently to his various track offices and became acquainted with her dad's secretary, Annette Caravetta. When in Florida, the two women often chummed around together, beachcombing and swimming.

Romance blossomed between O'Hare and the lovely Ursala Suzanne "Sue" Granata. Sister to both a Chicago politician and a prominent attorney, Granata was a refined young woman who was talented in the arts, particularly music. She had previously worked as a secretary at the track for O'Hare but more recently, like Caravetta, had become a full-time slumming buddy for Patricia O'Hare in Chicago. Marriage was on their agenda, as the pair reportedly was waiting for an annulment of O'Hare's first marriage before finalizing their own plans. Speculation pegged a spring 1940 wedding.

On Wednesday morning, November 8, 1939, O'Hare planned to wrap up track business and depart for Washington, D.C., to close a real estate venture before heading to New York state. O'Hare was contemplating a new track in Buffalo now that pari-mutuel betting was legal there. He was also culminating deals in both Florida and Massachusetts for new dog tracks. His ultimate destination was Florida for the winter race season there.

O'Hare, fastidiously dressed in a $100 blue suit and exquisite calfskin oxfords, stopped by his equally impeccable Sportsman's Park office one last time that season. Encased in his rich environment of thick midnight blue carpeting, rich mahogany furniture, and the finest prints of thoroughbreds and racing scenes adorning the walls, secretary Annette Caravetta, Johnny Patton, a track publicist, and a track auditor met with O'Hare to wrap up business and perhaps finalize an application for next season's racing dates as required by law. Concluding the agenda, only O'Hare remained in the office that afternoon. A little after three, O'Hare finished his business, climbed into his Lincoln Zephyr coupe, and pulled away from the track lot, heading north on Cicero Avenue then right onto Ogden Avenue, the main artery running northeast directly into the Loop, where he was scheduled for one last business meeting.

Nearly three miles up Ogden, he passed through tree-shaded Douglas Park. From a side street, another coupe, bearing one or possibly two passengers in the rear wearing dark felt hats, emerged to trail O'Hare. Sensing trouble, O'Hare accelerated to over fifty miles per hour. The mysterious coupe kept pace. Three blocks further up the road from Douglas Park, as the vehicles raced toward Talman Avenue, the second car pulled nearly even with O'Hare on his driver's side.

On the Ogden side of the Garden City Plating and Manufacturing Company at 1436 Talman, twenty-year-old employee Peter Szent was painting the front windows as the coupes raced by. Startled, he whirled around to see what all the hubbub was about. As the vehicles speeding abreast of each other approached Rockwell Avenue, the next block, a man on the passenger side of one of the cars raised a shotgun, "his elbow braced on the frame of the car," Szent recalled. "He apparently was pulling the trigger with his left hand. . . . There was about eight inches of the barrel protruding from the door." Two blasts fired at close range punched neat holes in O'Hare's driver's-side window, the buckshot striking his head and shoulder with horrific force.

O'Hare's coupe swerved out of control to the right, jumping over a short concrete curb, glancing off a street lamp, and continuing a short distance on the grassy median dividing Ogden and a parallel thoroughfare with trolley tracks before colliding with a trolley pole. The car's front end wrapped around the pole, and the rest of the vehicle crumpled behind it, the right-rear end coming to rest partially on the trolley tracks. Inside, O'Hare hit the steering wheel with such force that he bent the wheel and deflected the steering column almost to the ceiling. He came to a bloody rest, slouched down in the seat, his lower body partially beneath the steering column. A .32-caliber automatic lay unused on the seat beside him. The killers continued on their way, appearing to be in no particular hurry when the young painter lost sight of their coupe at Western Avenue.

At the outset of the investigation into O'Hare's death, Dan Gilbert, chief investigator for the state's attorney, told one reporter, "There might be a thousand angles to this case." Such an apparently typical gangland hit made the Nitto crowd the likeliest suspects. The inquiry focused on O'Hare's many business affiliations, past and present, with the Capone gang, as police speculated there might have been a quarrel over dividends. Personal belongings found on O'Hare, including a memorandum and paper notes with the names of various women as well as a steamy note in Italian referring to someone named "Margie," suggested other possibilities. The Sue Granata romance surfaced with the examination of his watch, which had the passionate inscription *"amor sempiternus"* (love eternal), on the back and "Ed-Sue" underneath. With at least two women in the picture, a lover's quarrel—no matter how far-fetched—entered the list of motives.

There was also the timing of it all to consider. In 1934, Bureau of Prisons authorities had transferred Al Capone from the federal penitentiary in Atlanta to Alcatraz. In November 1939, he was to be released on parole in a matter of days after serving seven years of his eleven-year sentence. The newspapers wondered whether his release might somehow doom O'Hare. That burning question received considerable fuel when, nearly a week later, an anonymous tip led authorities to a secret apartment kept by O'Hare on Sherwin Avenue. In one of the expensively decorated rooms they found a note from a mysterious "George," supposedly privy to words uttered by Capone and warning O'Hare of "remarks and threats" that Al Capone was making. More specifically, the letter said, "The Big Dago swears he is going to have Ohare [sic], or will see that some of his friends score for Eddie."

Perhaps based on this tidbit, one theory circulating around the news desks was that Capone had had O'Hare murdered because O'Hare was partly responsible for sending Big Al to prison in the first place. When word of this got back to Capone, so the story goes, he sought vengeance from behind prison walls. Talk of Capone's return to the rackets was also being bandied about, and some thought the murder was a mob present for Al.

The problem with this theory, though, is that O'Hare and most of the outside world had no idea about the true state of Capone's health. Capone was suffering from advanced syphilis, and mental decay was an unavoidable side effect. He may very well have uttered something about O'Hare, but by this point he was regularly drifting into and out of lucidity. Federal agents interviewing him on one occasion, perhaps to learn more about gang business, gave up after his babbling was reduced to mumbo jumbo. One prison guard on Alcatraz pronounced him "screwy as a bedbug."

Upon his release on November 16, Capone's family shuffled him off to Baltimore's Union Memorial Hospital for treatment. The specialist treating him was alarmed at the publicity given to Capone about the O'Hare murder and went so far as to call the FBI and assure them that Capone's extremely poor health made it "impossible for him to stage a comeback in the rackets"—or even a serious conversation, for that matter. There was to be no homecoming for Capone, and if Nitto really wanted to kill O'Hare for ratting out his boss (as well as himself), given his temperament, he would have done so much earlier. Still, something spooked O'Hare. Shortly after receiving the "George" letter, it was discovered he had taken out three insurance policies for himself.

Another theory about O'Hare's murder was based on the money needed to effect Capone's final release from prison. The family still owed the feds approximately $20,000 in fines and court costs that had to be paid before he could be released. Gossip suggested a Nitto mob collection drive was in progress in order to assist the Capone family and that O'Hare refused the charity drive. Another O'Hare note turned up, not from a possible romance but from secretary Caravetta, regarding a call from the local FBI. They wanted to ask him a few questions, likely in connection to the ongoing gambling investigation.

The state's attorney's investigation pressed forward, though apparently without vigor. The day O'Hare was buried, authorities simply pointed fingers in the direction of the "Capone racketeers." After a couple of days, reportedly satisfied that all to be found had been found, Chief Investigator Dan Gilbert wandered off to Iowa City to take in the Notre Dame-Iowa football game. State's Attorney Courtney laxly shrugged off any possibilities of finding the slayers: "Gangster killings almost invariably are followed by silence. No one will talk. There never is a scrap of evidence." The gangster possibility appeared to strengthen when police questioned Annette Caravetta. Out of character, O'Hare was visibly shaken, she said, as if his life were in peril; he was "extremely irritable, yelling out over trifles he wouldn't have noticed ordinarily. He was always outspoken against gangsters, but in the last three weeks he was more outspoken than I had ever seen him. And he seemed to always have them on his mind."

Yet no manifest effort was made to round up any of the gang, though it was known to at least one reporter that most of the gang's "torpedo men" were in Miami and Hot Springs. Two days after the murder, Frank Nitto checked into the Arlington Hotel in Hot Springs. None of the other mob big shots were to be seen around town either. A few days later, both Courtney and Gilbert announced to their satisfaction that the murder was the result of the Nitto Outfit. Courtney leaned toward the "O'Hare two-timed Scarface" theory, while Gilbert claimed to have inside information from street sources that said O'Hare had disputes with Nitto's company at the track. The lovers' quarrel theory had dropped to a distant third place possibility, but at least one highly regarded investigator close to the scene, as well as some of those in the print media, still regarded O'Hare's relationship to Sue Granata as the key to the puzzle. Gilbert's sources seemed to be closer to the truth.

Less than a week after the murder, leads in the case filtered into the FBI office in Washington from Miami and pointed to Nitto. One call came from a *Miami Daily News* employee who asked whether investigators realized that the Gulf Stream racetrack in Hollywood, Florida, had closed some time prior to O'Hare's death. The reporter had found that O'Hare had become involved in a deal to reopen the track and have the horses off and running as early as winter. This put O'Hare in direct competition with nearby Tropical Park. The owners of this track did not put Gulf Stream out of business only to see it reopen again. The reporter's source put at least

40 percent of Tropical Park's ownership in the hands of the Chicago mob, with East Coast gangster Owney Madden also having a slice. Others mentioned gambling magnate Frank Erickson and others. For the Chicago share, Frank Nitto and John Patton each owned roughly 8 percent through their Gables Racing Association. This may have been sufficient motive, the reporter said.

Any conflicts detected by Gilbert at Sportsman's Park may have provided sufficient motive. Nitto had, by some accounts, a 15 percent interest there as well. O'Hare had recently toughened his stance against his gangster friends, requesting that Glencoe police check license plates on cars around his house and keep hoods away from the track. His maid at his Glencoe home reported a bomb threat had been received there shortly after the murder.

Just the same, dog racing conflicts may have proved O'Hare's undoing. An FBI source close to the dog racing community understood O'Hare was reputed not to pay his obligations. John Patton also thought him to be "a ruthless business man" and described their relationship for the past year or so as "not pleasant." Unquestionably, any quarrel with Patton would be a direct affront to Nitto himself. Recently, O'Hare had seemed to go into hiding when Nitto visited the Florida tracks, in particularly the Miami Kennel Club. Nitto had a "free run" of the beach track offices, calling Chicago and his East Coast allies at his leisure. The motive for his death, according to Patton, who was perhaps deflecting attention from his own holdings, was possibly due to "angling for something in New York. He might have squeezed somebody." Should any of those deals cross Nitto allies in the east, it was just as good as stepping on Nitto. O'Hare's monopoly on dog racing notwithstanding, he simply seemed to have overestimated his power, and his philosophy regarding business dealings with hoodlums wore thin.

<hr />

Little did Nitto know that when he directed his mob into IATSE, they were skirting the edge of trouble almost from the outset. Since mid-1933, alarmed by their investigation into Tom Maloy, the feds began looking into racketeering complaints from members of other IATSE locals. Near the top of the list was Nitto ally Louis Kaufman of Newark Local 244. In August 1937, Assistant Attorney General Morris recommended prosecution of Kaufman and several other officers for tax evasion, and all were later found guilty.

In June of that year, complaints from St. Louis prompted investigation of IATSE First Vice President John Nick and his buddy Clyde Weston, rulers of Local 143, for salary kickbacks and racketeering in which the two coerced local theater owners to purchase audio equipment and services from companies in which they maintained interests. If a theater owner resisted, he found himself without projectionists. Background checks showed Nick had been arrested sixteen times on charges ranging from suspicion of larceny to robbery to murder. Weston, an Illinois native, was not nearly as accomplished as Nick, compiling a record that included deserting the U.S. Army and robbery. These might add up to minor incidents, but Nitto had to understand the feds were nipping at the IATSE's heels. It seemed Bioff's counsel to Nitto about the greed of "every Tom, Dick, and Harry" had proved correct, but Bioff forgot to include himself among the piranhas.

In California, everything seemed to run without a sputter for Nitto's mob. Bioff collected the annual $50,000 payments from the big producers with no problem, usually through small installments disguised as miscellaneous expenses to avoid potentially embarrassing and unexplainable large payments of cash. In mid-1937, Nick Schenck and Bioff worked a more oblique scheme that enabled the racketeer to collect from Loews. Schenck arranged for a Bioff-appointed representative to collect a 7 percent commission on the sale of raw film from the Smith and Aller film company as a ghost employee; Schenck, would then switch enough studio film purchases from primary vendor Eastman-Kodak to this firm (which sold DuPont film) to more than cover the original sum and the income taxes as well. Bioff then arranged for his brother-in-law to take the position, which later went to a trusted official from Local 2 in Chicago.

Then Bioff committed a series of faux pas. Soon after lending a hand to break the 1937 FMPC strike, Bioff eyed a large ranch in the San Fernando Valley, the asking price for which was about $100,000. Bioff couldn't afford to show that much income since he paid no taxes on any such amounts. To purchase it, he borrowed the necessary $5,000 retainer from an IATSE official. Further, since he helped break the FMPC that year, he turned to Joe Schenck at Loews for a favor. Schenck borrowed the full amount, wired it to his New York office, and then paid off the loan in Hollywood to make it falsely appear to be coming from New York when, in fact, a check for the amount was issued to Bioff through Schenck's nephew. Should anyone ask, they would merely call it a "loan." Bioff later explained the rationale for this subterranean maneuvering, saying that a more overt loan would make it "appear that we were too friendly," and supposed labor-management adversaries shouldn't be in collusion.

However, after a Schenck representative assessed the value of the ranch at far below the asking price, Bioff cancelled the real estate deal but kept the $100,000 tucked away in a safe deposit box. Not only did Schenck forget about the amount, but that fall, he bought Bioff over $36,000 worth of stocks, over half of which was stock in Twentieth Century Fox. Through Schenck, authorities suspected Louis B. Mayer of contributing an additional $29,000 in various stock purchases. The transactions did not remain off-the-record for long.

According to Louis B. Mayer, Willie Bioff helped solve the actors threat in 1937. The Screen Actors Guild was organized in 1933 to represent players in the production of motion pictures; the union was affiliated with, but not a member of, the AFL and negotiated studio contracts for some 2,000 or more members. By 1937, the membership was over 8,000 and consisted of three tiers of *dramatis personae*: Class A players, the stars, made $50 or more per day; Class B members earned up to $16.50 daily as "dress" extras appearing close up in scenes; and Class C extras, or simple background atmosphere players, made up to $5.50 a day (anyone with the right connections could become an extra if he or she paid for a union card). During the FMPC tempest, SAG used the occasion to press their cause: they, too, were due a new contract with producers and seriously considered a sympathetic walkout of their own.

As it turned out, they did not, and it was Bioff who intervened to make sure they didn't. Labor guy Bioff impressed at least some SAG members, who viewed him as an apparent ally in the Hollywood labor jungle.

That autumn, however, he proved quite the chameleon, changing from good guy to bad guy when SAG resumed contract discussions with the producers. Before the talks, IATSE Vice President Harlan Holmden appeared in Los Angeles announcing that his international union had jurisdiction over all movie-industry labor, including the actors, citing agreements stretching back to the mid-1920s. SAG always maintained these agreements did not include actors, directors, or writers and viewed this as the opening move of a hostile takeover. One evening, as SAG leadership met with Louis B. Mayer about contract negotiations, bully Bioff stalked in unannounced and threw such a scare into the producer that he settled with the actors. The producers agreed to a ten-year, no-strike SAG Basic Agreement. SAG rolls for extras remained open, but the initiation fee was doubled, and quarterly dues were raised threefold. Further, no player could work without a card paid to date in good standing. SAG leadership remained suspicious—and with good reason, for although they did not know it, it was during this period that producers bestowed upon Bioff their gifts of stock investments.

Shortly thereafter, the first pebble of the avalanche began rolling when Bioff attempted to collect from Harry Cohn at Columbia. The studio had received a pass on its original $25,000 levy because of their economic difficulties, but Bioff thought it was high time to collect some money. He consulted Louis Campagna, who relayed the word from Chicago to strike against Columbia and get the money whenever he saw fit. Bioff waited for some insignificant but legitimate tiff to use as a pretext and then called the strike on November 8.

The problem was that apparently nobody notified Johnny Rosselli. He and Cohn were buddies from the early days, and when Bioff struck at Columbia, Rosselli was furious at being left out of the decision. He called Bioff in for a dressing-down, and Bioff told him that if Cohn didn't pay, Rosselli would be responsible to Nitto. Rosselli promised a Cohn payment of $25,000 within a week, so Bioff called off the walkout. No cash materialized, and a couple of weeks later Campagna pressed him to get Rosselli onto Columbia for the money, but the suave mobster only informed Bioff that Cohn double-crossed him. Nothing more happened, and they never got the money, according to Bioff.

However, a state assembly subcommittee investigating labor conditions happened to be in town. They weren't probing Hollywood labor in particular, but the inexplicable wildcat strike at Columbia piqued enough interest for members to draw up a subpoena for this suddenly powerful Bioff character. To make matters worse, Carey McWilliams, a lawyer acting on behalf of rebel Hollywood union members (Local 37), filed a complaint with the California Speaker of the House to have the House's labor committee investigate IATSE and its bullying tactics. He fed the committee a complete dossier of news clippings and police records regarding this apparently unsavory union man Bioff, pressing the committee to look into the matter vigorously. Legislators also heard SAG's president, actor Robert Montgomery, who testified how the actors had staved off what they perceived as an informal IATSE takeover. He, too, had hired private detectives to scrutinize Bioff.

Legislators only gingerly confronted Bioff, telling him, "It has been alleged that the alliance is a racket and that a Chicago gang has been brought in here to enforce the racket." Bioff branded the whole thing a subversive Communist plot, and pandemonium broke lose. Suspiciously, almost as quickly as the whole matter surfaced, it was dropped. What eventually broke the Hollywood racketeering case wide open, remembered IRS agent Elmer Irey, was what the committee didn't do. Their investigation was "so bad," he recalled, a grand jury in Sacramento decided on a later inquiry into the possible corruption of state legislators. The FBI also reported the investigation as an apparent "whitewash." Revelations of IATSE payments—for legal services—to quash the investigation surfaced. The grand jury called Bioff again, and this time Joe Schenck was also summoned. The $100,000 item on Schenck's records turned up, but when asked about it, Schenck eluded questions, saying he "couldn't remember" or "had no recollection of" the amount to Bioff. The hoodlum lied as well. They might be able to pull the wool over the eyes of state people, but a red flag amounting to six-figures instigated a tax investigation by the SIU of both Schenck and Bioff.

The California state assembly investigation did, inadvertently, produce one enormous and damning tidbit for future use. Because of their scrutiny, Bioff temporarily rescinded the nefarious 2 percent assessment that had been imposed on IATSE members of Local 37 about December 11, 1937. Perhaps to make up lost income, Bioff critically blundered when he approached the producers before Christmas for an extra $20,000 contribution. Bioff slipped distinctively when pressing Harry Warner for the loot, explaining, "the boys in Chicago are insisting for more money." Producers were long used to the Bioff squeeze play, but apparently for the first time, if only vaguely, they now recognized just who backed the bully.

On December 22, the picture illuminated further when the *IA Progressive Bulletin*, an organ for dissident IATSE unionists shrieked: "BIOFF EXPOSED! POLICE RECORDS REVEAL PAST." The front-page extra laid out Bioff's unsavory past: arrests with West Side characters James Adducci and Phillip Mangano, and a more recent write-up in a Chicago paper after the murder of Louis Alterie noted that "police [were] hunting Willie Bioff and Joe Montana, West Side gunman." Accentuating the text were two choice photos of international union representative Bioff in police custody. Worse yet, in one instance, Nitto's name and mention of the Chicago mob appeared. An adjoining article urged repudiation of the current IATSE administration and a return of autonomy for the locals. The author noted the union collection of an estimated three-quarters of a million dollars without any substantial return outside of the usual 10 percent raise. Fiery script urged, "Brothers, we shouldn't be suckers any longer!"

So cocksure was he that he could defeat both state officials and the grumpy union ranks that Bioff squeezed producers for more money that winter. This time, Schenck announced the producers were in no position to dole out funds. For Bioff's information, Treasury people were nosing into producers' accounts, specifically

Schenck's and that $100,000 deal. Predicting that agents would eventually question Bioff in the matter, they agreed Bioff should disappear, if only temporarily, until they could grasp a solution. Separately, Nitto no doubt concurred. In February 1938, compliments of the studios, Bioff departed on a three-month long cruise for Rio de Janeiro and Europe. Harry Warner even sent a bon-voyage telegram.

Instead, the adversity only continued to accumulate. Within a month, United Features Syndicate columnist Westbrook Pegler unveiled the names of Bioff and Browne to the public. Pegler, an unabashed and dogged journalist, frequently addressed labor issues, the Red menace (communism) being a primary topic of concern during the Depression years. Examining the closed-shop agreement recently reached between SAG and the studios, he noted the only threat to industry and labor peace was Browne's IATSE organization. The actors, he reported, suspected that IATSE officials, with Bioff in the lead, might try to coerce the actors into their fold. With revelations of Bioff's past seeping out, the guild decided further investigation of both Bioff and Browne was necessary. Pegler announced he would investigate, too.

When Bioff made landfall in May, Browne and his lawyer in New York briefed him on the income tax investigations. Bioff's orders from Nitto were to stay low, except to drum up support for McLane's bid for international president. Amazingly, the mob pulled strings from the shadows, angling for "them actors." At the annual IATSE convention, held in June 1938, the leadership pushed through a resolution to call on the National Labor Relations Board to withdraw any protection sought by SAG earlier as well as to ask the AFL to withdraw charters from the affiliated actors unions. The appearance of impropriety grew when producer Sydney Kent took the stage to commend the virtues of IATSE.

The opening the mob saw was far too enticing. The crux of the matter, they knew, rested chiefly upon the vulnerable extra players. From the beginning, Class B and C players paid dues to SAG but were, under union bylaws, ineligible to vote in SAG matters. The lofty Class A stars ruled the union, and the increasingly voluble extras complained of "taxation without representation."

The heat cranked up a notch during the last half of 1938. SIU agents questioned producer Schenck at least three times, and each time his story of the $100,000 check to Bioff seemed to change a little. The agents found this suspicious and wanted to haul in Bioff for questioning. With the heat on, Nitto ordered his resignation from the international organization until the hubbub blew over. Officially, he was out for appearance's sake, salving the unionists and the public, but Bioff remained Nitto's union mover, with Nick Circella as an official close to Browne. Suspicion switched to another mob connection when, on October 26, *People's World* published two reproductions of stock certificates for 100 shares each of Twentieth Century Fox in the name of Bioff and went on to allege his ownership of 30,000 shares, payments for helping break strikes in 1937, they said—and the certificates were dated November 30, 1937. Additional reports of alleged collusion drifted about freely.

Amazingly, Nitto's leadership role in the Chicago mob toward the end of the decade has been called to question over the years by those who say that protégé Paul Ricca had, in fact, supplanted Nitto as leader of the Chicago mob. A February 14, 1939, *Daily News* article noted the rise of the mysterious figure Paul Ricca to leadership compliments of sponsor Frank Nitto. According to George Murray, in his *Legacy of Al Capone*:

> Ricca stepped out as Nitti's successor as the head of the Capone hierarchy.
> Power gravitates to the man strong enough to take it and hold it. Strength
> of personality won the approval of those present. Nitti from that time on
> was in second place.

It may have appeared that way because Nitto's stealthy leadership after Capone was little reported and understood by the press. Now with Hitler making rumblings in Europe, foreign policy dominated press ink, forcing all but the most sensational mob activities and revelations to the back pages, if they were reported at all. Except for the most well-informed crime beat reporters, the press was kept guessing about the leadership of the old Capone mob. The assertion that Ricca was leader is no surprise, but of course, if one examined the big picture and understood the mob's organizational mechanics from the past, the assessment was overstated.

Some have followed the notion of Ricca's leadership based on a single incident in the IATSE conspiracy that seemed to support the *Daily News* contention. The whole matter surfaced late summer 1939 amidst pressure on local gambling caused by the Annenberg investigation. Ricca and D'Andrea dropped out of Chicago and met Bioff in California. They discussed the danger of the current system of theater payments in Chicago to avoid the tax men, yet Ricca directed Bioff to start collecting money from all the producers again because the mob needed the money. The federal pressure had cut off the money tap, and in Bioff's words, "there wasn't much income at that time, only the one source [the Loews film deal]." Bioff deferred, though, citing the Treasury Department pressure.

Extorting producers directly presented a clear danger, but skimming union treasuries proved immensely less dangerous. Opportunity opened in that direction when the Associated Actors and Artists of America, an umbrella organization covering some 30,000 actors including SAG, vaudeville, variety, nightclub, and radio artists, looked to split apart after AAAA leader Ralph Whitehead came to believe a movement from within had developed to oust him. SAG had recently lost its NLRB protection, and IATSE thus looked to set up a new actors union based in New York. Whitehead talked to Browne in New York about a charter with the IATSE, bringing all his people over along with an AFL charter as the American Federation of Actors, led by vaudeville and stage actress Sophie Tucker. In this way, IATSE might also get the long-disgruntled extra players away from SAG as well.

In response, as Whitehead feared, a movement within the AAAA circulated a petition to strike; it might even drive a wedge between the producers and IATSE. Bioff, already on the ground by August 4, handled the situation in Hollywood. Browne, who feared that a split among the actors unions, including SAG, might cause too much commotion at such a sensitive time, consulted Nick Circella at his side. Nick called Nitto in Chicago about the matter, and he gave the go-ahead. Nitto would place handbook operator Charlie Gioe as watchdog over the AAAA. Circella reported back to Browne, "My people would like to get hold of that union." Bioff, always anxious to get "them actors," went along with the move, and Browne issued the charter. When a tempest of angry actor protests materialized at AFL headquarters, Bioff called Browne in New York to revoke the charter for safety's sake and was told by Browne, "Well, I cannot do that." Browne reasoned that Whitehead was a good friend and that he had stuck his neck out for him: "I have put myself in the position that I cannot very well get out now."

Bioff, protesting the hullabaloo it had caused, argued, "I do not care about Whitehead. I do not care about anyone. You revoke that charter."

Listening in behind Browne was Circella. He reminded Browne of mob orders and told him, "Don't revoke that charter."

Caught in the middle of the rhubarb between the mob men, Browne handed the phone to Circella, but he refused to talk to Willie directly, so Browne revoked the charter per Bioff's request.

When Nitto received word of the action from Circella, he raged at the insubordination and called a meeting in Chicago. Bioff found out through Ricca, who phoned him on the coast and told him "to drop everything, get on a plane and come in." Nitto, Ricca, Campagna, Circella, Browne, and Bioff met in Bioff's Bismarck Hotel suite. Nitto assumed a calm, businesslike demeanor when he opened the meeting, speaking directly to Bioff. "There are some complaints here about you that we have got to get straightened out, and it's important that we do it at this time. Nick tell your story."

Circella directed at Bioff, "You are trying to replace George Browne by issuing orders, it is embarrassing to George and me. Here we made a promise. . . . How does it make him look in the eyes of these people?"

Browne jumped in: "You tell me on the one hand to revoke the charter and Nick is in back of me pulling my coat not to revoke the charter." All he wanted to know was whose orders to follow.

Nitto turned a menacing look on Bioff and asked, "By what right did you have to order George to revoke the charter when you knew it was an order from us to issue a charter?"

"Well, I would like to explain that, Frank. Paul and Phil D'Andrea were out to my home." Bioff said he had told them about all the local publicity regarding racketeer Bioff stealing this and that and that investigations were going on. He told Paul: "It is causing us a lot of trouble. I want to know how important this actors union is to the Outfit." Ricca told him, "Why do you put that to me? It is up to you three, up to you, George and Nick. Whatever you see fit to do, go ahead and do it."

According to Bioff, this cleared him. After all, he recalled, " I was practically on trial there." He remembered everybody looked somewhat surprised that Ricca had acted in such fashion, but the meeting adjourned friendly and businesslike, with no problems.

This Ricca incident is measured by some as a coup d'état showcasing his eel-like emergence as Number One and Nitto's decline. Hardly—it was simply business. Nitto, busy ironing out gambling matters in Chicago, was not aware—nor did Bioff make him aware—of the acute situation on the ground in California. Ricca, who was on the spot, simply made a decision in the best interest of the mob. At worst, like the earlier Rosselli incident, it represented a communication breakdown. At best, he was setting himself up as the clear Number Two among his mob associates by acting only as a Number Two should, whether he was to be appointed by Nitto or Nitto had already appointed him as underboss.

The situation is not so different from the Capone-Nitto relationship of the late 1920s, except that the gang had now broadened its business far beyond Prohibition and Chicago. Nitto as leader directed the gang's vast empire and vision, with protégé Ricca and associates directing day-to-day activities. Nitto involved himself in local instances only when the need arose or, as in this case, to iron out differences in the gang. As long as Bioff had acted with some authority recognized by Nitto, it was okay.

As with the Capone-Nitto relationship years before, Ricca's increased visibility and discovery by the Daily News in 1939 may have had much to do with Nitto's frequent absences. In true Capone fashion, Nitto was reported spending most of the winter in Miami, returning to Chicago only to tend to important business. When in town, he took an apartment near Oak Park under the alias Frank Raddo. Summers saw him in Wisconsin at times, enjoying the north woods. Rumor had it that Nitto sponsored Ricca as "acting" boss in his stead. Nitto's health seems to have become problematic at this time as well, and heart troubles and stomach ulcers were rumored to plague him. He increasingly spent more time in and out of hospitals for these ailments, and he had never fully recovered from the Lang gunshots years before. Complications still bothered him. His protégé Ricca would naturally be the go-to man for the mob in Nitto's absence.

Nitto's poor health might also explain the dichotomy of his economic stratagems. Beginning in 1939, Nitto began divesting himself of some of his gambling interests while still apparently directing the long-range strategy for overall mob interests. For example, at the time the feds indicted Moe Annenberg, Nitto suggested to James Ragen a mob partnership in the wire service to corner a significant portion of nationwide gambling. The mob never wavered in this goal, but within months of O'Hare's murder, Nitto sold his share of the ancillary business, Sportsman's Park, for no apparent reason. A change of ownership should not have created any hardship for Nitto, whose portion was held in Johnny Patton's name, but Nitto's move prompted his partner to sell his shares too. Later asked why he would divest himself of such an asset, Patton replied that, after the O'Hare killing, he "just didn't like the atmosphere." As for Nitto, Patton didn't know his motive.

At the same time, the press suspected that, after the murder of wheel operator Walter Kelly in January 1939, the mob wanted in on the millions generated by the black wheels on the South Side. The move into the wheels supposedly gathered increased interest with the indictment of politician-gambler go-between Billy Skidmore and perhaps the most prolific wheel operators, the three Jones brothers, on tax evasion charges the following spring. The window of opportunity was now open, someone had to fill the void, and the mob thought itself best suited. These rumors continued throughout Nitto's reign.

Yet while Nitto was thought to be angling the mob for this slice of gambling, in a peculiar move, he sold his share of Ed Vogel's slots back to the slot king for a $10,000 gain, the income appearing on his tax returns as "vending machine income." Why sell out for such a paltry gain after he had been raking in, according to the Treasury people, at least $50,000 annually? When the grand jury investigating Annenberg, Skidmore, and Cook County gambling pronounced local law enforcement in that area, particularly that of Sheriff Tom O'Brien, a "colossal sham" (earning him the moniker "Blind Tom"), Illinois Attorney General John Cassidy brought in the state police. Nitto and his mob tried bribes of as much as $200,000 down and $8,000 a month to gain a pass but failed. The slots were reportedly routed, but this would only be temporary—no different than Courtney's war on handbooks the previous year, as Nitto certainly knew. Vogel stayed in, yet Nitto wanted out. However, Nitto retained an interest in at least a handful of the betting parlors.

Taken together, circumstances hint more of an eventual Nitto retirement than a Ricca takeover. The organization was much too businesslike with upper-level managers polished with great respect for any hostile action to come from within, especially for no reason. And no explanation has ever surfaced for the alleged Ricca power play. In fact, outside of Colosimo's obstinacy, such things did not happen in Chicago.

If gang leader Frank Nitto contemplated retirement, mob business would provide no such window of comfort. The following months would provide ample opportunity for management to revolt, yet Ricca and company backed Nitto to the end. The McLane trial and Nitto's deteriorating health late in 1940 provide a better scenario for a more obvious Ricca presence than the Bioff incident.

With one pickle after another, pressure mounted on IATSE from all sides in spring 1939. After further study and enough documentation to illuminate Bioff's checkered past and suggest what appeared to be a Schenck bribe to Bioff to break the FMPC strike, Robert Montgomery phoned local FBI offices on April 15 and asked if they would be interested in what SAG investigators had accumulated on corrupt IATSE officials. The answer was yes.

After quashing a state investigation in 1937, the IATSE sought to reinstate its 2 percent assessment on Local 37. To ensure compliance, Browne declared an emergency in Hollywood and tossed out dissident unionists. This added more fuel for the fire—local authorities in California, weary of continuous complaints against the IATSE, decided to launch a grand jury investigation of union activities. A subpoena for Browne was issued. Afraid of being served with the request for a court appearance in California, Browne directed IATSE action from nearby Arizona. Reports then surfaced of a pending nationwide IATSE strike ordered by George Browne as a means to pressure producers to exert influence to end the inquiry. Then, out of the blue, the inquiry was abandoned. Agents later noted that Schenck and IATSE reps met with the district attorney (without dissident reps), and local FBI agents requested immediate assistance to investigate. Failing locally, disgruntled members of Local 37 resorted to the state courts but lost the jurisdiction fight. They subsequently followed through by filing a complaint with the Anti-Trust Division of the Department of Justice, and only three days after Montgomery phoned the FBI, the Department of Justice authorized a full investigation of the IATSE.

To make matters worse, SIU agents caught up with Bioff about the Schenck "loan" on April 14, 1939. The response he gave was that the money was for investment purposes—an oil deal and stocks. The questioning then focused on the remuneration of the funds.

Q: "About how long after you received the cash did you do that [return it]?"

A: "It may have been a couple of days."

The investigators knew Bioff and Schenck's stories differed, so in June, Treasury department officials called Schenck, Bioff and their respective lawyers to Washington for a face-to-face conference to determine the true nature of the transaction. Referring to the money again only as a loan, this time, neither caved to provide a reason.

———※※※———

On September 1, 1939, Nazi Germany invaded Poland and embroiled the continent of Europe in war. Hollywood, thousands of miles away, was immediately impacted. Box office sales tanked and, like the Depression, the producers felt the financial pinch. At the bargaining table with the IATSE, producers now wished to negotiate a new Basic Agreement but without the usual 10 percent raise. Willie Bioff, however, was still around, happily imposing himself as the white knight of Hollywood labor. According to him, "There is an obvious way for producers to retrench without attempting to shave or withhold $2 or $3 a week from the paycheck of the little fellows who average less than a $1,000 a year." He then cited the salaries of the producers, some of whom, he said, according to the U.S. Treasury, drew salaries averaging $3,600 a week. Bioff continued by noting that of the sixty-three men who made $200,000 annually, forty were in the picture business. Said Bioff, "These are the men who would economize by taking $2.50 off the paycheck of the man making $25 a week."

———※※※———

Charles H. Carr, special assistant to the attorney general, met with FBI agents to determine the best angle from which to pursue the Bioff-Schenck issue. Three main avenues of prosecution appeared possible: 1) income tax violations; 2) antitrust racketeering; and/or 3) contraventions of collective bargaining. Carr, according to agents, appeared to lack confidence in any of these avenues except perhaps pursuing Bioff on tax matters—and about that he remained doubtful, given the lack of hard proof. On that point, FBI agents apparently concurred: reports from the Treasury department indicated little progress. Certain officials seemed hesitant to pursue the matter, perhaps because such a prominent man such as Schenck was involved. SIU agents in the field, led by crack agent Alf Oftedal, felt otherwise. Their determination might doom both men, and they pushed indictments against them both despite the lack of support from their superiors. Oftedal was determined to stand his ground "even though it went to President Roosevelt."

Meanwhile, agents tracked the Bioff payback story and hit pay dirt. An FBI field report dated November 14, 1939, reveals a timeline for the $100,000 transaction:

> June 17 Schenck borrowed $100,000 from his bank and transferred the money to NY
>
> June 22 Schenck pays off $100,000 loan above with currency and causes his LA books to falsely show this loan repaid from money from NY. June 23 Schenck pays Bioff $100,000 through his nephew.
>
> June 25 Bioff calls off the ranch deal.
>
> June 29 Bioff obtains currency for the $100,000 check and places it a safe deposit box.
>
> July 17 Schenck sails for Europe
>
> July 27 Bioff enters the safe deposit box for the first time since placing the money there.

The problem with Bioff's story was that Schenck did not return from Europe until September. There was no way he paid the money back "in a couple of days."

23

"WE WILL PROBABLY ALL WIND UP IN JAIL"

EORGE SANDERS, BUSINESS AGENT FOR the Chicago Waiters Alliance, fell out with Nitto labor marauder Danny Stanton. On April 5, he disappeared. When his wife asked union officials about his whereabouts, she was told he was out on a long drunk. Without an income, she was allowed a position on the union payroll. After a couple of months, and with no reappearance by Sanders, they dropped her to fend for herself. A year later, street talk alleging that her husband and been shot and buried in quicklime finally made it into print. His was one in a series of labor/racketeering murders and high jinks experienced by Chicago, news of which was mostly relegated to minor treatment in the press. But amidst the gambling revelations in 1939, crime seemed a worse epidemic than ever. The Chicago Crime Commission openly considered reinstating its public enemies list made famous nearly a decade before "unless there is some measure taken to stop this lawlessness." Ordinarily a job for the county's top cop, State's Attorney Thomas Courtney, relief instead came from the usual federal sources—and as far away as New York.

The most famous labor murder of 1939 was that of Nitto aide Louis Schiavone. He had worked side by side with Nitto in alcohol distribution during Prohibition, and since then, Nitto had placed him in charge of that operation, which stretched over the entire north end of the state. (Illegal alcohol was still profitable because the mob paid no tax on products.) Recently, the feds had investigated his activities.

On the night of July 5, Schiavone was driving east on Ninety-fifth Street between Crawford and Cicero avenues when a coupe sped up alongside. An occupant raised a 12-gauge shotgun and squeezed off two bursts of buckshot through Schiavone's open driver's-side window, virtually decapitating him. When police arrived on the scene, they found in his expensive car a recent audit covering the financial workings of Local 66 of the Elevator Operators and Starters Union run by Matt Taylor. The motive for his killing was never really understood, but the fact that papers from Local 66 ended up on his body was not a complete mystery.

According to Matt Taylor, a lawyer approached him in 1936 and said the Nitto mob wanted union funds, saying the mob understood the union treasury to be worth at least $100,000. Taylor, who had run the union and its 3,500 members for thirty-five years, said he would have nothing to do with gangsters. The lawyer set up a meeting and escorted Taylor to a bar where he met Nitto's man Louis Schiavone. The gunman informed Taylor that "you would want to be sick someday, and I would be a doctor. We want to put a man in your union." Taylor again refused.

The mob next tried a different tactic. Jerry Horan, head of the BSEIU at the time, invited Taylor to dinner in his Bismarck Hotel suite, where he introduced Taylor to Louis Campagna. Taylor was given to understand Nitto's strategy. Horan nominally ran the BSEIU for the mob, but Taylor's union belonged to another international. The BSEIU needed Taylor's local as leverage to wring payments from Loop building owners under threat of strikes. After dinner, Campagna laid a certified check for $50,000 in front of Taylor. "Matt," he said, "I want you to step out as president of the elevator operators union." When Taylor questioned selling out his union, Campagna offered a $500 per month ghost job as well. Taylor still refused, whereupon the gunman warned that Taylor was being a "damned fool" and would regret it someday.

When George Scalise succeeded Horan, he immediately went to the American Federation of Labor leadership and requested they transfer Taylor's local to the BSEIU. Successful in his request, Scalise craftily went about ousting Taylor, filing a lawsuit for an accounting of union funds. Sure to find some discrepancy, he would then have reason, according to union bylaws, to replace Taylor with a mob stooge.

A couple of days later, a lawyer visited Taylor and told him, "Matt, you are through now. Let us go to work and help you out on this. The mob is going to get you." Taylor knew the warning to be genuine. In addition to the Campagna threat, Taylor knew that whenever Scalise happened into town, he met with mob union stooges Mike Carrozzo, Louis Romano, and Tom Burke of Louis Alterie's old janitors union local. Recently, a group of masked men had robbed him and fired a couple of gunshots in his direction. Resigned to his fate, Taylor asked, "Well, what is it going to cost me? What is the fee on this thing?"

"You know you have given the mob a fight," the lawyer reckoned, "and it cost them money and they aren't going to let you down easy."

Taylor found out the cost in another meeting in a cocktail bar when a mysterious figure approached his table. "Taylor," he announced, "it will cost you about ten grand to get out of this. The setup is for Burke to take over the union and put in some new business agents."

Later, Tom Burke brought the official mob proposal to Taylor: "We want fifty percent of the union's money, a new executive board, and I want to put in a new treasurer." Asked whom they had nominated for treasurer, Burke replied, "It's going to be Schiavone."

Taylor agreed to the deal, sort of. To stave off personal threats and a mob takeover of the union he had nurtured for so long, Taylor began paying out small amounts of union funds, he says, to Tom Burke. When they wanted more, rather than steal further from the treasury built up by honest men, Taylor turned over $3,000 of his own money. Pressed for more in early July, Taylor was forced to dig into the union treasury for another $3,000 payment. Scalise then curtly dropped his legal action. For Taylor, the money was only a down payment. As long as he continued paying the mob parasites, they allowed him to live and retain the union—all the way to spring 1940, after over $30,000 in payments, when Taylor fell ill with tuberculosis. With Taylor bedridden, Nitto's mob ransacked the mob treasury. Six months later Taylor died.

Louis Schiavone never made it to union treasurer. Soon after the first money rolled in, he was shot down, a union ledger in his possession. As Nitto's go-between with Burke, Taylor guessed he held out some of the original money from his mob bosses, and though he had access to union business, the audit in his possession was never fully explained.

Only after the Schiavone murder did the name of George Scalise surface in Chicago newsprint as a union leader attempting to take over Matt Taylor's elevator union. Scalise's name became suspect far away in New York City as well. Aggressive New York District Attorney Thomas Dewey had put many of the city's marquee gang leaders to flight or in prison, and now George Scalise's local racketeering activities piqued his interest. Besides raking off union funds, Scalise and his hoods squeezed large sums of money from commercial building owners through threats of strikes or property damage. However, Scalise and his associates did so a little too noticeably when, on one occasion, they shut down 1,500 city buildings for two weeks. At the time, a Dewey assistant called union officers in for questioning, later keeping a wary eye on union activities there. The recent Schiavone-Matt Taylor affair only heightened their misgivings.

In due course, it came out that as a teenager, Scalise served four years in federal prison for pandering. Mortified at the revelation, Scalise scampered west to Chicago to inform Nitto of his intent to resign from the union. Nitto couldn't afford to lose him over such a petty disclosure. Under Scalise, the BSEIU was expanding its grip, by reason or force, throughout the country. Nearly 70,000 members now paid dues. Nitto ordered allies on the BSEIU executive council to not only refuse the resignation but also soothe Scalise with a shower of accolades as a great asset to the international and a swell and super organizer. The BSEIU crisis resolved only temporarily for Nitto in January 1940.

A rehabilitated Scalise then moved west to gather in a large San Francisco local by force. On the pretense of union irregularities, he suspended officers and took command. What he didn't count on was his own fourth international vice president, head of the union, electing to fight President Scalise in court. Testimony revealed Scalise as a despotic leader with unlimited access to top union funds. The court heard allegations that up to $300,000 was missing from the international union's treasury. Officials from Chicago were called west for embarrassing testimony, and union members in San Francisco gathered a reform faction within the international organization.

In New York, Dewey dug further. Scalise's name emerged linked with Nitto allies, racketeers Augie Carfano, Lepke Buchalter and Joe Adonis. The name of Scalise's East Coast international representative, Izzy Schwartz, surfaced in connection with New York Local 32B activities. Before long, the New York district attorney's office gave BSEIU reformers in San Francisco reason for hope. They put it in print in the first edition of the *Building Service News*, dated March 19, 1940: "SCALISE STOOGE EXPOSED: IZZY SCHWARTZ ARRESTED FOR EXTORTION." Following the exposé of crook Schwartz and an across-the-board censure of Scalise, at the bottom of the page appeared a four-inch-square ad reading:

KEEP GANGSTERS OUT OF OUR UNIONS
Attend the Joint Defense Committee
DANCE AND CARNIVAL
Saturday, April 6

Even worse than the internal revolt for Scalise and Nitto, Dewey put together a case, and on April 21, Scalise was arrested in New York on fifty-three counts of conspiracy and extortion for shaking down building owners there for more than $97,000. A month later he was indicted on an additional sixty counts of grand larceny involving missing BSEIU funds. Days later, the BSEIU executive council forced Scalise to resign.

Nitto's name cropped up connected to Scalise's rise. Closer scrutiny revealed easterner Scalise had been a virtual unknown until Nitto's sponsorship. In Chicago, the press, illuminated perhaps for the first time, named Nitto as "the present head of the old Capone gang . . . [which] is now said to be national in its operations." As layers of Nitto's operations were gradually peeled back to expose the boss, the illumination hurt the gang's interests.

⸺◦◦◦⸺

For over a year with no major outcry since the first ray of light exposed Bioff, it appeared Nitto's lie-low strategy might succeed after all. Columnist Westbrook Pegler did not forget—he couldn't. Since his first column questioning Bioff and the IATSE, anonymous letters, some from professed union members, had poured into his office stamping Bioff as a bad character. Pegler understood that accusations were one thing and sufficient proof for a conviction was another. Just the same, Pegler heard casual chatter regarding a Bioff pandering charge, but nobody seemed willing to risk owning up to the allegation. On the West Coast, Pegler bumped into Carey McWilliams, who had initially scrutinized Bioff. He, too, believed Bioff to be an expanderer but could provide no hard evidence.

Nagged by the continual flow of allegations, Pegler determined his next trip through Chicago would be a Bioff research expedition. Sure enough, among the items he discovered was a Bioff arrest in 1922 for pandering. A judge convicted him and sentenced him to six months in prison and a $300 fine. Further digging revealed the scandalous exclusive: Bioff served a few days and was then released pending appeal. A year later, a higher court turned down his case, but Bioff never reentered lockup. Moreover, his $5,000 bond was returned, not forfeited, and his fine remained unpaid. Pegler could not find out why Bioff didn't do the time.

On November 24, 1939, he broke the story in his column, "Fair Enough":

> Willie Bioff, convicted of pandering in 1922, who became the labor dictator of the entire amusement industry, arrived at his position of power in the guise of the bodyguard for George E. Browne. . . . [R]eceived $100,000 from a movie picture magnate in 1937 . . . never was a worker in any of the theatrical or moving picture trades or professions and never was elected to high office in the regular manner . . . and it is only now disclosed nationally to the members of the union which he rules that he still owes time on a sentence imposed in 1922 on proof that in a specific instance, he accepted from a woman $29 which she had earned that day by entertaining 13 men as a prostitute in a West Side dive.

Faced with the facts, State's Attorney Courtney had no choice but to extradite Bioff back from California to serve his time. A telegraphic warrant was sent to Los Angeles, where Bioff surrendered, posted a $1,000 bond, and was released pending an extradition fight. (The FBI file says Courtney's warrant was negated in court on a technicality, but Governor Horner signed another later.)

Pegler pursued Bioff and the IATSE in subsequent columns. By early December, national news magazines *Newsweek* and *Time* headlined columns "BELEAGUERED BIOFF" and "SWEET WILLIE," respectively. Small-time Chicago crime watch tabloid *Lightnin'*, published "every little while" and pronounced "the World's Humblest Newspaper" by publisher Elmer L. Williams, needed no prodding to jump on the case. Williams, who had plagued gangs and crooked politicians since Prohibition days, actually exposed the Bioff pandering record six months prior to Pegler. Also ahead of Pegler, he unmasked Browne's sometime disorderly past and exposed his international representative Nick Circella as a suspected gunman and bank robber. Of Willie, he suggested changing his surname to "Buy-Off."

Nitto now had more than just the Scalise affair to worry about. The matter unraveled further when, on January 11, 1940, U.S. marshals in Los Angeles arrested Bioff on two counts of tax evasion, based partially on his $100,000 transaction with Joe Schenck. According to George Browne, who was called back to Chicago, Nitto convened meetings of mob commanders Ricca, Campagna, and Gioe on nearly a daily basis to consider how to handle the IATSE. Browne said he believed the union could run in Bioff's temporary absence with no problem. For Bioff's tax predicament they called into the meetings lawyer Sydney Korshak.

In February, Bioff lost his extradition fight on the pandering charge after arguing the arrest was a "youthful mistake" and further noting he had lived in Chicago for fourteen years thereafter and nobody seemed to care. When the governor of California signed the papers, he made no friends in Chicago, commenting on Bioff's latter argument: " I feel constrained to take into consideration the fact that he lived in a community which has had a type of law enforcement that permitted a court's sentence to go unsatisfied for eighteen years."

When Bioff returned to Chicago, he became party to Nitto's meetings, usually at the Bismarck Hotel. It was at a Bismarck meeting with Nitto, Ricca, Campagna, Louis Greenberg, and Charlie Gioe that Bioff first met his mob messenger in legal matters. According to Bioff, Gioe brought Korshak in and made the introduction: "Willie, meet Sydney Korshak;, he is our man." Gioe explained he wasn't just another lawyer looking for a fee and added, "I want you to pay attention to Sydney when he tells you something, that he knows what he is talking about, any message he might deliver to you is a message from us." Bioff was told to lay low while Korshak devised a strategy for his tax evasion case.

On the pandering matter, local attorney and now state senator Abe Marovitz led a team in fighting for Bioff in his appeals. For two months they battled, until April 15, only a week before Scalise was indicted in New York, Bioff entered city jail for a five-month stay.

<hr>

The onslaught of bad publicity rained on Nitto's group. Pegler, a few days earlier, turned his pen on what he called "Mafia" operations in labor. Capone gangsters Bioff and Circella ran IATSE, while Scalise's unions "were positively crawling with criminals." A day later, he exposed Nitto's name for the first time directly as boss of the Miami bartenders and waiters unions. He pronounced Nitto "the most vicious criminal veteran of the hoodlum wars of Chicago," though he did not connect the dots to IATSE fully. In a column later in the month, he noted that Nitto was engaged in the wholesale beverage business in Miami and declared, "Mr. Frank Nitti . . . is outranked only by Capone in American crime."

The local press turned their pens on the IATSE and Nitto's remaining thug in the union, Nick Circella, as well as on Scalise. "Browne," noted one editorial, "seems to have a penchant for appointing dubious assistants." Picking up on Williams's *Lightnin'* revelations of the previous year, they noted Circella's record for robbery and also understood Local 110 was his to run. Browne, they noted, was no angel himself, and they brought up former First Vice President John Nick of St. Louis, who was also investigated for racketeering. (Nick and Weston were indicted on twelve counts of racketeering in June.) Scalise made good fodder for the papers, which pointed out that while the many scrubwomen, window cleaners, and chambermaids paid their dues while earning $13 a week, the union boss maintained a twenty-seven-room mansion in Connecticut. "I've been Peglerized," Scalise groused after the continued harassment by columnist Westbrook Pegler led to his downfall.

The union accepted Scalise's resignation from the BSEIU on May 7, 1940. Veteran BSEIU official William McFetridge of Chicago was elected president. Tom Burke, Nitto's original choice back in 1937, also desired the position, but this time he was told not to run or else.

Officials at the city jail caused mob men no great hardship in communicating with Bioff. An insider professed night and day visits "for hours at a time" by Nitto, Ricca, Campagna, Circella, and others, an account later confirmed by Bioff. For privacy in which to conduct mob business, Bioff said, they were given, of all places, the prison chapel.

Jail time served Bioff favorably in at least one sense: it forced the feds to postpone his tax trial. Then, as Bioff acclimated to the prison routine, the press cornered him and asked if he knew of Joe Schenck's indictment. The leader of the movie industry faced twenty-four counts of making false statements involving the Bioff loan and tax evasion to the tune of over $400,000. Schenck denied the charges. As for Bioff, when asked, he shrugged the Schenck affair off, saying, "That's something I have nothing to comment on. Let Mr. Schenck do the talking."

Shortly afterward, he received a visit from Sydney Korshak. Word had filtered back from the West Coast to Nitto that Joe Schenck was indeed talking—to the feds. In Bioff's words: "He [Korshak] told me I better get myself organized for an alibi in the defense of my income taxes, because the information they had is that Joe is talking; that Joe would be a good victim, for he is known as the play boy of the industry and the politician of the industry; to dump it into his lap, and think in that direction." Then Ricca visited him and told him, just in case things didn't appear to be working out, about a coffee plantation in Mexico so that Bioff could consider taking it "on the lam."

The heat made Circella's IATSE position untenable. Late one night, Nitto called Browne to a meeting. Gioe delivered the labor leader to a lonely spot on a country road outside the city where Nitto was waiting. He instructed Browne that Circella was to resign from the union; his presence might prove a liability with all the newspapers digging around. Particularly, he was afraid Pegler might find that Circella was never a U.S. citizen and blow the whole thing open. But, he told Browne, Circella's resignation was in name only and he was still the mob's authority in the union.

Charlie Gioe delivered the news of Circella to Bioff. The prisoner protested that if Circella resigned, the game was up; he and Browne wanted to quit. Gioe reported Bioff's sentiment to the mob. A couple of days later, Gioe and Campagna went to the prison and huddled with Bioff within the sanctity of the prison chapel.

Campagna whispered to Bioff, "I understand from Charley that you told him you are going to resign. Is that right?"

"Yes sir."

"Well, anybody resigns, resigns feet first. You understand what that means?"

"I do." Bioff did not resign.

In a stroke reminiscent of the Scalise affair, Nitto used an IATSE convention that June to soothe Bioff. Because he put Circella on the shelf, the mob boss sent unknown face Gioe to the convention in Louisville to oversee his interests. Browne used the platform to defend convicts Bioff and ex-Vice President John Nick of St. Louis. Bioff, he declared, performed "the most remarkable job any man has ever done for labor against terrific odds." The studio unions, he noted, refused his resignation earlier and demanded his representation "even if he had to do it from his jail cell." Further, he advanced a resolution of appreciation for Bioff:

RESOLUTION NO. 3

Resolution of Commendation in Appreciation of Brother William Bioff's Services

WHEREAS, Brother William Bioff has been unmercifully persecuted by unscrupulous interests . . . has been attacked in an unfair manner. . . . [He] worked untiringly to promote peace and welfare of our International. . . .

BE IT FIRMLY RESOLVED, This District in Convention assembled . . . does hereby reaffirm its belief in the honesty and integrity of Brother William Bioff and

BE IT FURTHER RESOLVED That the secretary . . . is hereby instructed to present this resolution for the favorable consideration of the general convention and that a copy be forwarded to Brother William Bioff.

Respectfully submitted by: The Hollywood Locals of the IATSE

The heads of twenty-three locals attached their names to the resolution, which passed.

Browne proceeded to perfume the union's other convicts as well. John Nick, who resigned as first vice president after his racketeering conviction, was lauded by President Browne for his "faithful and capable service." Outside convention proceedings, Browne defended both Bioff and Circella as particularly efficient and good union men. Of Bioff, he said, "Simply because they dug up an eighteen-year-old misdemeanor doesn't mean Bioff is wrong now." Of Circella's troubles, they were twenty years ago: "He is a good union man." Browne indicated that Bioff would return to work after he was released, and back in the convention hall, delegates voted Browne to a fourth term as IATSE president.

Bioff evidently didn't endorse Browne's offer for reinstatement. In mid-September, just a couple of days before his release, Browne met Bioff to brief him on transportation and plans after his release. He brought along airline tickets for an out-of-town destination. For reasons never made clear by either man, the meeting disturbed Bioff to the point that he told Browne to leave. Browne arranged a meeting with Gioe at Circella's swank Colony Club on the North Side and shoved the airline tickets at Gioe, saying, "Here. You can deliver the tickets. I have had enough of this. I try to do the best I can, and the best I get is abuse for it." Gioe assured the labor leader that he would deliver the tickets. Gioe reflected further, much to Browne's amazement, "I have never cared much about this labor business. I told the Outfit time and time again it is no good. We are making plenty of money elsewhere. . . . We will probably all wind up in jail as result of it."

The *Herald-American's* September 21, 1940, headline declared, "'CZAR' BIOFF FREED." A large sedan entered prison grounds, and Bioff emerged in a neatly pressed, double-breasted green suit and polished tan shoes. He snarled at cameramen as he ducked into the auto. Then, as promised, he gave reporters his statement. He tossed out a half-dozen neatly typed pages announcing he had paid "his pound of flesh" and sped off.

24

CRISIS MANAGEMENT MOB STYLE

JOE'S ESTIMATION THAT THE MOB members would end up in jail because of labor racketeering seemed distant at the time, yet one by one that summer, the Outfit's racketeers were sent away or were, at the very least, under intense scrutiny. Scalise was indicted in April and convicted of grand larceny and forgery a week prior to Bioff's release; he was sentenced to ten to twenty years in prison. With Bioff's tax evasion case pending, Big Mike Carrozzo, czar of Chicago's hod carriers and street workers unions, caught the suspicious eye of Internal Revenue agents. They discovered expenditures since 1937 far beyond his estimated $12,000 annual income. Big Mike apparently purchased a number of farms totalling about 900 acres. In addition to dairy income, he had developed a keen interest in breeding thorough-bred horses, which received nothing but the best from Mike, who outfitted the farms with stylish barns and constructed a half-mile exercise track on one of the proper-ties.

In June, as agents were developing their case, the Justice Department indicted Carrozzo and nine associates for labor racketeering. A month later, agents slapped a tax lien on him for evading nearly a quarter of a million dollars in back taxes. Mike put up over $277,000 in securities as a release, then two weeks later died of natural causes, thus depriving Nitto of yet another veteran racketeering figure. One paper noted an immediate benefit: the price for paving a city street dropped between 15 and 25 percent. Another announced his death was expected to strengthen Nitto's position in labor rackets, for he would name Carrozzo's successor. On September 18, John Nick and Clyde Weston of St. Louis were found guilty on eleven of twelve racketeering counts, and each received five years in federal prison and a $10,000 fine.

—⚬⁄⁊⁄⚬—

With potential disaster nipping at Nitto's mob from the IATSE and BSEIU scandals, the most acute threat developed in 1940 from George McLane and his bartenders union. When McLane returned in January from his temporary mob-imposed exile, Murray Humphreys and Local 278 dictator Louis Romano called him to Gibby's Ogden Grill for a meeting. They explained there were a "great many complaints about him" and reiterated their warning: McLane could stay and collect his pay as long as he went along with the program. Apparently with McLane back in town, his remaining supporters in the union looked to him for a solution to Romano. Word of these hopes seeped back to Romano, who instantly called a union meeting. Someone, he said, was talking too much, according to his sources. To stamp out any problems, Romano fired all pro-McLane officers as well as McLane, naming as the new agent in his place Thomas Panton.

A few days later Romano received a phone call from someone who wanted to meet with him. The next day, he stood face-to-face with McLane's wife, Christine. The gutsy woman asked about the union meeting and the meaning of Romano firing her husband that way. Nitto's mobster abruptly informed her it was none of her business.

"This is my bread and butter," she pleaded.

"Take your husband and get out of town," came Romano's terse reply.

She pleaded further, saying there was her family for which she was responsible. She couldn't possibly leave her home and her mother behind.

Romano gruffly grilled her: Whom did she value more, her family or her husband? "If you know what's good for your whole family, you and your husband will get out of town," he told her. They would call him if they needed him, and that was the end of the conversation. McLane packed up and left for Hot Springs.

Within weeks, something went strangely amiss. Romano called McLane back, telling him he needed him because news people had noticed his absence and had begun speculating that he had been murdered. McLane returned briefly to show his face about town. Then, out of the blue, Romano was pulled in for police questioning. They wanted to know about his unions, but he stonily denied any association with Dan Stanton and Frank Nitto. He insisted he was merely a good union man.

First-rate union President Romano proceeded to send out letters to his 4,400-plus members announcing a new hospitalization plan. The agreement, he informed them, was with the American Hospital on Irving Park Road and would cost members $10 annually. The problem for members was that the union enforced the policy retroactively to the first of the year, meaning that members would be forced to pay for a quarter-year's worth of the plan and receive nothing. Someone alerted hospital officials about the plan, but since they had made no such agreement, they notified the state's attorney's office. Romano's reaction to the disclosure was, "I don't understand why newspapers or other outsiders are sticking their nose in our business, anyway."

Believing McLane was responsible for leaking the phony hospital plan to the press, Romano axed McLane from the union payroll. To head off any procedural protests, he and his cronies rammed through a new set of union bylaws giving Romano command over every aspect of union functions. Determined to recover his pay, if not his job, the gutsy McLane matched his move. Instead of filing a grievance within the union or the local joint council—where he knew he would lose a kanga-roo court—he filed a civil suit in Circuit Court. The next day's headlines ran with the story. "UNION CZARDOM BY CAPONE GANG," declared the *Tribune*, while the *Daily News* reported, "UNION LEADER DENIES CHARGE OF GANG RULE."

McLane's thirty-two-page petition, filed along with his brother Michael and brother-in-law William Salvatore (both tossed out by Romano as well), named Nitto, Ricca, Campagna, Humphreys, Nitto finance man Fred Evans, Romano, Thomas Panton, Romano secretary-treasurer appointee James Crowley, and a bevy of union stooges as defendants. Filing his appeal before Judge George Rush, his lawyer pleaded for an urgent injunction, arguing, "George McLane is the only man who stands between the Capone Syndicate and the looting of the union funds." McLane declared in writing Nitto's plan to not only take over the union and ravish its treas-ury but also use its members to push Syndicate brands of beer and alcohol as well as mob bottled water, peanuts, music boxes, and linen services. The phony hospital plan only represented the latest outrage, he said.

He spelled out Romano's rule over Local 278 and the entire joint council of fif-teen related unions managed by Danny Stanton. He said his appeal to the interna-tional was pointless because mobsters had successfully softened up the leadership team of Ed Flore recently with a shower of expensive gifts, including diamond rings. Romano had presented Flore's secretary-treasurer Hugo Ernst with a rich wristwatch at Circella's Colony Club. Two vice presidents had received glitzy baubles as well. Flore denied any knowledge of such gifts, but ever since Romano's election to the joint council, he had showered officers of the international union with gifts. One vice president was given a beautiful sapphire surrounded by five carats of diamonds, and another was given a diamond-studded platinum wristwatch. In return, at least one vice president now found it suitable to shower Romano with praise.

The suit brought by McLane triggered sharp criticism of authorities. If true, one press editorial wondered how it was, with state and federal liquor commissions in place, that Nitto's mob took over breweries and distributors. The editorialist also wondered what role the Chicago Federation of Labor had played as gangsters absorbed unions, asking, "And what was the Chicago Police Department doing?" He continued sardonically, "Did the phony bartenders slip them a Mickey Finn, too? Or was it a golden fizz on the house?"

For Nitto, who was already dealing with the Bioff and Scalise calamities, McLane proved to be the biggest wrench in his plans. McLane's injunction not only froze all union books and accounts and brought to light his grand scheme, but now the feds were back on the scene again—U.S. Attorney William J. Campbell and Internal Revenue agent Clarence Converse of the SIU announced plans to have a look. Converse said he would check gangster incomes for signs of looted money. Even normally lethargic State's Attorney Thomas Courtney was shocked enough to send Chief investigator Dan Gilbert to union offices where he arrested and served grand jury subpoenas on Romano, Crowley, and twelve other union men.

McLane testified the next day. Nitto and Humphreys were key figures, along with Ricca. The name of Joe Fusco, who studied the booze business in the Capone days, came to light as the mob man behind Gold Seal Liquors. Over time, Courtney came to suspect the mob had swindled the bartenders union of nearly a million dollars. When Courtney's men raided the union office, he learned federal agents had beaten him to the punch as they investigated Nitto's activities in relation to a suspected $1.5 million missing from Scalise's BSEIU as well.

McLane emerged from his heavily guarded, middle-class North Side home a couple of weeks later to return as business agent for the union. Escorted by police from the state's attorney's office to union offices on North Clark Street, McLane rolled up his shirtsleeves for a fresh start only find the office barren. Commenting on his first day back on the job, McLane said, "There's little for me to do, because I can't find anything to work with."

Nitto immediately started diplomatic damage control. The mob couldn't get close to McLane, so they called on his wife instead. Mrs. Romano set the lunch date at Heinrici's, the city's oldest restaurant situated in the heart of the theater district. At a quiet table, Mrs. McLane faced off with Louis Romano. The self-styled union man ordered her to influence her husband to drop the civil suit.

Curtly, the spunky lady shot back what he had told her before: the union was "none of her business."

Romano ordered her to listen up: "You better talk to your husband. You know that I'm getting the blame for all this!" Unless she did what he ordered, "we'll dirty him up as much as anyone can be dirtied up." The chiseled-faced thug then laid out a plan for the people her husband was to meet. When she refused, Romano stormed out.

At long last, it appeared McLane might get back to valid union work. In midsummer, rumors floated that Nitto planned to ditch the bartenders, as the glare was drawing too much attention to other mob operations. Stanton's collection of the associated waiters union was in Courtney's spotlight, and a recent South Side murder fueled police suspicions that Stanton had assumed or planned to take control of twenty-nine local painters unions. Courtney found it politically expedient to begin knocking over handbooks again.

Authorities put the net out for Nitto, Humphreys, Stanton, and Cicero mob figure Claude Maddox. Through lawyers, Nitto was said to have presented a proposal to McLane: Nitto would release control of the union by having Romano, Panton, and Crowley resign in exchange for peace. When asked about the proposal, McLane upped the ante, posing a serious problem for Nitto. McLane declared, "I have no intention of running out on State's Attorney Courtney or United States Attorney

Campbell. Mr. Courtney came to my assistance when the gang was threatening me with death. . . . Without his help and that of Mr. Campbell, I wouldn't have dared oppose the Nitti gang." In reply to the rumored Nitto offer, McLane said, "Any settlement, if there is one, will have to be satisfactory to Courtney and Campbell as well as to Judge Robert Dunne." Dunne then placed the union into receivership until the legal matters played out.

Reminiscent of the Prohibition gang wars, recent conditions spurred the Chicago Association of Commerce to team with President Bertram Cahn of the Chicago Crime Commission, Courtney, and Mayor Kelly to formulate a "stop Nitti" drive. Unavoidably, from this point on, Nitto—just as Capone had been near the end of his tenure—became a lightning rod for publicity. The suit brought Nitto's name and the mob to light after nearly a decade of operating largely under the radar. As Europe braced for war, foreign policy headlines kept Nitto's name pushed to the back pages.

<hr />

September opened poorly for Nitto's mob. The day after Matt Taylor died (on the sixth), a sworn statement he had made to State's Attorney Courtney a month earlier found its way into print. Though he did not name Nitto, his revelations shed more light on the local racketeering with which his mob was associated. Romano's name appeared at the very moment the bartenders scandal was coming under scrutiny. With the abundance of names connected to Local 66 headquarters in Chicago, Courtney had no choice but to pursue indictments against Scalise. Most significantly, Taylor shed further light on George Scalise's racketeering beyond what Dewey had shown in New York. When the trial opened, witnesses were asked about notations in certain books, and one mark led back to Chicago. The initials "F R" were followed by a diamond shape to indicate $400 a month payments for nothing to Frank Diamond, and Diamond was now in the spotlight. With Clyde Weston and John Nick convicted, Taylor's letter forced Courtney to bring indictments against not Nitto, whose group hoisted Scalise to the top, but rather Scalise for plundering union funds. Nothing became of those charges. Still, on September 14, Scalise was convicted, and he faced state and federal charges of income tax evasion as well.

After the verdict, Courtney said, "Racketeers and gangsters must be forced out of Chicago unions, and this statement gives us a powerful weapon to that end." This was the second gift horse received by Courtney, but then politics reared its ugly head with mud slinging—and Nitto's name was the sludge.

Running as the Republican candidate against Courtney for state's attorney was Cook County Superior Court Judge Oscar Nelson. Unfortunately, Taylor's affidavit named Nelson as a key figure in arranging the move of Local 66 into the BSEIU; further, allegations arose that Nelson claimed $70,000 a year as the legal representative for Alterie's old janitors union. At the Scalise trial, at least four witnesses, backed by union transcripts, placed then-lawyer Nelson at the BSEIU meeting in which George Scalise was elected president of the BSEIU in 1937. Worse yet, witnesses claimed it was Nelson who presented Scalise's name to the BSEIU board.

Candidate Nelson then chose a series of radio broadcasts illogically entitled, given the circumstance, "Hypocrisy in Public Office," to claim the court evidence presented had been "manufactured." Yes, Nelson said, he knew Scalise "slightly" because he had been in the labor business for about thirty years. He then attacked Courtney. "George Scalise," he asserted, "became a big-shot labor man during Courtney's term of office, but Mr. Courtney did not become disturbed until Tom Dewey grabbed him and convicted him." Because the union was headquartered in Chicago, he went on, it was Courtney's job to prosecute him, not Dewey's. A former Courtney assistant fired off a salvo that Courtney's "lack of courage and leadership" caused him not to prosecute tough criminals. The record, they noted, shows thousands of successful prosecutions of what they termed "poor boys," those without political protection, but what about the vicious gangsters? they asked.

The next night Nelson implied the ultimate in malfeasance, revealing to the public that Captain Dan Gilbert, chief investigator for Courtney's office, had shared the same hotel in Hot Springs, Arkansas, with gang boss Frank Nitto. Gilbert had supposedly stayed there the previous April when authorities were, Nelson said, seeking Nitto for questioning. Nelson pressed the unpleasant picture of Nitto and Gilbert as daily golfing companions at the resort. The charges were never substantiated, and Gilbert deflected them, noting that Nelson "made Scalise. . . . He cannot lie his way out of this." Besides Scalise, the record, he said, illustrated Nelson's friendship with Capone and henchman Dan Serritella, and to top it off, he said, there had been no manhunt for Nitto in the first place. Nelson lost the election.

⸻⟨⦿⟩⸻

Exposés via political chatter notwithstanding, catastrophe threatened Nitto through McLane, his brother Michael, William Salvatore, and even McLane's wife, Christine, when they talked to the grand jury. Nitto worked to head off disaster. A stenographic record of a wiretapped phone conversation of Murray Humphreys's years later provides an insight into Nitto's leadership at such a critical period. Advising an associate about a crisis at the time, Humphreys relays a bit of historic advice: "If a —— general is out in the field with an army, and he's getting the —— beat out of him, he has to throw caution to the wind and try stuff; he can't just stand there and get shot down. . . . If we think we're gonna get beat anyhow, we have to take a chance."

The first effort to "try stuff" collapsed miserably when one juror made for the state's attorney's office to report what became the October 1, 1940, headline for the *Daily News*: "GANG PLOT ON GRAND JURY BARED." The juror swore he had received an anonymous threatening phone call telling him to vote a "no bill" in the bartenders racket case. The next evening, he received a call from a friend, a former co-worker, asking him to do the same. The friend claimed to be intervening for an acquaintance who was interested in the case. "But I'm only one person in twenty-three. What can I do about it?" the juror asked. "They got others," he was assured. "There are other connections that have been taken care of." Besides, his friend announced, the whole matter was simply a political fight, and "it would do you some good with the bartenders union" if it turned out that way. The juror was told to keep everything hush-

hush because "there will be no kickback."

The next day, the grand jury recommended that Nitto and the heart of the mob—Ricca, Campagna, and Humphreys—be indicted on four counts of conspiracy. Fred Evans, who was evolving into the gang's "financial genius," received the same indictment, as did Romano and union officer Thomas Panton. A judge issued arrest warrants and set bonds at $3,500 apiece. Romano and Panton came in, made bond, and were released. For the mob men, however, there would be no disgrace of a highly public arrest. Labor racketeer Murray Humphreys led the way, making "overtures" to surrender through his attorney. A day later, the dapper, fully suited Welshman greeted deputy sheriffs by appointment at Twenty-sixth and Kedzie. Quickly escorted to the criminal courts building and fingerprinted, Humphreys made bail and walked.

Frank Nitto made his appointment for the morning of October 9. Impeccably dressed in deep blue, the undersized gang leader met Chief Deputy Sheriff Joseph Lelivelt at the corner of Harlem and Chicago avenues in the suburb of Oak Park. Nitto was fingerprinted, and when asked his address, he gave the Ronga residence at 1208 McAllister. When asked his occupation, Nitto answered "salesman." Then in a remarkable display of humor given the circumstance, he laughed, "But don't ask me what I sell." Nitto remained affable throughout several hours of questioning at the state's attorney's office then left. When Fred Evans appeared at the state's attorney's office on the tenth, it left only Ricca and Campagna at large.

After the indictments, Bertram Cahn, president of the Chicago Crime Commission and spokesman for the Chicago Association of Commerce, declared, "Our greatest peril is in the indifference and complacency with which we look on the alliance of between politics and crime. If we tolerate deals between cheap politicians and racketeers, we are permitting our government to begin rotting." Worth noting, he said, was the Nitto character Lawrence Mangano and his rule over the West Side and maybe the North Side as well. Claude Maddox, according to Cahn, was another higher-up in the gang who was worth watching since he was rumored to be the power in bartenders Local 450 in Cicero. Authorities should have heeded Cahn's advice.

Nitto appeared in court on October 11 and went from the amiable character he had been only a couple of days before to snarling at the press photographers. The case was continued to the twenty-eighth. When he reappeared with his attorney, they were told the conspiracy trial was set for November 18. The pair quickly departed, Nitto not saying a word and his lawyer explaining only that the gang leader was suffering from ulcers. The mood was equally glum behind the scenes. Humphreys later recalled to a friend that when the mob was strong, "and all of us guys get indicted . . . Nitti was hollering like hell that . . . we gotta break through. We broke through." There was no hollering this time.

The gang was fighting a battle on two fronts. Soon after the indictment, bartenders union receiver Roy Keehn ousted Thomas Panton and two Romano allies from the organization "for the good of the service." Keehn also asked the court to dismiss attorney Harold Levy as union attorney based on McLane's statements that

Levy directed McLane to turn the union over to the mob. The receiver then drafted a measure to replace Romano's self-serving plurality election rules with rules based on majority rule. Trouble faced Nitto in another court when McLane filed a civil suit against the same group already under indictment. The linchpin in all matters was McLane.

The mob's strategy became apparent, if not comical, in civil proceedings when Harold Levy caused a stir by fetching a psychiatrist to observe McLane on the stand. Outside the courtroom, he announced the doctor's observations to be the basis for a Nitto mob defense that "McLane is crazy and subject to delusions of persecution." Intimidated to err on the side of caution, the prosecution called in a pair of its own experts the following day. The legal hype went up a notch when Levy added two more experts to his team. A couple of days later, the strategy appeared to lose credibility when, at the height of McLane's testimony—when he said Nitto threatened to kill him if he didn't go along—one of Levy's psychiatrists stirred the courtroom with an arousing snore. Summoned to consciousness, the doctor bolted upright, adjusting his glasses to "study position." After another defense doctor publicly declared McLane "undoubtedly sane" and left the proceedings without fanfare, the effort to prove him crazy was no longer considered viable.

Evidence that the Nitto group planned an end run at least in the civil matter surfaced when Louis Romano wailed that his union cronies had betrayed him. The fuss started when Romano, still president of the union pending outcome of the civil suit, discovered handbills promoting candidates for union offices for an election in January 1941. Much to his mortification, the endorsement for president went to secretary-treasurer James Crowley. Oddly, heading the opposition to Crowley, but for reasons far different from Romano's, was George McLane. Speaking from experience, he dubbed Crowley nothing more than a "candidate of Frank 'the Enforcer' Nitti."

After examining Crowley's past, the state's attorney's office concurred. Nitto again tried floating, through intermediaries, a proposal to McLane (practically admitting guilt, he bargained with what he had left in the union): he guaranteed McLane's safety provided all current legal matters were quashed and also pledged McLane re-election as business agent to a five-year term should Crowley also be elected president. Defense attorneys presented the motion before the court. If not successful, they expected a trial by December 1, and they still faced an unpromising battle to push Crowley's bid through. Receiver Roy Keehn questioned Nitto's audacity in guaranteeing McLane's election, saying he, Keehn, was there to purge the union of gangsters. He would have none of this Nitto deal; he wanted a genuine union election. The state's attorney's office also proclaimed the need for fair elections, as did a sizeable portion of union membership.

November 1940 marked a period in Nitto's life from which the fifty-four-year-old gang boss never recovered fully. Pressure from the year's close calls with Bioff and Scalise and now the legal entanglement with McLane induced ulcers, apparently sidelining Nitto with hospital stays or home care (giving rise to the need for Ricca and Campagna to remain at large to run mob operations). The first week of the month, a serious heart ailment sent Nitto to Presbyterian Hospital for treatment. At least Nitto could rely on father-in-law Dr. Gaetano Ronga to arrange for the best medical care.

As Nitto lay in a hospital bed, on or about the eleventh of the month, his young wife Anna fell ill in Miami and returned to Chicago. She had long preferred to spend most of her time at the couple's Di Lido Island home near Miami, where she enjoyed the nightclub circuit with friends. For a year, she had suffered from periodic spasms of abdominal discomfort, and when she was transported to nearby Mercy Hospital after her return to Chicago, tests confirmed acute ulcerative colitis, an inflammation of the large intestine and an ailment for which few curative medical treatments existed at the time—especially if the illness was in an advanced stage. Confined to his own bed, Nitto monitored her condition, which seemed to change little. Sunday, November 17, gave reason for hope as she rallied slightly, but suddenly during the following night, her condition deteriorated. Alarmed, Nitto was released early that morning to be at his wife's bedside, and Reverend Matthew Canning arrived to administer last rites. With her husband at side, Anna Theresa Nitto slipped away at 11:35 a.m. at the age of thirty-eight.

Friday dawned cloudy, and a throng of ordinary citizens, police characters, and politicians came to the funeral service at St. Charles Borromeo's Church on the West Side. Nitto, a pale figure in black, arrived wearing spectacles and accompanied by his six-year-old son Joseph. At least sixteen carloads of flowers attended the funeral procession out Roosevelt Road to Mount Carmel Cemetery in the Far West suburb of Hillside. The centerpiece of the floral arrangements was an enormous heart made of orchids.

The following Monday, a pale Nitto arrived in court to plead innocent to the McLane charges. A conviction on the most serious felony charges carried a potential sentence of between one day and five years in prison and a $5,000 fine. On the misdemeanor charges, the group faced up to one year in jail. No longer clothed in the rich, tasteful colors of previous appearances, Nitto was still dressed in black and looked "sick." After half an hour, the judge granted him leave. A reporter noted Nitto as "a wan figure" as he stepped to the bench. Jury selection proceeded without him, with talk from a close friend indicating Nitto's worsening health as the cause for his absence; the friend noted that Nitto probably wouldn't show his face in court until the actual introduction of evidence proceeded. Because he had not yet been served in McLane's civil suit, some thought he was playing tag with the sheriff's department.

Because State's Attorney Courtney was tied up in a bitter campaign against Oscar Nelson for the November election, he assigned to the McLane case two top assistants, Wilbert F. Crowley (no relation to defendant James Crowley) and William Crawford.

By the twenty-fifth, they had to reason to appear uneasy: McLane petitioned to remove the receivership, saying he had made "peace" with his unions foes. As for his other enemies, he had no worries since Keehn had ousted them. Worse yet for the prosecution, William Salvatore had disappeared the week before, as had principal union bookkeeper Margaret Meyers. Both were expected to be key witnesses in the case. Still, the prosecution felt McLane's testimony was enough to gain a conviction.

One report had Nitto seriously ill and holed up in a North Side apartment being tended by private medical staff when business agent McLane took the stand on the twenty-ninth. Crawford began the routine questioning for the state's case.

Q: "Your name?"

A: "George B. McLane."

Q: "Your age?"

A: "Fifty-two."

Q: "Your address?"

A: "Twenty-nine eleven Lunt Avenue."

Q: "What is your wife's name?" continued Crawford.

A: "I'll have to refuse to answer that on the grounds that it might incriminate me."

The prosecuting team exchanged puzzled looks as Crawford asked McLane whether he knew Nitto, Humphreys, Romano, and the others. No answer. Crawford continued, asking if McLane had not previously testified about threats made by the men. Again, McLane gave no answer. Crawford pressed about Romano's "dirtied up" comments relayed by his wife. Still nothing from the defendant; he simply hung his head even as the state's attorneys threatened him with contempt charges. Humphreys, Romano, and company broke into grins "a mile wide," as described by one of the state's attorneys.

Presiding Judge John Bolton put off until Monday morning a review of whether non-defendant McLane was within his constitutional rights to invoke the Fifth Amendment. The state's attorney would give him time to reconsider his position. Asked about the sudden silence of his client, McLane's lawyer acknowledged his client's fear of Nitto and what might happen to him. Rumors had indeed floated that McLane and/or his wife might be kidnapped if he talked. He assured the press that he felt his client "had overcome nine-tenths of his fear. If the gang's power does not head him off," his attorney continued, "he will tell the truth on Monday."

Monday also happened to be the last day for nominations of union officers to run in the upcoming election. If McLane was to take up Nitto's offer made weeks before, he could stall no longer. Speculation had the McLane faction of the union patching up differences with the Crowley faction. This presaged the underlying feeling McLane would not testify as his lawyer expected.

He did not. Throughout the ordeal, McLane had received around-the-clock protection from the state's attorney's office with two policemen assigned to him on eight-hour shifts. They made no difference. Nitto's gang broke through.

According to chief investigator Dan Gilbert later, Chicago police Sergeant William Miller, who was assigned to guard McLane, was a personal friend of the union man. One evening, the pair announced to the others on guard detail at the McLane house that they were going to the corner for a newspaper. Instead, they went to Cicero to meet mob man Claude Maddox. The gangster again outlined the plan to re-elect McLane if he would refuse to testify against Nitto and the other mob men.

Next, according to information collected by the FBI, Murray Humphreys outlined the legal strategy, covering all the bases. The racketeer successfully approached someone on the prosecution staff, McLane, and a member of the jury. McLane, Humphreys said, would continue to complain about Nitto, et al., but when he was sworn in and placed on the stand, he would refuse to testify. The motion for a directed verdict for acquittal would be introduced. At the very least, if the case went to the jury, they had that fixed as well. After being sworn in, the strategy went, McLane would be placed in "jeopardy" and thus the case could not be retried.

When the trial reconvened Monday morning, McLane again refused to give evidence, prompting an appeal by the prosecutor Crowley to Criminal Court Judge Bolton. The judge ruled he could not prevent McLane from standing on his constitutional right of self-incrimination. "Under the law," Bolton said, "he [McLane] is the best judge of whether certain testimony might incriminate him." Crowley announced, "That's our case. The state rests." Nitto's attorney moved for a directed verdict of not guilty, which the judge promptly granted.

Outside court, McLane exhaled in relief. He had been nominated for business agent at the union meeting the previous night. He told the press, "Now I can campaign for re-election as union business agent. Peace is wonderful."

The irony of the big picture was duly noted by one reporter: "Frank 'the Enforcer' Nitti, muscle genius of the old Capone mob, is free to return to the exercise of his genius as result of a pass given him in the Criminal Court yesterday within a couple of hours of the time State's Attorney Thomas J. Courtney was inducted for a third term amid as many flowers as they used to send to gangsters funerals." Bertram Cahn of the Chicago Crime Commission looked further: "The situation has a side to it that is most dangerous. . . . In this instance the parties involved took advantage of the situation to get out of court. Apparently McLane and Nitti and others settled their differences privately, and made peace, because they want to continue to operate as they have in the past." The *Chicago Daily Tribune* announced the next day in an editorial entitled "The Nitti Case" that the dismissal was "a danger signal to the decent people of Chicago. It is a signal that a criminal gang has proved itself more powerful than the law enforcement agencies of the community." Westbrook Pegler jumped on the subject as well, arguing that the fact that Nitti and clan walked away from the charges proved nothing had changed: McLane did not recant his revelations, and unionism was still at risk.

McLane soon found out the Nitto mob was hardly up to its end of the bargain. Forty members crowded the field for the January 6 election of twelve union officers (only three were paying positions), including five for McLane's business agent position. McLane now enjoyed the luxury of being promoted along with former McLane foe and the odds-on favorite for President, James Crowley (who was still named on McLane's civil suit). Shortly before Christmas, one of McLane's opponents dropped out, admitting he made a deal with McLane who offered to take care of him after the election. A few nights later, another candidate suddenly packed up his wife and children and left his apartment, explaining only that he was "going out of town for a while." The state's attorney's office no doubt held the Nitto gang responsible for his flight.

One more McLane opponent mysteriously dropped out by year's end, leaving him an apparent cinch in a race facing only a relatively new, unemployed bartender named Thomas McElligott. The election was held in the courtroom of Judge Robert Dunne under the eye of receiver Keehn. Early returns worried McLane allies when vote numbers suggested Crowley supporters refrained from wholeheartedly supporting the McLane portion of the ticket. By 2:30 in the morning, it became apparent McLane's chances of election were dimming, and in fact, the numbers the next day showed a disappointing loss by nearly a two-to-one margin to a virtual unknown. McLane's supporters later discovered McElligott was a secret friend of supposed McLane ally and suspected Nitto puppet President-elect James Crowley.

The final comment on the election was delivered by Dan Gilbert of the state's attorney's office. "The Nitti mob still is in control of the union," he acknowledged, "but I'm glad to see McLane defeated. McLane was a traitor to the forces of good government and . . . threw away his chance to clean up the union."

25

PERSONAL DECLINE

RONICALLY, ILLUMINATION OF THE GANG boss who had practiced and preached the *sub rosa* operating theory coincided with his personal deterioration. The McLane case awakened the public, confirming Frank Nitto as gang boss of Chicago, and illustrated just how powerful the gang under his direction had become after many supposed it impotent following Capone's departure. Gang boss Nitto, still holed up and plagued by reported heart ailments, missed the courtroom celebration, and immediate care of son Joseph fell more on widower Nitto's shoulders. Much like Capone in his later days as gang boss, Nitto, with the light now shed on him, became ever more the whipping boy for Chicago's ills.

Soon after the McLane debacle, the *Daily News* headlined newly discovered bogeyman Frank Nitto with an injunction from the police commissioner: "DRIVE NITTI FROM GAMING: ALLMAN." Long after the fact, they proclaimed Nitto had recently added gambling to his underworld résumé when Police Commissioner James Allman announced Nitto, Dan Stanton, and other "Capone-era" mobsters as the predominant figures in the racket. "I want every book in the city closed," he ordered, "and kept closed."

Sheriff "Blind Tom" O'Brien was forced into action as well because the whole gambling matter came as a result, not of local will to discourage gambling, but rather from an injunction obtained by the Illinois attorney general in a downstate Belleville

363

court to close gambling statewide. He marked an estimated 1,380 betting parlors would be closed in Cook County alone. Among those to be held in contempt of court if those places remained open: Harry Levin, Harry Guzik (Jake's brother), Charlie Fischetti and his brothers, Martin Guilfoyle, as well as old gambling hand from the 1920s James Mondi. Two state senators, one mob designate Dan Serritella, made the listing by virtue of his scratch sheet business. Even the corporate telegraph and telephone companies Western Union and AT&T were named for ostensibly supplying a service to illegal businesses. Of course at the top of the list—"the main beneficiary" according to one source—was Frank Nitto of 1208 McAllister Place.

When a reporter visited a sampling of known Loop parlors, he found them still standing room only. The announcement scarcely bothered bookies on the street either. "This will blow over," one declared. "Everyone knows that, so they're all operating." Another lay bare what he plainly suspected the heart of the matter: "The Democrats just don't want to give the Republicans a chance at this money." A few days passed and local papers counted only thirty-four summonses served by the Cook County sheriff. Pressed to explain how his law enforcement arm could find barely a handful of book joints, O'Brien termed the original state estimate as "phony."

Though Courtney thought the injunction idea "a fine weapon," it was two months before he publicly announced his own war on gambling. The *Daily News*'s February 5, 1941, headline announced: "COURTNEY TELLS AIM: DESTROY NITTI EMPIRE." Courtney maintained, "It is a matter of great public safety that Nitti be stopped from carrying on his illicit gambling activities." In the fight, he announced, "I'm with Commissioner Allman one hundred percent."

Handbook raids commenced, but the drive lapsed into inertia after three months. Calls for Nitto's ouster resonated from the Chicago Crime Commission, encouraging Courtney and the law to drive out the hoodlums. Commission President Bertram Cahn had earlier pronounced Frank Nitto as "the outstanding character of the racketeers and gangsters in Chicago." Police raids rekindled for another brief show in the Loop before sputtering out for the summer.

Skeptics then suggested the real reason behind the half-hearted crackdown was that another effort was being made in the Illinois legislature to legalize handbooks: the crackdown might be simply a political ploy to pass the bill, if in fact Nitto and the mob were booted out of the business (or at least the law gave the appearance of such). State budgets were tight, and the bill promised to alleviate some stress with new taxes. Previously, even officials of mob-infested Cicero considered enforcing a $5 annual tax on vending machines, a lucrative mob business in the county. Talk also reverberated about a new criminal-political setup to control the business since go-between Skidmore was heading to prison for tax evasion. Even Commissioner Allman retreated on his declaration some months before declaring, "It looks like Nitti is heir apparent to Capone."

Lack of apparent will by local law enforcement to enforce gambling laws was not Chicago's only problem. Judicial leniency came under fire from the Chicago Crime Commission and the state's attorney. Courtney noted the release of 158 bettors after a raid on a particularly pricey handbook in the Hamilton Hotel, even after a police captain had testified to the nuisance—the same joint had been raided at least two dozen times in the past year. Said Courtney: "No one is trying to unduly prosecute these persons who were arrested in the handbooks. The police department is not fighting them. It is fighting Nitti." With this type of adjudication of evidence, he wondered "what chance have the police or the people?"

Elmer Williams in his March issue of *Lightnin'* thought that if Nitto could be eliminated from Chicago, the city might yet be able to reclaim its fair name. Cynical to the end, he held out little hope; he prophesied it might take another ten or fifteen years at the current rate.

A Cruel Joke
A notorious nuisance named Nitti
Has battered for years on our city.
Our "Crime Fighters" say
They will chase him away.
Those fellows are certainly witty.

Williams asserted that the average citizen surely wondered why it was that the great forces of Chicago city and Cook County law enforcement, combined with powerful business interests, had, in all these years, been unable to take out "one little hoodlum."

He had caustically railed officials about Nitto since last summer's Carrozzo and Scalise fiascos before lumping some of the city and county's highest law enforcement figures into the scatterbrain category in a piece entitled "Nitti and The Nit Wits." It was particularly aimed at Courtney, as an example, he said. When he appealed to the Chicago Association of Commerce to help the plundered serfs of these regimes, a spokesperson answered, "We are cooperating with officials." Replied Williams, "God save us! The officials are in the racket with hoodlums." Williams wondered why the commerce association didn't notice that Tom Courtney's cousin had won a million-dollar asphalt contract with the city even though he didn't have an asphalt plant. Did they not know that Carrozzo had arranged the deal? He supplemented his contentions on another page, noting Courtney's inaction on the Scalise affair for nearly five months after its discovery by Thomas Dewey.

Now in the spring of 1941, in one of his last issues, Williams lashed out at Courtney's latest gambling-smashing effort, wondering who protects gambling in Chicago when the operations are exposed but no charges are filed. He recalled that Courtney's raids in 1938 were turned strictly to "fact-finding expeditions" when two important mob figures were arrested but not charged. Currently, only Nitto's highly visible Loop handbooks were being targeted, with the same results. Yet what about the numerous gambling dens and books in other districts run by the Democratic precinct captains? When Courtney and company prepared their list of targets, he continued, did they conveniently overlook those targets as well as the black policy rackets?

Williams noted:

AN OLD ROYAL CUSTOM
Nitti, Chicago's Whipping Boy

He explained that, in old Europe, a whipping boy was kept handy when the prince deserved physical punishment. Chicago, Williams thought, had practiced the same tradition for the past few years: "For a long time Al Capone was whipping boy for Chicago officials. Now it is Al's cousin [sic], Frank 'the Enforcer' Nitti. . . . When our professional 'crime fighters' are at a loss to explain the protected gambling or other rackets, they trot out Nitti, the whipping boy."

The summer droned on with Nitto appearing occasionally in the local papers. *Chicago Tribune* writer Lloyd Wendt penned a month-long weekend series, "The Men Who Prey on Labor," festooned with pictures of Nitto, Bioff, Browne, Romano, Scalise, and Caldwell. "CAPONE'S COHORTS CARRY ON," screamed the headline on the final full-page exposé.

In August, Nitto's handbooks were once again raided in the Loop, this time compliments of the county highway police on their first such foray into the city in perhaps forty years. A few days later, a *Tribune* reporter happened into the fashionable International Room of the Drake Hotel. Dining together were a chief from the county police and convicted (though out on appeal) gambling king Billy Skidmore, and the reporter snapped a picture. The chief resigned, and the crusade against Nitto's handbooks ceased.

Williams's lashing of Courtney for inaction proved at least partly true in 1941. One incident would have proved fatal to the mob if it hadn't been for Courtney, and this time, Courtney could not blame disobliging judicial conduct. Jake Guzik, the mob's money and connection guy for Loop gambling, had ensconced himself in a fashionable North Shore hotel as "Mr. Goodman." Neighbors noticed Goodman's work hours and the high number of nightly visitors he received, and one nosy couple asked the doorman one night about a particularly imposing character arriving out front. "He's a bigger gangster than your neighbor," he informed them. Later they discovered through the loose-lipped doorman that Goodman was actually Jake Guzik.

The couple left for a two-week vacation in September, and while they were away, management promised to refurbish their rooms. When the couple returned, they found the workers still at the job. Hotel management apologized for the delay and offered the old Goodman apartment as temporary lodging, Guzik having given up his lease in the interim. The wife seldom cooked, but one day decided to warm a coffee cake. When she opened the oven door, she found five yellow and one white loose-leaf ledger sheets rolled together and held tight by a rubber band. She notified the well-informed doorman in the event he knew how to locate the owner, and shortly thereafter, a stranger telephoned to offer $500 for the sheets.

In the interim, she bumped into a *Tribune* reporter and related the strange occurrence. He immediately persuaded her to turn the papers over to the newspaper for an exclusive story.

They revealed another headache for Nitto: the balance sheets turned over to the *Tribune* represented gambling business outside the city. Sheet one listed territorial collections of slots and gambling houses mainly from the suburbs, with Cicero, Chicago Heights, Blue Island, Melrose Park, and Morton Grove among those named. The second sheet listed payout to mob operators, an interesting find in that it attested to the Nitto gang's efforts to bring many remnants of the old Prohibition gangs into the fold. Vincent McErlane, brother of deceased killer Frank and an old Saltis hand, ran gambling near Palos Heights. Leo Mongoven ran part of the south county, with Marty Guilfoyle still managing the northwest. Sheet three provided the inclusive profit-loss statement. Number four listed capital expenses such as new slots or roulette wheels. The fifth sheet was a total recap sheet. The juiciest find was the last, a "kick out" or payoff sheet, to suburban officials. In all, it appeared the mob netted about $2.6 million a year from suburban operations. For a nearly a week, the revelation dominated the *Tribune's* pages.

Bertram Cahn called the news "astounding." He continued, "All are guilty of conspiracy. The proof seems to be there." He added, "State's Attorney Courtney can indict officers who permitted the laws to be violated and the slot-machine racketeers, too." The officer on whom the responsibility fell, Sheriff "Blind Tom" O'Brien, expressed astonishment when asked about the slots—he knew of no such things, he said.

Village officials of those suburbs named in the documents expressed surprise that such mischief went on inside their borders. The mayor of Melrose Park stood side by side with his police chief, saying, "Neither of us ever got a penny from any slot-machine syndicate." When they were asked why not, they said, "We don't pay attention to the machines because we have other duties we think are more important." The police chief of Franklin Park to the northwest proposed, "I am sure there are no slot machines in this vicinity now." That's because, he said, he leaves those matters to the state's attorney.

When the Chicago Crime Commission sent out investigators, they found Cicero to be the most notorious berg. Three complete casinos were located along one block of Roosevelt Road. At 2131 Cicero Avenue, in the old Ship gambling house, the first floor had been converted to a dance hall, while the second floor housed the Rock Garden Club, the most expensive and perhaps the most extensive gambling joint in Cicero. On one occasion a commission observer reported sheer impudence. While at the Rock Garden Club, a hundred or so patrons were told to go upstairs "for a few minutes" the manager said, until raiders left. He later discovered it was a fake sheriff's raid. They came in, looked around, left the gaming apparatus intact, and left. Bertram Cahn commented "These criminals seem so certain of protection they dare anything." He clarified the commission's stance: of gambling they would not preach from the pulpit, but they were concerned that an unchecked gambling syndicate could corrupt government.

The *Tribune* handed the documents over to State's Attorney Courtney "so that the full power of the law" might be brought to bear on county-wide grafters and gamblers. Courtney professed eagerness to punish any named individuals so that "the evil rule of the Guzik-Nitti gang may be broken." He shammed on, "I have fought Syndicate gambling and the gang leaders throughout my tenure in the state's attorney's office. I'm going to keep on fighting these gangsters. These papers may prove of great help." Courtney assigned Gilbert to dig up evidence, while he went before the grand jury to seek a "John Doe" docket and subpoenas for a case he trumpeted that may become famous as "the beginning of the end of a twenty-year reign by the Capone-Guzik gang." With the goods in hand, expectations were indeed high. Courtney's sermon turned out to be empty blabber, for after a week, the whole matter disappeared from public view with nothing accomplished. Chalk up another campaign to political expediency.

If anything, the episode served to take a little heat off Nitto, if in name only, and add to the historical gobbledygook. If only to hype sales, one paper headlined, "JAKE GUZIK IS NO. 1,"speculating that Nitto's poor health had caused the gang leader to abdicate. In the dark about the true extent of mob affairs, a week later a writer haphazardly crowned Guzik the new boss succeeding Capone and Nitto.

⎯⎯◦⁄◦⁄◦⎯⎯

Nitto appeared anxious to retrieve cash assets. The troubled gang boss divested himself of traumatic reminders. After the death of wife Anna, he distributed many of her valuable possessions, some through business associates in Florida, according to one account. While there in the spring of 1941, he arranged the sale of the Di Lido Island home and properties also, perhaps with the future of son Joseph in mind. On March 19, he sold all, including the home furnishings, for $45,000. Nitto also provided job security for his gardener, stipulating that the buyer keep him employed at $12 a week. The signatory was Lorraine Wills, wife of Nitto labor thug Max Caldwell. Nitto's associate received a special agreement stipulating monthly payments to Nitto until one-third was paid, then a warrant deed would be issued. If there was a default of thirty days, Nitto would take back the property.

Three weeks later, longtime physician and former Nitto father-in-law Dr. Gaetano Ronga, age sixty-six, suffered a fatal heart attack at his home at 1208 Lexington. Through all this adversity, Nitto attended to business, though perhaps the business was a bit more personal. Another instance of business seemed to indicate a retrieval of debts preparing for something unknown.

Pete Clifford, affectionately known as Petey to his friends, an entertainer and piano player, owned a piece of the Paddock Club in Miami Beach. On May 23, Clifford received an urgent phone call from a woman who asked to meet him at a spot on Jefferson Avenue. When Clifford curbed his car, a large black Buick pulled alongside and someone reached out and pumped five .38-caliber slugs into him, killing him instantly. Coincidentally, a house very close by happened to be a Guzik home.

One gang source reported Nitto found his wife Anna was having an affair with the entertainer. A longtime resident who frequented the area and knew the club well reported Anna was a frequent patron of the Paddock but that she usually left with a friend. Sometimes Petey would drive her to Di Lido Island, but "she wasn't looking," were his words. Investigations later showed a Clifford debt to Nitto for $30,000. Unwilling or unable to pay, any suspicions of an affair only supplemented the motive to kill him. The official suspect, though it was never proven, was Sam "Golf Bag" Hunt.

—⚜—

Nitto's mob still pushed Hollywood—business as usual on that front. Willie Bioff returned to the West Coast on IATSE business, cloaked by Browne's assertion that he represented a "valuable asset" to the union. The first order of business was the expiration of the IATSE Basic Agreement with the studios. Studio negotiator Pat Casey called for a renewal of the agreement, but Bioff, back in bully form, refused, pointing out that the producers still owed him $400,000 per the last agreement. Until they paid up, there would be no discussion and nothing but "a lot of trouble."

Since the first discovery of the $100,000, the U.S. Treasury assigned crack agent Alf Oftedal to look into the matter. Unfortunately, as SIU chief Elmer Irey recalled, Oftedal reported a weak case that might only prove to embarrass Joe Schenck. Probing beyond that single transaction with Bioff, however, showed, as Irey later said, "Joe was an out-and-out tax cheat" via the typical phony deductions and stock transactions for a number of years. In New York, they turned the evidence over to U.S. Attorney Matt Correa and his young assistant Boris Kostelanetz. Brother of composer Andre Kostelanetz, Boris started as number-cruncher for Price-Waterhouse before he was asked to assist the U.S. attorney's office. Little did he know the ride he was in for.

A matter of grave concern for Nitto's bunch, in June 1940 with Bioff already under indictment, Correa and Kostelanetz obtained indictments of Schenck and his bookkeeper for conspiracy to evade more than $400,000 in taxes. In addition, they charged Schenck with making false statements in regard to the Bioff transaction. When the trial convened in March 1941, Schenck at least cleared up the matter of the Bioff transaction, but limited cooperation served no good. He was found guilty and sentenced to an unexpectedly harsh term of three years in prison and a $20,000 fine. In short time, Irey remembered, the fifty-nine-year-old chairman of the board at Twentieth Century Fox Film Corporation sent for Correa and Kostelanetz, saying, "I'll talk gentlemen. I don't want to spend three years in jail."

Correa brought Schenck before the grand jury in New York to investigate his IATSE dealings. As a rule, the tax conviction of Schenck would have brought to a conclusion any further involvement of the Treasury Department and Irey's SIU—racketeering fell under the jurisdiction of the J. Edgar Hoover's FBI. However, after finishing the investigation of John Nick and Clyde Weston in St. Louis, the FBI closed its files, and a new request to investigate was turned away by Hoover. Now with the world at war, even without the United States, Hoover claimed his department was short of manpower coping with Japanese and German spies.

On May 19, Bioff probably thought he caught a break of his life when the pending California tax evasion case against him was postponed. The prosecution did not object when Bioff's attorneys implored his industry service was indispensable to the national defense for assisting in the "preparation of a certain film which was being prepared for the United States Army." A day later, Bioff received a troubling phone call from Johnny Rosselli: the suave gangster, along with many Hollywood producers, had been called to testify before the grand jury in New York (the feds were not aware of Rosselli's involvement at the time). He informed Bioff that "everybody is talking here, there is going to be a lot of trouble, all of the people you have done business with have squawked. . . . So conduct yourself accordingly." Rosselli set up a meeting to brief Bioff on his testimony.

On May 23, the New York grand jury returned indictments of both Bioff and IATSE President George Browne for two counts of racketeering and one count of conspiracy. If convicted, they faced a maximum of ten years in prison and a $10,000 fine on each count.

When Rosselli arrived back on the coast, he drove to Bioff's ranch home, where, in the piny den, Rosselli briefed him on his grand jury testimony, concentrating on the when, where, and how about Bioff—for most of this, Rosselli had lied. The key, he said, was that Bioff understood what Rosselli said so that he could testify to the same information and not cause a perjury indictment against Rosselli.

Bioff's phone rang a day later. It was mob lawyer Sydney Korshak in Chicago. He was flying west to meet him to begin arranging his defense. When they met at the Ambassador Hotel, Korshak asked what he knew of the indictments.

"All I know about them at this time," the thug replied, "is what I have read in the newspapers."

"Well, are you prepared with your defense?"

"No, not altogether."

Korshak laid out the line of attack, saying, " Well, Joe will be the next victim." He explained to Bioff that he had seen the Schenck tax trial transcripts. The government, he believed, left enough equivocation—too many unaccounted Schenck financial transactions—to allow Bioff to say he gave the extortion money to Schenck. Their reason would be that Schenck, as the leader of the industry, was taking it as a slush fund to fix things in Washington, D.C.

Bioff surrendered in California and quickly made $25,000 bail with a promise to appear in federal court in New York. On the way out east, he stopped into Chicago and met Paul Ricca and Charlie Gioe in Bioff's hotel room. Ricca asked about his defense, and Willie explained the scheme to pin the affair on Schenck. Expressing his misgivings that Bioff "didn't have a chance in New York," Ricca suggested he abscond.

"Well, I have enough time for that. If I do get convicted," Bioff told Ricca with an air of confidence, "I am sure I will get bond on appeal . . . and think of it in that direction." Ricca unenthusiastically endorsed Bioff's plan and reminded him that if he wanted to run, the organization had a coffee plantation in Mexico. Eventually, Ricca assured him, they would smooth out the indictment and he could return.

Privately, the mob wasn't so sure about their man Bioff going to New York. After George Browne surrendered and made bail, he, too, went to Chicago. The mob ordered him to meet Charlie Gioe in Antioch, a small Illinois town hugging the Wisconsin border. Gioe outlined his defense and offered to put lawyers at his disposal. Maloy's old Local 110 under mob domination approved financial support for Browne as well.

Gioe then got to the point. "What I am wondering though is about Willie. Do you think in this matter Bioff will stand up or do you think that he will squawk?"

Browne answered, "I would not know that. You people know him better than I do, and I would not care to pass that opinion on it."

———— ❧❧❧ ————

A local victory for one union's rank-and-file that summer unraveled Nitto's business web further. In early June, about 600 employees of Chicago's Hillman's grocery stores, enslaved by Max Caldwell's Local 1248, met secretly to plan revolt against the dictatorship of Nitto's labor agent. At a follow-up meeting, the number ballooned to about 1,000 as employees from area A&P and National Tea stores joined in. The revolt was at least partially spurred when, a few months earlier, Caldwell's goons slugged members of a rival union, including several middle-aged women, who were attempting to work stores organized by Caldwell. Angered as well by the apparent lack of substantial benefits for which they had long paid heavy union dues and perhaps emboldened by McLane's civil suit against gangsters, the insurgents hired a lawyer of their own and filed for an accounting of unions funds. They notified American Federation of Labor President William Green they would no longer recognize Caldwell as their representative and intended to form their own union.

To the court and state's attorney, the revolting employees divulged Caldwell's tactics. Part-time workers earning as little as $2.34 a day were forced to pay annual initiation fees of $25 along with $2 a month in union dues. All members were forced to buy the union publication *Over the Counter* at the $2 yearly subscription rate. Along the way, they were also coerced to buy fundraiser tickets at $2 apiece. When asked about union elections, one employee recited the usual procedure: " I would receive postcards on Monday notifying me of an election to be held on Sunday (the day passed)." Employees later promoted to store managers related how, even though they were no longer eligible for union membership, Caldwell forced them to pay dues to maintain their good health. store owners complained that if, even by chance, employees opted out of the union, Caldwell forced them (the store owners) to pay their monthly union dues in order to avoid vandalism and ugly harassments of customers.

By mid-summer, Nitto's name was splashed over the case as the master of Caldwell's leash and by the disclosure of Caldwell's rags to riches story. His checkered past included a sentence for bootlegging in Indiana (not served), ties to the old Capone mob, and several arrests for applying labor muscle. Having recently found his union bonanza, he was able to buy Frank Nitto's home in Florida. Authorities asked Caldwell about the mobster, but he denied knowing Mr. Frank Nitto and further failed to identify the mobster when shown pictures of him. When asked how he could afford monthly $450 house payments on a salary Caldwell insisted was $125 a week, the hoodlum had no answer.

Eventually a grand jury called in Caldwell and his brother Michael, a union official, for an explanation of the charges and to request the union's books, which Caldwell said were missing. The union secretary made off with them, he thought. Outside the courtroom, when a *Chicago Daily Times* photographer aimed his camera at Caldwell, Michael kicked the pressman in the stomach and slugged him. Separated by a bailiff, Caldwell, the man the feds now suspected of collecting $240,000 over the last five years, pulled his brother aside, gruffly marched to the court clerk window, and demanded his witness fee of $1.10.

Altogether, it was estimated the union collected $300,000 annually, yet after four years of Caldwell's rule, only $62 remained in union bank accounts. Not only that, but like Romano's scam with the bartenders, the retail clerks paid for a nonexistent hospital plan. To supplement his income, Caldwell was thought to have wrung tribute from other merchants by threatening to unionize their stores through one of three unions he claimed to represent—the unions, though, existed only on paper. A partial list of forty-eight airline trips paid for by the union over an eighteen-month period, mostly to accommodate Caldwell and his family on their trips to Florida, reached Courtney's office. The other names checked out by the state's attorney turned up two Nitto agents in the South Side policy wheel racket and two associated with liquor distributorships suspected of mob ties.

Under siege, Caldwell was forced out of the union business in Chicago; however, State's Attorney Courtney filed no charges. Only sixteen months later did Caldwell face charges—federal charges—for aiding the union secretary to abscond, not with the union books (as he had) but rather for evading a draft notice, whereupon the FBI arrested him.

⚜⚜⚜

The Bioff-Browne case was assigned to Federal Judge John C. Knox. Bioff learned up front the disposition of the judge they were up against. In an early hearing, prosecutor Correa made it known his preference to keep Bioff confined until trial because many of the witnesses proclaimed fear for their safety. Knox released Bioff on a higher bail but sternly warned the thug that he possessed no tolerance for violence: if any threat were made against *any* witness, he would lock up Bioff for the duration of the case—no question about it. Knox set the trial date for August 18.

Nitto's mob helped stall as long as possible. One of the key witnesses in the case was to be mob gunman, alias Browne assistant Nick Circella. Aware of the government subpoena, he fled. Citing Circella's absence, Correa obtained trial postponements, a delay that quickly induced Bioff's lawyer to proclaim to reporters the feds were employing a stall tactic.

Up to now, Nitto only needed to worry about Bioff, but in mid-September, New York's prosecutors subpoenaed Browne to produce the books from Chicago Film

Operators Local 110. They were confident figures would illustrate even more union money had been appropriated by Browne and Bioff on top of the producer extortion money. Information unearthed by U.S. Attorney J. Albert Woll in Chicago and State's Attorney Courtney trailed a $65,000 investment of union money into the swank café and gambling hotspot, the Colony Club, owned and operated by the Nitto Outfit. The club's manager was none other than Nick Circella, who they also discovered was the autocrat of Local 110. On September 30, Correa announced the indictment of Circella for conspiracy in the same racketeering case, along with Louis Kaufman in New Jersey. On that point, the prosecution team surely was well-read regarding Browne, Bioff, and Circella as Nitto underlings, but they had no proof to tie them in. In the meantime, Correa and Kostelanetz prepared for an early October trial date for Browne and Bioff.

Nitto discovered the extent of the government's case in the IATSE affair when Matt Correa made his opening statements in the Bioff-Browne case on October 8. Correa outlined the entire extortion scheme from the producers, how the Basic Agreement was made in exchange for payments, though at this point he could finger only about $550,000 exchanging hands. He asserted the mob had told the filmmakers, "You pay us or else we'll wreck your business!"

It took only three hours to empanel a jury, with, amazingly, only three potential veniremen being excused by way of having read Westbrook Pegler's exposé, which assuredly would have left a strong impression against the defense. Nick Schenck, brother of Joe and president of Loews, testified the first day, his narrative one that a reporter rated as high as "some Hollywood film thrillers." The slight Russian native related Bioff's first appearance on the movie scene announcing himself as "boss." Schenck also related how Bioff elected George Browne and then demanded $2 million from the studio heads. Schenck recalled exactly Bioff's swaggering response when he had protested: "I've thought the matter over and maybe two million dollars a year is too much—I'll take a million." Louis B. Mayer, chief of Metro-Goldwyn-Mayer, followed to confirm Schenck's testimony. Bioff's brother-in-law appeared on the stand to testify about the commissions on the film deals.

The earth-shaker for Bioff and Browne—and all of Nitto's mob, for that matter—came on Monday, October 20, when testimony, as the *Tribune's* headline declared, "REVEAL CHICAGO UNDERWORLD'S SHAKEDOWN CUT." Albert and Harry Warner of Warner Brothers Pictures reported the basic shakedowns as the others had, but this time with Bioff's crucial "boys" statement. Albert Warner related the instance when thug Bioff came stomping in around Christmas demanding money, claiming Warner was $20,000 behind in his payments. When the producer demurred, Bioff, as Warner testified, said he "must have it. You know it's not all mine—the biggest part of it goes to people in Chicago, and I must insist on getting it. I've got to have it; the boys are asking for it." Warner had hurriedly scrounged up $7,500 and turned it over to Bioff, who admonished him, "That's chicken feed, but it will help for Christmas." Warner's secretary verified that her boss left envelopes of cash to be handed to Bioff when he called. The same day, Correa queried Austin Keough, vice president of Paramount Pictures, as to why he would pay such great sums to Bioff. "I regarded the making of these payments to Bioff and other associates with him . . . to preserve my company against possible and very probable financial disaster."

On the twenty-seventh, it was Bioff's turn to take the stand. The racketeer showed up in a snappy, double-breasted gray suit with a blue handkerchief tucked in the breast pocket. He took the stand in his own defense, his lawyer Michael Luddy questioning him. Bioff explained he started out a poor boy and that when he became connected to IATSE, he met Nick Schenck on the East Coast. Sticking to the defense's plans, Bioff said it was Nick who wanted him to collect and transfer large sums of money from other producers to his brother Joe out west. Along the way, he collected sums in Chicago. Joe got every cent, he swore. The money, as Bioff understood, was the prorated share of the others to cover the costs incurred by the Schencks to influence legislation and get things done for the industry. Yes, he confidently said, he and Joe Schenck were close; Joe had loaned him money and bought stocks for him.

After two days of smooth sailing on the stand with his defense counsel, Bioff faced off with U.S. Attorney Matt Correa. Paul Ricca was correct in his estimation— Bioff had no chance. The prosecutor immediately jumped on Bioff's checkered past, asking why Bioff had explained his start in the labor racket yesterday as a Teamster business agent when, in fact, a year ago during his pandering hearings in Chicago, he had claimed his first employment was with labor racketeering boss Mike Galvin. "Wasn't the reason you didn't mention Galvin's name here," Correa roared, "is because he was a notorious labor racketeer in Chicago?" Correa pressed Bioff, asking why he had not testified to previous employment at the St. Joseph Valley Brickyard under President Phil D'Andrea, the same Phil D'Andrea who had acted as Capone's bodyguard and gunman in the twenties. The prosecution also asked for an explanation of his hobnobbing with gangland.

When Bioff attempted to distance himself from his gangland cronies, Correa produced police lineup photos of Bioff with West Side hoodlums. Bioff stammered, looked toward the ceiling, and rolled his eyes, denying knowledge of their background. Correa then produced a fistful of news clippings recounting their arrests and shady backgrounds. The prosecutor hammered away, asking why Bioff had used at least five aliases during his lifetime, especially on such innocuous items such as insurance policies—and even on his own marriage license. How many times had the defendant been married, he simply asked. One, replied Bioff. The prosecutor then produced evidence of two marriages, causing the tough bully to exclaim: "You're trying to smear me!" Bioff finally broke, admitting he had lied to the Internal Revenue Service and the California grand jury, but only, he said, "to protect Mr. Schenck."

Browne hardly fared better. A week later, the jury needed only a little more than two hours to find the pair guilty on all three counts. Disrupting Bioff's plans further, Judge Knox refused further bail and sent both men to lockup—no absconding to Mexico. On November 12, Bioff and Browne learned their fate—and it was worse than even Correa had sought from the court. Dubbing Bioff "a hardened criminal" and Browne the "weaker" of the pair, the prosecution asked for fifteen- and ten-year sentences on three counts, respectively. Instead, Judge Knox threw the book at the pair. He gave Bioff the maximum ten years on all three counts, with counts one and two to run concurrently, count three to run consecutively—a grand total of twenty years, plus a $20,000 fine. Judge Knox allowed for some leniency: he suspended count three and offered five years' probation, but only when the defendant had paid the fine in full. Browne was given the same sentence structure, but with eight years on the first two counts and ten on the third count—altogether an eighteen-year condemnation.

Understanding a greater conspiracy existed but had not been proven, Correa unsuccessfully questioned each in lockup, hoping to pry the names of gangsters from the pair. He did not give up. Neither did Judge Knox. Just after Christmas, the judge retained jurisdiction over the men's cases, meaning that, should circumstances arise, he could amend their sentences.

26

THE U.S. ATTORNEY VERSUS . . . ?

ALONG WITH THE INDICTMENT OF mob guy Nick Circella, part of the fallout of the Bioff-Browne affair was the indictment of Louis Greenberg associate and 2% Fund bookkeeper Izzy Zevin for perjury. Correa understood there was but had yet to uncover its full extent. However, just because Nick Circella had been a fugitive from justice since September didn't mean he was out of the labor racketeering business altogether. Nitto and Ricca saw to it that he was still collecting a share. Since his forced resignation as IATSE special representative, they passed Local 110 money to his chauffeur, who clandestinely transferred it to Circella.

On the morning of December 1, 1941, the tall, full-faced gangster stopped for breakfast at Shorty's Place, a small place far from his customary North Side haunts down near Cook County's southern rim. As he dined, agents of the FBI swarmed in and arrested him for a trip back to New York to face trial. If Correa rejoiced at the news, he was soon disappointed, for Circella quickly made bail. When the regular mobster appeared in court the following spring, he proved tighter-lipped than either Bioff or Browne as he pleaded guilty to the charges of racketeering. This plea was made to avoid having to give testimony on the witness stand and provide further clues for Correa to track. On April 7, 1942, authorities shipped him off to Leavenworth for an eight-year stay to keep Bioff and Browne company. His silence was rewarded by the mob. When Circella's union money courier approached Gioe and Ricca with his cash and asked about Nick, Gioe informed him, "Don't worry about Nick, we are taking care of Nick. He and his family will be taken care of."

U.S. Attorney Correa knew that great sums of money had been transferred to Chicago gangsters, but he had no names. Nitto and his mob were, for the time, insulated by the silence of prisoners Bioff, Browne, and Circella. Convictions and information obtained thus far resulted from investigations of income by the Internal Revenue Service. To move forward, any further investigation of criminal matters among the Chicago mob had to be made by the FBI, under whose jurisdiction this fell. Nitto received unusual and temporary relief thanks to the Japanese attack on Pearl Harbor; after the U.S. joined the war, the bureau's new priority was rooting out wartime spies, leaving limited manpower to devote to domestic racketeers. They did not turn a blind eye to the matter, but neither did they pursue it in the urgent fashion favored by Matt Correa. Unwilling to let such grave misdeeds possibly slip away unpunished, Correa petitioned the Treasury Department for the continued temporary services of SIU agent Alf Oftedal.

Securing a jurisdiction waiver from the FBI, in February 1942, Correa dispatched Oftedal to Leavenworth to concentrate on Bioff, who seemed to be the critical link between IATSE funds and the Chicago gangsters. Oftedal happened to be the perfect agent for the assignment. The sessions in the warden's office were not grueling, "bright light in your face" interrogations; they didn't have to be. "Alf," remembered prosecutor Boris Kostelanetz, "is the kind of guy you want to make executor of your will after meeting him once." Oftedal's superior Irey also thought him to be "the most skillful examiner of witnesses that they had in the unit." Oftedal visited Bioff twice. The soft touch didn't immediately work, but Correa understood if anybody could succeed, it would be Oftedal.

Knowing the IATSE 2% Fund to be a great source of money for the racketeers, Correa moved to retain Oftedal and pursue that angle while hoping to break Bioff or one of the prisoners. An April 7, 1942, letter from the commissioner of the Treasury Department to Attorney General Samuel O. Clark Jr., regarding the Correas' 2% Fund investigation read in part:

> Mr. Oftedal has already been directed to make investigations of these matters with a view of developing such evidence as may be available indicating violations of the income tax laws. He will be instructed to continue this work and in so doing to cooperate with Mr. Correa . . . as he has in previous investigations. These instructions are not intended to change Mr. Oftedal's status and he will continue to operate under the immediate direction of the Chief of the Intelligence Unit [Elmer Irey]. . . .
>
> I am sure that Mr. Correa will find the Bureau of Internal Revenue entirely cooperative in the efforts to administer justice in these cases.

Such a generous directive allowed for a simultaneous two-prong attack on the Nitto mob from both tax evasion and racketeering angles, but it also presented an obvious hurdle, at least for Correa as a member of the Justice Department: he was now more or less dependent on the Treasury Department for information. Alf Oftedal was also in the middle. In an internal memo from Oftedal dated April 7, he verified his position:

> It is understood that I am in no sense to work under the direction of the United States Attorney's office for the Southern District of New York. I am, on the other hand, to cooperate with and assist him, maintaining all the time, however, my identity with the Intelligence Unit and under the immediate direction of the Head of the unit.

Correa would not find the keeping of this promise to be the smooth sailing originally guaranteed.

The tiff—or the race to catch credit for the big prize—between the two government bureaucracies had evolved before April. Irey's SIU in Washington built strong tax evasion cases against certain Hollywood producers. Finishing the probe, they could now account for almost all the extortion payments through 1941—for their tax jurisdiction. Oftedal, however, reported back that his understanding was that Correa thought "some sympathetic treatment" should be afforded the producers given their previous testimony in the Bioff-Browne case—it was Warner's disclosure, he noted, that originally set the whole thing in motion—and by drawing attention to their testimony, he reasoned they might be needed in the Circella and Kaufman cases when they came to trial (this proved not necessary in Circella's case). Irey was not privy to any understanding and would consider what was in the best interests of his agency.

He also knew from Oftedal's work that the 2% Fund went to Chicago gangsters, and this would open several promising cases against hoods as well. Oftedal enthusiastically reported to his Treasury Department superiors "that a vigorous investigation of the racketeering activities in connection with the use of that fund of the IATSE would go a long way in breaking up control of the Chicago gangsters and possibly accomplish an effective cleaning up of the racketeering situation there." He also relayed the importance of "certain key individuals" who could provide invaluable leads once they cracked. Of course, he said, the magnitude of the investigation would require numerous agents scattered all over the country, and Irey agreed to supply them, placing Oftedal in charge of coordinating the effort.

Oftedal started his investigation by questioning Izzy Zevin, the gang's 2% Fund bookkeeper, regarding certain monetary transactions made through the federal mail, but Zevin refused to budge. In the meantime, Correa filed John Doe indictments in New York to initiate a grand jury investigation. Forcing Zevin's hand, he called him before the grand jury where Nitto's agent held firm, claiming no knowledge of any money passing hands. Correa slapped him with another perjury indictment and then issued subpoenas to Bioff and Browne in Leavenworth to appear in New York on April 30. Neither would return to Leavenworth. In New York, Browne remembered, he, sometimes with Bioff, spent nearly every day in the U.S. attorney's office with Correa, sometimes accompanied by Oftedal. The men were careful not to press the prisoners about the instant case but only to discuss the prospective evidence—and never with a stenographer present—in hopes of prying them open.

Oftedal, working the Correa side of the case, asked chief SIU agent in Chicago A. P. Madden about work performed concerning prominent Chicago gangsters; he was told by Madden that the SIU had not performed any work in that direction since the early 1930s. They were, however, he said, working on a comprehensive investigative program toward that goal.

The response to Oftedal's query fully illustrated how even an SIU agent, when working for contending interest U.S. Attorney Correa, did not receive cooperation from his own bureau. In fact, Internal Revenue was far from inactive in gangster tax matters, especially those of Frank Nitto. Since Nitto's 1930 tax-related conviction, agents made it a point to question him periodically about suspicious items on his tax returns. In 1937, an Internal Revenue agent questioned him in a Loop hotel over a curious "miscellaneous" item on his 1935 tax return in the amount of $59,500. "Nitti said," the agent explained, "that the money came from a gambling enterprise vending machine income. In his own words he was in cahoots with Eddie Vogel in the slot-machine racket in Chicago." But he told the agent, "He kept no books." Reportedly, he later amended the miscellaneous section to read "vending machine income" while he claimed to work as a salesman for the Roma Wine Company. Red-flagged by all the talk about "Chicago boys" receiving loot, agents now appeared to be looking, at least half-heartedly, in his direction.

More alarming, the SIU began peeking into the affairs of Nitto associate Louis Greenberg and his City Management, questioned his bookkeeper and confiscated Greenberg's books. This led them to the Symphony Theater interests, the same theater Nitto had mortgaged twice earlier for loans but which was now held in Greenberg's name. Agents also started a file compiling data from IATSE accounts attempting to track dispersal of the 2% Fund.

<hr />

Nitto might have been even more annoyed: Naval Intelligence agents began to investigate Nitto, his gang, and even Capone for possible subversive tendencies. Despite all that was going on around them, the mob command and control remained intact. Acting on Browne's behalf, lawyer Sydney Korshak relayed messages from the Nitto group to Browne in lockup, paid Browne's fines, and worked with Mrs. Browne to pay rents and take care of property.

Exactly to what extent, if any, Nitto understood the scope of the investigation of him and the gang at this time is not clear. But with Bioff, Browne, and Circella in prison, he must have at least suspected the worst. Neither is it known how far his health had deteriorated, though he was only fifty-six. Both factors appear to have influenced his actions concerning long-range care for seven-year-old son Joe.

Nitto had known former Edward O'Hare secretary Annette Caravetta at least since 1930, if not before. On May 14, 1942, widower Frank Nitto married the thirty-something Caravetta in St. Louis, Missouri. Presiding over the civil ceremony was district Justice of the Peace and alleged Nitto contact John Dougherty (who later became sheriff). When the couple returned to Chicago, they moved into an attractive, yet modest, brown brick bungalow on Selbourne Avenue in the quiet suburb of Riverside, two burgs west of Cicero and perfect for raising a family. Most neighbors got to know the couple, but few knew who he was. Upon moving in, he threw a large party and invited most of the neighbors. At the event, a reserved Nitto moved about introducing himself as a fruit and vegetable merchant and did not, as one guest recalled, partake in any of the free-flowing liquor.

Certainly a subject for later tax discussions, immediately prior to the marriage, Nitto promised to bestow upon Annette cash gifts of $75,000 and $50,000. Whether as an inducement to marry and care for son Joe or for whatever other reason he gave her the money is unknown. It doesn't, however, appear to be an inducement for she remained steadfastly loyal to him years later. Nitto also set his son up with nearly $30,000 in government bonds.

———◊/◊/◊———

A week before Nitto's marriage trip, the government perhaps edged somewhat closer. The SIU investigations of Hollywood producers caused enough concern to have agents investigate subsidiary New York and Chicago theater chains. In Chicago, the examination yielded enough evidence to plan prosecution of the Balaban and Katz theater owners. Presumably, investigators also examined burlesque impresario Nathaniel Barger, who could hardly explain payments to hoodlums. Barger related how, for the past several years, he had been forced to take on mob ghost employees, first mob heavyweight Frank Diamond and then Phil D'Andrea.

On May 7, Barger agreed to the SIU suggestion to fire D'Andrea and testify for the Treasury Department in front of a federal grand jury in Chicago. At first, D'Andrea tried to muscle Barger himself. Unsuccessful at this, around mid-summer he curiously brought along one of the Capone brothers, perhaps to capitalize on the fear factor in the name—now diminished but not forgotten. Amazingly with an investigation at hand, D'Andrea persisted in his attempts (which shows the gang was not completely in tune with what was happening), demanding $2,000 in back pay and upping the $200 weekly schedule to $600. D'Andrea threatened that if he wasn't paid, "The boys wouldn't like it." Barger, who had agreed to fully cooperate with the SIU investigation, refused and found his theater marquees smashed and his new drive-in picture screens damaged. The SIU could then add these two mob clods to their list of suspects.

———◊/◊/◊———

Outside of closed-mouth Bioff, Browne, and Circella, U.S. Attorney Correa possessed only testimony from studio officials. One individual above all seemed to promise a definitive link between the Chicago mob and the extortion case. Correa understood James Costen, Warner Brothers' manager of the Chicago area, to have been coerced into leasing Greenberg's Symphony Theater for the film giant. With a little work, he thought it might be possible to develop Greenberg as a witness. On

381

June 16, Correa sent a written request to Chicago's SIU to interview Costen toward that end. He received no reply.

Four days later SIU chief Irey wrote his agents in Chicago:

> The case as it now stands presents many interesting possibilities. . . . There is strongly emphasized in the evidence now available, however, two or more major conspiracies to violate the laws of the United States. The principal offenders that are still at large, of course, appear to be Frank Nitti, Paul Ricca, and Louis Campagna.

He noted, however, that these men "were constantly alert to the requirements of the income tax laws" and had carefully insulated themselves so as to avoid any legal entanglements.

By mid-summer, Irey was no further along than his New York counterparts. He, too, realized Bioff's testimony was necessary to break the case, but Willie had responded to crack agent Oftedal only marginally, careful to never finger Syndicate men.

The wheels of law enforcement stalled. Correa developed a list of names of potential witnesses—now including Chicago lawyers suspected of moving the extortion money for Nitto's mob—but he lacked the resources to investigate. Irey had the manpower but was treading delicately so as to avoid stirring any suspicion of his investigation. The FBI was nosing around enough to keep their finger on the pulse of the case but evidently provided little of use to either Correa or Irey.

Agent Oftedal said, in a letter to chief Irey dated July 7, 1942:

> I have no work here for Special Agent Emery. There isn't much for me to do either. . . . Our leads of information are nearly exhausted and we have not yet obtained direct evidence against any of the three principals, Nitti, DeLucia [Ricca] and Campagna. In fact the prospects for ever getting "the goods" on them seems extremely slim.

Oftedal added, "In view of this, I seriously question if we, of the Intelligence Unit, should not withdraw from the picture."

Frustration had turned into a bit of inter-governmental sniping. Evidently Oftedal turned to the FBI and received a lengthy bureau report only to discover, he claimed in a memo to Irey, that much of the information contained therein appeared to have been developed by his SIU agents. He noted the FBI had waived its interrogation rights for key prisoners. Oftedal noted, though, that when an FBI agent sat in on an SIU situation conference, the SIU declined to provide copies of certain confidential data for the bureau's use.

The FBI reportedly kept an eye on the Nitto home on Selbourne Avenue, possibly since the day he moved in. The bureau did not perform the work themselves but instead detailed the job to the Riverside police. The mobsters, no doubt, sensed prying eyes. That summer, the Chicago Crime Commission received a curious anonymous tip:

> I realize the handy cap [sic] you people are working against to try and rid
> the City of Hoodlums & Racketeers when the City, State, & County Offi-
> cials are working against your organization. . . . They are all involved in
> the Graft they have been taken in the past from these Hoodlums they are
> mentioning now such as Eddie Vogel, Frank Nitti, Louis Campagna & the
> rest. . . . The partys [sic] name I will give you . . . is one of the main cogs
> in the Capone outfit . . .if you people are sincer [sic] in apprehending this
> outfit, watch 1431 No. Ashland Ave RiverForest Ill Mr. Tony Accardo they
> are in and out of his home daily.

An opposing point of view and one that brought up Capone once again; Courtney shortly thereafter pronounced the Capone gambling syndicate as "crushed."

⟋⟍⟋⟍⟋⟍

During the first week of August, while in New York, Alf Oftedal sent a letter requesting the status of the Chicago SIU investigation of key individuals in Chicago and on
the West Coast. No reply was forwarded.

Impetus to break the investigational gridlock came from Correa, but he had to
wait nearly two months before he could organize a meeting with SIU special agents
A. P. Madden and Nels Tessem of Chicago. Kostelanetz was there for Correa. Kostelanetz was straightforward as he reported on October 6: "I attempted to determine
from the gentlemen present what progress has been made in Chicago in this investigation." Madden replied a great deal had been obtained, but when Kostelanetz
asked to review the data, Madden explained that unfortunately "it was in a great
many files scattered throughout his office." Kostelanetz brought to attention
Oftedal's inquiry last August, and Madden fumbled that he had the file in his brief-
case, but the file contained many irrelevant matters he wished to dispose of first.
Could Kostelanetz wait until tomorrow? Next, Kostelanetz pressed a laundry list of
potential witnesses, asking what work they had done in regard to those individuals.
When the meeting adjourned, he reported: "The result of this can be fairly stated
item by item." As listed:

> 5. Frank Nitti—No work done as to him directly . . .
> 6. Louis Campagna—No work done as to him directly . . .
> 7. Paul Ricca de Lucia—No work done as to him directly . . .
> 8. Frank Diamond—No work done as to him directly . . .

When Kostelanetz inquired why, in Diamond's case, nothing had been done
even though prior testimony from the Scalise trial indicated tax fraud on his part,
Tessem quite frankly reported he had not followed this up.

Madden sidestepped the issue of at least three lawyers pegged to have handled
a portion of early extortion money in Chicago, saying that one of them, Billy Parrillo, had local stature and one couldn't "'barge in' on him unless it had some very
good reason." But Madden rebounded by promising an investigation. Kostelanetz

humbled the tax man by kindly pointing out there was no need for a secret investigation—the payments were from 1934 and were, therefore, barred from investigation by the statute of limitations. Madden sank. The other two lawyers reportedly held positions as assistants in the Illinois attorney general's office in Springfield, and Madden felt he could not pursue the matter with them. Regarding Bioff's initial transactions with one, lawyer Ben Feldman, Kostelanetz asked about two payments totaling $36,000. Madden had interviewed him on one occasion about a phony $20,000 invoice but halted the examination when Feldman fumed at the line of inquiry. Kostelanetz wrapped up the meeting:

> I asked Mr Madden whether or not they have any real confidential informant. . . . Mr. Madden said that he had no confidential informant.
> I inquired whether or not any progress reports had been written . . . Mr. Madden said no.
> I inquired whether the Intelligence Unit in Chicago during this whole period had been able to establish a single fact indicating the culpability of any of the persons mentioned above and Messrs. Madden and Tessem said no.

The next day, Madden produced the file called into question the day before. Kostelanetz thumbed through it and noted, "The file appeared stripped of all papers other than the immediate correspondence shown to me." He then stumbled upon an obvious oversight on Madden's part: Oftedal's request last August, which remained unanswered. Attached to it was an SIU memo from the special agent in charge on the West Coast to Chicago dated August 31, 1942, in regard to subject Johnny Rosselli:

> Transmitting for your information copy of letter of Special Agent Oftedal dated August 27, 1942, and a copy of deposition of —— ——. In view of the present situation, no copy of the statement of —— —— is being sent the U.S. Attorney in New York.

The heads of the respective investigations entered the meeting. Correa pressed his inquiry on SIU chief Irey, asking why the Chicago office had not at least tried to question Louis Greenberg or James Costen. Irey and his assistants explained in their defense that any such questioning might "disturb" current Treasury examinations of the two. Correa then drew the dagger of his argument—the incriminating August 27 memo. Irey professed ignorance and promised an investigation "to see how such a thing could have happened." The main thing Irey said he wanted to do was alleviate any friction between the two agencies so that no future misunderstandings would arise. He apologized to Correa for any appearance that his Chicago office had been "holding out" on him and suggested Correa meet with the special agents present to work out a comprehensive program to examine witnesses.

When Correa brought up the subject of Oftedal's continued work, Irey gave him a shocker—Oftedal had recently retired from the SIU section of the Treasury

Department. For Correa, the news caused grave concern. Prisoners from whom Oftedal had cultivated confidence so carefully over the past ten months, who had slowly begun to release tidbits of information at the risk, perhaps in their own minds, of their personal well-being and that of their families, might now clam up. As it turned out, they did—and at a critical juncture. The eighteen-month life of the grand jury investigating the IATSE case was due to expire at the end of October, and Correa had no guarantee they would pick the case back up.

Worse, Irey's fresh offer of cooperation, if truly meant, was short-lived. With a measure of cooperation implied, Correa brought Barger and his principal assistant east to testify before the New York grand jury. In his office, Barger also related D'Andrea's recent threats against his person unless he resumed payments. In fear for Barger's life, Correa called upon the Chicago SIU for help:

> I feel that the situation is critical with respect for Barger's well-being. I believe that every effort should be made to safeguard Barger against harm if for no other reason than that his testimony will eventually be needed not only in the investigation but also in the event of any forthcoming trial. Also, I believe that Barger is willing to help the Government in the apprehension of the hoodlums. . . . Accordingly, I strongly recommend that an all-out effort be made through use of dictaphones or whatever other facilities you have available to catch these people "in the act."

Back in Chicago, Barger relayed to the SIU his offer to set himself up as a decoy and fund the entire operation to snare D'Andrea out of his own pocket because he was "sick and tired of the whole business." Madden relayed the message to Correa but deferred, suggesting other agencies of the Treasury Department (the Secret Service) were better equipped and staffed with personnel to handle the matter. He proposed as well the slim chance that this request would be granted by the Secret Service since they were busy with war matters and suggested the FBI.

Kostelanetz phoned Irey on October 22 regarding the urgency of the Barger situation. Irey suggested the FBI route as well but noted they would likely refuse given any potential conflict of jurisdiction. Asked what the SIU would do in the event the FBI refused, Irey deferred that decision to his superiors.

The very same day, the Chicago SIU office dispatched a letter to Correa in New York:

> I have carefully considered your proposal . . . and have discussed the matter in detail with Mr. Madden. I have reached the conclusion that I cannot satisfactorily cooperate along the suggested lines. . . .
>
> The question that is presented regarding protection for Mr. Barger . . . is quite often raised. The Intelligence Unit does not have the facilities for furnishing him or his theaters with protection.
>
> The Chicago Division feels that D'Andrea is a man who should be prosecuted and I am entirely in sympathy with that view. . . .

I may suggest that the Federal Bureau of Investigation has the equipment and the personnel to procure the evidence which you need. . . . . There is a strong probability, however, that an investigation by that organization would disturb sources of information which we plan to use in the near future.

Respectfully,

(signed) F. S. Peabody
Special Agent

With Barger's life possibly hanging in the balance, Correa moved to expedite the matter by conferring with FBI agents in the New York office. They revealed they had kept that investigative file open but described it as being more or less "inactive" for the past couple of months. They also deferred to higher authority. After a few days, Correa still had heard nothing from the FBI.

During the interim, Correa received word from the SIU that they apparently had had second thoughts about their FBI suggestion. An investigation of Barger by the agency, they argued, "would disturb sources of information which we plan to use in the near future." Correa replied, "So that I may properly appraise your statement, I would appreciate it if you would write to me and tell me just what sources of information . . . would be disturbed by your suggestion that the Federal Bureau of Investigation be used to develop the current Barger incident."

Hoping to uncap the case by loosening tongues on the inside, Correa indicted Nitto bookkeeper Izzy Zevin on nine counts of lying to a grand jury. Curious as to how Circella paid his bail with large sums of cash, Correa questioned Martin Hirsch and indicted him that same day for perjury. Hirsch was the individual who had paid Nick Circella's bail with $25,000 in cash and lied as to the cash's source.

Receiving no word from the SIU, Correa wrote again: "Since it appears that during the past year the Intelligence Unit in Chicago has done work other than that requested specifically either by myself or by Mr. Oftedal, it is my earnest desire to have either copies of all reports concerning your work done independent of requests originating from New York or if no such reports exist, a statement . . . would be appreciated."

A month after the original Correa request to the FBI, the New York office replied that, in the matter of Phil D'Andrea's racketeering practices, the facts of the case had been forwarded to Washington for consideration. Further:

in as much as these facts were related to a matter being investigated by the Internal Revenue Bureau of the Treasury Department, investigation on the part of this Bureau would result at least in a partial duplication of effort. . . . it is a long established policy of the Bureau . . . that the Bureau will not investigate matters wherein any Governmental agency is conducting an investigation.

With these facts in mind instructions have been received from the Washington headquarters of this Bureau to decline to investigate the matter.

The SIU followed a day later with their reply:

> Although intensive investigation has been made during the past year . . .
> the information gathered still is largely in the form of accounting work
> papers. . . . it is a virtual certainty that none of this material would be of
> any value to you.

They augmented their stonewalling by adding that the cost and time to duplicate such materials would be much too difficult and expensive to bother.

In follow-up correspondence at the end of November, Correa sensibly asserted that any information on the subjects was valuable in keeping with his practice of evaluating prospective grand jury witnesses before expending funds to transport them to New York. Pursuant to the practice, he requested that the Chicago SIU interview under oath Frank Nitti, Louis Campagna, Paul Ricca, and Louis Greenberg. He also asked that, after the interviews, the agents serve the four with the subpoenas contained therein to appear in New York beginning December 14. The SIU refused and returned the subpoenas.

Correa appealed one last time directly to Irey on December 2, noting the refusal of the FBI to help and asking if he would give further consideration to the matter. Irey replied on the eighth, citing difficulties in terms of budget and manpower. Furthermore, according to Irey:

> The matter does not appear to have any relation to income tax violations
> but relates to a class of crimes clearly within the investigative jurisdiction
> of another agency.
> We have consistently been desirous of helping you in every way we
> properly can in development of your case in New York, but I do not feel
> . . . that we can make the particular investigation in Chicago.

The U.S. attorney received one last call from the SIU on December 5 categorically opposing Correa's intention to call the subjects before the grand jury, arguing it would cause problems for the tax investigation now under way. Correa did not call the gangsters to New York.

—◁◦/◦/◦▷—

With the statute of limitations on a good portion of the charges set to expire in March 1943, and in light of the present state of bureaucratic mulishness, it appeared Nitto and his associates might escape the federal inquiry into their IATSE dealings after all. Adding to Correa's apprehension, another crisis developed. While it was his understanding that Nitto and company were unaware of the current tax investigations, they may very well have been informed of the IATSE investigation. Definitive reports of information leaks regarding the progress of the racketeering case and threats to informers landed on his desk.

Alarmed, a week before Christmas, Correa fired off a memo to Assistant Attorney General of the United States Samuel O. Clark outlining developments since October, focusing on the difficulties in correlating work between New York and Chicago and the uncooperative nature of the Treasury Department. He stressed that such action as desired by the SIU would amount to an "amnesty to major criminals" and ran contrary to the view of the Department of Justice. The leaks, he reported, have "never happened before to my knowledge in the three and one-half years that I have been investigating . . . IATSE. I am, therefore, greatly disturbed by this unfortunate development." The substance of subsequent Justice Department correspondence is not recorded, but when Correa approached the FBI in New York shortly after the New Year, they now agreed to "afford every cooperation and to provide an adequate staff for the prompt handling of the work."

27

THERE IS NO LIFE EXCEPT BY DEATH

ITTO SPENT PART OF THE 1942 holiday season with the Caravettas. To brother-
in-law Charles Caravetta of Pullman, Michigan, who visited the house, Nitto
appeared uneasy—"not acting right," he thought, and ailing. He understood that
Nitto suffered from stomach ulcers and heart trouble and, as a result, had been in the
hospital on several occasions for treatment. Anxiety of some sort, he noticed,
seemed to aggravate his brother-in-law's physical condition. Some later understood
cancer was part of the diagnosis, and it may have been. After the New Year, Nitto
bestowed upon his wife a gift of $75,000, explained as a promise he made to her
upon their marriage last May.

Correa's long-awaited breakthrough in the logjam of officialdom came in early January when the FBI's New York staff finally agreed to follow up leads in the case. He
now concentrated his efforts on coaxing open witnesses. For months, Correa and
Kostelanetz had questioned Bioff and Browne in New York about the criminal evidence but never about the case itself. Despite renewed efforts and rumors to the contrary, the stalemate remained status quo. The two convicts had talked to no one
recently, not even the Treasury people, so investigators only had Louis Greenberg
and possibly Ralph Capone as identifying witnesses.

Outside of Bioff and Browne, the only person they had access to who could connect crucial events was Nick Circella. Originally, he went to prison to avoid ques-

tioning and to protect his associates, but amazingly, prosecutors found prison life had eroded his determination. Circella would now talk. "He never agreed to spell everything out for us," said Kostelanetz later, "but there was a measure of coopera-tion." Nick Circella spent part of January in front of the New York grand jury. That Circella cracked changed everything, but the Chicago underworld had somehow picked up the word.

Nitto, though not 100 percent, was far from the end of his rope. His Syndicate immediately engaged damage-control procedures. First, mob emissaries approached Mrs. Circella, asking her to talk to her husband for them. In mid-January, while on a visit to New York that was ostensibly a wedding anniversary surprise for her jailed husband, Mrs. Circella met with Nick and pleaded with him to chatter no more. Nitto's group also located the wife of George Browne. She was told if her husband cracked, she would end up dead. Word was transmitted to Browne, who immediately lost all thought of a loose tongue. Bioff's spouse, on the other hand, evidently could not be traced by the mob. As the mob worked the Bioff problem, discouraging word filtered back regarding accomplice Circella. His wife's appeals apparently fell short, and Nitto and Ricca were seen conferring with associates in a downtown hotel room near the end of January. The mob would not act against Mrs. Circella, but there was someone almost as dear to the prisoner they could make an example of.

Since the mid 1930s, Nick had been cozy with an ex-waitress, a titian-haired beauty named Estelle Carey. An orphaned product of the Northwest Side and sometime model, Carey was waiting tables at a couple of restaurants when Circella took notice of her and installed her in his swanky hot spot, the Yacht Club, a com-bination casino and nightclub near Rush Street. Now a dyed blonde stunner, her job was managing one of several "26" dice tables, a simple form of gambling in many clubs and taverns. Usually, an attractive woman like Carey sat behind the green felt table entertaining patrons who usually wagered anywhere from a quarter on up to ostensibly win drink vouchers. In actuality, "26" was a come-on game for potential gamblers.

A client first selected his target number, one through six, from the dice cube. He placed his bet ($1 and up was common at high-end joints) then took a leather cup with ten cubes and rolled them out thirteen times; each time, the hostess counted and marked the number of times his payoff number came up. The payoff odds depended on the final tally: totals of ten or less and thirty or more paid the highest, while odds with twelve or any number between fourteen and twenty-five were losers.

The key to Carey's job was her ability to work with sweetly amusing flirtatious gentlemen and lonely drunks, building a rapport and keeping them gushing to ensure their future return while relieving them of perhaps $10 or more each night. (Carey was credited with swindling $800 and up from certain customers.) The lat-ter was achieved through skillful manipulation of the dice—switching loaded dice unsuspectingly into the game or quickly swiping the cubes from the table and marking a false tally in the house favor. A sharp eye, she directed the obviously well-heeled clients to the upstairs casino so that their pockets could be lightened even further.

Carey was such a moneymaker for the club that Circella made her manager of the "26" games and may have given her 25 percent of that take. Later, he moved her over to the ritzy Colony Club on Rush Street, where she increasingly handled a considerable portion of Circella's funds, some of it thought to be extortion money for which Circella was responsible. Among the club's crowd, he relished her company, and she became his paramour, adorned with $175 gowns accented by handkerchiefs at $90 a dozen while earning $200-$500 a week. Not bad for a hard luck ex-waitress.

Carey's bubble of fortune burst in 1940 when police raids shuttered the Colony Club. Then her benefactor Nick Circella was indicted in the movie extortion case in 1941. When the FBI finally nabbed him, the obvious notion was that Carey had spilled the beans on his location; his friends "have not liked Miss Carey since," one reporter wrote. Never the one-man woman, since then, she rendezvoused with several men about town; with one she vacationed to Florida. Notably, she remained well-dressed, not hurting financially after his capture. Talk turned to the missing extortion money; one writer theorized that she was safeguarding Circella's money in his absence. Any mob suspicions regarding her role with the feds in building the extortion case proved to be well-founded, for they were indeed looking at her as prospective witness. Further rumors of collaboration with Internal Revenue didn't help her position.

Whatever the truth of the matter, the mob caught up with Carey on the afternoon of February 2, 1943, in her Addison Street apartment on the North Side. When the killer departed the scene, he ignited a fire, the smoke from which finally alerted neighbors. The fire department was called, and upon crashing through the front door, firemen found Miss Carey on the floor partly beneath an overturned chair, her legs consumed by flames. She had been battered with a blackjack and kitchen rolling pin, slashed by a saw-like bread knife, and strangled. Most of the carnage had been applied to her face. She died not by this assault but more gruesomely, the coroner later determined, from second and third-degree burns from the fire.

The initial investigation focused on jealous lovers. She had plenty of suitors from her club days, evidenced by letters of worship stowed in her bedroom. A search revealed two missing fur coats; perhaps the fire was set to cover the robbery. But if robbery was the motive, why did the thief neglect to seize the obvious and easily pocketed $2,500 in jewelry in the bedroom? Police rebuffed both theories as more of Carey's connections to Circella surfaced. Ultimately, they hauled in mob guys Ralph Pierce and friend Les "Killer" Kruse as suspects, but lacking solid evidence, the pair was released.

At first, it appeared the mob strategy might succeed. When news of Carey's death flashed to New York, Kostelanetz lost Circella as a witness. "As soon as she was killed," the prosecutor later recalled, "that was the end of it. He turned off, boom, just like an electric light." Aware of the threats against Mrs. Browne, Kostelanetz immediately sequestered her in a hotel room under twenty-four-hour watch by U.S. marshals. Nonetheless, the Carey example reinforced her husband's lost nerve, and Correa lost another witness.

The murder of Estelle Carey, however, boomeranged Willie Bioff, who immediately called on Kostelanetz. "We sit around in jail for those bastards," he said, "and they go killing our families. To hell with them. What ya want to know, Boris?" Not only did Bioff completely divulge what he knew in the Hollywood extortion case, he also buzzed information to Treasury agent Alf Oftedal, presumably for the tax cases Internal Revenue had long aimed at the hoodlums. Perhaps Bioff's example ignited a flicker of courage within Browne, for bit by bit he became more cooperative. The cooperation came even when Kostelanetz could offer neither man any guarantees in return regarding lighter sentences or amnesty from their current predicament. The only promise made to Bioff and Browne was that their families would be protected.

Riverside police watched the Nitto house for months at FBI request. Expensive cars came and went—there was an especially noteworthy parade of them one night shortly after Carey's death. The mob chiefs conferred deep into the night before departing, talk no doubt centering on what to do about main sieve Bioff after seeing their own pictures splashed across the papers and reading stories claiming, "RACKETS 'BIG 5' IN FEAR OF U.S. AGENTS—WILLIE BIOFF MOST HELPFUL." Frustrated that they had never located Mrs. Bioff, with her husband holed up in New York, most time-tested tactics in the mob arsenal were useless. Killing Bioff seemed the only option, though.

Tremendous pressure developed on Nitto to do something—this was a federal rap; no penny-ante local jail time faced at them this time. Later word had a last ditch, desperate effort aimed at killing Bioff via mob prisoner and old Nitto acquaintance Lepke Buchalter. He was under a death sentence for murder and in the same prison, they thought. He had nothing to lose, so they wondered if he would grant his Chicago associates one last favor. Whether the story was true or not, no action materialized. Underworld buzz picked up by one reporter had frantic last-ditch attempts by Nitto to bypass the Bioff problem by going straight to the feds. A prominent attorney reportedly made a trip, first to New York, then to Washington, D.C., to fix the case, failing dismally at both locations.

With these failures, mob strategy was essentially bankrupt. By the end of the month, they surely knew Louis Greenberg and Ralph Capone had received summons to appear before the grand jury—even the New York press had reported the story. Bioff was there, and Browne appeared twice. In a week, even George McLane was there in a limited way.

A February 11, 1943, headline in the *Daily News* reported, "JURORS 'HIT PAYDIRT,' TRACE CAPONE MOB FUNDS TO CHICAGO SOURCES." The story noted that the "investigation started back in 1941 with Harry Warner's testimony of Bioff's demands for a Christmas present for the 'boys in Chicago.' Those identities are now near."

On February 19, 1943, another paper's headline read, "N.Y. FILM RACKET PROBE MAY SOLVE 3 MURDERS HERE." The story stated that the "Carey, Maloy, and Osterberg murders point to the Capone mob. The Bioff-Browne dealings are essentially a Chicago operation."

Unable to stop the hemorrhaging of information from New York, Nitto called on attorney Anthony Bradley Eben and asked if he would represent Nitto in the case when it came to trial. Eben agreed that he would. As to the looming charges, Nitto protested his innocence during a tête-à-tête with the attorney, saying he was a legitimate businessman, an investor. Nitto then quit Chicago for Florida. He signed his Di Lido Island home over to a secure third party (Max Caldwell's wife, who later defaulted, enabling Nitto to regain the property), no doubt to avoid seizure in the tax matters sure to arise later. He arrived back in Chicago early March and emptied his bank accounts of a further $50,000, which he gave to his wife. The previous year, he had invested nearly $30,000 in bonds for his son Joseph. He met Eben on several more occasions in the lawyer's LaSalle Street office. Around Riverside, Nitto frequently took long, solitary strolls, perhaps contemplating his prospects. To Berwyn Police Sergeant Charles Rudderman who observed Nitto there, "He looked like a shadow." The sergeant had known him to be a sick man for some time. Others in law enforcement also knew crime boss Nitto to be significantly fading in health.

Nitto would have paled further had he known what Correa had amassed as of early March. He pegged their direct extortion of the movie industry by various methods to the tune of slightly more than $1.1 million. In addition, of the estimated $1.5 million collected for the IATSE 2% Fund, only $75 remained in the union account. Correa had Nitto and eight associates as the primary culprits—six of the eight were Chicago men. Correa was further contemplating a super roundup with possible indictments against strong-arm "lesser lights" Charles Fischetti, Tony Accardo, Bob McCullough, Joseph Imburgio, and Louis Romano.

In this respect anyway, the Chicago mob lucked out: to avoid statute of limitation complications, immediate action was requested. A letter dated March 17, 1943, from the U.S. attorney general to Matthias F. Correa, Esq., read:

> Pursuant to the provisions of Section 420C Title 18, U.S.C., you are hereby expressly directed to institute prosecution under sections 420a-420e, Title 18 U.S.C., of the following persons:
>
> Frank Nitto
Louis Campagna
Paul de Lucea, et al.

Also to be charged per the letter's "et al." were Phil D'Andrea, Frank Diamond, Charlie Gioe, Ralph Pierce, Johnny Rosselli of Los Angeles, and Louis Kaufman of New Jersey. Indictments charging violations of the federal anti-racketeering, mail fraud, and conspiracy statutes were to be opened Friday morning, March 19. The *Chicago Tribune* caught wind of the goings on in New York the night before and ran the following headline: "THREE CAPONE MOBSTERS BOSS EXTORTIONISTS—NITTI, RICCA, AND CAMPAGNA RULE." Predictions of ten mobsters facing indictments were partially correct—for the court of public opinion, the paper published everything: photos, mobographies, everything.

From the beginning, all this publicity apparently chafed the U.S. attorney in Chicago, J. Albert Woll, as much as it did the mob. When Woll called upon Assistant Attorney General Clark to inquire about progress in the New York case, Clark asked him the source of the news leaks in Chicago. Woll said he knew of no such leaks and in a statement symptomatic of professional jealousy announced "he would not add further publicity to the prosecuting New York attorney." Woll then admitted a certain amount of displeasure that this young attorney was prosecuting Chicago criminals; further, he said, the whole matter might tip off his prosecution of the tax matters.

———⌁⌁⌁———

The timing appears off—and if it occurred, evidence suggests it was probably the noteworthy meeting in February after the Carey murder—but later accounts supposed one last mob meeting under Nitto's direction held the night before the indictments were to be unsealed. It may have convened at Nitto's home, and the principals in attendance were said to be Nitto, Ricca, Campagna, D'Andrea, and up-and-coming lieutenant Tony Accardo. Ricca spoke for the others present, saying of the coming indictments, strategy for mob leader Nitto was limited. The core of the conversation was thought to have focused on the following line of reasoning from Ricca to Nitto: "When Capone got us in income tax trouble he took the full rap. You'll be smart to do the same. You got us into this; you brought in Willie Bioff and shoved him along, you were behind him in the movie operators union and in the bartenders union."

"This is a conspiracy charge," Nitto protested, "I can't take the rap alone."

The two hotly debated tactics back and forth before ending with Ricca's snap: "They can't convict us without your testimony. It's necessary for you to get out of the way. Will you take care of that yourself or shall we do it?"

If Ricca's argument can be taken as fact, it was obviously faulty from the get-go for he had apparently forgotten that it was Nitto, not Capone, who first went to jail over tax matters, and it was Nitto who surrendered to take the heat for the bartenders case back in 1940, as a leader should—not Ricca or Campagna, who absconded. Nitto was correct; a conspiracy case simply wouldn't dissolve because one individual turned himself in.

Perhaps Ricca more logically argued for the "Circella solution" as the best chance to beat the rap and keep the organization intact. Nitto should plead guilty and go to prison to avoid testifying. He might not survive a prison term because of his health, but the mob would take care of his dependents. If expiring in prison seemed unbefitting a mob boss, the only other alternative for the leader, as Ricca was thought to have envisioned it, was death. As the story goes, when Campagna and D'Andrea chipped in support for Ricca's position, with Accardo silent on the sideline, Nitto stood alone. Late that night the assembly broke up, and for Nitto there were no agreements and few alternatives.

Whatever the truth of the details, the tenor of mob discussion around that time, said one close enough to know, was that Nitto was "handed a gun to shoot himself— or else he didn't even have to do it himself." Was there a coup d'état in a highly structured crime organization now bowed in desperation, or was it Nitto's failing health and the possibility of a long prison term? In any case, the prospects presented a tremendous jolt to Al Capone's successor, the man who had galvanized the mob after the 1920s, completed the takeover of Cook County, and expanded the mob's business into a variety of interests nationwide. It was endgame for Frank Nitto in Riverside, Illinois.

—◦/◦/◦—

Friday, March 19, 1943, dawned miserably—the temperature was in the thirties, heavy overcast clouds blanketed the daylight, and a cold drizzle fell intermittently. Nitto's phone rang late that morning. It was lawyer A. Bradley Eben in the Loop. Word had come from New York; the indictments were unsealed earlier. On three counts of racketeering, the mob men faced a maximum of ten years in prison and/or a $10,000 fine for each. On three counts of mail fraud, the sentence was a maximum of five years and/or a $1,000 fine. Given their reputation, the gang leader no doubt expected the worst. Eben asked him to make arrangements to surrender. Certainly, said Nitto. Eben's office would inquire about the bail amount to be expected. Nitto said that was fine and supposed he would meet him in the afternoon sometime and hung up.

About 1 p.m., Nitto sent his wife to make a novena for him—his illnesses, his legal troubles—at Our Lady of Sorrows on Chicago's West Side near Garfield Park. After Annette departed, Nitto, the man who only judiciously imbibed the vice of his Prohibition trade years earlier, poured out a few gulps of grain alcohol. He moped a while, probably wrestling with his future. Fifteen, even ten years in a federal penitentiary seemed like an eternity to a fifty-seven-year-old man in declining health. He might not even survive the experience. He might have figured parole into the equation, but given his experience with parole boards years before, Nitto had no reason to think optimistically. On the other hand, if he didn't plead guilty and tried to fight the charges . . . either way, his career was finished. Braced by alcohol, he stepped out into the cold air for a walk. He dressed well for the occasion; a brown plaid overcoat topped his gray checked suit with thermal wear beneath. He arranged a blue-and-maroon plaid scarf around his neck. A brown fedora protected his head. Nitto then wandered off.

Although is was approaching 3 p.m., the day's faint light was quickly giving way to gray darkness, the heavy clouds obscuring the low sun. Now that the light rain had stopped, it looked more like a bleak winter afternoon than the beginning of spring. Illinois Central Railroad conductor William J. Seebauer and switchmen Lowell M. Barnett and Edward H. Moran were riding in a caboose in a line of freight cars slowly backtracking south along a spur line in the Chicago suburb of North Riverside. To Seebauer, who was a weathered hand with an elongated, rubbery, jovial face, the course was routine: make a stop at the torpedo plant in North Riverside and continue down to the main Illinois Central line. En route, they were to flag traffic at the unprotected crossing at Cermak Road, then make the necessary switches at the plant further south. However, there would be no normalcy for Seebauer this trip.

As the train crept south toward the bustling street, Seebauer and Barnett observed a man weaving down the tracks a block or so away, his back to the train.

He was staggering past the Municipal Tuberculosis Sanitarium on Cermak Road, in the vicinity of the Gage Farm and Nursery to the east of the tracks. Both trainmen were worried for the safety of the man, who appeared to be so drunk he "was hardly able to stand up." As they crossed Cermak Road, Seebauer was relieved to see the man had at last heard the train's approach and stumbled off the tracks to the left down into the soggy, calf-high grass along the embankment near the farm. Seebauer remained on the caboose platform as it drew even with the man's position and carefully watched him. Nitto stood beside the six-foot chain-link fence that ran parallel to the Illinois Central's right-of-way when Seebauer called out, "Hi there, buddy!" Nitto turned and drew a gun. Seebauer dove into the caboose for cover as a shot was fired. Assuming the bullet was aimed at them, Seebauer warned the others, "That guy's shooting at us!"

Moran, who saw the first shot clearly enough, said, "No, he's trying to kill himself." Moran jerked the signal to stop the train and held his cover with the others as another shot was fired.

Moran was correct. Nitto's shaky first shot had missed the mark, piercing his brown felt hat just above the band but failing to even wound him. Four or five seconds later, a dazed Nitto, standing unsteadily perhaps only four to five feet from the fence, once again raised a .32-caliber Colt revolver toward his temple and pulled the trigger. This shot also a missed and passed harmlessly through the top of his hat— close enough, though, to lodge a lock of hair in the exit hole. The shock of the blast caused him to lose balance, wobble, and fall backward against the fence, his head resting at a ninety-degree angle against his chest.

When the train stopped, the men in the caboose were six to eight car lengths past the man. Seebauer and Barnett decided to dismount and investigate further. As they crept forward, Seebauer had the idea of rushing the man and taking his gun. Barnett, however, thought better of the plan, saying, "If you think I'm going to rush a man that is drunk and with a gun, you are crazy. I've got a wife and family." The switchman's instincts sealed Nitto's fate. Nonetheless, the men cautiously inched up the tracks toward Nitto. Barnett described the gangster's last moments:

> We kept walking slowly until we got within twenty feet. We got so close you could see the man's eyes rolling. I hollered at him. He looked at me and rolled his eyes. I said, "Well, if he tried to kill himself, he didn't do a good job." We stopped. I stayed where I was and Seebauer crawled through the cars to get on the side of the train away from the guy and be able to crawl up closer and look at him from under the car. . . . Suddenly, the fellow raised himself to a sitting position, put the gun to his head and pulled the trigger. There was a shot and the man fell back against the fence.

At that moment, Seebauer closer to Nitto than the others heard the man let out a last, "dying gasp." Nitto still clasped the revolver in his right hand; his perforated hat lay in the wet grass nearby. No more indictments, no thoughts of tax problems, no more troubles.

Seebauer walked to the sanitarium to have a call put in for the Riverside police. Barnett and Moran remained at the scene, though warily keeping their distance from Nitto's lifeless body. When Riverside Chief Clarence Neuschaefer and two squads arrived to take control of the scene, the three railroad workers returned to the train without knowing whose death they had witnessed until alerted by the media. It was Sergeant William Crowe of the Riverside Police Department and Chicago Police Sergeant Martin Joyce who identified Nitto, both remembering him from the old days.

The North Riverside police and the Cook County sheriff responded to the call as well—a possible suicide, they were told, along the Illinois Central spur line south of Cermak at approximately Twenty-fourth Street. Alerted, the press homed in on the scene, and the Cook County Coroner arrived. Weighted down by a thick overcoat, he trudged over to the scene with daylight fading fast. He studied Nitto's revolver in the glare of the photographers' lights; three bullets remained. Examination of the dead man's pockets revealed a wallet bearing "Frank" in gold letters, $1.03 in coins, a pack of cigarettes, a pencil, a solitary key, a single stick of Clove chewing gum, and a rosary. A draft registration card aided positive identification; another document gave the name of Lucy Ronga at 1208 Lexington as a contact.

The veteran and the young officers crowded around the supine Nitto. The looks on their faces showed either resigned disgust or astonishment, perhaps even wonder, as they recognized the man whose name rang wide and powerful on the streets of Chicago, now lying in a disheveled heap of rain-soaked clothes, streaks of trickled blood on the lapel of his overcoat. Suicide seemed so drastic a measure, nearly unheard of in the powerful underworld. They were likely all wondering why.

"Frankly, it doesn't surprise me," chimed Chicago Police Captain William Drury, a veteran of many tangles with mobsters. He knew Nitto to have been in ill health for some time. "He probably figured he was due for prison, and that he couldn't get the express medical care that he desired—so he took the easy way out." Berwyn Sergeant Charles Rudderman concurred, "with the New York indictments returned he might as well do it the easy way." Markedly less reflective was Chief of Detectives John L. Sullivan's summation. The manner of his death was no surprise to him, he asserted; guys like Nitto "can dish it out, but they can't take it."

Annette returned home about 3:30 p.m. and found her husband absent. Neighbor Mrs. W. J. Meyer witnessed her arrival, saying of Mrs. Nitto, "She looked so happy." She continued: "Whatever they say, she knew nothing about it." Riverside police arrived not long after she did to notify her of her husband's fate. Grief-stricken, she finished her weepy discourse to the officers, while outside, reporters lay siege to the bungalow, a couple managing to question the sobbing widow. In between endless phone interruptions, Annette told the police she and her husband knew something was amiss. Strange cars had staked out the house in recent weeks—they (she never specified who) were hounding him. All Nitto wanted was to be left alone to raise his son. He was a wine salesman, she said. Nitto enjoyed the neighbors and they liked him; theirs was quite the friendly, all-for-one, one-for-all neighborhood. She disclaimed any knowledge of his illegal activities, "Poor Frank! He never did a wrong thing in his life." So ended the interview.

Nitto's death provided a banner day for the Chicago press, with papers featuring lengthy articles about the man, his death, and the indictments. On March 19, 1943, the *Daily News* ran a headline—"NITTI FOUND SLAIN HERE AFTER U.S. INDICTS MOB"— and an extra—"EXTRA: CAPONE'S CHIEF, 6 OTHERS CITED"—on Nitto's death and the indictments. Déjà vu 1930-31; once again, it took federal agents to clean house.

The indictments were by far the greatest single blow to Chicago organized crime, their negative impact felt throughout the mob's business organization. With Nitto dead and the mob's top echelon under siege, what would be become of the mob? Their usually lively gambling and nightclub business slumped, and owners complained for weeks, but everyone had packed up and was lying low. Even Cicero, long a mob stronghold, remained eerily silent. The temporary economic chaos was now something for Nitto's successors to solve. One local newspaper wondered in their editorial page about the impact on the alliance of crime and politics and observed this was most inopportune for Mayor Kelly. A mayoral election was only weeks off, and Mayor Kelly and his clique, who had allowed the Nitto mob to terrorize the citizens of Chicago for so long, must be worried. Kelly won the April election, but by the fewest votes of any previous win.

The coroner's inquest into the death of Frank Nitto was anti-climactic, with witnesses and answers fewer than at the mortal scene. Only the conductor Seebauer and a police sergeant of the highway patrol testified about the death. Seebauer related the incident as he saw it, and the police sergeant told of the response and what they found upon arrival—very cut and dried. Annette, still distraught from the experience, did not show herself. Instead, her brother Charles Caravetta was called to provide the jury with some insight into Nitto's affairs and state of mind. Intentionally or otherwise, he was not very helpful. He really didn't know much, he told the jury. Caravetta knew Nitto to be a physically sick man and appeared at that time not to be in a good state of mind. With the testimony and the evidence cited by Coroner Brodie as to the wound, the jury retired for a few minutes before concluding the death was a suicide due to temporary insanity. The death certificate was filled out as a genealogist's nightmare, with most of the information requested of Nitto answered "unknown." Charles Caravetta signed it and claimed Nitto's body.

In distinct contrast to his father was Joseph Nitto. "Joe was such a shy boy when he first came here," reflected one neighbor. "He was just beginning to warm up and be friendly. Now this had to happen," she continued. Another sadly reflected his misfortune because "you wouldn't want a better-mannered child than little Joe." Last autumn, another recalled sympathetically, the solitary, withdrawn boy had wandered over simply to gaze endlessly into the sputtering flames of a slow-burning pile of leaves. It was heartrending.

By Monday morning, the nine-year-old boy was the only person accessible to the press at 712 Selbourne. There, a reporter found the forlorn child outside with a pair of metal roller skates strapped to his shoes, periodically coasting over the rough cement sidewalk in front. For the writer, he stopped. Tugging at his brown lumberjack jacket with his gloved hands, the spectacled boy's large blue eyes blinking in the bright morning sun, he proudly announced his name, Joseph Nitto. The quiet, pale boy volunteered: "My father died. That's why I'm not in school today." About his dad: "My daddy was nice. He gave me these skates a long time ago, maybe a couple of years, when I was little." For his own future, with a world war still on, he proudly wanted to become a marine flier. Until then, he said, who knows? He tightened up the skates and glided a short distance, then paused. Thoughtfully, he announced, "I don't know whether I'll go back to school or not. My mother's awful sad right now. I think maybe I'll stay home and take care of her. I'm big enough to—really."

Newspapers speculated the funeral would be held sometime about mid-week, but undertakers and the family conspired to avoid publicity with an early burial. The move caught the Mount Carmel Cemetery staff in the western suburb of Hillside unprepared, but they quickly pressed a hodgepodge eight-man crew to work. Shortly after Joe Nitto's morning interview, a handful of mourners, numbering no more than two dozen, hastened to bid Nitto a graveside farewell just inside the cemetery's south entrance. The day was a dreary overcast of dark gray as they filed graveside. Annette, cloaked in a black Persian lamb coat, sobbed with Joseph at her side. The rest of the mourners were mostly women cloaked against the cold. Surely among the group were Nitto's sister, Anna Vollaro, and Dr. Ronga's widow, Lucy. Of the very few men in attendance, none were recognized members of the mob—not that they necessarily deserted him at the grave; putting in an appearance was just too dangerous. Not even lower level gang members risked a police pick-up and press spotlight in view of the circumstances. Only one press photographer made it to snap a bleak picture or two.

Funeral home owner Guy Iarussi issued a few brief words of sanctification, and then a group, with the photographer pressed into service, lowered Nitto's $5,000 bronze coffin into the cold earth. Iarussi then directed the mourners: "That concludes the ceremony folks; please return to your cars." The floral display left behind showed little in the way of quantity or extravagance—no farewells, no hearty send-off from gang friends, only a heart-shaped pillow of red and white roses from the widow, a floral pillow of fragrant gardenias from the father-in-law, and some lesser unmarked baskets. Attached to one of the largest pieces was a large ribbon inscribed "Dear daddy."

The bright gray marble monument dominated the proceedings. The center portion, perhaps six-feet tall and maybe two-feet wide, towered above two lower sections connected to either side. A cross, shadowed by ornate carvings, extended within the center portion, and at its base was the name NITTO. To the right side, Nitto had buried his second wife, Anna, three years earlier below the inscription on the stone's top edge: "THERE IS NO VISION BUT BY FAITH." Frank 'the Enforcer" Nitto was lowered into the ground to her left. Above him, on that section's top edge, Nitto left his parting reflection: "THERE IS NO LIFE EXCEPT BY DEATH." The words carved upon Nitto's monument proved most prophetic, the Nitto name most resilient.

"Uncle Sam is not yet through with the case of Frank 'the Enforcer' Nitti"—the *Tribune*'s declaration was the most egregious understatement of the era. The matter of *U.S. Internal Revenue versus the Estate of Frank Nitto* troubled his widow and son for years in several aspects. Upon his death, agents combed through files, preparing a claim for federal estate taxes. The State of Illinois had its claim as well. They long knew Nitto and mob men were wisely keeping their assets covered, burying them in legitimacy to avoid the bulk of taxes. For Nitto, that was at least part of Louis Greenberg's role all along, and Greenberg had done an exceptional job. Annette Nitto understood this, but she was not about to divulge it. Like most hoods, Nitto left no will. Thus, this was no easy task, no quick solution for the tax men. Until such time as the layers of camouflage could, if ever, be peeled away, rumor of Nitto's "millions" persisted. Five months after his death, investigators were still stumped.

Secondly, his death only served to hasten Internal Revenue efforts to bring to a conclusion questionable issues on previous tax returns. Since 1932, Nitto duly filed and paid income taxes. Studying the matter for some time, Internal Revenue suspected he had short-changed them. His tax returns illustrated an alarming decline of net income from 1938 to 1939 and again from 1941 to 1942. The press speculated this was due to his waning influence, while others offered new and complicated government bookkeeping measures stifling gang efforts to skim cash here and there as the cause. Certainly his poor health had diminished his influence to a degree, but for that exact reason, his reduced income was *his* doing.

To the U.S. Treasury agents, however, the crux of the matter they long studied remained taxes and penalties due on his share of the alleged Hollywood extortion money. Just how much of that money had Nitto received? That would be determined during the trial of his fellow conspirators.

Rounding up Nitto's cronies in the Hollywood case proved no easy task. Johnny Rosselli, who had joined the Army as a patriotic ploy, surrendered the day of the indictments, complete in his U.S. Army uniform. The rest dodged authorities. Nearly a week later, rumor circulated Charlie Gioe would surrender in the case as a "guinea pig" to determine the size of bonds the feds would require. He did not. Instead, interim leaders Ricca and Campagna surrendered late on the twenty-fourth, paying $50,000 in bail apiece, despite the U.S. attorney's arguments for $100,000 bail bonds. Gradually, they all filtered in. The next day, Ralph Pierce and Gioe turned up; bail was set at $50,000 each. Frank Diamond came in March 30 and Phil D'Andrea on April 1, both shaken by sudden $60,000 bail demands, which were later reduced to $50,000. With the exception of Diamond, who failed to make arrangements for his bonds, the rest paid and were released.

They appeared again in preliminary hearings before identifying witness Ralph Capone and, in Gioe's case, Nitto friend Louis Greenberg. Obviously terrified, Greenberg hesitated on the stand. Defendant Pierce, standing alongside Gioe, stared him down, saying, "Answer him, you bum. What are you waiting for?" In early June, they returned to court to answer charges for the second indictment, mail fraud. They were fingerprinted, photographed, and released on another $50,000 bail.

The same day, Assistant U.S. Attorney Matt Correa, who was entering the armed forces, recommended to the U.S. attorney general his replacement in the case—his assistant, Boris Kostelanetz. His appointment as special assistant to the attorney general was viewed as the key to the successful outcome of the case: "Successful prosecution depends to a very large extent upon the personal relationship, particularly the trust and confidence existing between certain key witnesses who are in mortal fear of gangster reprisals upon themselves and their families and myself as the official of the department in charge of the case." Kostelanetz interviewed Greenberg and Bioff personally. The attorney general concurred with Correa's assessment.

———

Annette Nitto unavoidably set in motion events late that summer that would give her little respite from the lingering tax affairs of her late husband. In August, she filed for administration of the Nitto estate in Probate Court. The court approved her and adopted son Joseph Nitto as the only direct heirs to the estate. Nitto's only blood relation, sister Anna Vollaro, made no claims. Neither did Marie Capezio, wife of mob member Tough Tony Capezio. Her maiden name was Nitti, and her alleged relationship as "the late Frank Nitti's sister" had surfaced the previous spring when she emerged from Civil Court victorious in defeating a lawsuit brought by an Oak Park doctor regarding a car accident three years earlier. Her identity was perhaps the most critical misconception that would be perpetuated over the years.

With the case CR# 114-101, *U.S. versus Nitto et al.*, scheduled to be heard in early October, Annette swore in an affidavit for the court that her deceased husband and the Nitto in the title of the case were in fact the same person. That ended the criminal matter. Nolle prosequi was entered. Headings of the indictments now became *U.S. versus Campagna et a.*

Back in Chicago, Annette filed an appraisal of all Nitto's visible possessions in court. The unremarkable list shows a mix of both his unpretentious lifestyle and cunning:

REAL ESTATE
None.

PERSONAL PROPERTY

1.	Avails from sale of real estate in Florida lots	$12,500.00
2.	Cash on deposit in Berwyn National Bank checking account	$5,317.05
3.	Avails from note paid, as per money order #20629	$1,587.42
4.	Contract for sale of stock in Gables Racing Association, Inc	$50,000.00
5.	Personal property as per Bill of Appraisement	$5,086.00
	TOTAL PERSONAL PROPERTY	$74,490.47

So much for the millions. The trifling amount hardly stirred an inch of press. The Selbourne address was never in his name; the Florida home also appeared to be in a limbo of undetectable real estate transactions. A home in Hot Springs was alleged. On the personal property list for Nitto were several items of jewelry, the most grandiose of which were his star ruby and a star sapphire rings, both in platinum mountings. Among the clothes and miscellaneous were several $30 suits, a couple of $1 hats, and a $15 golf set. Subsequently, Annette collected the standard $5,700 widow's award in the form of Nitto's jewelry with the balance in cash. All documents were signed duly as Annette Nitto. As for the remainder of the estate, the government now had a starting point for collecting taxes due.

As for business assets, Nitto like Capone, never owned the resources of the organization in his name. When he exited the business, the nightclubs, handbooks, and the like from which he had extracted income simply continued on under the direction of others. There was, though, the matter of his hidden investments with Louis Greenberg, namely his share of the Manhattan brewery. That investment was not the mob's; a portion truly belonged to Nitto. Even before Nitto died, Annette negotiated with Greenberg to make an accounting of his ventures. He acknowledged Nitto's brewery interests, but according to her, the Russian only hemmed and hawed on the compensation. For later meetings, she brought in attorneys to loosen roadblock Greenberg, all to no avail.

This was perhaps because Greenberg was up to his neck in federal troubles beyond the extortion case—he might need the capital from Nitto's investments for his own legal fees. The feds were investigating the methods by which he obtained properties at exceptionally low figures. For years, they had suspected his connections with two Illinois Assistant Attorneys General in the tax division of that office who were thought to be working with Greenberg's City Management Realty in foreclosing distressed properties. Officials were also looking into Greenberg's tax returns for the years 1935-41. Until relieved of these difficulties, he proved to be just as durable a headache to the widow as the feds.

<hr />

In New York, Kostelanetz fully understood not only the gravity of the case but also just whom he was dealing with:

> Typical of Chicago hoodlums, their records reveal few convictions and a great many arrests and indictments involving, in the case of particular defendants, serious charges including murder and the kidnapping of a judge. The record is replete with instances where juries have disagreed, and it is consistent with their reputation that some attempt may be made in this case.

Taking no chances, a month before the trial, he solicited the FBI to scrutinize the jury panel. The government would try the extortion indictments first since they carried the stiffest penalties. Pending the outcome, they could bring to court the lesser mail fraud indictments at their time of choosing.

The extortion trial began October 5, 1943, and was expected to last several weeks. The prosecution called over thirty-five witnesses. The star was, of course, Willie Bioff. The pudgy bully never flinched on the stand, boldly recounting in detail the activities of Nitto's organization from the beginning: the soup kitchen, the meetings in Riverside, the names and dates, the money drops. George Browne, on the other hand, perceptibly shaken by the presence of the mobsters in the docks, testified to a much lesser extent; he was often forgetful, unsure, but just sure enough to buttress Bioff's account. Ex-bartender business agent George McLane was there to recount the defendants' previous and acute extortion methods. Nervous, unsteady, even more so than Browne, he helped little. The studio moguls detailed money events similar to those Bioff had cited. Lesser witnesses and evidence solidified the case further. On November 24, 1943, the prosecution rested its case. Among the laundry list of facts disgorged:

Campagna and Ricca each collected part of $^2/_3$ of $1 million
D'Andrea received over $48,000
Diamond received over $13,500
Gioe participated in direction and control
Rosselli profited and performed certain duties
Kaufman received extortion funds

The evidence given did not implicate Ralph Pierce in the money exchanges, and the defense won a rare victory when they made a motion to dismiss the charges against him and he was freed.

In their turn, attorneys for the defense made the movie moguls the perpetrators, saying it was they who bribed their clients for services in labor affairs. The principal crook was union man Bioff; the defendants were merely intermediaries, they argued. They attacked Bioff as a criminal and liar whose testimony could not be trusted and accused Bioff of lying now to convict their clients and shorten his own term. Why, they asked him, did he now, all of a sudden, desire to turn state's witness? Willie explained a sudden infusion of patriotism: "Pearl Harbor did something to me. I want to cut my prison term down so I can help fight the Axis."

About his previous jury testimonies, Bioff explained he had committed perjury: "I lied and lied and lied." When defense counsel asked why he lied about Schenck, he replied, "I know. I am just a low uncouth person. I'm a low type sort of man. People of my caliber don't do nice things."

After calling thirty-six witnesses, the defense rested its case. None of the defendants testified but rather sat solemnly throughout the proceedings, with the exception of Frank Diamond, who peered down, shaking his head seemingly in a daze, incessantly mumbling in Italian. Toward the end, Ricca, Rosselli, and Diamond claimed illness and missed much of the proceedings. Not to be hoodwinked, Kostelanetz requested a government physician examine the men.

Then he counterattacked the defense's claims. Bribery is the "voluntary" payment for services, he reasoned, but the Chicago group wasn't asked to come in to perform services—they muscled into the industry. Further, Bioff could not have carried the entire scheme on his shoulders alone. On the touchy matter of Bioff's character, Kostelanetz acknowledged Bioff's past, saying that, yes, he was a criminal, a gangster, and a liar before the trial, but the attorney skillfully argued that none of this meant that "when he confesses he is lying further."

After deliberating almost twelve hours, the jury agreed with the government, returning guilty verdicts on all counts. On New Year's Eve 1943, all except Louis Kaufman received the maximum sentence of ten years in prison and $10,000 fines (Kaufman received seven years plus the same fine). The Chicago mobsters, minus an obstinate Frank Diamond, shipped off to the Atlanta federal penitentiary the following March; Kaufman went to the federal prison in Lewisburg, Pennsylvania, in July. Kostelanetz also indicted old Nitto chauffeur Harry Hochstein and accountant Izzy Zevin for lying to the grand jury in September. Nearly the entire 1930s upper echelon of the Chicago mob was behind bars. For Chicago, however, the glory of victory would be fleeting.

⸺◈⸺

One year to the day after Nitto's suicide, the city's political icon of the Roaring Twenties, Mayor Big Bill Thompson, a recluse in his Chicago hotel suite, died of pneumonia at age seventy-six. His antithesis, William Dever, had passed on years before, in 1929, at age sixty-seven.

Through 1944, Annette Nitto jockeyed back and forth to Florida tending to affairs while caring for minor Joseph Nitto. They still resided at the Selbourne address in Riverside. In Florida, she reacquired the Di Lido Island house—in her name. Nearby, she owned 2/25ths interest in the land on which the Miami Beach Kennel Club rested which she supposedly obtained through the estate of O'Hare. She finally got Greenberg to pay the money owed to the Nitto estate and the trust for son Joseph. Greenberg paid with two checks: one in the amount of $64,500 for balance due on a Nitto loan prior to his death, the other in the amount of $100,000 to be paid to the trust of Joseph Nitto, a guarantee made in 1934. Afterwards, the parties inked two agreements releasing Greenberg from further payment to the estate and to the trust of the boy. He thought himself free and clear.

The civil net of the movie extortion case was finally cast down on Annette Nitto when the racketeering convictions were upheld by the U.S. Court of Appeals and the defendants denied hearings by the U.S. Supreme Court. Facts divulged Frank Nitto's share of the extortion cash as roughly equal to that of his principals Campagna and Ricca. Comparing those figures with previous tax returns, Internal Revenue determined the amount due. Agents inventoried the gangsters' assets lest there was any mob trickery. Sure enough, they discovered Campagna and Ricca both owned suburban homes as well as large farms outside Cook County, jointly listed in their wives' names. No such real estate was listed for Frank Nitto; he had recognized this possibility prior to his death and disassociated his name from the Florida

404

property. Nonetheless, agents prepared to move with simultaneous jeopardy and transferee assessments against all parties including Annette "so that no one of these individuals will be put on notice and thereby have an opportunity to make further disposition of such assets as they may have on hand."

On November 7, 1945, the Collector of Internal Revenue slapped Annette with a claim for taxes, penalties, and interest due against the Nitto estate in the amount of $427,400.03. Ricca and Campagna were hit with claims of $141,631.72 and $370,583.02, respectively. Lawyers for the latter two immediately sat down with government agents to clear up the matter while they appealed the amounts to the U.S. Tax Court. In less than a year, both defendants settled their tax claims for pennies on the dollar. In accepting the offers, U.S. agents opined, "it was doubted whether sufficient proof could be shown in the event the case went to trial." To do so entailed bringing in Bioff and Browne, of whom those agents claimed to be uncertain of their location. Oddly, the U.S. would not grant Annette Nitto the same reservation: perhaps because they were suspicious of her accounting all along or because she refused to cooperate, the feds planned to drag her to court.

28

"AS STRONG AS THE UNITED STATES ARMY"

A N INSIDER MADE THE ABOVE estimation of the Chicago mob as the United States emerged from World War II more powerful and more prosperous than ever before. As it had after the disastrous tax investigation that snared Capone years before, the mob organization administered by Frank Nitto not only survived a greater leadership catastrophe but, as a result, flourished even more than it did in 1932. "When Capone got sent up," recalled a Nitto associate, "Frank took over the Outfit and really consolidated all the rival gangs, stopped all the wars, and made room in the Outfit for guys of all nationalities, but we Italians, you know, the made guys, called the shots. When Prohibition went out, we branched into other rackets. We not only got into unions, but we ran the politics in that city, and we had plenty of juice in Springfield. Frank deserves much of the credit for moving the Outfit into these areas." Transactions immediately following the extortion trial undeniably showed that his successors achieved an even higher pinnacle.

The unusually quick tax settlements by Ricca and Campagna demonstrated their desire to extricate themselves from prison as soon as possible—they had no intentions of serving ten years in prison, much less in a location as undesirable as the federal penitentiary in Atlanta. Conditions were not to their liking, and the warden was less than amicable, unaccommodating of their desires. He disciplined D'Andrea and Ricca for conniving with others about prison diets. On August 8,

1945, Ricca, Campagna, D'Andrea, and Gioe successfully petitioned to be transferred to the Leavenworth federal penitentiary, claiming it was closer to their point of eventual release. For medical reasons, D'Andrea later shuffled to the federal prison hospital in Springfield, Missouri. Johnny Rosselli moved to the Terre Haute federal prison. Some wondered how such notorious hoodlums could pull off transfers en masse.

In Leavenworth, the defendants focused on obtaining release, even though they still faced the mail fraud indictments. Attorneys for both sides previously agreed to postpone the matter until final disposition in the extortion case, and the last part of April 1947 marked the end of what the feds legally interpreted, under the circumstances, as the two-year limit from which the government could elect to try the defendants upon discovery of new evidence. Logically assuming such notorious characters stood little chance of early release, U.S. Attorney Kostelanetz recommended the move to nol-pros the indictments:

> The prison sentences imposed are currently being served and the fines, other than Kaufman's, have been paid and the government would not be warranted in spending the large sums of money required to bring the case to trial, particularly where such action may be coupled with a possibility that, upon conviction, concurrent jail sentences may be imposed by a Court which may regard the activities covered by the two indictments as essentially one course of conduct.

On May 6, the motion was hurriedly entered by other attorneys and approved. With back taxes erased, obstacle number two toward gaining freedom was now removed. By summer, the group's core was eligible for parole and progressed through the normal application process. Members of the three-man parole board interviewed the men in July, and while all prisoners were entitled to such review, in and of itself did not guarantee release. The hoods needed a favorable vote from the parole board, and this they obtained with astonishing speed on August 7. Even then, release might normally be held up for a couple of months due to bureaucratic reviews and paperwork, but not for this Chicago bunch. The defendants, with the exception of Diamond and Kaufman, walked out of prison as parolees on August 13, 1947, after serving nearly the absolute minimum of their original sentences.

Freedom for some of the most notorious hoodlums in the country naturally met with cutting skepticism and suspicion back home. The *Tribune* on August 16, 1947, ran an editorial entitled "Who Fixed This One?" that said, in part:

> There is nothing in their records to give the slightest hope that they have been rehabilitated. . . . Since there was no normal reason for granting them parole, the assumption must be that some one put in a fix on their behalf. Atty. Gen. Clark's department of justice had already been shown to be a protector of criminal vote thieves in Kansas City. Now it appears as a patron of even more vicious gangsters.

Words from the Chicago Crime Commission were equally acerbic and more brusque; this group called the paroles "an outrage and national disgrace." Though he enjoyed no legal authority to do so, Chicago Police Commissioner Prendergrast advocated barring the hoods from Chicago. Infuriated, Illinois Representative Fred E. Busbey pledged a swift investigation.

Kostelanetz (now in the public sector) had opposed the paroles from the start. Presiding over the original case, Judge John Bright also thought the defendants should serve out their sentences: "I know of no better way for the suppression of this kind of activity than severe punishment." In fact, in June 1946, when legal representatives approached the judge about reducing D'Andrea's sentence because of health concerns, he turned them away just as Kostelanetz had done a year earlier. U.S. Attorney General Tom Clark promptly muzzled both men, as well as the entire Justice Department, pending, he said, the outcome of an FBI investigation. In September, the House of Representatives Committee on Expenditures in the Executive Departments formed a subcommittee of five members, including Illinois Representative Busbey, determined to probe into the seamy affair.

Over a six-month period, the committee questioned more than fifty witnesses, including members of the parole board, lawyers, U.S. district attorneys, and even the defendants themselves. The timeline of events put together by the committee suggests the critical actions wheeling toward the paroles began not long after Missourian Harry S. Truman became president and centered on three key figures: 1) St. Louis attorney and Truman's senatorial campaign manager in St. Louis, Paul Dillon; 2) Dallas attorney and long time Clark friend, Maury Hughes; and to a lesser degree, 3) Truman appointee, Attorney General Tom Clark.

It was Dillon who, on May 12, 1945, wrote the U.S. Bureau of Prisons superintendent requesting the transfer of Ricca, Campagna, Gioe, and D'Andrea to Leavenworth. According to the Acting Superintendent of the U.S. Bureau of Prisons, Dillon's letter began with the weighty reminder, "I managed the senatorial campaigns of President Truman in St. Louis." The transfers were made over the vehement objections of the warden in Atlanta. Though he kept no offices in Chicago, Maury Hughes chatted with Clark's assistants in Washington about the mail fraud matter. A stranger who looked "like an Italian" hired him. The man said one of the defendants wanted the charges disposed of, and in a matter of days the indictment was dropped.

The U.S. Parole Board, whose task it was to review federal parole cases, came under intense scrutiny, with the committee wondering how they could vote for such action in the first place, *unanimously* no less. The chairman of the parole board was T. Webber Wilson of Mississippi, and the other two members were recent appointees of Attorney General Clark: Fred S. Rogers, a Texas neighbor of Clark's who was appointed in January 1947, and B. K. Monkiewicz of Connecticut, appointed just weeks before the paroles were approved. Wilson interviewed three of the parolees; Rogers interviewed D'Andrea only. Monkiewicz, the newcomer, said he had been busying himself out of town catching up with his caseload. On August 7, attorney Dillon called upon parole board chairman Wilson requesting the release of the four men, and that same day, the board elected to discharge the men.

Clark at first deflected responsibility for the parole board's actions, claiming the body was, in his words, "autonomous." They could and did act without consulting him, he insisted. The investigating committee pointed out to the attorney general, however, that ever since the scandal broke, members of the board were unable to talk to anyone without consulting Clark first. He was also responsible, they reminded him, for two of the board appointments in the first place. Clark, however, would only admit to subduing an FBI report on the matter.

When questioned, B. K. Monkiewicz explained his vote as the result of a hurried review of the case, and since the other two already voted in favor, his vote didn't mean a thing anyway (only a simple majority was needed). Rogers and Monkiewicz both claimed never to have heard of the old Capone gang and viewed the subjects only as middle-aged criminals who could be rehabilitated. Chairman Wilson did not appear before the committee. He had resigned from the parole board a little more than two weeks after the men went free and retired to his Coldwater, Mississippi, home, where the press caught up with him. Asked to explain what he knew of the Capone gang and the subject case, Wilson simply stated he knew about the gang from the papers but "didn't believe all he read." As to the case, he was under the impression that Bioff and Browne were the real culprits. Busbey lashed at Wilson's justification as "childish." Wilson died that winter before the committee could question him formally.

Busbey then presented an embarrassing illustration of the parole board's irregular methods. How was it, he asked, that these men with numerous records of arrests, convictions for conspiracy, investigations on income tax fraud, and indictments for mail fraud could be released on parole, while former Chicago gambler William R. "Big Bill" Johnson, guilty only of income tax evasion and serving a much lighter sentence, had been refused parole this past April? Busbey wondered whether it was because he had not employed the services of Dillon or Hughes as counsel.

The Chicago press quarried locally for specifics, and the tidbits they uncovered painted a more sinister picture. The previous fall, reporters from the *Tribune* had heard tales of voter manipulation in preparation for the Cook County elections. Republican leaders in five wards, predominantly Italian, were being asked to swing constituents to Democrats "to help out the boys." They did. Those wards, noted the press, presented the only noticeable deviations from previous election voting patterns. Word also had it that Guzik was to raise $300,000 as payment for the mobsters' release; others called in with a figure of $250,000, and one claimed it went to Dillon. Busbey advised Hoover in the FBI of the ugliness: "There are nasty rumors in Chicago that somebody got a lot of money to let these desperate gangsters out of prison." The FBI looked into the matter, but turned up little information useful for prosecution.

Dillon said he received no payment for his inquiries to Washington and branded the rumored six-digit payoff pure "fiction." He had made his decision as a favor to a friend, a Missouri congressman who had been approached by Mrs. Campagna. (After the committee adjourned, it was learned Dillon submitted a bill to Mrs. Campagna for $10,000; the bill was paid.) Perhaps more embarrassing, the investigating committee heard of Dillon's connections to Willie Heeney, Campagna's partner in a few Cicero gambling spots.

Meanwhile, the FBI learned from St. Louis of his contentious and unsavory reputation as a lawyer. Dillon was tied up with the powerful Pendergast machine running Missouri. He often defended hoodlums, including the deceased Kansas City crime boss and Nitto ally John Lazia. He had defended St. Louis Sheriff John Dougherty—the same Dougherty referred to as Nitto's connection to St. Louis in the IATSE matter. Locals also understood Dougherty to be tied to East St. Louis gambling. Dillon was often seen in the company of former labor racketeers in St. Louis and had been overheard bragging about his high political connections in Washington. Hughes, it was learned, received $15,000 from the mysterious Italian-looking stranger for approaching Clark's staff on the mail fraud indictments, but he could not recall either the man's face or the name.

It smelled awful, but in the end, the committee concluded: "While the hearings have disclosed the use of considerable money and the employment of individuals in a position to exert influence with those in authority, the committee has been unable to discover any violation of federal law." It looked as if the Chicago hoods had put one over on federal law enforcement—something they had been unable to do previously. With considerable egg on its face, the U.S. government was motivated to stay after Campagna and the rest to the very end.

⚜⚜⚜

The State of Illinois filed suit against Nitto's estate for personal property taxes in 1947. The amount was a comparatively paltry compared to the amount for federal taxes, and state collectors were not likely to see anything. By the time the federal matter came before U.S. Tax Court, Annette pleaded poverty. The *Tribune* announced her sorry financial state to the world on September 13, 1948, in a headline proclaiming, "NITTI MILLIONS GONE; WIDOW, SON ARE BROKE." The Bureau of Internal Revenue placed jeopardy liens on Joseph's trust fund as well as on the remainder of the money Nitto left his wife before his death. She had paid all of Nitto's outstanding debts as well as his 1942 taxes out of that pocket. Now, the bristly widow complained, she was forced to take fourteen-year-old Joseph out of military school and put him into public school. The boy had been a close friend of the late naval flying hero Butch O'Hare and hoped one day to follow in his military footsteps. There was nothing else, she declared. If Greenberg held any money for son Joseph, she knew nothing about it. As for the movie extortion cash Nitto was said to have received, she replied, "If I learned there was any extortion money in the estate, I'd throw it into the Chicago River."

The government would have nothing of her assertions of penury; their claim for over $400,000 in taxes and penalties remained fixed. Bringing the full weight of the tax codes down even further, agents targeted Nitto's gifts of $125,000 to his wife as part of the estate, making them taxable. Additional digging uncovered nearly $70,000 of unreported income from his slot-machine business with Ed Vogel during the 1930s, $14,880 in dividends from the Gables Racing Association, and additional potential liability to the tune of another $29,970 in bonds bought by Nitto for his son Joseph in 1942. Other technicalities on returns might add to the total. To make clear their intentions, the government subpoenaed Willie Bioff and George Browne to Chicago, something they were unwilling to do in the Ricca and Campagna tax matters.

Nitto's stylish yet unsmiling widow arrived in tax court with veteran attorney James A. O'Callaghan, who had handled the estate from the beginning. She sat stoically as he submitted his first order of business to the presiding Judge John W. Kern: lift the liens placed on the widow and adopted son. "It is our contention this money was set aside for the adopted son prior to the time the government says Nitti received the money from the Hollywood producers," he claimed. The judge reserved opinion until the evidence was presented.

O'Callaghan's strategy thereafter was aimed primarily at the issue of the extortion money. He argued again that "the government alleges Nitti's share was more than $400,000, but it can't trace one penny to Nitti's pockets." In summation, Nitto never received the money, but if he did, extortion money is not taxable; if the feds did collect on what they claimed, it would leave Nitto's widow and son destitute. The last argument hardly mattered, but the "not taxable" line of reasoning left government counsel chuckling. They recalled the tax case of Murray Humphreys back in 1935 regarding the $50,000 he received from the alleged ransom of a kidnapped local labor leader. Humphreys admitted no guilt in the crime, but they noted he paid taxes on that sum.

On September 29, the government whisked Bioff and Browne into Chicago under round-the-clock watch. For safety concerns, authorities shifted the tax trial from U.S. Tax Court on Lake Shore Drive to the more secure U.S. Customs Building on Canal Street, where the pair was ensconced. Platoons of agents guarded the location under strict mandate to inspect all persons entering and leaving the site. Identities were checked, and photographers waited outside, the only pictures they managed to snap were of the elegant widow and her attorney.

One well-heeled reporter did manage to get inside and interview Browne. Federal agents inside and outside the room monitored the journalist, who asked a few questions before soliciting for a photograph. The former union leader refused: "I'm established in my community. I don't care about myself, but my kids are in school. People have stopped wondering about me. If they saw my picture, I'd have to move."

The headlines covering the trial over the next few days tell the story. On October 1, 1948, the *Sun-Times* led with "BIOFF TELLS HUGE NITTI FILM SHAKEDOWN CUT." Nitto's widow listened impassively most of the day as the bespectacled labor thug rehashed his 1943 testimony. From the beginning, Nitti received 50 percent, then two-thirds of the extortion money, but Bioff related only one instance in which he personally handed Nitti money—a $12,000 payment. Bioff's quote of the day followed: "This was chicken feed though, in comparison to the money coming in those days."

The next day's headline in the *American* declared, "DRURY LINKS NITTI TO KILLING OF CERMAK." On this day, Browne testified in generalities, saying nothing really useful. Both he and Bioff wrapped up their testimony and left the city. Depositions from others were read, including one from local theater man John Balaban. Other witnesses called included Chicago police lieutenant William Drury and former chief investigator for the state's attorney's office Dan Gilbert. Neither shed any light on Nitto's income, but they spiced up the proceedings a great deal. Drury related a tangle with Nitto in 1933. Hauling him to the station, Drury had mentioned the Newberry and Cermak deaths. Nitto, he reported, boastfully replied: "I've got a good alibi. . . . Besides, those two guys were no good."

The *Tribune's* headline for that same day read: "BARE GANG'S ORDER TO NITTI TO SLAY BIOFF—LEADER CHOSE SUICIDE RATHER THAN OBEY." In his testimony, Dan Gilbert offered little other than his familiarity with Nitto's last mob conference. "Ricca, Campagna, and the others were demanding that Nitti kill Bioff to prevent him from testifying against them," he said. "They demanded that Nitti shoot Bioff, even if he had to do it in a crowded courtroom."

The October 5, 1948, headline for the *Daily News* read, "NITTI TAX DECISION RESTS WITH JUDGE." On the last day of the trial, the defense called those who had prepared Nitto's tax returns for the years 1935-40. One, a certified public accountant, claimed no knowledge of extortion money from their discussions. The other, a lawyer, claimed Nitto simply dropped by with numbers. He never showed him receipts or papers; Nitto "would come to my office and tell me his income." He filled out the forms and that was it.

The final witness, Annette Nitto, took the stand. Neatly dressed in a beige suit and black hat, to reporters she still appeared heartbroken over the loss of her husband. In a soft voice, she gave her address as 712 Selbourne Road, Riverside, Illinois. She and her husband had wed in May 1942, and he had given her two wedding gifts totaling $125,000. She did not know that any of her husband's money came from the extortion scheme, and if it did, she assured the court, she would have nothing to do with it. It was the movie moguls who made false statements against her husband. When asked what kind of man her husband was, she replied; "He loved his home, loved his boy, and I hope me."

Judge Kern gave O'Callaghan ninety days to file further briefs in the court. When O'Callaghan did, he claimed, "The record is devoid of evidence that Nitti received and did not report" the extortion money claimed. Ten months later Judge Kern disclosed his rulings. While the government had failed to provide convincing verification as to the amount of extortion money Nitto received, "we do know that he did receive and did personally retain some of the proceeds. Any other conclusion would be beyond the pale of reasonable belief." Annette was liable, but only for what the bureau had previously determined as unreported extortion income—$137,000. As for the proposed penalties, fraud with intent to evade taxes must be shown before they could be assessed, and so far, this had not been proven.

Nitto's widow was found liable for other items: deficiencies totaling just over $70,000 for amended returns, unreported racing dividends totaling $14,880, and money gifts to her amounting to $125,000. The burden of the total tax for these items was not fixed. Still, the verdict signified victory for Annette amounting to a reduction of nearly $300,000 on the extortion portion alone. O'Callaghan promptly announced a fight to the end in order to reduce the figure further. On January 26, 1950, the tax court refused to hear the appeal and determined a total tax bill of $138,075.99 for the years 1935-40.

Unmercifully, the feds kept up the pressure. A year later, they filed an additional claim for back taxes in the amount of $46,028.77; this was the straw that broke the widow's back. Lawyers' bills had devoured tens of thousands of dollars already; Internal Revenue had received some payments, and now they wanted the rest. All that visibly remained were two bank accounts totaling $25,222; by order of the Probate Court, Internal Revenue acquired $24,191, and the lawyers received the rest. The action rendered the estate insolvent, and on April 4, 1951, the estate of Frank Nitto was closed at last.

Annette retired from the Chicago spotlight with Joseph, perhaps to Florida for a time. In early 1956, she briefly reopened the estate. According to Annette, while making a final sift through the remainder of her late husband's papers, she discovered two dividend checks in the name of Frank Sasso in small amounts from 400 shares of stocks purchased in the mid-1930s. She devoted considerable time and travel over several weeks to prove that Sasso and Nitto were one and the same. The accumulated dividends and eventual sale of stock amounted to over $10,000. Once again, lawyers and taxes claimed a considerable portion. Two weeks later, the estate of Frank Nitto was shuttered again.

━━◁◦/◦/◦▷━━

After Nitto, leadership of the mob would have passed to Paul Ricca, but his trial, jail time, and the intense scrutiny of his probation due to his shady release from prison necessitated that leadership pass to the most capable of the lieutenants, Tony Accardo. Any shakeup in leadership brings change to the status quo, and the primary local business objective of the mob under Accardo in the mid-forties was to claim absolute control over all forms of local gambling. Before doing so, the mob restructured existing staff.

As early as April 1943, the new mob leadership attempted to make such an alteration. "So long as Nitti lived, Stanton retained power," one police lieutenant said. Longtime South Side hulk Danny Stanton was seated at a bar in the 6100 block of South Halsted when a loyal adherent ran in and whispered a warning. Stanton departed quickly. Four strangers soon entered, ordered beer, searched the place from top to bottom, and then left.

Two weeks later Stanton fell not far from the place of his origin. About 11:30 p.m. on May 5, 1943, Stanton was with friend and recent U.S. Army outcast Louis Dorman in Harry's 6500 Club, a tavern occupying a corner lot at Sixty-fifth and South May streets. Police had long considered the location a Stanton outpost. The pair had dropped in two hours earlier, bellied up to the bar, and downed six beers apiece. Now Mrs. Harry Preyner, the owner's wife, was serving up round number seven. Stanton had positioned himself at the rear of the bar so as to observe the comings and goings; fatally, however, an innocuous service door directly behind him led out the side to May Street.

414

Ten minutes later, as he tilted back the bottle of beer for a drink, the door opened and shotguns poked through and blasted. The first salvo killed Dorman instantly. Stanton had just enough time to lumber toward the rear of the bar for cover when another blast caught him in the head and torso. A final salvo downed another Stanton man. As a touch-up for the carnage, the assassins circled around front and put three revolver shots through the front windowpanes. The forty-six-year-old Stanton died twenty minutes later at nearby St. Bernard's Hospital.

"There are any one of a hundred reasons why Stanton might have been killed," observed one investigator, "and they are all connected with gambling." Stanton owned handbooks in the region and of late had been developing a wire service and protection racket to which numerous murders were connected. In this, he was looking to rake off a greater portion of the fattening paychecks received by locals in South Side factories that had geared up for war production.

The two witnesses in the bar could provide little to police. Mrs. Preyner was in the back office when the blasts echoed, her husband upstairs in their apartment. Still, police had a fair idea whom to question. Suspects included Martin Quirk, James "Red" Fawcett, and Sam Hunt, all with good cause. Stanton had tried to kill Quirk a few years ago, but he recovered favor and became a minor part of Stanton's ring. Stanton had even sent Quirk to kill a couple of leftover Saltis hands, including Willie Neimoth in a gambling matter, but Quirk double-crossed Stanton.

Fawcett, long thought to be Stanton's bodyguard, claimed only to be a local steel mill employee, yet police heard of a recent Fawcett-Stanton squabble. What's more, Hunt and Fawcett were known to be friends, and the style of both the attempt and the actual murder hinted at the Hunt killing methodology. Also, Hunt had labor interests in Cicero with Claude Maddox and was thought to be angling for Stanton's South Side interests. At the same time, police heard about a Stanton drive to make himself absolute ruler of those unions, putting him at odds with Maddox as well. Stanton had to go. Ultimately, talk had Quirk as Stanton's killer with the thought that perhaps he might be awarded Stanton's gambling realm; instead, the mob killed him on September 8. Fawcett was murdered in the spring of 1945, conspicuously leaving Maddox and Hunt the lone men standing.

The restructuring of gambling rights after Nitto continued for a year and a half in other parts of town, sending at least seven victims to the city morgue. Political feuding exploded into a gunfight, claiming Nitto's "friend" in the black South Side and Stanton gambling-labor racketeering associate J. Livert "St. Louis" Kelly in April 1944. Stanton's brother-in-law retired after surviving an ambush later that year.

In the early morning darkness of August 3, 1944, Lawrence Mangano, the Near West Side vice and gambling magnate under Nitto, returning to the city from a long night at the mob's Paddock Club in Cicero. In an odd twist, he chauffeured bodyguard Michael Pontillo and Pontillo's girlfriend in a maroon 1941 Mercury. It was a jolly cruise, with the car radio blasting dance music as they whisked up Blue Island Avenue toward the city's center. As they neared the intersection with Taylor Street, however, the occupants noticed a black sedan following them.

Mangano, assuming an impending police matter, curbed his car. As the pursuer slowly approached, Mangano exited his vehicle to bribe his way to freedom and was hit by buckshot and .45-caliber slugs. The assailant's car sped off, turning at the next block. Immediately, Pontillo and girlfriend went to retrieve the fifty-four-year-old Mangano, when, out of the dark, the assailant's car rounded the corner from behind for another pass. This time, a shotgun blast felled Pontillo as the pursuers raced off for good as the blaring melody from Mangano's car provided background music for the entire episode. The hit was never really understood by police. The former Public Enemy Number 4 had been quite content with his piece and told them he never desired to be on top of the gang. He never feared his "public enemy" tag either. Once, while bailing Tony Accardo out of jail on a bombing charge, he boasted, "Us public enemies have got to stick together." So much for loyalty.

The numbers (policy) racket in the South Side black neighborhoods raked in millions of dollars for the kingpins there. During Nitto's waning years, the mob was thought to be initiating an intrusion into the racket after the killing of chief Walter Kelly in 1939 and the indictment of the three Jones brothers on tax evasion in 1940. Stalled because of McLane and the movie extortion crises, the mob under Accardo renewed the campaign in earnest in the mid-forties. The principal holdouts remained brothers Edward and George Jones and Theodore "Teddy" Roe. In 1946, the mob solved the Jones problem by kidnapping Edward. His brother George negotiated his release for $100,000, and the men soon fled to Mexico. Teddy Roe persevered, though his take of the business dwindled. By 1951, a number of indictments by the state's attorney thinned the remaining lower ranks, leaving Roe as the sole survivor. In June, the mob disastrously attempted to kidnap him, and a ferocious gun battle erupted, killing one. A little more than a year later, they ambushed him for good and got their share of the lottery racket.

The organization under Frank Nitto made major inroads in their effort to control racing information services for handbooks through Guzik and Serritella but was never quite able to jostle James Ragen out. Nitto's successors found Ragen to be equally difficult. They tried freezing his local Midwest News Service out of prime space at the Cicero racetracks and sent Cicero police in to interrupt his business there. When these maneuvers failed, the mob determined to obtain racing data by circumventing Ragen. When Ragen learned of this, he planned to cut off his service to them completely.

In March 1946, the mob incorporated *Trans-American News* as a direct competitor to Ragen's *Continental Press*, with Tommy Maloy's former bully, Ralph O'Hara, as one of the leads. They systematically went about forcing Chicago handbook operators to drop *Continental Press* in favor of *Trans-American*. Those who continued to stand by Ragen were slugged or killed, but Ragen held fast. He appealed to a local political power and even went to the state's attorney, with no success. Bodyguards now followed him on his daily travels from his South Seeley Avenue home to his office in the Loop. He safeguarded his family, confining them to their home, fully knowing the mob was prone to kidnapping as a popular means of obtaining their desired results. With Ragen's heels dug in and all other means of takeover exhausted, a mob warning filtered back to him at the funeral of his older brother (Frank Ragen died in March 1946): get out of town in twenty-four hours or be killed. He refused.

In April 1946, the mob made their first attempt on Ragen but had to abort it when he outraced a vehicle containing two unknown men to the Morgan Street police station. Given a police escort home and a detail for home security, Ragen dismissed them in short order thanks to his selfless and noble reasoning that it was unfair to make the taxpayer shoulder the cost of his security in a business he fully knew to be fraught with danger. The following month, he dictated in the state's attorney's office what he hoped would be an insurance policy of sorts—a complete statement of what he knew of mob activities and their affairs. The original was held in safekeeping in the event of any harm befalling him, while he leaked a copy to the mob via Dan Serritella as a warning that should anything happen to him, the original would be released to law enforcement. Humphreys then met Ragen and bluffed the mob's position, telling him that most of what Ragen knew was about Frank Nitto, and Nitto was dead. Regardless, the organization could ill afford to have talk of their affairs bandied about.

On June 24, Ragen was driving home with his usual tail of bodyguards. They were motoring in the 3800 block of South State Street when a car in front of Ragen suddenly slowed, causing him to brake. Pulling up alongside him was a small delivery truck, the rear of which was open but covered by a heavy tarpaulin. Two shotguns poked through the tarp and blasted Ragen. At least one of his bodyguards returned fire as the truck sped away, but the shots only managed to obliterate a nearby tavern window. Wounded, Ragen was taken to a nearby hospital where he recovered over the course of the next few weeks, though not without losing the use of his shattered right arm. Police guarded the entry to his room, the hallway, and even the fire escape outside. His continued progress was widely reported from the fortress, when, suddenly on August 14, he died.

An autopsy revealed the cause of death as a chronic kidney inflammation complicated by mercurial poisoning. How much mercury was present in his body the coroner did not note, but he explained its presence away, labeling it as an ingredient in the blood plasma. At least one authority on plasma transfer rebuffed the explanation, and suspicion remains. Thereafter, the mob obtained favorable news distribution rights from *Continental*, and inside a year, their own *Trans-American News* folded. The whole matter was a continuance of Nitto's vision and looked ahead to handbook potential in Las Vegas. Ragen's former multimillionaire boss, Moe Annenberg, had preceded him in death, having succumbed to pneumonia at the age of sixty-four on July 20, 1942, just a month after his release from federal prison.

James Ragen was never a great believer in Frank Nitto. "At the time, he was supposed to be Al Capone's successor in charge of the Chicago Syndicate-but that, of course, was a laugh. It was Capone," he insisted, "not Nitto that ran the mob." Ragen surely possessed great knowledge of his news information services and had some interaction with the Nitto crowd, but his estimation of the mob's leadership situation was far off base. Capone had long been mentally incapacitated by neurosyphilis, and after his release from prison, he retired to the Florida sun of his Palm Island estate. His mental and physical health steadily declined, and on January 25, 1947, Nitto's Brooklyn neighbor suffered cardiac arrest and died in bed at age forty-eight.

The family returned him to Chicago for burial in Mount Olivet Cemetery on Chicago's Far South Side. Before long, thanks to the ever-popular Capone legend, endless sightseers trampled the spot, and the Capone family moved his grave (along with those of his father and brother Frank) to Mount Carmel in the western suburb of Hillside. The parallel course of two men that began so long ago continued, for when finally interred, Al Capone lay virtually across the road from his valued enforcer, Frank Nitto.

Death claimed Sam, the last of the Genna brothers who were Nitto's primary adversaries in the Prohibition alcohol racket, in December 1951; Jim had succumbed in 1931, and Pete had passed on in 1948. George Moran, last leader of the once powerful North Side Gang and intended target of the St. Valentine's Day Massacre, gradually faded into obscurity. The 1940s found the aging Moran resorting to bank robbery until his arrest and incarceration in the Ohio State Penitentiary and later Leavenworth federal penitentiary, where he died of cancer in 1957.

<hr />

On October 20, 1950, Ed Kelly, Chicago's mayor during Nitto's heyday as gang boss, visited his doctor for a routine checkup. He had experienced heart difficulties the previous spring but told his doctor, "I've never felt better in my life." While scheduling an appointment for a return visit, the seventy-four-year-old Kelly collapsed and died.

Three years earlier, Martin H. Kennelly succeeded Kelly as mayor. The Chicago mob found it no more difficult to operate under Kennelly and those after him than under previous administrations. According to Chicago mob historian John Binder, the 1950s represented the mob's zenith. Locally, they monopolized gambling and the nightclub industry, and certain labor circles still bowed to their influence. Beyond city and county, they held considerable sway in Milwaukee, Dallas, New Orleans, and Los Angeles and were generally recognized as the primary organized crime power west of the Mississippi River. And though the Chicago mob did not invent Las Vegas, during the fifties, they invested in it as one of its main players.

<hr />

A great number of Nitto's associates exited the mob during the fifties, not all as a result of domestic house cleaning. Charlie Fischetti died of a heart attack at age fifty in April 1951. Phil D'Andrea's health declined while he was serving his extortion term, and he never quite recovered. When Chicago Police Commissioner Prendergrast laid out the unwelcome mat for the extortion parolees, D'Andrea, his appearance now aged far beyond his actual years (one paper referred to him as "a little old man") assured those present, "They won't have any trouble with me." In September 1952, D'Andrea died quietly in Riverside, California, after an extended illness. He was sixty years old.

After his release from prison, Charlie Gioe's gangland prestige and affluence diminished, but he never appeared to hurt for money. He lived at Louis Greenberg's upscale Seneca Hotel on the Near North Side and may have owned a piece of it. He had sundry interests in restaurants, nightclubs, taverns, and real estate and may have retained some handbook interests. Because of his parole status, however, he claimed only to be in the legitimate construction business, building a boom of drive-in theaters.

Nonetheless, in the late 1940s, the feds briefly revoked his parole. Though he had been questioned in three murders since his release, he generally stayed out of trouble. The clownish, balding gangster always appeared at FBI offices for questioning when required, yet he cooperated very little. That may have changed in the early 1950s when immigration officials decided to double-check personal information he had given authorities. They found sufficient discrepancies to begin deportation hearings, and talk then began to circulate that he was dealing with the feds to avoid deportation.

Coincidentally, Senator Estes Kefauver's committee was coming to town to investigate crime. Tony Accardo reportedly told Gioe to take leave and "go over with Lucky," meaning exiled New York gang leader, Lucky Luciano. Rumor had it that the mob was pushing him out of his local interests, but Gioe resisted and was thought to be living in fear. To others, though, he appeared more brazenly ambitious. In late summer 1954, his buddy Frank Diamond freely blabber-mouthed to police that Gioe had approached him about muscling some labor unions. In fact, when a local restaurant which he was fronting was bombed prior to its grand opening, he approached a mob associate in a rather abrupt manner about fixing the matter.

Authorities involved in the movie extortion trial doubted the acuity of Frank Diamond's mental processes. Pure hardheadedness had prevented him from obtaining parole with the core of the Chicago group. In the beginning, he was so made at the government that he refused to deal with it in any manner. After his conviction, he ignored legal advice to serve time and earn credit, and he instead refused to enter prison until his appeals were exhausted. As a result, Boris Kostelanetz later remarked to authorities, "He did . . . a year and a half for free, you might say."

Both the feds and the mob probably viewed his extended stay favorably. Ricca and his old mob knew management of Diamond had been problematic even in his best days, and now Tony Accardo was in charge. When finally released, Diamond started off on the wrong foot. Noted one crime beat reporter, the same old Frank Diamond began pushing people around like a real "wild man." Gioe seems to be one of the few who appreciated this side of Diamond when he wanted into the unions, but the graying bully rebuffed him, saying Gioe was simply trying to exploit him for his own gain.

In 1952, police questioned Diamond regarding the murder of a local union official. The man had given Diamond $10,000 to buy some property, but the check bounced—the wrong thing to do to anyone, much less a savage. Like Gioe, he was thought to be the subject of immigration investigations. Diamond was also known to have a loose tongue, and his gang income could surely be better applied to more trusted and useful mob personnel. Besides, a new gang face had been elevated as mob representative in many labor matters during Diamond's incarceration, ostensibly ordinary trustee of taxi cab drivers union Local 777, Joe Glimco.

In late summer 1954, the mob rid themselves of both vexatious old-timers. They caught up with Gioe on the night of August 18, 1954. He had just entered the driver's side of a friend's car parked on the Near Northwest Side, but before he could insert the keys into the ignition, Gioe was shot five times, one bullet drilled through his head. He slumped down across the front bench-style seat, dead at age fifty. Three nights later, Frank Diamond eased his car into the driveway of his home at 710 South Keeler and left the vehicle to open the garage door and park his car within. As he returned to the auto, assassins jumped from the shadows of a nearby alley and blasted him with shotgun and pistol fire. The sixty-one-year-old was DOA at Bethany Hospital.

Two weeks later, Nitto's local labor vandal Max Caldwell suffered a fatal heart attack while lying on a couch in his Miami Beach home, dying at fifty-seven. Having won an appeal of his conviction for aiding the flight of a draft evader, the mob had sent him to Florida as a muscle man. As late as 1952, he was in the spotlight regarding the murder of a union official of the Carpenters Council of Miami.

"Little" Louis Campagna's reputation among his associates no doubt soared well above his stature after his conviction. Even before his scandalous parole release, he was the subject of a Bureau of Internal Revenue investigation. However, Campagna (and Ricca) greatly benefited from a false assumption held by the main of law enforcement. Unaware of the shadowy machinations working to obtain their early release, an agent suggested the following:

> Under ordinary circumstances it is believed the evidence in this case would warrant a recommendation of criminal prosecution. However since the taxpayer is now serving a long sentence in a Federal Penitentiary on another charge, it is believed the effort of the government should be concentrated on collecting its taxes rather than upon a new prosecution. It is, therefore, recommended that no concentration be given to a criminal prosecution.

Instead, civil proceedings were instituted. Campagna's attorney worked the case to a compromise, and via a letter dated October 11, 1946, the lawyer sent Internal Revenue a check in an amount that was equivalent to almost twenty-four cents on the dollar. The outrage eventually hit the papers full steam, but less than a year later, Campagna was free and could boast of having rubbed the government's nose in it twice.

Like all the subjects of the parole scandal, the feds hounded Campagna, aiming to fling him back into jail on some technicality of parole violation. In 1950, the government threatened Campagna for not fully explaining where all of his tax settlement money had come from. The explanation was vague. People, he said, just kept coming into his lawyer's office to deposit money for Louis. Authorities could prove nothing. Despite his on-again, off-again difficulties, he remained high in the mob hierarchy. May 1955 found Campagna vacationing in Florida with a lawyer friend, enjoying a little sun, a yacht excursion or two, and deep-sea fishing. They were trolling the waters off Miami when Campagna hooked a thirty-pound grouper. As he was reeling it in, he suffered a heart attack and died at age fifty-four.

❦

The mob never forgets.

A year after the conviction of Ricca, et al., Willie Bioff and George Browne were given a reduction in sentence and modified parole for aiding the government. In 1945, they were released with new identities. After the pair departed, prosecutor Boris Kostelanetz rationally assessed the pair's grim future: "They would be objects of revenge on the part of the convicted men and their families and associates for the balance of their natural lives." The two dropped completely from the radar screen, only appearing under extreme security to testify in Nitto's tax case and vanishing back into their protective covers as quickly as they had resurfaced.

On the morning of November 4, 1955, William Nelson of 1250 East Bethany Road in northeast Phoenix, Arizona, bade good day to his wife Laurie at the front door. They lived in one of the finest neighborhoods in town, a former citrus grove turned subdivision. It was a bright day, and he was headed into town on business. He climbed into his pickup truck, parked directly in front of the attached two-car garage, and waved goodbye to his wife. Mrs. Nelson waved then returned to her kitchen and domestic affairs.

When Nelson engaged the ignition, the truck exploded with a concussion heard across the desert for a mile. Truck parts were scattered over a 300-foot radius, and shards of metal were embedded in the Nelson house. The garage door was blown in, devastating their new Mercury inside. All the south windows of the Nelson house were shattered. Other homes as far as 150 feet away were damaged. Dishes were knocked from shelves at twice that distance. All that remained in the driveway was a twisted wreck of truck metal and a 1½-2-inch depression just below the truck's starter. Nelson's singed body was hurled thirty-six feet from the truck and landed at the base of a small grapefruit tree. His right leg was blown off at the knee, his right hand above the wrist, his fingers so mutilated the only fingerprint available came from his left ring finger. Nelson's watch stopped at 10:55 a.m. Maricopa County lawmen had long known William Nelson and Willie Bioff to be one and the same persons.

Evidence collected by the Maricopa County sheriff—including sash cord of the type used for Venetian blinds, fragments of paper and cardboard, and the dimensions of the driveway depression—suggested an explosive device consisting of six to eight sticks of dynamite placed in a small cardboard box that was wired to the starter and held in place by the cord. (The paper turned out to have belonged to the truck's owner's manual.) Given the sensitivity of the subject's background, the FBI was notified, and they assisted with lab tests, but local authorities retained jurisdiction over the matter.

Few doubted the real reason for Nelson/Bioff's murder. Chicago authorities sent Phoenix information regarding suspect hoodlums, presumably including known bombers, and the investigation soon focused on Clarence Michael Campbell, a known Chicago and St. Louis character who may have used a previous alias to rent a car at the Phoenix airport two days before the murder. Officials were anxious to locate him and obtain a handwriting sample to match against the one found at the Phoenix car rental, but before they could nab Campbell, he was blown to pieces while attempting to plant a bomb in Chicago on May 25, 1956. Of the four signature samples of his that remained, none was sufficient to connect him to the rental.

There the case ended, but just how the mob found out where Bioff lived remains hazy. According to residents, Bioff had arrived in the neighborhood about eleven years ago. A pleasant man, they thought him to be in the cattle feed or cotton business, which is why they believed he used the truck. Some thought he dabbled in stocks and bonds. The Nelsons were quiet and stayed close to home, according to his wife.

Westbrook Pegler, the same reporter who had brought Bioff down years earlier, determined to solve the murder mystery. About all he unearthed was a mildly embarrassing rapport Bioff had with local law enforcement that allowed him access to their firing range, as well as his acquaintance with U.S. Senator from Arizona, Barry Goldwater. (Goldwater did not know him as Bioff at the time.) Chatter had Bioff as an informant. More interestingly, Pegler reported that Bioff's activities extended to the Phoenix-Las Vegas gambling set. Other talk had Bioff as an investor in a Reno casino. Popping up among the gambling crowd, a business heavily infiltrated by hoods, was far from wise. He was probably in danger in Phoenix the whole time. Maricopa County officials understood that Tony Accardo had checked into town on at least one occasion. His visit, along with those by several mob associates from time to time, was regarded as normal given the long-term incarceration of Jake Guzik's son there on moral charges. Bioff could have compromised himself at any time.

Nearly two years later, Senator Goldwater received a warm and sincere letter concerning a presidential pardon for "Bill." He forwarded it to the FBI for consideration. An agent returned the letter to the Honorable Senator suggesting a more direct avenue for the matter. The "Bill" to whom the letter referred was, in fact, Willie Bioff, and the letter was thought to be from his wife Laurie. She had sold their home, but in 1957 she was still living in the Phoenix area. Whether she ever succeeded in her quest to get her husband pardoned is unknown.

<hr>

For more than a decade after Nitto's death, his mentor and financial man Louis Greenberg successfully tiptoed between the mob and legitimacy, leaning more toward the latter but hewing to the former when necessary. "He would like to break away," said one associate, "and he is having a hell of a time doing it." A multimillionaire, with

Nitto's passing, he owned 85 percent of the stock in the Manhattan brewery, which reaped $10 million a year in sales. Besides the Manhattan, he owned at least a portion of the Prima-Bismarck Brewing Company on South Archer. Other Greenberg interests included Capone's old Hawthorne Hotel in Cicero, the Town Hotel, the Seneca Hotel, Ace Distributing, and the old Lawndale Enterprises. He had long acquired properties through his City Management Realty, whose offices were conveniently tucked within the Manhattan Brewing Company complex on South Union Street.

On February 10, 1947, presumably because of the gangster stigma attached to the Manhattan and the need for legitimacy to compete with surging mainstream brewing giants, Greenberg changed the brewery's corporate name to Canadian Ace Brewing. Among the promotions the following year was one featuring Greenberg hamming it up with popular comedienne Joan Davis. The sales strategy still consisted of forceful tactics in the form of high-pressure sales to humble tavern owners on the nearby South Side. On one occasion in 1949, their shady methods cost them when the state liquor commission briefly yanked the company's wholesale permit because of false statements on its renewal application.

Greenberg had appeared as a material witness in the movie extortion case, but since 1943 he had lain low, demonstrating nothing but loyalty to the mob. Long known to be their financial connection to legitimate enterprises, he offered nothing of value to either the House subcommittee investigating the parole scandal in 1948 or the Kefauver Committee in 1950. In the latter, he skillfully evaded the questions put to him.

Q: "Did Nitti ever help you in connection with the sale of your beer?"
A: "No sir."
Q: "Do you know Tony Gizzo?"
A: "Yes."
Q: "And he subsequently became your distributor in Kansas City?"
A: "No sir."
Q: "Now, Gizzo was quite closely associated with Nitti; was he not?"
A: "I do not know, sir."

When Gioe was murdered, police questioned Greenberg in the hope that he would shed some light on the case, but he immediately slammed shut the discussion: "If I knew who did it, which I don't, I wouldn't tell you. . . . He was a nice fellow."

The allegiance on both sides appeared to have worn thin by 1955, however. Greenberg had applied for a liquor distributorship, perhaps seeking to expand his holdings beyond the beer trade. This may have run contrary to veteran mob favorite Joe Fusco and his booze portfolio and may have even bucked mob plans for beer distribution in Chicago proper. Matters relating to Frank Nitto's estate were also alleged to have cropped up. In October 1955, Nitto's adopted son Joseph turned twenty-one, and one story had Frank Nitto's friends prodding Greenberg for additional payment to the son's trust fund even though legal agreements had ended the claim years before. Greenberg refused. Combined with Bioff's recent murder, perhaps all this drudged up troubling memories of 1943. In any event, something disturbed him. In the weeks following Thanksgiving, he seldom traveled alone, often towing his wife Pearl about as a likely defense since Greenberg was fully aware the mob almost never harmed family who were detached from business affairs.

At the end of work hours on December 8, 1955, Greenberg and his wife left the old Manhattan brewery and drove toward home, the Seneca Hotel on the Near North Side. Traveling north on South Union only a couple of blocks from the brewery, impulse overtook them: why not stop for dinner at the Glass Dome Hickory Pit Restaurant? It was along the way at the northwest corner of Union and Twenty-eighth streets, and it was *the* South Side gathering spot for baseball fans attending games at nearby Comiskey Park. They had passed the restaurant time and again but had never dined there. Greenberg curbed their 1953 coupe almost at the front door facing west on the Twenty-eighth Street side of the restaurant.

Inside, the restaurant was teeming with as many as one hundred patrons, despite the baseball off-season. The couple enjoyed a couple of whiskey sours before washing down their shrimp and chicken dinners with coffee. The young waitress presented the bill of $6.18, and Greenberg tendered $7.00, waving off the change as a tip. It turned out to be Greenberg's last supper.

The couple exited the restaurant shortly before 7 p.m. Greenberg graciously opened the passenger door for his wife. As she climbed in, two men ran up to Greenberg and had a swift, faint conversation with him that concluded with Greenberg saying fearfully, "No, no." One of the men pulled a revolver and put two slugs point-blank into the millionaire, who instantly crumpled to the sidewalk in plain view of his wife as the two assailants dashed east across Union. Greenberg somehow recovered and slowly pulled himself to his feet with the aid of the open car door. Amazingly, he staggered off after th men. He had reached the middle of the Union crosswalk at the north side of the intersection when the assailants wheeled around for a look. Startled at the gritty energy of their victim, one of them fired three more rounds, one of which struck Greenberg above the left eye, dropping him for good. The men continued their exodus east before ducking into an alley. The "Jekyll and Hyde existence" of sixty-four-year-old Louis Greenberg ended on the bloody pavement in the middle of Union Avenue.

The family concluded the murder had been a botched robbery attempt and were so firm in their belief that they offered a $5,000 reward for information leading to the arrest of the perpetrators. It was never collected. The press, on the other hand, suspected a Syndicate hit, and Police Commissioner O'Conner suspected a connection with the string of murdered Capone men that had been building during the last eighteen months. When the department's lower ranks inspected the scene, they, too, leaned toward the robbery theory, noting the amateurish aspects of the murder. The bullets were the ordinary lead and copper .38-caliber type, rather than the professionally preferred steel-jacketed .45-caliber bullets, and experts would not put themselves in a position to have to escape on foot rather than via a getaway car. One police captain familiar with mob hits also pointed out that pros would have seen to it that "he went down and stayed down."

Nonetheless, word soon went out to bring in Tony Accardo and Jake Guzik for questioning. Ricca happened to be in Florida, and Joe Fusco came and went within fifteen minutes. By virtue of his courtroom threat against Greenberg back in 1943, Ralph Pierce ranked high on the pick up list. A couple of days later, he wandered in voluntarily and said of his whereabouts at the time of the murder, "I can tell you, but I don't care to." On the advice of counsel, he refused a lie detector test. He was an oil speculator, Pierce said—what would he have to do with a murder? He then walked out. Few seemed to note the similarity in *modus operandi* between Greenberg's killing and the Estelle Carey murder—both looked like robberies. Pierce was a suspect then, too. Further, this was the only way to hit Greenberg and avoid hurting his family in the process, so it looked like a delicate but businesslike mob hit.

Six months after the Greenberg murder, the Syndicate had its customers place beer orders by calling Premium Beer Sales and "ask[ing] for Jackie." The man thought to be in charge of Syndicate beer sales was Tony Accardo protégé Jackie Cerone. When officials scrutinized Tony Accardo's tax return a year later, the mobster listed his main income as being derived from activities as a sales agent for Premium. He was responsible for Chicago distribution of Foxhead 400 beer, a product not of Greenberg's hometown brewery but rather of the Foxhead Brewery of Wisconsin. This all indicated a clear motive for Greenberg's murder in that the mob now had a more active role in product selection and beer sales than Greenberg may have desired.

—◈—

Bioff's partner and former IATSE President George E. Browne seemed a little worse for wear when he emerged from federal prison. Internally sour, he stubbornly clung to his conviction that, all along, he was doing good work for the labor movement. In the flesh, Browne had shed much of his prior, decadent physique; in 1944, he looked more like a pathetic form of the bespectacled Farmer John type than the confident, burly union leader he had been. Sensibly, when released, Browne resettled where he blended superbly—in Dubuque, Iowa, as the very ordinary John Vernon. There he bought a house and established his wife and three daughters. Nearby, the Merchant's Hotel and the Page Hotel also served as part-time lodgings.

He remained unemployed, though not without money. (Ironically, the Internal Revenue cases against Browne and Bioff were dropped for their cooperation in the criminal case.) A close friend acted as his personal bank, sheltering large sums for him and delivering cash when necessary—precautions to keep Browne as invisible as possible. Burrowing further, Browne seldom stirred from the locale, preferring to pass much of his time—long, solitary hours—slurping drinks at the Page Hotel bar, relieved, if nothing else, that Chicago hoodlums supposed him to be somewhere in Mexico or South America.

Browne's blasé existence abruptly ended in 1955. His personal guardian learned of a former gang chauffeur, an Italian, now possibly living in town. Their paths never crossed, but it was close enough. In November, newspapers revealed Bioff's murder. Afterwards, the FBI notified local authorities of the possible danger to

Browne's life. A month later, Greenberg's death made headlines. His friend reported that Browne believed "he is living on borrowed time and expects to be killed at any time." An overwhelming and natural suspicion, but with the mob, it was hard to tell how accurate such suspicions were. Browne, though he did business with the mob, was never a member of the gang, as was the case with Bioff, and had none of the business links Greenberg did. And unlike Bioff, Browne testified reluctantly at best. As one columnist noted, "killing him would prove of no real value." Nonetheless, in January 1956, the FBI received a last word that Browne had shuffled off to Burlington, Iowa, his address unknown. Anonymous for the remainder of his life, somewhere untouched by the mob, he was thought to have died later that year.

Nitto associate Nick Circella also disappeared into a twilight zone of sorts. When the mob's heavy hand eliminated girlfriend Estelle Carey, Nick served out the remainder of his eight-year sentence in Leavenworth with little thought of premature release. This amounted to six years, counting time off for good behavior only—no parole. The matter was entirely his doing. In 1944, he received from Hollywood friend Sophie Tucker a letter of recommendation urging parole. Nick ignored it. When he became eligible for parole on December 6 that year, without a word he declined to apply. It was not until a year later that he finally stirred, and in February 1946 he was given a parole hearing. The matter was continued until May, when the parole board refused to grant his release, no explanation given. He would do his time the hard way, and he did so, serving the longest term of any of the Chicago mob hierarchy in the case.

By this time, quite possibly, Nick didn't want to appear eager for release. The core of his associates was now among the prison's population, having been transferred there from Atlanta. The shift alarmed Atlanta's warden, who notified the Bureau of Prisons of the possible danger to Circella. Also troubled, Mrs. Circella wrote Kostelanetz for help. She would soon travel to visit her husband and wanted assurance from Kostelanetz that her husband was "not being forgotten." He tried, but as he was now in the private sector, there was little he could do. Only when an Illinois congressman, a Chicago reverend, and his wife petitioned the prison was Circella at least transferred to serve the remaining time in the less confining space of the Leavenworth Honor Farm.

When Circella's term finally expired, he returned to the Chicago area. The mob left him alone, but U.S. Immigration officials were another matter. It seems they had no record of his citizenship, and by virtue of his conviction, they were set to deport him back to Italy. In the end, they agreed to let him leave the country for a point of his choosing as long as he paid the bill. On April 21, 1955, Nick and his wife boarded the SS *Del Norte* for Argentina, far from the North Side cabarets and nightclubs to which he was accustomed. Eventually, they returned closer to home, Mexico City. The last that was heard of him, he had bought several shrimp boats and prospered, never to return to Chicago.

Despite thirty years of gang numbers floating from end to end in his brain and a pushover appearance to boot, roly-poly Jake Guzik remained politely stone-lipped to the end. The following is indicative of his entire testimony before the state's attorney regarding the James Ragen murder.

Q: "Don't you have any partnership arrangement with anybody in the city of Chicago?"

A.: "No sir."

Q: "None whatsoever?"

A: "No sir."

When he was reported kidnapped in April 1944 and it was said he allegedly paid between $25,000 and $100,000 for his freedom, the ex-pimp feigned to solve the mystery for the press—it was only a stickup. The men got *only* $1,700, he groaned. Few believed it. He was equally uncooperative when Senator Estes Kefauver called him before his investigating committee. In 1950, he was living well in Chicago's upscale South Shore area as a self-professed "retired gambler." A month after he confidently walked away from police questioning in the Louis Greenberg murder case, he dropped into St. Hubert's Old English Grill, his daily stop in the Loop. While there, he collapsed from a heart attack and died at the age of seventy.

Sam "Golf Bag" Hunt was perhaps at his murdering busiest during the Nitto years. His reputation always preceded him. Seemingly hauled in at just about every mention of a murder, Hunt became so annoyed with police that he customarily checked in at the nearest station whenever a lead-filled body turned up. As late as 1942, he stood accused of killing a motorist and wounding the passenger over a petty traffic accident. The state's attorney tried the case four times before Hunt was finally acquitted. After questioning in the Stanton murder, it is believed that he shared in Stanton's labor and gambling domain while still performing useful contracts for the mob. In August 1956, six months after Guzik passed on, Sam Hunt checked into a Schenectady, New York, hospital while visiting his niece. Pneumonia and heart ailments caught up with him there, and he died at age fifty-five.

In December 1956, Johnny Patton, former village president of Burnham for more than forty years and Nitto's front man for his racetrack interests, died at his farm home in Indiana at age seventy-three. He had been retired since the late 1940s and plagued by ill health for the past three years.

Old habits die hard. Sixty-year-old former BSEIU President George Scalise pled guilty in 1957 to two counts of conspiracy in a union welfare scam which netted him and his associates nearly $300,000. The judge, in pronouncing a one-year sentence, rejected pleas of ill health, declaring Scalise nothing more than a "Tripoli pirate who moved in on any fat ship which was defenseless."

Outfit heavyweight and St. Louis native Claude Maddox remained a figure in suburban labor racketeering after helping engineer the deal that freed Nitto and company in the 1940 McLane incident. He was thought to have remained a power in Local 450 of the Hotel and Restaurant Employees Union as well as a collector of minor gambling interests. Quite wealthy as result, he enjoyed an extensive stable of horses and rubbed elbows with the lofty equestrian set as the sophisticated "Mr. Moore." Snared by the law in the late 1950s for failing to register a gambling device, he served ten months of a one-year sentence. Shortly thereafter, on June 21, 1958, fifty-eight-year-old John Edward Moore, alias Claude Maddox, died in bed at his lush suburban Riverside home.

Nitto accomplice in the bartenders union takeover bid and "financial wizard" Fred Evans, age sixty, was about to climb into his 1958 Cadillac when he was pulled aside and gunned down by two men on August 22, 1959. He had recently dominated the city's linen business, controlling uniform and rag cleaning, linen supplies, and diaper services. Unglamorous as it may seem, the business was good for as much as $250,000 a year. He was subject to two federal investigations, one of which was a tax investigation into mob labor agent Joey Glimco. His murder was attributed to any one of these angles.

After he was double-crossed by the mob and voted out of his union in early 1941, George McLane wisely never tried to regain the stature he once had. Despite the damning testimony against Nitto and company that at one time put him one step from his grave, the mob let him be. He retired to the North Side of Chicago with his wife, two sisters, and a brother, living out a quiet life as a humble bartender in a neighborhood liquor store. Three days after Fred Evans was gunned down, George McLane died quietly in nearby Edgewater Hospital at age sixty. His elected successor in Local 278, Joseph McElligott, retained McLane's old position until his death in 1967.

In November 1959, the mob's last Prohibition era competitor, Roger Touhy, was released from prison on parole after serving twenty-five years for kidnapping. That same year, he teamed with Chicago *Sun-Times* journalist Ray Brennan to write his biography, namely his account of the Factor kidnapping that landed him behind bars. In it, Touhy never claimed to be an angel, but he always declared this charge to be a phony rap contrived from both sides of the law. The Nitto mob notwithstanding, according to Brennan, Touhy fingered the top three persons responsible as former detective Dan Gilbert; Jake Factor, California millionaire real estate man; and former state's attorney Courtney. As result of his conviction, those in the underworld who stood to gain the most were members of Nitto's organization.

Of those who now remained, mob fixer Murray Humphreys was recognized as the man with the most to lose if Touhy continued with his crusade.150 Over the years, Humphreys settled into relative obscurity while still running certain mob affairs, and he wanted to keep it that way. The venom between the two that was expressed when they were clashing over the union rackets years ago remained concentrated. As of late, Touhy blamed the mob for muscling distributors to avoid carrying his book.

Perfectly aware of his precarious position as a parolee, Touhy hired retired policeman Walter Miller (the same cop who was at the center of the McLane deal) as a bodyguard so that no one could slip a phony parole violation rap on him. This, he exclaimed, was his only real fear. As extra insurance, Touhy resided with his sister at 125 North Lotus Avenue near Oak Park, keeping his forays about town to a minimum. His ever-watchful sister also insisted that he return home at least a half-hour prior to his 11 p.m. curfew, just to be sure. Otherwise, he went about his business never really fearing the mob would "hit" him.

During the week of December 6, a retired rabbi interrupted a stranger in the basement of his apartment building at 120-122 North Lotus, across the street from number 125. The man had shoved aside an old refrigerator that blocked access to the basement window looking out across the street, and the window ledge appeared to have recently been cleaned. A building janitor later found a litter of cigarette stubs and food remnants in the same location.

On December 16, Touhy and Miller spent the evening in the Loop with biographer Ray Brennan. The writer left the group about 9:30, and Touhy and Miller returned to North Lotus about 10:15. Seven concrete steps led from the walk to the porch, an open attachment to the brick home. As the pair hit the last step, two men jumped from the dark below and unloaded five shotgun blasts into them. Miller managed to squeeze off three shots at the fleeing men before collapsing. Touhy buckled, bleeding profusely from a fist-sized wound in his upper left leg and a multitude of pellet-sized wounds elsewhere. By the time the ambulance arrived, his blood cascaded down nearly the entire length of the concrete steps, but Touhy was still conscious. He assured policemen and attendants, "I'll be alright; I'm okay." Less than an hour later, he was no longer an irritant to anybody.

At the time of the murder, Jake Factor was dining in a posh Near North Side restaurant. When asked, Factor elaborated on his heart-felt sadness for Walter Miller and his enormous hospital bills (he survived), and then about Touhy, he offered a somewhat uninspiring, "It's not my way of life. I feel very badly. It's too bad for any human being to be cut down like that." He had instituted a $3 million libel suit against Touhy and his book upon release, and events did not alter his legal plans. Gilbert knew no reason for Touhy's murder. He blandly speculated that he had held out on his pals a portion of the ransom money collected so long ago.

Of course, the mob was suspect. The gunmen and the lookout across the street hinted at a professional job—especially since the mob was long noted, as in the case of Bioff, for waiting as long as it takes to get their man. Managing director of the Chicago Crime Commission Virgil Peterson also suspected organized crime. Other investigators surely pointed out that Touhy, in prison, "was just another convict," but outside prison walls, he was bad publicity for the crime syndicate. One press editorial summed it up:

> In a world where there are few roses, Roger Touhy did not pretend to be one, but his finish emphasizes that even a man who was not so good may be the victim of men who are worse.

Roger Touhy was sixty-one when he died.

Thomas J. Courtney remained state's attorney until 1944. The following year, he attained a position as a Circuit Court judge, a post he held for twenty-five years. He died in 1971.

Courtney's chief investigator, Dan Gilbert, had a thirty-plus-year résumé in law enforcement when he became the Democratic candidate for Cook County sheriff in the 1950 election. By and large, the nomination represented a sure-bet winner. Three weeks before the votes were cast, however, Senator Kefauver brought his organized crime committee to Chicago, and Gilbert testified before them behind closed doors. The committee only said afterwards that Gilbert testified to amassing a fortune through market speculations, but the press quickly dubbed him the "world's richest cop."

Somehow a transcript of his testimony made its way to the *Chicago Sun-Times*, which printed it in its entirety just days before the election, and the answers to questions about Gilbert's fortune were seen to be on the edge of the believable, given his regular policeman's salary. When his tax returns were scrutinized, they disclosed gambling income. Counsel for the committee inquired as to the source of his gambling, saying, "That's not legal betting is it?" Gilbert fumbled, "Well, no, it is not legal"—this from the man who campaigned to eradicate Cook County gambling in six months. Angry voters went to the polls and elected last-minute Republican candidate John E. Babb by more than 370,000 votes, at which point Gilbert retired from public life.

Jake Factor withdrew to California, where he prospered as a real estate speculator, soon reaching millionaire status. Pardoned by President John Kennedy in 1962 for any misdeeds in the past, he died in 1984 at age ninety-one after a long illness.

Nitto's name resurfaced in early 1957 when Annette reopened the estate yet again. Perhaps due to the yarn of Greenberg's financial holdout as a possible motive to his murder, Annette Nitto filed suit in the Superior Court of Cook County against the estate of Louis Greenberg, the individuals and co-executors as given by his last will and testament. She formally outlined the Nitto-Greenberg financial trust and alleged that over the course of years, she believed in excess of $2 million was passed to Greenberg. While he was alive, Greenberg had procrastinated about making a full accounting, and it was only with the filing of his estate inventory and the disavowal of such a trust by the family that she was now forced to make a claim. The two legal agreements clearing Greenberg years before were exhibits to the filing; nonetheless, the action moved forward.

The battle played on for the next couple of years as a series of mundane legal delays while the two parties haggled over technicalities. In the end, both sides agreed that neither could make an accurate accounting of the labyrinthine finances of the two characters. In December 1959, rather than fight for all the money she claimed rightly for the estate, Annette reconciled to conclude matters once and for all for a mere lump sum of $35,000. On May 4, 1961, eighteen years after his death, the probate of Frank R. Nitto was duly closed for good. By then, Annette had ducked completely from view.

Thanks to this final case, a touch of incongruity energized further misinterpretation of the history of Frank Nitto. For some reason, perhaps bending to press accounts from the very beginning, Annette Nitto filed the legal action as Annette Nitti. The claims were made in the name of the estate of Frank R. Nitti—an *i* for an *o* once again—and for history this misspelling seemed destined to remain.

Further events continued to baselessly engrave the *i*-for-an-*o* name in the history books as well as in enduring talk. When the television series *The Untouchables* was launched in 1959, veteran actor and perennial heavy-hitter Bruce Gordon appeared as Frank "the Enforcer" Nitti. Of the show's script, not of Gordon's portrayal, Johnny Rosselli reportedly commented to an up-and-coming hood at the time:

> Let me tell you something. . . . They make Capone and Nitti look like bloodthirsty maniacs. The guys that write that —— don't know the first thing about the way things were in those days. Eliot Ness, my ass. The tax boys got Al, not Ness. And what did he ever have to do with Frank Nitti?

The latter question was probably in reference to the show's portrayal of the Enforcer's death in which, after a chase by Ness, Gordon's character is run down in a Chicago subway.

On February 22, 1964, the *Daily News* reported Nick Nitti was in partnership with Tony Accardo's son in a suburban travel agency. The venture folded late that year, but Nick resumed an interest in the travel business through his Nitti Travel in River Grove with John and Michael Nitti. Because of the apparent abundance of mob bookings at both offices, some suspected of this Nitti clan a high mob pedigree. On August 14, 1965, the *Tribune* reported the arrest of Salvatore Nitti, fifty-one, for operating a gambling wire room. Police announced Nitti as the nephew of the late Frank "the Enforcer" Nitti, and the FBI suspected Frank Angelo Nitti to be a nephew of Nitto as well.

Of all these proposed Nitto relationships, almost certainly none are fact. Joseph and Virginia Nitti begat son Frank Angelo circa 1911, and Frank's siblings begat nephews Michael, Salvatore, and Nick Nitti, who then begat John and Nick Jr. a generation later. When twenty-two-year-old Rich Nitti was arrested in connection with a 1984 murder and pronounced the great-grandnephew of the Enforcer by a *Sun-Times* reporter, Nitti's attorney disgustedly waved off the supposition, saying, "Don't believe it." In this, he was correct. Rich, likely the third generation, lived at the Melrose Park address of Nick Nitti. He was indeed the great-grandnephew of Frank Nitti—Frank Angelo Nitti, not Francesco Raffele Nitto. Of Plan-It Travel, the Nitti-Accardo venture, many seemed inclined to place the reason for the mob traffic there on the Nitti name rather than on the obvious importance and current overbearing presence of mob boss Tony Accardo's kin. The same thing again occurred with Nitti Travel, where the most overlooked name allegedly connected with the place was up-and-coming Chicago mob boss Jackie Cerone.

As to the relationship of this Nitti clan to Frank Nitto, the supposed ties surfaced only well after Nitto's death. Their roots may date back to the matter of Marie Capezio's 1943 arrest and claim to be Nitto's sister. Her maiden name was Nitti, and she was possibly a distant relative of the aforementioned Frank A. Nitti clan. The clincher against any relationship seems to be that Frank Angelo Nitti was born twenty-five years after Nitto to a couple who never appear in the Nitto record, and his police record began only in 1929, when Judge Lyle sentenced him for larceny of an auto. Long after this arrest, Frank A. Nitti was still running up a lengthy record of arrests, thanks to petty-larceny projects. Surely, Frank Nitto, Capone's mighty Enforcer in 1929 and leader of the mob through the 1930s, would not permit a relative to lead such a paltry and risky existence.

In 1982, a *Tribune* reporter attempted to discover the relationship between Frank "the Enforcer" Nitto, John and Nick Nitti, and the Nitti Travel Agency. When he reviewed the birth records, adoptions records, and other vital information, he discovered absolutely no connection. Nitto, he concluded, had only one adopted son, who never used the name Nitti. In any event, Frank Nitto's only sibling, Anna, bore no children. All this investigation was necessary because, though Frank Nitto never used the name Nitti, somehow the press did. Outsiders who didn't know better perpetuated the wrong name, and in time this simple mistake blew out of control.

And the myth goes on. As late as 1979 the press reported that the recently murdered ex-con Robert "Cherry Nose" Brown was, somehow, the great-grandnephew of Frank "the Enforcer" Nitti.

The 1960s carried away both Nitto associates and landmarks. Venerable labor racketeer Murray Humphreys expired in 1965, while moon-faced politico and sometime front man for Nitto's scratch sheet business Dan Serritella passed on in 1967. Fellow conspirator in the movie case and New Jersey connection Louis Kaufman died in February 1965. Lacking mob appeal, he withered away in prison, serving the maximum length of his seven-year sentence. Part of his lengthy stay in prison was due to the fact that he could not pay the adjudged $10,000 fine. The Treasury Department could have informed the Justice Department of his supposed penury. In the 1930s, they battled Kaufman for six years to collect $6,000 in back taxes, the last of it as $200 per month installments. Finally, the Justice Department agreed upon a payment plan to pay his fine, and since 1949, Kaufman paid the U.S. government sums between $10 and $30 a month toward that end. When he passed away, the bill still registered a balance of $8,725.

Nitto's legacy, the Manhattan brewery, outlasted nearly all other rivals in the venerable brewing town. After the name change to Canadian Ace Brewing and Greenberg's death, the pressure of the large national brewers forced sales into a slow decline. Many similar breweries feeling the pinch went belly up. In a desperate measure to reinvigorate sales, executives at Canadian Ace selectively bought up a handful of local brewers and introduced new labels. Without Greenberg and mob influence, however, the death knell finally came in 1968 (leaving Meister Brau as Chicago's last brewer). As of the late 1990s, all that remained of the once mighty Manhattan brewery at Twenty-ninth and Union was a small, indiscernible brick segment. Auctions that regularly feature Manhattan memorabilia often contain the Nitto/Nitti name in the catalog line to stir up interest. The scarcest of cans from the brewery remains perhaps Manhattan Bock. In Nitto's time, Manhattan Bock was chiefly a bottled product and, according to one expert, only a single small shipment of cans was produced as a special order in 1937.

———※/※/※———

Harry Hochstein, Nitto's sometime chauffeur and aide, drifted along in an inoffensive way. In 1956, the worst that could be observed of him was his supposed association with Capone's old dairy enterprise, Meadowmoor Dairy. Through the sixties, he still could be spotted at mob-attended weddings. He died in 1971. Thomas Burke remained head of Local 25 from the day of Alterie's death in 1935 until 1973. He died three years later.

Coarse, graying, ex-bartenders "union official" Louis Romano remained a secondary figure in mob circles after Nitto's demise. He once sued the police force for $100,000 because they arrested him in his later years for "no good reason," he said, bringing upon him great disgrace by associating him with the Capone name. In 1954, he was appointed as a labor consultant for the Chicago Restaurant Association. The lawyer who appointed him by way of recommendation claimed that Romano, as former head of the bartenders union, "performed exceptionally well in his capacity as labor advisor and expert." Later, in language resonant of the early Hollywood stereotypical gangster, Romano told a congressional committee investigating improper activities in the labor fields "the whole bunch of youse are wrong." Finally out of the public eye, he spent part of his later years in Coral Gables, Florida, surviving into the late 1970s.

After his movie extortion conviction, Nitto's protégé Paul Ricca fought a cat-and-mouse battle with the feds, who were anxious to put the subjects of the scandalous 1947 parole back in prison. More often than not, he bamboozled authorities and, thus, always remained high in the mob chain of command. Like Campagna, Internal Revenue computed an extensive Ricca income unreported during the movie extortion years, with taxes and penalties amounting to over $141,000. He settled the case for a petty twenty-six cents on the dollar.

As part of its efforts, the government continued to scrutinize him for any possible parole violations. He was picked up in 1948 but released. In November 1950, he was rearrested for parole violations that included failure to reveal the source of the money he used to pay back taxes and misleading parole reports regarding expenditures during January 1948, in particular the extravagant spending for his daughter's wedding reception at the Blackstone Hotel in Chicago. Of his wealth, he later explained that betting on horse races was part of the answer: "I can't help it if I win, in thirty or sixty days, $91,000." Nearly two years and numerous hearings later, Ricca won round two with the feds.

U.S. Immigration, in turn, took their best shot. They dissected his naturalization papers and discovered his original Paul Maglio immigration story was phony. He was, in fact, Felice DeLucia of Naples, Italy, where, in 1917, he had served two and a half years for murder. Four years later, he was tried in absentia for another murder and sentenced to twenty-one years in prison. By this time, however, he had obtained a duplicate passport as Paul Magio and entered the United States. On the basis of the new information, U.S. District Court Judge Walter LaBuy in 1957 ordered Ricca's citizenship revoked and issued deportation orders. The cunning Ricca managed to stall the order.

While appealing the decision, Ricca was found guilty of tax evasion. He never took the stand in his defense and accepted the prospects of a prison sentence—at least he would be in the U.S. In the summer of 1959, he surrendered to serve a term in the federal penitentiary at Terre Haute, Indiana. When he emerged in 1961, he readied himself to face the leftover immigration matter. Ricca avoided deportation rather simply: a person can only be deported provided the destination country accepts them. In Ricca's case, he cleverly provided officials of target countries with a complete summary of his unsavory background in the United States; surely no country wanted a scoundrel, and as long as they refused, he remained in the United States.

Ricca never left, and through the 1960s, he served as a valuable mob go-to answer man, ever shrewd and succinct. The aging chief appeared on the surface as much the balding and loving grandfather as a hard-nosed mob boss. By 1971, his health began to gradually give way, and the following year, he entered Presbyterian's St. Luke's Hospital for treatment. Still in the hospital mid-October, he died of an apparent heart attack at seventy-four.

Ralph Capone passed away in November 1974. Of the Capone brothers, other than Al, Ralph was probably the most familiar to Nitto. Though he never again ranked as high as he did during Prohibition, the mob gave him odds and ends to sustain himself and the family. Gradually, Ralph's career faded to obscurity, and he died at eighty-one.

By July 1976, Ralph Pierce, a suspect in the Estelle Carey and Louis Greenberg murders and a recent South Side boss, had spent nearly five weeks in the intensive care ward of a local hospital before he expired at age seventy-two.

The sole surviving member of the convicted movie-trial defendants, Johnny Rosselli, returned to California after his release and continued to be an important figure in mob circles. Highly regarded in many underworld fields of endeavor, he served as a suave ambassador of sorts, consorting with mob chiefs from Chicago to New Orleans to Florida. He played key roles in the mob's gambling efforts in Las Vegas and Havana, Cuba. The mid-1970s found him splitting time between California and Florida, where his sister lived.

In 1975, the U.S. Senate formed a Select Committee on Intelligence Activities, named the Church Committee after its chairman, Senator Frank Church. Their focus was on overseas assassination plots by the Central Intelligence Agency. One key part of the inquiry included the plots to kill Fidel Castro and the mob's alleged aid in them. The underworld watched with interest. In June 1975, previous mob boss Sam Giancana was murdered in his home, and at least part of the reason was ascribed to his upcoming appearance before the Church Committee.

The key mob witness, according to one senator, then became Johnny Rosselli. He testified before the committee, but in a delicate way so that he felt he didn't compromise anyone. For a year, Rosselli went about his business, then in the summer of 1976, he received two warnings from friends, vague notices of mob contracts on his life. Rosselli insisted everything was fine, but on July 28, he went missing from his sister's Florida home. Ten days later, two fishermen trolling the shallow waters of the Inter-Coastal Waterway near Miami observed the top of a fifty-five-gallon steel drum breaking the surface. Through openings in the side, it appeared as if clothes were within. They man called police, and when the drum was opened, the body of seventy-one-year-old Johnny Rosselli was found inside. The official cause of death was asphyxiation, though he had been shot, stabbed, and later hacked apart to fit in the drum.

Nitto's slot-machine partner Ed Vogel continued to rake in millions from the machines long after Nitto's death—about $2.5 million annually, according to one estimate. When the young guns of the mob eased him out in the 1950s, he was allowed to keep the vending-machine business. He cornered the coin-operated amusement and game machine business, including jukeboxes and pinball and cigarette machines, imposing a $1 tax per machine under his Apex Amusements Company. A later complainant charged that he used police to enforce jukebox locations and to force out all competitors in Cicero. A multimillionaire, Vogel's wealth permitted him to maintain three ex-wives while living in a $100,000, ten-room lakefront apartment complete with household staff. Prosperity also allowed him to slum part-time in Palm Springs, California. It did not, however, permit the eighty-one-year-old relief from the leukemia to which he succumbed on June 12, 1977.

Of the two policemen accused in the 1932 shooting of Nitto, Harry Miller retired to California. Friendly, he never discussed the episode with anyone and survived into the seventies. His partner Harry Lang disappeared soon after the shooting. In the 1930s, he was reported to be working as a minor labor agent and litigating to get his detective job back. He apparently never did.

Robert Larry McCullough, who was arrested with Nitto in 1925, remained active after Nitto's death as a strong-arm terrorist and handbook operator associated with Paul Ricca, Frank Diamond, and Ralph Pierce. He also served Johnny Patton at Sportsman's Park as the chief of track police. Later investigations pegged him as managing the parking lot concessions at Sportsman's Park while working winter months at the Miami Beach Kennel Club. He outlasted nearly all of Nitto's primary contacts, dying on January 24, 1989, at age ninety-seven. Only Tony Accardo, who passed away on May 27, 1992, at eighty-six, survived him.

When Hollywood resurrected *The Untouchables* as a motion picture in 1987, Frank Nitto's character was portrayed as an oily, debonair weasel—hardly menacing. The fiction continued when Eliot Ness eventually tossed the character off a rooftop, during Prohibition no less. Mercifully, a year later, writers from the *Chicago Tribune* set Nitto's demise straight. Then Leonard Hill Films released *Nitti the Enforcer*, a Nitto biography starring actor Anthony La Paglia as perhaps the most convincing Nitto to date. The movie, mostly accurate, emphasized the Nitto name. Unfortunately, Nitto's epic biography was only ninety-four minutes long and was syrupy with sentimentality.

One of the most recent Nitto portrayals was seen in the early 1990s when an updated weekly version of *The Untouchables* series appeared. It revealed a very businesslike Nitto; however, when the show folded after a run of a couple of years, the last episode ended with a hint at yet another fairy tale: Nitto somehow conniving with the feds to put Capone in prison so he could take over.

Few of Nitto's bloodline lived to see the portrayals. Brother-in-law Vincent Vollaro had died long before, on October 2, 1942. Nitto's one and only sibling, sister Giovannina "Anna" Vollaro, passed away March 4, 1960, at nearly eighty years of age. Both died in Brooklyn. At the time of her death, the majority of their middle-aged children still could be found at 104 Garfield Place, unmarried with no offspring of their own.

Of Nitto's half-brothers, Raphael Dolendo died in March 1973, while Genaro, a retired business agent, expired in Florida six months later. The years gradually carried away most of Frank Nitto's twelve nieces and nephews, with a couple of them surviving into the 1990s. The last of Anna Vollaro's sons, Frank Nitto's blood nephews, died in New York in 1995. At the time, the 104 Garfield Place address in Brooklyn was still in the family's name after seventy years.

After Lucy Ronga, the widow of Nitto's father-in-law, Dr. Gaetano Ronga, died in the early seventies, among the items left to be administered was the property that had seemingly been in the family's name forever, the house at 1208 Lexington (then McAllister). In the end, it was family friend Annette Nitto who administered the sale the following year after a half-century of possession.

Annette apparently remained in the Chicago area through the seventies. When she passed away in May 1981, she retained to the end, despite the long-simmering Nitti/Nitto confusion, the genuine name, Nitto.

Perhaps putting to rest the theory that Greenberg's murder had anything to do with benefiting him—or if it did, he was washing his hands of the whole affair— twenty-one-year-old adopted son Joseph officially signed that he would have nothing more to do with the estate of his late father and perhaps his name. In the Probate Court of Cook County, regarding the estate of Frank R. Nitto, deceased, dated March 12, 1956:

> I, JOSEPH NITTO, the sole surviving son of the above named decedent, hereby sell and assign to my mother, ANNETTE NITTO, any and all claims that I might have in connection with the above described estate.

> (signed) Joseph Nitto

The young man disappeared, surfacing only once more to sign a public record in the matter. He routinely signed the document "Nitto," but then, perhaps to make it official, superimposed an *i* over the *o*, as the new document incorrectly listed Nitti as the official name. He then dropped from view, married, and raised three children, unbothered to this day and thought to have assumed his original birth name.

Landmarks of Nitto's life, vestiges that embraced his existence, have also largely disappeared. In New York, the Navy Street tenements with which he was familiar in his youth vanished many years ago; however, Garfield Place where his sister once lived remains much the same, and now is even upscale. His Di Lido Island home remains. In Chicago, urban blight claimed the Four Deuces and the Metropole Hotel decades ago, and Cicero's Twenty-second Street landmarks of the Prohibition days are long gone. Interstate 90/94 slices through the Near West Side Little Italy area of his Chicago arrival, and much of the rest of the area has been developed as part of the University of Illinois-Chicago campus. A high-rise Cook County office building occupies the former site of Nitto's Capri Restaurant headquarters, and the Lexington Hotel was demolished in 1995. The site where Angri, Italy, native Francesco Raffele Nitto decided his fate—and thus ended the Nitto family in bloodline and name once and for all—beside the railroad tracks that overcast March day in 1943 has long been urbanized and paved over as the North Riverside Park Shopping Mall; most shoppers are oblivious to the history of the ground on which they tread.

In 2003 the Town of Riverside's preservation commission debated about naming Nitto's 712 Selbourne address as a historical site. Nitto's last home received the nomination under the selection criterion as having belonged to a famous person. A supporter reasoned, "It's preserving history. We have to remember the good and the bad." The commission rejected the notion, 8–1, perhaps wishing to purge that part of its history much as the City of Chicago did when it denied historical status to Capone's home a few years earlier.

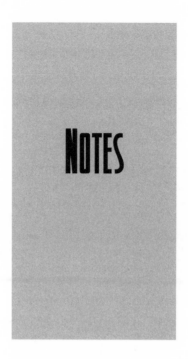

NOTES

EXPLANATION OF NOTES AND SOURCES

Every attempt was made to locate original sources to get the most concise picture of Frank Nitto's life, since what little that has been written about him over the years has oftentimes proved unreliable or incomplete. George Murray, the only author to really tackle Nitto and the successors in the Capone mob, did not use footnotes in his *The Legacy of Al Capone*. In an interview with Mr. Murray, he told the author that while he used some original sources, he relied heavily upon newspaper clippings from the publisher at which he worked. Much of what he wrote concerning Nitto was verified as coming from such; still other information could not be corroborated in any case.

Even on a few government documents the information Nitto provided sometimes did not stand up. For example, Nitto gave the name *Guerra* to federal bureaucrats as the ship on which he traveled to America. Apparently federal agencies thought it was not sufficiently important to confirm it. The press picked up the detail and used it later. However, the author's search for such a ship turned up empty. In reality, the name of the ship was one that sounded like *Guerra*, and was in fact the *Werra*. Nitto's name is plainly on the manifest with his mother and sister. Certainly Nitto, three decades after arrival, simply couldn't recall the exact name of the ship. It wasn't important to him either.

When multiple sources are cited in the notes, they are listed in order of the degree the text relies upon them; however, in cases, where multiple sources provide the same data, I refer to the most contemporaneous source or the account I felt was most reliable—such as a book containing footnotes to identify sources rather than one that did not. Further discussion of various sources may occur to clarify discrepancies and/or provide the reader with additional information regarding the event.

Books are cited by author's name followed by page numbers: "Binder 77" refers to page 77 of John Binder's *Images of America: The Chicago Outfit*. To differentiate multiple books from the same author, I cite the author's name followed by a major word of the relevant title, then page number: Nelli *Chicago* 95 refers to Humberto Nelli's *Italians in Chicago, 1880-1930: A Study of Ethnic Mobility*; whereas Nelli *Crime* 134 refers to *The Business of Crime: Italians and Syndicate Crime in the United States*. In cases where a book with two authors is frequently used, their last initials are provided with a page number. For example: W&K *Big Bill* 102 refers to Wendt and Kogan's *Big Bill of Chicago*, page 102.

Official documents, especially those originating within a court system, are first listed by their complete title, case number, and other references; then abbreviated with case number only. Certain abbreviations found in the bibliography are given such as "FBI" referring to the Federal Bureau of Investigation, because they are used so frequently; case, serial, and page numbers usually follow.

Newspaper and other periodical sources are listed with abbreviation and date: DN 5-11-21, for example, refers to the *Chicago Daily News* for May 11, 1921. Often multiple dates for the same paper are given, separated by a comma. Every effort was made to obtain multiple newspaper sources for major events noted in this book. In cases of single sources, the source may have been the only publication that chose to report those facts. For instance, in the Nineteenth Ward Powers-D'Andrea battles to which Nitto was no doubt familiar, not all newspapers chose to cover the various killings there since they were so common an event. Also, in some cases of microfilm research, most commonly, the portion of film for the relevant date was either damaged or otherwise unreadable. For those enthusiasts double-checking newspaper sources, you may find a reference does not appear in the microfilm version (I found this out the hard way, too). In some cases I was able to view and make notes from original news clippings of some papers that covered the event in an early edition but dropped it from a later edition—the only one that made it to microfilm, thus the void. In the case of magazines, most are identified by full title in the notes such as *Time, Lightnin'*, and *Collier's*, followed by the date. Some that were used more frequently may be found abbreviated in the bibliography.

ARCHIVE SOURCES AND ABBREVIATIONS

BOP   **U.S. Bureau of Prisons**
CCC   Notes from the files of the **Chicago Crime Commission**
DOJ   **Department of Justice** documents other than those originating at the FBI
FBI   **Federal Bureau of Investigation**
HHPL   Documents from collections of the **Herbert Hoover Presidential Library**
IIA   *Investigation of the Improper Activities in the Labor or Management Field: Hearings Before the Select Committee*, Senate, 85 Cong.1 Sess.–86 Cong. 1Sess., Feb. 26, 1957–Sept. 9, 1959
IMW   *Investigation as to the Manner in Which the United States Board of Parole is Operating…: Hearings Before a Subcommittee of the Committee on Expenditures in the Executive Departments*, House, 80 Cong. 2 Sess., Sept. 25, 1947–March 11, 1948
INS   **Immigration and Naturalization Service** records
IOC   *Investigation of Organized Crime in Interstate Commerce: Hearings Before the Special Committee*, Senate, 81 Cong. 2 Sess.–82 Cong.1 Sess., May 26, 1950–Aug. 7, 1951
TXC   **The Tax Courts of the U.S. Reports.** Vol 13., Dockets 8840–8842. Tax Court
#111   #111, July 1, 1949–Dec. 31, 1949
USvC   *United States vs. Campagna et al.* Transcripts of the trial courtesy Boris Kostelanetz

Page CHAPTER 1
3   **Luigi Nitto**: BOP #38021 Frank Nitto gives Louis, and FBI #62-24090-22 Frank Nitto gives the original as Luigi.
3   **village of Angri**: On both his Declaration of Intention #129102 and Petition for Naturalization #64355 Nitto lists the village as Angri while other sources in his BOP records list the village variously as Angori or Ancori, the Greek versions or possibly recorded incorrectly by the staff; Glazier and Filby in *Italians to America*, 1993 lists Angri under villages of Italy; at any rate Nitto was not Sicilian as claimed by Murray 28, 289.
4   **history of Angri**: *The Angri Page* web site www.geocities.com/Athens; Amifthetrof 148 quote and for banditry and much of the history of the southern region.
4   **"not a nation"**: Ibid. 154; the North's exploitation of the South and high taxes: Nelli *Immigrants* 20-24.
5   **Angri development**: *The Angri Page* www.geocities.com/Athens.
5   **rural villages**: Nelli *Immigrants* 21; "consisting of one room" from Carlo Levi's, *Christ Stopped at Eboli*.
5   **marry Rosina Fezza**: State of New York Death Certificate #235, July 27, 1915, gives her father's name as Luigi Fezza which was corrupted through translations on American documents later; Anna Nitto's Brooklyn marriage license #4691 gives mother's maiden name as Fazzi; son Gennaro Dolendo's Florida death certificate #73-087955 gives it as Rose Fezzia.
5   **his sister's birthdate**: State of New York, Kings County Surrogate Court. Records #5212-45 and #6840-60 gives her name as GiovanninaVollaro nee Nitto; her age: 1900 U.S. Census she was counted twice, first on June 4, 1900, at her mother's Navy Street residence where she listed her age as 19, ten days later at her Garfield address she listed her age as 20; the 1915 N.Y. State Census lists her age as 36 and on four of the first five birth certificates of her children her age is consistent with 1879 or 1880; her name is listed on many records variously as Joanna, Annie, or Anna; Frank later wrote to her often from prison listing her on the record as simply Anna.
5   **Francesco Nitto born**: BOP #38021 Application for Parole Biographical Sketch, his 1942 driver's license as reported in S 3-20-43, and most cases when Nitto recorded his age on official documents such as marriage certificates are consistent to this date; INS #751-C1919944 letter dated 1-04-32 in relates to a Nitto interview on 11-1-32 in which he gives Jan. 27, 1886; Nitto's headstone in Mt. Carmel Cemetery lists 1888, this however was probably based on the what little knowledge his last wife possessed of his life before he came to Chicago.
5   **Nitto's lost children**: 1900 U.S. Census she says only 4 of 12 surviving, see notes below for names.
6   **"If I could have"**: Nelli *Immigrants* 42.
6   **steamship companies**: Amifthetrof 159-160.
6   **father Luigi died**: BOP #38021, Application for Parole Biographical Sketch and FBI #62-24090-22.
6   **married Francesco**: 1900 U.S. Census his age as 48, hers as 40, the years married as 12, but their name as Nitto; the same census within the same family, daughter Anna curiously gives her name as Dolent; also within the same census Rosina and Francesco claim two children directly, Raphael born in 1895 and Genero born in 1897, Brooklyn Birth Certificate #1518 for Gennaro Dolendo clearly gives the name Francesco Dolendo for the father, Gennaro's Florida death certificate gives his father's name as Dolendo; in America the name was most often corrupted to Dolendi or Dolent (phonetic, Do-len-tee)
6   **talent as a painter**: Passenger manifest of the Prince Line *Elysia* arrived arrived New York July 31, 1890, curiously it has his name as Dolente.

6   **none of the new arrivals:** Rosina in the 1900 U.S. Census lists only 4 of her 12 children surviving which at that time were Francesco and Giovannina Nitto with Raphael and Gennaro Dolendo; on Gennaro's birth certificate Rosina lists him as her third child presumably in the U.S. leaving nine born in Italy of which only Francesco and his sister survived.

6   **July 1890 ... Dolendo departed:** Passenger manifest of the Prince Line *Elysia;*according to *Immigrant Ship Information* www.fortunecity.com/littleitaly, the Elysia was built in 1873 for the Anchor Line and immediately served the London-New York run where she completed over 50 round-trip crossings. Later she was re-fitted with new engines and served many like Dolendo in the Mediterranean before she was scrapped in June 1898.

7   ***Werra* details:** Ibid. The *Werra* could accommodate 125 first and 130 second-class passengers as well; built by the John Elder & Co. in Glasgow, Scotland for North German Lloyd in 1882. She was later chartered to a Spanish company and finally scrapped in 1903. Most likely Rosina's husband sent her the tickets prepaid weeks in advance. This, according to Heaps 25, was common as one quarter to one half of all immigrants arriving at that time received tickets in this fashion.

7   **their passenger numbers:** Passenger manifest of the North German Lloyd liner *Werra* lists the family as: Rosina Fezza, Giovanna, and Raffaele; Rosina traveling without husband, used her maiden name as most Italian women in similar situations did at that time; Nitto lists the vessel as the steamer *Guerra* on Declaration of Intention #129102, Petition for Naturalization #64355, and two documents within BOP #38021; clearly Nitto, 30 and 40 years after the fact, couldn't remember the exact name of the ship; a check of the *Morton Allen Dictionary of New York Arrivals* reveals no record of vessel named *Guerra* leaving Italy, nor does *Italians to America,* curiously, no federal agency researched his claims.

7   **Capones left Italy:** Schoenberg 17.

7   **Nitto date of arrival:** *Mortan Allen Dictionary of New York Arrivals* and *Italians to America* list the Werra's date of arrival, though not its port of embarkation; that is listed only on the ship's manifest; Giovannina's Kings County Naturalization Record   #296-214 gave her date of arrival as Aug. 12, 1893, a check of liners received in New York that day came up empty; on Nitto's Declaration of Intention #129102, Petition for Naturalization #64355, and two documents within his BOP #38021 Nitto gave the date variously as spring 1890 or 1891, May-July 1890, and May 1890; as in most similar cases, the discrepancy is easily explained—in those days, remembering dates was simply not a life priority; again no federal agency thought this important to double-check.

8   **processed at Ellis Island:** A check of Ellis Island records came up empty. It is known that a fire at the original station (information below) destroyed many original documents dated 1893 and prior. However, the author was able to prove the Werra's passengers processed through the station by locating records in the Ellis Island archive for several other Werra passengers arriving that same day also listed in the Morton Allen Dictionary of Arrivals.

8   **the first Ellis Island:** Benton 36-38;"It looks like a latterday" observation originally appeared in the Oct. 24, 1891, issue of *Harper's Weekly;* this inceptive Ellis Island station burned to the ground in less than three hours on June 14, 1897, only one day after full completion, though it had operated since 1893.

8   **the regimen:** Ibid. 38-39 as well as the process 3 to 4 hours; sum of $50: Heaps 87; arrived with $17: Amfitheitrof 160.

8   **Harrisson, New Jersey:** BOP #38021, Application for Parole Biographical Sketch.

9   **Brooklyn conditions-accomodations:** Nelli *Immigrants* 57, 65; Weld 137.

9   **Union and President streets:** Ibid.   .

9   **at number 113 Navy**: Certificate of Birth, Brooklyn #1518 for Gennaro Dolendo.

9   **rent ... $3.00-$4.50**: Kobler 17, also for neighborhood description, festivities, and "odd little" quote; *Trows* Brooklyn Business directories lists the church at 24 Lawrence, "Father Gioachino Garofalo" presiding.

10   **spattering of ethnics**: Street check of the 1900 U.S. Census.

10   **"The Navy Yard was"**: Balsamo interview Sept. 18, 1997.

10   **Sands Street**: Kobler 22-24; *Trows* Brooklyn business directories for saloons, etc.

11   **scavenging junk**: 1900 U.S. Census gives his illiteracy as well.

11   **Public School #14**: BOP #38021 Application for Parole Biographical Sketch; the address of PS #14 and administrator's name confirmed through a check of the 1898 Brooklyn City Directory; BOP he also confirms working after school.

11   **Vincenzo Vollaro arrived**: Manifest Navigazione Generale Italiana liner *Montebello*, arrived June 10, 1893; according to www.ellisisland.org the *Montebello* was built by James Readhead & Company in Shields, England in 1887 and originally named the *Charters Tower*. The same year, she was sold to serve the Italian flag and renamed. She was torpedoed and sunk off the coast of Spain during World War I.

11   **his skills**: Shoemaker: Ibid. as does his Certificate of Marriage Brooklyn #4691 and most Brooklyn directories however Certificate of Birth, Brooklyn #11458 for son Luigi Vollaro he lists his profession as a barber.

11   **marriage to Anna Nitto**: Certificate of Marriage, Brooklyn #4691 Oct. 21, 1894; their relocation: Certificate of Birth, Brooklyn #11458 dated 1895 for Luigi son (Luigi) Vollaro lists their address as 73 Van Brunt Street; family demographics: Gennaro Vollaro: 1900 U.S. Census confirmed by Social Security Death Index; Raphael Dolendo: 1900 U.S. Census confirmed Social Security Death Index; Gennaro Dolendo: 1900 U.S. Census confirmed by Certificate of Birth, Brooklyn #1518 dated Feb. 8, 1897 (names as given on documents)

12   **the Capones**: Schoenberg 19-21.

12   **142 Navy Street**: 1900 U.S. Census.

12   **"had to work"**: BOP #38021; Application for Parole Biographical Sketch and for age he left school.

12   **Nitto's miscellaneous jobs**: Ibid. Bowling alleys specifically from 1900 U.S.Census with at least 4 in the area confirmed by Trows Brooklyn directories; Nitto's school performance cannot be verified, a search for records came up empty; according to the New York Board of Education, when PS #14 closed, its students and records were moved to PS #67; a check with the school secretary revealed their records for PS #14 date back only to World War I.

13   **Nitto picked up barbering**: Speculation as reasoned in the text; skills of LaFernina from the soundex card for Vollaro's Naturalization Certificate of Kings County dated May 5 1899, to which LaFernina was witness; *Trows* Brooklyn Business Directory for 1900 lists 5 Italian barbers within a couple blocks of his Navy Street address; served as interpreters: Weld 137.

13   **youth gangs**: Balsamo int.; he explained why kids might join gangs at that time; activities and progress: Schoenberg 22-23; Becker 22 for 'the chance to make money" and "we all knew" quotes

14   **Navy Street Boys**: Balsamo int. including errands for the "big guys" and his understanding that Nitto led the group then.

14   **Capone's birth**: Schoenberg 18-19.

15   **"Nitti hung around"**: Balsamo int. including Al as "the mascot" older Capone boys."

15   **"One day a local Irish..."**: Balsamo int.; the event was related to him by a woman, who though in her 90s, was of very sound mind and speech; a similar incident was related

in a 1990s Capone biography with Capone, not Nitto in the lead role; I was assured by Balsamo this is incorrect and the dateline appears to rule out Capone's lead role— about the date, Balsamo guessed no later than 1907 since "Al was 7 or 8 years old tops." In fact, the event likely occurred no later than 1905 since most reliable accounts of the Capone family state the oldest son Vincenzo, also known as James, ran away from home circa 1905 and by 1907 the family had moved to Garfield Place. It's hardly imaginable that Al then at age 6 or 8 would be leading his older brothers or Nitto, 13 years his senior around in a neighborhood fight.

15   **"good standing"**: S 3-20-43 retrospective has him as a member of the Five Points Gang and the quote; T, DN 03-20-43 as a member of the gang; however, FBI #62-24090-28 their investigators in 1930 doubted such a membership for reasons given in the text.

16   **Nitto's departure**: BOP #38021 Application for Parole Biographical Sketch; as for reasons he was in disagreement with his stepfather, Nelli *Immigrants* 137 notes elder male frictions.

16   **moved in with sister**: Ibid. 1905 New York State Census shows the Dolendo's at 142 Navy Street without Frank Nitto; the Vollaro's at 34 Garfield Place: Certificate of Birth, Brooklyn # 23352 for son Sebastiano Vollaro, Oct. 15, 1904, gives the address; Certificate of Birth, Brooklyn #36965, Nov. 10, 1898, for son Vincenzo Vollaro gives 19 Garfield Place; other sources during the intervening years place them on Garfield or right around the corner at 473 Fourth Ave. or 373 Fifth Avenue.

16   **work at shoe factory**: BOP #38021 Application for Parole Biographical Sketch gives it at 48th Street & 3rd Avenue.

16   **Capones on Garfield Place**: Schoenberg 21.

17   **Torrio's place**: Ibid. 27-28.

17   **Capone "answering a call"**: Ibid. 22, 28 and for his early gang days.

CHAPTER 2

19   **left New York**: BOP #38021 Application for Parole Biographical Sketch of a residential history Nitto gives a Navy Street address until 1911with a subsequent move to his sister's at 104 Garfield Place, however, records indicate that the Vollaro's, though in the area, were not at number 104 until the early 1920s. Other addresses given on this record, where they could be checked against his given time frame, with the exception of one in 1930, proved inaccurate or inconclusive. Suffice to say his memory may have been imprecise for such seemingly insignificant details, which may have been many indicating a very transient lifestyle not uncommon at the time, one rental to another. Nitto at the time of his incarceration was eager for release and quite cooperative in freely, but minimally admitting his misdeeds to BOP officials when required. Of course, one cannot discount deliberate and self-serving testimony to at least partially cover his tracks.

19   **absent from New York**: A search of the 1910 U.S. Census incomplete but reveals Nitto to be neither on Navy Street nor the Vollaro's at 15 Garfield Place; the 1915 New York State Census yields the same search results, but with the Vollaro's at 296 First Street near Garfield Place; city directories yield nothing as to Nitto's whereabouts either under the Nitto name or variations thereof. Unfortunately, Illinois did not participate in a census during the years in question. Chicago City Directories provide no listings for Nitto, Levitt or variations thereof.

20   **sister's citizenship**: Kings County Court #296-214 and #296-215 naturalization papers for Anna and Vincenzo Vollaro respectively, dated May 5, 1899.

20   **Nitto's marriage**: State of Texas, County of Dallas Marriage Certificate #4973 gives her name as Rosie Levy, Nitto later on his Petition for Naturalization #64355 and

Declaration of Intention #129102 gives it only as Rosa; INS #751-C1919944 an inter-view with Nitto, he admits her actual name to be Rose Levitt; subsequent divorce papers in Superior Court, Cook County #28S480155 gives the name variously as Rose Levitt or Rose Leavitt; a search for 902 Evergreen in the 1917 Dallas City Directory and a search of years 1914-18 for the couple under many spelling variations of their names proved fruitless. For the text, I give it as Rose Levitt.

20   **James Capone ran away**: Kobler 383; a later Nitto associate referring to Louis Cam-pagna, FBI #58-2000-8.

21   **unable to register**: Nelli *Immigrants* 107.

21   **Rose Levitt**: S 3-19-43 report mentions her; hints of her background from Cook County #28S480155 in which a witness says she left for New York after their divorce. Was she from there?

22   **proximity of nationalities**: Nelli *Italians* 8-9, 43; street analysis of the 1910 and 1920 U.S. Census for South Halsted, a main artery of the Italian community; number 700 through number 900 block south consisted mainly of Greeks, Russians, and Italians.

22   **"no city on the continent"**: This and following quotations: Paynter Wilson 7, 14.

23   **Nitto arrived ... 1913**: Petition for Naturalization #64355 dated June 12, 1924, Nitto is specific about the date; one might claim that he could have been deliberately dis-honest, but he probably was not for two reasons; first, already deep into his criminal career in 1924 and still an alien, he risked being deported upon arrest, no questions asked; secondly, he had no reason to lie, the man was trying to become a legal citizen and I suspect he didn't really want to botch it up on a paper technicality, though the date given may not be accurate, safe upon citizenship, he could not be deported regardless of the circumstances, except for an unchronicled prior conviction. Also key is the testimony from his first divorce trial, Cook County #28S480155, of one prose-cution witness Sydney Gottloeb claiming to have known Nitto at least 16 years prior to 1928, this places Nitto in Chicago at least by 1913, possibly even 1912; IOC 1348 Greenberg claims to have known Nitto "about 30 years" prior to Nitto's demise this also puts his arrival near 1913; S 3-20-43 puts it at 1913; at any rate, Nitto did not fol-low Capone to Chicago as many would have it, he was there long before the Big Guy.

23   **habitation limited to**: Nelli *Chicago* 22-32 for patterns of early Italian settlement.

23   **First Ward boundaries**: W&K *Lords* 8 map of 1890 and 1943 borders, for more see Asbury 100, 122, and W&K 25-26.

23   **Big Jim Colosimo**: Asbury 312-315.

23   **residential attraction diminished**: Nelli *Chicago* 29 for the local development forcing them out of the First Ward; professor Humberto Nelli performed extensive research utilizing census and city property records.

24   **Nineteenth Ward boundaries**: Ibid. *Chicago* 102 map shows borders for both 1898 and the redistricting of 1914.

24   **major Italian communities**: Ibid. 31 and Schiavo 33- 35.

24   **Johnny Powers**: W&K *Lords* 38-39.

24   **smell linking politicians**: Asbury 3 made the analogy .

24   **"either you go along"**: W&K *Lords* 40.

24   **the ward's vice district**: Lindberg 125.

24   **protection price list**: Peterson 75-76 sourcing *Harper's* Jan. 22, 1898.

25   **"worst housing"**: Nelli *Chicago* 32-34; Schiavo 34.

25   **where Nitto gravitated**: Inference based on proximity of friends.

25   **reverted to barbering skills**: See the many sources below indicating the career; never licensed as a barber: INS File #751-C1919944 letter from the Secret Service dated 11-3-32 claims he apparently never obtained the state barbering license as required by

Illinois law since 1910, a later memo dated 12-29-33 states that certain information indicates he never was a barbering the first place.

25   **barbering ranked**: Nelli *Immigrants* 76; "thought to possess": Schoenberg 21.

25   **Italian employers**: BOP #38021 Parole Biographical Sketch, Nitto lists employers R. Russo and L. Esposito but only back to 1919, probably self-serving to cover the relevant years being investigated; S 3-20-43 gives barbering as his first occupation; addresses: 1910 U.S. Census and Chicago directories.

25   **Mack Ronga**: 1913 City Directory listed Mack with Gaetano Ronga, physician.

26   **Joseph Vicedomini**: BOP #38021, Parole Biographical Sketch, Nitto provides his name as well as the theatre and intimates employment therein; a check of city directories failed to turn up the theatre, however, in 1914, under Vicedomini's name he gives the theatre address as 914 S.Halsted and in 1917 he gives it at 815 W. Taylor, FBI #58-2000-273-10 lists the 1920 address at 914 W. Taylor; U.S. 14th Census in 1920 gives his address as 909 S. Bishop, his occupation as a theatre manager and his age, 35.

26   **major German and Irish**: Nelli *Chicago* 103   .

26   **friends ... German couple**: Superior Court, Cook County #28S480155 testimony of Sydney Gottloeb.

26   **Russian-Greek populace**: Nelli *Chicago* 103 also for Russians second in number to Italians in the ward   .

26   **Nitto's first barbering job**: S 3-20-43, Harrison gives he Factor version.

26   **Factors (originally Factorovitz)**: The history of the Factor family is hazy at best; original family name: McConnell 19 in which he cites Jake's immigration papers as a source; NYT 8-31-38 (Max Factor obituary, a half-brother) and *The Concise Dictionary of American Jewish Biography*, Volume 1 list their home town as Lodz. The brothers apparently came over at different times and may or may not have come in contact with each other thereafter. Jake was thought to be in Chicago circa 1910-15. T 2-3-43 has the Halsted area where Factor grew up. Halper 73 finding of the facts of a later Factor case for his early employment.

27   **remembered Nitto**: IOC 1348 Greenberg testimony gives the location, a check of city directories 1913-14 indicate the shop at 712 South Centre whose street name changed to Racine owned by one Joseph Antoniello; IOC 1348 for quote.

28   **Greenberg description**: FBI #62-75201 memo dated 3-9-44 gives physical traits; additional descriptions from photos in T, ST 12-9-55   .

28   **Louis Greenberg bio**: ST 12-9-55, A 12-20-55 as a millionaire; no consensus on the exact date of birth nor place; on his Petition for Naturalization #38887 Greenberg claims its March 5, 1891,in Esvanawa, Russia; more recent FBI #62-75201 and various sources in CCC file give it as Dec. 10, 1891, in Yanove, Russia; the same CCC gives Greenberg's Petition for Naturalization info providing the date of arrival as April 11, 1906 and port of embarkation; as a machinist: IMW 792; Greenberg at his uncle's: IMW 792; quote "taking a percentage": Murray 25; Chicago ... in 1909 or 1910: IMW 792-793 Greenberg mentions uncles and cousins already there on the West Side; a check of the 1910 U.S. Census proved inconclusive and a check of the 1920 U.S. Census shows a Greenberg family on Avers Avenue, though no evidence of him being there.

28   **settled across the river**: IMW 793 Greenberg gives the location of the restaurant and saloon as being in that same area Van Buren and Market Streets; started as a swamper: Murray 26-28 also for the chores and his promotion.

28   **acquainted with Morton**: CCC memo dated 11-9-50, DN 5-19-44; though neither specify an exact date; Schoenberg 70 for Morton born Markowitz; Morton's deeds: Asbury 343 for organizing neighborhood toughs and suspect in several murders; Burns 87 as murder suspect.

29   O'Banion background: Burns 81-82; Pasley *Capone* 43-44; Asbury 342-343 especially for jackrolling drunks; Murray 26 for the technique; police record: CCC memo dated 7-20-22.

29   **Weiss background**: DN 10-15-26, T 10-13-26.

29   **Greenberg intro to O'Banion**: This whole affair is rather ambiguous at best. CCC. memo 2-9-48 gave the saloon blossoming into the bond business, while memo 11-8-50 and DN 5-19-44 claim it was Morton making the introduction, with CCC giving the date about 1915-1919; Murray 26-27 asserts a chance meeting between Greenberg and O'Banion in alleys while jackrolling a drunk very early on 1909 in the Market Street area which could be—Greenberg was there until circa 1914-15 by his IMW testimony; 1915-16 appears more likely given Greenberg opened a North Side saloon then Greenberg according to his IMW testimony; if Morton made the introductions, a later meet 1919 is even possible since prior to 1912 O'Banion was in and out of jail and by 1917-18 Morton was off fighting in the war and that time O'Banion worked diversely as a newspaper slugger, safecracker, etc.; to be sure, Greenberg became more familiar with O'Banion after his move to the North Side and their business became more embroiled.

30   **business split**: Murray 27.

30   **Greenberg's bar**: Ibid. 28-29 gives the start up procedures, political costs and supplies of stolen booze; Murray also states O'Banion and Weiss in attendance for some vague amount of time which follows information from the CCC; the location: IMW 793 Greenberg states he was there about 5 years from 1909.

30   **"Greenberg was the kind"**: DN 12-12-55; Murray 27-29 describes his money lending schemes.

30   **residence and family**: IOC 1348-1349 Greenberg stated he lived around McAllister Place at the time his first child was born in 1913 and some time thereafter; CCC file gives date of marriage as only 1912 probably out of state, as neither the CCC nor the Feds could turn up a certificate; 1920 U.S. Census confirms the birthdate in 1913; his Declaration of Intention #50534 dated Feb. 6, 1915, gives his address as 4346 Lincoln Avenue on the North Side.

30   **nearby Ronga residence**: IOC 1348-1349 Greenberg testimony for McAllister Place in 1913; 1910 U.S. Census and City directories give Ronga's address.

31   **expand his operation**: CCC memo dated 11-9-50 of a government investigation into Greenberg's activities gives the date of business from 1915 to 1920 and location at Lincoln and Montrose; Declaration of Intention #50534 dated Feb. 6, 1915, gives his address as 4346 Lincoln Avenue, which is at Lincoln and Montrose; City directories 1916-17 provide the location of his second saloon as 1558 South Lawndale way out on the West Side Lawndale District; 1920 U.S. Census clearly lists the Greenberg's at 4346 Lincoln near the intersection of Montrose; Murray 29 provides for both, but incorrectly identifies the Lincoln Avenue address as that of a South Side street whose name was later changed to Wolcott Avenue; after all, why would Greenberg develop close ties to O'Banion on the North Side if he lived way down on the South Side? Certainly, if Murray's assertion was true, Greenberg would have developed ties to someone much closer to home.

31   **Factors may have lived**: City directories 1912, 1914, and 1915 put the Factors at 3132 W. 14th Place, Spaulding, and 1524 S. Central Park respectively—the only definitive address for Jacob Factor's shop is at 3855 W. 12th in the 1916 directory; all are near Cicero, and coincidently only blocks from Greenbergs. The question: Are these the same Factors?

31   **quit barbering-jewelry fence**: INS #751-C1919944 letter dated 03-26-31 reveals one

unidentified source who said he was selling jewelry for commission, but does not indicate as whether it was stolen or not; S 3-20-43 reported he worked as a barber during the day and a jewelry fence at nigh; the same INS letter above reveals their investigation determined at least at the time of his application for citizenship in the early 1920s Nitto was probably not a barber as claimed.

31   **Dr. Ronga background**: Schiavo 194 and Cook County Death Certificate #10123 give Nola, Italy in 1874; 1920 U.S Census confirms 1874 and gives 1887 as the arrival date: Schiavo 194 provides a detailed educational history and a rare photograph of the doctor in his early years; at 1204 McAllister: Chicago City directories 1914-15; the 1910 U.S. Census lists him at number 1208; city directories 1916 and 1928, the 1920 U.S. Census, and Schiavo in 1928, all list him at number 1200: when he died years later his address was still at 1200; His businesses: City Directories 1912-17 provide the his business addresses.

32   **She may have had family**: Though one can't prove it 100 percent beyond a reasonable doubt, 1920 U.S. Census reveals a Hymann Leavit living with some Greenberg's at 1433 Avers in the Far West Side Lawndale District and both the Greenberg family and Hymann are listed as tailors. Coincidently, and significantly Declaration of Intention #50534 dated Feb. 6, 1915, Alex Louis Greenberg listed as his initial occupation as being a tailor.

33   **Nitto's mother**: New York State Record of Death, Certificate of Death #235, July 27, 1915, for all information regarding Rose's death; *Newsday* dated 4-7-98, a local publication provided by New York genealogist Rhoda Miller for information regarding King's Park State Hospital; according to Rhoda, 3 institutions existed out Long Island at that time: Kings Park State Hospital, Central Islip State Hospital, and Pilgrim State Hospital, the area then was quite remote, no more than a nice, peaceful, wilderness area 25 miles east of the Queens: to possibly indicate the severity of Rose's condition, according to Rhoda, "It was no short term place to be." Unfortunately, at the time, she said they were known to be "huge, huge dumping grounds." More recent downsizing has caused the state to lump the populations of the three into one facility.

CHAPTER 3

35   **Italian bankers**: Nelli *Crime* 140-141 for complete details on these private brokers.

35   **"the means by which"**: Nelli *Immigrants* 162 also notes Prohibition rescued many from poverty.

36   **"as free from organized"**: Asbury 309 for quote, and 303-309 in for closingthe Levee and a detailed account of the Levee history during this time; Colosimo's closing: 308.

36   **Harrison's defeat**: W&K *Big Bill* 96.

36   **Thompson's "rascality"**: Kobler 60.

36   **Thompson background**: W&K *Big Bill* 15-26,46-48, 101-105; "Just who is this": 101; "Babe Ruth": Sullivan 191: dichotomy of platforms for instance pro-Wet among saloons while pro Dry among the church crowds and "no harm in a friendly": W&K 103-105.

36   **Sweitzer's support**: Ibid.100, 106 for Democratic controlled offices, vice bosses.

37   **betting favorite**: Ibid. 100, 113.

37   **"for the bowwows"**: Ibid. 113 and election results.

37   **Thompson's beginnings**: Ibid. 119, 123, 128-130; "I guess the only thing": 128; "Don't forget to": 130; "kind words for him": 123; reference to bottled beer: Skilnik 99 for an excellent history of brewing in Chicago.

37   **Anti-Saloon League**: Dobyns *Amazing* 229, 239-240; Sinclair 102-105; bullying Mayor Busse: Skilnik 95

38   **Webb-Kenyon Bill**: Dobyns *Amazing* 240-241.

38   **"manufacture for sale"**: Ibid. 242-243, also for their lobbying efforts.

38   **war years and Prohibition**: Sinclair 175-177 noted the number of men away at war would reduce resistance to Prohibition ideas, also for the Dry arguments in the name of patriotism; Gompers…direct jobs lost: Dobyns *Amazing* 238 and Sinclair 180-181,185; cessation of ardent spirits: Skilnik 107, this outlaw of alcohol was the first step towards drying up the country.

38   **Greenberg's saloons**: Murray 29 lists his Market Street venture in addition to a saloon at 16th and Lawndale out west and 4346 Lincoln Avenue

39   **stocked with illegal**: Ibid. 29.

39   **"questionable friends"**: DN 12-9-55 gave hijackers and fences; CCC memos dated 2-9-48, 11-8-50 claim O'Banion and Weiss were good acquaintances of Greenberg's, both noted thieves of just about anything at the time.

39   **forged paperwork**: Murray 33; CCC memo 1-24-49 notes his arrest on May 21, 1921, on suspicion of running a major underground liquor ring; bloated supplies: Murray 29-30 also says Greenberg began to fence the extra stuff himself.

39   **Nitto involved**: CCC memo dated 11-8-50 derived from IRS data states it began in 1918 as a liquor business; same memo reviews Superior Court of Cook County #57S-2335, *Annette Nitto vs. the Estate of Alex Louis Greenberg*, in which she claims the fiduciary relationship lasted in excess of 25 years prior to Nitto's death seems to support it, Greenberg denied any connection in his IOC testimony.

39   **liquor specifically**: Ibid. Irey 45 says Nitto worked "cooking alcohol" while not barbering.

39   **Dr. Ronga's involvement**: Ibid.

40   **"no single disease"**: Dobyns *Amazing* 287.

40   **medicinal restrictions**: Ibid. 290-292.

40   **Ronga's pharmacies**: Chicago City Directories 1913-15.

40   **agents found pharmacies**: Dobyns *Amazing* 294.

40   **physicians dilemmas**: Ibid. 291; three dollars a pint: 290, 292.

41   **Johnny Torrio**: McPhaul 104-122, 459-460; Landesco 910.

41   **roadhouse definition**: T 12-18-59.

41   **Prohibition / Volsted Acts**: Sinclair 176-179, 184-189; Kyvig 1-13 ,23; "law does regulate" quote: Kobler 69.

42   **"booze" as slang**: DN 5-12-21.

42   **Thompson's re-election**: W&K *Big Bill* 164-170; Lewis & Smith 392-394; and for the numbers.

43   **brewer options**: Skilnik 115-118, 122-123.

      "larceny in their hearts": McPhaul 141; Torrio and Stenson: Landesco 912.

44   **Schaffner's Manhattan**: Murray 17, 30 for Torrio's purchase; Skilnik 122 for background and brewery history; CCC memo dated 1-24-49 confirms Greenberg's involvement early on with "reliable" sources mentioning his management of the place; the same memo confirms the brewery was incorporated under the name Malt Maid Products on Dec. 31, 1919, and operated as such through Prohibition; "booze business put": T 12-10-55; CCC memos dated 2-9-48 and 12-28-48 confirm those associations.

44   **Roosevelt Finance**: Murray 32 gives it as Roosevelt Finance Company in the early 1920s, it was officially incorporated on 1-13-26 according to CCC memo dated 1-20-49, they were unable to trace it prior to 1926.

44   **Capone's early days**: Schoenberg 35, 53.

45   **New Years Day activities**: HE 1-1-20.

45   **January 17 pronouncement**: T 1-17-20 also for the reaction.

45 Will Rogers quote: Kvvig 16.

45 bootlegger quote "Just ...": Sullivan 137 quoting Dion O'Banion.

45 local police enforcement: Pasley *Capone* 94-95; W&K *Big Bill* 192; Asbury 347; Asbury and Pasley for one district's examples; Lindberg 163 for half the force on the take and quotes "It was such" and "It came".

46 federal enforcement: Dobyns *Amazing* 273, 313 also for Volsted penalties.

46 Torrio "knew exactly": McPhaul 156.

46 beer price and usage: Ibid. 164, 181.

46 whiskey prices: Per fifth: Sinclair 196; per shot glass: McPhaul 165 .

47 Colosimo and his death: T 5-11,12-20; DN 5-11-20; HE 5-12-20; Asbury 312-313; "jackals": Kobler 70; death: headline: T 5-11; see HE for nice photo spread.

47 Capone's increased wealth: Pasley *Capone* 18.

47 description of Four Deuces: Asbury 319, T 2-9-36; photo in spread here.

48 Torrio expansion: McPhaul 119, and 168 for number of speakeasies.

48 brewery ownership: Landesco 912-913 names the West Hammond, Manhattan, and Best breweries with silent interest in several others; Manhattan brewery and Greenberg's ownership: CCC memo dated 1-24-49; geyser from: T, DN 5-22-24; number of barrels moved: McPhaul 181.

48 location of Nitto's friends: Chicago City directories 1915-17; 1920 U.S. Census; the Gottloeb address from Superior Court of Cook County #28S480155 gives the friendship of the Gottloeb's and the Nitto's.

CHAPTER 4

51 embattled epicenters: DN 3-10-21 list the streets and conditions.

52 "Conditions ... Nineteenth": Landesco 951.

52 "If I got out of bed": DN 3-10-21.

52 "Dead Man's Tree": Pasley *Capone* 79 for location and description.

52 "Flats are vacant because": T 5-13-21.

52 Marzano and Esposito: T 3-9-26; T 3-22-28 detailed much of Esposito's early life; Burns 216 for quotes.

52 Powers building support: Nelli *Italians* 95, 103, 110 gives his methods: .

53 *La Tribuna Italiana Transatlantica*: Ibid. 103-104 quotes from the paper and conditions.

53 D'Andrea background: Birthdate and came to Chicago: DN 2-19-21; University of Palermo in T, DN 5-11-21 with HE 5-12-21 specifying studies in priesthood; DN 2-19 and HE 5-12 for scholar and linguist; HE 5-12 for macaroni factory at 2132 Archer; DN 5-11, HE 5-12 for physical description; Burns 200 for law studies, children, and popularity among Italian citizens; Red Cross and other benevolent societies: DN 5-11-21, T 5-11-21.

53 Other manifestations: Nelli *Crime* 134 his source is the autobiography of early Italian American crime figure Nicola Gentile, who lived in Chicago during D'Andrea's most potent years; Sewer and Tunnel Miners: DN 5-11-21, T 5-11-21, and HE 5-12-21; International Hod Carriers: Landesco 949 while T 5-11-21 simply states the Hod Carriers' Union; Water Pipe Extension Laborers: DN 5-11-21, T 5-11-21 gives D'Andrea as leader of this union; Macaroni Manufacturer's Union: Landesco 949.

54 Unione Siciliana: "certain elements" in DN 2-19-21; Much confusion seems to have developed over the years concerning this organization and its connection to the Mafia or whether they were in fact one and the same. Nelli in *Business* 134-135 seems to separate D'Andrea's recognition as community leader or ranking Mafioso from his leadership of the Unione. The Unione was originated there as a benevolent organization, collecting membership dues in order to assist fellow countrymen in time of

need, and Sicilian nativity seems to have been a prerequisite for membership. However, such a significant domain of members and a like treasury may have had corrupting effects. Eventually D'Andrea was able to work his way in as its head and likely used it to his advantage. In that sense the Unione was just *one tool* he used to exert his personal influence over certain elements of the community as an old-home Mafia-like figure. D'Andrea the reigning figure would rake off what he desired from the Unione treasury. He was already doing just that from *pisans* as head of certain unions. It seems that successor heads of the Unione became more closely affiliated with the emerging and predominant organized crime establishments, always all-powerful throughout their community, while maintaining certain Unione criterion, but apparently ancillary to crime bosses, representing their concerns. Therein is where the two become somewhat intertwined and muddled. T 5-17-21 names D"Andrea as the Unione's first and current president; Landesco 950, Asbury 240, Peterson 115, and Nelli *Italians* 105 all recognized him as president as well; its intended purpose see Murray who printed a picture of the incorporation papers for the Chicago branch, it was incorporated in the State of Illinois Sept. 17, 1895, for the purpose of aiding those "members towards the other in case of illness." None of the signatories are D'Andrea's; FBI #58-2000-240 a check of records in January 1939 indicates a name change to the Italo-American National Union chartered in Illinois in 1895 for the purpose of organizing Americans of Italian extraction, providing both insurance and sociological work.

54   city's *Capo Mafioso*: Nelli *Crime* 134 from Nicola Gentile's memoirs.
54   "long lorded over": Landesco 949.
54   **Italian-American Educational Club**: T 5-11-21, DN 5-26-21 give it at Taylor and Miller streets; T 6-28-21 says D'Andrea founded the club.
54   "shining light": Asbury 239.
54   county commissioner: HE 5-12-21, Landesco 949.
54   D'Andrea criminal record: HE 5-12-21, DN 2-18, 19-21.
54   connected to ... forgers: HE 5-12-21 gives the details; according to a U.S. Secret Service in 1902 Chicago flooded with phony 10-cent pieces. The agent traced some of the coins to D'Andrea's macaroni factory and then raided his home only to find D'Andrea's wife stashing some of the loot.
54   red light ... unfrocked: Landesco 949; HE 5-12-21 says he became mixed up in the "restricted district in the 22nd Street area."
54   " To make an accusation": Landesco 949.
54   rally his supporters: Burns 202 notes the boomerang effect amongst D'Andrea's supporters who "fought as savagely to elect him."
55   Lombardi gunned down: DN 2-22-16, Landesco 949 for event details; DN quotes his daughter that D'Andrea "brought about the shooting" .
55   "invaders": Landesco 948 drawing distinction of their respective Italian followers.
55   offering political office: HE 5-12-21,Landesco 950.
55   election overruled: HE 5-12-21 and the possible double-cross—it seems logical enough for such vicious ward politics.
55   bomb at Powers's home: T 9-29-20, HE 5-12-21, Landesco 950; T says reverberations broke windows up to 6 blocks away.
55   "no quarter asked": Nelli *Italians* 106.
55   D'Andrea wrangled: DN 2-19-21 notes D'Andrea's liberal donations to donations to the Thompson machine.
56   bomb at 854 Blue Island: T 2-18-21, T 5-11-21.
56   Joseph Spica bombing: T 2-18-21 gives the details, Spica a lieutenant of D'Andrea's, lived in the rear of the building; Landesco 951 gives his address as 1028 Newberry Avenue,

says Spica's son-in-law, a D'Andrea lieutenant was there and implies him the target.

56   **Powerss' reward**: Landesco 951.

56   **"If the system of bombing"**: Nelli *Italians* 108-109.

56   **Dr. Ronga's role**: DN 5-12-21 as D'Andrea's physician; Nelli *Italians* 106-107 as a staunch supporter, he provides a portion of the text and date of the letter; Nitto as well informed, a supposition based on the fact of their business, they had known each other long before this election.

56   **voting irregularities**: Nelli *Italians* 110 both sides participated without a doubt; DN 2-22-21, HE 3-9-21 noted 400 policemen; T 2-23-21 reports on a squad of 25 to clean out the ward and lists the number of arrests.

57   **election results and quote**: Nelli *Italians* 111 for quote and margin of victory as 381 and for final election tally 3,984 to 3,603 in Powers' favor.

57   **Nitto at 922 South Halsted**: Declaration of Intention #129102 Superior Court of Cook County.

57   **"Move or die" sign**: DN 2-23-21 intended for those at 727 Forquer.

57   **D'Andrea's recount**: HE 3-10-21, DN 5-11-21.

57   **"Old accounts ... settled"**: Landesco 951.

57   **secret D'Andrea meeting**: HE 3-10-21, police had information regarding a meeting that 25 politicians of the 19th Ward were marked for death, but gives no names; later HE 3-16-21 gives the reward and suspects Gambino and Amatuna collecting money; DN 6-13,15-25 and T 7-10-25 for Genna family history; T says the brothers numbered 7 with one unnamed sibling staying in Italy; Gambino and Amatuna occupations: HE 3-16-21; importing gunmen: DN 3-10-21.

57   **Esposito incident**: One of those obscure murders for which seemed to be little reported. HE 3-9-21 and Burns 206 both agree he was shot and pitched out of an auto, Chicago P.D. homicide record #5962 confirms details in text.

58   **Labriola murder**: DN 3-8,9-21, T and HE 3-9-21; quote from Burns 203; Amatuna and Gambino: HE 3-16-21, T and DN 5-13-21; vote margin: DN 3-8; threats, murmurs to wife: Burns; "I hear" quote: DN 3-8, T 3-9-21.

58   **Raimondi murder**: CCC memo dated 1921 providing details from the coroner's report, Chicago P.D. homicide record #6866 confirms details and 910 Garibaldi address, DN 3-8, 9-21, T 3-9-21, HE 3-9,10-21; DN 3-8, same murder crew; Raimondi background: "blood brothers" in Burns 205; olive oil and cigar business: DN 3-8; T for Raimondi reaction; "Madre di Dio! from DN 3-8.

59   **subsequent events**: DN 3-10-21 for "You are on it" as well as the unidentified victim dumped in the alley; HE 3-12-21 reports the alley murder as the third victim; Landesco 952 reports the gunfight in the grocery store; murder of Tony Marchese: T 7-24-21, chronologically this appears to be a separate murder from the alley man above and did not make the late edition news pages that day.

59   **"See, no gun"**: DN 3-10-21 and HE 3-13-21; HE 3-10-21 says extra police squads sent the ward to search any suspicious characters; "See, no gun." and ward silence in DN 3-10-21.

59   **Greenberg's lesson**: Murray 30 that he complained so vehemently about the price of freedom which makes all the more sense if he was an alien which he was; his Declaration of Intention #50534, Feb. 6, 1915, and Naturalization Petition #38887 in Circuit Court of Cook County finalized June 30, 1921.

60   **Nitto's Declaration**: Declaration of Intention #129102 Superior Court of Cook County dated March 9, 1921.

60   **Gardino and Nuzzo**: HE 5-13-21, T 7-24-21; HE and DN both report an earlier attack on Gardino as well.

60   **"You're going to take"**: Burns 207; the incident evidently went unreported.

60   **April raid**: T 5-11-21 reports it happening on April 12 with gambling and concealed weapons charges filed against the men including a weapons charge against D'Andrea, while HE 5-13-21 and DN 5-26-21 have it on April 10 with DN reporting charges of disorderly conduct filed against 16 men including D'Andrea, Angelo Genna, and Michael Licari.

60   **Wolfson note**: DN 5-11-21, T and HE 5-12-21 all agree on the the the wording and dif-fer only in punctuation; T and HE 5-12 D'Andrea thought they were Black Handers; T for Wolfson moving out May 1; HE put the move on May 4 and noted the move of the neighbors upstairs.

61   **in Amato's restaurant**: DN, T 5-11-21 and HE 5-12-21; DN and HE mention Amato's by name being at Halsted and Taylor, with DN stating D"Andrea was playing cards with bodyguard Joseph Lapisa; later HE 5-13-21 gives the card players as Iarussi and "another friend"; T only that he returned from a dinner at a Neopolitan restaurant at Taylor and Halsted and that 2 men accompanied him home and dropped him there at 2 a.m.; see Burns 208 for "There's no danger" and "dynamite" quotes.

61)   **George King-the apartment**: DN and T 5-11-21 for King's observations: photo in T 5-12-21 for exterior apartment depiction.

61   **D'Andrea shooting**: DN, T 5-11,12-21, HE 5-12, 13-21 and Burns 208-209; curbing the vehicle: photo-diagram in T 5-12-21 indicates the near curb and as do the police in T 6-28-21 however HE 5-12 diagram and Burns 208 adhere to the far curb story to support the notion of a traitor providing an expanded killing field for the assassins, but given the breadth of distance between the near curb and the front steps, it wouldn't seem necessary; sources all differ as to the number of wounds, but report near of more than a dozen: where he fell: DN 5-11 and T 5-12 photo-diagram: according to DN 5-11 and HE 5-13, D'Andrea squeezed off 5 shots, 3 hit the window as seen in T photo; escape route: DN and T, HE 5-12 report they escaped out back to a rear alley with DN; hats found: DN, T 5-11 and HE 5-12 give the details of the hat none however support Burns 209 contention that they contained a $2 bill and *figlio di un cane* (son of a dog) slur, in fact the press reported the note as "Flowers for D'Andrea" with $20 attached.

62   **hospital treatment**: DN, T 5-11, 12-21 and HE 5-12-21; HE, DN 5-12 for Dr. Ronga's medical actions and HE for quote; Burns 208 "God bless you" quote.

62   **"a new force attempting"**: T 8-16-21, police suspected a power vacuum.

62   **Tanzillo and subsequent episodes**: Body in drainage canal: HE 5-15-21 and T 7-24-21; DN 5-14-21 for Tanzillo episode; Licari's death: CCC memo dated 1921 provid-ing details from coroner's reports and DN 5-26-21; Prior to D'Andrea's death he bought a saloon out of the Nineteenth Ward. The question remains: Was he shuck-ing his responsibilities to his comrades?

63   **Lapisa murder**: CCC memo dated 1921 providing details from the from coroner's reports, T 6-27,28-21, DN 6-27-21, Burns 210-212; home near Death's Tree: T lists his home at either 712 or 715 South Loomis; as a contractor: T 6-28; Lapisa as pres-ident of *Societe Di Mutuo Soccorso Ventimigilia*, a charity picnic for children to be held July 25: CCC file and T 6-27; final position of the car: photos and diagram in T 6-27, this source also notes the position of church shadows over Lapisa; T 6-27 for Father Gian-bastiano's speech.

63   **motives for his murder**: Sources vary, however in T 6-28 police note Lapisa picked up his two passengers at the Italian-American Educational club, now in Genna con-trol, this is the strongest evidence supporting their involvement in the killing; surely they suspected him of treachery from whispers of the far curb admission; Landesco

953 also gives Lapisa swearing to avenge D'Andrea's death; "take care of Genna": T 6-28-21 for Angelo as one of D'Andrea's closest friends and quote; still Diamond Joe Esposito, despite remained neutrality in the Powers feud.

64   **Sinacola ambushed**: DN and T 8-16-21 both give the police explanation as he was ready to talk; in DN police advise this event occurred the day after Lapisa was gunned down; relationship to Lapisa in DN and Burns 212; swore reprisal: Landesco 953.

64   **Orlando killed**: T 7-22-21.

64   **"Two-Gun Johnny"**: T 7-24-21 for the whole incident and his history; T gave his name as Gardino, D'Andrea gave him the names of those to execute: HE 5-14-21.

64   **Sinacola murder**: T, DN 8-16-21, Chicago P.D. homicide record #6996.

64   **Guttillo and others**: DN 8-26-21 for Gutillo details; Pasley *Capone* 96 called him a "Powers henchman"; Pasley 97 lists Joseph Marino a D'Andrea man, see Chicago P.D. homicide record #6527 for date; Pasley lists Nicola Adamo, a Powers man on November 26.

64   **suspects Amatuna and Gambino**: T and DN 5-13-21.

64   **Angelo identified**: T 5-13-21: T 10-8-21 found innocent of the murder; Ronga's testimony in the matter: CCC trial observer notes in Criminal Court of Cook County Case #24369, *State of Illinois vs. Angelo Genna*.

65   **Genna's arrest**: HE 6-15-25; Pasley *Capone* 97 gives Jim arrest and acquittal.

65   **Mike Merlo**: T 6-15-25, Burns 98, and Asbury 347 for head of the Unione; Burns and Asbury for his rule, i.e., abhorred violence, etc.

65   **Esposito's power**: Asbury 345 for "special pets" quote; T 3-22-28 and Burns 217-219 for "who's who" quote and clientele; political connections: T 3-9-26.

66   **Galveston-Nitto**: Galveston history in 1915-19 city directories; quote and Galveston's reputation: Sinclair 217 quoting an official in the Wickersham Report, a congressional report on Prohibition enforcement; S 3-21-43 retrospective states a possible arrest there; Nitto's acquaintance there: BOP File #38021 lists one D. M. Cleary Route 1, Box 233, Galveston, Texas; according to Galveston directories as far back as available (1919) this was one Daniel M. Cleary, he also listed as his address the Nellie Dairy at 6015 Avenue Q; FBI #60-2149-166, page 60 for Sam Maggeo as a Nitto connection and well-known Galveston gangster; inquiries to the Galveston Police Department to check for a Nitto arrest record were futile.

CHAPTER 5

69   **"the biggest alcohol"**: T 6-16-25.

69   **Heitler's scheme**: T 2-18-21, DN 3-8-21.

70   **Will Roger's quote**: Sinclair 217.

70   **Genna's old habits**: James and Angelo early Prohibition offenses: Schoenberg 128; Angelo's stolen jewelry arrest: Landesco 1078; involvement in John Notti case: HE 6-15-25; Mann Act case and quote: HE 6-15-25; "Little Mike" the youngest: DN 6-17-25, but as for ages of the rest, several sources give conflicting data; Mike's arrest as part of a stolen car ring and part in the Adamo murder: HE 6-15-25; occupations of Jim, Sam, Pete and Tony plus quote: T 7-10-25.

71   **Genna's alcohol [start]**: DN 6-15-25; T 11-14-25 specifically that Samoots started Angelo in the business; Burns 132 adds Nerone below assisted as well.

71   **evolution of their business**: Henry Spingola and tenement production: Asbury 346; "soft snap" quote and earnings: T 7-10-25; flavorings and labels: Pasley 93; alcohol plant details: T 6-16-25; importing families from Sicily: T 7-9,10-25 specifically T 7-9 for the Marsala Club.

72   **business roles of brothers**: DN 7-9-25 has Tony as a building contractor while according to Chicago Detective Capt. Stege in DN 7-8-25 he arranged flats for new-

comers and was "quite active" in the business; "Bloody Angelo": HE 5-27-25; T 7-9-25 for enforcing decries.

72　**financial aspects, payouts**: Burns 131 for gross and net income, Pasley *Capone* 94 lists specific payouts.

72　**Genna temperament**: Burns 130 for quote also.

72　**Amatuna**: Spelling of last name follows contemporary newspaper sources; tried killing musicians union BA: DN 11-11-25; killing the horse: Kobler 89; splashy wardrobe: Pasley *Capone* 111 and Burns 141; as most generous: T 11-14-25.

72　**Tropea**: Burns 145-146, Kobler 89; T 2-16-26 says he was greatly feared by the community and preyed upon it; T 2-17-26 adds the Gennas imported him.

72　**Nerone**: Burns 132-133 gives name, quoted sobriquet and personal details; Pasley *Capone* 109 gives "The Cavalier" and that the Gennas imported him based on his abilities solely as a gunman.

73　**Anselmi and Scalise**: Kobler 89 for quote; descriptions see T 6-13-25, as members of the Marsala Club: T 7-9-25.

73　**"allies to be handled"**: Kobler 162.

73　**O'Banion career**: Amalgam. "sunny brutality" quote: Pasley *Capone* 45; Chief Collins attributed 25 bodies: Pasley 23; impromptu hijacking: CCC Bulletin #38 and #45 dated 4-5-26 and 11-17-28 respectively give Drucci and O'Banion records; 1918 list of robberies in T 1-22-24; dated alcohol thefts, Schoenberg 71 who accessed original court records, higher end thefts described in Burns 83 and Pasley 47; Cragin alcohol plant: T 6-16-25; top three bootleggers: HE 11-11-24.

74　**appearance of**: Burns 85-86 especially the quote; and HE 11-11,12-24 for married, residence, acquired a working interest in the florist business, and florist quote; Burns 98 notes soothing effect on the hood.

74　**Weiss**: Quote and unlawful maturity, good with guns: DN 10-12-26, Pasley *Capone* 24, 51, and Asbury 352; never convicted: DN 10-15-26 nor do any other of the sources mention a conviction; "mental hawk": DN 10-12-26; brightest: Pasley 24; long hours hustling: DN 3-5-24, 10-15-24; O'Banion deferring and quote in DN 10-15-26; appearance, way with women: DN 10-15, "dying" quote: DN 10-15; a follies girl: Burns; kind to his mother: Asbury 352: his brother's quote DN 10-15.

75　**Alterie**: Name according to family in T 7-20-35, HE 7-19,20-35; T 7-19 for his adoption of Alterie name; "I make no boast": HE 11-13-24; "poppycock": HE 7-19-35; Captain Stege's observations and quotes: DN 2-25-26; age: T 7-19-35 as about Aug. 2, 1885, corresponds with coroner's notes in CCC; origins: DN 2-25-26, T 7-19,20-35; Two Gun alias given in HE 7-19; ranch name: T 7-19, HE 11-13; Alterie out west and Denver Stockyards rodeo: HE 7-19-35; pictures and filming: HE 11-13-24.

76　**criminal activities**: Jewel robbery: T 7-19-35; local mischief: Murray 69; murder charge and pleading insanity Murray with pic of him in hospital bed; killing horse: HE 11-13-24 and T 7-19; Webster hotel incident: Pasley *Capone* 52; union activities T and HE 7-19,20-35.

77　**George Moran**: Name in HE 11-15-24; Pasley *Capone* 246 describes him as smart enough to shy away from cops but with a lengthy criminal past; pic in T 7-9-25 show him handsome early on; originally nicknamed as "big Joe": HE 1-12-26 and more accurately "Big George" in DN 10-15-26; quoted exchange with police: X *Marks* 23; initiation of "Bugs" moniker and explanation in Lyle 201fn.

77　**Gusenbergs**: Burns 51; photos in Helmer and & Bilek; descriptions, quote from Schoenberg 210.

77　**Drucci**: Pasley *Capone* 23, 51; HE 11-15-24 for name Vincent Drucci, Schoenberg 80 for his real name as Di Ambrosio; "Schemer" nickname: HE 1-12-26; police record in

CCC Bulletin #38 and #45 dated 4-5-26 and 11-17-26.

78 **Torrio generally credited**: Burns 44 that he established the organized bootleg industry dividing the groups into territories, Pasley *Capone* 42 hints as much.

78 **O'Banion-Greenberg finances**: CCC memos dated 2-9-48 and 11-8-50 give loans and amounts to O'Banion's family, and interest in the brewery; CCC memo 1-24-49 references indictment #12457, *U.S. vs. Malt Maid* in which witnesses observed O'Banion and Alterie at the brewery on a number of occasions.

78 **independents killed**: Landesco 927.

79 **Dever's plurality**: Schmidt 72; his background: 6, 13-14, 29, 72.

79 **"I wish the good people"**: Ibid. 88.

79 **Collins's raids**: Schmidt 76, 79-80, 85-86.

79 **political change disrupted**: Landesco 910-911 explains the disorder in the underworld caused by the 1923 election.

79 **"Who you buying ...?"**: Burns 48 and Spike's high-pressure methods, .

80 **Jerry O'Conner killed**: Landesco 924 attributes it to the Torrio gang; Saltis was an ally, and Saltis reacted first to the incursion.

80 **September 12, Dever**: Schmidt 85.

80 **Meegan and Bucher**: Landesco 924; according to Schmidt 85-86 what galled Dever most was that suspect Dan McFall was an employee of the sheriff's office and this reflected poorly on his efforts to clean up the town.

80 **soda parlor raids**: Schmidt 86.

81 **Capone's income**: Pasley *Capone* 18.

81 **Internal Revenue**: Schoenberg 79.

81 **1922 accident**: Ibid. 78. with Pasley *Capone* 20-21, quoted boast from Schoenberg.

81 **Dale Harrisson report**: S 3-20-43.

82 **Nitto businesslike**: The author did not uncover any trace of indulgence on Nitto's part in any newsprint or periodical. Interview 9-25-95 with contemporary news photographer Anthony Berardi, he remembered seeing very little of him, but when he did, Nitto struck him as the serious businessman type.

82 **the gang "as formed"**: Landesco 1012.

82 **Greenberg "They never"**: Murray 30 along with 25 percent piece of the brewery

82 **no Mafia rituals**: Conclusion formed through discussions with Chicago organized crime researcher John Binder. Besides there are no contemporary accounts even hinting of such and as given in the text, how could one explain the presence of Guzik, Ed Vogel or later non-Italians in high standing including Welsh blood in labor racketeer Murray Humphreys?

83 **Nitto's initial duties**: Feds investigating his activities later in DOJ #5-23-259 and INS #751-C1919944 letter dated 3-26-31 pegged it mainly in the alcohol racket with 'probably" quote in INS letter; DN 3-20-43 pegged his initial duties as a collector and bookkeeper earning $250,000 a year—perhaps based on later income figures; S 3-20-43 also says a collector for the Capone mob, but specifies start in Cicero.

83 **reference to "triggerman"**: Kobler 145, with all due respect to a magnificent writer—this was apparently not so.

83 **"his worst enemy"**: Irey 45.

CHAPTER 6

85 **"Nightly raids"**: Landesco 860.

85 **Torrio's bribe attempts**: Asbury 337, Kobler 113-114.

86 **Gambling "absolutely dead"**: Landesco 900, also for "find a cheater" quote.

86 **Cicero history**: Asbury 332 Burns 38; Asbury notes beer supplied by the O'Donnell's; Tancl: Landesco 909; Hawthorne Park description: Lyle 101.

87 **Vogel bio**: Physical description: T 4-19-59; background: ST 6-15-77 also for "the first to discern"; date of birth: CCC file; T for full history; and ex-wife's quote.

87 **Vogel's business**: ST 6-15-77 dispersed funds, reached the top without firing a shot; T 4-19-59 for "common, ordinary", quote that upset him; run-ins with law: T; Vogel's slot machines: Peterson 297-298 for incident.

87 **October 1923**: Burns 39 and Asbury 332 for details.

88 **Vogel's mark of approval**: T 4-19-59.

88 **Hawthorne Hotel**: Pasley *Capone* 62-63 for a complete description; bulletproof blinds: Burns, 39.

88 **Twenty-second Street**: Burns 38; Binder 21 contemporary picture for estimated width, traffic flow and parking as well as width of walk.

88 **Nitto's responsibilities**: S, DN 3-20-43 as appointed a collector; S expressly states in Cicero; "in the booze racket": INS #751-C1919944 letter dated 3-26-31.

89 **collection methods**: "frank and to the point": *USvC* Bioff testimony 212; "If a debt": P 10-31-30; "He got" quote: RD September 1932.

89 **"rapid" rise**: T 3-20-43.

89 **reform threat**: Landesco 1011 for pre-election situation in Cicero; Capone accepted: Schoenberg 96-97.

89 **mobilized the troops**: Landesco 1010-1011; Burns 40 for one patrolman who foolishly intervened.

90 **police move in**: T 4-2-24.

90 **Frank Capone shooting**: T 4-2-24; his funeral services: T 4-6-24.

90 **nobody bothered operations**: Landesco 910 for names of authorities as well as tip-offs.

91 **St. John episode**: Kobler 151-157, Schoenberg 100-101 for quotes "Let the kid alone" and "Take the Ship"; Ralph as mean crude etc.: Schoenberg 96; St. John's recovery and Capone's take over: Kobler.

92 **Capone quote "I tell 'em"**: Schoenberg 101.

92 **Nitto's characteristics**: Tony Berardi int. 9-25-95 for "banker-like" and "appeared very intelligent" quotes and timid observations; "moderate drinker": BOP #38021; George Meyer int. March 1993 corroborated Schoenberg's quote "You couldn't pay him" Meyer retired quietly to Texas after spending most of his adult life in prison .

92 **Nitto smoked**: BOP #38021.

92 **Cicero in 1923 wide-open**: DN 9-21-23; Landesco 900.

93 **Pete Penovich**: A UPI photo in Spiering.

93 **Frankie Pope**: HE 3-7-34 picture for description; Pasley *Capone* 65 for quote; Landesco 900: son of a gambler, millionaire; partners with Penovich: T 10-15-31 suggests he ran a gambling joint with with Penovich at least to May 1924.

93 **owners of the Ship**: Landesco 900, 1012 and for most of them as Loop veterans.

93 **exacted 25-50 percent**: Pasley *Capone* 41 he accurately describes the methods used as completely autocratic.

93 **takeover of Penovich**: Spiering 145, Penovich testimony for Ralph's actions; T 10-15-31 for all quotes.

93 **Hawthorne Smoke Shop**: Spiering 129 Leslie Shumway statement.

93 **Mondi takeover**: DN 10-13-31 including quote of cashier Fred Ries.

93 **the Subway**: Spiering, 129-130 Leslie Shumway statement describes the setup.

93 **migratory concerns**: DN 10-13-31; the Radio Inn: HE 11-13-24 gives the name and address, also mentioned in T 10-8-31, Spiering 185.

94 **the Ship**: Nelli *Crime* for contemporary picture complete with sign and address; Pasley

Capone 39-40 for its location near the El lines and "Monte Carlo" quote; Ship's profits: T 10-17-31, Nelli *Crime* 177 gives the Ship's take at a half million dollars.

94   **graduated to gaming books**: *Illinois Policeman and Police Journal* May-June 1947 courtesy of the CCC.

94   **daily routines in houses**: Spiering 130-131, T10-8-31; the house bank retained $12,000: T and Spiering 171.

95   **Nitto's likely residence**: BOP #38021 Biographical Sketch and Petition for Naturalization #64355.

95   **citizenship**: Petition for Naturalization #64355.

96   **location of alcohol plants**: T 6-16-25 gives addresses for both.

96   **Genna booze quality**: Burns 93 as well as price and pushing it into O'Banion territory, but *X Marks* 15 reports that the Irishman pushed into Genna markets first, clearly their was some divergence on alcohol market share.

97   **Torrio diplomacy**: Ibid.

97   **O'Banion hijacked**: Asbury 347

97   **Mike Merlo's dictum**: Burns 98-99 also provides a short Merlo bio.

97   **Sieben Brewery incident**: Landesco 913-914, Burns 95 for account in detail.

97   **Early November meeting**: A hazy episode at best. Text follows the most contemporary source DN 10-12-26 which gives those 3 names, amount and cause of Genna's debt, but no firm date, only implying that it was not long before O"Banion; s death; most later recitals of the meet follow in some fashion the *Illinois Policeman and Police Journal* May/June 1947, this source specific about the date as November 3, but names Nitto, Capone, Rio, Frank Diamond, O'Banion, Weiss and Drucci in attendance with no mention of Torrio—all of which are realistic and make sense, for example: Would Torrio and O'Banion travel about, particularly O'Banion to Cicero, without at least some top associates? The journal article in fact provides no sources for that account, so we really don't know. Curiously, DN is not without its flaws. For example, it claims that O'Banion and Weiss earlier just walked in and muscled Torrio for 25 percent of the Smoke Shop and the Ship in early 1924—highly unlikely with Capone and a retinue of gunmen running the show. But that Torrio might award him with points there for one or both the reasons in the text seems probable and that Genna would refuse payment in the first place based perhaps on the earlier O'Banion hijacking would make sense. DN also states, interestingly, that talk around town had Torrio indifferent to the demise of either party since—with Genna refusing to pay a gambling debt—both now exemplified treachery, but as events unfold clearly Torrio sided with the Gennas.

97   **Merlo's floral tribute**: Burns 99 for wax/floral effigy and amounts spent.

97   **Schofield's shop**: Photo in the John Binder collection for exterior description; interior inventory from Burns 100.

98   **O'Banion murder**: HE 11-11-24 and headline; Burns 101-102; Pasley *Capone* 55-56; gang suspects: Burns 103.

98   **Louis Alterie proposal**: HE 7-19-35.

98   **Weiss's shots at Capone's car**: Pasley *Capone* 75.

98   **Torrio's court matters**: Schoenberg 123.

99   **shooting of Torrio**: Burns 109-110; Pasley *Capone* 75-76; Torrio's lockup: Burns 111; Schoenberg 127; his abdication: Burns 111-112.

99   **Fed appraisal of Ralph**: "never much of a power": T 10-25-31; "stupid": Irey 27.

CHAPTER 7

101   **Nitto citizenship**: Superior Court of Cook County Certificate of Certificate of Naturalization #1919944, Nitto officially changed his name simply to Frank Nitto though

he often used the Americanized "Ralph" as a middle name.

101   **South Marshfield**: CCC copy of Nitto's April 1925 arrest report.

102   **2146 South Michigan**: description: T 4-8-25 picture; the Carleon Hotel was on the northwest corner of 22nd and Wabash at number 2138 South Wabash and only a block away was the New Wabash Hotel.

102   **"Dr. Ryan"**: DN 4-7-25, HE 4-8-25 both give Ryan as the name, though DN specifies Frank while HE gives John S. Ryan; T 4-7-25 did not report any specific name; Pasley *Capone* 69-70 writing in 1930 gives the Al Brown version that was cultivated over the years.

102   **office description**: T, DN 4-7-25.

102   **"surrounded by towering"**: DN 4-7-25 also typewriters and clerks.

102   **hoodlum memos, lists**: T 4-7-25, DN 4-7-25, HE 4-8-25.

103   **reproduced booze page**: HE 4-8-25 was the only paper to print details; note the total is 50 cents off.

103   **contents of records**: T, DN 4-7-25, and HE 4-8-25 all agree on records for alcohol and disorderly resorts: "disgustingly accurate" and amount as $25,000 monthly: DN; $10,000 a week: HE; quality testing: T and DN; phone records: T.

103   **names of attendees**: T, DN 4-7-25 and HE 4-8-25 names of 8 men and cash.

103   **Birmingham's Squad 1A**: CCC copy of Nitto's April 6, 1925, arrest report. ammunition and shells: HE 4-8-25.

104   **county sources, contents**: T 4-7-25 claimed the records represented a significant portion of operations which included well known businesses.

104   **Torrio's bottled water**: HE 4-8-25.

104   **Patton's bribe**: T 4-7-25 gives it as $5,000, DN 4-7-25 reported it as $15,000.

104   **Nitto arrest recorded**: Copy of police arrest report in which he gives his occupation as manager; HE 4-8-25 reported his refusal to elaborate.

104   **"SUPERTRUST BARED!"**: T 4-7-25 and for "minor heads" quote; other papers announced: DN 4-7-25 and HE 4-8-25.

105   **speculation as to contents**: T, DN 4-7-25.

105   **federal agencies interested**: T, HE 4-8-25.

105   **Birmingham served**: HE 4-8-25.

105   **"the law forced me"**: T 4-12-25 also quote "no federal cases"; " direct refusal": T 4-11-25; knocked the bottom":DN 4-11-25 also quote for "peculiar procedure."

106   move to Metropole: Pasley *Capone* 68-69; "a central headquarters": Schoenberg 170; booked rooms: T 10-10-31.

106   **"Prominent criminal"**: Pasley *Capone* 69; all activities described in DN 12-9-27, probably his source; expand to fifty rooms: Pasley *Capone* 68-69 .

106   **cafés**: Little Florence Italian Grill: Drury 166 for critique and quote, Amato's, mentioned here because of its geographical proximity; Drury 173 gives atmosphere, restaurant details and Maglialuzzo; John Citro's Café: *Lightnin'* 5-20-25 mentions Amatuna as well as proximity in Little Italy; Drury 174 gives restaurant details; Bella Napoli: T 3-9-26 details including sale to Coscioni .

107   **Felice DeLucia**: DN 7-10-43, DN 10-12-72 and page 312 of a transcript of Virgil Peterson's IOC Testimony gives Nitto credit for discovering Paul DeLucia though neither pinned down the date; *Collier's* 10-7-39 reports it as 1925 which seems right as Nitto was in with Capone circa 1923 and once established, perhaps a year or so he could recruit for himself. Place of meet in question: the above restaurants are a possibility –though in one instance Ricca himself tells the FBI in #58-2000-274-6 the place in which he met most of his gangland acquaintances was the Bella Napoli –he claimed employment there from 1923-26.

107 **Ricca background**: FBI #58-2000-273, 10-15 gives it complete with police record; physical description: Chicago PD arrest photo dated 1927 with standard Bertillion information attached.

107 **South Side beer war**: Landesco 924-925.

108 **Gennas as foremost**: T 7-10-25 their dominant operation in Little Italy.

108 **Tony Lombardo**: Burns 229 for Lombardo bio information, wholesale house and mention of tough tactics; Aiello partnership as cheese merchants and commission brokers: Pasley *Capone* 101; the two supplying Genna's operation: Landesco 1079; Lombardo a "level–headed man": Burns.

108 **Capone's strategy**: Pasley *Capone* 101-102 discusses logical motives for Capone to desire elimination of the Gennas.

109 **Angelo Genna murder**: Author cites DN 5-26-25 and HE, T 5-27-25; particular details; down payment version: T; Pasley *Capone* 102 gives the alcohol plant—probably based on DN reporting police found on Angelo a black book for Genna business.

109 **murder suspects**: HE 5-27-25 quotes Chief of Detectives Schoemaker for suspects as "not Italians"; belief that O'Banion's remnants killed him: DN 6-13-25.

109 **ambush Moran and Drucci**: DN 6-13-25, HE 6-14-25, T 7-9-25 gives the ambush at Congress and Morgan; names of North Siders: learned by Chief Schoemaker according to T.

109 **Mike Genna's death**: DN 6-13-25 and T, HE 6-14-25; see T for excellent photos and diagram of the scene.

110 **treachery of Scalise**: T 7-10-25 also for Anselmi; Schoenberg 130.

110 **Tony Genna's murder**: HE 7-9-25, DN 7-8-25, T 7-9-25 text generally follows HE; number of assailants remains in question, but perhaps key in T—witnesses described them as looking like Italians   .

110 **Genna aftermath**: Schoemaker quote: T 6-14-25; T, HE 6-14,15-25 report police raids and quantities of booze; brothers fleeing: DN 7-10-25; retiring: Burns 131.

111 **suspects Tony's murder**: T, DN 7-9-25 gave the range of motives; DN 7-8-25 reported an initial police search for Moran and Drucci; worth noting, Pasley *Capone* 102 pegged the elimination of the Gennas solely on Capone for reasons given in the text earlier, i.e., treacherous, as does T 7-10-25 which believed the murders the work of the "Chicago Mafia"; also, HE 7-9-25 noted Weiss was serving a short stint in jail ostensibly for the Sieben Brewery affair.

111 **Tony Campagna**: T, DN 7-16-25 and T 7-17-25; also gives Campagna and Novello as dangerous Genna men; Sam Lavenuto and James Russo: *X Marks* 24 for details, and Landesco 927.

112 **Samoots Amatuna**: DN, T 11-11-25, with DN 11-11, T 11-12,13-25 noting his engagement to Merlo's sister; DN 5-26-25 and HE 5-27-25 reported him to be Merlo's successor; $22,000 in the hole: T 11-14-25.

112 **his murder**: DN, T 11-11-25; T 11-12,13,14-25 for his condition; Burns 143 noted friends in doubt whether he would end up on stage or the gallows some day.

112 **Zion and Goldstein**: Pasley *Capone* 112, Landesco 1080.

113 **murder suspects**: Burns 144 for North and West Siders, the latter probably based on the rumor in T 11-11-25 that Amatuna hijacked a truckload of alcohol in their territory; however T reported witnesses claiming shooters to be "dark of skin".

113 **Nitto's new charge**: DN 9-22-30; Wilson & Day 41-42 names Cicero, Little Sicily, and the West Side also supported by DOJ #5-23-259; according to the Feds they name Nitto as "chief" of Capone's alcohol subsidiary, that he organized and derived great income from Melrose Park and Bellwood.

113 **Melrose Park**: HE 7-9-25 for bootlegging situation; Pasley *Capone* 196 reports Espos-

ito sales there; Taddeo as boss: HE 7-9 and T, DN 9-28-25 with DN describing him as a "Genna henchman"; Amatuna's stills: HE.

113　**Taddeo murder**: T, DN 9-28-25 for details; Campanille murder: T, DN 1-8-26; successor: Landesco 1078 for Joe Montana in Melrose Park, also gives him as a previous Genna alky cooker; DN 9-11-28 for Montana as Lombardo-Capone ally.

113　**Orazio Tropea**: Burns 145 says he was appointed the lead position; contemporary press sources acknowledge his lead.

114　**Spingola murder**: HE, T 1-11,12-26.

114　**Morici brothers**: T, HE 1-28-26 and T, HE 1-29–26; Antonio died a day later; T 1-28 claims they sold sugar and yeast to the Gennas which would seem to make them Lombardo's competitors; Agostino testified for Genna: CCC observer notes for Criminal Court of Cook County Case #24369.

115　**Tropea murder**: T, DN 2-16-26, quote from T; T 2-21-26 for pocketing proceeds and amount; about the community revenge theory, would any persons outside the gangster realm dare confront a gunman like Tropea? Worth noting, T 2-16 reported a few Sicilians consulting police about the truth of Tropea's death, fearful, they wanted to make sure "the Scourge" was actually dead. This was not the type of character ordinary denizens were willing to tangle with.

115　**murder of Tropea aides**: Vito Bascone: T2-22-26; Ed "the Eagle" Bardella: T, DN 2-24-26, the spelling of the name from those original news sources; Joseph Calabrese: T 3-7,8-26 including quote, Gnolfo's auto, and mistaken identity; CCC numbered list of murders for 1930 and Burns 156-157 for Gnolfo's fate.

CHAPTER 8

117　**Murray noted "found"**: Murray 19.

117　**corporate setup**: DN 10-8-31 including quote; that it was not a true board –they did not elect officers etc. – analysis from crime researcher John Binder.

117　**revenue division**: Ibid. as does T 10-25-31.

118　**"Big Four"**: Quote from HE 11-15-30, the four as such according to cashier Fred Ries testimony in CCC trial observer notes dated 11-14-30; Guzik BOP #41276L parole hearing dated 12/12/33 he admits Al, Ralph and Nitto as partners.

118　**Louis Schiavone**: Personality: DN 7-6-39; helped in alky sales reflected in DOJ #5-23-259, DN which pronounced him a "major Capone executive" in the alky business and T 7-6-39; his drug company: T 7-7-39; lost an eye:; lost an eye: DN; CCC Scalise-Anselmi file notes his arrest with Scalise on 8-4-27.

118　**Louis Cowen**: T 10-28-33.

118　**Frank Rio**: FBI #69-180-152 letter dated March 20, 1935, T, HE 2-24-35 and DN 2-25-35.

118　**Robert McCullough**: CCC memo dated 5-3-44.

119　**"Mops" Volpe**: DN 9-22-30 as a key bodyguard; Landesco 1040 for abilities, and Pasley 195-196 for Esposito's favors.

119　**Jack McGurn**: CCC memo dated 9-2-33 for his history and criminal record; T 2-15,16-36, Pasley *Capone* 166-168 also for coroner's quote.

119　**Phil D'Andrea**: FBI #58-2000-273 -17, 19, 21 and IMW 868 for his background and record; marksmanship: Kobler 146.

119　**Louis Campagna**: FBI #58-2000-273, 1-9 gives his CPD and FBI records, criminal history, and background; IMW finding of the facts also IOC 296.

120　**Nick Cricella**: Chicago PD record, *Lightnin'* August 1939, T 9-30-41.

120　**"know it legally"**: Landesco 840 quoting a prosecutor.

121　**"war to the hilt"**: Landesco 832.

121　**raids and press coverage**: Pasley 132 and *X Marks* 28; alky stills destroyed: T 5-4-26;

suburbs: Burns 175-176; the $80,000 incident: DN 2-27-36; overall damage estimate: Burns 175-176.

121 **quoted warning to saloons**: Landesco 836 as coming from the Capone gang. indictments against: Ibid.

121 **West Side Report**: Sammons' bond paid by Weiss's mother: T 5-5-26, this certainly signaled to Capone interests of some cooperation between the two parties, while Schoenberg 165 also notes she put up the bond for McErlane in a murder case –completing the Weiss-Saltis-O'Donnell circle; Klondike and Sammons arrest: X Marks 28-29; Jules Portuguese: one of those murders which seems to have a no lack of suspects, T 7-14,15-26, pointing to Weiss; Portuguese was taken for a ride and dumped on the Far Northwest Side, perhaps fortifying the Weiss theory; T 7-15 reported Myles O'Donnell as suspect.

122 **South Side Report**: Landesco 925; Frank Conlon death: T 7-24-26.

122 **Frank Cremaldi**: T 5-22,23-26, DN 5-22-26; he was taken for a ride and killed 20 miles west-northwest of the Loop; X Marks 29 thought him a Genna hand, T 5-23 notes him in frequent company of Mike Carrozzo, a South Side labor agent and ally of Capone; Landesco 928 simply concluded he was an Italian out of territory.

122 **Rossi disappearance**: Burns 185-186, Lyle 116 for details .

123 **Standard Oil Building**: Landesco 928 gives the date as August 10; Burns 186 and Pasley *Capone* 121-123 for details.

123 **Hawthorne Hotel**: T 10-12-26 briefly mentions it as does Landesco 928 who dated it September 20; Burns 187-188 and   Pasley 115-120 for details of shooting.

123 **peace conference**: DN 10-12-26; DN gave Weiss's demands as Mops Volpe and Frank Clementi as some concrete form of sincerity for peace whereas X Marks 30 (1930) names Volpe and Frank Rio while Burns 188-189 (1931) gives Anselmi and Scalise; author follows original source believing 1) Weiss would demand them because of the personal affront, 2) he most likely identified them as the gunners, and 3) they were available, whereas Scalise and Anselmi were still in police custody; moreover, Landesco 928 *fn* also notes that Weiss's demand was for the attackers at the Standard Oil Building to be "put on the spot" – obviously not Scalise and Anselmi.

124 **wasn't a killer type**: Capone FBI #62-39128-124 memo dated 12-6-39 regarding an interview with underworld links who stated Nitto wasn't a killer type; "What had Nitti" quote from RD September 1932.

124 **things done in a hurry**: DN 6-17-32 and RD September 1932   .

124 **Nitti originated ambush**: Police opinion in STLPD 6-17-32, also in DN 6-17-32 and RD; they reinforce it by observing most ordinary gangsters were too dull to think of new ideas; "alley rat" and cement head analysis while actually praising Weiss: DN 10-15-26—altogether with reasons given in the text and Nitto's personality, it is quite a possibility; "perfect" quote: X Marks 30-31, " ... perfection in the art. It was the most masterfully planned and executed of any ganglands crimes including even the Valentine Massacre, which was to come after."

124 **machine-gun nests**: T 10-12,14-26 for details on 740 North State including renter's name Lundin and date, with Pasley *Capone* 125-126 giving the same; both Pasley and Burns 190 give the Superior Street rental.

125 **Weiss ambush**: DN, T 10-11,12,13,14-26; excellent diagrams in DN and T 10-12.

125 **agreed upon territories**: Pasley *Capone* 141-144 for details; Landesco 928.

125 **O'Donnell, Sammons ... **: Schoenberg 170-171 citing T 3-6,13-27; "put a quietus": Pasley *Capone* 135.

126 **Saltis retreated**: Hollatz, 97 for complete details of his Wisconsin activities and sanctuary; Landesco 929 notes Salits and McErlane in trouble with authorities combined with Capone backing of their adversaries greatly strengthened Sheldon's grip in the south.

CHAPTER 9

127 **in Thompson's HQ**: W&K *Big Bill* 268-269 demands by Capone's organization: 250-251; DN 12-6-27 recognized the investment nature of these contributions.

127 **Thompson's victory**: Ibid. 243-251, 271.

128 **Thompson's appointees**: Ibid. 276; DN 12-6-27 Serritella's association with Capone was only known later according to W&K.

128 **Drucci's death**: Pasley *Capone* 159-160.

128 **Martin Guifoyle**: Landesco 930.

128 **Claude Maddox**: *X Marks* 38; background and record: S 8-16-46, S-T 6-23-58.

128 extent of Nitto's business: DN 12-6-27 and DN 9-22-30; 20,000 speakeasies: Pasley *Capone* 144; DN 12-6 for "Law and order", "see the light" and corporal punishment quotes; DN 9-22 gave Nitto operating stills and the extent of the contributing allies.

129 **1927 alky murders**: Fiori: T 3-14-27; Castenaro: T 5-14-27, and a numbered list of 1927 murders compiled from the coroner's reports found in the CCC, Landesco 929 gives his independence while Pasley *Capone* 176 says he might be an informer; Celebron: Pasley 176; Hitchcock: T 7-27-27, DN 7-28-27 with T explaining he owned a Capone joint the Arrowhead Inn which was raided and closed that he might have tried to reopen without permission .

129 **"Nitto got his bread"**: DN 2-27-36; T 3-6-31, 4-3-32 also rated him as a partner; HE 11-15-30 as a one of the principle owners of the Ship and Subway; all backed by notes from Guzik BOP #41276L Parole Hearing and CCC trial observer notes Jack Guzik tax trial dated 11-14-30, witness Fred Ries testimony.

129 **sophisticated procedures**: CCC trial observer notes Guzik dated 11-14-30 witness and bookkeeper Fred Ries gave details including "mixed up" quote; bookkeeper Leslie Shumway described details in Spiering 171.

129 **profits**: Ibid. "I would say not." quote from HE 11-15-30.

129 **booze mobs turned to**: Landesco 902.

129 **strain on Cicero's gambling**: Ibid. as well as "Who's going" quote.

130 **Chicago gambling**: DN 11-22-27, Landesco 901-902 and for Tennes wire service including rates.

130 **Capone's lecture**: W&K *Lords* 344-345.

130 **Mondi dictated**: DN 12-6-27; W&K *Big Bill* 280 gave "We'll get" quote, though Landesco 903 gives the rate at 25 percent

130 **Smith and Hyland**: Primarily STLGD 11-9-39 including quotes; also HA 11-17-39; Madison's kennel club: BND 5-15-26, 7-30-27.

131 **Edward O'Hare**: Amalgam. STLGD 5-14-23, 11-9-39; STLPD 11-9-39 DT 11-9, 13-39; T 11-9-39; particulars, never swore or seldom drank liquor: STLGD, DT, T 11-9; **athleticism**: DT 11-13; St. Louis U.: STLGD 11-9; STLPD 11-9; bootlegging clients: T 11-9.

131 **O'Hare incorporated**: STLGD 11-9-39, HA 11-17-39, DN 5-20-43, TD July 1941.

131 **pari-mutuel system**: Landesco 903-904.

132 **O'Hare's local problems**: BND 6-14-27, 7-30-27; TD July 1941 gives local dog tracks closing in 1927; that he went to Chicago: though the chain of events is somewhat vague, HA 11-9-27 estimates about this time; T 11-9-39 states Capone invited him up, however, according to O'Hare's lawyer in HA 11-17-39 this was not the case; O'Hare was in the area by 1926, according to a trial witness in T 5-10-40 and suggested in DN 8-9-27 and 6-12-29; "doctored" dogs: DN 8-9-27.

132 **opened in Thornton**: DN 8-9-27, DT 11-9-39, HA 11-17-39; DN says Thornton ran in 1926; in HA, O'Hare's lawyer explains the move to Chicago in detail, he opened in Thornton because he could not immediately get the political pull to open out west; Thornton ruled by Ellis: T 6-12-29, Virgil Peterson memo dated 6-9-50.

132 **Lawndale Kennel Club**: Though the history of the track has muddled over the years, T 5-10-40 for background of this club given by Ed Wait, a pro gambler, an original club investor, and witness in the later trial of Big Bill Johnson.

132 **Hawthorne Kennel Club**: Ibid. also noted the competition though it is unclear exactly when the Hawthorne opened; Wait also recalled the saturated market.

133 **O'Hare deal**: Amalgam of TD July 1941; HA 11-9, 17-39; T 5-10-40; HA 11-17 mentions O'Hare's control of hounds through his International Greyhound Racing Association; Egan's Rats: HA 11-17; "If I can't" quote: TD; the track merger: clearly given in great detail in T 5-10-40 by Wait; HA 11-17 gives the added benefit of a St. Louis alliance.

133 **Nitto handled the deal**: T 11-18-30 mentions the accountant: Nitto's money transaction and money collected: DOJ #5-23-259, it gives the date of the Nitto deal as March 1927.

133 **Laramie Kennel Club**: DOJ #5-23-259, it and the Hawthorne were one and the same; T 6-12-29, DN 5-20-43 noted the location explicitly at 35th Street and 52nd Street (Laramie Ave.) while others sometimes list incorrectly 22nd or 23rd streets; the Laramie name was probably a corporate title used until 1928 or 1929 when 6-12-29 newspapers covering police raids there clearly refer to it as the Hawthorne, they also report the number of area tracks reduced to the 3.

133 **Patton, McCullough, etc.**: Guzik BOP #41276L Parole Hearing dated 12-12-33 he names them as does Peterson 284-285; Barton and deposits: T 10-14-31.

133 **gang receipts**: Text relies on list in Pasley *Capone* 60.

133 **"A racket"**: Hostetter & Beesley 4.

133 **trade association racket**: Ibid. 4-14; Eisen's Meat Peddler's: Pasley *Muscling* 64-65; Master Cleaners: name from Pasley *Muscling* 76, though the exploitation of the linen industry is told in many sources.

134 **numbers of rackets**: Hostetter & Beesley 13, 25 also for bombs exploded; affected services: Landesco 980 names many more as a "partial list".

134 **"scarcely a commodity"**: Pasley *Muscling* on fp Robert I. Randolph quote.

134 **special assessments**: Hostetter & Beesley 16.

134 **"The more you give"**: Pasley *Muscling* 73.

134) **Carrozzo**: Ibid. 70; also recorded in April–June 1940 papers.

134 **Stanton in city hall**: Ibid. 70-71 also for the Plumbers' union.

134 **Barker-White-Humphreys**: Ibid. 16-17; Barker's recurrent jail stints: Chicago Bureau of Investigation record dated 5-2-30; White's frequent jail stints: State's Attorney's Office record dated 5-2-30; White: Pasley named White as Barker's chief aide; Pasely *Muscling* 12-16 credits these two for horning in on the Chicago Coal Teamster's union; they evolved amongst the West Side O'Donnell according to Pasley 76; "superintendent of transportation.": HA 10-20-48; Humphreys: FBI #CG 92-348 Section 7 pages 180-187 outlining press reports and T 4-5-36 for an superb account of laundry rackets; *X Marks* 27 gives White as an O''Donnell gunman early on while T 4-19-36 entitled *Bullets, Bombs, and Blackmail* offers an excellent accounts of all three with Klondike O'Donnell invading unions with Capone's "moral backing"; cost 25 percent: Pasley 58.

135 **Humphreys quote**: T 4-16-36.

135 **cost of racketeering**: Pasley *Muscling* 16-17.

135 **Aiello family**: Pasley *Capone* 171-173 and also gives "banner year"; Pasley and DN 11-22-27 note the rivalry.

135 **Jack McGurn**: McGurn's criminal history dated 9-2-33 in the CCC .

135 **Torchio murder**: Chicago PD homicide report # 9176, specifies one Tony Tochio age 32 of Bellwood, New York; Pasley *Capone* 169 for "professional killer" .

135 **poison plot and response**: T 9-8-28 specifies both Capone and Lombardo.

135 **Dominick Cinderello**: Numbered list of 1927 murders found in the CCC, also mentioned in McGurn's arrest for such in his 9-2-33 CCC criminal history report.

135 **Russo and Spicuzza**: Ibid. for details including St. Louis origins; alky cookers: Landesco 929; T 9-8-28 gives the reward.

135 **Sam Valenti**: Ibid. for details; an Aiello agent: Pasley *Capone* 169 and Burns 228.

135 **Sheldon's perfidy**: Burns 228.

136 **Aiello alliances**: DN 11,26,27,29-27 and T 11-24, 27-27; DN 11-29 for Mondi demands and double payments; T 11-24 suggests the outcomes for Aiello, Moran, and Skidmore.

136 **La Mantio episode**: DN 11-21-27, HE 11-22-27.

136 **detective bureau siege**: HE 11-22,23-27 and DN 11-22-27 with quote from DN; police escort: HE 11-23-27

137 **Aiello nervous breakdown**: DN 11-23-27, T 11-24-27; to New Jersey: DN 1-5-28.

137 **Capone—Minerva Club**: DN 11-22-27 including "roscoe" quote.

137 visit to Skidmore HQ: HE 11-23-27; joint at 823 West Adams: DN 11-29-27 including number of patrons.

137) **"Don't quote me"**: Pasley *Muscling* 71.

137 **"Mayor of Crook County"**: W&K *Big Bill* 280.

138 **Belcastro called in**: DN 11-23-27.

138 **Thompson's aspirations**: W&K *Big Bill* 281.

138 **Sgt. Lynch incident**: DN 11-23-27, T and HE 11-24-27; DN gave the names of those in the squad.

138 **November 23 raids**: Ibid. mainly HE for Pete Genna and T for O'Conner quote.

139 **Nitto arrest November 24**: The entire story an interesting example of how pieces of research come together since no record exists in police files. The first clue came from Nitto's FBI File #62-24090 which contains a poor quality copy of a Nitto line-up photo. The author then discovered and obtained a reference copy of the same photo from the Chicago Historical Society with the date given, but with a sleeve of one other person shown. A check of papers did not give Nitto's name, but gave the round ups of gangsters at the time. The author found in Capone's FBI #69-180-153 a letter dated 4-12-35 in which agents reference the early lineup photo of Nitto with Coscioni. A later FBI field report in Nitto's file dated 10-11-30 reveal that the reason this incident fails to appear in police records is that Nitto had the records plus the original photo legally destroyed.

139 **Walker-Berienbach fight, raids**: T, DN 11-26-27 give the names of those taken; T 11-27 for Aiello's brother and DN 11-28 for Esposito's pull and "lock and key" quote; Pope taken: T 11-29-27.

139 **police close gambling**: DN 11-29-27 and for Capone's suburban operations; HE 11-23-27 gave a city wide estimate of the loss due to gang warfare.

139 **Spingola bombings**: T 11-25,26-27; other bombings in T, DN 11-29,30-27 .

140 **bombing losses**: DN 11-23-27.
   "some Christmas money": DN 11-29-27.

140 **Capone meeting pols, police**: DN 11-29-27 heard it and reported the location as a suburban Hillside tavern.

140 **Capone left to hunt**: T, DN 11-29-27 with quote from T.

140 **further bombings**: T, DN 11-29,30-27 .

140 **Ferraro murder**: DN, T 11-30.27.

CHAPTER 10

141 **Capone down time**: Wisconsin: IOC interview of Ralph found in the CCC, says they were often there, sometimes with Nitto; residents at the time interviewed by Hollitz

70-72 remembered them; T 11-29-27, 12-5-27 mention a Capone hunting trip there; Florida: T 10-13-31, DN 10-21-31 for leasing the place; DN 10-9-31 for the Palm Island deal.

141   **Nitto-operation manager**: *X Marks* 40 reinforced by articles appearing as notes for text later in the chapter.

141   **Guzik ill**: T 10-10-31 mentions his illness that winter.

142   **130 gang murders**: W&K *Big Bill* 307; certainly the numbers during Prohibition were high and troubling for city leaders, but problematic because of the widely disparate numbers previously published hence the author's use of "unofficial" .

142   **bombings**: T 12-17-27; W&K *Big Bill* 307.

142   "The rulers of the city": Peterson 42.

142   **bombing Thompson allies**: DN 1-26-28 reports the incidents as clearly part of the criminal-political gambling fracas, Landesco 904 for quotes.

142   **warnings to Diamond Joe**: DN 3-22,23-28 including the murder of his brother-in-law, quotes in DN 3-22.

142   **Esposito's murder**: T 3-22-28, DN 3-23-28.

142   **Deneen-Swanson bombings**: W&K *Big Bill* 304-306 for details .

143   *"The rockets' red glare"*: Ibid. 304.

143   **election violence**: DN 4-10-28 also for voting irregularities.

143   **Aiello men killed**: CCC list of murders for 1928 compiled from coroner's reports in which investigators believed these men to be Aiello men .

143   **Yale backing Aiello**: T 9-8-28.

144   **Yale murder**: Pasley *Capone* 242-245, Burns 224-228.

144   **Dominick killed**: CCC list of murders for 1928 lists his death; Canale's death: CCC list gives the date as July 25.

144   **move to the Lexington**: DN 8-1-28; accommodations in DN 10-29-31.

144) **Nitti recognition**: DN 8-1-28 including quote.

144   **901 South Halsted**: BOP # 38021L Nitto admits to half ownership of the place while Superior Court of Cook County #28S480155 summons dated 7-10-28 police note he frequents the place usually between "5 and 6 p.m."; operated by Coscioni's: 1928 City Directory lists Louis Cascioni, Naples Restaurant, 901 S. Halsted; episode regarding theft: Municipal Court Case #46758, it was dismissed on advice of the prosecuting witness Louis Coscione on 3-16-28, this also lists Coscioni as owner; CCC memo 3-26-44 lists Joseph Coscioni a Capone agent.

144   **Nitto at the Congress**: DN 8-01-28 gave the address only.

144   **Nitto in Wisconsin**: Ralph admitted: IOC interview found in the CCC; residents remembered: Hollatz 105, the quote from a resident though it may have been at a later date it is used here to illustrate a rarely exposed side of Nitto.

145   **income estimates**: Nitto's income to a Cicero bank: DOJ #5-23-259 and U.S. District Court for the Northern District of Illinois Ind. #21246; T 4-3-32 reported about $70 million passed through Nitto's, Guzik's and Ralph's accounts.

145   **commodity prices**: DN 4-7-25 ads.

145   **thought prior income**: INS #751-1919944 memo dated 3-25-31.

145   **1926 total income**: DOJ #5-23-259, Ind. #21246.

145   **Ralph's early encounters**: Irey 28-30.

145   **Guzik filed forms**: T 11-19,20-30.

145   **Nitto's new banking deal**: DOJ #5-23-259 memo dated 3-20-31 prepared by Assistant U.S. Attorney Dwight Green details the method—that some change occurred about the time of Ralph's initial IRS encounters clear by the decrease of Nitto income found in 1926; Irey 46 notes the procedure as legal at the time.

146   Yellow Cab stock: FBI #62-24090-21; periodic cab wars did erupt.

146   George Meyer: Meyer 13, 19-20; Nitto business at the track: DN 8-1-28; "three hundred" quote: Meyer 20; the number of men questionable, in a Frank Loesch letter to the U.S. Senate Judiciary Committee dated 3-23-32 found in the HHPL he states an "unimpeachable witness" with whom he was familiar stated that Capone admitted at one time to having about 185 men on his payroll at $300-$400 a week; Nitto's "I'll handle it" quote from Schoenberg 246.

146   Nitto divorce: Superior Court of Cook County #28S480155 *Rose Nitto vs. Frank Nitto* including settlement, divorce granted 7-30-28.

146   Anna Ronga: Age: 1920 U.S. Census; marriage and divorce: Superior Court of Cook County #27S451073 *Anna Chesrow vs. Eugene Chesrow.*

147   Lombardo murder: T, DN 9-8-28; he was age 37.

147   Pete Rizzito: T 10-28-28; CCC list of murders for 1928.

147   It was "Frank Nitti": DN 2-3-30.

CHAPTER 11

149   Charles Dawes: Hoffman for his background; as great-great grandson: 11; his career; 25-27; pushed for Fed intervention 30-31.

150   Dwight Green: Casey 118-119.

150   Chicago Association of Commerce: Plan war on crime: HE, P 9-9-26.

150   Oct. 18, 1928: HHPL Capone file Treasury Department memo dated 3-19-30; department chosen: Irey 26.

150   two methods: Spiering 67.

151   agents keeping books: Casey 118-119 for quote and clipping articles.

151   publisher Knox: Irey 26; followed by Loesch: Hoffman 51.

151   taxpayer fraud history: Irey ix.

151   Madden in charge: Ibid. 29 with assistants; Wilson from Baltimore: Wilson & Day 30; Converse in Hollywood: DN 2-27-36; stars names: Messick *Secret* 167.

151   checked for returns: Irey xii.

151   "Ralph was stupid.": Ibid. 27; quote blaming Ralph: 28-29; the entire Ralph Capone case outlined in Irey 28-31.

152   Chicago Heights: T, HE 1-7-29; "center of" quote from T .

152   police chief murder: HE 1-7-29 and for Basille; other murders attributed: T 1-8-29.

152   Chicago Heights raid: HE, T 1-7-29, T 1-8-29.

153   Pasqualino Lolordo: T 1-8-29, HE 1-10-29 with descriptive details from photo in Binder 35   .

153   headline: HE 1-10-29.

153   Moran complicity: Pasley *Capone* 236-238.

153   his Fairview Kennel Club: T 5-18-29 without permission; low attendance evident in June 1929 raids reported in T, DN 6-12-29—suggests it never really was popular; bombing (while it was Laramie) reported in BND 9-1-27, it said the bomb occurred in a vacant lot 200 feet away thought only to scare patrons while Kobler 245 gives arson at the Hawthorne apparently later.

153   attempts on McGurn: McGurn criminal dated 9-2-33 in CCC with dates of the incidents.

153   headline: DN 2-14-29.

154   Massacre details: Helmer & Bilek 97-99.

154   defections: *X Marks* 59-60 names both Newberry and Foster.

154   Nitto marriage: State of Missouri, City of St. Louis License #316957.

154   Guinta as Unione leader: HE 5-9-29 for background and arrest with Scalise.

154   **treachery of the trio**: *X Marks* 55.

154   **elimination "Nitti's idea"**: S 234 quoting George Meyer and later for Meyer recalled quote; bodies found: HE 5-9-29.

155   **Atlantic City**: T, DN, HE, NYT 5-18-29 for general events; Nitto and 3 others named in Wolf *Costello* 89-91; Messick *Lansky* 35-36 mentions booze as a topic, whereas T gives the Massacre and peace as key issues; Moran there: HE, NYT; Aiello and Saltis by proxy: T; Torrio mediating in Chicago: DN; "signed": T.

155   **Nitto went back east**: DN 5-18-29, T 5-20-29.

155   **Capone-Rio arrest**: T 5-18-29.

155   **Nitto confers with Capone**: T 5-20-29 speculated arrangements as given in text.

155   **speculation (as to leader)**: "Torrio Coming Back": DN 5-18-29; as "Racket King": 9-9-29; Ralph in charge T 5-20-29; Guzik –"field marshall" and Ralph from the Cotton Club: HE 5-17-29; Ralph's Montmarte Café: Ness 115-122.

156   **regarded "Frank Nitti"**: T 5-20-29 including quoted continuation.

156   **Eliot Ness**: Ness 93 including tip that Nitto called the meet. In his book, Ness seldom mentions Nitto while seemingly placing more emphasis on Ralph Capone as the important gang figure carrying out orders in Al's absence. This might be explained: 1) Ness was fixed on the Big Guy, and 2) Ralph, his brother, was much more easily located than Nitto, who learned to keep an extremely low profile.

156   **competitors**: Moran in Evanston: DN 9-9-29; Alterie: BND 9-1-27.

156   **North Siders killed**: *X Marks* 59-60.

156   **Sheldon—tuberculosis**: Ibid. 47.

156   **McErlane casualties**: Ibid. 54; Saltis made peace: 47.

Chapter 12

159   **endorsed by Nitto**: Irey 45-46.

159   **"breaking down ... partners"**: DN 4-2-30.

159   **Nitto got "careless"**: Irey 45.

159   **Druggan-Lake 1926**: T 1-19-26.

160   **Ralph's $3,200 check**: Irey 31; Carroll account with aliases: Ibid. 31-32 also gave amounts.

160   **nameplate matched**: DN 4-18-30   .

160   **Ralph's arrest—prizefight**: DN 10-9-30, Irey 34; DN gives bond reduction.

160   **Tessem assigned to Nitto**: Wilson & Day 40, Irey 45-46.

160   **Nitto's records destroyed**: FBI #62-24090-25 field report dated 10-11-30 is also specific to the date.

161   **Tessem tracking the check**: Irey 46-47.

161   **Nitto "retired"**: INS #751-1919944 letter dated 12-29-33.

161   **aggregate income**: DOJ #5-23-259 memo dated 3-20-31; Treasury Department letter dated 3-8-30 gives an account of the checks and "higher ups" estimation:

161   **"gross income"**: Ibid.

161   **largest business accounts**: Ibid. particularly a letter dated 3-8-30 which lists many of the check makers, Schiavone and Mondi clearly listed, the author opted not to reveal the name of the businessman involved.

161   **"evasive in their answers"**: Ibid. that other witnesses clammed up and "if" quote: T 3-26-61 retrospect by Frank Wilson.

161   **Julius Rosenheim**: DT 2-1-30, DN 2-3-30; McGurn arrest: DT and CCC memo 9-23-33 outlining his arrest record.

162   **Nitto's sobriquet born**: DN 2-3-30 this was the earliest "Enforcer" mention the author recovered   .

162   "Not a 'pineapple'": DN 2-7-30; "Beauty squads": DN 4-18-30.

162   **terrible city conditions**: DN 2-6-30 also gives the number of murders, Dawes quote, and Rosenheim reward offer.

162   **Secret Six**: *St. Louis Star* 11-22-32 in Robert Isham Randolph Papers at the Chicago Historical Society; Malone- the best undercover agent from T 3-26-61.

163   **Hoover determined**: HHPL Capone file contains many updates for Hoover from the Treasury Department, the attorney general, and interested Chicago individuals dated March 1930 regarding the tax prosecutions of Chicago gangsters, particularly Capone.

163   "Nope. Bottles goes": Irey 34 including Ralph's attempt at a deal.

163   **attorney general reported**: Quoted from HHPL Capone File letter 3-25-31.

163   **legal questions—tax statutes**: BOP #38021L Attorney Parole Report dated 9-15-31 U.S. Attorney George E. Q. Johnson explains in detail the difficulties facing the prosecution in those days given the myriad of tax laws that had yet to be entirely tested through the court system.

164   **Lucas letter**: DOJ #5-23-259.

164   **grand jury witness**: Ibid. letter dated 4-13-31 name of the witness (not a gang member) withheld by the author; "poor character from BOP Parole Report.

146   **indictments**: U.S. District Court, Northern District of Illinois, *U.S. vs. Frank Nitto*, Case #21246.

146   "no secret": Recalled by Irey 46; subpoenas, even from material and identifying witnesses all returned unexecuted in #21246.

164   **headline**: HE 3-23-30.

165   **initial search found no one**: DN 3-22-30 also hinted the Lexington and reported the raid netted men and liquor; HE 3-22-30 reported Johnson's plea for help.

165   **warrants for Fischetti**: Subpoenas in case #21246.

165   **Capone and associates**: Schoenberg 265-266.

165   **retained Mattingly**: Ibid. 260, quote from 254

165   **new Nitto warrant**: Subpoena in case #21246 .

165)   **Nitto in Florida**: FBI #62-24090-21 field report dated 10-3-30 the information given to the FBI by the U.S. attorney's office by word they received in April.

165   **Florida arrests**: Schoenberg 266.

165   **CCC public enemy list**: The original displayed in the CCC dated 4-23-30.

165   *Daily News* **list**: DN 6-18-30.

165   "uncertain ... territory": Irey 34.

166   **Ralph's trial**: Irey 34-35; evidence as "remote": HHPL Capone file letter dated 4-28-30 describing Ralph's trial; "one thing to argue' quote from Green 119; quoted observation of Ralph's attorneys from HHPL letter; Ralph's sentence from Irey also in HHPL and DOJ summary memo dated 3-25-31.

166)   **Parrillo fix**: Originally found in Murray 152, considerable support given in HHPL letter dated 3-23-32 from Frank Loesch of the CCC to Hon. William S. Borah, Chairman of the Sub-Committee of Judiciary Committee of the U.S. Senate outlining racketeering, politics and organized crime in Chicago relates Parrillo as an assistant U.S. attorney and gives the "partisan" quote used in text, Loesch further notes his primary responsibility as handling Prohibition cases; key is Tessem in a memo dated 10-8-42 in DOJ #5-2742 recalled their suspicion of Parrillo and his proximity to the grand jury room which was later altered .

167   **customary business**: DN 6-3-30.

167   "chief" and "arch killer": DN 6-18-30; Plescia, Monistero, Ferrari: *X Marks* 60 and a list of 1930 murders found in the CCC.

167   **Fox Lake Massacre**: DN 6-2,3-30.

167　**Lingle's death**: Boettiger 15-18 and Burns 289-292.

167　**attributed to Zuta**: Ibid. 102-107, 326-327, 41 gives the original police suspicions noting Lingle hated both Zuta and the Aiello's; DN 10-24-30 gives the Newberry angle.

167　**Zuta's death**: Ibid. 105-107, Burns 302-303 including first attempt on his life in the Loop; DN 10-24-30 gives Newberry as suspect in that shooting, while Stanton is credited by witnesses with the hit in Wisconsin, .

167　**Foster as suspect**: Boettiger 75-82 and Burns 296.

168　**Nitto's involvement**: Leo Brothers cropped up: Boettiger and Burns; Meyer 11 points the finger directly at Nitto as the person who arranged for Brothers to take the fall— Nitto and the Capone gang did have strong business ties in St. Louis to arrange such a setup; the Red Forsythe theory: Boettiger 70-72 gives the initial tip pointing to him, they followed it up and suspected it origins with the Capone gang; FBI #32-15941 found in Capone FBI file, an anonymous letter dated Nov. 26, 1930, also gives Forsythe as the killer ordered by Nitto—Forsythe eventually allied with the Capone gang.

168　**warrants again returned**: Ind. #21246.

168　**"Ash Can Pete" killed**: CCC list of 1930 murders compiled from coroner's reports classified an Aiello man by an investigator.

168　**Smokeshop ledger**: Wilson & Day 46-47 and search for Shumway.

168　**Dunbar checks and Ries**: Ibid. locating Ries in St. Louis: Irey 4 says Wilson's tip came from a hoodlum, Spiering 140 claims it was O'Hare; STLPD 9-25-32 retrospect piece had him working for local gambler; his arrest: Wilson and Irey, and STLPD; letter from Guzik relative was Louis Lipschultz with instructions to flee to Mexico.

168　**Ries agreed to testify**: Irey 47-48 and Wilson gives the jail site, that he agreed to testify in the Nitto case and the date are clearly given in dated notes from a hearing regarding Ind. #21246, the warrant was issued that day, on September 4 Ries was remanded to the custody of Frank Wilson for safekeeping.

169　**Johnson ... to the FBI**: FBI #62-24090 memos and field reports in serials 1-19 and dated 9-3-26 illustrate the conflict with the FBI over the Ries matter, Johnson's appeal to apprehend Nitto and in particular Hoover's quote from a memo dated 9-18 regarding a telephone call to agent H. H. Clegg of the Chicago bureau; Johnson's "overshadowed" plea as related per Clegg memo to Hoover dated 9-18; that Johnson went over the top clear from Hoover memo dated 9-19 in which he refers to Johnson meeting Assistant Attorney General G. A. Youngquist outside the presence of the FBI; the FBI requested and received Nitto photos and data from letter dated 10-3.

169　**tracing Nitto's family**: FBI field report dated 10-11-30.

169　**staked the Roamer Inn**: FBI field report dated 10-18-30.

170　**Judge Lyle**: Background, quoted comments and judicial temperament from *La Critique*, Vol. 5, No. 1 printed at the University of Chicago dated November 1930, the Chicago Bar Association they noted recommended against his retention; HE 1-10-26 also noted his high bond requirements.

170　**raid on the Lexington**: T 9-19-30.

170　**Carleon Hotel raid**: DN 9-25-30, T 9-26-30; "subterranean passage" in DN, other raids in T including Barton's capture.

170　**Guzik arrest**: BOP Guzik #41276L, Irey 48.

170　**"if we could catch [Nitto]"**: Irey 48; DN 9-19-30 for "desultory" search.

170　**Nitto might flee**: Rumor in T 10-25-30 because of the reward offered.

170)　**wanted posters**: T 10-3-30 and A 10-31-30.

171　**Nitto might surrender**: FBI #62-24090 field report dated 10-3-30.

171　**Johnson turned to Wilson**: Wilson & Day 41 he implored Wilson to uphold good government and find Nitto, quite likely because of Wilson's tenacity and Johnson's frustration with the FBI and local efforts; Wilson 34-35 and Irey 46 both held Malone as the key to locating Nitto and that Irey recalled him spotting Nitto twice at "Camp Capone"; the party events have been considerably jumbled over the years, but the text primarily follows Wilson 34-35 and his retrospect piece T 3-26-61– he was the man on the ground in Chicago—he gives the first as a Nitto birthday party in the Lexington—to place a timeline if in fact it was a party for Nitto, it was belated to 1930 or in advance of 1931 since Nitto's birthday was January 27 and must have occurred between Al's release March 1930 from Philadelphia and October 1930 (as we'll see); worth noting, it could not have been January 1929 as Al was in Florida avoiding the soon to be St. Valentine's Day Massacre (and sometime thereafter) and by May he was in jail for ten months, it would not have been 1928—before the IRS investigations began—and 1931 would be far too late; Wilson then mentions a second party –without specifying a salutation—this one at the Little Florence; Irey 58-60 (in 1948) mentions only one party, an incident at the Little Florence and has it as a going-away party for Al, (undated, but would make it summer 1931) supposedly celebrating the idea he would get off lightly on his tax charges without any indication it affected the Nitto case and would be far too late anyway; key perhaps is a more contemporary STLPD 9-25-32 retrospect piece gives the revelry at the Little Florence as a celebratory party for Guzik who was released on bond (without specifying date) probably after his late-September arrest which makes more sense; this second party is mentioned here since Spiering 96-98 (in 1976) relates an incident in which Malone thought his cover blown at a Nitto birthday party, but at the Little Florence, and that while attending this event (Spiering 98 relates), Malone gleaned some loose talk about Nitto's bank accounts and passed it to Wilson—though Spiering did have access to IRS files, he did not note his sources completely and his version appears to be a blend of Wilson and Irey; the author respectfully disagrees with the Nitto bank account talk for 1) it's hard to imagine that gangsters already on notice would bandy about such information, 2) neither Wilson nor Irey mention tax information obtained through these encounters and most strongly 3) by establishing a timeline for such (March-October 1930), the Nitto case was already made by agents Tessem and Converse, the indictment filed, all they were trying to do was *locate* fugitive Nitto; Irey 46 does note one simple key item: Malone reported back that he had spotted Nitto and that he changed his appearance; reporter quote on his appearance: HE 11-1-30.

171   **Rogers and O'Hare**: Wilson & Day 32 seems clear that O'Hare merely desired to distance himself from the Capone name, there was no deal to get his son in.

171   **the Greenberg trail**: HHPL Capone file, memo dated 4-28-30 for Madden's quote; STLPD 6-7-33 relates the pursuit.

172   **events leading to Nitto's capture**: Amalgam, since no one version previously related, even by those involved, appears absolute; some gave details-others did not, and sometimes there are obvious exaggerations. The text relies on the more contemporary Irey 48-50, Wilson & Day 41, Boettiger 186-187, T 3-26-61, STLPD 6-7-33, and out-of-town news articles found in Robert Isham Randolph Scrapbooks in the Chicago Historical Society; Wilson & Day 41 and his account in T 3-26-61 give the core basics— the reporter tip of Nitto's car, Malone's watch for the car with Wisconsin plates, tailing Mrs. Nitto, and the stake out across from the apartment. "Don't look for him" in T 3-26-61; Irey 48-49 simply relates Malone knew from his undercover work that the suburbs served as popular residence for gangsters and that Malone elected to search in that direction armed with a photo of Mrs. Nitto (also given in T 3-26-61), the car chase beginning with a chance incident as do Wilson in T 3-26-61 and STLPD 6-7-33—the STLPD specifying a test drive, Irey adds that apparently Mrs. Nitto tried

to lose Malone in the suburbs; both Wilson and Irey mention the trip lasted several hours; Berwyn apartment: STLPD relates the agents recognized the place as previously visited by Greenberg, with T 3-26-61 for her opening the window; Wilson quote to Irey: Spiering 100 ostensibly from a memo; surveillance: Irey mentions the belfry only, Wilson in T 3-26-61 gives the apartment building across the street as does Robert Randolph as reported in Detroit News 1-31-31, *St. Louis Star-Times* 11-22-32—Randolph as member of the Chicago Association of Commerce helped put up the Nitto reward money; as postal inspectors: Wilson in T 3-26-61; STLPD 6-7-33 related the fire hydrant ploy with the agents going inside and representing themselves as police officers to an elevator operator to pass the word to Mrs. Nitto whereas Irey wrote they called in an alarm and let the firemen contact Mrs. Nitto—from the ruse the agents learned the alias Belmont; the apartment number not given here and in doubt: Irey identified it as 3-D, STLPD as number 402, Boettiger (in 1931) gave it as the third floor; Greenberg arrived apparently on the evening of October 30: DN 10-31-30, T 11-1-30; Irey, STLPD, and Randolph in the Detroit *News* relate agents observed Nitto *inside* the apartment; the call to Roche's office including quote: in Boettiger—STLPD and T gave the call well after midnight; Roche's busy night: T and P 10-31-30 for the Sammons arrest; Belmont exchange: Irey and STLPD, though open to speculation –they were the only two nearly matching accounts, except STLPD had Mrs. Nitto answering the door, as did Boettiger—Wilson claimed after seeing him enter the building, they followed him in and knocked on the door, but does not give who answered only that Nitto presented a business card and that he later gave up, the problem not one news report mentions Frank Wilson on the scene; DN 10-31-30 report runs close to Irey, T and P report him taken while in bed, but T 4-2-31 in retrospect gives the confrontation at the door, A 10-31-30 says he surrendered, but adds a ammunition found; interestingly lavish apartment furnishings in DN and P 10-31.For the record: Nitto's arrest in the CPD Office of Detective Division dates his arrest on October 30. The date is off. Irey and Wilson both note early a.m. the 31st as do all contemporary newspapers which carried the story on October 31 noting the arrest early that morning, i.e., after midnight. Maybe some bureaucrat heard it as having occurred that night, assumed p.m. and hence marked it the 30th.

174   **Aiello away on business**: T 10-24-30 gives his control of the Unione and names the suburbs; meeting with Moran: HE 10-25-30; HE 10-26 mentions the Newberry angle.

174   **Spano killed**: Chicago PD Homicide record #11124, he was ambushed by rifle and shotgun fire.

174   **Presto apartment**: DN 10-24, 25-30 for shortened version of name and his business with Aiello.

174   **Aiello's family visited**: HE 10-25-30, DN 10-24-30.

174   **tenants in 202 Kolmar**: T 10-24-30; DN 10-24-30 gives the efficiency rooms and also the men as pleasant and courteous.

174   **in 4518 West End**: T 10-24-30.

174   **Mexico destination**: T 10-24-30; HE, DN 10-24-30.

175   **Aiello murder**: T, DN, HE 10-24-30: slug count: DN 10-24-30 had the count at 55 and the cumulative weight as about a pound while noting 60 found their mark, T had it as 35 and Burns 305 had it as 59; Aiello's age from a list of 1930 murders found in the CCC.

175   **Kipling's work**: T, DN 10-24-30.

CHAPTER 13

177   **wanted for questioning**: DN, P 10-31-30.

177)   **Madden and Green**: A 10-31-30, HE 11-1-30.

177) INS grilled him: INS memo dated 3-7-31, the visit: November 1.

177 Headline: T 11-2-30.

177 "first of his lieutenants": HE 11-1-30.

177 supposed rift with Capone: DN 10-9-30.

178 strained finances possibility: DN 11-3-30.

178 Naples Restaurant raid: P 11-5-30, T 11-6-30; Pierce as Humphreys protégé: FBI #92-3088 reports the two were friends and that Pierce acted his bodyguard.

178 "Nitto stood in court": HE 11-1-30.

178 judge "did not show": P 11-7-30.

178 Chamberlain's observation: T 11-2-30.

178 Grand Central: DN, P 11-8-30, P 11-11-30; bond surety business: DN 11-8-30.

178 "a great a menace": Ibid.

179 arrest on vagrancy charge: Chicago PD rap sheet in BOP, HE 11-8-30 Nitto quote and name gaff from HE, which claims the mistake in reverse "o" for an "i."

179 Nitto-Rio ordered back: P 11-11-30.

179 bond technicality: CCC observer notes Municipal Court Case #1060074 and widely reported in the papers on 11-12-30; Lyle's quote to Nitto an amalgam from T, DN 11-12.

179 Tony Berardi: Interview September 25, 1995, he recalled the event including Judge Lyle's reprimand, his Nitto photo appeared in T, A 11-11-30.

179 another property bond: HE 11-15-30.

179 tussle number two: CCC observer notes Municipal Court Case #1060074; A, DN 11-18-30, DN for Lyle quotes.

179 paid $10,000 bond: Ibid., T 11-18-30.

180 fix for Guzik: HHPL Capone File, letter dated 4-13-31 from Assistant Secretary of the Treasury Arthur Ballantine to the Herbert Hoover's Presidential Secretary Walter H. Newton with accompanying memos relating the entire incident.

180 Guzik trial: CCC observer notes dated 11-14-30: Guzik's defense: DN 11-19,20-30; prison sentence: BOP Jack Guzik #41276L.

180 government deal: Johnson outlined it in detail in Nitto's BOP, Attorney Parole Report dated 9-15-31, quotes are from that report; aiming for other corrupt officials: HHPL Capone File memo dated 3-24-31.

181 Nitto in court—plea: Appearance: T 12-21-30; his lawyer's quoted objection: DN 12-20-30; P 12-20-30 reported the strategy to keep the civil end open .

181 "while the sentence": P 12-20-30.

181 Nitto's statement: While several papers had portions of it, *Time Magazine* 12-29-30 gave the entire statement as given in the text; T 12-21-30 gave the "educated man" observation, it did impress quite a few and may very well have articulated Nitto's views, but probably with eloquence contributed by his attorney: T also gives Nitto's "get it over with."

182 Nitto as a sacrifice: Mentioned by HE 12-21-30 and *Time Magazine*.

182 possible maneuvers: George E. Q. Johnson's term was to expire in February noted as coincidence, he was retained.

182 Murray's conclusion: Murray 154; probably based on the timing of later events (1932) as we shall see, certainly a possibility, .

182 capable men left: DN 12-20-30.

183 Nitto to Leavenworth: HE, T 1-11-31; HE for quoted conversation.

183 BOP became: Leavenworth Area Development Homepage, November 2002, *United States Penitentiary: History of the USP 1896-2002*, www.lvarea.com/data/usp; the reorganization became effective May 14, 1930; 11 prisons at the time: www.bop.gov March 2004

183 **USP Leavenworth history**: Ibid. also 1998 The History Channel series *The Big House* installment entitled *The Big Top—Leavenworth* and Leavenworth Area History page www.lasr.net particularly; 3 regional prisons in www.bop.gov; details of the prison, "marvel" quote and identification center: www.lavrea.com.

184 **regulations**: Primarily www.lavrea.com; haircuts: T 10-25-31; T says control was tight, which may have been the rule, but Nitto's BOP record illustrates otherwise.

184 **prison population**: Ibid.

184 **processing new arrivals**: Nitto's BOP and T 10-25-31.

185 **Nitto correspondence/visitors**: BOP Correspondent List, January-March 1931 and Visitor Registration; address of Coscioni's given on his BOP as 5253 Quincy, a check of the 1928 Chicago City Directory provides the tenants as Hugo and Joseph Coscioni though the 1931 Chicago Phone Directory provides only Joseph's name at the address. The connection to one William Coscioni not clear. A William Coscioni appears at the address in 1928 through at least 1933 according to the same sources. Amazingly, William is listed at 922 S. Halsted in 1923, the same address Nitto claimed only a year or earlier.

185 **aim of exchanges**: Conjecture based on the alignment of communication dates from Visitor's Register and Correspondent List with events in Nitto prison record; Anna's double visits noted in the register as well as meetings allowed in warden's office "with permission" as noted in the record; names of Marzano and Colianni appear as references in the Trusty Prisoner's Agreement in the record—their backgrounds from 1923 and 1928 Chicago city directories and *Lightnin'* June 1940.

186 **work assignments**: Recommendation of Psychiatrist report and parole interview dated July 3, 1931.

186 **CCC suggested deportation**: INS letter dated 12-13-30 from the Naturalization Service to the CCC, the quote from a summation previously given (as given in the letter) in response to the CCC request dated August 29.

186 **on November 25, 1930**: INS letter dated the same from District Director Fred J Schlotfeldt to Chamberlain requesting information from the CCC; deportation criteria reported in DN 3-3-31, T, HE 3-4-31.

186 **sweep of illegals**: T 1-11-31; Volpe as reported in T, HE 3-4-31.
March 7, 1931, letter: INS File #751-C1919944.

187 **headline**: HE 3-4-31.

187 **Cermak background**: Details in Gottfried 15-18, 50-53, 78; quote: 78.

188 **further political career**: Ibid. 78-82, 88-95   .

188 **County Board**: Ibid. 105-108, 146; "Mayor" quote, patronage: 128.

188 **sought mayor's chair**: Ibid. 134.

188 **Wet stance**: Ibid. 140-142; "personal liberty" quote: 150; "conspicuously" and Dever's slim margins: 151.

189 **he maneuvered**: Ibid. 170-175.

189 **Thompson's wane**: W&K *Big Bill* 306 including quotes.

189 **wrestled control**: Gottfried 191-198 plus vanquishing his enemies.

190 **Thompson's declarations**: W&K *Big Bill* 323-324; beat Lyle: 329.

190 **campaign against Cermak**: Ibid. Particularly, casting himself as fit to be Fair mayor: 323; "You want a Bohunk": 331; campaign ditty: 329-330; "I won't take ... Chairmock": Gottfried 205; "biggest crook": W&K 331; "Saving Tony": Gottried 205; "I expect to win": WK 332.

190 **Cermak reaction**: Lyle dubbed: Dobyns *Underworld* 106; higher taxes and unemployment: Gottfried 219, 241.

190 **Serritella-Hochstein**: DN 4-30-32, CCC Trial notes dated 4-28-32.

190 **Cermak support**: T 4-3-31 for Dunne's plea; Gottfried 208-209; "Your own common sense": 213; "salvaging": 219; protecting business: 210-211, 228; Cermak's "pack up": LD 4-18-31; hoodlum support: Gottfried 212-213.

191 **Thompson support**: Ibid. 217.

191 **forecast and quote**: T 4-5-31.

191 **election details**: T4-8-31, W&K *Big Bill* 332.

191 **Thompson "skunk"**: Stuart 471; quotes from civic leaders: T 4-8-31; out of town reaction: Stuart 471.

CHAPTER 14

193 **O'Hare and Rogers visit**: BOP Visitor's Register; O'Hare fingering Shumway: Schoenberg 299.

194 **April 7 visit**: Frank Patton and town given as recorded in the BOP Visitor's Register; Serritella's activities: DN 10-24-31.

194 **Wilson and Tessem**: BOP Visitor's Register with their business described in a letter from the Deputy Commissioner of the Naturalization Service to the Treasury Secretary dated 12-29-33 in Nitto's INS file; fingerprint records sent: letter from Kansas City District Commissioner of Naturalization to the commissioner in Washington, D.C., date May 7, 1931, in Nitto's INS file.

194 **Form 7-1926**: BOP File.

195 **Parole Board history**: Department of Justice, U.S. Parole Commission official homepage www.usdoj.gov/uspc/history.

195 **Capone's indictments**: Schoenberg 309-310, T 6-13,14-31.

195 **Zarter inquiries**: Letters to Chicago PD dated 4-25 and 4- 27-31, to U.S. Marshal's Office dated 5-21.

195 **Board letter**: BOP File with Zarter's reply dated 6-25-31.

196 **Forest Dairy**: Letter dated 6-29-31.

196 **Dire and Marzano**: Letters dated 6-29-31.

196 **Anna Nitto's plea**: Letter dated 6-29-31.

197 **Nitto's evaluations**: Work Report To Board of Parole dated 6-30-31.

197 **parole hearing with Tucker**: Report of the Hearing of Frank R. Nitto dated 7-3-31 includes quotes and conclusions.

199 **Capone's rumored deal**: T 2-23-36 and Schoenberg 311.

199 **legal status of hoodlums**: T 6-13-31, 10-18-31.

199 **trustyship revoked**: BOP record dated 9-15-31 notes the revocation, but nothing exists in Nitto's file to explain the action.

199 **Loesch-Hoover exchange**: Loesch letter dated 6-29-31 as member of the National Commission on Law Observance and Enforcement in D.C. to Hoover at the HHPL, Hoover's reply (probably a draft) not signed, but dated 7-1-31.

200 **Wilkerson refused**: T 2-23-36 gives the specifics and Wilkerson's sermon; T 6-14-31 reports that Capone's team attempted a compromise cash settlement as a means to avoid criminal indictment which was not out of the ordinary at the time.

200 **gang rank and file**: FBI #69-180-95 field reports for December 1931 concerning hoodlums in and out of Capone's county lockup, especially Ricca, Rio, and Campagna; McGurn: T 10-18-31, DN 5-4-32;; Hunt arrested: 10-10-31, 3-23-32; Ted Newberry: 10-29-31; Heitler murder: T 5-2-31, CCC summary of coroner's reports providing autopsy details and age; the secret letter surfaced in DN 9-18-31.

201 **Nitto's appeals**: Nitto letter dated 9-20-31 and 10-15-31; Timmon's letter 10-15-31; Nitto's communications to Anna and lawyer Epstein in BOP Record of Correspondents for the period September-November; Anna visited Johnson: Anna Nitto letter dated 11-23-31.

201 **Johnson on Nitto's behalf**: Letter dated 10-15-31 from Johnson to Timmons; quote from Johnson in Form 792, the Parole Report by the U.S. Attorney.

202 **legal gray area**: Johnson gives an explicit explanation of the sentence in his Form 792 as 1 year and 1 day minus time off for good behavior only provided Nitto met certain criterion. No doubt he could not supplant federal law and deny Nitto a parole hearing if that were the official sentence, so it is likely that is the reason he let the 18-month sentence stand officially. Johnson's "I have" quote from letter to the Parole Board dated 10-21-31; "If his conduct" quote from his report Form 792.

202 **Nitto petition**: Letter to Parole Board dated 9-20-31.

202 **clumsy appeal [the fine]**: Letter to Parole Board dated 10-15-31

203) **Woods "should a change"**: Letter from Wood to Nitto dated 10-20-31.

203 **Capone bribe attempts**: Schoenberg 316.

203 **tax trial**: Compilation of DN, T 10-7 thru 10-18-31 and Schoenberg 309-325; specifically Johnson's quoted summation in T 10-18-31; details of sentence T 10-18-31 and Schoenberg 324-325; Capone allowed to run his business: FBI #69-180-95 field report 12-17-31 investigating the allegation.

204 **Matt Kolb**: Touhy 72-81, T 10-18-31, DN, T 10-19-31; wounds and age from numbered list of 1931 murders from coroner's reports in the CCC.

205 **Johnson wrote**: Letter dated 10-21-31 to the Parole Board.

205 **Irey phoned**: Handwritten BOP message dated 10-29-31.

205 **"I am doubtful"**: Handwritten BOP message dated 10-24-31.

205) **Wood's response**: Letter to Nitto dated 10-30-31.

205 **plight of Guzik, Ralph Capone**: Guzik: U.S. District Court Northern District of Illinois case #22080; Capone: U.S. District Court Northern District of Illinois case #21117.

205 **Nitto's fine paid**: Receipt signed by Clerk of the U.S. District Court in Chicago, Charles M. Bates dated 11-20-31.

205 **Anna'a appeal**: Letter dated 11-23-31.

206 **Johnson wrote**: Letter dated 11-30-31.

206 **appeal denied**: Formal notice of denial signed by the three board members and dated 11-30-31; others denied: letter dated 12-2-31 from board secretary H. C.Heckman.

206 **high marks**: Work record: Progress Report located in Recommendation of Psychiatrist Remarks; communications: Record of Correspondents; Annette Caravetta background; 1920 U.S. Census.

207 **Irey face-to-face meeting**: Parole Board Memo dated 1-20-31 for all details.

207 **McCaul report, quotes**: INS File letter dated 11-30-31.

207 **Schlotfeldt wrote**: INS File letter dated 1-4-32.

207 **checked Chicago records**: INS File letter dated 1-14-32 from Schlotfeldt toDistrict Director in Dallas, Texas, asking to check marriage records there.

208 **last correspondence**: Record of Correspondents.

208 **release and money**: Certificate of Release dated 3-24-31 signed by Nitto.

208 **results of INS investigation**: INS File a last letter dated 12-29-33.

208 **Nitto in town**: P 3-25-32; a meeting: DN 3-24-32.

CHAPTER 15

209 **"Without the Volstead"**: T 10-26-31 editorial speculating on the future of Capone's gang with the boss going away

209 **headline, and fed quotes**: T 10-25-31 including speculations.

210 **headline**: DN 5-5-32.

210 **headline**: HE 5-9-32 for paragraph as well, except DN 5-5-32 for Coroner Walsh and DN 6-17-32 for Barker and Humphreys uniting.

210   organizational chart: HE 5-22-32.

211   **New York's say-so**: Messick *Lansky* 60-61, The whole episode in his book appears based upon an event occurring on April 19, 1932, when Ricca, Luciano, Lansky, and Sylvester Agoglia were indeed arrested outside the Congress Hotel. A police lineup picture was taken of the men and T 4-20-32 recorded the event in a tiny pres clip (minus the photo). The photo disappeared from bureau files and the incident forgotten until the *Chicago Sun-Times* discovered a copy and printed it on Nov. 15, 1953. The story attached says the group (and others) was discussing leadership of the Chicago mob. Most of the rest of Messick's text, including their nominations for boss of Chicago, was probably fashioned from the fact that Ricca and others were thought to be Capone's contacts with New York during their Castellammarese War while he was in Cook County Jail. As such, no doubt, they would be the more familiar faces to Luciano et al., not Nitto who was in Leavenworth at the time. Of Nitto's alleged belligerence —who knows? The author contacted Hank Messick however, he disposed of his notes long ago and did not wish to discuss Nitto or anybody else.

211   "so well organized": T 10-25-31, the Feds having as much info as anybody recognized the fact.

211   **Frank Rio as a candidate**: Gambling File in the Virgil Peterson Papers in the Chicago Historical Society, Peterson wrote that Rio was "heir apparent" but failed, so Nitto replaced him. His source appears to be HE 5-9-32 and an article in T 2-9-36 outlining the mob's command listing Rio as head with Nitto as 2nd VP.   .

211   **Hal Andrews**: RD September 1932 "Gangsters Grip on Chicago" his *X Marks the Spot* credit as given under the author's name in RD.

212   **pessimism**: Much speculation at the tiume due to simple lack of knowledge and inevitable end of Prohibition; "fall to pieces": DN 5-5-32; "the band of criminals" alluding to Lucifer leading Capone: DN 5-4-32 editorial; credit Hal Andrews in RD for observing multiple threats to Nitto's group, but he identified them as more gangs.

212   **change of tactics**: FBI #62-39128-124 including "muscle" quote, what they got from a veteran reporter close to the underworld. As the reader shall see, the mob during Nitto's reign reserved murder as a means primarily to rid itself of troublesome *internal* members.

213   **mob's organization**: Except for notes below, much of the text about the Nitto organization from street-level sources (as they understood it to be) developed by CCC in 1951. Those sources believed the departmental type of mob in place at that time. As for leaders: CCC notes coincide with witness testimony in *USvC* and various Chicago news articles from May to November 1932, and September-October 1940; Nitto's Manhattan brewery: CCC memo 2-9-48, derived from the Alcohol Tax Unit shows that Greenberg and the mob owned it, with a cover corporation to run it, and Superior Court of Cook County Case #57S2335, in which a claim was made that Louis Greenberg admitted Nitto owned a "very considerable portion" of the brewery; Joe Fusco: CCC memo 1-10-49; Nick Circella's role speculative, he apparently emerged a mob favorite, according to *USvC* testimony and February 1943 articles later owned various nightclubs; Loop gambling and Skidmore's role: *Lightnin'* May 1941 and *Collier's* 10-7-39 "Too Much Fun" by John T. Flynn, after quite a study, he wasn't sure of the gambling set up either; gambling agents: Mangano and DeGrazia named by Flynn, Guifoyle in DN 6-17-32 as having interests, while Heeney named in FBI #58-2000-622 and key Cicero figure in Binder 58; Capezio as a gang manager: HE 1-11-32 while T 1-11-32 has him as leader of the old Circus gang with Maddox; Stanton: T 5-6,7-43, DN 5-6-43; Newberry: T 7-3-32, HE, DN 1-7-33; Winkler a Newberry operative: FBI #7-77 letter dated 9-26-33 as did T, HE 10-10-33; McGurn and associates: McGurn's police record in a CCC memo;

Ralph Pierce: FBI #92-3088-178 Humphreys File Section 7 claims Humphreys, Hunt and Pierce in booze business late 1920s; politicians: Peterson 246.

214 **Ricca's quote**: Messick *Lansky* 62.

214 **Newberry's retirement**: DN 5-23-32.

214 **Red Barker's business**   : Barker history from T 4-19-36, state's attorney record of his arrests in CCC, except, T, HE 6-18-32; Barker-Galvin feud: DN 6-17-32.

215 **Barker ambitions**: Gambling and beer: DN 6-17-32; setting himself up: T 6-18 and DN 6-20, Schoemaker quote from T.

215 **Barker murder**: DN, T 6-17,18-32; diagram of murder in HA 3-9-50; *hit* by 36 bullets according to T, DN 6-17, the number extracted reported much less; clerk's quote: DN 6-17; Barker's age: list of 1932 murders found in the CCC.

216 **weapons and descriptions**: DN 6-17-32.

216 **suspects—headline**: Ibid. and HE 6-18-32. DN recognized the ambush as an old Nitto technique; DN for 3 on pick-up list and DN 6-20-32 for tracing the guns; "Sicilian" quote in T 6-17-32 and "too much ambition" in T 6-18-32.

216 **"The great problem"**: *Collier's* 7-13-40 "These Our Rulers."

216 **Chicago's economics**: Gottfried 241-247.

217 **Cermak personality**: Ibid. 244-245 including quotes except Stuart 502 for "master of detail"; identify enemies, minions 245.

217 **job cuts**: Ibid. 259-260; 272 for quote.

217 **crime cleanup**: Ibid. 280-281 including quote on 281.

217 **Thompson resurgence**: Ibid. 307, W&K *Big Bill* 338-340; W&K 338,340 for Thompson quotes; Gottfried for "Anton the First."

218 **policy wheels**: Gottfried 280; Biles 89-94 for layoffs, raids, number of arrests and newspaper quote "Cossacks" from the Chicago *Defender*; W&K *Big Bill* 341-342 for question and "More Democrats"; Biles notes that while Republicans received 84 percent of the black vote in 1931, by 1935 they garnered only 19 percent .

218 **1932 election**: W&K *Big Bill* 340-341, Stuart 500, Gottfried 307-308, 313 for Cermak's virtual control of Illinois.

218 **Cermack to shake things up**: Gottfried 280 including "suppression" quote: W&K *Lords* 350-351 for his intentions to clean up the town before the World's Fair.

219 **personal command, allies-enemies**: Gottfried 280-281 from September 1931 Chicago newspapers for his absolute command and use of investigators; Skidmore: Murray 171; Johnson and Newberry: Stuart 502 also noting that Cermak, in his opinion, dealt closer to the underworld "than any mayor in Chicago's history"; Roger Touhy's good graces: Lyle 260-261; Guifoyle in A 12-2-32 and Stuart; Cermak explained away crime and quote: Gottfried 281.

219 **headlines and arrests**: "Arrest Ten" headline: HE 11-2-32 with "at home" quote and events also in T 11-3-32; Hump's arrest: HE 3-23-32; Police Round Up More headline: DN 11-2-32; Hunt's arrest: HE 3-23-32.

220 **headlines and arrests**: "Gangsters Fleeing" headline; HE 11-3-32; "Crime Incorporated": HE 11-11-32 with Adducci and Bioff details from HE and T 11-11.

Chapter 16

221 **Callahan illness**: Cook County Indictment #68043 testimony 4-6-33 and CCC observer's trial notes regarding Ind. #68750 testimony 9-26-33.

221 **Brandtman ... office details**: DN 12-19-32, HE, T 12-20-32; furnishings: original photo in author's collection and photo in HE.

222 **Nitto use of office**: HE 12-20-32 except alcohol samples and map in T 12-20-32, and taking bets from Nitto testimony in CCC observer notes regarding Ind. #68750.

222 **Nitto's time of arrival**: Approximate. Nitto testimony Ind #68043 dated 4-7-33 says it was 11 a.m. with the raiders entering about an hour later while on 9-26-33 in CCC observer trial notes regarding Ind. #68750 he puts his arrived at 1 p.m. The text however relies on Nitto's earlier testimony, which seems to coincide with Detective Miller's assertion that he met Lang about noon to initiate the raid.

222 **Lang and Miller**: CCC observer trial notes Ind. #68750 and T 4-8-33 trial notes for lengths of service and Browne interview September 1995 for comment of Miller; T for meeting at the Sherman House and Lang's request for certain squads.

222 **the raid ... Nitto wounds**: Amalgam of Ind. #68750 trial notes from CCC, DN 12-19-32, T and HE 12-20-32, T 4-6-33; the event somewhat murky mainly as to location of Nitto and his men during the raid; HE diagram seems to show Nitto shot in smaller inner office, the men lined up in the larger room and Lang apparently shot out in the hall, but the other sources especially Callahan testimony in #68750 indicate Nitto was removed from the smaller inner office DN 12-19 and Callahan as reported in T 4-7 gives the number of hoodlums in the large office as 4 with Nitto and 2 others in the inner office; T for "Spit it out" quote; T 9-27 and testimony #68750 for "What's your name?"; wounds: DN only gave neck, chest, and abdomen while HE gives the second and third shots as nicking his lung and lower, lodging near his spine, T as below shoulder and puncturing a kidney; explaining the wounds Dr. Ronga as reported in DN 12-21 thought the first shot caused Nitto to twist around the other shots then fired during the motion seem to coincide with Nitto's later explanation (CCC Trial Notes #68750 9-26-27) that he turned to prevent Lang from firing again and Callahan (T 4-7-33) that he "staggered" around when he got hit twice more. All news sources give Lang's wound to the left arm, though not specific. As for the note, it was sent to the Northwestern University crime lab for analysis. Transcripts of the decipherable portions were given in T and HE 12-21-32 and read fairly unremarkable, HE 12-20-32 and later S 3-20-43 report it contained information regarding a Nitto train trip. A photo of the note appears in *True Detective Stories* magazine August 1933. As to what became of the note after analysis, it seems to have vanished.

223 **headline**: HE 12-20-32 as well as Lang's account.

223 **salutation to police**: DN editorial 12-21-32.

223 **meritorious bonuses**: T 4-13,14-33.

223 **Nitto's condition**: DN 12-19-32 and HE 12-20-32 reported his grim chance to live with "weaker" quote in T 12-20-32.

224 **in the Bridewell**: Description of room and Nitto from DN photos; questioning by authorities in DN 12-19 and HE 12-20; photographer episode in DN; condition of Nitto, ibid. and T 12-20; doctors: Schiavo lists Ronga as Chief of Staff, while HE 12-22 and T 12-25 refer to him as "head"; Dr. Charles J. Besta reported in HE, on DN photos of Nitto taken at the Bridewell and T 12-26-32—Besta treated Nitto for only 5 more days when on December 24, he was struck dead by a cerebral hemorrhage at age 36; HE, A reported Ronga's medical advice and DN for Ronga calling in the best surgeons.

224 **Anna's vigil**: T 12-20-32 including Dr. Ronga's quote.

224 **"I'm going"**: DN 12-20-32, also for doctors upping his chances.

224 **legal troubles**: CCC notes regarding HC #22196 Nitto's court hearing and T 12-21-32; Jefferson Park Hospital strategy in HE, DN 12-21-32 with quote in DN; bond and release in CCC notes, HE, DN.

224 **names of associates**: DN 12-19-32, T and HE 12-20-32, A 12-21-32 with lineup photo in T; federal agents: T 12-21-32 with T 12-20 announcing McGee's confession; charges in DN, A 12-21, $1,100 bail in T, A 12-21.

225   **story of bedside meetings**: Murray 177 whose source seems to be *True Detective Mysteries* dated August 1933.

225   **Cermak's determination**: T 12-21-32; following events: robber gunned down by Miller in HE 12-22 and T 1-1-33—T also gave 2 robbers and bandit with in 2 weeks, Martin Sanders in T 12-28, Agoglia and Costello, and Mangano's place in T 12-30; T 1-1-33 reported Cermak's war on speakeasies all along —to bring them back under his political domination: HE.

225   **headline**: HE 12-22-32 and quote.

225   **New Year's message**: T 1-1-33 and quote.

226   **Johnson and Skidmore**: Peterson 159.

226   **Lang protected**: T, DN, A 12-21-32.

226   **Nitto to survive**: HE 12-24-32 first reported the likelihood.

226   **Ted Newberry**: T 1-8-33 except his indictment in Peoria, Illinois on Prohibition violations as reported in T 7-27-31, P 11-3-31; gambling: names of places in T 1-8-33 and A 1-16-33; handbook business: DN 1-7-33; quote "to get out" in DN; that he might pick up at least part of the booze business: conjecture, the raid on Quality Flout apparently a command center for North Side distribution suggests some possible plot; possible threat since Christmas: T 1-8, Peterson 161.

226   **his death**: DN, A 1-7-33 and T 1-8-33; see map in T for location of body, DN gave only an approximate distance from Michigan City, though A described the nearby town of Baileytown, Indiana; tread mark indications in DN, and quote in T.

227   **Public Enemy List**: T 1-10-33 with headline.

227   **Nitto slipped out**: DN 1-20-33 gives address also.

227   **legal matters inching**: Reported mostly in snippets of print, DN 12-29-32, A 1-4-33, and T 1-11-33 used here.

227   **triumph in tax case**: A, STLPD 1-24-33, T 1-25-33.

227   **January 27 ruling**: T 1-28-33 source for quotes as well.

227   **scheduled bond**: Sworn statements and copies of property records dated 2-1-33 found in Ind. #68043; Nitto apparently split his recovery time among 1206 McAllister where he was served a summons, 1200 McAllister which he lists on some documents as a residence (both near Dr. Ronga) and 36 North Menard which he maintained for most of the year—all found in Ind. #68043 and #68750. Of D'Allesio as Nitto's aunt, the listed relationship was not a bloodline, but possibly rather by marriage if anything.

227   **Nitto's summons**: Summons in #68043; physical description from T 2-3-33 and photo in T 2-10-33.

228   **Manhattan Brewery**: Renamed in April according to CCC memo dated 1-24-49.

228   **Lueder as president**: CCC memo 12-30-48; the Adonis associate according to CCC memo 2-9-47 was Phillip J. O'Hara—he stayed on 4 or 5 months.

228   **racketeering squad**: T 5-9-33 names Humphreys and O'Donnell as leaders in the field also naming Diamond in T 5-11 and O"Donnell ally Sammons in T 5-23.

229   **February 2 shooting**: As reported in T 2-3-33, however, Touhy in HA 3-13-50 claims his men the victims.

229   **"I'll shoot you in the head"**: DN 3-20-43.

229   **racketeering campaign**: Brass marbles method and valued damage in HE 5-13-33; Belcastro named in DN 5-2,4-33; number and type of businesses from list compiled by the CCC dated 2-1-33 to 5-1-33.

229   **brewery agents**: T 4-3-33 includes quotes "You'll take beer from us" and "Buy our beer or."

229   **legalization of beer**: Ibid. including named breweries and orders.

230   **Roosevelt's itinerary**: Picchi 1-10; description of Bayfront Park and amphitheater from photos on page 94.

230 **Cermak's strategy**: Amalgam: A 2-16-33 reports school funding while Alderman Jacob Arvey quoted Cermak as wanting "cash to meet all our payrolls" - both are widely written later on; patronage jobs: Gottfried 316-318 citing Stuart in *The Twenty Incredible Years* (1935) notes Cermak's absolute control over state offices from the governor on down except federal patronage which was allotted to Senator Hamilton; Biles 14, Gottfried 301 note Cermak's reluctance to support FDR in the beginning and for that reason lost favor with FDR which he then sought to regain.

230 **the shooting**: Picchi 14-15 who accessed most Miami papers; Cermak's wounds from diagram in A 2-16-33.

230 **Cermak's condition**: A 2-16-33 fit and 50-50 chance; Picchi 41 for 80-20 chance and suspicious symptoms, HE 3-2-33 for specifics, and Picchi 134 for his death.

231 **Zangara**: Sentences: Picchi 120-121, "stingy" quote on 121; doctor's diagnosis: 110; superintendent's quote: 215; "Pusha da button!": 191; fortieth man to be executed in electric chair: HE 3-20-33.

231 **financial crisis**: HE 3-6-33, T 3-7-33.

231 **Nitto's March court appearance**: Ind #68043 for petition; appearance: photo in T 3-21-33 and DN photos in author's possession; departed to Florida: T 4-4-33, obvious from photos of next court appearance—he was well-tanned; Fischetti alongside: Murray 182.

231 **mob meeting**: Murray 182-183 names several principles, plausible especially Frank Erickson, with whom Nitto would hook up with in a couple Florida race tracks.

232 **April trial**: Nitto appearance from photo in T 4-4-33, and DN photos in author's possession; jury selection: CCC trial notes Ind #68043, T 4-4, 5-33; Lang-prosecutor dialogue: T, DN 4-6-33 as is the account of the court room scene; Dougherty's "not well": T 4-7-33; "WAS a policeman": T 4-6; Callahan testimony and dialogue: DN 4-6, T 4-7; Miller testimony and dialogue in T 4-7, DN 4-6; verdict: Ibid.

233 **grand jury testimony**: T 4-7-33, DN 4-7, 8-33; Nitto's quote: T, DN 4-7.

234 **headline**: T 4-7-33.

234 **Courtney wondered**: T 4-8-33.

234 **Lang's "wreck the ... party"**: T, DN 4-8-33.

234 **incensed Courtney**: T 4-7-33; Dougherty's quote: T 4-8-33.

234 **Courtney's quotes [to protect the brewers]**: T 4-3-33.

234 **headline**: T 4-7-33.

235 **bombing next morning**: Prima event and quotes: DN 4-8-33; CCC memo dated 12-28-48 for Manhattan brewery incident; fault Touhy: author's supposition given mob ownership of the Manhattan, and later the Prima brewery, it probably had as much to do with Touhy's beer sales efforts and the ongoing Teamster ruckus.

235 **Touhy's Florida time**: FBI #7-77-169 Field Report dated 9-26-33, arrest record within notes Touhy arrest in Titusville, Florida on 3-15-33 for possession of a machinegun.

235 **Sass-Goldberg**: DN 5-1-33, T 5-2-33; ultimatum quote in DN.

235 **May bombing campaign**: DN, T 5-1, 2, 3-33; the teamster allied with Touhy.

235 **coal strike**: T 5-9,10-33 DN 5-10,11-33; TNT trial: Ibid.

236 **new mayor**: Biles 6, 17-19 including change of selection process.

236 **Fair schedule changed**: DN 5-2-33.

236 **Kelly's relaxed attitude**: DN 5-1-33.

236 **bombings "acute stage"**: T 5-2-33; CCC notes on events dated 5-1 listed racketeering related bombings for the worst years as 88 in 1929 and 80 in 1930.

236 **theft and ridicule of police**: Theft and "probably" quote in DN 5-3-33 with caricatures in DN 5-4-33.

236 **headlines**: DN 5-4-33 and DN 5-5-33 respectively.

236 **objects of investigation**: Ibid.

236 **Kelly changed his tune**: DN 5-10,11-33 describes his efforts in breaking up the coal strike.

236 **potshots at Touhy ally**: T 5-17-33 reports James Lynch, teamster business agent, claiming the White group fired 3 shotgun blasts at his home early this morning.

CHAPTER 17

237 **Century of Progress**: A Century of Progress: Report of the President to the Board of Trustees dated 3-14-36; exhibits: *A Century of Progress Official Guide 1933-1934*, postcards and photos in the author's collection and a labeled aerial view in T 5-21-33; attendance and revenues; Report of the President above.

238 **"whole place sewed up"**: Murray 182 allegedly quoting Charlie Fischetti that the mob collected off nearly every food, drink, and ride franchise—accuracy unknown, however, a United Press report in T 7-20-33 editorial claimed hoodlums owned 40 concessions; Humphreys popcorn: Murray, while Lyle 268 and Peterson 167 had him lining up certain rides; beer concessions: Peterson 168.

238 **Mondi and gambling**: Lyle 268; Cicero's availability: Peterson.

238 **Humphreys**: Documents located in BOP #45760L including his FBI record, parole report by the U.S. attorney, and Record of Commitment in *U.S. vs. Murray Humphreys alias etc.* #27428.

239 **Capone's soft spot**: Karpis 151.

239 **kidnappers in the city**: FBI #7-77-650, memo dated 5-4-36 and Peterson 169-170.

239 **Nitto's suspicions**: Karpis 149-153; Verne Miller's death: HE 12-3-33.

240 **mob kidnappings**: Ritchie for $50,000: FBI #92-348 reporting Murray Humphreys as suspect; Petrillo in HE 12-2,3-33 and DN 12-3-33; the risk noted in T 12-18-59.

240 **Touhy-Hamm case**: FBI #7-77-74 field report dated 7-29-33.

240 **Factor kidnapping**: Headline: A 7-1-33; the kidnapping events: A 7-1-33 and T, HE 7-1,2-33; ransom in text: T 7-2; wide range of speculation in all newspapers.

240 **Jerome's kidnapping**: HE 4-16, 17-33 also T 7-2-33; T reports family claims no payment made, but HE 4-17 reported the $50,000 payment; HE 4-17, T 7-8 give both Sam Hunt and Humphreys.

240 **suspects**: A 7-1-33 speculated Factor as an easy target for Touhy with Humphreys gone and reports on the initial search for the Touhy gang; Touhy's initial interview in A 7-13, his alibi and account in Touhy 95-96; Factor's release from T, DN, A 7-13-33.

241 **Factor ransom—his account**: $50,000 in text: DN 7-13-33 whereas T 7-13-33 speculates a $75,000 compromise based on earlier, larger demands; Arvey's involvement and quote in DN, A 7-13-33, the amount, if paid, was never cleared up; Factor's interview: A 7-13: couldn't identify his captors: T, DN 7-13, T 7-18-33; half million dollars and number of captors also in T.

241 **"Do you intend"**: DN 7-13-33 as well as Factor reply.

241 **inconsistency of Factor's**: **"to avoid remarks"**: A 7-13-33; appearance: Halper 76, his suit was slightly wrinkled, but clean, however, DN 7-13 says it was "moldy" while T 7-13 had it "soiled", photos show no major spoilage; descriptive quote: Halper.

241 **headline**: T 7-8-33.

241 **Factor's legal trouble**: T, HE 7-8-33; T, DN, A 7-13-33; battle in U.S. courts: DN 12-4-33, HE 12-6-33; British suspicions: A 7-13-33; October hearing: T 7-9-33.

242 **suspects**: All listed in T 7-15-33.

242 **Touhy arrest**: FBI #7-77-74 field report dated 7-29-33 and T 7-21-33, Halper 77.

242 **lineup**, Courtney quote: T 7-22-33.

243 **Touhy's optimism**: Touhy 121-122; speculation as to presence of Gilbert and Factor, 126-127   .

243   **Hamm trial-Factor quote**: Ibid. 118-121, "wouldn't hurt a fly" quote 127.

243   **Supreme Court decision**: DN 12-4-33, HE 12-6-33; finding of facts before Judge Barnes in Touhy 260-261.

243   **first trial**: Capone gang frame-up: T 1-24-34; Factor's changed testimony: Halper 76-78; hung jury; DN 2-2-34, T 2-2-34.

244   **second trial**: Witnesses Costner and Banghart, and Factor's identification of the pair: T 2-14, 17,18, 20-33; as Touhy men: T 2-14, though Touhy in an interview for HA 3-14-50 claims never to have talked to Banghart in his life; priest unable to testify: T 2-16-33. Costner received a 30-year sentence for mail robbery. He was paroled by 1950, but was later arrested for felonious assault. He later signed a deposition admitting he perjured himself, according to HA 3-14-50.

244   **Touhy's claim of "swindle"**: Quote and opinion: Touhy 186; his theory: 228.

244   **Factor for a phony kidnapping**: HA 3-14-50.

244   **possible Nitto connection**: Hamm kidnapping: FBI #32-15941-7; interest Factor in a brewery in FBI #7-77 field report dated 9-26-33.

244   **Judge Barnes's conclusion**: Touhy 255-266; for all Judge Barnes' findings and quotes. It must be noted that Courtney, Gilbert, and Factor were put on the stand during the hearing before Judge Barnes, all denied knowing of any conspiracy to frame Touhy. Other witnesses, however, came forward admitting they were pressured by the men to testify against Touhy.

244   **Factor extradition lapses**: Halper 85.

245   **his subsequent troubles**: T 2-3-43 for his unsavory deals and conviction Gilbert as witness: DT 2-21-40; mail fraud, sentence and deal with Humphreys: DN 2-9-49.

246   **Nitto-Drury incident**: A 10-2-48 and 11-4-48 related by Drury; quotes from A 11-4; disorderly conduct and subpoena T 7-20-33 and HE 7-29-33.

246   **Nitto's vagrancy warrant**: T 9-12-33.

246   **Nitto's appearance**: HE 9-27-33.

246   **irony of legal teams**: T 9-28-33.

246   **defense opening statement**: CCC observer notes from the trial and T 9-26-33, quotes from T.

246   **Miller testimony**: Ibid., T, HE 9-27-33, quotes regarding Cermak: HE; T noticed the absence of the Newberry story.

247   **Nitto testimony**: Ibid. Q and A from HE 9-27; Q and A cross-examination from Murray 178 is similar to CCC notes; "no ill-will" in HE.

247   **Callahan**: CCC observer notes

247   **Lang testimony**: Ibid. T, HE 9-28-33, Q and A from both newspapers.

248   **other witnesses**: CCC observer notes, HE, A 9-28-33, DN 9-27-33.

248   **prosecution closing**: Ibid., T, HE 9-28-33; quotes: HE.

248   **defense closing**: Ibid., quotes: T 9-28-33.

248   **jury and outcome**: Ibid.; "case as strange": HE; sentence: HE and T agree Lang faced 1-14 years and the misdemeanor as up to one year, but differ on the fine; Lang quote from T though HE had it somewhat different though the gist is the same; Lang's discharge: T 11-25-33; new trial CCC notes dated 12-29-33, DN, T 12-29-33; "Don't thank": T 12-29.

249   **postponements**: Cook County Case #68750 Memorandum of Orders.

249   *True Detective* account: *True Detective Mysteries*, "Cermak was put ON the Spot" dated August 1933.

249   *Real America* account: *Real America* 3-part series by Lester Freeman dated September-November 1933, quotes: November.

250   **Chicagoans about the shooting**: Frank Loesch: DT 8-1-44; Connelly and Drury in

HA 11-4-48; Judge Lyle's reasoning from T 4-14-57 and Lyle 267-268; McPhaul in ST 2-10-63.

250 **opposite views**: Gottfried and quotes from 324, except 'Gangsters" quote on 323; Blaisé Picchi's examination from his book *The Five Weeks of Giuseppe Zangara* 85-89, "lone wolf" on 216, and "utterly" quote from 221; Schoenberg argument from 359. Perhaps the last surviving person to have known the intimate details of the case was the Honorable A. L. Marovitz. Later appointed to the federal bench, the author interviewed the Honorable A. L. Marovitz three times in his chambers during 1993-94. He disclosed absolutely nothing of the case. He said he knew the men involved, as well as other hoodlums such as Winkler and Newberry, but when asked to elaborate, he deferred: "Why do you want to write about bad things? There are so many good things to write about." .

253 **Teamster outcome**: T 4-19-36 article *Bullets, Bombs and Blackmail* a complete history of the Chicago Teamsters' to date; a last attempt to muscle in T 2-20, 21,22-34.

253 **North Side gambling**: Winkler's clubs and Lebensberger: HE 10-7-33; Capone muscled: HE 10-8-33; club description: HE 10-7; McLaughlin: T, DN 10-7-33; Skidmore: HE 10-8-33; the additional club: T.

253 **Winkler not ideal**: Nebraska bank robbery: HE 10-8-33 and n.p. 10-30-31; indictments DN 10-7-33 and HE 10-8-33, DN mentions the percentage gained: McLaughlin and McFadden: DN 10-9-33

254 **Lebensberger's death**: HE 10-7, 8-33, T 10-8-33, DN 10-9,10-33; "financial" quote: T; rumor of Nitto's visit in DN while HE 10-8 reports of a mob court but no names.

254 **Winkler's bond**: HE 10-7-33 and McLaughlin.

254 **Albert Bregar's death**: T10-23-33 also for "if the police" quote.

254 **Winkler's death**: Largely from HE 10-10-33 except description of the distributing company from photo in A 10-19-33 and number of shotgun slugs given here from A 10-30-33 quoting the coroner's verdict directly; all quotes and boy's accounts from HE, the boys thought the vehicle a white coupe, but police after talking to other adult witnesses were satisfied with the green truck as other papers reported; age: STLPD 10-10-33 based on an arrest record in St. Louis.

255 **suspects and investigation**: Italian men: T, DN 10-10-33; T 10-20-33 names White, O'Donnell, and Capezio as suspects; Weber and his business: A 10-24-33 says it was dominated by hoods; Alterie's presence: A 10-23-33 and DT 10-30-33; T, DN 10-10 for his beer business at the Fair; the gambling investigation: T, A 10-30-33; Skidmore's testimony and quote: HE 10-24-33; slot machine business: A 10-24, this would give Nitto even more reason to liquidate the men given his partnership with Vogel and aim no doubt to dominate the business county-wide; HE 10-27 for police knowing nothing of gambling.

255 "CHICAGO HONEYCOMBED": A 10-30-33

255 "STOP GAMBLING": T 10-31-33.

255 **press opinions**: Winkler's gambling as reason: HE 10-11-33 and T 10-20-33; "speed" quote DN 10-10-33.

255 **to question Nitto**: T 10-20-33; noting the "speed and accuracy" and as a rep of the syndicate quote.

255 **Nitto "out of town"**: T 10-30-33.

256 **Louis Cowen**: Diamond nickname: T 10-30-33; his fortunes: T 10-28-33, HE 10-29-33; owned the Cicero paper and Sportsman's Park: T 10-28; influence: HE 10-28-33; new dog track: T 10-28; new split HE 10-29-33 and new management in T 10-28, HE 10-29.

256 **Cowen's death**: T, DN, HE 10-28-33; suspected inheritors of Cicero gambling among others in T 1-26-34.

256   **repeal of Prohibition**: DN, HE 12-4, 5-33; "a break" quote: DN 12-5; hotels and "bigger than": DN 12-4; women and prices: HE 12-5; headaches and quotes: DN 12-5.

257   **White's personal life**: T, DN 1-24, 25-34; except length of hiding: DN 1-25 and T 1-27; honeymoon: T 1-27-34.

257   **White's murder**: T, DN 1-24-34, HE 1-25-34; wounds: sources initially reported as many as 3, but with T 1-26 amending to one each in the chest and left arm; age variously given as 42 or 44.

258   **theories**: T, DN 1-24-34 reports the possible federal connection based on the FBI meeting, and the Sammon's theory; fear of the Touhy gang: DN 1-26, T, HE 1-27 with Purvis quote from DN; dark skinned strangers: T, DN 1-24 while T, HE 1-26 report the identification of O'Donnell and Humphreys; T 1-25 reports the Maddox-Looney connection given their labor interests; HE 1-25 reports the two as suspects via the TNT trial.

258   **Frankie Pope**: DN, A 3-7-34, "too low" quote in A

259   **J. George Ziegler**: T 3-21-34, DN 3-24-34 with quote from DN.

CHAPTER 18

261   **"If It Isn't Booze"**: Collier's 11-26-32

261   **Torrio credited**: McPhaul 282-289, Messick *Lansky* 72-73; McPahul also notes Burton Turkus and Sid Feder in *Murder, Inc.* first published in 1951 reprinted Da Capo Press 1979 pages 98-99 with Torrio as the mastermind.

261   **Frank Costello looked**: Messick *Lansky* 72.

261   **1934 meetings**: McPhaul 289 also for Chicago attendees: worth noting here in *State of New York vs. George Scalise*, Ind. #224300 (dated 1940) and later in T 10-11-47 and other papers, Murray Gurfein, New York lawyer and former head of the New York District Attorney's racket bureau during the thirties intimated at the time the birth of the gangsters national organization in 1934 centered on a meeting in the Capri Restaurant, Chicago; it may have appeared so in 1940 since it may have been the first instance which surfaced a New York racketeer (Scalise) working with the Chicago mob for division of spoils, but that it was key in determining a national syndicate appears to be far overstated.

262   **Nitto's track ownership**: TXC #111 Ruling #1950-16-13397 and IOC interview of Patton.

262   **General News history**: Collier's 1-27-40 "Smart Money" for complete details of General News, Moe Annenberg, and the handbook business; tossing losing tickets: Biles 105.

262   **Nationwide News**: U.S. District Court, Northern District of Illinois, *U.S. vs. Moe Annenberg, et al.* Ind. #31762; Collier's 1-27-40 for "which side would win."

262   **Nitto moved in**: Approached Lynch with deal: S 9-26-46; meet with Ragen and deal: S, T 9-26-46, Peterson 278; "forceful" from Peterson.

263   **price for General News**: *U.S. vs. Moe Annenberg* #31762 statement of facts.

263   **a new company**: Ibid. with Collier's 1-27-40 for description of printed publications, scratch sheets, etc.

263   **$850,000 check**: *U.S. vs. Moe Annenberg* #31762 statement of facts.

263   **Ragen met Nitto**: Peterson 278 including in $100 bills.

263   **"Some men has plenty"**: *Lightnin'*, May 1939.

263   **associations and cost to public**: CCC racketeering memo dated 11-25-30; *Commerce* "Racketeering ... Its Causes and Cures" March 1932.

264   **Capri Restaurant**: City directories plainly give the address as 123 N. Clark, though for some reason, perhaps typos, Murray Gurfein gave 133 N. Clark, Peterson gave 135 N. Clark, others did the same; chefs that managed the place listed in *N.Y. vs. Scalise* #224300 memo dated 8-23-40 investigation of the restaurant in great detail;

third-floor description and "long table" quote: *USvC* Bioff 300; a labor leader quote: T 10-18-40 also mentions the third-floor loft.

264 **beneficial venture**: *N.Y. vs. Scalise* #224300, Peterson 173.

264 **BSEIU history**: *N.Y. vs. Scalise* #224300 memo dated 11-15-34.

264 **east ... undeveloped**: Ibid. Isadore Schwartz trial testimony 60.

264 **Carfano proposed**: Ibid.

264 **Scalise background**: Ibid. New York PD record and investigative files dated 5-7-40, 6-6-40, 10-15-43.

265 **contacted Carfano**: Ibid. Scalise's elevation into the BSEIU: Schwartz trial testimony 52-57 including split with Nitto's mob.

265 **20,000 new members**: Ibid. Van Heck testimony 11; strike info: T 3-5-36.

265 **"a lot of money"**: Ibid. Schwartz testimony.

265 **Lawndale Enterprises**: CCC memo dated 1-24-49 regarding Greenberg's investments names the theater

265 **Symphony Theater**: IOC interview of Greenberg found in the CCC.

265 **Ricca-World Amusement**: FBI #58-2000-273-11 for details.

265 **Tom Maloy-Local 110**: Personal and Local 110 history: T, HE 2-5-35 and especially 3-29-36; early extortion: T 5-26,27-21; union wages: T 3-29-36; Gusenberg's, Capone and Stanton: T 3-27-33, 3-29-36; theater bombings: October 1931 papers with list in T 3-27-33: Belcastro as suspect: T 10-14-31; Jacob Kaufman incident: T, DN 6-21-31, including suspect Stanton.

266 **two-man booth extortion**: U.S. District Court, Northern District of Illinois, *U.S. vs. Thomas Maloy*, #28674 and DOJ #5-23-333.

267 **$5,000 vacation ...** : T 3-29-36.

267 **George Browne**: BOP #58945L, *USvC* 1015-1016 testimony; appearance from various photos.

268 **contacts and arrests**: *USvC* Browne testimony 1017,1298, *Lightnin'* August 1939; police record in BOP #58945L, *Lightnin'* and *USvC* testimony 1304-1306.

268 **with Big Tim Murphy**: *Lightnin'* August 1939.

268 **speakeasy business**: *USvC* testimony 1300-1304 including quote "best customer", important to note Browne made it clear this implied because he paid for what he drank—which he remembers many of his friends were served "on the house" – not because as has been implied elsewhere, that he drank unusually excessive quantities; *Lightnin'* May 1939 gives the number of Browne's saloons in the Loop as 3 and that this naturally put him in touch with Capone's outfit.

268 **elected IATSE VP**: *USvC* Browne testimony 1017.

268 **conditions of Local 2**: Ibid. 1017-1019; pay cuts, pay dwindled: Bioff 114, 432 and Browne 1023 testimony.

268 **Fulton Street Market**: Ibid. Browne testimony 1020-1021, 1292-1294.

269 **introduced to Bioff**: Ibid. Bioff testimony 109, 761-764 and name of association.

269 **Bioff physical features**: BOP #58944L for specifics and various photos.

269 **early mob associates**: *USvC* Bioff testimony 105 for all names and duties; work with Zuta: T 3-8-40.

269 **pandering arrest**: Police record located in FBI #60-2149-29 field report dated 4-21-39: also CCC observer notes from trial dated 3-21-22; intercession of Galvin and Zuta: DN 3-6-40, T 3-8-40; did not serve time: Bioff's BOP File #58944L.

269 **further arrests**: Police record in FBI #60-2149-29 field report dated 4-21-39 and serial 123 report dated 5-31-41 give among others two arrests in 1921 for burglary, BOP File #58944L, *Lightnin'* May 1939.

269 **with Mangano**: *USvC* Bioff testimony 109, 760-764.

270   **"Some weeks" interview**: *Saturday Evening Post*, 1-27-40, "All Right, Gentlemen, Do We Get the Money?" by Florabel Muir—she was granted one of the few one-on-one interviews with Bioff, .

270   **Browne's run for president**: According to Browne, *USvC* testimony 1023, 1145, and 1294, the soup kitchen evolved out of his benevolent efforts to gain votes, he also gave its official name; election margin: testimony 1018.

270   **Century of Progress work**: *USvC* Browne testimony 1144-1145 including "nimble" and Bioff 114, 432, for split of income.

270   **California strike**: Ibid. Browne 1034.

270   **Balaban and Katz chain**: Recalled in T 3-8-71 Barney Balaban obituary.

270   **restoration of pay**: *USvC* Browne 1026 including Balaban's offer   .

270   **negotiations**: *USvC* Browne 1026-27 and Bioff 120; Bioff's "frame of mind" quote: 1026; Bioff's demand: Bioff 120 remembered it as given in text, whereas Browne waffled in his later testimony 1027 saying he did not remember who made the demand, but thought it as $20,000; Bioff 120 for "How about" quote.

271   **fictitious lawyer bill**: *USvC* Bioff testimony 121, 464 reveals the setup; DOJ #5-2742 memo dated 12-18-42 names Parrillo and Feldman; memos dated 10-6-42 and 10-8-42 also cite both men.

271   **events at the 100 Club**: *USvC* Bioff 122-123 and Browne 1029, 1207 testimony; the bill: Bioff 122 quoted as "very substantial", asked what he meant, was it $5, $10, or $500, he replied: "Closer to $500, sir, than $5."

271   **Circella's visit**: Ibid. Bioff 124.

271   **Bioff reported the call**: Ibid. Browne 1031 along with "They're all right."

271   **Carleon Hotel and Outer Drive**: Ibid. Bioff 125 and Browne 1029-1033, 1211.

271   **Browne did not reveal**: Ibid. Browne 1033.
    Nitto visited the kitchen: Ibid. Browne 1034.

272   **"We want 50 percent or else."**: Ibid. Bioff 130, 802; Bioff told authorities later: "I understand what 'or else' means, coming from him."

272   **"couldn't lock horns"**: Ibid. Bioff 134.

CHAPTER 19

273   **Serritella ... Senator**: Peterson 272.

273   **Hochstein errand boy**: *USvC* Bioff 135-136 he acted as a chauffeur: rented the Riverside house: Summation 3639   .

273   **mid-April 1934**: Ibid. 135-136, 574 Bioff gives the date and place.

273   **"small living room"**: Ibid. 575-576 also for those present and why.

273   **mob agenda and speakers**: Ibid. Bioff 138-139 and Browne 1036 both agree Nitto and Rio had lead roles; Nitto laid out the rules and quote: Bioff 138; why Browne failed: Browne 1036; clean background and Nitto's plan including quote: Bioff 139-141; Horan and Carrozzo: Bioff 141; convention date and place: IATSE report of minutes dated 6-8-36 found in the Pegler Papers.

274   **Lepke meet in May**: Ibid. Bioff 581 and Browne 1037-1038, 1226 both agreed Fischetti drove; drinks served: Bioff 583.

274   **Nitto-Lepke exchange**: Ibid. Bioff 145, 583 and Browne 1038-1039.

274   **Bioff's "million dollars"**: Ibid. oddly Browne 1039 remembered it, Bioff did not; it was Rio not Nitto as Murray 263 had it.

274   **Nitto and Rio instructed**: Ibid. Browne 1040-1041 including names in text.

274   **continuances in Lang case**: Cook County #68750; Nitto "too ill" and in Arkansas: T 6-1-34; Oak Park infirmary: CCC memo dated 6-24-52; nol-prossed: case #68750.

275   *Louisville Courier-Journal*: Messick *Secret* 172.

275   "delegates'" presence: *USvC* Bioff 146-147 and Browne 1226; suites next door: Bioff 912; Circella and Lepke: Bioff 471; unanimous election: Bioff 146.

275   Diamond incident: *USvC* Summation 3639-3640.

275   celebratory meet: Ibid. Browne 1043   .

275   Nitto's instructions: Ibid. Bioff 149 and Browne 1042, quote from Bioff; split of money: Browne 1044; Circella appointment: Bioff 149, 747 and Browne 1043.

276   new federal law: Ibid. Summation 3713 it was enacted June 18, 1934.

276   recover lost jobs: Ibid. Bioff 152-153 and Browne 1045-1046.

276   meeting Rosselli: Ibid. Browne 1045-1046 also recalls Circella hung over and furious that morning; quote "This is our man": Bioff 152-153.

276   Johnnie Rosselli: Rappleye & Becker 28-33.

276   on Casey's payroll: *USvC* Bioff 152-153, 802-803; "It seemed" quote by Browne 1045-1046 and that Casey would help.

276   chat about McGurn: Recalled by Browne 1043-1044 including quotes.

277   Kaufman to testify: T 6-21-31.

277   postal telegraph: DOJ #5-23-333 file on O'Hara and Maloy activities.

277   Maloy "as a racketeer": Ibid. memo dated 3-8-34 for quote though they had investi-gated he and the union for 3 years   .

277   SIU investigation: Ibid. gives the detail of the probe; "M. T. Expense": memo dated 10-23-35; money handled: memo dated 3-8-34; quote to broaden the study also in 3-8-34 memo.

277   newspaper reported gifts: T 10-25-34; the Maloy probe was no longer a secret.

278   O'Hara perjury: U.S. District Court, Northern District of Illinois, *U.S. vs. Ralph O'Hara*, #28664 dated 1-18-35.

278   Korte went to Ricca: *USvC* Summation 3675 including quotes.

278   Maloy's age: Numbered list of 1935 murders compiled from coroner's reports found in the CCC.

278   problems cropping up: Indiana home robbed: T, HE 2-5-35; mob threats and fundraiser: T 3-6-60 a retrospect of Local 110; doubled his guard: HE 2-5-35.

278   "causing severe": Quoted from DOJ #5-23-333 memo dated 1-14-35.

278   Maloy indictment: *U.S. vs. Maloy*, #28674 dated 1-25-35.

278   Dr. Quinn: HE 2-5-35; routine to get car in T 2-5-35   .

279   Maloy's murder: T, HE 2-5-35, list of 1935 murders found in the CCC; quote and O'Connell: HE   .

279   Browne to assist Courtney: HE 2-15-35.

279   future decided by Nitto: *USvC* Bioff 233 names those present at the meetings; Browne 1102 for "As I understood" quote.

279   Browne—emergency decree: Ibid. Browne 1103 for 50 percent kickback; Circella's quoted order: Browne 1051; Browne's suggestion: 1105-1106.

279   Nitto's approval of Korte: Ibid. Summation 3675-3676 noted Korte's meeting with named mob men and that Nitto's word was needed; also for quotes; no indication why Nitto was laid up.

280   system to install family: Ibid. Bioff 236-237 also for "elsewhere" quote; salary kick back: Browne 1103; O'Hara as ghost employee: DOJ #5-2742 memo dated 3-6-43; names mob men who installed family: Bioff 236-237 and a CCC memo dated 3-26-44 notes their relationship.

280   Rio died: T 2-24-35.

280   services-Nitto led: Noted in DN 2-25,27-35.

280   raked IATSE expense fund: *USvC* Bioff 160-161 also that Nitto sent them.

280   use Maloy's old scheme: Ibid. Bioff 166-169, 171; demanded the extra man: 166-167; $100,000 demand: 171; "kill grandma" quote: 169.

280   **meet with Coston—agreement**: Ibid. Bioff 170-172, 542; ruinous actions: *USvC* Summation 3642; pro-rated shares 171, 177-178.

281   **phony lawyer bills**: Ibid. Bioff 174,176, 887 and Browne 1059.

281   **move IATSE headquarters**: IATSE report dated 6-9-36 in Pegler Papers.

281   **conversation with Nitto**: *USvC* Bioff 155-156 and Browne 1049-1050.

282   **demands on Barger**: Ibid. Bioff 293-300 for his prosperity; Nitto's 50 percent demand: Bioff 294-296; Barger at Gibby's: Murray 246; according to Browne, Gibby's was known as the place where the theater crowd congregated; Circella's quoted conversation: Browne 1074-1075.

282   **"Hello partner"**: A 10-3-48 while Messick *Secret* 175 for a more colorful version.

282   **amounts Barger paid**: *USvC* Summation 3686.

282   **Bioff reported the $200**: Ibid. Bioff 300-301 and DOJ memo dated 12-18-42; Nitto's quoted response: Bioff 302; Diamond on payroll: 304; D'Andrea replaced him: Browne 1077 and DOJ #5-2742 memos dated 10-29-42, 12-18-42 Diamond evidently left when he became more involved in the BSEIU; D'Andrea as replacement: IMW 878; his sister: *USvC* 1077.

282   **Bioff "revision of profits"**: Ibid. Browne 1053-1054.

282   **substance of the meeting**: Ibid. Bioff 182-183 for speakers and Nitto quote; Nitto erupted quote: Browne 1055 remembered it; in a separate room: Bioff 183; however the author could find no source to back Murray's 277 assertion that Nitto nearly shoved Browne out a window.

283   **2 percent tax—rationale**: United States District Court, Southern District of New York, *U.S. vs. Isadore Zevin*, # C133-160.

283   **accountability**: Aller 102-104 and for union membership

283   **Zevin appointment**: *USvC* Bioff 192-193 for Nitto's order: classified ad: Browne 1061; the introduction: Bioff 193: Zevin from the brewery: Summation 3681.

283   **salaries for Fund reps**: Ibid. Bioff 926.

283   **Local 306, the largest**: Ibid. Browne 1184.

283   **emergency decree**: IATSE report dated 6-9-36 in Pegler Papers.

293   **contract talks**: *USvC* Browne 1064 including quote "not my."

284   **theater disruptions**: Aller 82-83 recalled the name of the movie and several incidents that outraged customers.

284   **execs paid $150,000**: *USvC* Bioff 201; 518 for division of spoils.

284   **Browne ... after the money**: Ibid. Browne 1052 for ignorance of payment and 1059 for hardly handling money; Bioff 884 noted his drinking problem and quote; the author could find no source for Murray 245 claim of 100 bottles of beer a day.

285   **$12,000 to Nitto**: ST 10-1-48 including "chicken feed."

285   **Arkansas home**: T 9-13-48.

285   **Anna Nitto**: Resident Hy Saxe interview with Robert Schoenberg Jan. 22, 1989, recalled her nightclub days; her gambling activities: T 9-13, 28-48, according to chief counsel for the IRS Charles Oliphant at a congressional hearing.

285   **to adopt a baby**: T 9-13-48 and IOC interview of John Patton.

285   **Joseph Ralph Nitto**: Carland County, Arkansas Adoption Order #3542.

285   **impact on Anna**: Interviews above both indicate her night life extended to 1940.

285   **$100,000 trust fund**: IOC interview of John Patton and A 9-27-48.

CHAPTER 20

287   **Courtney's record**: DT, HE 3-25-35; his Maloy investigation: HE.

288   **assassination attempt**: T, DN, DT, HE 3-25-35; headline and his 'mob' quote: T; "on the run": DT; "It wasn't gambling": T; Kelly backed him: HE 3-27-35; Spike O'Donnell:

DT 3-26-35; reward: DN, DT 3-27-35; he backtracked: DT 3-27.

288   **machine guns no longer**: DN 7-19-35, also notes they were more expensive.

289   **Kelly re-election**: T 4-3-35 for complete story and election numbers.

289   **the payoff**: T 8-10-40 gives samples of Nitto's power.

289   **name of Local 278**: Rubin 267; known simply as the Bartenders' Union

289   **George McLane persona**: Rubin 267 including "regular guy", "drunkard" and "habitual violator" ironically, from Louis Romano interview in *Lightnin'*, September 1940; Red Light district: *Lightnin'*; disorderly conduct and assault charges: notes from police record in CCC.

290   **news hawk account**: HE 8-23-23 including quotes and nest egg.

290   **weakness of union**: Newell 85; for gambling and investigation activities: Rubin 267-268; name change: T 3-27-33.

290   **applicants for jobs**: Ibid. notes number, pay, and Wittwer's quote/ .

291   **Nitto's expansion**: Gold Seal Liquors: CCC memo dated 1-10-49 and T 10-18-40; Tony Gizzo: *USvC* Bioff 241; Iowa agents and Wisconsin: CCC memo 1-24-49; Cady 182 for Cream Top Ale made in Wisconsin as a Manhattan product (also in T 10-18) shipped primarily to the South.

291   **F. R. Nitto Beverage Co.**: FBI #60-2149 memo dated 8-8-41, DN 12-27-40 Pegler column also mentions a Nitto distributorship; Roma Wine Company: T 9-28-49.

291   **forceful sales**: CCC memo dated 1-24-49   .

291   **acquired rivals**: Ibid. Lists names of the breweries, for example the Prima and Bismarck breweries.

291   **17 percent retail market share**: Murray 202, reasonable given their saloons, etc.

291   **Manhattan's "lousy beer"**: CCC memo dated 1-24-49.

291   **recommend a mob product**: Rubin 275 recognized the advantage the mob could exercise if they controlled the bartenders; also for "just as good" quote.

292   **union dues collected**: Transcript of Romano interview by police dated 2-16-40 in CCC files; DN 5-31-40 put it at $250,000.

292   **"Our first trouble"**: T 6-3-40.

292   **umbrella group**: Rubin gives the official name of the international.

292   **Stanton demand**: CCC observer notes dated 11-29-40 and T 10-18-40 including quote; Derby results from T 5-5-35.

292   **LaSalle hotel meet**: Ibid. "shot in the head": T, similar versions in HA 10-17-40 and DN 10-21-40.

293   **Capri Restaurant**: *USvC* McLane testimony 2321and T 10-18-40; in most instances in recalling 1935 events, McLane also named Humphreys and Guzik present, however, both were still in federal prison serving time for tax evasion—Guzik released late that year, Humphreys released early in 1936; guns on table: DN 10-21-40; Nitto's demand and "dumped" threat: CCC observer notes 11-29-40 and DN.

293   **"Give us the names"**: T 10-18-40; McLane and Nitto quotes: T 12-7-40.

293   **July meet—Fred Evans**: CCC observer notes dated 11-29-40, and T 10-18-40.

293   **"What ... stalling for?"**: Conversation: T 10-18-40, except "blow your head off" : CCC notes dated 11-29-40 and HA 11-29-40   .

294   **Romano introduction**: T 10-18-40; police record: Romano interview by Chicago PD dated 2-19-40; "he'll go along": T and CCC notes.

294   **Auditorium Hotel**: T 10-18-40, DT 10-20-40: T lists products; Nitto quote about fair trade in both T and DT.

294   **Local 450**: IIA exhibit #12856 a copy of the charter.

294   **Bismarck Hotel meet**: T 10-18-40 including quotes.

295   **ancillary businesses**: Tavern fixtures: CCC memo 1-24-49; Humphreys' linen business

based on FBI #92-3088, Section 7 synopsis summing up his control of the linen industry; Ralph's business: DN 5-31-40, T 11-27-40 with T giving the name; John's Havanna company, value, and "good idea ... boys drop in": T.

295   **Wagner Act**: law as of July 5, 1935

295   **reporter observation**: T 7-21-35; Bioff quote: *USvC* Bioff 606-607.

295   **Alterie's union dealings**: Ash Haulers': DN 7-19-35; Local 202: T 7-19-35.

295   **studio apartment**: T 7-19-35, location and registered name.

296   **Alterie refused to pay**: *N.Y. vs. Scalise* #224300 notes.

296   **Scalise elevation**: *N.Y. vs. Scalise* #224300 Schwartz testimony, minutes of the BSEIU board meeting 4-30-37; Thomas Burke: Schwartz testimony and file memos.

296   **Local 25 ... with theater strikes**: HE 7-19-35; generally, a strike by any one of the several unions required to operate a theater (i.e., musicians, operators, stagehands, cleaning persons, etc.) induced a show of sympathy from the others, thus closing the theater altogether.

296   **Alterie in Florida**: T 7-19-35.

296   **the ambush lookout**: DN, T 7-19-35; "loving care of": DN; "model roomers": T ; bullet proof vest: n.p. 7-19-35 reprinted in *Building Service News* dated 3-19-40 in files of Ind. #224300

296   **Alterie murder**: DN, HE, T 7-19-35; killed at 10:05 a.m. according to synopsis of coroner's report in the CCC; Mrs. Alterie in lobby and Alterie quote: HE.

296   **Nitto as key suspect**: T 7-21-35.

297   **Alterie burial**: T 7-21-35 with T 7-19-35 giving his sister's town.

297   **movie making unions**: Number of unionists and guildes: FBI #60-2149-51 field report dated 8-5-39 and serial 65 field report dated 11-14-39, *Saturday Evening Post* 1-27-40, Muir 9; pre-strike IATSE members: *USvC* Bioff testimony 210 says and Aller 104; number of internationals originally in the Basic Agreement: FBI #60-2149-54 field report 8-25-39; membership down to 158: FBI #60-2149-74 Bioff statement 4-19-39, Muir 82 reports 159—trusting Bioff here.

298   ***Thirteen Hours By Air***: *USvC* Bioff 203-204, Aller 88: the BSEIU issue: Browne 1215; the IBEW absorbed: FBI #60-2149-54.

298   **Balaban and negotiations**: *USvC* Bioff testimony 205 and Browne 1080-1081.

298   **theater strike**: Ibid. Browne testimony 1234 recalled the timing of the Paramount conference; Illinois strike details: T 12-1-35 while Aller 89 recalled it spreading to other cities; strike in Chicago: T 12-2-35.

299   **Drake Hotel meet**: *USvC* Bioff testimony 207-210; Balaban recalled, "financial collapse": A 10-3-48.

299   **Browne-Casey ...** : Ibid. 211, Aller 109.

299   **Guzik's release**: BOP #41276.

299   **Ricca, Campagna handled**: *USvC* Bioff testimony 222.

299   **Campagna's candidate**: Ibid. Bioff testimony 239-240; "all right": Browne 1106.

299   **Circella's sister**: Ibid. Summation 3688.

299   **Humphreys release**: BOP #45760L.

299   **Genaro murdered**: T, DN 12-20-35, quote from DN.

300   **McGurn [Mann Act]**: CCC copy of McGurn's criminal history and police record, details also in T 8-27-33, T 2-15-36.

300   **golf talents**: DN 7-17-33, T 8-27-33; T with pictures of him at the Western Open; HE for rumor of his death

300   **"How can I get ... trouble"**: T 7-18-33 for entire conversation.

300   **225 Club**: T 6-21-34; padlocked as a "resort": T 6-23-34.

301   **McGurn's hard times**: T 7-15-35 for details, except jewelry: HE 2-16-36.

301 **Prignano**: McGurn sought him: HA 12-30-35, HE 2-17-36; pal of Capone's: DN 12-30-35, HA 10-28-48.

301 **Nitto favored Pacelli**: DN 12-30-35; support and quote: HA 10-28-48.

301 **attempts on Prignano**: T 12-30-35; clash with Mangano in T, DN 12-30-35.

301 **Carmen Vacco**: DN 12-30-35.

302 **Prignano murder**: T 12-30-35 for details; HA 10-28-48.

302 **McGurn called police**: T 2-16-36.

302 **McGurn murder**: DN, T 2-15-36; DN details wounds.

303 **comic valentine**: HE 2-16-36; T 2-16-36 provides a picture of it.

303 **anachronism**: T 2-16-36 remarks the gang held him "useless"; age: police record dated 11-24-30 in CCC put on July 2, 1902, DN 2-15-36 had it as July 2, 1903.

303 **Demory murder**: T 3-3-36.

304 **Rep. Bolton murder**: T 7-9,10-36; handbook incorporation: T 7-2-35; contemporary sources seem to think legislation favored the mob, later HA 10-29-48 theorized it favored legit investors at the expense of the mob.

304 **"He's a solid kid"**: HA 10-23- 48.

304 **estimations of Nitto's mob**: "miserably lessened": T 2-16-36; "more powerful" letter: FBI #32-15941-34 with "1000 percent stronger" in FBI #32-15941-35.

304 **Nitto's business interests**: TXC #111 except for Sportsman's Park interest: IOC interview of John Patton; and beachfront house: *USvC* 212 Bioff testimony.

CHAPTER 21

305 **IATSE meet**: *USvC* Browne testimony 1175.

305 **Capone's or Nitto's home**: Ibid. Bioff testimony 212 and Browne 1177.

305 **Bioff to take charge**: Ibid. Browne 1085.

305 **put Rosselli on payroll**: Ibid. Bioff 212, 829; Bioff's "sore thumb" and Nitto's quoted reply: 212; Roselli's pay: 245-246.

305 **Bioff's cruise**: Ibid. Bioff 651, 830.

306 **Basic Agreement history**: FBI #60-2149-54 field report dated 8-25-39 and serial 101 field report dated 9-2-40 chronologically lists all the contracts.

306 **wanted 33-100 percent raises**: *USvC* Bioff testimony 935.

306 **trumped local charters**: FBI #60-2149-51 field report dated 8-5-39.

306 **"as ... Schenck goes"**: *USvC* Bioff 621, reinforced by Albert Warner's testimony 5-16-41 regarding Bioff, Warner was asked why Nick Schenck was contacted in regard to Warner's own company. Warner replied, "No, except that Nicholas has always assumed a domineering, commanding position in the industry, and the rest ... just let him go ahead."

306 **Browne softened Schenck**: Aller 96-97.

306 **Bioff's demands**: *USvC* Bioff testimony 216, 623 while FBI #60-2149-123 field report dated 5-31-41 gives $1-2 million demand; though in *USvC* 216-217, he says $2–3 million; Schenck quote: FBI #60-2149-123 testimony of Nick Schenck 5-15-41; close down theaters: 216-217; Bioff quote: Aller 97   .

306 **they appealed to Browne**: *USvC* Browne testimony 1090 including quotes.

307 **at Pat Casey's office**: Ibid. Bioff 935 and Browne 108; named studios and producers: FBI #60-2149-123 memo dated 5-20-41; Bioff and Browne roles and Browne quote: Ibid., except Bioff's "den of hyenas" from *Saturday Evening Post* 1-27-40 by Florabel Muir; studio economic health: FBI #60-2149-123, executive Austin Keough testimony dated 5-15-41 and Sydney Kent affidavit dated 5-15-41.

307 **"We all ... sold out"**: *USvC* Bioff testimony 935.

307 **agreement—$1 million**: Ibid. Bioff 225-226; pro rata shares: Bioff 219-220 and

Browne 1094, while executive Sydney Kent testimony of 5-15-41 (FBI #60-2149-123) had Bioff demanding $200,000 from each. Kent says that the major producers came up with the figures given, negotiated with Bioff, who then informed the other studio heads; in exchange 10 percent raises: Bioff 892; no change in conditions observed by Aller 99.

308 **began paying tribute**: *USvC* Bioff testimony 221-222 and Browne 1095, and evidence introduced at the 1943 for locations; amounts paid: Ibid. and testimony of Sydney Kent and Nick Schenck in FBI #60-2149-123; "sums lying around": Aller 98; Warner's sum and later payouts: testimony of Albert Warner in FBI #60-2149-123; the producers 1941 testimony agreed the money was NOT paid immediately, but later in the year.

308 **"What did Bioff say ... "**: FBI #60-2149-123, testimony of Austin Keough; Warner's reply: testimony of Albert Warner.

308 **split with Nitto's gang**: *USvC* Browne testimony 1100, Browne carefully explained that Bioff was the principle contact with Nitto's mob.

308 **2 percent tax raked**: *Saturday Evening Post* 1-27-40 by Florabel Muir bases the take on $3 per member and Hollywood membership up to 6,000 (Bioff 655-656 thought it at 5,000); IATSE membership increased: Aller 104.

308 **Kansas City convention**: Held June 9, 1936, Auditorium Hotel: minutes from the convention in Pegler Papers; mob attendance and activities: *USvC* Bioff testimony 241-243 and Browne 1108 including Bioff's appointment.

308 **"I would like for your"**: *USvC* Bioff testimony 630-631, 655, FBI #60-2149-65 report dated 11-14-39 for the whole RKO episode; the FBI also reports Bioff charge to IATSE for the carpets.

309 **Bioff's routine trips**: Ibid. Bioff 258-259 and Browne 1116-1117.

309 **FMPC problem**: FBI #60-2149-51 field report dated 8-5-39, and serial 54 field report dated 8-25-39, *USvC* Bioff 668, 892-893, Rappleye & Becker 88-89.

309 **the strike**: Nitto and Rosselli directing: Rappleye & Becker 88-89; FBI #60-2149-51 field report dated 8-5-39 reports Bioff employed about 20 gunmen; street action reported by Muir in *Saturday Evening Post* 1-27-40; actress quote: Rappleye & Becker 89.

310 **Bioff pushed the deal**: *USvC* Bioff testimony 894, FBI #60-2149-51 field report 8-5-39 for agreement details as well as serial 54 field report 8-25-39 for new IATSE membership and for those who did not go along.

310 **"to accomplish ... selfish"**: *USvC* Bioff testimony 908.

310 **Schenck's appreciation**: FBI #60-2149-74 from Bioff statement on 4-14-39 and Schenck statements on 5-23-38.

310 **"them actors"**: *Saturday Evening Post* 1-27-40, by Florabel Muir, who reported on the spot from Hollywood.

310 **July 1936 headline**: T 7-10-36 and "Camorra" speculation.

311 **Nitto-Campagna arrest**: T 8-12-36, weak smile from back page photo; recovering from wounds: HA 10-29-48.

311 **714 West Di Lido**: Dade County Recorder of Deeds warranty deed #17283 dated 4-29-37 signed Anna Ronga.

311 **description of property**: Exterior and interior: T 7-19-41; ocean frontage, palms, pool, and wall: T 10-23-42; Carfano nearby at 508 West Di Lido: *N.Y. vs. Scalise*, #224300, Carfano interview dated 8-6-40.

311 **Campagna-Pierce visit**: *USvC* Bioff testimony 274-275.

311 **sprinkler systems**: Ibid.

311 **Kaufman episode**: Ibid., Bioff 256-258 including Nitto and Bioff conversation and quotes.

312 **Scalise nomination and rise**: *N.Y. vs. Scalise*, Ind. # 224300 specifically, Isadore Schwartz statement dated 8-19-40 and trial testimony; Scalise reports Thomas Burke affidavit.

312 **Bioff ordered east**: *USvC* Bioff testimony 357-358.

312 **Scalise elected**: Minutes of the BSEIU General Executive Board dated 5-11-37 found in the Ind. #224300.

312 **Cuba trips**: *N.Y. vs. Scalise*, Ind. # 224300.

312 **Romano contacted**: Notes from CCC file regarding McLane.

313 **Nitto called McLane**: *USvC* Bioff testimony 356-357 for place and names .

313 **Flore run the union**: Rubin 276.

313 **"We will make you"**: *USvC* Bioff testimony 357; Nitto assured McLane: Quoted from HA 10-17-40; McLane nitpicked: *USvC* McLane testimony 2377; Nitto's "Bioff will get": HA 10-17-40 supported in substance by *USvC* McLane 2377; testimony; made Cararazzo: T, DN 12-5-40; in "an alley": T, DN.

313 **nationwide distribution**: DN 12-27-40 Pegler column; Chicago Federation of Labor: DN 12-5-40; tavern association: T 10-22-40.

313 **Nitto's slush fund idea**: T 12-3-40.

313 **candidate McLane**: Recalled by Rubin 275-277 including "reconsider it": 277; and "strongest opposition" analysis: 284.

314 **Ed Flore as soft**: Ibid. 284, Newell 85-86; resistance out east: Ibid. 279-280, 293 also for Dewey; mysterious ... persons": Ibid. 284.

314 **McLane's convention frills**: Ibid. 284.

314 **thugs beat a Flore nominee**: Ibid. 285, the man ,as it turned out, was elected.

314 **San Fransicsco police**: Newell 86.

314 **convention speeches**: Rubin 299-301, also quoted in Newell 86-87 who accessed the convention's stenographic records.

315 **vote margin**: Newell 87.

315 **Nitto ordered McLane**: T 12-5-40 gives the Congress Hotel and McLane's drinking as a problem and Nitto's "get on" quote.

315 **after Robert Stanchi died**: CCC McLane file for Nitto orders and action including Humphrey and Evans at the Capri.

315 **Chicago Joint Council**: Newell 84 provides a complete list of the 14 locals comprising the council, though some sources put the number at 15; "to Cicero":T 12-5-40.

315 **"I'm taking over"**: The entire incident an amalgam of T 6-1-40, 10-18-40, 12-8-40 and CCC McLane file; "taking over" and "shut your eyes": T 10-18; "take a trip": CCC McLane file; Levy's reply: T 10-18; "I can go to sleep": T 12-8; Humpreys "That is the trouble": T 12-8 and warning to obey: T 6-1; a live bullet and quote: T 7-15-58; McLane packed up: CCC.

316 **Seeger's resignation**: T, DT 9-12-40; "want muscle": DT; "Take this": T.

316 **Trades and Crafts Council**: Newell 88, according to Newell this was short-lived and disappeared about 1938 probably because of political pressure.

316 **15 South Side unions**: DN 5-4-43 naming Stanton an Kelly.

316 **painters unions**: 1940 CCC file memo outlining the violent history of the union.

317 **Mike Carrozzo**: T 4-14, 15,16, 20-40, DT 4-16-40, DN 11-3-40; "secret income": n.p. dated 4-14-40 in CCC.

317 **Max Caldwell**: T 6-7-41, T 7-9, 18, 31-41; n.p. 11-22-42 and memo noting arrests dated 5-20-40 in Pegler Papers including "legs broken"; union dues, fees and hospital plan from Local 1248 letterhead mail to membership dated 2-8-39, 3-29-39, 4-25-39.

317 **"Whenever crime"**: *Collier's* 7-13-40.

318 **"Gambling and its agencies"**: FBI #32-15941 in an anonymous communication dated 11-26-30.

318   **gambling staple**: DN 9-29-39, *Collier's* "Too Much Fun" by John T. Flynn for subsequent quotes.

318   **to open a joint**: Ibid. and *Collier's* 10-7-39; Flynn notes only the highly organized Nitto mob could handle the intricacy of lining up the details and services   .

318   **city-wide setup**: *Collier's* 10-7-39 including quote describing Johnson; payoffs-Skidmore and amounts: *American Mercury* February 1940; his junkyard: DN 2-20-41; Skidmore quote: *Collier's*; timing of payoffs and split: *American Mercury*.

319   **Annenberg supplied 80 percent**: *Liberty* 8-5-40.

319   **scratch sheets**: Ragen's sheet failed: Ragen statement dated 5-2-46 in the CCC; Flannigan sheet: DN 6-3-40.

319   **Moe didn't like losing**: DN 6-25-46.

319   *Green Sheet-*Guzik: Ragen statement and DN 6-25-46   .

319   *Red Sheet* **decline**: Annenberg discount to Nitto: DN 6-25-46; threats and recruiting: T 5-26-39; subscriptions: DN 6-3-39.

320   **Nitto's national plan**: A 6-26-46 also for Ragen's end up "in an alley."

CHAPTER 22

321   **Courtney-Kelly animosity**: Biles 67.

321   **"Syndicate controlled"**: DN 9-6-38.

321   **politically charged—"Fighting Tom"**: Moniker and general campaign information from Biles 67-68; handbook casualties: Chicago papers September and October; policy wheel crackdown: DN 8-29-38.

322   **"part and parcel"**: *Collier's* 7-13-40; political opportunism: Biles 68.

322   **"OLD CAPONE MOB" exposé**: DN 2-14-39.

322   **Nitto received word**: FBI #62-34299-24A, an anonymous letter dated 2-16-39 certainly a dubious source, but that Nitto would have directed support for Kelly is obvious in part by Courtney's harassment (political or not, better to stick with a known entity) and from ensuing and absurd election totals in mob wards.

322   **primary victory margin**: Biles 70.

322   **Green's campaign**: Ibid., and T 4-5-39 also for money spent; mob money for Kelly: T, while a nameless source in FBI #62-34299-24A says about $50,000.

323   **mobilize unions**: T 7-7-39 including sample letter in text.

323   **election results**: T 4-5-39 gives ward totals also noted in Biles 73.

323   **gambling back to normal**: DN 6-7-39 including detailed observations.

323   **Annenberg-Skidmore**: DN 6-1-39 for investigations.

324   **Nitto scurried for cover**: DN 6-5-39; "We're shut tight": Ibid.

324   **lawsuit by Flannigans**: DN 6-3-39.

324   **Nitto's offer to settle**: Ragen statement 5-2-46 in the CCC including tailor shop meet and Ragen quote.

324   **Annenberg indictment**: United States District Court for the Northern District of Illinois, *U.S. vs. Moe Annenberg et al.*, Case #31762 outlines the individual tax evasion indictment The federal probe resulted in indictments against Annenberg, many of his associates, and businesses far too extensive to cover in detail here except to say that it comprised much of his vertical and horizontal interests.

324   **James Ragen indictment**: Case #31764 specifying tax evasion for years 1933-36 (inclusive), synopsis in DOJ File #5-23-1205.

324   **William Johnson**: DN 3-1-40.

324   **policy kings**: T 3-6-40.

325   **Nitto playing golf**: *USvC* 3626 summary.

325   **"can make money"**: T 11-9-39.   .

325   **O'Hare's interests:** FBI File # 62-39128-120, memo dated 11-20-39 including John Patton as active in the tracks.

325   **Nitto's ownership:** TXC #111 Ruling #1950-16-13397 for the first two; IOC interview of Patton specifies Miami, both give Patton as cover for Nitto; ST 9-28-48 gives 1 Ohio and 2 Florida tracks.

325   **O'Hare's worth:** T 11-9-39.

325   **his family:** STLGD, HA 11-9-39, DN 5-20-43.

325   **Sue Granata romance:** Ibid. and TD 7-41 speculating a spring wedding.

326   **November 8 business:** DT, T, HA, 11-9-39; DN 11-13-39; O'Hare's wardrobe and office description: TD 7-41.

326   **murder episode:** T 11-9-39, DN 11-13-39; witness quote: DN.

327   **investigation:** T, DT, HA 11-9-39; "a thousand angles": DT; the "Margie" note and watch inscription: HA.

327   **Capone's name:** T, DT 11-9-39.

327   **secret apartment:** DN, DT 11-13-39, TD 7-41; "George" note: TD.

327   **sending Capone to prison:** STLGD 11-19-39.

       a mob present: Schoenberg 345-346.

328   **Capone's health:** Schoenberg 345-346 including "screwy" quote; agents questioning him: FBI #62-3198-101 memo dated 10-26-39; and serial 121 memo dated 12-1-39 for the specialist quote.

328   **insurance policies:** DT 11-14-39.

328   **collection drive theory:** DT 11-12, 13-39; FBI call: T, DT, HA 11-9-39.

328   **authorities point to:** "Capone racketeers" and Gilbert's action: DT 11-12-39; Courtney quote: DT 11-13-39; Caravetta quizzed: HA 11-17-39, STLGD 11-19-39; quote: STLGD.

328   **"torpedo men":** DT 11-17-39.

328   **Nitto in Hot Springs:** *USvC* 3626 summation, S 12-3-43.

328   **result of the Nitto outfit:** DT 11-17-39 Gilbert and Courtney theories; quarrel theory dropped: FBI File #62-39128-124.

329   **Florida track premise:** *Miami Daily News* tip: FBI File #62-39128-110 memo dated 11-16-39; Frank Erickson: Peterson 285; Nitto and Patton interest explicit in TXC #111; O'Hare's ownership in Tropical Park and others reinforced by FBI File #62-39128-120.

329   **O'Hare's toughened stance:** DT, T, STLGD 11-19-39.

329   **O'Hare's reputation:** Chiefly IOC interview of Patton except FBI #62-39128-120 memo dated 11-20-39, a source claimed that O'Hare refused obligations.

329   **Feds targeting IATSE:** Louis Kaufman: DOJ #52742 Section 3.

329   **John Nick-Clyde Weston:** FBI #60-2149-3 and serial 61, among the first IATSE men to be investigated; also Circuit Court of St. Louis, Missouri, Case #30641 February 1940; criminal records: St. Louis PD file in FBI #60-2149.

330   **Bioff's oblique scheme:** *USvC* 262-264 Bioff testimony, FBI #60-2149-123 field report dated 5-31-41 and Louis B. Mayer testimony dated 5-16-41.

330   **$100,000 loan:** Ibid. 286-287, 676-678 and FBI #60-2149-65 field report dated 11-14-39; "too friendly" and stock gifts including Louis B. Mayer: FBI file.

331   **SAG affair and background:** FBI #60-2149-51 field report dated 8-5-39 and serial 59 field report dated 10-16-39; that Bioff solve the actor problems: Louis B. Mayer testimony dated 5-16-41; Bioff's "parading": FBI serial 57 memo dated 10-6-39; Bioff threw a scare: serial 51.

331   **Columbia incident:** Ibid. of Campagna: Bioff 279; November 8 strike: Bioff 279-280, Browne 1121. FBI #60-2149-65 field report dated 11-14-39; Rosselli-Bioff exchange: Bioff 282-283; double-crossed: Bioff 284.

332   **state investigation**: Ibid. Bioff 692, FBI #60-2149-57 memo 10-6-39.

332   **legislators heard**: FBI #60-2149-57 and *Saturday Evening Post* 1-27-40, by Muir; "white-wash" and alleged IATSE payments: FBI #60-2149-57.

332   **"It has been alleged"**: Rappleye 7 Becker 93 from an *Los Angeles Times* piece.

332   **Elmer Irey remembered**: Irey 283-284 including "so bad" quote and that it initiated a tax investigation.

332   **"couldn't remember"**: FBI #60-2149-51.

332   **2 percent tax rescinded**: FBI #60-2149-51 field report 8-5-39.

332   **"the boys in Chicago"**: Rappleye & Becker 107.

332   *IA Progressive Bulletin*: Vol.1, No. 11, dated 12-22-37 includes Bioff's police photo and record, names of Nitto associates and fiery 'Brothers" quote.

333   **Bioff squeezed—Schenck**: *USvC* 713-714 Bioff testimony.

333   **Rio de Janeiro**: Ibid. 718 including Warner's farewell.

333   **Pegler first exposed**: Pegler column n.p, n.d, but marked March 1938 "first Bioff" found in Pegler Papers.

333   **briefed on tax inquiry**: *USvC* 721-722 Bioff testimony.

333   **the convention**: FBI #60-2149-51 field report dated 8-5-39; Kent spoke: serial 74.

333   **vulnerability of extras**: Ibid., and serial 59 field report dated 10-16-39; crème of extra calls: serial 51.

333   **Schenck questioned**: FBI #60-2149-57 memo dated 10-13-39

334   **Nitto ordered ... :** *USvC* Browne 1122, reports of Bioff's resignation filtered out by September 1938.

334   *People's World* **report**: FBI #60-2149-51 field report 8-5-39. other alleged collusion: FBI #60-2149-74.

334   **Nitto lead questioned**: DN 2-14-39, 6-6-39 placed Ricca at the top; Murray's claim on 288.

334   **Ricca, D'Andrea met Bioff**: *USvC* 304-305 Bioff testimony also gives tax dangers; "wasn't much income": 326-327.

335   **AAAA episode**: Many confusing reports given the many Hollywood organizations and their acronyms, the text relies on from FBI #60-2149-51 field report 8-5-39, serial 65 field report dated 11-14-39 and *USvC* Browne 1124-1125; Bioff-Circella exchange from *USvC*.

335   **Nitto called a meet**: Ibid. 323 Bioff testimony

335   **mob discussion**: Ibid. 323-324.

336   **"practically on trial"**: Ibid. 325.

336   **Nitto spending time out**: *Collier's* 10-7-39; DN, 2-14-39, 5-1-41; T 3-20-43 all give his return to Chicago mainly for important business; "Frank Raddo": DN 2-14; Wisconsin evident from arrest record compiled by the FBI reflecting an arrest in Racine, Wisconsin.

336   **wounds-complications**: DN 5-1-41.

337   **Nitto sold his share**: IOC interview of Patton also his "atmosphere."

337   **wanted policy wheels**: Peterson 180 supported by T 3-6-40

337   **Nitto sold his slots**: TXC #111; shown as vending income: T 9-28-48.

337   **tried bribes**: T 9-16-48 including "sham" quote.

338   **Montgomery phoned**: FBI #60-2149-29 field report dated 4-21-39.

338   **Local 37 tiff**: FBI #60-2149 serials 25, 29 field report dated 4-21-39, serial 57 field report dated 10-6-39 for the entire affair including Schenck.

338   **agents questioned Bioff**: FBI #60-2149-57 memo dated 11-13-39 and serial 51 field report 8-5-39.

338   **meeting in Washington**: Ibid. reinforced by FBI #60-2149-77.

338   **Bioff quotes during bargaining**: FBI #60-2149-64 citing L.A. paper n.p. dated 11-17-39 article "Film Shutdown Appears Likely."

339 **avenues of prosecution**: FBI #60-2149-57 memo dated 10-13-39 gives appraisals of various officials—hesitancy to prosecute not fully explained; Oftedal's stance and quote in FBI #60-2149-57 memo.

CHAPTER 23

341 **George Sanders murder**: T 6-3-40, HA 6-4-40 with quote from Murray 189.

341 **"stop this lawlessness"**: CCC labor racketeering bulletin dated 4-30-41.

341 **Louis Schiavone murder**: T, DN, HE 7-6-39.

342 **Matt Taylor's union**: T 9-7, 8-40, DN 9-7-40 Taylor's statement outlining mob attempts at his union; Schiavone quote: T 9-7 .

342 **meet with Campagna**: T 9-7-40 including quotes.

342 **a lawyer visited Taylor**: Ibid.; including quoted dialogue and meet at bar.

342 **mob proposal 50 percent**: Ibid.; including 'Its going to be Schiavone..."

343 **Taylor's payments**: T, DN 9-7-40 somewhat convoluted in the articles as to timing of certain funds paid prior to Schiavone's murder, but that he held out as Taylor suspects possible, Taylor says he paid out of his own pocket first and a list of union payments in T shows 4 payments made prior to July 5.

343 **motive for Schiavone's murder**: Ibid. Taylor's belief.

343 **Scalise's name surfaced**: T 7-8-39; in New York: *N.Y. vs. Scalise* #224300 outlines the charges made against him with details of strikes T 3-5-36, 1-28-40.

343 **revelations of his past**: T 1-28-40.

343 **BSEIU membership**: T 4-28-40.

343 **Nitto ordered**: *N.Y. vs. Scalise* #224300 memo dated 6-6-40 also reported in T 4-28-40; accolades: T 1-28-40.

343 **attempts in San Francisco**: T 4-27-40.

344 *Building Service News*: The original issue found in *N.Y. vs. Scalise*.

344 **indictments**: Conspiracy indictments in *N.Y. vs. Scalise* #223974; larceny charges listed in #224300.

344 **"national in its operations"**: T 4-28-40.

345 **Bioff research expedition**: DN 11-28-39.

345 **Bioff's pandering sentence**: CCC observer notes dated 3-21-22, Bioff's BOP file #58944L, FBI #60-2149-67 memo dated 1-9-40.

345 **Pegler broke the story**: DN 11-24-39.

345 **criticism of Courtney**: Pegler column DN 11-28-39.

345 **Bioff extradition**: FBI #60-2149-67 memo dated 1-9-40 explains the entire extradition process via a telegraphic warrant; also in Bioff's BOP File #58944L.

345 **national magazines**: *Newsweek* and *Time* columns appeared 12-4-39.

345 *Lightnin'*: It first appeared circa 1925; he exposed Bioff in the May 1939 issue; "Buy-Off": August 1939 issue; *Lightnin'* seems to have disappeared by the mid-1940s.

345 **Bioff-tax evasion**: U.S. District Court for the Southern District of California, *U.S. vs. Willie Bioff*, Case #314233-RJ and FBI 60-2149-74 field report dated 1-24-40.

345 **Nitto convened meetings**: *USvC*, 1126-1127 Browne testimony.

346 **"I feel constrained"**: DN 2-17-40.

346 **Bioff's Chicago meetings**: *USvC*, 328-329 Bioff testimony, also for Gioe's quote "meet Sydney ... ."

346 **Bioff's appeals**: In numerous Chicago papers from 2-21-40 to 4-14-40; they also mention Abe Marovitz as his attorney .

346 **Pegler's crusade**: "Mafia" and "crawling" observations: DN 4-2-40; Nitto as "the most vicious": DN 4-3-40; Nitto "outranked" and Miami activities: DN 4-19-40.

346 **Browne's penchant**: DN 4-24-40 names those individuals.

346 Scalise's extravagances: DN 4-16,18-40; *Lightnin'* 9-40, some supported by expenses found in *N.Y. vs. Scalise* #224300.

346 "Peglerized": DN 4-22-40.

346 Scalise resignation: DN 5-7-40; McFetridge as successor: DN 8-5-40; Burke told not run: T 8-17-41.

347 Bioff's visitors: *USvC* 331-332, Bioff testimony including chapel as the meeting place; insider quote: nameless letter to CCC dated 8-13-40 mentioning mob visits.

347 postpone tax trial: BOP File #58944L Parole Report dated 12-4-41.

347 press cornered Bioff: HA 6-4-40 including Bioff quotes.

347 Korshak and Ricca advice: *USvC* 917-922 Bioff testimony.

347 Nitto called Browne: *USvC* 1128-1129 Browne testimony; Bioff 332.

347 "resigns feet first" and meeting: *USvC* 332 Bioff testimony; Browne 1130-1131.

347 Gioe sent to the convention: Ibid. Browne 1128.

348 Resolution No. 3: HHPL Pegler Papers Collections

348 Browne defended ... : IATSE Convention Meeting transcripts and T n.d; 'Simply because" and "good union man": T 6-3-40.

348 Bioff disturbed: *USvC* 1131 Browne testimony.

348 Browne and Gioe meet: Ibid. 1131-1132; Gioe quote: 1132.

348 headline—Bioff release: HA 9-20-40; quote from T 9-21-40.

CHAPTER 24

351 Scalise conviction: *N.Y. vs. Scalise* #224300.

351 Mike Carrozzo case: DN 3-27-40, 6-24-40, 7-25-40; price of asphalt: T 9-15-40.

352 Nitto to name successor: DN 8-6-40.

352 McLane returned: CCC trial observer notes 11-29-40, DN 5-31-40; quote from DN; Newell 88 relates all officers fired

352 Romano and Mrs. McLane: CCC trial observer notes 11-29-40, HA 11-29-40 352 police interview Romano: Chicago PD report dated 2-16-40.

352 union hospital plan: DT 4-23-40; the DT was the only paper to carry the story leading Romano to suspect later that McLane leaked it because of a friend of his worked there.

353 new union bylaws: DN 6-1-40, T 6-2-40.

353 headlines: T 6-1-40 and DN 6-2-40.

353 McLane's petition: Amalgam of DN and T papers 6-1, 2-40; "the only man": T 6-1; syndicate brands: DN 6-1; 15; joint council: HA 6-3-40; expensive gifts: DN 6-11-40 and n.p. 7-28-40 in found in Pegler papers: Flore's denial: T 6-1, DN 6-2.

353 criticism: DN 6-4-40.

354 investigation and mob: Fed investigation: T, HA 6-2; state's attorney inquiry: T, DN 6-4-40; men named by McLane: T, DN 6-4-40, DN 6-5-40.

354 nearly $1 million: T, DT 6-6-40.

354 Courtney's late raid: T 6-7-40, also his peek into the Scalise affair.

354 McLane return to work: HA 6-2-40 including quote.

354 Romano ... Heinrici's: CCC trial observer notes 11-29-40 including quotes; Heinrici's restaurant from Drury's "Dining Out."

354 Nitto to ditch the bartenders: T 7-20-40.

354 Courtney investigation: T 7-8-40 for his interest in Stanton; T 7-20-40 for attention to labor operations; painters' unions: T 8-14, 17, 18-40; handbook raids: T 8-17,18, 24,27-40.

354 dragnet for Nitto ... : T 7-21-40; reported Nitto proposal: Ibid., also McLane quote.

355 Bertram Cahn quote: T 8-13-40.

355   initials "**FR**": *N.Y. vs. Scalise* #224300 and DN 9-20-40.

355   "**Racketeers ... forced out**": T 9-8-40.

355   **Oscar Nelson episode**: Involvement in Local 66 and as a legal rep for the janitor's union: DN 9-7-40; present at BSEIU meet and Scalise's name: DN 9-20-40, T 9-21-40; his broadcasts DN, T 9-26-40, T 9-27-40; attack on Courtney including quotes: DN 9-26.

356   **about Captain Gilbert**: DN, T 9-26-40, T 9-29-40; Gilbert's reply: T 9-27.

356   **Humphreys's advice**: FBI #58-2000 Elsure File a transcript of a wiretap in which he mentions Nitto and an incident that reflects the circumstances of what almost certainly appears to be the McLane case.

356   **headline**: DN 10-1-40.

356   **jury tampering**: DN 10-1-40, T 10-2-40 including "But I'm only" and "They got others" quotes; "do him some good": T 10-3-40; "no kickback": T 10-2.

357   **the indictment**: Cook County Criminal Case #40-1468, CCC observer notes and DN, HA 10-3-40 for particulars; the files of the criminal case are no longer available having been auctioned off to a private collector in 1993. The author was permitted by the auctioneer to obtain a few notes from the file prior to the auction.

357   **Fred Evans as "financial wizard"**: T 10-10-40.

357   **Humphreys's surrender**: T, HA 10-4-40.

357   **Nitto's surrender**: DN, HA 10-9-40, particularly DN for quotes.

357   **Bertram Cahn speech**: T 10-7-40.

357   **Nitto in court**: T 10-12-40 and photo; health: T 10-29-40.

357   "**Nitti hollering like hell**": FBI #58-2000 Elsure File.

357   **receiver Keehn's actions**: T 10-10, 29-40 and DN 10-18-40; "for good of service": T 10-10-40.

358   **defense strategy**: HA 10-18-40, T 10-18,19-40, DN 10-18,21,28-40; "McLane is crazy": T 10-18; last doctor snoozing and final diagnosis: DN 10-28.

358   **James Crowley**: T 10-26,27-40, 11-13-40; "candidate" quote: T10-27; Nitto's proposal outlined in T 11-13.

359   **Nitto in hospital**: T 11-20-40.

359   **wife Anna's death**: Cook County Death Certificate #32093 gives the details and the date (November 19), much of the press had the wrong date; fell ill in Miami: T 11-20-40, also gives Nitto's condition

359   **funeral**: HA 11-22-40 and T 11-23-40 reported it but with some conflict over details such as flowers and value of such.

359   **charges-potential penalties**: HA, DN 11-25-40; notes from Ind. #40-1468.

359   **Nitto in court**: HA 11-25-40 for looked "sick": "wan figure": DN 11-25-40; granted absence: DN 11-26-40.

359   **playing tag [civil suit]**: T, HA 11-27-40.

360   **witnesses disappeared**: T, HA 11-25-40.

360   **Nitto holed up**: HA 11-29-40, but does not give an address.

360   **McLane testimony**: CCC observer notes 11-29-40 and HA 11-29-40; startled responses: DN, HA 11-29-40; smiles "a mile wide": DN.

360   **threats to McLane**: T 12-1-40 including his attorney's quote.

360   **feeling ... not testify**: Ibid.

361   **mob deal with McLane-court strategy**: Amalgam of sources. Gilbert's version in T 10-4-48; information in CCC files provides the deal to re-elect McLane if he refused to testify, both also give Maddox as the contact; FBI Humphreys File #CG 92-348 Section 8 says they gleaned info that Humphreys made approaches all around, but does not give name of his high legal contact, only that he tried the state's attorney

and his assistant but failed. They were also informed Humphreys advised the mob strategy to McLane.

361   **Monday court events**: DN 12-2-40, T12-3-40; Judge Bolton quote from T.

361   **"Now I can campaign"**: T 12-3-40.

361   **Nitto-Courtney irony**: DN 12-3-40; Bertram Cahn observation: Ibid.; "The Nitti Case" editorial: T 12-4-40.

361   **Pegler observation**: DN 12-27-40.

362   **bartender's election**: T 12-3-40, DN 12-6-40; those dropping out: DN 12-6, 13-40; "going out of town": T 12-18-40, another dropped by year's end leaving only McElligott; election in the judge's court: DN 12-9-40; results: T 1-7-41, T 1-8-41; discovered McElligott as Crowley friend: 1-7.

362   **final comment**: Dan Gilbert quote: T 1-8-41.

CHAPTER 25

363   **Nitto's court absence**: DN 12-2-40

363   **headline—proclamation**: DN 12-14-40 including Allman quote.

363   **injunction**: DN, T 12-4-40 including Nitto as "beneficiary; number of parlors: DN 12-14-40.

364   **bookie reaction**: DN 12-4-40 and for quotes.

364   **O'Brien arrests**: DN 12-14-40 including reply.

364   **"fine weapon"**: DN 12-4-40.

364   **headline–quote**: T 2-5-41.

364   **CCC jumpstarted**: DN 5-1-41; Cahn's evaluation of Nitto: T 2-21-41; raids sputtered out: T 5-19-41.

364   **raids as apolitical ploy**: DN 5-1-41; Cicero's tax consideration: DN 12- 17-40.

364   **"it looks like Nitti"**: DN 5-1-also for talk of new alignment.

365   **judicial leniency**: T 2-5-41 also for Courtney quote "fighting Nitti."

365   **Cruel Joke**: *Lightnin'* 3-41 also for "one little hoodlum."

365   **"Nitti and The Nit-Wits"**: Ibid.; "in the racket ... hoodlums": *Lightnin'* 9-40. criticism of Courtney: *Lightnin'* 5-41.

366   **Nitto as whipping boy**: Ibid. including quotes.

366   **Lloyd Wendt series**: *Tribune* from Aug. 8 to Aug. 31, 1941.

366   **Drake Hotel incident**: Peterson 191.

366   **Jake Guzik incident**: Reported daily in T 10-25 thru 10-31-41; some of the details: Cahn's "astounding" in 10-27; O'Brien response in 10-26 as are the reactions from various suburban officials; Cahn's "dare anything" and concern in 10-28; Courtney's reaction in 10-31.

368   **"Jake Guzik is No. 1"**: T 10-25-41, later crowned Guzik: T 10-31-41.

368   **Nitto divest himself**: Anna's personal property: IOC interview of John Patton; sold Di Lido island property: Dade County Recorder of Deeds sale dated 3-19-41; home furnishings: T 8-21-41; gardener: T 10-15-41.

368   **Dr. Ronga's death**: Cook County Certificate of Death #10123 and T 4-7-41.

368   **Pete Clifford**: His murder recounted in MH 7-1-48; IOC interview of John Patton recalled it happened in front of the Guzik home; motive and suspects: Patton heard Nitto's wife thought to be having an affair, while long time Miami resident at the time Hy Saxe recalled just the opposite for Robert Schoenberg in an interview Jan. 22, 1989; Hunt: MH

369   **Bioff's return—business**: *USvC* 334-335 Bioff testimony including 'a lot of trouble"; quote "valuable asset" in T 4-30-41.

369   **Schenck investigation**: Irey 284 including "tax cheat" quote

369 Kostelanetz background: Interview.

369 charged Schenck: DN 6-3-40, HA 6-4-40, Irey 285; sentence: Irey and T 5-24-41; "I'll talk" quote in Irey 285.

369 brought to grand jury: Irey 286

370 Bioff tax break: Bioff's BOP File #58944L, Parole Report dated 12-4-41 and for "preparation of certain films" quote.

370 Bioff-Rosselli chat: *USvC* 335-336 Bioff testimony including quotes.

370 racketeering indictments: Bioff's BOP File #58944L, T 5-24-41.

370 Korshak defense strategy: *USvC* 337-340 Bioff testimony including quotes; slush fund: Ibid. 347.

370 Bioff made bail: T 5-25-41, DN 5-27-41.

370 meeting with Ricca: *USvC* 345-346 Bioff testimony including quotes.

371 Browne meet with Gioe: Ibid. 1132-1133 Browne testimony including quotes; support from Local 110: DN 5-27-41.

371 Caldwell—Local 1248: T 6-7, 9, 17-41, 7-9-41; quote about election: T 7-9.

371 Caldwell's past: T 7-19-41; denied knowing Nitto: T 8-20-41, as well as analysis of apparent insufficient income.

372 grand jury incident: T 8-15-41; alleged income: T 7-19-41.

372 his union collected: T 6-7-41, T 8-31-41 also gives the $62 remaining; phony hospital plan: T 7-19-41; airline trips: T 7-31-41; Nitto agents: T 8-21-41.

372 Caldwell faced federal charges: ST 9-6-54.

372 Knox and trial dates: T 6-13-41.

372 trial developments: T 8-19-41 gives Circella's absence as a reason and defense retort; subpoena Local 110 books: T 9-21-41, also for Colony Club money; Circella-Kaufman indictment: T 9-30-41.

373 "You pay us or": T 10-9-41 and for amount of money.

373 Nick Schenck testimony: T 10-10-41 including quotes.

373 Louis Mayer: T 10-16-41.

373 headline—Warner's: T 10-21-41 including the "must have it." quote.

373 testimony: "chicken feed": Ibid. also recounted in S 11-6-43; "to preserve my company": T 10-23-41.

374 Bioff's defense: T 10-28,29-41.

374 faced against Correa: T 10-29,30,31-41; " smear me!" and "protect Mr.Schenck" quotes in T 10-30.

375 sentencing: T 11-13-41 outlines what Correa sought and his analysis of the pair; actual sentences: Bioff's BOP File #58944L and Browne's BOP File #58945L ; BOP files also give Knox's jurisdiction decree.

CHAPTER 26

377 money to Circella: *USvC* 3678-3680 Summation.

377 Circella arrest: *Harper's* June 1944 , "Who Killed Estelle Carey?" John Barlow Martin; T 2-3-43 gives the date.

377 his sentence: FBI #58-2000-61 and 194.

377 Gioe "Don't worry": *USvC* 3680 Summation.

378 limited FBI help: Irey 286 explains the spy priority; the FBI did not ignore the IATSE problem however, they maintained a file since Dec. 5, 1935.

378 Correa petitioned: Irey 286; DOJ #5-2742 contains several written correspondence to and from Correa.

378 Oftedal to Leavenworth: Bioff BOP #58944L, *USvC* Bioff testimony 773, DOJ #5-2742 memo dated 10-7-42 —he visited him twice; "Alf" quote from DOJ.

378 **text of letter**: DOJ #5-2742 dated 4-7-42.

379 **Oftedal letter**: Messick *Secret* 179.

379 **cases against producers**: DOJ #5-2742 memo dated 4-6-42.

379 **"sympathetic treatment"**: Ibid.

379 **Oftedal's quoted report**: DOJ #5-2742 memo dated 4-6-42.

379 **Izzy Zevin**: U.S. District Court for the Southern District of New York Ind. *U.S. vs. Zevin* in DOJ #5-2742.

379 **subpoenas to Bioff-Browne**: U.S. District Court for the Southern District of New York Ind. #CR 114-101/102 dated 4-22-42; N.Y. detention and no return to Leavenworth: Browne and Bioff BOP records; every day with Correa: *USvC* testimony Bioff 580, Browne 1179.

380 **Madden—no work**: DOJ #5-2742 memo dated 10-7-42.

380 **agent questioned Nitto**: T 9-28-48, 10-4-48 with Nitto quote from T 10-4; Roma Wine Company in T 9-28   .

380 **SIU studied Greenberg**: DOJ #5-2742 memo dated 10-7-42.

380 **Naval Intelligence**: CCC memo dated 4-14-42.

380 **Korshak's work**: *USvC* Browne testimony 1229, 1317-1319.

380 **Nitto's marriage**: State of Missouri, City of St. Louis, Recorder of Deeds License #438050 signed by Dougherty.

381 **712 Selbourne**: S 3-20-43 says they moved in shortly afterwards, the home they reported was worth $15,000; a check of property records shows nothing in either of their names (as one might expect); party: S 3-20.

381 **promise of gifts of money**: TXC #111 also for son's bonds.

381 **to prosecute producers**: DOJ #5-2742 memo dated 4-6-42.

381 **Barger-D'Andrea**: Ibid. memos dated 10-29 and 12-18-42 for the entire investigation; additional info in IMW 878; "The boys" quote and vandalism: 10-29 memo; Capone brother: IMW.

381 **leasing the Symphony**: Ibid. memo dated 10-7-42.

381 **Correa sent to the SIU**: Ibid. he mentioned the letter and date with no reply.

382 **text of Irey letter**: Messick *Secret* 179-180.

382 **"constantly alert"**: Ibid.

382 **lawyers moving money**: DOJ 5-2742 memos dated 10-6, 10-8 and 12-18-42 naming Ben Feldman and William Parrillo.

382 **text of Oftedal letter**: Messick *Secret* 180 including "In view" quote.

382 **FBI sat in on SIU meet**: Ibid. 180-181 from an Oftedal memo.

382 **eye on Nitto's home**: T, S 3-20-43 reported it, but reports in Nitto's FBI file apparently addressing this issue are inked out citing FOIA exemption b7D (could reasonably expect to disclose the identity of a confidential source, including State, local or foreign agencies ...)

383 **anonymous tip to CCC**: Letter to CCC dated 8-8-42.

383 **Courtney's "crushed"**: T 10-4-42 he apparently knew nothing or had little knowledge of the fed investigation.

383 **Oftedal's August request**: DOJ #5-2742 memo 10-6-42 with no reply   .

383 **Kostelanetz report**: Ibid. including quoted material and partial list.

384 **Madden produced the file**: Ibid. memo dated 10-7-42 including the stripped file quote and the quoted 8-31-42 letter.

384 **confronts Irey**: Ibid. with Irey's "to see" and "holding out" quotes.

385 **grand jury life**: Ibid. memo dated 12-18-42.

385 **Correa called upon the SIU**: Ibid. memo dated 10-29-42 by Correa—a sequential accounting of correspondence of the case through December with the quoted portion

of that letter given, also for Barger's "sick and tired" quote and Madden's suggestion that other agencies might help.

385 **Peabody letter**: Ibid. dated 10-22-42.

386 **FBI case inactive**: Ibid. memo dated 10-29-42.

386 **Correa received word**: Ibid. memo dated 10-29-42 relating the SIU quoted "disturb" reply and Correa's "I may appraise" retort.

386 **Hirsch-Zevin indictments**: U.S. District Court for the Southern District of New York Ind. *U.S. vs. Hirsch* and *U.S. vs. Zevin* in DOJ #5-2742; Hirsch supplied Circella's bail: DOJ #5-2742 memo dated 12-18-42.

386 **Correa wrote again**: DOJ #5-2742 memo dated 12-18-42 with quote.

386 **FBI reply**: FBI letter dated 11-27-42 in DOJ #5-2742.

387 **SIU reply to Corera**: DOJ #5-2742 memo dated 12-18-42 with quote.

387 **Correa requested SIU**: Ibid.

387 **Correa-Irey correspondence**: Ibid. including 12-8 "desirous" quote and one last call on the fifth.

388 **memo to Samuel Clark**: Ibid. including 'amnesty" evaluation and the question of leaks with quote.

388 **FBI cooperation**: Ibid. Clark memo from Assistant Attorney General Samuel O. Clark dated 1-12-43 recalling his talk with Correa, he notes Correa was prepared to lodge a complaint against obstinate Treasury officials, but let the matter drop when the FBI came through.

CHAPTER 27

389 **Nitto's holiday**: Testimony of Charles Caravetta in Cook County Coroner's Report #80-March 1943, Frank Ralph Nitto, Inquest #192202; cancer: DT 3-21-43; money to his wife: TXC #111.

389 **previous cooperation**: *USvC* 1014, 1179 Bioff testimony and 1320 Browne testimony; murmurs: HA 2-5-43.

389 **Greenberg and Capone**: U.S. vs. *Campagna et al.*, CR#114-101 affidavit dated 4-13-43.

390 **Kostelanetz quote**: Rappleye & Becker 107 confirmed by author's interview with Mr. Kostelanetz, March 1995.

390 **Circella in grand jury**: A 2-3-43.

390 **mob threats to wives**: Mrs Circella: A 2-4, 13, 16-43 based on an interview with her; Mrs. Browne: *USvC* 930-931 Browne testimony; known to authorities "previously" in DOJ #5-2742, teletype dated 2-9-43 from Correa to the Attorney General's office; word of a mob meeting, anonymous tip: T 2-12-43.

390 **Estelle Carey**: Personal data: amalgam T, S 2-3-43, A 2-4-43; her ability to swindle: T 2-11-43; handled his money, A 10-4-48: extortion cash: Romer 109-110; his paramour: Roemer as did HA 2-5-43 calling her in the gentle vernacular of the day "his sweetheart"; clothes: T 2-11 and salary DN 5-19-43.

390 **"26" dice game**: Procedures, rules, odds as given in the text, many thanks to the knowledge and research of former Chief of Cook County Sheriff's Police, Arthur Bilek. According to Mr. Bilek, the game was popular in Midwest taverns and bars, particularly Chicago, from roughly 1920 to 1960. He noted a few variations of the game played throughout the city such as "Fourteens" and "Bingo." Perhaps these explain the somewhat imprecise versions of "26" that appear in Murray 299-300, Martin, *Harper's*, June 1944, "Who Killed Estelle Carey?" and T 2-3-43. According to Mr. Bilek, the games apparently disappeared due to an change in public attitudes towards open gambling and political pressure.

391 **Colony Club closed**: S 2-3-43.

391   **rumor that she informed**: Roemer 110; "have not liked": S 2-3-43; never a one-man woman: A 2-4-43; to Florida: HA 2-5-43; well-dressed: T, S 2-3-43; about extortion money, a Lee Mortimer column in n.p. from HHPL Pegler Papers probably early 1950s; Carey as a prospective witness: DOJ #5-2742 teletype dated 2-9-43; aid Internal Revenue: A 2-4-43.

391   **Carey's death**: T, S 2-3-43, DN 5-19-43; cause of death: summary of the coroner's report found in the CCC.

391   **theories**: Jealousy: S 2-3-43, HA 2-5-43; robbery T, S 2-3-43 both give 2 furs missing—both list considerable jewelry remaining; suspects: DN 5-18-43.

391   **lost Circella**: Rappleye & Becker 107-108 including quote confirmed by interview with Mr. Kostelanetz.

391   **protecting Mrs. Browne**: DOJ #5-2742 teletypes dated 2-9,11-43 from Correa to the Attorney General.

392   **effect on Bioff**: Kostelanetz quote in Irey 287; though Bioff recalled in *USvC* 930 that he began having doubts when Browne's wife had been threatened; began talking: *USvC* 535, 774 Bioff testimony; Browne wavering: *USvC* 1280; Bioff relates Oftedal's guarantee for safety only, *USvC* 578 and 3634; Kostelanetz interview in March 1995, there were no promises of lighter sentences, regardless of press speculation. He then kindly showed the author a copy of the Practice Manual for U.S. Attorneys dated April 1935. Section 6(b) reads "No Assistant is authorized under any circumstances, to make any representation or statement as to what the government's recommendation will be: a. as to sentence after plea or conviction." .

392   **watch on Nitto's home**: S, T 3-20-43 reported it, however FBI reports of this timeframe in Nitto's file are blacked out.

392   **headline**: A 2-4-43.

392   **Lepke Buchalter**: T 10-3-48, Chief Investigator for the State's Attorney Dan Gilbert testifying what he heard; Lepke was executed in New York, March 1944.

392   **attempted fix**: DT 3-21-43.

392   **bankrupt strategy**: Greenberg and Capone: *U.S. vs. Campagna et al.* CR#114-101 affadavit dated 4-13-43; Bioff and Browne: *USvC* 774 and 1280; McLane: Ibid. 2325; New York press: *New York Herald Tribune* 2-19-43.

392   **headlines**: DN 2-11-43 includes "boys" quote; headline and contents: DT 2-19-43.

393   **Nitto's actions**: Eben as attorney and discussions: FBI #58-2000-141, Eben interview by FBI dated 9-26-47, T 3-20-43 and DT 3-21-43; Florida property, Warranty Deed dated 2-27-43 Dade County Recorder of Deeds; his $50,000 gift and bonds for his son: TXC #111; walks: T 3-20 according to neighbors and wife Annette, and Charles Caravetta testimony in Coroner's Report #80-March 1943, Inquest Frank Ralph Nitto,#192202; policeman's quote and that others knew of his health problems: S 3-20-43.

393   **facts and targets**: DOJ #5-2742 memo from Correa to the Attorney General summarizing status of investigation, including the names of whom he referred to as the "lesser lights"; the total extortion of Hollywood film industry: Statement of Facts, Item #17, provided to the U.S. Court of Appeals for the 2nd District; 2% Fund total: DOJ #5-2742 memo dated 3-6-43.

393   **official letter**: *U.S. vs. Campagna et al.* CR #114-101.

393   **headline**: T 3-18-43.

394   **chaffed Mr. Woll**: DOJ #5-2742 memo to file by Assistant Attorney General Samuel O Clark dated 2-24-43 regarding his conversation with U.S. Attorney Woll, Clark records Woll's defensive posture, obviously not pleased with either being left out of the case entirely or deprived of throwing the first punch so to speak—Woll's office

was preparing to prosecute the tax matters against the defendants. In the same file, another Clark memo dated March 13 records Woll's displeasure that the decision to prosecute the indictments in New York rather than Chicago. Clark explained to him the nature of the money exchanges justified trial in New York. One suspects, Woll might have been the source of the Correa's difficulties getting cooperation in Chicago all along.

394 **last meeting**: The first mention of an alleged last mob meeting appears courtesy Clem Lane in DN 7-10-43. The second comes from wire service baron James Ragen in a statement to the state's attorney in May 1946. The third comes from chief investigator to the state's attorney Dan Gilbert while testifying in October 1948, safe to say Gilbert's account appears to be a rehash the Ragen statement. The basic text of conversation is similar in all three accounts. The only difference between the three is that Clem Lane had the meeting at Ricca's home on Lithrop Drive in River Forest; the other two insist it was at Nitto's home. Murray 289 apparently followed Clem Lane's account, but takes considerable liberty in reporting the dialogue and places the meet at Nitto's home. The reason the author believes a climatic meeting probably occurred much earlier: Why would the group wait until the very last minute to arrive at such a decision? They certainly knew from February papers the high probability of their indictment. The conversation in the text here consists of Ragen's account (as reported in S 6-26-46) since he had a working relationship with the Nitto crowd, he might know better than the other two; the meeting at Nitto's house (likelihood): police observations of meetings there reported in T, S 3-20-43 suggest it.

395 **"handed a gun"**: IOC interview of John Patton; he did not relate the event, but only what he understood the situation to be at the time.

395 **Eben conversation**: T, S, DN 3-20, DT 3-21; indictment particulars CR #114-101-102; Eben in DT 3-21 dismisses reports that Nitto appeared before the grand jury in New York which was supported by an interview with prosecutor Kostelantetz in March 1995 in which he denied Nitto being there saying "You would never tip off a defendant by doing that."

395 **novena**: Wife to make novena follows Annette interview in T 3-20-43.

395 **alcohol**: Coroner's Report #80-March 1943, Inquest #192202 contains a signed handwritten note by Dr. William D. McNally reporting Nitto's blood alcohol level at 0.23 percent grain alcohol. As to where he took his last drinks, no source says, except Clem Lane in DN 3-19-43 who states he stopped at a number of saloons along the way. Lane also reports a number of incorrect details, such as Nitto shooting at the train first, and later in DN 7-10-43, of all things, that Nitto picked up a copy of the DN along the way to read the headlines. Nitto likely took the drinks at home, if for no other reason than no one ever came forward to support Lane's saloon assertion and nothing is mentioned in official reports about any liquor containers on or near his person.

395 **clothes**: T 3-20-43 aided in by DN photos from the Chicago Historical Society.

395 **Nitto's death**: On March 20, 1943, multiple articles of Nitto, his death, and the indictments appeared in DN, DT 3-19-43, T, S, DN DT 3-20-43. Accounts of his death vary slightly among the three railroad men, especially what was said, but generally they give the same picture. All quotes from the men in T 3-20-43. T, S have excellent diagrams to reference location; Seebaurer to the sanitarium: T; two policemen who identified him: S; the look on their faces from DN photos; contents of pockets from photo in DT 3-21 and generally the same in other accounts; Lucy Ronga: DN 3-19 and T 3-20.

396 **description of shots fired**: from Seebauer in T and S; photo of hat: T; also given in testimony before the coroner's jury the next day in Coroner's Report #80, March

1943, Inquest #192202. Five holes were found in the hat, the last critical shot through the hatband and entered his head just above the tip of his right ear. The slug lodged on the left side and did not exit the hat.

396   **route taken**: No one ever speculated or claimed to witness the route of his walk and how he came to wandering south on the Illinois Central tracks. However since he walked the neighborhoods frequently as of late apparently seeking stillness, he may have continued north on quiet and secluded Selbourne Avenue, which curves close to the Illinois Central main line. He may have well wandered onto the tracks and north to the spur line before backtracking south again.

397   **police quotes**: All from S 3-20-43.

397   **Annette arrived**: T, S 3-20-43; arrival time in T; neighbor's quote in DT 3-23; Annette's quote from S.

398   **headline and business**: Headline: DN 3-19-43; economic chaos: DN 3-20 editorial: T 3-22-43; election results: T 4-5-43.

398   **inquest**: Coroner's Report #80-March 1943, Inquest #192202.

398   **Joe Nitto**: DT 3-21, 23-43 including all quotes; DT 3-23 for photo of Joe.

399   **funeral**: T 3-22,23-43 and S, DT 3-23-43; particularly T 3-23 for Annette and her son, photo on back page to estimate the number of mourners; *Sun* and *Daily Times* photographers made it late snapping a shot of a worker filling the grave; details of the headstone from author's photos, apparently added later are small stones flush with the ground. The right announces: Mother Anna Theresa Nitto 1902-40. A matching stone to the left reads (incorrectly), "Father Frank Nitto 1888-1943." The birthdate is off, probably due to the lack of knowledge of whomever placed them there. When Nitto died, in his pocket was his driver's license giving his birthdate as Jan. 27, 1886.

400   **"Uncle Sam is not"**: T 3-24-34.

400   **Nitto's tax matters**: Ibid. for federal estate matters, A 8-17-43 for millions quote; short-changed Feds and income decline in TXC #111 ruling #1950-16-13397; speculation as to decline: T 3-24-43.

400   **"guinea pig"**: T 3-24-43 .

400   **surrender dates and bonds**: warrants of apprehension for each subject located in *U.S. vs. Campagna et al.*, CR#114-101 also #114-102 for mail fraud bonds and news accounts from DT 3-24, 25-43.

401   **"Answer him, you bum"**: S 4-15-43, T 12-9-55 as quoted.

401   **Kostelanetz and quote**: DOJ #123-51-18, letter dated June 8, 1943, from Mathias F. Correa to Attorney General Francis Biddle; of Kostelanetz personal contacts with the subjects; Kostelanetz interview.

401   **probate filing, claims**: Probate Court of Cook County # 43P5267; Marie Capezio, incident and alleged relationship: A 4-1-43.

401   **nolle prosequi**: for Nitto affidavit dated 9-24-43 in *U.S. vs. Campagna et al.*, CR#114-101, the motion was granted on 10-5-43.

401   **estate inventory**: Probate Court of Cook County # 43P5267.

402   **inch of press**: S 10-12-43 seems to have been the only one to report it.

402   **real estate given**: Property records Doc #319729T, #1307102 and 03 in the Cook County Recorder of Deeds covering the period he was there do not show Nitto's name on the Selbourne address at any time; records in the Dade County Recorder of Deeds show his Florida home remained in the name of others since February 1943; Hot Springs home: T 9-13-48.

402   **personal property**: Probate Court of Cook County # 43P5267 business with Greenberg: Superior Court of Cook County #57S-2335, *Annette Nitti, as administrator for the estate of Frank R. Nitti, deceased vs. Ida Schultz, et al.*

402   **Greenberg investigations**: Real estate inquiry in DOJ #5-2742 memo dated 10-8-42 from Internal Revenue, relates that the two Illinois officials in question were also two of the lawyers who handled local extortion money for Bioff; income tax trouble: CCC memo dated 11-8-50, Internal Revenue determined he owed over $75,000 in additional taxes for years 1935-41.

402   **"Typical of Chicago"**: DOJ #123-51-18, letter dated 9-7-43 from Kostelanetz to the Asst. Attorney General Samuel O. Clark and return letter dated 9-14-43 from Clark authorizing the action.

403   **extortion trial—prosecution**: Substance of testimony from *USvC*; description of witnesses from interview with Mr. Kostelanetz; facts of the case from Statement of Facts, Item #5 provided to the U.S. Court of Appeals.

403   **defense strategy**: *USvC* 3617 Summation; attacked Bioff and his sudden patriotism with quotes: Irey 286, 288; ill defendants: Absent Waivers in CR #114-101; Kostelanetz requesting a physician, DOJ #123-51-18 letter dated 12-17-43 and DOJ Form 25-B requesting reimbursement dated 1-11-44.

404   **Kostelanetz counter**: On Bioff's character and quote: *USvC* 3632 Summation, also DOJ #5-2742, teletype dated 11-9-43 shows Kostelanetz prepared to call an expert to counter claims that Bioff was a psychopathic liar.

404   **sentences**: Judgment and Commitment statements for each defendant in *U.S. vs. Campagna et al.*, CR#114-101, Hochstein indictment CR#115-271, Izzy Zevin indictment CR#113-162.

404   **Thompson and Dever**: Thompson: W&K *Big Bill* 15, 356; Dever: Schmidt 6, 175.

404   **still resided**: Selbourne address from various documents in Probate Court of Cook County # 43P5267; regained Di Lido Island home: Dade County Recorder of Deeds Book 2431 dated 10-23-44; Miami Beach Kennel Club: T 12-21-50 reporting on the Kefauver hearings questioning of H. B. Benvenuti in which he described Annette's interest in the property.

404   **Greenberg payments**: Copies of both checks in Probate Court of Cook County # 43P5267, legal agreements: attached to paperwork regarding 57S-2335 in file.

405   **IRS strategy**: FBI #58-2000-453; joint ownerships: serial 273.

405   **IRS claims**: Amount due by the Nitto estate from Probate Court of Cook County #43P5267, the Final Report filed Feb. 13, 1950; Campagna and Ricca figures and settlements from FBI #58-2000-274 and serial 453 field report also for quote. No source gives a definitive answer as to why the feds pressed Annette so hard. The Chicago media by 1950 was wondering the same with no explanations. One is led to believe, they were suspicious all along of her various transactions, the Di Lido real estate switch and Kennel Club land purchase for example.

CHAPTER 28

407   **"strong as the United States army"**: Copy of Ragen Statement made Thursday, May 2, 1946, the complete quote as follows: "For your information, they are probably as strong as the United States Army is at the present time."; Roselli quote: Demaris *Last* 122.

407   **prison time**: FBI #58-2000-274 interview with Ricca on 10-1-47 page 9; disciplined: IMW 40, exhibits 34-F and 35-D; D'Andrea's transfer: IMW an undated Leavenworth medical report before the committee suspects moderate anginal syndrome, thus his transfer to Springfield 1-13-47.

408   **Nolle prosequi**: FBI #58-2000-145x pages 7-8 from the Attorney General's office.

408   **parole fury**: Editorial headline: T 8-16-47; T 5-13-48 gives a chronology of events, including quote; Busbey to investigate: T 9-18-47; opposition by Bright and Kostelanetz:

exchanges listed in FBI #58-2000-458; Bright's quote: IMW 41; specific opposition to D'Andrea by Judge Bright in a lengthy letter to the Parole Executive dated 6-5-47 in IMW 43-44 and in FBI #58-2000-458 memo dated 10-3-47; Clark actions's: IMW 330-334 regarding efforts to get information.

408   **centered on**: T 10-4-47; Dillon's and Maury Hughes actions and quotes: T 5-13-48; on Hughes: IMW 336.

408   **actions of parole board**: IMW 37-39 particularly a memo to the committee by Fred S. Rogers explaining Dillon's appearance on behalf of the applicants, also in T 5-13-48 as well as Clark's actions.

410   **Wilson's quote**: T 5-13-48 including Busbey's reply and comparison.

410   **Chicago tidbits**: Guzik to raise money: FBI #58-2000-622 memo dated 12-13-47; purported $250,000 to Dillon: FBI #58-2000-4 memo dated 9-19-47 an interview with Chicago reporter James Doherty relating what he found; "help out" and Busbey quote: T 5-13-48.

410   **focus on counsel**: Dillon and Hughes payments: T 5-13-48 and IMW 285; Dillon's reputation and background: FBI #58-2000-3 summary dated 9-18-47 and FBI #58-2000-4 memo dated 9-19-47, except Pendergrast and crime boss Lazia in T 10-1-47; "fiction": HA 3-2-48.

411   **committee conclusion**: Rappleye & Becker 115; coincidentally, one year after the scandalous release of Campagna et al., in August 1948 according to the U.S. Parole Commission website, the Attorney General increased the Board of Parole from 3 to 5 members because of "a post war increase in population." .

411   **State of Illinois filed**: Probate Court of Cook County #43P5267.

411   **Annette's poverty**: Headline: T 9-13-48; liens: T 9-28-48: paid debts and Joseph's schooling: T 12-7-49; knew of no Greenberg money: T 9-13-48; 'If I learned" quote: DN 10-4-48.

411   **government claims**: TXC #111; subpoena Bioff and Browne: ST, T 9-28-48 and DN 9-29-48.

412   **Annette's defense**: T 9-28-48; O'Callaghan's quotes: A 9-27-48; summation of arguments T, ST, A 9-28-48; fed response and Humphrey example in HA 9-28-48.

412   **Bioff-Browne security**: T 10-1-48 including the trial site and security; Browne interview and quote: DN 9-30-48.

412   **headline "BIOFF TELLS"**: ST 10-1-48 including content.

413   **headline "DURY LINKS"**: A 10-2-48; except Balaban depositions in ST, T 10-3-48.

413   **headline "BARE GANG'S"**: T 10-2-48 including content.

413   **headline "NITTI TAX"**: DN 10-5-48; preparer's also in ST 10-5-48.

413   **Annette on stand**: DN 10-4, 5-48; testimony and "He loved": DN 10-5.

413   **"the record is devoid"**: T 2-20-49.

413   **Tax Court decision**: TXC #111 865-869, reasonable belief quote on 866.

414   **O'Callaghan's fight**: ST 1-8-50 and final tax bill in Probate Court of Cook County # 43P5267.

414   **additional tax levy**: Probate Court of Cook County # 43P5267 , Final Report dated April 2, 1951, and T 3-22-51.

414   **Frank Sasso stocks**: Probate Court of Cook County # 43P5267.

414   **primary objective local**: Peterson 291.

415   **Stanton's death**: "So long" quote and first attempt on his life: S 5-7-43; death: S 5-6-43, T 5-6, 7-43; wounds, age from synopsis of coroner's report found in CCC.

415   **motive**: Handbooks and "hundred reasons": S 5-7-43; rake off fat paychecks: DN 5-18-43.

415   **suspects**: Quirk: T 10-1-43; Fawcett as bodyguard: T 5-11-43; squabble with: S 5-

6-43 and DN 5-18-43; friends with Hunt: S 10-6-43; Hunt's style: S 5-7-43; labor activities: S 5-7-43; link with Maddox: T 5-7-43; Quirk's murder: T 10-1-43; Fawcett's death: DN 5-26-45.

415   **other gambling deaths**: Peterson 359 fn; J Levert Kelly in T 4-8-44.

416   **Mangano's death**: DN 8-3-44, T 8-4-44: quote and age: DN.

416   **policy racket**: Initiating takeover: DN 6-29-40; killing of Kelly: Peterson 181; Jones indictments: T 3-6-40; Teddy Roe: Peterson 292, 319 and Binder 82.

416   **moves against Ragen**: Ragen Statement made Thursday, May 2, 1946, and Peterson 280-281; O'Hara role in Trans-American: DN, A 6-25-46, T 6-26-46, ST 11-14, 15-50; Ragen's appeals in his own statement; protecting his family: A 6-25, 26-46, the warning: A 6-26-46.

417   **Ragen shooting**: First attempt: A 6-26-46; his statement and mob response: A 6-26-46; coroner report: T 9-23-46.

417   **Moe Annenberg**: T 7-21-42.

418   **Capone**: Ragen quote on Nitto: DN 6-25-46; death, burial: Schoenberg 355, 365.

418   **the Gennas**: ST 12-23-51.

418   **Bugs Moran**: Binder 72, Schoenberg 358.

418   **Ed Kelly**: Biles 151.

418   **1950s zenith**: Binder 77-78.

419   **Charlie Fischetti**: T 4-12-51.

419   **D'Andrea's death**: T 9-21-52 obituary; T 8-19-54 reported he was ill since his release; quote from DN 8-15-47.

419   **Charlie Gioe's affairs**: Diminished: T 8-20-54; at the Seneca: ST 8-19-54 he owned a piece: T 8-20-54; fiscal interests: ST 8-19-54, T 8-20, 22-54; construction business: DN 8-19-54; questioned in murders: T 8-19-54; at FBI offices: FBI #58-2000-61 report dated 10-3-47; federal investigations: T, ST, DN 8-19-54; Accardo told him: ST 8-19; the mob pushing him: ST 8-19 and T 8-23-54; approached Diamond: T 8-23-54; fix the matter: T 8-20-54.

419   **Frank Diamond**: His sanity in question: T 8-22-54; he refused to accept prison time: judgment and commitment statements for defendant in *U.S. vs. Campagna et al.*, CR#114-101 and reported in T 8-23; Kostelanetz quote: IMW 550, explanation of the system in IMW 56—usually those judged guilty will elect to enter prison and serve time while their case is being appealed because if they lose, the time served will be applied toward the sentence; wrong foot and "wild man": T 8-23; bounced check: T 8-22; subject of investigations: T 8-23; Joe Glimco: T 8-29, 9-1,2-54.

420   **murder of Gioe**: T 8-19-54.

420   **murder of Diamond**: T 8-22-54.

420   **Max Caldwell**: Death: ST 9-7-54; history: T 1-29-44, CCC memo dated 11-26-47.

420   Louis Campagna: FBI #58-2000-453; final settlement: serial 274; surveillance of the 4 parolees: FBI # 58-2000-635 memo dated 12-23-47; sources of money: ST 11-14-50; Cicero connections: T 6-25-55; death as reported in T 6-6-55.

421   **"they would be objects"**: T 11-5-55; on the modification of their sentence: Browne BOP File #2151-SS and Bioff BOP File #2150-SS, their trial judge retained jurisdiction of their cases and subsequently modified their sentences on 12-22-44 to time served plus 5 years probation.

421   **Bioff's end**: FBI #95-61386-1 investigative report from the Maricopa County Sheriff dated 11-9-55 including autopsy report supplemented by details in T 11-5-55; finest neighborhood, explosion heard and dishes knocked from shelves; watch stopped: FBI file, serial 9, memo dated 11-4-55; examination of evidence and conclusion: above FBI source with FBI Laboratory Work Sheets dated 11-18-55.

422   **real reason**: Numerous Chicago papers fingered the mob as did the WDN 11-5-55 and New York investigative reporter Victor Riesel in typed piece titled "Inside Labor" in which he sent to the FBI (File #95-61386) dated 11-7-55.

422   **Clarence Campbell**: FBI #95-61386-24 memo dated 8-16-56, field reports dated 8-30-56 and serial 25 field reports dated 9-11-56, 10-2-56, serial 26-27 dated 9-21 and 9-26 26 respectively; FBI #95-61386-5 memo dated 11-14-55 suggested an investigation into the revenge motive reporting that theory has "substantial foundation"; Campbell's ironic death—he fell on 3 sticks of dynamite: T 5-26-56.

422   **how they found Bioff**: his occupations: T, ST 11-5-55, close to home: WDN 11-5-55; Pegler's investigation: FBI #95-61386-18 interview with Pegler in the Phoenix on 3-16-56 and a copy of his article appearing in the Arizona *Republic* dated 3-26; Goldwater did not know: Pegler interview; an informant: FBI #95-61386-22 and NYJA 3-26-56; the gambling world: NYJA; investor in Reno: A 11-5-55; mob figures in Phoenix: ST 11-6-55.

422   **letter to Goldwater**: FBI #95-61368-28 has a copy of the original letter addressed to the Honorable Senator dated 4-1-57 with references only to "Bill" and the sender's name redacted, but with the handwritten note "Bioff" visible at the side. Also in file is a letter from the senator on his official letterhead dated April 3 seeking FBI help, but providing no names. The agent's return letter to the senator is dated April 8 with a note at the bottom that Bill and Bioff are one in the same.

423   **Greenberg's interests**: Quote: DN 6-26-46; percentage of stock: T 12-20-55; sales: T 12-11-55; owner of Prima Bismarck: CCC memo dated 2-21-44; other holdings from same CCC memo; change to Canadian Ace: CCC memo dated 12-28-48; promo picture: A 12-9-55; high pressure sales: ST 2-10-49.

423   **his mob loyalty**: Questions from IOC 1352-1353; quote in Gioe questioning: ST, DN 12-9-55.

424   **worn thin**: Liquor distributorship: ST 12-9-55; rumor about the Nitto estate: Murray 35-36 writes it as fact based upon coincidental actions later discussed; never traveling alone: T 11-11-55.

424   **Greenberg's death**: ST, T 12-8-55, A 12-9-55; Jekyll quote in A 12-9; award and press suspicions: ST 12-9-55; O'Conner first suspects: T 12-9-55; amateurish analysis and quote: ST 12-9; suspects: ST 12-8-55; Ricca: DN 12-12-55, Fusco in A 12-10; Pierce: T 12-10, DN 12-9, quote in DN 12-12.

425   **"ask for Jackie"**: CCC memo 5-28-56 a confidential witness heard it; Accardo's role in.

425   **Premium**: Roemer, 202-203, 209.

425   **George Browne**: Appearance: photo as BOP #2151-SS; doing good union work: summary of psychiatric report dated 2-11-42, BOP # 58945-L. which also notes: "He appears to present a fairly clear picture of a man whose judgment has progressively failed." Burlington, Iowa: FBI File #95-61386-8 memo dated 11-23-55 and serial 15 memo dated 12-22-55 but some still thought him in Dubuque; the Italian there, it may be Lew Farrel real name Ferrari who represented Greenberg's brewery interests locally, CCC memo dated 2-9-48; friend's quote and FBI warning: FBI serial 8; "killing him" from Victor Riesel's *Inside Labor* found in FBI #95-61386; last FBI info on him: serial 15 memo dated 1-5-56; death: Investigative Reports: *Movies and the Mob*, 1995, Bill Kurtis Productions for BBC / A & E Network.

426   **Nick Circella**: Prison time and parole status: FBI #58-2000-451-7 field report dated 10-2-47; alarmed Atlanta's warden: IMW 90 memo dated 5-1-45; Mrs. Circella: FBI # 58-2000-458 page 2 memo dated 10-3-47; the prison farm: FBI #58-2000-451; returned to Chicago: A 10-5-48; final destiny: Murray 297-298, later Roemer 108 reported the same, according to Circella's brother.

427   **Jake Guzik**: T 4-14-44, 12-19-50, 1-14-56, ST and DN 2-22-56.

427   **Sam Hunt**: Activities in S 5-7-43, 10-6-43 and T 8-21-56; Accident: T, DN 7-6-42; death: T 8-21-56.

427   **Johnny Patton**: T 12-24-56.

428   **George Scalise**: T 5-9-57.

428   **Claude Maddox**: T 6-22-58, ST 6-23-58.

428   **Fred Evans**: T 8-23-59, ST 8-25-59.

428   **George McLane**: T, ST, DN 8-26-59.

428   **Joseph McElligott**: T 3-9-67.

428   **Roger Touhy**: 3 men he fingered: ST 12-18-59; Humphreys most to lose: T 12-21-59; their venom: T 12-20-59; muscling distributors: ST; sister and Walter Miller in ST; basement observatory: T 12-18-59; shooting of: T 12-17-59 and photo in Binder 88; quote: T.

429   **reaction of Factor**: T 12-18-59; also for mob as suspect and editorial.

430   **Tom Courtney**: *Tribune* obituary located by Jeff Thurston.

430   **Dan Gilbert**: Peterson 260-262.

430   **Jake Factor**: *Capone's Mob Murdered Roger Touhy* by John W. Tuohy, Barricade Books, 2001.

430   **Annette's lawsuit**: Superior Court of Cook County #57S-2335; amount won and date closed: Probate Court #43P5267.

431   **filed as *Nitti***: Superior Court Cook County #57S-2335.

431   **Rosselli's comments**: Demaris *Last* 122 talking to Jimmy Fratianno.

431   **on the Nitti family**: family tree in CCC, DN 2-22-64 and T 8-14-65; Nick Nitti and Accardo as partners: Demaris *Captive* 81; "Don't believe it": ST 9-12-84; Rich and Melrose Park address: ST 1-6-84; alleged Cerone connection: CCC Nitti File notes; *Tribune* investigation into the Nitti relationships: CCC memo dated 3-9-82; Brown as Nitti great nephew: T 9-26-79 and ST 9-27-79.

432   **Humphreys-Serritella**: Humphreys: Schoenberg 357; Serritella: T 10-31-67.

432   **Louis Kaufman**: *U.S. vs. Campagna et al.* CR #114-101 memo dated 5-21-65 the Department of Justice Claims Unit to the Civil Division outlining Kaufman's history; tax payments: DOJ #5-2742, Folder 2, correspondence dated 6-21-39.

433   **fate of the Manhattan**: Skilnik 199; rarest of cans according to Lew Cady in 1981, a brewery sleuth, he knew one who had the original invoice for the shipment.

433   **Harry Hochstein**: Later days noted in CCC Nitti File; his death: T 1-11-71.

433   **Thomas Burke**: T 7-23- 73, T 4-10-76.

433   **Louis Romano**: Arrest and Capone quote: ST 7-21-49; appointed labor advisor; T 10-13, 17-54; quote "the whole bunch": Binder 88; retirement: notes from the CCC Nitti File; obituary in T 2-7-78.

434   **Paul Ricca**: Tax settlement: FBI #58-2000-274 page 30 and serial 452 pages 6-7; picked up in 1948: DN 11-28-50; parole violations in 1950: DN 11-28,29-50, ST 11-29; "I can't help " quote: T 10-12-72; won round two: ST 8-22-52; phony naturalization: T 6-13-58, DN 10-12-72; income tax case: T 7-22-59, DN 10-21-61; death: DN 10-12-72.

434   **Ralph Capone**: Schoenberg death 362.

434   **Ralph Pierce**: T 7-8-76.

435   **Johnny Rosselli**: Rappleye & Becker 308-310 for Sam Giancana; of Rosselli's testimony: 312-313; warnings and his death: 4-5, 318-320.

435   **Ed Vogel**: T 4-19-49 and ST 6-15-77 .

435   **two policemen**: Harry Miller from interview with Harold Browne, September 1995. Browne got to know Miller when the latter looked him up after he saw Browne's credit

on the 1968 movie *The St. Valentine's Day Massacre* starring Jason Robards. They then got together to chat occasionally. Of Miller, Browne said he retained his police officer mannerisms, but never even mentioned Nitto. Harry Lang elected business agent for the Hebrew Butchers' Association: T 8-25-34, litigating: T 11-17-36.

436 **Robert Larry McCullough**: CCC memos dated 5-1-44, 5-10-44, 5-14-48.

436 **Tony Accardo**: Roemer 429.

436 **Nitto movie**: *Nitti The Enforcer*, 1987 by Leonard Hill Films.

436 **sister and brother-in-law**: Vincenzo Vollaro from Surrogate's Court of King's County File #5212; Giovannina Vollaro from Surrogate's Court of King's County Probate Petition #6840-60.

436 **half-brothers, nephews**: Raphael Dolendi Social Security Death Index, brother Genaro, Office of Vital Statistics, State of Florida #73-087955 clearly gives the matching birthdate and mother's name; of Nitto's nieces and nephews most traced through the Social Security Death Index where birthdates clearly matched.

436 **Lucy Ronga**: Property Doc #23502117 in the Cook County Recorder of Deeds.

436 **Annette Caravetta**: Cook County Medical Examiner Certificate of Death #81-029405.

437 **Joseph Nitto**: Records in Probate Court #43P5267; used original family name from CCC memo of *Tribune* investigation dated 3-9-82, though the he could not recall the name, the author out of respect to Joe's privacy did not print his name.

437 **Nitto's home**: ST 5-29-03 courtesy of Jeanette Callaway of the CCC.

BIBLIOGRAPHY

Aller, Herbert. *The Extortionists*. Beverly Hills, Ca.: Guild-Hartford Pub., 1972.

Amiftheatrof, Erik. *The Children of Columbus: An Informal History of the Italians in the New World*. Boston: Little, Brown, 1973.

Asbury, Herbert. *Gem of the Prairie: An Informal History of the Chicago Underworld*. Garden City, N.Y.: Garden City Pub., 1942.

Basten, Fred E. with Salvatore, Robert & Kaufman, Paul A. *Max Factor's Hollywood: Glamour, Movies, Make-Up*. Santa Monica, CA: General Publishing Group, Inc., 1995.

Benton, Barbara. *Ellis Island: A Pictorial History*. New York: Facts on File Pub., 1985.

Biles, Roger. *Big City Boss in Depression and War: Mayor Edward J. Kelly of Chicago*. Dekalb, Ill.: No. Ill. U. Press, 1984.

Binder, John J. *Images of America: The Chicago Outfit*. Chicago: Arcadia, 2003.

Boettiger, John. *Jake Lingle: Chicago on the Spot*. New York: Dutton, 1931.

Burns, Walter Noble. *The One-Way Ride: The red Trail of Chicago Gangland from Prohibition to Jake Lingle*. Garden City, N.Y.: Doubleday, 1931.

Cady, Lew. *Beer Can Collecting (New Revised Edition)*. New York: Charter Communications, Inc., 1981.

Casey, Robert J., and Douglas, W.A.S. *The Midwesterner: The Story of Dwight H. Green*. Chicago: Wilcox & Follett, 1948.

Dobyns, Fletcher, *The Amazing Story of Repeal: An Expose of the Power of Propaganda*. Norwood, Ma.: The Plimpton Press, 1940.

_____. *The Underworld of American Politics*. New York: priv. prntd., 1932.

Demaris, Ovid. *Captive City*. New York: Lyle Stuart, Inc. 1969

_____. *The Last Mafioso*. New York: Times Books, 1981.

Drury, John. *Dining Out*. New York: John Day, 1931.

Gottfried, Alex. *Boss Cermak of Chicago.* Seattle: Washington U. Press, 1962.

Heaps, Willard. *The Story of Ellis Island.* New York: The Seabury Press, 1967.

Helmer, William J. and Arthur J. Bilek. *The St. Valentine's Day Massacre: The Untold Story of the Gangland Bloodbath That Brought Down Al Capone.* Nashville: Cumberland House Publishing, Inc., 2004.

Hoffman, Dennis E. *Scarface Al and the Crime Crusaders: Chicago's Private War against Al Capone.* Carbondale and Edwardsville, Ill.: S. Ill. U. Press, 1993.

Hollatz, Tom. *Gangster Holidays: The Lore and Legends of the Bad Guys.* St Cloud, Mn.: North Star Press, 1989. .

Hostetter, Gordon L. and Beesley, Thomas Q. *It's A Racket!* Chicago: Les Quinn Books, Inc., 1929.

Irey, Elmer L. as told to William J. Slocum. *The Tax Dodgers: The Inside Story of the T-Men's War with America's Political and Underworld Hoodlums.* New York; Greenberg, 1948.

Johnson, Malcom. *Crime on the Labor Front.* New York: McGraw-Hill Book Co., 1950.

Karpis, Alvin, with Bill Trent. *The Alvin Karpis Story.* New York: Coward, McCann & Geoghegan, 1971.

Kobler, John. *Capone: The Life and World of Al Capone.* New York: Putnam's, 1971.

Kyvig, David E. *Repealing National Prohibition.* Chicago: U. of Chicago, 1979.

Landesco, John. *Organized Crime in Chicago: Part III of the Illinois Crime Survey 1929.* Chicago: U. of Chicago, 1929; 1968 edition.

Lewis, Lloyd, and Henry Justin Smith. *Chicago; A History of Its Reputation.* New York: Harcourt, Brace, 1929.

Lindberg, Richard C. *To Serve and Collect: Chicago Politics and Police Corruption From the Lager Beer Riot to the Summerdale Scandal.* Praeger: New York, 1991.

Lyle, John H. *The Dry and Lawless Years.* Englewood Cliffs, N.J.: Prentice-Hall, 1960.

McConnell, Thomas Chalfont. *Luck and Witless Virtue vs. Guile: In Which an English Clergyman Proves the Nemesis of John ("Jake the Barber") Factor, Alias J. Wise, Alias H Guest.* Chicago: Chicago Literary Club, 1943.

McPhaul, Jack. *Johnny Torrio: First of the Gang Lords.* New Rochelle, N.Y.: Arlington House, 1970.

Messick, Hank. *Lansky.* New York: Putnam's, 1971.

_____. *Secret File.* New York: Putnam's, 1969.

Meyer, George H. as told to Chaplain Ray and Max Call. *Al Capone's Devil Driver.* Dallas: Acclaimed Books, 1979.

Murray, George. *The Legacy of Al Capone: Portraits and Annals of Chicago's Public Enemies.* New York: Putnam's, 1975.

Nelli, Humberto S. *Italians in Chicago, 1880-1930; A Study of Ethnic Mobility.* New York: Oxford U. Press, 1970.

_____. *The Business of Crime: Italians and Syndicate Crime in the United States.* New York: Oxford U. Press, 1976.

_____. *Immigrants to Ethnics: The Italian American.* New York: Oxford U. Press, 1983.

Ness, Elliot, with Oscar Fraley. *The Untouchables.* New York: Julian Messner, 1957.

Newell, Barbara Warne. *Chciago and The Labor Movement: Metropolitan Unionism in. the 1930's.* Urbana, Il.: U.of I. Press, 1961.

Pasley, Fred D. *Al Capone: The Biography of a Self-Made Man.* New York: Ives Washburn, 1930.

_____. *Muscling In.* New York: Ives Washburn, 1931.

Peterson, Virgil W. *Barbarians in Our Midst: A History of Chicago Crime and Politics.* Boston: Atlantic Monthly Press/Little Brown, 1962.

Picchi, Blaise. *The Five Weeks of Guiseppe Zangara: The Man Who Would Assassinate FDR.* Chicago: Academy Chicago Pub., 1998.

Rappleye, Charles and Ed Becker. *All*

American Mafioso: The Johnny Rosselli Story. New York: Doubleday, 1991.

Roemer Jr., William F. *Accardo:The Genuine Godfather.* New York: Donald I. Fine, 1995. .

Rubin, Jay., and M.J. Obermeier. *Growth of a Union: The Life and Times of Edward Flore.* New York: Historical Union Association, Inc., 1943.

Schiavo, Giovanni E. *The Italians in Chicago; A Study on Americanization.* Chicago: Italian American Pub., 1928.

Schmidt, John R. *The Mayor Who Cleaned Up Chicago: A Political Biography of William E. Dever.* DeKalb, Ill.: No. Ill. U. Press, 1989.

Schoenberg, Robert J. *Mr. Capone: The Real – and Complete-Story of Al Capone.* New York: William Morrow and Company, Inc., 1992.

Sinclair, Andrew. *Prohibition: The Era of Excess.* Boston: Little, Brown, 1962.

Skilnik, Bob. *The History of Beer and Brewing in Chicago, 1833-1978.* Self, 1999.

Spiering, Frank. *The Man Who Got Capone.* New York: Bobbs-Merrill, 1976.

Stuart, William H. *The Twenty Incredible Years.* Chicago: M.A. Donohue, 1935.

Sullivan, Edward Dean. *Chicago Surrenders.* New York: The Vanguard Press, 1930.

Touhy, Roger with Ray Brennan. *The Stolen Years.* Cleveland: Pennington Press, 1959.

Weld, Ralph Foster. *Brooklyn is America.* New York: Columbia U. Press, 1950.

Wendt, Lloyd, and Herman Kogan. *Big Bill of Chicago.* New York: Bobbs-Merrill, 1953.

_____. *Lords of the Levee: The Story of Bathhouse John And Hinky Dink.* Garden City, N.Y.: Garden City Pub., 1943.

Wilson, Frank J. and Beth Day. *Special Agent: A Quarter Century with the Treasury. Department and the Secret Service.* New York: Holt, Rinehart & Winston, 1965.

Wilson, Samuel Paynter. *Chicago and Its Cess-Pools of Infamy.* Chicago: Self, 1910.

X Marks the Spot (Anonymous). The Spot Publishing Co., 1930.

INDEX